TEACHING MATHEMATICS IN THE ELEMENTARY SCHOOL

David J. Fuys
BROOKLYN COLLEGE

Rosamond Welchman Tischler
BROOKLYN COLLEGE

Little, Brown and Company
Boston   Toronto

Library of Congress Catalog Card No. 78-61739

ISBN 0-316-29720-8

10

MV

Published simultaneously in Canada
by Little, Brown & Company (Canada) Limited

Printed in the United States of America

ACKNOWLEDGMENTS

Illustrations by Lily Yamamoto

Material in this book was prepared for use in elementary, early childhood, and special education mathematics education courses in the Performance-Based Teacher Education Program at Brooklyn College of the City University of New York.

Page 4: "One of these things is not like the others . . ." © Jonico Music Inc. Used by permission.

Pages 67–68. Extracts from *The Child's Conception of Number* by Jean Piaget. Reprinted by permission of Humanities Press Inc., New Jersey, and Routledge & Kegan Paul.

Page 123: The bottom diagram is adapted from Chapter 1, "Sprouts and Brussels Sprouts," in *Mathematical Carnival* by Martin Gardner (New York: Alfred A. Knopf, 1975). Reprinted by permission.

Page 217: The diagram is adapted from material by Robert Wirtz. Reprinted by permission from Curriculum Development Associates, Inc.

Page 231: The worksheets are adapted from activities in *Individualized Computation* by Robert Wirtz (Washington, D.C.: Curriculum Development Associates, Inc., 1974). Reprinted by permission.

Pages 571–572: "Ten Basic Skill Areas" is reprinted from an NCSM Position Paper on basic mathematical skills by permission of the National Council of Supervisors of Mathematics.

PREFACE

This is an activity-oriented book intended to help prospective and practicing teachers develop and strengthen their background in mathematics content and methods of teaching elementary school mathematics. It evolved from materials we prepared for undergraduate courses combining mathematics content, learning theory, methods of teaching mathematics, and field experiences in elementary schools. We believe that to teach mathematics effectively, a teacher must be able to synthesize knowledge in the following three areas which are interrelated throughout this book:

1. *Mathematics:* content in the elementary school mathematics curriculum and background mathematics which provides perspective on the school curriculum;
2. *Learning theory:* how children learn and rationales for commonly used teaching methods;
3. *Methods of teaching:* general strategies and approaches as well as specific methods and activities for teaching topics in the elementary school mathematics curriculum.

The book consists of eleven chapters that are organized around major topics in the elementary school mathematics curriculum and instructional materials. The heart of each chapter is an initial section of hands-on math lab activities that provides interesting, enjoyable, and challenging experiences in learning mathematics. The activities are at an adult level, yet can be modified for use with children. The activities serve as a basis for subsequent Discussion Questions and Comments, and Follow-up Sections in each chapter. These sections deal with the mathematics underlying the activities and methods in various teaching situations.

A major emphasis of the book is on "learning by doing." By doing initial activities, the readers (or "doers") not only learn mathematics but also experience first-hand methods for teaching children. This approach is based on the belief that "teachers teach as they are taught," and hence some of their learning experiences should be models for teaching mathematics to children. Effective classroom use of activities generally requires that a teacher adapt them for particular teaching situations. To help readers develop this ability, each chapter includes both a discussion of ways to modify activities and exercises on planning and using activities with children.

Throughout this book, readers are encouraged to *interact* with the material presented. In the activities much of the interaction is on a concrete level through the use of manipulatives. In the sections that follow, the reader is constantly encouraged to review or provide further examples of the ideas presented, and to respond to the very real questions that arise when one teaches elementary school mathematics. Answers to selected exercises are given at the end of the book. This interaction encourages readers to create their own references for subsequent use in teaching mathematics to children. The book also encourages students to interact with one another through small-group activities or through questions in the chapters to stimulate class discussion.

To help readers pursue their particular interests in teaching mathematics, the book includes Further Readings and Projects sections and an extensive bibliography of articles from professional journals and books about mathematics, learning theory, and strategies for teaching mathematics.

This book can be used in a variety of elementary school mathematics teacher training situations. It is suitable for a three- or four-credit, one-semester course that combines mathematics content and methods of teaching and that may include math lab and lecture/discussion sessions. The book was field-tested for several semesters in courses for early childhood and elementary school (regular and special education) teachers. Since considerable mathematics can be derived from many of the chapters, the book can be used in a mathematics content course for elementary school teachers. An instructor's manual contains suggestions for using the book in these different teacher education settings, as well as commentary on chapters and testing materials.

We would like to acknowledge our colleagues, students and reviewers who have used or commented upon these materials as they were developed. In particular, we would like to thank Dr. Dorothy Geddes, who was largely responsible for setting up the mathematics education program in which we taught, for her support and advice. Dr. Howard Munson at Winona State University in Minnesota reviewed and field-tested the materials, and, along with his students, provided many useful comments and suggestions. In addition, we appreciate the assistance of Jewell Garner, California State University, Los Angeles, and Henry S. Kepner, Jr., The University of Wisconsin, Milwaukee, who reviewed the manuscript. We would also like to thank colleagues at Brooklyn College who field-tested the materials over several semesters, in particular, Drs. C. James Lovett and Thalia Taloumis, and Fredda Friederwitzer, Deborah Levine and Nina Martorano, and their students, who gave much useful feedback on the materials. We would also like to thank the editorial staff at Little, Brown for their help and cooperation. Finally, we thank our respective spouses for their encouragement and patience.

D.J.F.
R.W.T.

CONTENTS

INTRODUCTION

How can we help children learn mathematics? Few people believe that there is an exact recipe for good mathematics teaching, yet most agree that the most vital ingredient is the teacher. An effective teacher must understand the mathematics to be learned, be sensitive to children's needs and the ways they learn, and be acquainted with a variety of strategies and methods for teaching. The purpose of this book is to help you develop these prerequisites for being a good elementary school mathematics teacher.

Each chapter of this book combines material on mathematical content, principles of learning, and methods for teaching mathematics, all growing out of your experiences with an initial set of activities. This book is not meant to be simply read — it is a "doing" book that invites you to become involved in an active problem-solving way with mathematics and with methods for helping children to learn mathematics. As you do the activities, ask yourself the following questions:

> What mathematics is involved here? That is, what concepts or skills are involved, and what types of mathematical thinking?
>
> Could these activities be used to help children learn mathematics? Could they be modified for use with children at different grade or ability levels?
>
> Which of the activities do you enjoy? Why? Which might children enjoy?

Organization of the Chapters

Chapters in the book are organized around activity sets that lead in a natural way to mathematics content, methods of teaching, and learning theory that supports the methods. Each chapter has six sections: Introduction; Activities; Discussion Questions and Comments; Follow-up Sections; Test Your Understanding; and Further Readings and Projects.

The Introduction presents a brief overview of the chapter. You should read it before you begin the set of activities.

The second section, Activities, will give you experience with a variety of materials — everyday objects, such as coins, beans, and popsicle sticks; specially designed manipulatives, both homemade and commercial (such as Cuisenaire rods and geoboards); and diagrammatic materials such as a number line. Activities in a set are generally meant to be done in sequence, although some activity sets offer you a choice. Most chapters include optional activities that can be done at home or that present particular challenges.

The activities are at an adult level and yet are generally of a type that you can modify for use with children. Your active participation in these hands-on activities is particularly important for several reasons. First, your experiences should convince you that you can do lots of interesting and challenging mathematics by thinking both with your hands and your head. Second, doing the activities will help you gain insight into how mathematics is done at a concrete or manipulative level, much in the same way that children approach such problems. Finally, these experiences should help you plan and use similar activities to help children learn mathematics.

Most of the activities are designed to be done in small groups of two to five students. However, there are also activities to be done individually, as well as some for a whole class to do, with each student contributing a piece of information and participating in the discussion. These experiences should indicate to you how to implement similar activities with different groupings of children. Also, by your working in small groups you should have many opportunities to discuss answers and solutions, raise questions, and share ideas with others in your class. Interacting in this way can help you clarify and strengthen your own understanding as well as suggest to you how children can learn not only from their teacher or textbook but also from each other.

The third section, Discussion Questions and Comments, develops and reinforces mathematical content and methods directly related to the activities. Questions, such as "What mathematics do the activities involve?", "How does this mathematics fit into the elementary school curriculum?", and "How can the activities be used with children?" are discussed.

The fourth section of the text is called Follow-up Sections. It contains information that deals with additional mathematics, learning theory, and methods. Some of the information develops background topics in mathematics and includes practice exercises (often with answers that you can check, if you want). Some sections present material on learning theory and its implications for teaching mathematics. Other sections deal with ways to help children learn mathematics — both specific methods for teaching important topics in the elementary school mathematics curriculum (for example, identifying and using materials to teach a particular topic, such as perimeter or addition of two-digit numbers with exchanging) and general strategies that apply to teaching many topics (for example, planning guided discovery activities, diagnosing difficulties children might have and recommending appropriate instruction to prevent or remedy these difficulties). Also, some general classroom practices are discussed, such as providing children with feedback about their learning or motivating instruction. These strategies and practices can be used in teaching many subjects, not just mathematics. The examples of activities for children, which illustrate the use of these methods and strategies, will probably need to be modified for use with a particular group of children. To help you do this, suggestions are included for adapting and sequencing activities for children at different age and ability levels and in different classroom settings.

The fifth section, Test Your Understanding, helps you review the material in the chapter. The last section, Further Readings and Projects, extends the ideas presented in the chapter. This section can offer you some direction in following up your own particular interests in teaching mathematics.

Interacting with the Book

Throughout the book you will be asked to interact with the material you are reading. Sometimes you may write or draw something to answer a question; you may act out problems with manipulative materials; or you may just reflect about a question that has been posed. Some questions have clear-cut answers and sometimes answers are provided (at the end of the book) so you can check yours if you want. Many of the questions can be answered correctly in different ways and you may want to compare and discuss your answers with other students or in class.

Questions are included for several reasons. They may help you learn better than just by reading, since responding to them requires you to think about the material and to use what you are learning. They enable you to check your own understanding and also reinforce it. They stimulate your thinking and encourage you to raise questions on your own, in particular about using activities to help children learn mathematics.

In some cases, the questions in the book and those you raise, like many of the questions encountered when teaching, may not have simple answers. The willingness to ask these difficult and challenging questions and to search for possible answers, individually and with the help of others, is one characteristic of a good teacher.

CHAPTER 1

ATTRIBUTE MATERIALS AND MATHEMATICAL THINKING

INTRODUCTION

Find the missing faces in the array below. Draw them. Try to describe them in words.

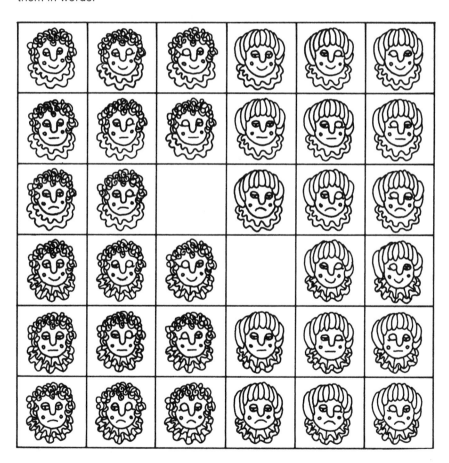

How did you find the missing faces? Perhaps you noticed that the faces have two kinds of hair, curly and straight. Maybe you identified other characteristics or attributes of the faces besides the kinds of hair, such as the shapes of the mouths. What other characteristics do the faces have?

Did you find the faces in a systematic or logical manner? Might young children, such as preschoolers or kindergarten students ages four to five, be able to find the missing faces? (If you can, try this with a child. If the child cannot draw the faces, you might present a selection of drawings of possible faces from which the missing faces can be selected. Ask the child to explain the reasons for his selection.)

Suppose that instead of drawings of faces, these were photographs of 34 different children. Do you think that you could now find and describe the two missing faces? Why?

This chapter concerns two types of materials that you can classify or sort: an organized "attribute set" such as the faces drawn above, and a more random collection of objects such as the faces of real children or a collection of buttons or seashells. Activities with a particular attribute set of colored shapes are designed to give you first-hand experience with its use in a variety of mathematical situations. Doing these Activities will orient you to a way in which children can experience and learn mathematics — that is, learning by doing. These Activities, with appropriate modifications, can be used to help children develop classification skills, acquire and use mathematical concepts and vocabulary, and gain experience with a logical or systematic way of thinking.

Discussion Questions and Comments focus on the mathematics that children can experience by using the attribute set of colored shapes, particularly in free-play situations, and on ways to adapt the activities for children at different age or grade levels (and even in other subject areas).

In the Follow-up Sections examples of other attribute sets and collections of objects are presented along with their uses for teaching several mathematical topics, including classification. Some sections concern how children learn concepts and offer methods for teaching them. Another section presents a brief overview of Piaget's work on the development of intellectual abilities in children, in particular their ability to classify. The final section deals with one area of background mathematics relevant to teaching elementary school mathematics: sets. Basic set concepts are reviewed and the controversy about the role of sets in the elementary school curriculum is discussed.

Note: This chapter is intended to be used with a set of attribute pieces that can be made easily from colored oak tag in four colors (red, blue, green, and yellow), two sizes (small and large), and four shapes (circle, square, triangle, and diamond), but other sets can also be used. (Activity 10 may need to be modified if a different set is used.) For each color, cut each of the pieces shown here. You should have 32 pieces, all different.

ACTIVITIES

Activity 1. Generating the Set

Students can be introduced to the attribute pieces through this activity in which they are challenged to discover the pieces in the set. The teacher can show students a covered box containing the attribute pieces, shake it, and ask, "Can anyone guess what is in here?" After students offer some guesses, the teacher can show one or two pieces and ask, "What are these?" Then after students describe the pieces in their own way, the teacher says, "Now try to tell what other pieces are in the box." As the students suggest appropriate pieces, the teacher brings them out and continues until all of the pieces have been displayed and described.

You might role-play this activity in a group with four to six students. One person is the teacher, and the others are the students.

Activity 2. Play, Play, Play

Play with the pieces. Create something.
What did you create?
What mathematics arose in your play?

Activity 3. Game — What's the Missing Piece?

Place all the pieces on a table for all players to see. One player removes one piece while the others have their eyes closed. Then the others try to guess the missing piece. The winner is the first person to identify the missing piece. The piece is returned and the winner then gets to remove one.

Try the game two different ways: allowing players to arrange the pieces to help them find the missing one, and without allowing players to arrange the pieces to help them find the missing one. Which of these two ways was easier for you? Did you use some strategy or method for arranging the pieces and then finding the missing one? If so, describe it.

Activity 4. Organizing and Sorting Pieces

1. Work with a partner. Arrange the pieces in some organized way. Describe how you organized the pieces.
2. Sort the pieces into exactly four piles. Describe or name the piles.

   ——————— ——————— ——————— ———————

3. *Game — Guess My Rule.* One player sorts the pieces one at a time into piles according to a secret rule while the other player watches and tries to guess the rule. One person has sorted nine pieces so far,

   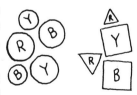

   as shown here. Where will $\boxed{Y}$ be placed?
        Another way to sort the pieces is into two piles using the rule: All large in one pile, and all small in another. When a player thinks he knows the rule, he completes the sorting while the other player checks. Play this game. What was your secret rule?

Activity 5. *"One of these things is not like the others . . ."* *

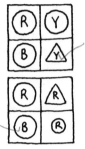

1. Arrange these four pieces. Which piece does not belong?

2. Arrange these four pieces. Which piece does not belong? (List other possible answers.)

Activity 6. Attributes and Values

1. In Activity 4, you might have sorted the pieces by color, or size, or shape. Suppose you sorted them by color. How many piles would you get? _____ How many pieces are in each pile? _____ Fill in the table below. (Depending on your set of pieces, you may find either three or four ways to sort.)

SORT BY	HOW MANY PILES?	HOW MANY IN EACH PILE?
Color	4	4
Size	4	4

2. Size and color are two *attributes* or characteristics of these pieces. Small and large are the *values* of the attribute size. What are the values of the attribute color? How many attributes does each piece have?
3. How many attribute pieces are there altogether in your set? Did you count them one by one? If you used a short-cut method, describe it.
4. There are many kinds of commercial attribute sets. One set has pieces that come in two sizes, four shapes, three colors, and also a fourth attribute, texture — pieces come in rough and smooth. How many pieces are in this set?

* You might recognize this as the song for a game on the television program *Sesame Street.*

Activity 7. Patterns

Fill in the spaces in each pattern below.

A a B b _____ _____ _____ . . .

add added bite _____ _____ caught _____ . . .

Make up some pattern with your attribute pieces. Draw it.
Have your neighbor tell what three pieces will come next.

Activity 8. Trains

1. *One-difference Trains.* A one-difference train of pieces is shown here.
   In this pattern, or train, an arbitrary piece is selected as the first "car"
   — here, a small yellow circle. Then a second car is added where the

   second car differs from the first car by exactly *one* attribute. Here
   the second car, a large yellow circle, differs from the first car by the
   attribute ___Size___. The third car differs from the second by
   the attribute ___Shape___. The train is made longer by adding
   appropriate cars.
   Making a one-difference train can be played as a game. With a
   partner, take turns adding cars to the train. You win if your opponent
   cannot add another car to the train or if your opponent makes a mistake. Players check each other's cars as the game is played.
   a. Play the game with a partner. Draw the first six cars in your one-
      difference train.

   b. Did you use all of the pieces in your train? If not, try to.
   c. Did your train exhibit a pattern? If so, describe it.
2. *Two-difference Trains.* In a two-difference train, each car must differ
   from the preceding car by exactly *two* attributes. Play a two-difference
   train game with a partner.
   a. Did you use all the pieces in your two-difference train?
   b. Is it possible to make a two-difference train with all of the pieces,
      where the small pieces all come before the large pieces?

Activity 9. Differences — A Discovery Activity

1. Take a large red circle and place it to your left. Next to this piece, make a pile of those pieces that differ from the given piece by exactly one attribute. In a second pile, place those pieces that differ from the given piece by exactly two attributes. In a third pile, place those pieces that differ from the given piece by exactly three attributes.

    Try to organize the pieces within these piles in some systematic way. Record in the table how many pieces are in each pile.

2. Select a different original piece and repeat the activity. Compare your results with your neighbor's. What do you notice?

Draw Original Piece	Number of Pieces Differing by One Attribute	Number of Pieces Differing by Two Attributes	Number of Pieces Differing by Three Attributes
Ⓡ			

Activity 10. Loops

1. *Two Loops.* Take two loops of string. Label one RED and the other LARGE. Put all the red pieces inside the loop labeled RED, and all the large pieces inside the loop labeled LARGE. Everything else is LEFTOVER. Leave these pieces outside both of the loops.

    In the space provided, draw a picture to show how you arranged the loops and draw one piece in each section of the loops.

    Refer to your placement of the pieces to complete parts a, b, and c.

a. You probably made the RED and the LARGE loops overlap. The pieces that are in both the RED loop and the LARGE loop are in the *intersection* of these two loops. How many pieces are in the intersection? _____
Find the pieces that are RED but not LARGE. How many are there? _____ How many pieces are LARGE but not RED? _____
How many pieces are in one, or the other, or both loops — that is, RED, or LARGE, or both RED and LARGE? _____ These pieces are in the *union* of the two loops.

b. Suppose that the two loops were labeled RED and NOT SQUARE, as shown here. In what section (a, b, c, or d) would you place the following pieces?
    Small red circle _____
    Small blue circle _____
    Large blue square _____
    Large red square _____

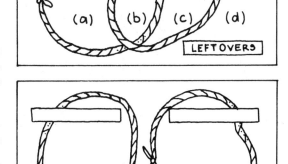

c. In part a, the two loops labeled RED and LARGE overlapped: there were some pieces in their intersection. The loops labeled RED and NOT SQUARE in part b also had pieces in their intersection. Label the two loops in the space provided, so that their intersection contains *no* pieces.
    Can this be done in another way? If so, describe it.

2. *Game — Guess the Labels.* One player thinks of labels for the two loops and places the pieces one at a time in appropriate sections of the loops. The other player tries to figure out what labels belong on the loops. (This game is like Guess My Rule in Activity 4.) You can use labels like NOT RED or NOT SQUARE to make the game more difficult.
    Try this game with your neighbor. Use string loops. Select labels for the two loops. Place some of the pieces in each of the sections of the loops. Then show the arrangement to your neighbor and see if he can guess the labels.
    Then fill in the labels in the diagram and draw one piece that belongs in each section.

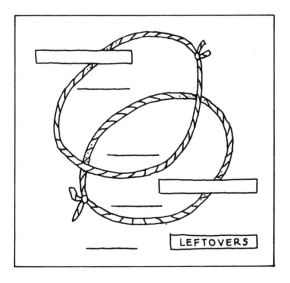

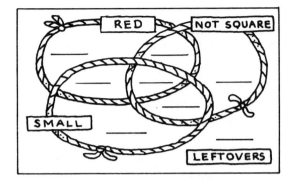

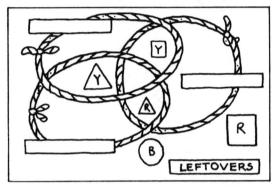

3. *Three Loops.* The two-loop activities above could be done with three loops. Work with a partner or in a small group and arrange the loops as shown here. Put in all of the pieces.

   In the blanks on the loop diagram, write how many pieces belong in each section. Use the information below to check your answers. (This information applies to the attribute set described in the Introduction of this chapter.)

   The RED loop has 8 pieces.

   The intersection of the SMALL loop and the NOT SQUARE loop has 12 pieces.

   The intersection of all three loops has 3 pieces.

   The union of the RED loop and the SMALL loop has 20 pieces.

   There are 3 LEFTOVERS.
4. Guess the labels for the loops in this diagram. ***Note:*** Only some of the pieces have been placed.
5. (Optional) Play Guess the Labels for three loops with a partner.

Activity 11. Difference Arrays (Optional)

1. Arrange the small pieces in the 4 by 4 array on the top of page 9 so that the pieces in *rows* (across) differ by one attribute and the pieces in *columns* (down) differ by two attributes.
2. Try to extend this array so that you use *all* of the pieces.

Activity 12. Squares and Roads (Optional)

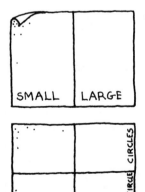

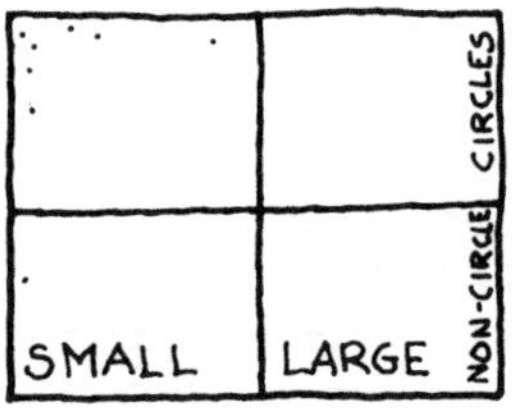

1. Suppose the two loops in Activity 10 were labeled SMALL and LARGE instead of RED and LARGE. Would there be any pieces in their intersection? Would there by any LEFTOVERS?

   Here is another way to represent this situation. Draw a line down the middle of a piece of paper. Label one side SMALL and the other LARGE. How many pieces are on each side? Can you think of another way to sort the pieces into two nonintersecting sets?
2. Perhaps you thought of something like CIRCLES and NOT CIRCLES. We could draw another line across the piece of paper and label the top and bottom, as shown here. Write how many pieces go in each section. (Check: The numbers, in some order, are 4, 4, 12, 12.)

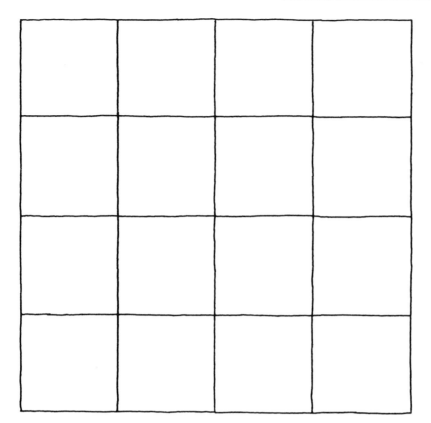

3. How do the four sections of the square diagram correspond to the four sections of this loop diagram?

   How could you make a "square" design that corresponds to a three-loop diagram?

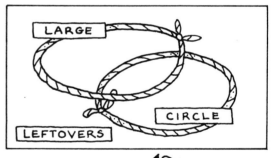

4. Here is still another way to sort the attribute pieces. Imagine that the pieces are going down a road that has many forks, all of which are labeled with road signs. See where some pieces go on this map. How do the four branches of this map correspond to the sections of the square diagram in part 1?

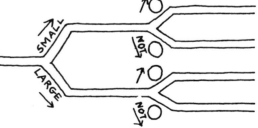

Activity 13. One-difference Puzzles (Optional)

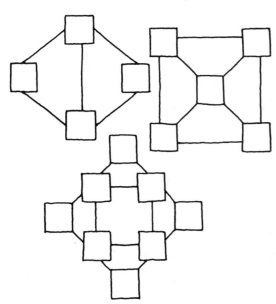

Can you place a piece in each box so that the pieces in the connected boxes differ by exactly one attribute? If so, sketch your solution. (Some may not have a solution.)

Note: These puzzles could be done as two-difference puzzles, or with the connecting lines being labeled 1, 2, or 3 indicating how many differences between boxes.

Activity 14. An Attribute Game (Optional)

Materials: Attribute pieces; die with 1, 2, or 3 dots on each face; three attribute spinners

Directions: Play this game with two to four players. Place all of the attribute pieces on a table for all players to see. In this game you pick up pieces as determined by the outcome of spinning one, two, or three spinners, as described below. The player collecting the most pieces is the winner.

1. Throw a die to determine how many attribute spinners to spin. For example, if you roll a 2, you can choose any two spinners to spin.
2. Spin the spinners you chose and pick up all the pieces determined by your spin. For example, if you roll a 2 and then spin a red on the color spinner and a triangle on the shape spinner, you would pick up all the red triangles remaining on the table.
3. Play until all of the pieces have been taken.

Which would you rather throw on the die — a 1, 2, or 3? Why?

DISCUSSION QUESTIONS AND COMMENTS

Attribute Pieces: What Mathematics Do Children Learn?

Do you think of the activities you did with attribute pieces as "mathematical"? In what way?

The faces in the Introduction to this chapter and the pieces you used in Activities 1–14 are two examples of attribute sets. Commercial attribute sets involve everything from geometric shapes to cartoonlike characters to types of plants and animals. What is the point of these attribute materials? What mathematics are children supposed to learn from them?

Perhaps you thought of the activities as "mathematical" because the attribute pieces are in the shapes of triangles, squares, and circles. Or maybe you saw the pieces as a material for learning about the union and intersection of sets, as in Activity 10 (Loops). However, there is more mathematics in the activities than identifying shapes or understanding the meaning of union and intersection. Doing mathematics involves a variety of processes — from recall of definitions and facts and understanding of concepts to higher order processes, such as organizing and classifying, finding patterns, reasoning logically, formulating and verifying hypotheses, and solving problems. Activities 1–14 were primarily intended to provide you with opportunities to experience these mathematical processes in activities that you can use with children, possibly in a modified form, as will be discussed later in this chapter. For example, giving directions orally to a small group of children, you could have them do the first part of Activity 4 that involves organizing the pieces in different ways. How the children organize the pieces depends on what they understand about the pieces, not on directions from the teacher to organize them in a specific way. Children as young as two or three years old may show ability to organize the pieces by arranging them in lines or stacks (such as by color), sometimes before they are able to name the pieces. Or children may organize the pieces by matching small pieces with corresponding large ones, but not really by sorting the pieces as "large" and "small," as shown here. Older children may invent other ways to organize the pieces, such as by making towers, alternating small and large pieces of a certain shape.

Some of Activities 1–14 involve sorting or classifying. Children can be asked to sort things by one attribute — for example, by shape or color, as in the second part of Activity 4 or in Activity 6. Activity 10, Loops, involves sorting by two, and then three, attributes at the same time. As we shall see later in this chapter, children develop the ability to classify gradually, first by one attribute and then later by two or more attributes at the same time.

Games such as Guess My Rule and Guess the Labels can challenge children to formulate and test a hypothesis about the rule for sorting. Activity 9, Differences — A Discovery Activity, may also be used to create a situation in which children form and test hypotheses. Some children may be able to give a logical explanation, informal of course, for why the same numbers appear in the table, no matter what piece is chosen. Others may try to verify the hypothesis by checking that it holds for a few different pieces.

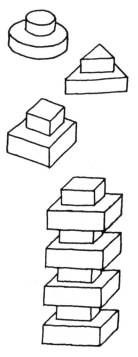

Several of the activities involve finding patterns. For example, in Activity 7, Patterns, you discovered the relationship between successive objects in a sequence. Perhaps you also invented patterns in your free play (Activity 1) or noticed some patterns when making one- and two-difference trains (Activity 8). If you tried some of the optional activities, Activities 11–14, you probably sensed that they involve some kind of problem solving. Perhaps you found that you could use a strategy to solve them.

You, and children also, may enjoy doing these kinds of activities because they make you think or because they challenge you in some way. The activities in this chapter and many in subsequent chapters reflect the point of view that learning mathematics is not only a matter of acquiring computational skills and knowing terminology, but also of developing the ability to think mathematically. Now your challenge as a teacher is to build upon your experiences here and provide children with appropriate activities to develop their thinking skills in mathematics as well as in other subject areas where similar skills are needed.

Why Free Play?

Did you enjoy the free play with the attribute pieces? Did you create something interesting? Did you learn something about the pieces by playing with them?

If you answered yes to these questions, you may sense that there are several reasons why children should have an opportunity to play with the pieces. First, free play allows the children to learn about the characteristics of the pieces by actually handling them. This hands-on experience is particularly important for young children who learn by doing. Second, free play provides a situation in which children can indirectly learn and use the vocabulary of size, shape, and color when sharing pieces with other children or talking about their creations with classmates or the teacher.

Third, while playing with the pieces, children may experience and investigate aspects of mathematics other than those directly involved in the planned activity and thus enrich their mathematical background. For example, a child might discover that shapes can be formed from various pieces. Sketch how a large square can be made from four small squares, a diamond from triangles, and a large triangle from four small triangles.

Children may organize the pieces in free play by making a design or a picture that uses certain kinds of pieces, such as all squares and triangles to make a tower. Children may also make or copy various patterns in their free play. For example, these designs might have been made by two children with one child copying the smaller version from the larger one. To do this task, children must find the smaller version of each piece in the large figure and then match its position exactly. A teacher may find it appropriate to comment on or question a child about the mathematical aspects of his design in order to bring these aspects to the child's attention.

Fourth, free play can be fun. The attribute pieces are attractive to children and may seem to be playthings. Children who do not have sufficient opportunities to play with the pieces and, in a sense, "get the play out of their systems" may find it difficult to join in later activities when it is important to follow instructions and use the pieces appropriately.

Finally, free play gives children a chance to "do their own thing" with the pieces, create whatever interests them, and be unconcerned about "the right way." While free play benefits the children, it also allows the teacher to observe them in the process of working with the pieces and to note their interests that can be incorporated into follow-up or other classroom activities. Also, during free play a teacher can evaluate young children informally in a natural and nonthreatening situation. For example, a teacher might notice that a child is having difficulty copying simple patterns, as shown here. Such a difficulty may simply indicate that the child needs more opportunities to do such copying tasks, or if it continues for an unusual period of time, it could indicate some kind of learning disability, perhaps calling for diagnosis by a specialist.

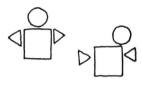

Modifying Activities for Use with Children

Throughout this book you will be asked to consider the use of the activities at the beginning of each chapter with children at varying ability levels and with varying interests, in different classroom settings (such as small group, whole class, individualized), and even in other subject areas. Such use will often require that you modify these activities or invent variations of them. This section focuses on various modifications of activities involving attribute pieces.

Modifications for Different Ability Levels, Ages, and Interests
Do you think that you could use Activity 1 (Generating the Set) with young children of ages four to five? Even if the children know the names of the shapes and the colors, playing the game with all the pieces may be too complex for them. One modification is to use fewer pieces, perhaps just the large pieces or maybe the large red pieces. Another modification is to arrange the pieces in a systematic way as they are generated in the game (see right). This will help children identify other pieces not yet displayed.

Both of these modifications can apply to Activity 3 (What's the Missing Piece?). In addition, a teacher might want to plan a sequence of games, first simple ones and then more complex ones, for those children who may find some games too difficult and become frustrated. Which of the following might be done first? _____ second? _____ third? _____

Most of Activities 1–14 assume that those doing them are already familiar with the pieces and their names. Children not having these prerequisites may first need to do activities such as those below which involve naming of shapes.

Hop Over the Puddle

(To be done by a teacher with a small group of children.)
Goal: Given an attribute piece, the child names the piece. Several attribute pieces are laid on the floor. Pieces are "puddles" on a trail. Children walk

along the trail and hop over the puddles, naming them. If they name it incorrectly, they fall in the puddle.

Making Men

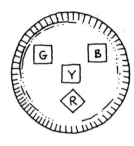

(To be done by a teacher with a small group of children.)
Goal: Given a description of an attribute piece, the child can find pieces of that type and arrange them in a specified pattern. The teacher arranges all of the large squares on a large paper plate. "This is Mr. Square. Can you make Mr. Triangle?" Other questions might include the following: "This is Mr. Red. Can you make Mr. Blue?" or (giving the child a smaller paper plate) "Can you make Mr. Square's little boy?"

A teacher might find it necessary to modify a game to make it more complex and challenging, to meet the needs of more capable children in a class or at a higher grade level. Activities like Difference Arrays (Activity 11), One-difference Puzzles (Activity 13), or those below can be used for this purpose. These activities can be written on activity cards or game boards and placed in a challenge file for individualized use by children.

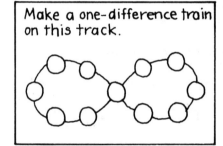

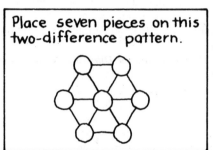

One source of attribute activities is a commercial set of activity cards. However, these sets may contain mostly challenging activities or those with several prerequisites. Some cards are designed to be read aloud by a teacher or by the children themselves, if they have appropriate reading skills. As a result, a teacher may have to select cards from these sets carefully, to present them to children orally, or to rewrite them in simpler language, if they are to be used with lower elementary students or with poor readers.

You may also want to modify the material itself or the format of an activity, in particular for younger children. For example, children might place large cardboard attribute pieces inside large loops on the floor. Or, children who find the idea of being inside a loop (as opposed to inside a container) too abstract might sort objects by placing them in boxes.

Attribute pieces can also be drawn or glued on cards, making a deck that can be used in card games where players should not see each other's attribute pieces. This deck can be used to play a game like "Concentration." All the cards are placed face down. Taking turns, children turn over two cards and take them if they have the same shape. If they do not, the cards are turned back over. You might have other rules for matching — difference only in size or only in color. The game continues until all the cards are taken, and the winner is the child with the most cards. Perhaps you can think of another game using this deck.

Modifications of the attribute pieces might also be suggested by the children's desire to play games with other kinds of materials. Real objects or teacher- or student-made attribute sets can also be used in many attribute activities.[1]

Modifications for Different Class Groupings

Activity 10, Loops, was designed for one person to do, individually or with a partner. However, this activity can be modified and done with a small group or even a whole class.

Loop Races

A first grade teacher divided the group into two teams. Each team races to place attribute pieces (felt cutouts) in their team's loop diagram (each made with two loops of yarn on felt boards). Team members take turns drawing a piece from their team's grab bag and placing it in the loop diagram. The team that finishes first scores five points, and each team receives one point for each correctly placed piece. The loop diagrams are checked by the children and discussed after each race.

Do you think that children would enjoy the race aspect of this game? Why or why not? Would it be a good idea to have the boys race the girls?

One difficulty in playing games, even in small groups, is that some children may not be consistently involved. This difficulty could arise in the game, What's the Missing Piece? However, you can modify this game to increase children's involvement, as described below.

Game for Four Children

Have four children sort attribute pieces by color, with each choosing pieces of a particular color. (A child might say, "I'll be Ms. Blue," and take the blue pieces.) Have the children close their eyes while you remove one piece from each child's set. Then each child tries to guess his own missing piece. (The game can also be played by taking particular shapes.)

Modifications for Other Mathematics Topics and Other Subject Areas

1. Find which one doesn't belong in each game below, and explain why.
   Note: There may be more than one possible answer.

Mathematics

5+1=	3+3=		33	222
7−1=	2+5=		45	66

Science

dog	cat
fish	horse

Geography

New York	Rhode Island
Chicago	San Francisco

2. Complete the following language arts games that have been derived from some games using attribute pieces.

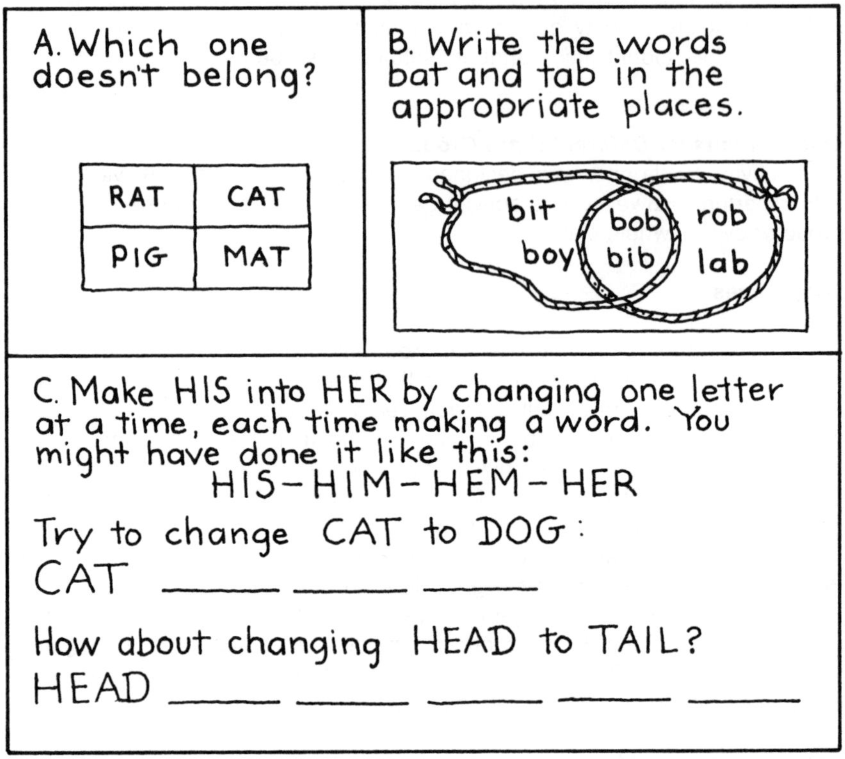

A. Which one doesn't belong?

RAT	CAT
PIG	MAT

B. Write the words bat and tab in the appropriate places.

bit   bob   rob
boy   bib   lab

C. Make HIS into HER by changing one letter at a time, each time making a word. You might have done it like this:

HIS — HIM — HEM — HER

Try to change CAT to DOG:

CAT ____ ____ ____

How about changing HEAD to TAIL?

HEAD ____ ____ ____ ____ ____

3. These various games can be used to motivate the opening of or follow-up to a lesson. These games can be incorporated into homework assignments also. Make up one game for a nonmathematical subject area.

Patterns

Pattern problems such as those below are included in some mathematics materials for kindergarten children. Circle the piece that comes next in each pattern.

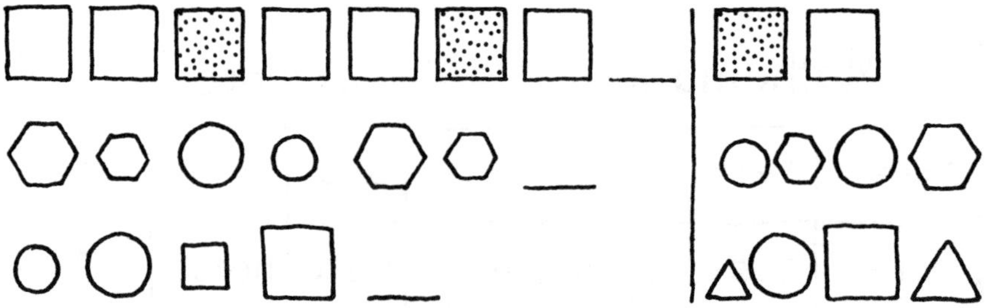

Kindergarten children who recognize and can name the shapes may be unable to solve problems like the last one. One difficulty might be that the problem does not provide enough information to allow the child to see the pattern small, large, . . . One remedy is to give more information, as in the first two problems. A second difficulty might be that the child does not perceive the shapes as a sequence from left to right, and hence might be unable to ask himself, "What comes next?" One remedy for this difficulty might be as follows:

> Cover the large circle and the two squares with your hand and ask, "What shape is this?" Uncover the next shape and ask, "Now what shape is this?" Uncover the next piece and ask, "What's this? Can you guess what's next?" Show the next one. "Now what might the next piece be like . . . which one of these could it be?"

Why is the uncovering of the pieces one at a time and the related questioning critical in this remedy?

This difficulty might have been prevented if the child had solved similar problems with real objects (for example, attribute pieces in a pattern as in Activity 7, Patterns) before doing the more abstract workbook patterns. The concrete activity provides the child with mental imagery needed to do the semiconcrete or picture patterns where the placement or sequencing of objects must be done in the child's mind rather than with real objects.

Loops, Sorting, and Concept Learning

Do you think that the attribute pieces could be used to teach children about squares? Read the following description of a simplified one-loop activity to be done with a kindergarten or first grade child.

> The teacher takes the attribute pieces one by one from their container and sorts them in front of the child, putting squares in a loop (or box) and the other shapes outside. The teacher says, "This is a square," as the square is placed in the loop and "This isn't a square," as it is placed outside. After sorting several pieces, the teacher says, "Now, please find the other squares and put them in this loop."

While this sorting activity would help the child learn the term *square* and discriminate square pieces (large and small) from the other pieces, it would not really help this child gain much understanding of what makes a shape a square. The child may think of a square as a piece that looks like ☐. Using this notion of square, the child might correctly sort the attribute pieces but might incorrectly identify shapes A and C below as squares and not identify B as a square. Of course, it is not reasonable to expect a child of this age to

develop a full understanding of what a square is. However, upper elementary children who are capable of developing this understanding often make these same kinds of errors in identifying squares.

Attribute pieces were not designed to teach the concept of square or triangle. However, a sorting game with appropriate materials, like the one below, could help older children learn the concept of a square. Notice how the shapes used and the special kind of sorting format below focus the child's attention on the characteristics that define a square.

Materials: Yarn or string to be used as dividers; a set of four-sided shapes (made from cardboard) that come in various sizes and have the following characteristics:

sides — all sides of equal length
           not all sides of equal length
angles — all angles of equal size
            not all angles of equal size

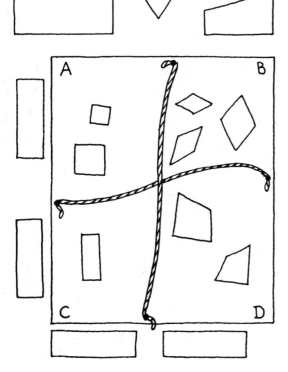

Directions: The teacher sorts the pieces into four piles as shown here. Children try to guess where the pieces go and to find a rule for the sorting.

    1. In which section would you place each of these shapes?

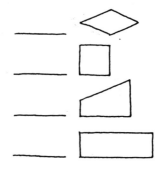

2. The rule for placing shapes in the top row is "All the sides are of equal length." Labels (to the left of the diagram) for the top and bottom rows could be as follows: (top row) ALL _____ EQUAL; (bottom row) NOT ALL _____ EQUAL. Fill in all four labels.

3. There are different ways to label the left-hand column. Can you think of a way different from the one you wrote above? What are the shapes in this column called? _____ (Do you think of all squares as rectangles?) What are the shapes in section B called?

Square is a concept that can be built from other concepts — a square is a shape that has four sides; all sides are of equal length; all angles are of equal size. Shapes that have these three characteristics are squares. Do you see why the three characteristics are essential? *Square* is an example of a *conjunctive* or *and* concept — a concept that is determined by two or more characteristics which must all apply at the same time. Small red triangles can be thought of as the conjunction of three concepts: small, red, and triangle. As we shall see later in this chapter, when Piaget's research into children's thinking is discussed, children acquire the ability to consider two and then more characteristics of a situation at the same time gradually over a period of years.

Two-loop activities can give children experience with *conjunctive* or *and* concepts. For example, informal loop activities such as those below can arise in classroom situations and can be used to help children develop their ability to classify by two attributes. Here children might fasten name tags in loops on a bulletin board display or write their names in loops drawn on a chalkboard, where the loops are used to describe *and* situations involving the children.

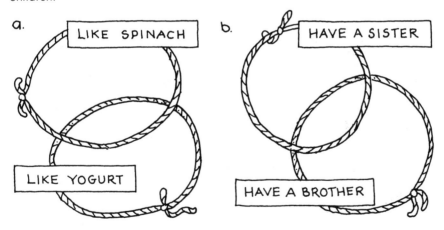

a. LIKE SPINACH / LIKE YOGURT

b. HAVE A SISTER / HAVE A BROTHER

A discussion of who goes in both loops provides experiences with the language of *conjunctive* concepts and develops the children's ability to work with *and* situations. Loops such as (c) can be used to provide a teacher with information about children that day. A teacher could also use this to take attendance. Loops such as (d) can lead to the development of concepts in other subjects — for example, What animals live on land and in the water?

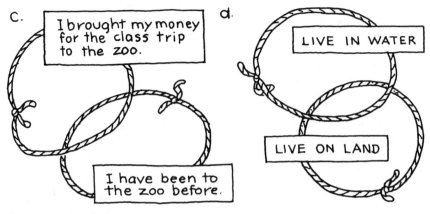

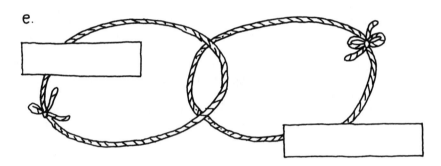

Add your own labels.

FOLLOW-UP SECTIONS

Other Attribute Sets and Their Uses

Attribute sets such as those illustrated here can be designed to help children learn specific mathematical concepts or reinforce previously learned concepts. Of course they may also be used in attribute activities similar to Activities 1–14.

Look at the pictures of some pieces from each set, fill in the blanks under the pictures, and then use the available information to determine how many pieces are in each set.

Children can sort the Dot Cards by number of shapes to practice recognition of one to three objects. If shapes are textured (perhaps felt shapes glued on cardboard), children can sort them by touch with their eyes closed or blindfolded. Children can also play card games with these Dot Cards.

A set like People Pieces was developed by the Elementary Science Study as part of its materials for classification and is available commercially.[2] A teacher can have children describe the People Pieces, identify their attributes and values, and organize them in different ways. Children might be

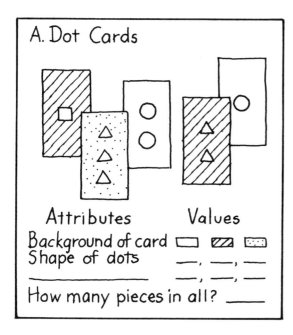

A. Dot Cards

Attributes   Values

Background of card ▭ ▨ ▱

Shape of dots ___, ___, ___

_____ ___, ___, ___

How many pieces in all? _____

B. People Pieces

Attributes   Values
Sex of person   Male, Female
Age of person   Child, Adult

_____ ___, ___

How many pieces in all? _____

asked: "How can you pair People Pieces in a natural way?" Are the People Pieces easier or more difficult to describe than the colored shapes you used in the activities? Why? Can you imagine making one-difference lines with the People Pieces?

Some pieces are missing from this attribute set. Can you describe them? Did you have any trouble finding a way to name the attributes and values in this set? Children may be able to sort these pieces in different ways even though they cannot name the shapes and describe their properties. Developing precise language and terminology is a desirable goal of many mathematics activities; however, lack of vocabulary or verbal skills may not indicate a lack of understanding. When given a chance to *show* rather than *tell*, children may demonstrate unexpected knowledge. As a teacher, you may find that attribute materials provide a vehicle for nonverbal communication, especially with children who have language difficulties.

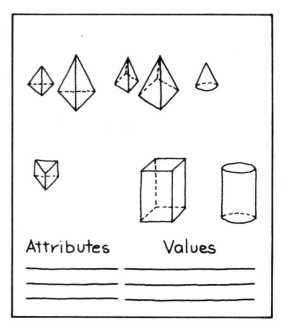

Attributes   Values
_____ _____
_____ _____
_____ _____

A first grade teacher might have a small group of children sort these attribute pieces to help build up their intuitive understanding for types of solids. These children do not need to know the names for the solids, but will generally be able to sort them and describe the sorting in some way (such as "These pointed ones go here."). A sixth grade teacher might use the pieces in a different way, by playing Generating the Set with the solids as an introduction to a chapter on solids. This activity gives children an opportunity to describe the solids in their own words. Then the teacher could have the children try to name the shapes they know (perhaps cone, pyramid) and also come up with appropriate names for the other shapes (for example, triangular pyramid, square prism).

Buttons and Other Materials

Preschool and kindergarten teachers often have collections of things for children to sort, such as crayons, paint brushes, eating utensils, or other real world objects such as buttons or seashells. Many mathematical experiences, including classification, can arise naturally from children's use of these materials.

Describe some ways you could sort this collection of buttons.

Is it easier to sort these buttons than the attribute pieces? Why or why not?

Buttons can be used for some of the same activities as attribute pieces, (for example, sorting) but not for others (for example, Generating the Set or What's the Missing Piece?, unless you select your collection of buttons very carefully). This is because the attribute pieces have exactly one piece for every possible combination of values of the attributes. This is why it is possible to tell just how many pieces there are in the set if you know how many values each attribute has. However, most collections of buttons have some duplications and many gaps. For example, how do you know that you will have a large red button with four holes?

Buttons do have some advantage over the attribute pieces as a material for sorting. For one thing, it doesn't matter if one or two buttons are lost from time to time because the collection can always be supplemented by whatever buttons show up. Also, with the wide variety of buttons in most old button collections, children can have much more choice about how to sort, such as by color, number of holes, shape, texture, material (like metal, wood, or plastic), or decoration. This can be more fun but also more difficult. Collections of buttons as well as toys, plastic eating utensils, or bottle caps may be more familiar to some children than the geometric attribute shapes. Sorting them may come closer to the type of real-world sorting we do. Everyone in the class can contribute to these collections and be involved with them in a personal way.

In addition to being useful for classifying, buttons can provide mathematical experiences that involve processes, such as matching, comparing, and ordering, all of which underlie the concept of number. Children often use these processes in everyday classroom situations, such as lining up for lunch in pairs, passing out milk, seeing who is taller, or seeing who has the shorter pencil. Appropriate comments or questions from a teacher can often direct children's attention toward mathematical aspects of these situations. However, children also need structured tasks to develop these processes. Below six activity cards are shown that a child could do with a collection of buttons. A teacher could read the directions to the child who would place buttons on the card. Next to the activity cards are given descriptions of the mathematical processes they involve and examples of everyday experiences involving these processes. Write another everyday situation for each.

Matching or *one-to-one correspondence:* the pairing of objects in one set (here empty buttonholes) with objects in another set (here buttons).
Everyday experiences: arranging cups on saucers; giving each child one cookie.

Many-to-one correspondence: the association of some fixed number of objects in one set (here two buttons) to things in another set (here toy animals).
Everyday experiences: giving each child three carrot sticks for a snack; passing out a fork, spoon, and knife to each child.

Comparison: the comparison of some measurement of two objects (here width of buttons and width of buttonholes).
Everyday experiences: which child on a seesaw is heavier; who is taller; who has the longer hair.

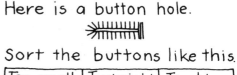

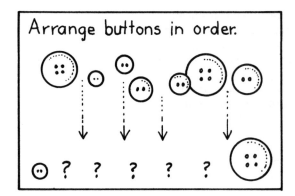

Seriation or *ordering:* the arrangement of a set of three or more objects in order by some measurement (here the diameter of buttons). Seriation tasks vary in difficulty, depending on how many objects are to be ordered.
Everyday experiences: stacking up a nested set of kitchen bowls; arranging members of a family in order of height.

Patterning: the perception of some sort of regularity of objects and their placement, and copying or extending this regularity.
Everyday experiences: setting a table according to a certain plan; decorating a cake or a picture frame.

(**Note:** There are three types of patterning activities indicated: copying a complete pattern, such as the face; seeing a repeating pattern and identifying what comes next; and making up a new pattern.)

In the activity cards above, there was some overlap of mathematical processes involved. For example, when putting "eyes" on the animals (Many-to-one correspondence), the child may use some patterning also such as deciding where eyes usually belong. Or, when finding buttons for the jacket (Matching), the child will probably sort or classify the buttons to get some that go together. In making the face with buttons (Patterning), a child may make the mouth by seriating buttons or perhaps sorting buttons to get a red mouth, and comparing buttons to get the same size eyes. These processes seldom occur in isolation.

1. Which of the processes above could children experience in a natural way by using attribute pieces?

2. Which of the activity cards suggest uses of buttons that would be real to children? Which do you think kindergarten children would enjoy the most? the least? Why?

3. One material that is always available in a classroom is the children themselves. Which of these mathematical concepts could you develop using this resource?

Many materials besides buttons have the same sort of mathematical potential. If you live near the seaside, you may be able to collect a large variety of shells. Below are described some activities that children might do with such a collection. Which activity (if any) involves one-to-one correspondence? _____ many-to-one correspondence? _____ comparison? _____ seriation? _____ patterning? _____ classification?

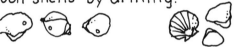

a. Children notice that some shells have small holes in them as if they had been drilled into. They investigate how the holes were made and find that a type of snail kills such shells by drilling.

b. Children notice that some shells such as mussels come with two attached pieces; however they often get broken apart. Children try to put the pairs back together again.

c. Children use shells they have collected to decorate boxes or picture frames.

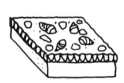

d. Children learn that as the animals grow, so do their shells. They find a collection of shells all of one type and arrange them to show stages in the animal's growth.

Can you think of other easily available natural materials that could be used in the same ways as the seashells?

e. Some children start their own collections and decide how to keep them in display boxes (shoeboxes with partitions).

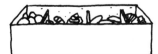

Concept Learning and Creature Cards

run	desk
hit	after
think	green
catch	animal
dream	city
jump	at

This section deals with a general method for helping children learn concepts in mathematics as well as in other subject areas. This method encourages a child to make observations, share them with others, and then formulate his own definition, generalization, or rule. To see an example of this method, examine the list of words shown and then decide which of these words belong in the left-hand column: kick, inside, see, cat, read, beautiful.

This list of words might be written on the board by an upper elementary grade teacher as part of a language arts lesson intended to help children develop the notion of verb. The teacher might write the words in columns for Guess My Rule (Activity 4), where the *objects* sorted into *piles* are words familiar to the children. The teacher could begin the game by telling students that they are to guess why some words are written in the left-hand column and others in the right. After saying and writing a few words (for example, run, hit, desk, think, after), the teacher might just say a word, for example, *catch,* and then ask the class, "Where should I write it?" After additional examples, once most of the children seem to be sorting the words correctly, the teacher can ask them to explain how the sorting was done. Then the term *verb* may be introduced and children may add a few more words to each column.

In using this method, the teacher supplies examples and nonexamples or *positive* and *negative instances* of the concept *verb* and encourages each child to identify characteristics that distinguish positive instances from negative ones. This method could be presented in another format that depends very little on the participation of the teacher — namely, by specially designed materials such as the creature cards. Try cards 1 and 2.

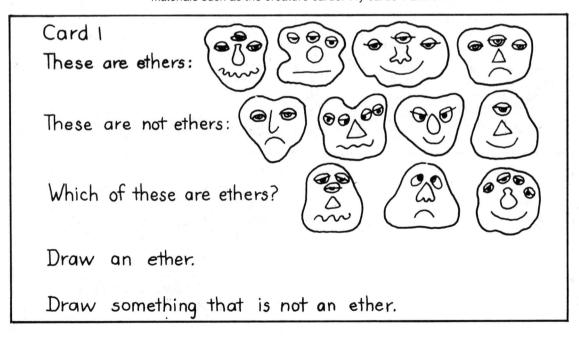

Card 1

These are ethers:

These are not ethers:

Which of these are ethers?

Draw an ether.

Draw something that is not an ether.

Card 2

These are nopes:

These are not nopes:

Which of these are nopes?

Draw a shape that is a nope and one that is not a nope.

What is a nope?

Card 1 may appear to be simply an enjoyable nonsense type of activity. However, it can provide children with practice of recognition of sets with one, two, and three objects. After children have drawn "ethers" (the funnier the better), they could go on to make other types of creatures — maybe "enos," "wots," or "rufos."

Card 2 deals with the mathematical concept "open curve." This concept could be introduced to a child by the card above, or it could be introduced to a whole class through a "positive and negative instance" activity similar to the language arts lesson.

Cards 1 and 2 resemble the Creature Cards that were designed not to teach concepts but rather to help children develop concept learning skills. The cards give practice in identifying characteristics related to a concept and in formulating verbally, pictorially, or in writing, descriptions and definitions of the concept.

The teacher-directed language arts lesson and the creature cards illustrate the positive and negative instance method for teaching concepts. Use of this method is supported by research on how concepts are learned, as described in *A Study of Thinking* by Bruner, Goodnow, and Austin.[3] Their research on concept learning involved various tasks like Guess My Rule done with an attribute set similar to the Dot Cards shown on page 21. Bruner and his colleagues characterized concept attainment as a decision-making process by which the learner formulates, checks and then reformulates hypotheses about the "critical characteristics" that define a concept. When you do a creature card or play a game like Guess My Rule, you are practicing this sort of decision-making process.

The inclusion of both positive and negative instances is an essential feature of this method, helping the child identify and then test characteristics

related to the concept. Above only positive instances of a "nyet" are given. Can you describe a "nyet" just from these examples? Below are some negative instances of a "nyet." Examine them and then try to describe a "nyet."

This activity with "nyets" should convince you that the positive and negative instance method is more effective for developing a concept than a method that uses only positive instances.[4] Another name for a "nyet" is convex set, and the negative instances are nonconvex sets.

The positive and negative instance method can be used to introduce concepts to children or to provide practice of previously learned concepts in an interesting and challenging way. Since the method encourages children to express their own definitions, it is particularly useful for introducing a concept to children before they encounter it formally, as written in their textbook. For example, a teacher might display a giant version of card 2 on a bulletin board a week before the class formally learns about that concept. Or, a teacher could sort positive and negative instances of open curves displayed by an overhead projector at the beginning of a lesson on types of curves.

Many concepts, both mathematical and nonmathematical, that are included in the elementary school curriculum can be introduced and reviewed by this method. Some of these concepts are given below. Add some of your own.

Mathematics — closed curve; right triangle; parallelogram; odd or even number; polygon; isosceles triangle; obtuse triangle; convex

Other
subject
areas
— noun; regular and irregular verbs; singular and plural; silent "e"; living and nonliving; liquid

Make up a creature card and try it out on your neighbor. Was your neighbor able to identify and describe your creature? If not, why not?

Piaget: A Perspective on the Intellectual Development of Children

To function in the everyday world, each of us must somehow make sense out of a tremendous variety of stimuli — persons, events, and objects around us. If it were not for the ability to categorize or classify, we would be over-

Creature Card

These are _____:

These are not _____:

Which of these are _____? a.   b.   c.

Draw a _____:

What is a _____?

whelmed by the complexity of our environment. How do we develop this ability to classify? Do children classify in the same way as adults? These two questions are related to the general question of how our intellectual abilities develop, to which the child psychologist Jean Piaget devoted over fifty years of research. Both the results of Piaget's research and his methods for observing children are interesting and important to teachers. This section presents a brief discussion of some aspects of Piaget's theory of intellectual development — first the development of the ability to classify, and then the stages of intellectual development in general. In later chapters, other aspects of Piaget's work will be related to children's learning of various mathematical topics (for example, number, measurement) in the elementary school curriculum.

This book reflects the point of view that teachers can become more effective if they are able to translate principles of learning theory into practice to help children learn. In this book, the treatment of learning theory — such as that of Piaget — is necessarily brief and limited in scope. You are encouraged to refer to the Bibliography* in order to learn more about learning theory and its implications for teaching.

Some Classification Tasks

Piaget investigated children's ability to classify by presenting them with various classification tasks and observing what they did and said. In some of these tasks, children worked with a set of shapes similar to those in the attribute set partially drawn on page 30.

* See references to Piaget in the Bibliography, pp. 577–584.

1. Fill in the table to indicate how you could sort the pieces in different ways.

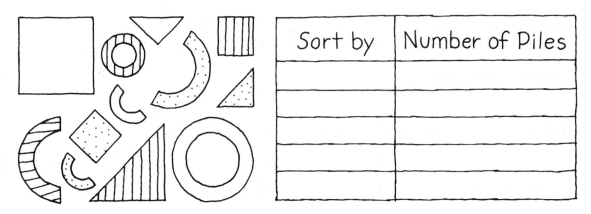

2. Suppose that these pieces came in four shapes (ring, half-ring, square, triangle), three shades, and two sizes (large, small). How many pieces would the attribute set have? _____ How many triangles? _____ squares? _____ straight-sided pieces? _____ curved pieces? _____

3. Suppose the pieces had been sorted into two piles or classes (straight-sided and curved) and that each of these two classes then had been sub-divided into two subclasses, as shown here. The diagram also describes this sorting of the pieces into classes and then into subclasses.

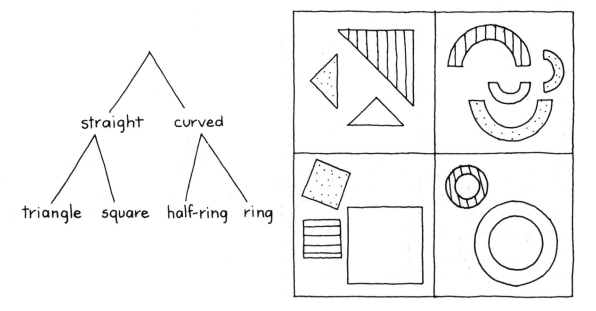

The following two questions concern relations between the classes and sub-classes of the whole set described above:

Are there the same number of triangles as straight-sided pieces?

Are there the same number of triangles as squares?

4. Do you think that first graders could describe ways to sort the pieces as you did in the table in part 1 just by looking at the shapes drawn on the page?

Actually, most first graders would be able to sort the pieces in different ways, if they used real pieces that they could sort physically. However, many children in grades 2–4, about seven to ten years old, would have difficulty answering the questions relating classes and subclasses, even if they had sorted the pieces as shown in the diagram. These children might say that there are as many triangles as straight-sided pieces.

The Development of Classification

Children's performance on various classification tasks indicated to Piaget that a child's ability to classify develops gradually, as the child grows older, and in a certain ordered way. However, there can be considerable variation in the rates at which these abilities develop in different children.[5]

When children about the ages of two to five are given objects and asked to "put together things that are alike" or "put them so that they are all the same," they use several methods for grouping the objects, but do not really form classes using all of the objects. One method is to group some objects that are similar and then include some that are not similar, as shown here. Another method is to organize the pieces by constructing a form or picture like a tower or a face. However, the requirements of the picture, not the characteristics of the objects, determine the arrangement of the pieces here. These children arrange objects unsystematically, with no over-all plan related to the characteristics of the objects.

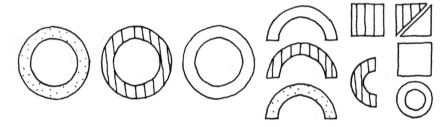

Older children about the ages of five to seven develop the ability to sort objects into classes (straight-sided and curved) and even into subclasses (triangle and square within straight-sided). However, these children do not understand aspects of relations between classes and subclasses (referred to as "class inclusion" relations). For example, a child might say that there are as many squares as straight-sided pieces. Here the child is comparing the subclass "squares" with the subclass "triangles" rather than with the whole class "straight-sided." This incorrect conclusion arises because the child focuses on the subclass "square" and cannot at the same time consider the whole class.

Children about the ages of seven to eleven are eventually able to construct classes and subclasses and also understand the relations between classes and subclasses. However, Piaget found that their classification is "concrete" — that is, they classify and understand class inclusion relations for objects that they can see and manipulate, but cannot do this when classes are described to them verbally. Only later do they develop the ability to classify formally or abstractly, as you did when you answered the questions above about sorting and class inclusion relations.

Piaget found that other kinds of abilities also develop gradually and in a certain sequence, such as the abilities to form one-to-one correspondences between two sets of objects, to arrange objects in some order (for example, from shortest to tallest), and to duplicate a spatial arrangement of objects. As discussed in the next section, Piaget characterizes intellectual development in general as occurring gradually in ordered, age-related stages.

Stages of Intellectual Development

Piaget's research on intellectual development has been influenced by his many early interests — biology, epistemology (a branch of philosophy that concerns questions, such as "What is knowledge?" and "How is knowledge acquired?"), psychology, and psychoanalysis — and by his work on intelligence testing. After receiving a doctorate in zoology at the age of 21 and then studying psychology and psychoanalysis for two years, Piaget worked on the development of French standardized intelligence tests. While administering these tests individually to children, Piaget noticed that various kinds of incorrect answers were given by children at different ages, leading him to revise his notion of intelligence in terms of the kinds of thinking used by children at different ages. This experience and subsequent work with abnormal children who had difficulties expressing themselves verbally suggested to him that researchers should study a child's thinking by carefully observing what the child does and says when faced with certain tasks. Throughout his research on intellectual development, Piaget used and refined this method, which has also been employed by those who replicated his interview tasks with children.

One major conclusion of Piagetian research is that there are fundamental differences between the mental abilities of children and adults. As discussed below, children of different ages also differ in their abilities and ways in which they view the world and explain it to themselves.

Piaget identifies four basic stages or periods of intellectual development that are related to the age levels of children.[6] Although these stages and substages within them are not reached at the same time by all children, Piaget maintains that they are attained in an invariant sequence.

Sensory-motor period: birth to about 2 years
Preoperational period: about 2 to about 7 years
Concrete operational period: about 7 to 11 years
Formal operational period: about 11 years on to adulthood

Sensory-Motor Period. During the sensory-motor period, an infant interacts with his environment, initially in an unorganized manner and then gradually with some systemization. The infant quickly learns to recognize various features of his environment (such as the sound of mother's voice) and to modify his behavior according to the demands of his surroundings. By the time the infant is about 12 to 18 months old, he attempts to find new ways to deal with a problem — for example, pulling a rug to bring an object within reach. Toward the end of this period (about 18 to 24 months), the infant begins to think about a problem and develop solutions on a mental rather than physical level. The child begins to form mental images — for example, imagining the action of an adult whom the child can now imitate without the adult being present. This development is gradual, and throughout it the infant is active — he seeks contact with his environment and responds to the contact by interpreting it in terms of his previous experiences.

Preoperational Period. During the beginning of this period, from the ages of about two to four, children develop their ability to represent or symbolize things that they have physically experienced, using objects, pictures, and words. Children also exhibit first signs of reasoning, sometimes drawing conclusions from what has occurred in the past. For example, seeing his mother begin to boil water, a child may conclude, "My mother is making coffee." This reasoning from one particular situation to another like it is typically based on the child's past experience.

During the preoperational period, children also begin to develop intuitive thinking that is based on their perception: the interpretation they attach to their physical experiences of touching, moving, feeling, seeing, and hearing. Often a child's perception of something will be quite different from an adult's.

Preoperational children use their perceptions to make judgments about number, size, or shape. However, their perceptions can fool them and lead them to make incorrect judgments. For example, suppose an interviewer asks a child to place as many black balls on a table as white balls placed by the interviewer. A child might line up nine black balls as shown here. Here the

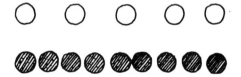

child focuses or *centers* on one aspect (length) of the arrangement of balls and ignores another (the number of balls). This reflects the preoperational child's general inability to consider two or more characteristics of a situation at the same time. In the previous section, we saw how this inability affects children's work with class inclusion relations.

1. Which path of toothpicks might a preoperational child think is longer? Why?

2. Which arrangement of tiles might a preoperational child interpret as covering more area?

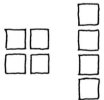

These tasks involving balls, toothpicks, and tiles concern the child's ability to *conserve* number, length, and area, respectively. Each of these tasks tests the child's ability to recognize that some property (such as number, length, or area) remains the same when objects are rearranged or transformed.

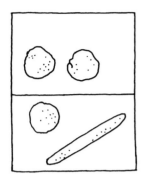

Compare the responses of two children to the following Piagetian task. In each case, an interviewer proceeds using the following format: First, show the child two balls of clay (as shown in the top diagram) and ask Question 1: "Is there more clay in one piece than in the other, or is there about the same amount of clay in each?" Second, transform one ball into a sausage by rolling it on the table (with the child watching), and then ask Question 2: "Is there more clay in one piece than in the other, or is there about the same amount in each?"

	Child A	Child B
Question 1.	About the same.	About the same.
Question 2.	More in this one (pointing to the sausage).	Still the same. This one is longer but it's thin. It can be rolled back into a ball too.

Child A cannot conserve quantity, but child B can because he is able to focus on two characteristics of the clay at the same time — length and thickness. Child A centers on just _____. Child B is able to reverse mentally the action of rolling the clay into a sausage. Child A cannot. This general inability to reverse an action mentally is another characteristic of the preoperational child.

Concrete Operational Period. During the concrete operational period, from the ages of about seven to eleven, children acquire the ability to focus on several aspects of a situation simultaneously, and to reverse an action mentally. The child begins to think logically, basing his judgments on reason, not simply on perception as does the preoperational child. For example, he may reroll the clay sausage into a ball or say that this can be done to explain why the amount of clay in both pieces is about the same. Or, the child may explain class inclusion relations by referring to the objects that he sorted into classes and subclasses. However, the child still is not able to do this when the objects are not present. Thus his thinking is still limited in a sense because it is concrete. But during this concrete operational period the child begins to depend less and less on manipulating objects as a way of knowing.

Formal Operational Period. Children in the formal operational period are able to think abstractly without reference to actual objects or actions in the real world. They can form concepts on an abstract level and solve problems mentally. The formal operational child can imagine that many things might occur and that several interpretations of a situation are possible. Thus, before solving a problem, he is able to analyze it and try to develop hypotheses about what would happen if he did different things. He becomes "capable of reasoning not only on the basis of objects, but also on the basis of hypotheses." [7] Now the child's thinking resembles that of an adult.

Some Implications for Teaching Mathematics

Although Piaget formulated a theory for the intellectual development of children, he did not derive from it guidelines for helping children learn. However, many educators have interpreted his work and have drawn implications from it for teaching children, especially at the early childhood level.

Probably the most important implication of Piaget's work for teaching mathematics at the elementary school level (grades K–6) is that children, who for the most part are in the preoperational and concrete operational stages, should be given ample opportunity to learn mathematics by doing — that is, by manipulating real objects. These hands-on experiences help a child acquire mental imagery needed to build up an understanding of mathematical concepts and to work with them later on an abstract level.

The importance of having children engage in mathematics *actively* — that is, by manipulating objects rather than just watching and listening — is stressed by many educators, in particular Z. P. Dienes and Jerome Bruner. As we shall see in later chapters, Dienes and Bruner recommend strategies (consistent with Piaget's work) for teaching mathematics to children. Basically these recommendations direct the teacher to gear instruction to the child's stage of intellectual development. Children at different stages have different ways of looking at the world, explaining it to themselves, and learning from what they experience. In order to gain insight into how a child thinks and what interests him, a teacher can follow Piaget's example and carefully observe and listen to that child. Teaching should begin with consideration of what a child knows, how he interprets the world, and how he builds on this experience and knowledge to learn new things.

Sets

Set Concepts in the Elementary School Mathematics Curriculum

The topic "sets" was probably ranked as number one in importance among the new topics incorporated into the "new math" elementary and secondary school mathematics programs developed in the 1950s and 1960s. Today mathematics programs place much less emphasis on set concepts than did the "new math" programs. The set concepts listed below are commonly included in upper elementary mathematics texts, and sometimes treated informally in grades K–3. Set concepts are also found in teachers' guides as background mathematics. In fact, the following was taken from a teachers' guide for a first grade text!

> set, one-to-one correspondence, cardinality,
> empty set, subset, union, intersection.

While the text did not intend that the concepts and terminology be formally presented to first graders, it did expect that the spirit of the set concepts be presented. For example, by classifying or sorting objects, children learn about the concept of "set" — a collection of objects. The text includes problems asking children to "find how many are in a set," "match objects in two sets by drawing lines between them," and "tell which set has more." By combining objects in two sets, children experience the union of two sets, which the text links to addition of whole numbers. In order to present set concepts at an appropriate level to children, a teacher must first understand the concepts themselves and their relationship to other mathematics topics and, second, be able to design activities for informal teaching of the set topics.

Mathematics texts for grades 4–8 generally include formal material on set concepts and their application (as a language) to other topics, such as common multiples and divisors, solution sets, and geometry. There exists much controversy about the formal teaching of set concepts, especially at the elementary school level. Critics of some current mathematics programs propose to do away with sets completely.[8] Others criticize current texts for their wordy and abstract formalizations of set concepts. Some feel that the problem is not so much a matter of the content, but rather one of the method for presenting it to children. For example, students may have difficulty understanding the formal definition for the intersection of two sets if a teacher just writes the definition on the board, gives a few examples, and then assigns students exercises in the text. These students may have no difficulty with the definition and its use if more appropriate methods (as described below) are used to enable students to build up their own definition of intersection.

While the controversy will go on, there is general consensus about the treatment of sets in the elementary school curriculum. First, symbolism such as $A \cap B = \{x : x \in A \text{ and } x \in B\}$ is considered unnecessary and undesirable at the elementary school level. Second, less formal use of sets and set notation has a place in the curriculum, especially if set language is appropriately and consistently used by pupils in connection with topics such as solution sets of equations ($\square + 2 = 6$, $3 \times \square = 12$) and inequalities ($\square + 3 < 8$).

Developing Set Concepts

The following pages are designed to help you build up (or possibly review) your background in set concepts and terminology. Subsequent chapters will show in more depth how these set concepts relate to other topics in the elementary school mathematics curriculum.

You will work with three different models for sets: listing, Venn diagrams, and regions. Examples of how each model can be used to illustrate three set concepts (union, intersection, relative complement) are given. This illustrates a "guess-my-rule" method of teaching — that is, providing several examples of a concept and having the student formulate his own definition before being given one. You can use this approach to develop various set concepts with upper elementary children, although they will undoubtedly need several examples and probably should work with only one model at a time.

First study the examples, then complete the related exercises, and finally write your own definitions for union, intersection, and relative complement. Check your definitions against corresponding ones given on page 39. Definitions need not be worded in just the same way; however, they should have the same meaning. Test your understanding of these definitions by doing the exercises on page 39 and checking your answers against those at the back of the book.

TYPES OF MODELS	INTERSECTION	UNION	RELATIVE COMPLEMENT
↓	These diagrams all show the intersection of sets A and B, written as $A \cap B$	These diagrams all show the union of sets A and B, written as $A \cup B$	These diagrams all show the relative complement of B in A, written as A/B
1. Listing a Set A set can be described by listing its elements or the things that belong to it, in brackets. (Note the special type of brackets.) $A = \{ \bigcirc, \square, \triangle, \diamondsuit \}$ $B = \{ \bigcirc, \bullet, \square, \blacksquare \}$	↓ $A \cap B =$ $\{ \bigcirc \square \}$	↓ $A \cup B =$ $\{ \bigcirc \square \triangle \diamondsuit$ $\bullet \blacksquare \}$	↓ $A/B =$ $\{ \triangle \diamondsuit \}$
2. Loops (Venn Diagrams) This model relates closely to Activity 10, Loops. Set A can be thought of as all things to be placed inside the loop labelled A. We can indicate the set by shading.	$A \cap B$	$A \cup B$	A/B
3. Regions of a Square In this model the set is represented by the shaded part of a square. One might show a square on an overhead projector and indicate the set by a piece of transparent colored plastic.	$A \cap B$	$A \cup B$	A/B

Set concepts can be related to other mathematical topics, situations involving classification, and other subject areas, as illustrated by the exercises on page 38. Children can do exercises like these informally without using set notation and still experience the flavor of the set concepts and their use. Try these exercises involving the three models for sets.

1. *Listing a Set.* Consider the following sets: A = {1, 2, 3, 4, 6, 12} and B = {1, 2, 4, 5, 10, 20}.

Fill in the following: A ∪ B = _____ A ∩ B = _____ A/B = _____.

Did you notice anything about the sets A and B? In fact, set A is the set of all *divisors* of 12, and set B is the set of all divisors of _____. (We say that 4 is a "divisor" of 12 because it "divides" 12 evenly, which means that 12 divided by 4 leaves no remainder.)

The set A ∩ B is thus the set of all numbers that are divisors of both 12 and 20, or in other words, the common divisors of 12 and 20. Which element in A ∩ B is the greatest? _____ This number is called the G _ _ _ _ _ _ _ C _ _ _ _ _ D _ _ _ _ _ _ of 12 and 20. (Complete the words.)

2. *Loops.* Let B be the set of people with brothers, and let S be the set of people with sisters. Put an X where you belong in the diagram on the left. Then shade in the indicated regions in the other diagrams.

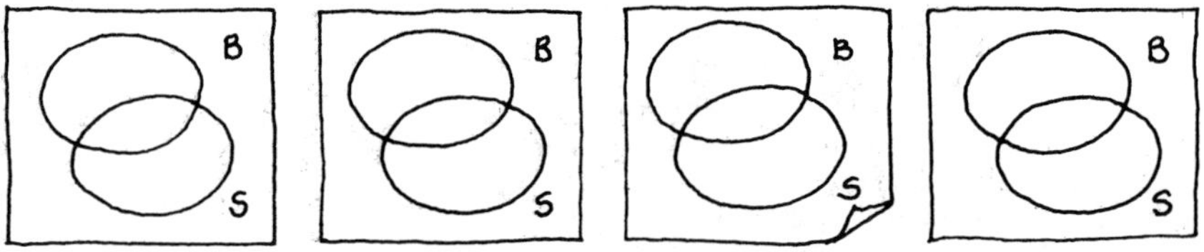

Where are you?   B ∩ S   B ∪ S   B/S
What can you say about people who fit in these regions?

People in B ∪ S have _____.

People in B ∩ S have _____.

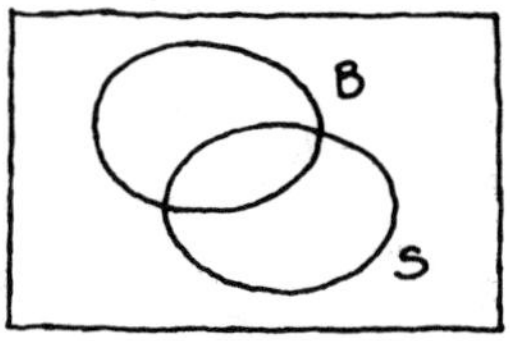

People in B/S have _____.

Use the set diagram provided to solve the following: There are 25 children in a class. A class survey indicates that 8 were an only child, 10 had brothers, and 11 had sisters. How many had a brother and a sister?

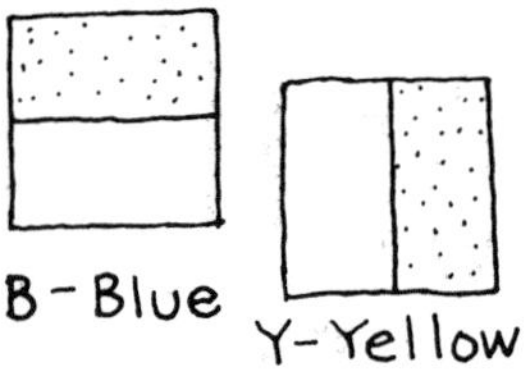

B - Blue
Y - Yellow

3. *Regions of a Square.* Suppose that you are using the "regions-of-a-square" model for sets on an overhead projector, and that your sets are as shown here. Shade in the sets below, and describe them in *color*. (Remember that when the primary colors blue and yellow are mixed, they yield _____.)

B∩Y   B∪Y   B/Y

Color(s): _____   Color(s): _____   Color(s): _____

4. Now write your own definitions.

The intersection of sets A and B is the set _____ .

The union of sets A and B is the set _____ .

The relative complement of set B in set A is the set _____ .

Set Definitions and Examples

Several definitions involving sets and set operations are given below on the left. Read the definitions and fill in the column of examples on the right. To check your answers, see p. 41.

Definitions

1. The *universal set* or *universe* is the complete set of objects under consideration in a given situation. (It is often symbolized by *U*.)

2. A *set* is a group or collection of objects (called *elements* or *members* of the set) often defined by some common characteristic or attribute. Sets can also be described by a listing of elements in *set brackets* {- - -}.

3. The *empty set* (or *null* set) is a set with no elements. It is denoted by ∅ or { }. (The set of hexagons in our collection is the empty set.)

4. The *cardinality* of a set is the number of elements in the set. The cardinality of set S is written as n(S).

5. Two sets are *equal* if they have exactly the same elements.
Two sets are *equivalent* if the elements of the two sets can be matched up in a one-to-one fashion.

6. The *union* of two sets A and B (written A ∪ B) is the set of all elements that are in A, in B, or in both A and B.

7. The *intersection* of sets A and B (written A ∩ B) is the set of all elements that are in both A and B. If the intersection of two sets is empty, one says the two sets are *disjoint*.

8. The *complement* of set A (written A′ or Ā) is the set of all things in the universal set that are *not* in set A.

9. The *relative complement* of set B in set A (written A/B) is the set of all elements of A that are not in set B.

10. Set B is a *subset* of set A if every element of B is also an element of A. (In other words, there are no elements of B that are not in A.) "B is a subset of A" is written B ⊂ A.

Examples

The following is the collection of pieces that we will use for examples:

$$U = \{\ \bigcirc\ \square\ \triangle\ \lozenge\ \bullet\ \blacksquare\ \blacktriangle\ \blacklozenge\ \}$$

If S is the set of squares in our collection, then

$$S = \{\qquad\qquad\}$$

If W = { ○ □ △ ◊ },
describe W in another way.

n(S) =   n(W) =
n(U) =   n(∅) =

If T is the set of triangles in our collection, then

$$T = \{\qquad\qquad\}$$

Is T equal to S?
Is T equivalent to S?

S ∪ T =
S ∪ W =

S ∩ W =
S ∩ T =
Are S and T disjoint?
Are S and W disjoint?

S′ =
W′ =
U′ =
∅′ =

W/S =
S/W =

Is S a subset of W?
Is S a subset of *U*?
If E is the set

$$\{\ \bullet\ \blacksquare\ \blacktriangle\ \},$$

find all eight subsets of E.

Practice Exercises on Sets

The exercises below are intended to help reinforce and extend your understanding of set concepts. As you do them, look for patterns and try to make generalizations. These types of exercises suggest that practice need not consist of lists of repetitive exercises that tend to be dull and do not lead to new understanding of the concepts involved.

1. *Listing a Set and Patterns*
    Let the universal set be the set of letters in the alphabet.
    Let A = the set of letters in "science":   A = {s, c, i, e, n}
    Let B = the set of letters in "math":   B = _____
    Let C = the set of letters in "music":   C = _____
    a. Fill in the following:
        A ∪ B = _____   A ∪ C = _____   B ∪ C = _____
        A ∩ B = _____   A ∩ C = _____   B ∩ C = _____
    b. Now complete:
        n(A) = _____   n(B) = _____   n(A ∪ B) = _____   n(A ∩ B) = _____
        n(A) = _____   n(C) = _____   n(A ∪ C) = _____   n(A ∩ C) = _____
        n(B) = _____   n(C) = _____   n(B ∪ C) = _____   n(B ∩ C) = _____
        Do you see a pattern here? If so, describe it.
        Does the union of two sets always correspond to addition? Does it sometimes correspond to addition? Comment.
    c. Thirty children had milk or juice for breakfast, 24 had milk, and 3 had milk and juice. How many had juice?
    d. On page 39 you saw that the set {●, ■, ▲} had eight subsets. The set {●} has two subsets, itself and { }. (Does { } contain any elements that are not in {●}? If you check the definition for subset on page 39 you will see that this means that { } is a subset of {●}.) Find all the subsets for the sets shown in this table and fill it in. How many subsets does the set {●, ■, ▲,◆ , ●} have? _____

Set	Number of subsets
{●}	2
{●, ■}	
{●, ■, ▲}	8
{●, ■, ▲, ◆}	

2. *Sets and Properties*
    Let the universal set be the set of counting numbers 1 through 9.

    $$U = \{1, 2, \ldots, 9\}$$

    Let A = set of even numbers: A = {2, 4, 6, 8}
    Let B = set of divisors of 8:   B =
    Let C = set of numbers less than 5:   C =

a. Write the numbers in this Venn diagram.
b. Find: $A \cup B =$
         $A \cap B =$
         $A/B =$

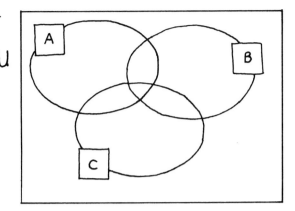

c. $B \cup C$ is the set $\{1, 2, 3, 4, 8\}$. $C \cup B$ is the set _____.
   Did you find $C \cup B$ without referring to the diagram or to the listings
   for sets C and B?
d. Part c suggests that for any two sets, P and Q, $P \cup Q$ is the same
   as $Q \cup P$. Is $P \cap Q$ always the same as $Q \cap P$? _____ Is P/Q always the same as Q/P?
e. The statement $P \cup Q = Q \cup P$ is true for any sets P and Q, and this
   is one property of union of sets. Another is $P \cup \emptyset = P$, since it is
   true for any set P. Give informal explanations for why these two
   statements are always true.
   Describe some other properties of union or intersection of sets.
f. (Optional) The statements $P \cup Q = Q \cup P$ and $P \cup \emptyset = P$ are true
   for any sets. Set statements can be always true, always false, or
   sometimes true and sometimes false. For example, $P \cup Q = P \cap Q$
   is true when sets P and Q are the same, and otherwise false. Underline statements below that are always true. For statements that
   are sometimes true and sometimes false, give examples of each
   case.

(1) $P \cap \emptyset = \emptyset$ (5) $P/\overset{\bullet}{Q} = Q/P$
(2) $P/\emptyset = P$ (6) $P \cup P' = U$
(3) $P \cup P = P$ (7) $P' = P$
(4) $P \cap Q = P$

(**Note:** Properties of union and intersection of sets are sometimes
treated in texts for grades 5–8. Children can compare these properties to those for operations on numbers, such as addition. However, knowing such properties is far less important for children than
trying to discover them or even trying to explain informally why they
hold.)

3. *Sets and Squares*
   Let the universal set be the whole square region. Sets A, B, and C are
   shaded (page 42). Refer to them to shade in the other squares. Find
   names for the shaded regions in the last two squares.

Examples

The following is the col-
lection of pieces that we
will use for examples:

$U = \{\bigcirc \square \triangle \diamondsuit \bullet \blacksquare \blacktriangle \blacklozenge\}$

If S is the set of squares
in our collection, then

$S = \{\square, \blacksquare \quad\quad\}$

If $W = \{\bigcirc \square \triangle \diamondsuit\}$,
describe W in another
way.

$n(S) = 2$ $n(W) = 4$
$n(U) = 8$ $n(\emptyset) = 0$

If T is the set of triangles
in our collection, then

$T = \{\triangle, \blacktriangle \quad\}$

Is T equal to S?   no
Is T equivalent to S?   yes

$S \cup T = \{\square, \triangle, \blacksquare, \blacktriangle\}$
$S \cup W = \{\blacksquare, \square, \triangle, \bigcirc, \diamondsuit\}$

$S \cap W = \{\square\}$
$S \cap T = \{\quad\}$

Are S and T disjoint?   yes
Are S and W disjoint?   no

$S' = \{\bigcirc, \triangle, \diamondsuit, \bullet, \blacktriangle, \blacklozenge\}$
$W' = \{\bullet, \blacktriangle, \blacklozenge, \blacksquare\}$
$U' = \{\quad\}$
$\emptyset' = U$
$W/S = \{\bigcirc, \triangle, \diamondsuit\}$
$S/W = \{\blacksquare\}$

Is S a subset of W?   no
Is S a subset of U?   yes
The eight subsets are:

$\{\quad\} \; \{\bullet\} \; \{\blacksquare\} \; \{\blacktriangle\}$
$\{\bullet, \blacktriangle\} \; \{\bullet, \blacksquare\} \; \{\blacktriangle, \blacksquare\}$
$\{\bullet, \blacksquare, \blacktriangle\}$

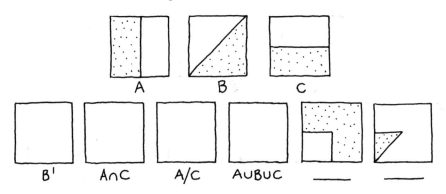

TEST YOUR UNDERSTANDING

1. Suppose that you have a set of attribute pieces that are pictures of

   cars. They come in three models ( ), three colors (red, blue and green), and also have numerals on them (1, 2, 3, or 4). How many pieces are there if the set is complete?

2. Here are some pieces from a teacher-made set of attribute materials. What are attributes? How many pieces are there in all?

3. Fill in five more pieces in this one-difference train.

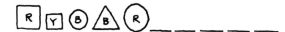

   What kind of a train is the one at left? Fill in five more pieces.

4. In this loop diagram, four pieces have been placed incorrectly. Mark them with an X. (Not all of the pieces have been put in the loops.)

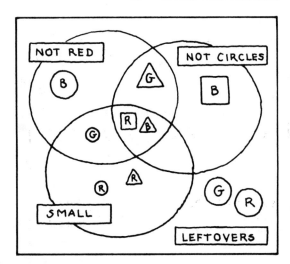

5. Provide labels for the loops. (Only some of the pieces are shown here.)

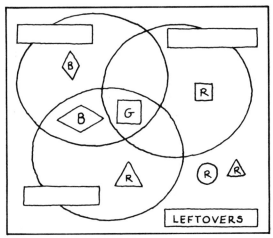

6. What mathematics may children experience by doing activities with attribute pieces?
7. Cite four reasons why a teacher should allow children to play with materials like the attribute pieces before beginning structured activities with the material.
8. Explain how to view "rectangle" as a *conjunctive* or *and* concept. How does Activity 14 involve *and* situations?
9. Describe how some collections of objects (other than buttons or shells) can be used to provide children with experiences related to classification, one-to-one correspondence, comparison, seriation, and patterning.
10. Describe two differences between attribute materials and a random collection of objects (for example, buttons or bottle caps).
11. Describe some important features of the positive- and negative-instance method for teaching concepts. Name two concepts that could be taught by this method, one in mathematics and one in another subject area.
12. Piaget characterizes a child's intellectual development as proceeding through four age-related periods: sensory-motor, preoperational, concrete operational, and formal operational.

    a. In which period are most kindergarten children? most children in grades 2–4?
    b. Characterize the preoperational period.
    c. How do children in the concrete operational stage differ from those in the formal operational stage?
    d. Describe two implications of Piaget's work for teaching children.

13. Describe the controversy that exists about the teaching of sets at the elementary school level.

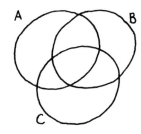

A   B

C

14. a. List the elements in sets A, B, and C below and write them in the diagram provided.

A = set of letters in the word "attribute"

A = {a, t, r, i, b, u, e}

B = set of letters in the word "pieces"

B = _____

C = set of letters in the word "set"

C = _____

b. Refer to the diagram above and answer true or false.

___ Set B and {u, n, i, o} have the same cardinality.

___ A ∩ B is a subset of the set of vowels.

___ B ∪ C = {t, i, e, s}

___ If the universal set is the set of letters in the alphabet, then C′ has exactly 20 elements.

___ B/C = C/B

___ (A ∩ C) ∪ (A ∩ B) = {e, i, t}

___ (C/A) ∪ (C ∩ A) = C

c. Fill in the table. Do you see a pattern that you could use to tell how many two-element subsets a set with 10 elements would have?

Set	How many two-element subsets?
{● ■}	
{● ■ ▲}	
{● ■ ▲ ◆}	

FURTHER READINGS AND PROJECTS

1. Show a set of attribute pieces (commercial or homemade) to a young child (ages four to seven) without giving any directions. Observe what the child does with the pieces. Note whether the child does anything "mathematical." You might show the set you used in this chapter, or the one described in "Making and Using Attribute Materials" by James Bruni and Helene Silverman, in *The Arithmetic Teacher,* 22:2 (February 1975), pp. 88–95.

2. In the Follow-up Section, Buttons and Other Materials, you saw how a collection of objects such as buttons can be suitable for a range of mathematical activities involving classification, comparison, seriation, one-to-one correspondence, many-to-one correspondence, and patterning. Gather such a collection, and describe an activity for each of these processes using your collection.

3. Often sets of activity cards are produced commercially for mathematics materials such as attribute pieces. One such set is "Problem Cards — Attribute Games and Problems" (St. Louis: Webster Division, McGraw-Hill Book Company, 1968). It includes activity cards for Attribute Pieces, People Pieces, and Creature Cards. Examine these activity cards and the comments about them in the accompanying Teachers' Guide. Could you use some of the activities with young children (grades K–2)? If so, how? With children in grades 4–8? If so, how?

4. Examine *Mathematics Their Way* by Mary Baratta-Lorton (Menlo Park, California: Addison-Wesley, 1976). It describes an activity-centered mathematics program for early childhood. Activities for grades K–2 are presented with photographs of children engaged in them. Some sample lesson plans are included, and questions asked by teachers about the activities are answered. Look at Chapter 1 (Free Exploration), Chapter 2 (Patterns), and Chapter 3 (Sorting and Classifying). Which of the activities described would you like to try with children? Did the sections called "Questions From Teachers" contain any questions you might have had?

5. In *Let's Play Maths,* Michael Holt and Zoltan Dienes (Harmondsworth, Eng.: Penguin, 1973) present a rationale for playing mathematics games with children. They also describe a variety of games including several that are similar to ones you did in the Activities. Examine the sections on "Sorting Games," "Ping-Pong Puzzles," and "Linking-up Card Games." Which of these games, or modifications of them, would you like to try with children? Why? Which resemble the Activities you did?

6. Classifying, comparing, and ordering are three processes that underlie the concept of number. Examine Chapter 5, Experiences for Young Children by E. Glenadine Gibb and Alberta M. Castaneda, in the 37th Yearbook of the National Council of Teachers of Mathematics, *Mathematics Learning in Early Childhood* (Reston, Virginia: NCTM, 1975). This article discusses these prenumber processes and activities related to them. Some of the activities can arise incidentally in the classroom. Can you think of other such activities?

7. In "Pattern Recognition Training: A Key to Math and Language Skill Development," (*Teaching Exceptional Children,* 7:2 (Winter 1975), pp. 61–63), Les Sternberg states that pattern recognition skill development is an extremely important instructional strategy for readiness experiences with mathematics and language concepts and for enhancing the reasoning and abstract conceptualization abilities of children. Examine the sample pattern tasks described in the article, and suggest how you could use attribute or classification materials described in this chapter in similar activities with children.

8. How should teachers teach? In "Mental Growth and the Art of Teaching," (*The Arithmetic Teacher,* 13:7 (November 1966), pp. 576–584), Irving Adler responds: "on the basis of an adequate theory of learning." Read the article. It describes three types of learning theories and then focuses on Piaget's theory of mental growth. According to Adler, what are the two major misinterpretations of Piaget's theory? Which of the implications of Piaget's theory do you think are most important for teaching mathematics? Why?

9. Can a child learn about sets in a natural way? Should they learn about sets, and if so, how? Read "Sets — Natural, Necessary, (K)nowable?" by

Dorothy Geddes and Sally Lipsey (*The Arithmetic Teacher,* 15:4 (February 1968), pp. 337–340). How do the authors of this article answer these questions? Does the material in this chapter reflect their point of view on the use of sets in the elementary school? Do you agree with them?

NOTES

1. James Bruni and Helene Silverman, "Making and Using Attribute Materials," *The Arithmetic Teacher* 22:2 (February 1975), pp. 88–95.
2. People Pieces, Attribute Pieces, and Creature Cards are materials in the Elementary School Science unit, *Attribute Games and Problems* (St. Louis: Webster Division, McGraw-Hill, 1967).
3. Jerome Bruner, Jacqueline Goodnow, and G. Austin, *A Study of Thinking* (New York: John Wiley, 1956), p. 54.
4. For more about the use of positive and negative instances, see Richard Shumway, "Students Should See 'Wrong' Examples: An Idea from Research," *The Arithmetic Teacher* 21:4 (April 1974), pp. 344–348.
5. These experiments are described in Jean Piaget and Barbel Inhelder, *The Early Growth of Logic in the Child* (New York: W. W. Norton, 1959).
6. Jean Piaget and Barbel Inhelder, *The Psychology of the Child* (New York: Basic Books, 1969) contains a detailed description of each substage.
7. Jean Piaget, "The Stages of Intellectual Development of the Child," *Bulletin of the Menninger Clinic* (May 1962), p. 126.
8. For example, see Morris Kline, *Why Johnny Can't Add: The Failure of the New Math* (New York: St. Martin's Press, 1973).

CHAPTER 2

NUMBER AND ITS USES

INTRODUCTION

Numbers, numbers, read all about them.

The Gotham Gazette
NO MORE NUMBERS!

Could you go for a whole day without using numbers? List five or ten different types of situations in which you use numbers. Compare your list with a classmate's. Can you classify your uses of numbers?

Most of us take numbers for granted. We use numbers every day to describe, name, and quantify things around us. But what exactly is a number? In what ways are numbers used? How can one teach children about numbers and their uses?

The Activities in this chapter will give you examples of various uses of numbers. They introduce themes and topics that will recur in later chapters, and that can be integrated throughout the elementary school mathematics curriculum. As you do the Activities in this chapter, try to relate them to the topics described below.

Applications. An important theme in this book is that mathematics should be useful, and that children should be able to apply the mathematics that they learn in some way — whether to real-life situations, games, puzzles, or simply in investigations that interest them. The question above reflects this concern for presenting numbers as an integral part of a child's life.

Estimation and Number Sense. Estimating about how many or how much is an important aspect of many applications of mathematics. Children should develop a sense for the reasonableness of a number being used to describe a given situation.

Grouping and Place Value. When counting large numbers, it is helpful to use some sort of grouping procedure, probably by tens, hundreds, etc. This strategy of counting by grouping is fundamental to our place-value system of writing numbers.

Pictorial Representation or Graphing. Numbers become most useful when relationships can be seen between them. There are various ways in which numerical relationships can be pictured — one important tool is graphing.

Probability. Sometimes numbers are used to describe something that has been or is now occurring, but often they are used to predict the future or the unknown. The use of numbers to describe things that are not certain — probability — is a relatively new strand in many modern elementary school mathematics programs.

Number Patterns and the Exact Use of Number. While many uses of number call for approximations or estimations, many intriguing patterns depend on an exact count. These number patterns arise in many types of situations, at many different levels.

Discussion Questions and Comments after the Activities concern classification of uses of numbers and the meaning of whole numbers. The main focus in this chapter is on the whole numbers 0–100. (However in some activities, especially those dealing with measurement and probability, fractions will arise.) Teaching the meaning of other types of number — larger numbers, fractions, decimals, integers — will be dealt with in later chapters, as well as the operations of addition, subtraction, multiplication, and division.

Further sections in this chapter discuss ways to teach counting; Piaget's study of how children develop the concept of number; and developing a sense for numbers through grouping. A section on teaching inequalities describes a sequence of activities for introducing the symbols $<$ and $>$. In later chapters, this sequence will be seen to apply also to other symbols. Behavioral objectives are related to teaching and evaluating the learning of number concepts. Sections on graphing, probability, and number patterns give a brief introduction to these topics that can be integrated throughout the elementary school curriculum, as they will be integrated throughout this book.

ACTIVITIES

Activity 1. Thirty Seconds . . .

1. When the second hand of your watch (or the wall clock) is on 12, close your eyes for what you think is 30 seconds. Open your eyes when you think 30 seconds have elapsed and immediately check the actual time elapsed on the clock. Time elapsed was _____ seconds. Did you overestimate or underestimate the 30 seconds?
2. Make a graph to show how the whole class did. Use a large grid on the chalkboard. Each person's estimate of 30 seconds should be marked with an X in a square. Decide on how the scale should be marked along the bottom.

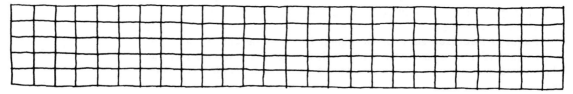

Did anyone estimate 30 seconds exactly? Did the class in general overestimate or underestimate? Explain how you determined this.

3. Did you use any method for counting off 30 seconds (for example, "1 potato, 2 potatoes, . . . , 30 potatoes")? If so, describe it.

4. (Optional) Try it again. This time to see if any particular strategy helps you estimate, the class might split up into groups, each trying a different method.

   Time elapsed on the clock was _____ seconds. Now did you over-estimate or underestimate?

   Make a graph of the class results again. (Use different colors for the different groups, if you tried different methods.)

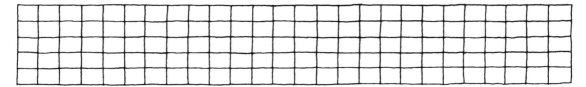

Compare these results with those for the first trial. Did the class improve as a whole? Explain your answer.

(Which counting method seems to be most effective, if you tried different methods? Explain your answer.)

Activity 2. Cents Sense

1. On the average, how much money in coins does a person in your class have in his or her purse or pocket? Make a guess. _____¢

2. Without looking, how much change do you think *you* have with you? First guess, then count the amount of coin money you have.

   Guess: I have about _____¢ in coins.

   Count: I have _____¢ in coins.

   Do you have more or less than the amount shown above?

   Do you have more than one dollar or less than one dollar? Write the amount in terms of dollars. $_____.

3. (Optional) Gather the actual count of coins from everyone in your class. List the amounts.

   a. What is the least amount from a classmate? _____¢ the greatest amount? _____¢

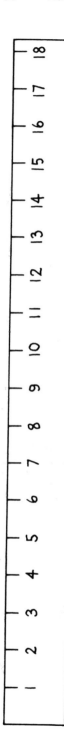

b. How could you make a graph of these numbers to see how they are distributed? It would be inconvenient to use a scale fine enough to show the exact amounts, and it is more practical to round the amounts to the nearest dime before graphing. 83¢ would be rounded to 80¢ because 83¢ is closer to 80¢ than to 90¢. 76¢ would also be rounded to 80¢. What about 65¢? This is 5¢ more than 60¢ and 5¢ less than 70¢ — for convenience we will agree (as most people do) to round 65¢ up to 70¢. This means that if you rounded your change to 70¢, you could have had any amount from _____¢ to _____¢.

c. Make a graph of the rounded amounts of change. Shade in a rectangle for each student.

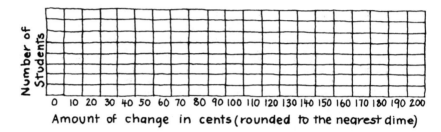

Amount of change in cents (rounded to the nearest dime)

Activity 3. Handspans

1. Look at the diagram showing a handspan. How wide is your handspan? Use the ruler, extending it if necessary, to measure your handspan.

   First, look at your hand and estimate how many units your handspan will be. Then measure it.

   Guess: About _____ units
   Measurement: About _____ units (Use whole numbers.)

2. Suppose the ruler were marked in ½'s so that you could measure your handspan more accurately. What measurement would you get? _____ units.

3. What measurement would you get if the ruler were marked in ¼'s? _____ units.

4. (Optional) Make a graph for the handspan measurements (to the nearest ½ unit as in part 2 above) of everyone in your class.

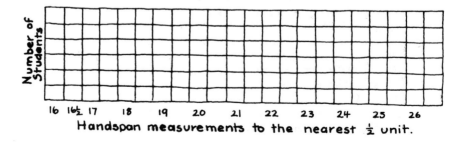

Handspan measurements to the nearest ½ unit.

What was the smallest handspan? _____ units. The largest? _____
units.

What was the most frequently occurring handspan? _____ units.
(**Note:** This number is the *mode* of the distribution of handspan measurements — to the nearest $1/2$ unit — in your class.)

What was the *average* handspan measurement? (Use a calculator if
you desire.) _____ units.

Is the mode the same as the average in this case?

5. Is your right handspan larger than your left? Guess first, then try it.
Are you right- or left-handed? Do you think this has anything to do
with it? How could you investigate this further?

Activity 4. Beans

Materials: Jar of dried beans, egg carton, spoon,
assorted containers

1. *Spooning Beans.* Take as large a spoonful of dried beans as you can.
Guess, how many are there? Count the beans in the spoonful by putting 10 beans in each cup of an egg carton.

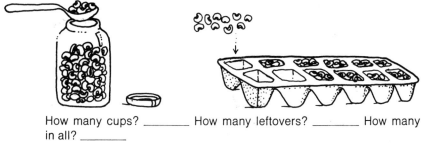

How many cups? _____ How many leftovers? _____ How many
in all? _____

2. *Beans in a Jar.* Have you ever tried to guess how many jelly beans
were in a jar? If you make the best guess of how many beans are in
the glass jar, you may win a prize.

Look at the jar of beans. Guess, how many are there?

Then use the other containers and your result in part 1 to approximate
how many beans there are in the jar. Your approximation is _____
beans.

Describe your method.

How could the class make an *exact* count to see who gets the prize?

Activity 5. Game — Guess the Color

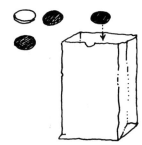

Materials: Colored cubes or chips of two colors,
say red and white; bag big enough to reach your
hand into, and in which you cannot see the contents

Directions: Play this game with three or more
players. One person secretly selects four cubes
or chips of any color combination desired (for

example, three red and one white) and hides them in the bag.

The bag is passed around from player to player. Players (except the cube hider) take turns reaching into the bag *without looking,* and drawing out one cube or chip. The player holds it up for all to see, and then drops it back into the bag.

When someone thinks he knows *exactly* what chips are in the bag, he makes a claim. The cube hider says whether the claim is right or wrong. If he is wrong, the player who made the claim loses a point and play continues. If he is right, he wins a point and the round is over. Then the winner gets to select the cubes or chips for the next round. The winner is the first to get three points.

You may find it easier to remember what chips have been drawn if you keep a tally or make a graph.

Variation: Try using five or six chips.

Activity 6. Building Towers

1. ***Materials:*** Wooden cubes

   a. How many blocks can you pile up to make a tower? Guess: _____
      Try it: _____
   b. Now try with two towers side by side. Do you think that you can build higher with two towers, as shown, than you did with one tower? Try it. How many "stories"?
   c. You can make a tower with two colors of cubes. You could make it easy to count your tower by making every tenth cube blue and the others of another color. Suppose your tower had two blue cubes and four more different colored ones on top of the last blue cube. How many cubes in all?

2. ***Materials:*** Assortment of bottle caps, jar lids, etc. (This activity can also be done with an assortment of blocks of different sizes, or with a large collection of real or play coins.)

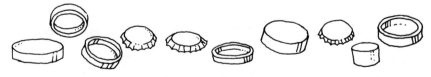

Try this game with two or more players. Take turns selecting a lid and adding it to a tower. The first player to make the tower topple loses!

Variation: Have each player make a tower as high as possible, counting the pieces as they are added. The player with the most pieces wins. Which lids would you put on the bottom?

Activity 7. Counting Squares

1. There are more than 25 squares of different sizes in the large square shown here. How many squares can you find?
   If you have difficulty beginning to count all of the squares, see page 54 for some hints. Describe your method for counting the squares.

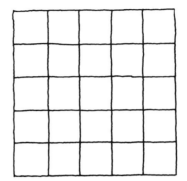

2. How many small squares of the same size (like □) are there in this diagram?
   How did you count them?

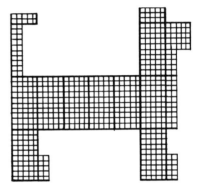

Activity 8. Throwing a Bean

Materials: Paper, milk carton, scissors, and a bean
Directions: Use a copy of the square shown here for a game. Trace the square, cut it out, and put it in the bottom of a half-pint or quart milk carton that has been cut to make an open box about two inches high.

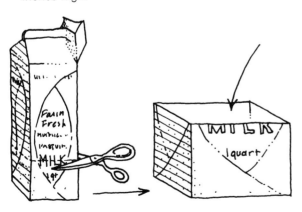

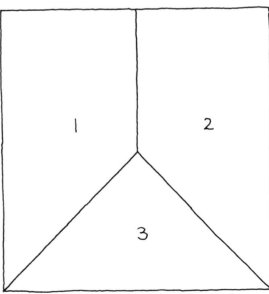

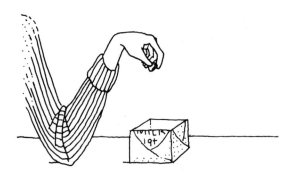

1. Throw a bean from at least one foot above the box. Perhaps you could rest your elbow on a table and drop the bean, as shown here. (If your bean lands exactly across a line, try again.) Before trying it, guess in which region the bean will land most often? region _____ least often? region _____ Throw the bean ten times and record your results. region 1 _____ region 2 _____ region 3 _____ What result would you predict if the bean was thrown 100 times? Why? region 1 _____ region 2 _____ region 3 _____ (Optional) Collect the results for the whole class. How many tries were there? _____ region 1 _____ region 2 _____ region 3 _____ Is this about what you would have predicted?

2. **Variation:** Do the activity in part (1) with *two* beans. Find the *sum* of the numbers of the regions in which they land. What sum do you think will be most common? _____ Why? Try it 20 times. Which sum was most common?

3. (Optional) Design your own game. Make a shape in a square the size of the bottom of a milk carton. Cut it out and put it in the bottom of a milk carton. Predict how many times out of 20 tries your bean will land *inside* the shape. Try it. Were you close?

Hint for Activity 7:

How many 1 × 1 squares like this are in the original 5 × 5 square? _____

How many 2 × 2 squares are there? (Begin counting in the upper left corner.) _____

How many 3 × 3 squares are there? _____

DISCUSSION QUESTIONS AND COMMENTS

Types of Number Questions

Imagine that you are a second grader. Read the number questions your classmates have formulated and write an answer to each of them. Then add two number questions of your own to the list.

NUMBER QUESTIONS WE ASK   Grade: 2
  1. How old are you?   Room: 103
  2. What is your height?   Date: September 12, 19 —
  3. What is your phone number?
  4. How much do you weigh?
  5. How many brothers or sisters do you have?
  6. How long do you spend eating dinner?
  7. On what floor of your building do you sleep?
  8. How many teeth do you have missing?
  9. What television channel do you watch the most?
 10. Where do you come in your family — first (oldest) child, second, . . . ?

 11.

 12.

A list of number questions such as these could be added to by the children and displayed on a bulletin board. These questions reflect children's personal uses of number concepts and number language.

The questions above illustrate different ways in which number is used. Think of one number question for each of the following types:

1. A question such as 5 or 8 that asks "how many" and is answered by counting objects in a set (such as members in a family).
2. A question such as 2 or 4 that asks "how much" and is answered by some kind of measurement.
3. A question such as 3 or 9 in which number is used as a code or name.
4. A question such as 7 or 10 that asks "which one" in a sequence and is answered by first, second, third, etc.

Which questions *could* have fractions as the answer? _____ Which could have zero as the answer? _____ Do any of the questions require large numbers (that is, greater than 100) as answers? _____ If not, write such a question suitable for second graders.

Questions 5 and 8 involve *rational counting,* that is, they involve actual counting of objects. *Rote counting* in contrast is simply a verbalization of counting words: "one, two, three, . . ." in English, "uno, dos, tres, . . ." in Spanish, or "un, deux, trois, . . ." in French. Children as young as two years old may have learned to rote count from one to ten (especially if they are daily viewers of *Sesame Street*). However such children may not be able to count a set of objects correctly. They may not realize that the sound pattern must be associated to the objects in a special way.

Do any of the questions 1–10 involve only rote counting?
Have you ever played a game in which you rote counted from one to ten? (For example, "One, two, three, . . . ten, ready or not, here I come!") If so, describe it.
Does the rhyme "Ten Little Indians" concern mainly rote or rational counting?

Does this rhyme concern rote or rational counting?

One, two, buckle my shoe,
Three, four, shut the door,
Five, six, pick up sticks,
Seven, eight, shut the gate,
Nine, ten, start over again.

Refer to the Spanish words for numbers one through ten: "uno, dos, tres, cuatro, cinco, seis, siete, ocho, nueve, diez."

First *say* them in order from "uno" to "diez." (**Note:** Are you rote counting? Try to memorize the sound pattern so that you can rote count.) Then rationally count (in Spanish) each set below.

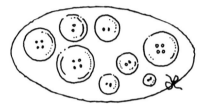 

Whole Number — What Is It?

The list of questions which might be asked by second graders showed that we use number concepts and number language in different ways for purposes of describing objects and events in the world around us. Numbers enable us to quantify "how much" and "how many," to indicate "which one" in an ordering, and also to simply name something (such as a phone number). Second graders most commonly find use for whole numbers, although some fractions and decimals are part of our everyday usage (half hours, quarter of a dollar, $.30). This chapter deals primarily with whole numbers — that is, the numbers {0, 1, 2, 3, . . .}.

Charades and Counting

Suppose you are playing charades. How can you communicate to your team the number of words in your phrase, *diamonds are forever?* One easy way to do this is to hold up three fingers to indicate that there are as many words in the title as fingers held up. From a mathematical point of view, holding up three fingers indicates a one-to-one correspondence between fingers and words, and shows the *cardinal* number three. The cardinal number of a

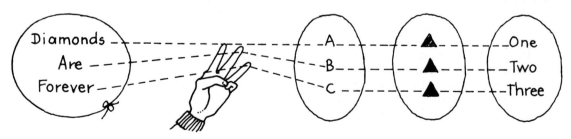

set describes how many objects are in that set. Two sets have the same cardinal number if they can be matched in a one-to-one correspondence; in particular, a set is said to have cardinal number three if it can be matched with the set of words {one, two, three}. By experiencing many situations involving the number three, we gradually detach "threeness" from any particular set and form a generalized notion of threeness. We come to think of three in terms of an unlimited collection of sets each showing threeness. The diagram illustrates this mathematical notion of the cardinal number of a set. Suppose that two sets cannot be matched by a one-to-one correspondence; could they have the same cardinal number?

Return to the game of charades now. Suppose that you have successfully communicated to your team (via fingers) that there are three words in the phrase. Now you want to give clues about the third word *forever*. Again you might hold up three fingers — this time, however, meaning not "three words" but "third word." Here number is used not in the sense of cardinal number that measures how many things are in a set, but in the sense of *ordinal* number that refers to the order of objects and indicates "which one" in a particular sequence.

In statements such as "Willie Mays's number is 24," or "My phone number is 686-2377," numbers are used in neither a cardinal nor an ordinal sense, but rather in a *nominal* sense. The symbol "24" is a baseball uniform code for identifying Willie Mays, and 686–2377 is a symbol for identifying motions of dialing — we could just as well use "NUM–BERS." (Do you see why? If not, look at the dial of your phone.)

Symbols such as the word "three" or the numerals "3" and "III" name numbers. This distinction between numbers (a concept) and numeral (a symbol) was given considerable emphasis in some "new math" programs for grades K–2, and gave rise to some cumbersome number–numeral language, such as "Find the numeral which names the number of objects in the set." While maintaining the spirit of this distinction in an informal way, current mathematics programs have replaced this heavy language, which was subjected to much caricature and criticism, by simpler language, such as "Write how many," or "Write a numeral to tell how many."

Return to the game of charades once more. Suppose that you have now communicated that you want to give information about the third word of the three word phrase, *diamonds are forever.* You hold up first three fingers, then one finger, then four fingers. What do these actions mean?

Counting and Measurement

Young children learn through play that some materials hold their shape and character (such as coins or cubes) while other materials flow, squash, or can be separated into many smaller pieces (for example, water into droplets, string into shorter lengths). When we ask questions about quantity, our use of number depends on the material: "How *many* coins?" or "How *many* cubes?" but "How *much* water?" or "How *much* string?"

In the first "how many" type of question, number is used in a *discrete* sense. Objects are matched in a one-to-one correspondence with the set {1, 2, 3, . . .}. This is called *counting*.

In the second "how much" type of question, number is used in a *con-*

tinuous sense. A unit of some kind is chosen and the number of these units corresponding to the object is used to describe the object. This is called _measurement_.

Some materials can be viewed in both discrete and continuous senses. Two children might compare their pencils. "How many does each have?" is a question of a _discrete_ or counting type. "Who has the longest?" is a question of a _continuous_ or measurement type.

The Activities at the beginning of this chapter involved various materials and uses of number. Activity 6 (Building Towers) was discrete in nature in that cubes were _counted_. Activity 3 (Handspans) was primarily continuous or measurement in nature. In Activity 4 (Beans) you _counted_ the beans that fit in a spoon, and then _measured_ the contents of the whole jar with the spoon and other containers. Here you used number in both discrete and continuous senses.

The process of measurement leads naturally to fractional numbers. In Activity 3 (Handspans) you probably found that your handspan did not fit _exactly_ next to some whole number of units. There was a little bit left over that you might have described as $1/2$ or $1/4$ unit, or perhaps some other fraction if you tried to be more exact. Fractions also arise in discrete or counting situations. For example, in Activity 5 (Guess the Color), you may have counted the occurrences of various colors and concluded that probably one out of four were red, or $1/4$ were red. Some mathematics textbook series focus almost exclusively on the discrete model for number; others provide a balanced presentation involving both discrete and continuous or measurement models. Children who have experienced only the discrete model in the early grades might have difficulty later when a measurement model is used to develop fractions, as is most commonly done. In later chapters we will examine how children learn about fractions and decimals in both discrete and measurement models. This chapter focuses on teaching whole or counting numbers.

FOLLOW-UP SECTIONS

Teaching Counting, Number, and Numeral (0–10)

What might a first grade teacher ask about teaching counting, number, and numeral? The following are three questions that might arise: (1) How are number topics sequenced or developed in textbooks or curriculum guides for grade 1 and how do these topics relate to later number topics? (2) How do children come to understand about number, and what difficulties might be anticipated? (3) What materials and methods can be used to teach the topics? This section concerns these three questions, mainly within the context of grades K–1.

Different Ways to Present Number Topics to Children

Number topics can be presented to children in many different ways. Many schools structure their mathematics programs about a text or workbook series, but there are various alternative and supplementary ways to present the same subject matter. Here are several ways that children can do tasks related to the following goal: identify a numeral from 1–5 and count that many objects or pictures.

1. A textbook exercise (shown here).
2. A puzzle made from paper plates cut in two as shown — one for each number being learned.

3. An activity where children take small boxes labeled with a numeral and fill them with the corresponding number of buttons.

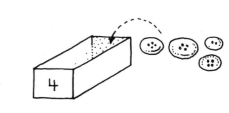

4. A card game where children take turns spinning a spinner to choose a numeral and then select a card with the corresponding number of pictures from a display of picture cards (if possible). Children can keep the cards they select, and the child with the most cards at the end is the winner.
5. A cooking activity where a fruit salad recipe calls for "4 🍌." A child reads the numeral and counts out the correct number of bananas.

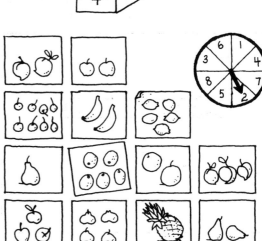

When choosing activities to teach a given concept, you should consider many factors. Answer the following questions about the examples above: Which would children enjoy most? _____ Which would help a child to correct a wrong answer himself? _____ Which would provide the most practice? _____ Which is easiest for a teacher to use? _____ to make? _____ Which type of experience should come first? _____

Additional examples of different ways to present numbers will be given in the following pages. The workbook exercises are discussed first, simply because they show clearly the type and sequence of number topics appropriate for young children. However later discussion questions will indicate why children's experience should originate with manipulation of objects as in (3) and (5), and should not be limited to the semiconcrete or pictorial mode of presentation as in (1), (2), and (4) above.

Workbook Number Exercises

Number exercises like those below appear in mathematics workbooks for kindergarten and first grade. (If you examine actual workbooks, you will find that bright colors make them more appealing and eye-catching.) They are presented here in a sequence typically found in curriculum guides for grades K–1.

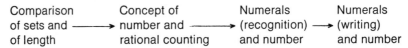

| Comparison of sets and of length | → | Concept of number and rational counting | → | Numerals (recognition) and number | → | Numerals (writing) and number |

Number exercises similar to exercises 1–15 below are introduced at the kindergarten level and are also included at the first grade level. At the kindergarten level, directions to most exercises are read by the teacher to the children who make appropriate oral or written responses. For example, in exercise 5 below, the teacher might say, "Which sets have two members? Point to these sets. Then make an X next to the sets with two members."

As you answer these number exercises (verbally, by making an X, by drawing a ring, or by writing an answer), notice how they follow the sequence described above.

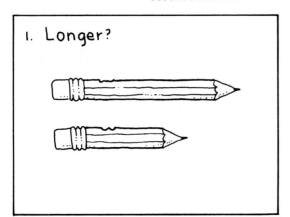

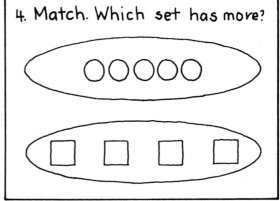

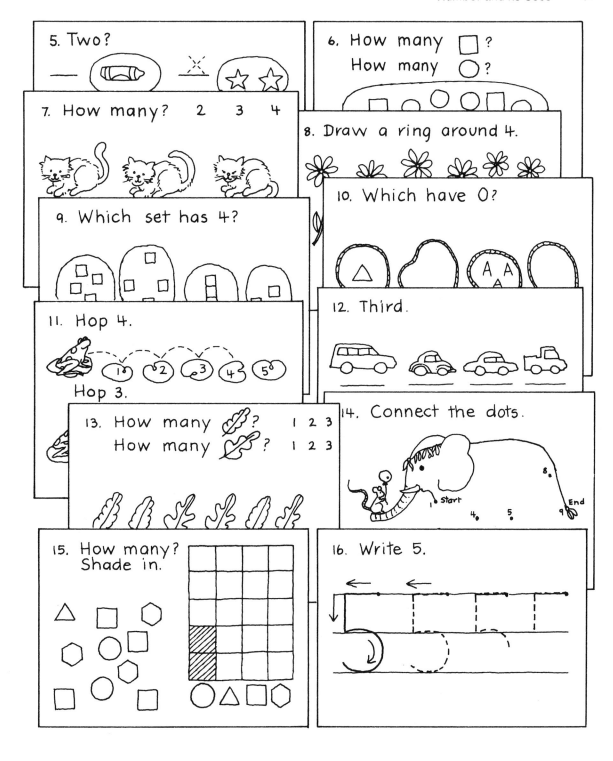

5. Two?

6. How many ☐ ?
   How many ◯ ?

7. How many?   2   3   4

8. Draw a ring around 4.

9. Which set has 4?

10. Which have 0?

11. Hop 4.
    Hop 3.

12. Third.

13. How many 🍃 ?   1 2 3
    How many 🍂 ?   1 2 3

14. Connect the dots.
    Start   End

15. How many?
    Shade in.

16. Write 5.

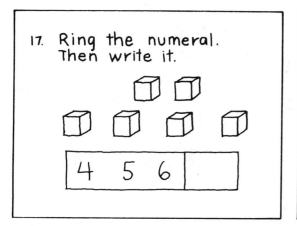

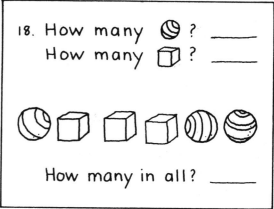

Note that exercises 1–6 involve the concept of number but not written symbols for numbers. Beginning with exercise 7, numerals are used. Does a child have to be able to count rationally to answer exercise 2? _____ 3? _____ 4? _____ 6? _____

In which exercise does "0" first appear? _____ The relatively late appearance of zero is not accidental. Young children sometimes have difficulty with the number zero. They have much experience with empty boxes or empty glasses, but this is not the same as thinking of zero as a number. Children may find the image of a container with nothing in it helpful when they work with zero.

The sequence by which texts introduce the numbers 0–10 varies from series to series. Usually the numbers 1–5 are introduced first, then 0, and later 6–10. Some texts pause and do a considerable amount of work with the numbers 0–5 before proceeding to the numbers 6–10, while others essentially do all of them at once. Some teachers feel that it is easier for children to start formal work with numbers with two (rather than one) because so many things in life come in pairs — eyes, hands, shoes, and so forth.

Notice how some of these early number exercises prepare children for later work, or are related to some other mathematical concept. For example, exercises 13 and 18 could be regarded as addition problems, although of course there is no symbolism "+," or even use of the words "add" or "plus." Exercise 15 relates to graphing.

1. In the preceding sequence of number exercises, which receives major emphasis, the cardinal or the ordinal concept of number? the discrete (counting) or continuous (measurement) use of number?
2. Is the nominal use of number embodied in any of these exercises?
3. Does exercise 11 involve rational counting? Do any of the exercises involve *only* rote counting? If so, which?

More Materials and Methods for Teaching Early Number Topics

The preceding exercises all come from workbooks. Children usually work on these alone at their seats, with paper and pencil. Many of these number topics can be presented using materials other than a workbook and calling for modes of response other than pencil and paper. Described below are four general types of materials and activities that deal with whole number topics (0–10).

1. There are structured mathematics materials designed for teaching specific number topics. The first three materials shown below are available commercially. You will find additional examples of such materials in catalogues of educational supply companies.

Slabs-on-pegs. Wooden or rubber slabs with holes fit over wooden pegs. There is one slab with one hole, two with two holes, etc.

Beads-on-pegs. Large colored beads fit on wooden pegs. Notice how the heights of pegs match the numbers. There is one bead of one color, two of another color, three of a third color, etc.

Number Puzzles. There are various types. Each set has pieces for 1–10. They are made of plastic, wood, or heavy cardboard.

Poke-through Cards. A problem is presented on a card with possible answers under punched holes below. The child selects the answer, pokes a stick through the hole, and turns the card over to see if the answer is correct.

Which of the materials above could you make yourself?

2. There are structured mathematics materials with many uses. These materials might include the following:

These materials can be used for various tasks. A few examples are given below. Initial tasks might involve only numbers 1–5.

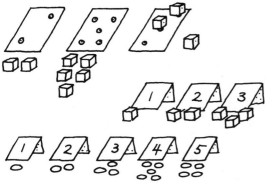

Put out the dot cards. Have children put out blocks to match. (They can put blocks on top of the dots if necessary.)

Have children put out the numeral cards in order, and arrange blocks to match.

Describe another way for children to put out the materials.

Game — What Did I Do? Have children close their eyes; the teacher or one child changes something in the correctly arranged array (as shown here.) The other children figure out what was done.

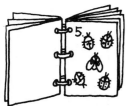

Children can make their own picture cards (perhaps from file cards) by drawing pictures or by pasting on pictures cut from old workbooks or magazines. They could also fasten picture cards together to make a number book, with one page for each number 1–10. (This book could later be added to, or children could take it apart and use their cards in other ways.)

Children might find the following activities, essentially the same as the ones above, more interesting because they can relate real-life situations to the objects to be counted. You can probably think of many others.[1]

Trains. Children first put cars marked with numerals in order, and then load them with cubes.

Cars. Children put toy cars marked with varying numbers of dots in the correct garages (made from cardboard boxes).

Vases. Children put paper flowers into vases marked with dot patterns according to the number of petals. (This works best for 3–6 petals.)

3. Many traditional games that children play for other reasons can be structured to give practice with number topics.

Dominoes. Use commercial ones, or make special cardboard ones.

Count Me Out. This is a circle game to choose a leader or to determine a line-up. Children stand in a circle. A special number is chosen, say seven. Children count in turn "one, two, three, . . . seven." Whoever says "seven" drops out and the next child starts again at one. The last one left is the leader.

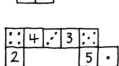

Stepping Stones. Rubber mats with large numerals are scattered on the floor (not too far apart). Children must try to step or jump from 1 to 2 to 3, . . . to 10 without touching the floor, or "falling in the lake."

Name another traditional game that could provide good opportunities for counting. (**Hint:** Think of card games, board games, or outdoor games.)

4. There are classroom situations and materials that can be used to give incidental number experiences. The following involve the children themselves:

Attendance. When the children line up, have girls on one side and boys on the other. Have each pair hold hands. How many are left over? Are they boys or girls?

Have children count how many are in school and figure out who is missing.

Names. How many letters are in your name? Make a graph. Here are two types.

1	2	3	4	5	6	7
M	A	R	Y			
D	A	V	I	D		
J	A	M	E	S		

		JAMES
	MARY	DAVID
3	4	5

How many syllables are in your name? How could you make a graph of this?

Clothes. Ask questions like the following: "What type of shoes are you wearing?" Classify the children's shoes and make a graph showing how many are wearing each type. "How many buttons are you wearing today?" Think of another number question about children's clothes.

Think of something else about children that can be used to give incidental number experiences.

The following questions involve a classroom material:

Check the crayon boxes. How many are in each? Which box has the most? fewest?

When giving out crayons, have a child from each table come up to get a red crayon for each child at that table. Have another child come up to get a blue crayon for each child, etc.

Ask each child to name his favorite color. Make a chart showing everyone's favorite color. Have the children check to see which color crayons are shortest. Why?

Think of another classroom situation or material around which you could design number experiences.

Situation or material:

Some number questions:

Workbooks and Alternatives

One drawback to most workbooks is that children do not get immediate feedback about the correctness of their responses unless the teacher is right at hand. Many other materials, such as listed in the preceding section, can provide immediate feedback, and when children play games they will often correct each other. Also, when children make an error with pencil on paper, they must erase it. This can be frustrating. However, when children make a mistake in a task involving arranging objects, they can easily correct it by simply moving something.

Another difficulty that children may have with workbooks is due to the semiconcrete mode of presentation. Some children may be able to count real objects rationally if they can move them in a way to prevent overcounting or undercounting, but they may not yet have developed a strategy or organized way of counting in a semiconcrete situation (especially when the pictures to be counted are not arranged in a row or orderly pattern, or when they are tightly crowded together). It is important for young children to have many experiences counting real objects before pictures of objects to build confidence and understanding of the counting process. Also, children may find numbers more relevant to their needs and experiences if they count familiar objects. Finally, children enjoy the more varied sensations, such as texture, weight, and sound, in these physical activities.

Most workbook activities involve only the sense of sight. Many of the activities described above also involve touch. One can plan activities involving several senses. A first grade teacher could use the following multisensory activity with small groups of children:

Children sit in a circle. One child bounces a large ball a certain number of times, while the others remain silent, and then rolls it to another child who must then say the number. (If a child says the wrong number, he rolls the ball back to the bouncer, who then has another turn.) The child who received the ball then repeats the action.

You can try several variations of this game: Children close their eyes and just listen to the bounces. Children keep their eyes open, and the child with the ball silently moves it up and down instead of bouncing. Then he rolls it to another child. Instead of bouncing a ball, one child drops pennies one by one into a bowl, so that the number can be checked later by counting. He then points to another child, who is to say how many.

Write a brief description of a multisensory activity you would use for the following goal: Given a set of 1–10 objects, the child writes an appropriate numeral for the set.

Recognizing Number Without Counting

The examples of activities in this section have dealt primarily with numbers 1–10. Most people learn to recognize these relatively small numbers without counting. Children often develop this ability in games where it is important to count quickly. Recognizing the number of a set of dots by eye is easier if the dots are arranged in some pattern, as they are on dominoes, dice, and playing cards. Some number materials for young children use regular patterns, such as the pattern boards developed by Catherine Stern.[2] These are

trays in which children insert cubes in the patterns shown. Children learn to recognize a certain formation as six and do not need to count the cubes each time to be sure. This pattern or structure of numbers is helpful in developing later arithmetic by the Stern approach.

Piaget and the Concept of Number

Matching tasks (for example, exercises 2, 3, and 4 on page 60) are included in the K–1 mathematics curriculum because matching two sets in a one-to-one correspondence (or showing that the two sets are equivalent) underlies the concept of cardinal number. From his experiments in which children matched sets of objects, Piaget concluded that children develop the concept of number in three stages as described below. In this experiment, children were shown six egg-cups and were initially asked to get as many eggs as there were cups. The experiments are quoted from *The Child's Conception of Number* by Jean Piaget.

Stage 1.

The child cannot form equivalent sets.

Interviewer: Take just enough eggs for the egg-cups, not more and not less, one egg for each cup. (The child made a row the same length but containing far too many eggs.) Is there the same number of eggs and egg-cups?

Fra: (4;3): Yes.

I: Well then, put the eggs in to see whether they're right. (He did so.) Were they the same?

F: No.

I: Are they the same now?

F: Yes (removing the extra eggs).

I: Now we'll take all the eggs out (making them into a heap in front of the egg-cups). Are they the same now?

F: No.

I: Why?

F: There are more egg-cups.

I: Are there enough eggs for the egg-cups?

F: I don't know.

I: (The egg-cups were put closer together and the eggs spread out.) Look, now is there the same number of eggs and egg-cups?

F: No, there are more eggs.

I: Are there enough egg-cups for the eggs?

F: No, I don't know.[3]

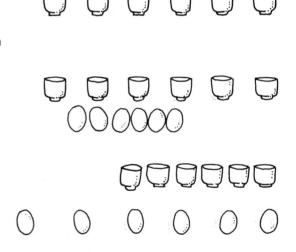

The child does not match sets one to one. Instead, he thinks that "same amount" means that the arrangements have the same length. In Piaget's terms, the child centers on one aspect of the situation — length — and ignores another aspect, number.

Stage 2.

The child constructs two equivalent sets but cannot *conserve number*, that is, recognize equivalence when the sets are rearranged.

Dum (5;8) . . . took 6 eggs to correspond to 6
   egg-cups and put them in himself. When
   they were taken out and put in a pile in front
   of the egg-cups, Dum thought they weren't
   the same.
Interviewer: Why?
D: Because you did that (making a gesture to
   indicate closing up).
I: Are there enough eggs for the egg-cups?
D: No.
I: (The egg-cups were put closer together and
   the eggs further apart.) Are they alright
   now?
D: No, because there are more eggs.[4]

The one-to-one correspondence is not fully understood. Dum's understanding is perceptual — that is, he sees that one row is longer and this perception deceives him. Also, the child cannot yet mentally reverse the action of grouping the eggs together. This is to be expected from preoperational children.

Stage 3.

The child can form equivalent sets and conserve number.

Bet (5;8) . . . with the eggs grouped together
   in front of the egg-cups.
Interviewer: Is there the same number?
B: Yes.
I: Why?
B: Because they're like that (making the ges-
   ture of grouping together).
I: And now (with eggs spaced out and egg-
   cups close together)?
B: Yes.
I: Why?
B: If you spread the eggs out, it's the same
   number.[5]

The ability to conserve number is gained when children enter the concrete operational stage, and they can consider two aspects of the situation at once and can mentally reverse the action.

These experiments show that you cannot assume that children think of numbers in the same way that adults do. Children may have very different ways of thinking, depending on their stage of cognitive development. It is important to talk to children and watch how they do tasks to discover just how they think and what they mean.

Do you think that this three-year old, Jeff, has developed the concept of "three"?

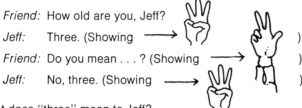

Friend: How old are you, Jeff?

Jeff: Three. (Showing ⟶   )

Friend: Do you mean . . . ? (Showing ⟶   )

Jeff: No, three. (Showing ⟶   )

What does "three" mean to Jeff?

Children often enter kindergarten able to rote count and count rationally from 1 to 20. Some of these youngsters, however, may not yet be able to conserve number. (Test some children if you can, to see if this is the case.) There are differing viewpoints about trying to teach a child to conserve number. Some teachers feel that one should just wait for the natural maturation process (after all, almost all adults have learned to conserve number without being taught). But others feel that at certain critical stages, the process can be helped by exposing a child to experiences that will help him progress to the next stage. For example, a child in Stage 2 above might be given experiences that show him the conflict between his perception (which set is greater, eggs or cups) and subsequent action (matching eggs to cups). Some examples of such experiences are given below.

Matching. Have a child set a cup on each of a set of saucers; put a toy car in each "garage" (box); give a piece of paper to each child at his table; or match small attribute pieces to large ones. Have a discussion of these actions with the children by asking the following questions: "Are there enough garages for the cars? Does every saucer have a cup? Are there too many pieces of paper?"

Rearranging Sets. Give children five toy "cups" (buttons) and a collection of cards with four to six circles (or "saucers"). Have children check — by placing buttons — which cards can be covered exactly with the buttons. There should be several cards with five in different arrangements.

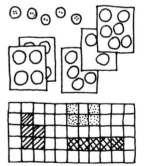

Give children five cubes and have them arrange them in different ways. They can then color the arrangements on squared paper, or record their patterns by gluing on paper squares.

The work of Piaget might alert teachers to the possibility that certain types of tasks or text exercises can cause difficulties for young children who are easily fooled by their perceptions. For example, why might children have trouble with these problems?

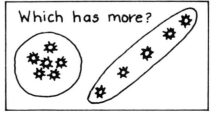

Counting Larger Numbers and Developing Number Sense

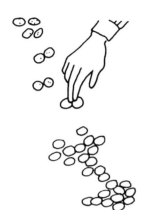

Counting — Word Patterns

When we count larger numbers, some sort of grouping helps us to get a feel for the quantity. How do *you* go about counting a pile of pennies, say over 50? Some people might count by twos (2, 4, 6, 8, . . .), others might count by fives (5, 10, 15, 20, . . .), while others might make piles of 10 pennies and count the piles (10, 20, 30, 40, . . .). All of these methods for counting are useful and children should practice them. For example, one counts by twos when counting children who are lined up in double file, and by fives when counting minutes on a clockface. Counting by tens is fundamental to our way of describing larger numbers, and children should be adept with the verbal pattern. Children usually learn to rote count from 1 to 10 by memorizing the ten unrelated words, "one," "two," "three," . . . , "ten." They might also be taught to count by tens in the same way, however they can also be helped here by noticing the pattern in the words:

twenty, thirty, fo[u]rty, fifty, sixty, seventy,
eighty, ninety

Only three words do not sound according to the pattern. (Some teachers recommend having children begin with "twoty, threety, fivety" for these, and then later switch to the standard names.) It should be emphasized that the "ty" is an abbreviation for "tens." Children can use a counting frame to push over rows of 10 beads as each word is spoken.

Once children know how to rote count from 1 to 10, and by tens from 20 to 90, they will have no trouble seeing the pattern and forming names for numbers 20–99. But our language is less rational in the spoken names for the numbers 11–19. Unfortunately, we do not use the pattern used for larger numbers for the teens — that is, we do not say "onety-two" for 12 — but we have in part a different pattern, and also two unique words. These names are learned by rote, but again children can be helped by hearing the pattern.

eleven, twelve,[6] thirteen, fourteen, fifteen,
sixteen, seventeen, eighteen, nineteen

Of course six*teen,* meaning "six and ten," is unfortunately easy to confuse with six*ty,* meaning "six tens."

Number Sense

While the names for larger numbers are often learned by rote or pattern, some physical meaning should be attached to them as early as possible so that children develop their "number sense" — a feeling for just how these larger numbers relate to things around them.

How well developed is *your* number sense? Can you describe situations where these numbers would arise?

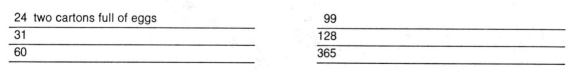

24 two cartons full of eggs	99
31	128
60	365

(You might try this with children; do they have a realistic sense of these numbers?) Children learn to associate large numbers with situations through many counting experiences. They can count collections in their classroom — perhaps buttons, crayons, books, or beans in a jar — or personal collections — perhaps marbles, stamps, or pennies in a piggy bank.

Many different structured models for large numbers are used in school, and they will be discussed in more detail in Chapter 7, Place Value. In the next pages, we will first examine textbook exercises and then concrete activities, both dealing with counting numbers 10–100.

Workbook Exercises

Here is a sequence of exercises typical of those found in first grade math workbooks. Do exercises 1–7 and 9. List the different ways in which ten is shown in exercises 1–7.

A Sequence of Sample Exercises on Place Value from a Grade 1 Workbook.

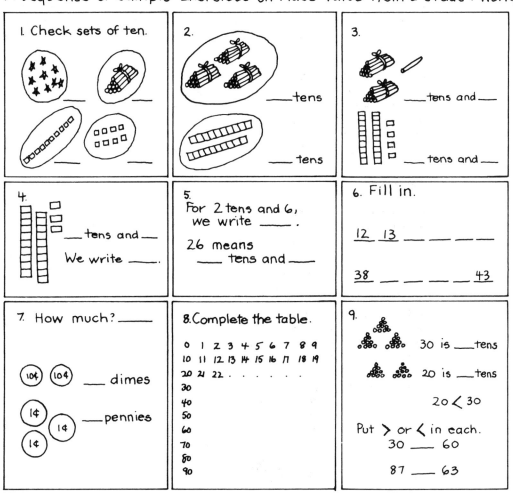

Which group in exercise 1 is the most difficult to recognize as a group of ten? _____ Without counting, would you *know* that there were ten circles in ⚬⚬⚬⚬ ? If you made a bundle of sticks and tied them up, would it look like 🪵 or like 🪵 ?

Children may have several problems with the semiconcrete representations in these sample exercises. Some problems may be *perceptual.* Do you think a child would *see* the diagram 🪵 as a bundle of ten sticks? Also, the picture of sticks may not be *meaningful* or *relevant* to a child who has not had experience bundling sticks. (Even if he has, he may recognize that it is an unnatural picture!) In such a case, where the objects shown in the diagram are foreign to the child's experience, the semiconcrete representations may not help the child to learn.

Even if the material shown in the picture is real to the child, the picture may not help the child to learn if he does not understand some aspect of the material. For example, the child might recognize a dime as a familiar coin, but not know that a dime is equivalent to 10 pennies.

Some workbooks use pictures of other manipulative materials that children use to learn about place value. However pictures such as 🫘 ::: may not be meaningful to children who have not handled the material shown. Did you recognize it as the homemade material bean sticks, made by gluing dried beans on popsicle sticks? These bean sticks make a pleasing tactile model for numbers, and as discussed in Chapter 7, Place Value, they can be used to develop arithmetic of two- and three-digit numbers.

Activities

Most appropriate for young children are materials that they themselves can count and form into tens. Before grouping into tens, they should have earlier experiences with grouping into smaller numbers — that is, making sets all with the same number (as will be described further in Chapter 7, Place Value). Such experiences might include packing crayons in boxes, putting pebbles in bags, or making bundles of straws.

On page 73 are four activity cards that illustrate counting two-digit numbers by grouping. (Notice that Spooning Beans is similar to the first part of Activity 4, Beans.) Similar activities can be used to prepare children for the workbook exercises. They also motivate counting by grouping where one wishes to count more quickly and accurately (as in Trains of Cubes); to check a guess (as in Picking Pegs); and to win a contest (as in Spooning Beans).

How many squares are in the marked rectangle in Counting Squares? How many pegs have been put in the board in Picking Pegs?

Which activity or activities would be easiest to do with an entire class? a group of 10 children? individual children? Which one do you like best?

Do any of the activities provide experiences that could help a child to deal with pictures of 10 that are used in the sample workbook exercises, such

as 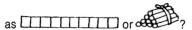 ?

TRAINS OF CUBES
Materials: Unifix cubes
Make a long train of Unifix cubes.
Count them. How many? _____

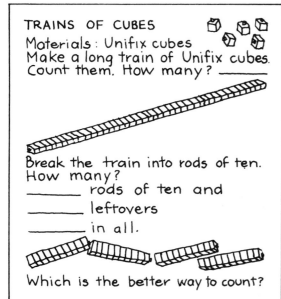

Break the train into rods of ten.
How many?
_____ rods of ten and
_____ leftovers
_____ in all.

Which is the better way to count?

COUNTING SQUARES
Materials:
    Squared paper
How many squares
of this size ▢ ?
Count them. _____

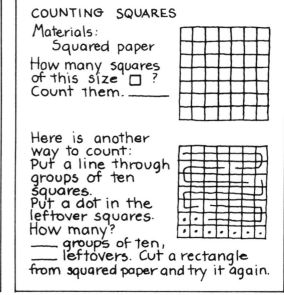

Here is another
way to count:
Put a line through
groups of ten
squares.
Put a dot in the
leftover squares.
How many?
___ groups of ten,
___ leftovers. Cut a rectangle
from squared paper and try it again.

PICKING PEGS
Materials: Pegboard, pegs

How many pegs can
you pick up in one
hand? Try it.
Guess how many? _____

Put your pegs in the pegboard
like this:

How many full rows?

How many left
over?

How many in all?

SPOONING BEANS
Materials: Jar of beans, 1 spoon
and 1 egg carton for each
person
Each person takes a big spoonful
of beans.
Guess how many? _____

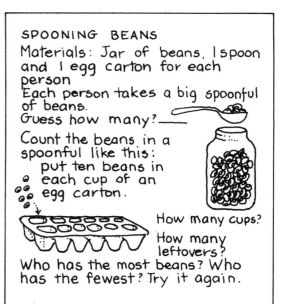

Count the beans in a
spoonful like this:
    put ten beans in
    each cup of an
    egg carton.

How many cups?

How many
leftovers?
Who has the most beans? Who
has the fewest? Try it again.

Perhaps you feel that Trains of Cubes could relate to ▭▭▭▭▭▭▭▭ ;
however none of the activities really relate to ⬚. Describe an activity
similar to the sample ones with a material that would help children understand ⬚.

The four preceding counting activities all involve two-digit numbers — most of the experiences yield numbers between 10 and 100, if the rectangles of paper, spoons, and trains are all chosen to be of the right size. Manipulative experiences need not be restricted to numbers under 100. Children can learn that a full pegboard holds 100 pegs; that if 10 rods of 10 Unifix cubes each are put in a can there will be 100 cubes; and that if all cups of a 10-section egg carton (cut off the extras) are filled with 10 beans each, there will be 100 beans. They can then count the materials shown below. How many are shown in each?

A small group of children could play the following game, using the materials above. Have the children start with some large number, then take turns adding one peg, bean, or cube to the collection, and say aloud how many in all. (Later, they can add three, five, or any specified number.)

Where Do Counting Topics Appear in the Curriculum?

The scope and sequence of number topics introduced at grades K–3 in a typical text series is shown below.

Grade	Number	Numeral
K	Matching; concept of more, less, same number; numbers (0–10) of sets; ordinals 1st–5th	Identifying numerals 0–10
1	Numbers (0–20) of sets; place value (tens and ones) and counting 1–99; ordinals 1st–10th; greater than >, less than <	Identifying and writing numerals 0–99
2	Place value (hundreds, tens, and ones) and counting 1–999; counting by 2's, 3's, 4's, 5's, 10's, 100's	Identifying and writing numerals 0–999
3	Place value for numbers to millions	Identifying and writing numerals to millions

Text series differ somewhat in their scope and sequence. You might examine one to see how it differs from this. Note in particular that counting over 20 objects (rather than recognizing a picture of bundles of tens) is seldom done in a workbook context. It is usually up to the teacher to make sure that children have some concrete experiences with large numbers. Also note that one first grade topic that we have not yet covered is inequalities, or greater than and less than. The next section concerns this topic.

Teaching Inequalities

The problem shown here might appear in a first grade workbook. Children often have trouble with inequalities, especially at the symbolic level. They may know that three is less than four, but have trouble writing this symbolically as $3 < 4$. The sequence of activities below will help children to understand the concept greater than or less than and to use the symbols $>$ and $<$. This sequence also applies to helping children learn other symbols and related mathematical concepts.

> Write: $<$, $=$, or $>$.
>
> 2 ◯ 3
>
> 6 ◯ 4
>
> 7 ◯ 5

Introducing the Concepts of Greater Than and Less Than

Clearly children cannot learn to use the symbols $>$ and $<$ unless they understand what it means for one whole number to be greater than or less than another. Actually young children have many experiences involving inequality, arising from matching. A teacher can help them to develop the language to express the concept. The following are some examples:

> When playing with toy cups and saucers, children match them up and find that there are cups left over — so there are *fewer* saucers than cups.
> At snack time, every child has a cookie and some are still on the plate — so there are *more* cookies than children.

Provide another example.

Children can also use structured mathematics materials to develop the concept of greater than or less than, as for example in this game using Unifix cubes (colored plastic interlocking cubes).

Game — Cube Grab

Materials: Unifix cubes

Directions: This game is for two players. Each player reaches into a box full of cubes with *one* hand and takes as many as he can. Then players compare handfuls, make rods from the 2 cubes and compare the heights, or put them back, one at a time each, and see who runs out first. The player who has more wins a cube.

Variation: Use a cube marked *more* on each of three faces and *less* on each of the other three faces, as a die. After players have drawn their cubes, the die is rolled. If it shows *more*, the player with more cubes wins; if it shows *less*, the one with fewer cubes wins.

Children can also work with this concept semiconcretely. For example, they might play the card game described below.

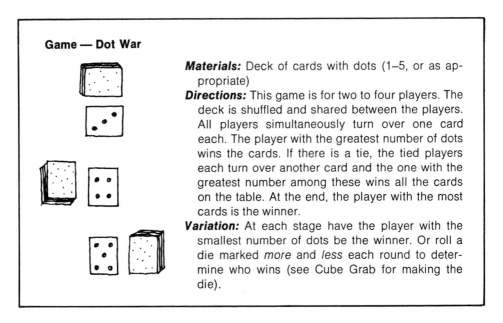

Game — Dot War

Materials: Deck of cards with dots (1–5, or as appropriate)

Directions: This game is for two to four players. The deck is shuffled and shared between the players. All players simultaneously turn over one card each. The player with the greatest number of dots wins the cards. If there is a tie, the tied players each turn over another card and the one with the greatest number among these wins all the cards on the table. At the end, the player with the most cards is the winner.

Variation: At each stage have the player with the smallest number of dots be the winner. Or roll a die marked *more* and *less* each round to determine who wins (see Cube Grab for making the die).

Tying Symbol to Concrete Experience

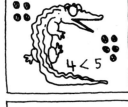

Children are sometimes asked to learn the symbols < and > while they are still having trouble writing numerals — writing ∂ for 6 and ⌐ for 7. Reversal of numerals is a fairly common problem that often goes away without much comment. As far as communication goes, both child and teacher know what ∂ or ⌐ means. But the symbols for inequality present more difficulty because when the symbol is reversed the meaning is changed. It is thus particularly important to give some visual meaning to the symbol. One procedure is to introduce an alligator who just loves to eat cookies. Children will decide that if he has the choice between two piles of cookies, he will eat the pile with the greater number. The teacher can display two piles of magnetic markers on the board and have a child place the hungry animal in the right direction, and explain why. Children can later write the numerals for the sets with the symbols < or > corresponding to the mouth. Children can use a cutout alligator (or possibly a fish, which is easier to draw) as long as they need to before writing the symbol alone. They may then be able to visualize the symbols < and > as mouths open towards the greater number.

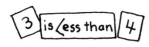

At a more verbal level, children might work with a card, as shown here, to associate "3 is less than 4" with "3 < 4." (Can you design a similar card for >?)

Practice With Symbols Alone

Eventually children should be able to work symbolically without reference to sets of objects or a movable alligator. However this should not be rushed and children should be able to refer back to the concrete experience as often as is needed. The game below provides practice with forming symbolic phrases.

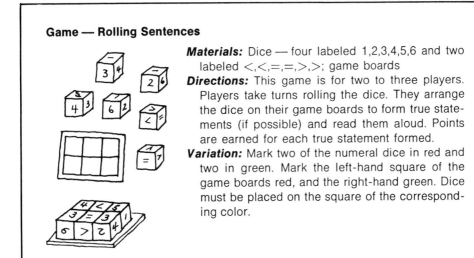

Game — Rolling Sentences

Materials: Dice — four labeled 1,2,3,4,5,6 and two labeled <,<,=,=,>,>; game boards

Directions: This game is for two to three players. Players take turns rolling the dice. They arrange the dice on their game boards to form true statements (if possible) and read them aloud. Points are earned for each true statement formed.

Variation: Mark two of the numeral dice in red and two in green. Mark the left-hand square of the game boards red, and the right-hand green. Dice must be placed on the square of the corresponding color.

Behavioral Objectives and Their Uses

Suppose you are a student teacher in a first grade classroom and that your teacher wants you to do a small-group lesson on a number topic. She will give you the goal for the lesson and let you take it from there. Which goal below would best help you to plan the lesson?

Goal 1: to learn about numerals.
Goal 2: to understand numerals and sets.
Goal 3: to identify a numeral for a given set of objects.
Goal 4: to identify a numeral (1–9) for a given set of objects.
Goal 5: to point to the numeral 4 on a piece of paper when shown 4 fingers.

Goals 1 and 2 are vague and general, and convey little information about what should happen during the lesson — that is, exactly what the children should be doing or learning. Goal 4 is more precise than Goal 3 and rules out two-digit numerals. Goal 5 describes one particular task, and one would hope that the lesson would accomplish more than this.

When communicating your teaching plans to others and when clarifying your own ideas, it is helpful to have a clear statement of the main focus of your lesson, such as Goal 4 above. These statements can help you to evaluate the effectiveness of your lesson, pinpoint learning difficulties, and identify other activities to help children learn the same topic. A statement of what the child

is to learn in terms of an observable behavior — that is, what the child is supposed to do or say — is often called a *behavioral objective.*[7]

Which of the following activities would be appropriate for the behavioral
objective written as Goal 4?

> The teacher calls a number aloud, and children hold up that many fingers.
> A bingo game. The teacher holds up a number of fingers, and children
> cover the corresponding numeral on their own bingo cards.
> At snack time, a child is asked to count the number of children at his
> table and ask for an appropriate number of milks.

(Two of the activities above are *not* appropriate for the stated behavioral objective. Write behavioral objectives for these two activities.)

Which of the following is the *primary* behavioral objective for game Cube
Grab? Try to improve on it.

> Child counts how many cubes he can pick up in one hand.
> Child counts a collection of concrete objects.
> Child describes which of two sets of concrete objects has more and which
> has less.
> Child identifies which of two numbers is greater.

One activity may have more than one behavioral objective. In the game
Cube Grab, comparing two sets of concrete objects is the main goal; but, if
children were also asked to count (although the activity is not described that
way), you would say that both the second and the third behavioral objectives
shown above are behavioral objectives for this modified activity.

Behavioral objectives can help you to evaluate what children have learned
in your lesson, and to plan appropriate further instruction. Evaluation can take
many forms — observation of children doing activities, oral questions, or written work. Match each behavioral objective below with an appropriate evaluation. (There is more than one evaluation for one of the behavioral objectives.)

Behavioral Objective:
1. To rote count from 1 to 10.
2. To identify the larger of two sets (1–10 objects or pictures).
3. Given a set of objects or pictures (1–10), to write the corresponding numeral.
4. Given a numeral (1–10), to identify a set with that many.

Evaluation:
(a) How many? ___
(b) 5? 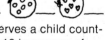 ___ ___ ___
(c) Teacher observes a child count-ing from 1 to 10 in a game of hide-and-seek.
(d) Teacher writes a numeral and asks children to hold up that many fingers.

Write an evaluation for the behavioral objective above which is unmatched.

Picturing Number — or Graphing

Children can investigate many numerical aspects of their surroundings, and often their findings become more meaningful if they are pictured or presented visually in a graph. Graphing is given formal emphasis in the mathematics curriculum at the upper elementary level, yet many kinds of graphs can be constructed by younger children. Graphing can provide practice of other skills, such as classification or counting. Following the sequence below, young children can learn to make bar graphs, first at the concrete level, then at a semiconcrete or pictorial level, and finally at a more formal, abstract level.

Note that one graphing situation — fall leaves — is used here to show all levels. However children would not do the complete series for any one topic. Also, young children should start with simpler situations at the concrete level, perhaps involving only two categories instead of five.

Situation 1: One day during the fall a first grade child brings his teacher a bunch of colorful leaves. This present motivates an activity in which children bring their favorite leaf to class. Children discuss ways to classify their leaves (such as color, length, shape). One such way to sort leads to the following graphs.

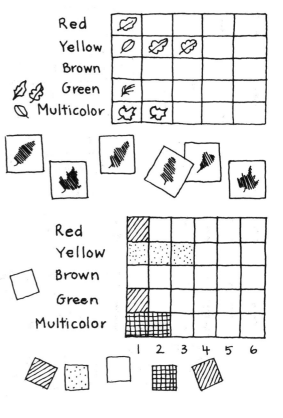

1. Graphing at the concrete level. Children pin their leaves in spaces on a large chart on a bulletin board.

2. Graphing at the semiconcrete or pictorial level. Children see that their leaves will soon wilt. To make a more permanent display for their bulletin board, they each take a square of paper and make a rubbing of their favorite leaf with the appropriate color of crayon. These squares are then pasted to a large chart that looks like the one in part 1.

3. Graphing at a more abstract level. Children see that it is easier to replace the pictures of leaves with a more abstract symbol. They might color in squares instead of pasting on pictures. Each child colors a square in the appropriate row, and the columns are numbered. (**Note:** This coloring can take young children a long time. The teacher could shorten the activity by preparing small squares of the colors involved, which children would then glue in place. Later children could use squares or press-on dots all of the same color.)

4. Formal bar graphs. These should be done only after graphing at the

levels discussed is well understood. Children simply count the number of red leaves and color in a bar that long.

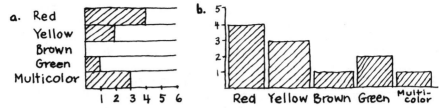

This sequence of graphs leads to a horizontal bar graph (a) above. It is just as appropriate for children to construct graphs leading to the vertical format (b) above.

Situation 2: One day a first grader comes to school very excited about her family's new kitten. The teacher asks the class: "Who has a kitten or a cat?" "Who has a dog? a bird? a fish? . . ." "How many pets do you have?" Do you see how the two types of questions can lead to two different types of graph? Could you make "pet graphs" at the concrete level? Why? Write your own situation involving something else that a child might bring to school or be excited about that could lead to a class graph.

Once children have had experiences with concrete or semiconcrete graphs, there is no end to the questions that lead naturally to counting and graphing. Opinion polls can be taken on all sorts of subjects. Questions can grow from children and their families, homes, and interests. Add some more questions to the samples below. Do you see how each could lead to a bar graph?

What is your favorite color?
How many children are in your family?
How tall are you?
How many pets does your family own?
How far do you live from school?

Children can use these pictorial representations of numbers to observe patterns and see relationships. For example, a graph of fall leaves might show that red leaves were brought in most often and green ones least often. Children should be encouraged to interpret their findings and try to explain them. Perhaps there were more red leaves because a particular tree near the school turned a brilliant red, or perhaps one type of tree is common in the area. When children use observed data to notice patterns, and then apply them to predict some unknown or future event, they are laying the foundation for later, more formal study of probability and statistics.

Probability

Probability, the mathematics of chance, was in the past studied only in high school, or perhaps the upper elementary grades. However, many new curriculums include probability as a strand throughout elementary school. Of course, early study is informal, mainly using terms "more likely," "less likely," or "equally likely"; only later will children learn to apply ratios and define the probability of an event exactly. Early work with probability can provide practice with other mathematical skills — counting, graphing — while introducing children to an important everyday use of number.

Two Approaches

In general, there are two ways to approach the study of chance: the empirical or experimental, and the theoretical. An empirical or experimental approach calls for performing an experiment a certain number of times, observing what happens, and then using this information to predict what will happen in the future. For example, in Activity 8, Throwing a Bean, you might have found that your bean landed in region 1 seventeen times; in region 2, fourteen times; and in region 3, nine times out of thirty. You might have concluded that you were less likely to get a bean in region 3 than in region 1 or 2.

Often the situation can be analyzed and the results predicted without an experiment. For example, in Activity 8 you might have recognized that regions 1 and 2 have the same area, but region 3 has less area (as shown in this diagram), and so predicted that on the average out of eight tries, three would land in region 1, three in region 2, and two in region 3. (Do you see why?) This is an example of the theoretical approach. It ignores some aspects of the actual experiment. For example, perhaps you were aiming the bean in some direction, or perhaps your table was slanted so that the bean tended to roll in some direction. Children should have experience with both approaches — experimental first — and compare these results with what might reasonably be predicted. Perhaps you did this sort of comparison in Activity 5, Guess the Color. You tallied the results of the experiment, perhaps finding that seven reds and two whites were drawn, and thought that this was close to the theoretical result if there were three reds and one white (that is, three times as many reds as whites would be drawn).

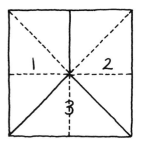

Choice Devices

The choice devices that are used for games provide many opportunities for the study of probability. It is useful for you as a teacher to be aware of the special features of various chance devices and of how they can be adapted to meet special needs. This chapter and some later ones use Throwing a Bean because it is easy to provide the device on the printed page, but there are many other ways to produce a chance number. The following are some examples.

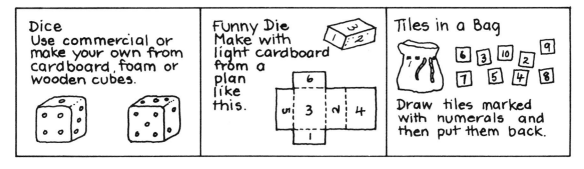

Pointer-type Spinner	Top-type spinner	Six Lima Beans
Fasten a pointer loosely to the middle of a piece of stiff cardboard so that you can spin it.	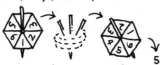 Cut a hexagon from stiff cardboard. Push a pencil or pointed stick through a hole in the middle. Spin it by twirling between two fingers.	 Paint dried lima beans red on one side. Use a small container as a shaker. The score is the number of red sides up.

What Numbers Can Result from Each of These Devices? The set of possible results from a standard die is {1,2,3,4,5,6} (or actually the dot patterns corresponding to these numerals). This is called the set of *outcomes* for the experiment of tossing a die. A Funny Die and a Pointer-type Spinner both give the same set of outcomes. What is the set of outcomes for the other devices?

Tiles in a Bag _____ Six Lima Beans _____
Top-type Spinner _____ (Be careful! It is *not* the same as for dice.)

Which device could be modified easily to choose numbers {1,2,3,4,5,6,7,8}? How? Which devices are easy to make? Which would be most fun to use?

When Are Outcomes Equally Likely? If a die is "fair," one would expect each of the outcomes 1,2,3,4,5,6 to be equally likely. That is, one would roll a 5 about one time out of six. A child found that after rolling a die 60 times, this was the result:

Outcome	1	2	3	4	5	6
Number of Times	12	10	9	13	9	7

Do you think that this was a "fair die"? How could the child find out?

Would you expect all results to be equally likely for the Funny Die? _____ Tiles in a Bag? _____ Pointer-type Spinner _____ (Look closely at the picture!) Top-type Spinner? _____ Six Lima Beans? _____ How could you test your guesses?

(Optional) Try throwing some lima beans and record the results. If you do not have painted lima beans, you could use six pennies and count heads and tails. You may be surprised.

What is Probability?

Probability is a number assigned to an *event* — or a particular set of outcomes, such as "3 is on top" or "an even number is on top" when a die is thrown — that indicates how likely that event is. There are two ways to determine the probability of an occurrence or event. First, a theoretical approach applies in a situation where all outcomes are assumed to be equally likely, or where there is some other reason to assign equal likelihood. For example, in Activity 8, Throwing a Bean, it would seem reasonable to assume that it is equally likely that the bean will land in any one of the eight triangular regions. The probability of an event is given by a fraction — the number of outcomes satisfying that event divided by the total number of outcomes. Some examples are given below.

Experiment 1: Throw a standard die and count the number of dots on the top.

Probability of getting a 3: 1 way to get 3, 6 possible outcomes, so the probability is 1/6.

Probability of getting an even number: 3 ways to get an even number, {2,4,6}, 6 possible outcomes, so the probability is 3/6 or 1/2.

Probability of getting a 7: 0 ways to get 7, 6 possible outcomes, so the probability is 0/6 or 0.

Probability of getting a number < 10: 6 ways to get a number < 10, {1,2,3,4,5,6}, 6 possible outcomes, so the probability is 6/6 or 1.

As you can see, the probability of an event is a number between 0 and 1. If the probability of an event is 0, then it never happens, and if the probability is 1, the event is certain to happen.

Experiment 2: Draw a tile from a bag (see page 81, Tiles in a Bag) and read the numerals. List the ways each event could occur. Find the probabilities.

	Ways the Event Could Occur	Probability
Probability of getting a number < 5:	{1,2,3,4}	4/10
Probability of getting an even number:		
Probability of getting a 10:		
Probability of getting a 0:		

The other approach to determining probability is *experimental*. An experiment is performed a large number of times, and the probability of an event is found by dividing the number of times it occurred by the total number of trials.

Experiment 3: Toss the Funny Die and keep a record of the numeral that appears on top. Suppose the results were as follows:

Outcome	1	2	3	4	5	6
Number of times	1	5	11	15	6	2

Probability of getting a 3: 3 was obtained 11 times, there were 40 trials (1 + 5 + 11 + 15 + 6 + 2 = 40), so the probability is 11/40.

Probability of getting an even number: an even number was obtained 22 times, so the probability is 22/40. (Do you see why it was obtained 22 times?)

Find the following for Experiment 3:

Probability of getting a 5: _____

Probability of getting an odd number: _____

Probability of getting a number < 10: _____

Of course, probability obtained in this way is approximate, because another experiment of throwing the same Funny Die 40 times can have somewhat different results. If, however, there are a large number of trials, the results will probably be close.

Number Patterns

While much everyday use of number is approximate, it is sometimes appropriate to make exact counts, and these often lead to interesting patterns (such as in Activity 7, Counting Squares). A few examples of patterns in sequences of numbers are given below. Young children can form these geometric patterns and practice counting; while in the upper grades these activities can provide novel and challenging situations that reinforce a wider range of number topics.

Arranging Chips

Materials: Chips, bottle caps, pennies, or pebbles

Use your materials to make each arrangement shown below. Continue the pattern, draw the next two arrangements, and fill in the spaces indicating how many objects are needed for each arrangement.

The numbers arising from Pattern I are called *triangular* numbers. Fill in the first 10 triangular numbers. It will help you to also fill in the spaces indicating the differences between successive numbers.

What is an appropriate name for the numbers in Pattern II? Fill in the first 10 numbers, and also the differences between successive numbers.

Lines in Circles

Draw all possible line segments between points drawn on the circles. (These line segments are called *chords*.) Fill in the table below.

Number of points on circle	2	3	4	5	6
Number of chords			6		

How many chords would there be for 7 points? _____ for 10 points? _____
Have you seen this pattern before?

Shapes

1. Use the triangular grid to the right to find triangles of different sizes. Draw them below. How many small triangles are in each? Fill in the number pattern.

   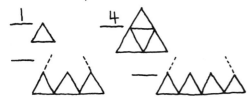

2. Use the diamond grid to the right to find diamonds of different sizes. Draw them below. How many small diamonds are in each? Fill in the number pattern.

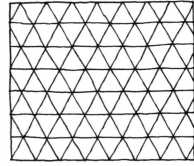

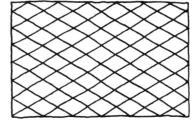

3. Have you seen the number patterns in parts 1 and 2 before? What number comes next in these patterns? Do you get the same number pattern if you look for squares in a square grid?

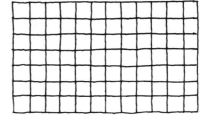

Secret Agent Teams

Ms. Nefus needs to select a two-agent team for a top-secret mission. She has seven secret agents (001, 002, 003, 004, 005, 006, and, of course, 007) to choose from. How many different two-agent teams could she form? Before you try to answer this problem, consider these simpler questions.

1. If she had two secret agents to choose from, how many two-person teams could she form?
2. If she had three secret agents to choose from, how many different two-person teams could she form?
3. What if she had four secret agents to choose from?
4. Do you see a pattern? Can you now answer the problem above?
5. {1,2}, {1,3}, and {2,3} are the different two-element subsets of the set {1,2,3}.
   How many two-element subsets are there for the set {1,2,3,4}? List them.
   How many two-element subsets are there for the set {1,2,3,4,5,6,7}?

You should have found that all of these counting activities give rise to one of the two patterns in Arranging Chips. Number patterns are hidden in a great many different situations. The first three of the preceding activities show that geometry and number can be closely related. In a later chapter, we will see how the study of number patterns can provide children with an opportunity to investigate and discover new relationships, and also to review and practice previously acquired skills.

TEST YOUR UNDERSTANDING

1. Describe two examples each where number is used in cardinal, ordinal, and nominal senses.
2. As you saw on pages 58–59, there are many alternatives to workbook exercises. Examine exercise 7 on page 61. Write a behavioral objective for this exercise and describe activities of the types listed below which involve the same objective. Activities using:
   a. a structured mathematics material.
   b. the materials described at the bottom of page 63.
   c. a traditional or modified game.
   d. a classroom situation.
   Were your activities self-checking?
3. Describe some difficulties that children might have with workbooks, and how these difficulties might be avoided with other types of materials.
4. Describe a test to see if a child can conserve number, and three stages that children go through in performing this task. Suppose that you discover that a first grader does not conserve number. What are some implications for teaching this child number topics?

5. Describe three different materials that children could group to show the number 138.

6. What difficulties do children have with the symbols < and >? Describe a sequence of activities to help children learn to use these symbols.

7. For each of the activities described below, write a behavioral objective.
    a. Stepping Stones, page 64.
    b. Exercise 6, page 71.
    c. Picking Pegs, page 73.
    d. Dot War, page 76.

8. Sketch an activity or describe a lesson for the following behavioral objective, and describe a way to evaluate it: Given a set of numeral cards (1–10), children arrange them in order.

9. Describe four different types of graphs (as on pages 79–80) that children could make about the types of shoes they are wearing to school.

10. Suppose that you spin the Pointer-type Spinner shown here. What is the probability of getting an even number? a "2"? a "3"? (**Hint:** Draw in a line so that the square is made up of eight congruent triangles.)

11. How many rectangles do you see in these diagrams? (Remember that a square is a rectangle.)

Use your results to predict the number of rectangles in this diagram:

FURTHER READINGS AND PROJECTS

1. Examine a kindergarten or first grade workbook to see if the exercises given on pages 60–62 are representative. Are there any types of exercises omitted? Is the sequence similar? What difficulties might a child have with the problems? Does the scope agree with the chart on page 72?

2. Examine the booklet *Piaget, Children and Number* by Constance Kamii and Roberta DeVries (published by the National Association for the Education of Young Children, Washington D.C., 1976). The authors describe Piaget's research relating to number, derive certain principles about how young children should be taught about number, and describe some appropriate situations in

which you can teach children about number. Do you agree with the principles of teaching listed? Can you think of other situations to add to their listing?

3. On page 63 were shown a few structured materials designed to teach number concepts. Examine some educational supply company catalogues and look for other materials that might give young children experience with counting. Evaluate the materials you find described. Would children enjoy them? Could you make a substitute yourself? Are they self-checking? Can they be used in a variety of ways?

4. Interesting and challenging counting materials need not be expensive. In fact, we are surrounded by inexpensive or junk materials that can form the basis for attractive games and puzzles. Examine the book *Workjobs* by Mary Baratta-Lorton (Menlo Park, California: Addison-Wesley, 1972), and also the article "Teacher-made Materials for Teaching Number and Counting" by Helene Silverman (*The Arithmetic Teacher,* 19:6 (October 1972), pp. 431–433). These should give you ideas for starting your own collection of homemade counting materials.

5. On page 70, it was suggested that young children should have plentiful experience with counting large sets of objects. The article "Let's Do It: Making Counting Really Count" by Mary Montgomery Lindquist and Marcia E. Dana (*The Arithmetic Teacher,* 25:8 (May 1978), pp. 4–11) provides many ideas for interesting counting experiences for children. The authors suggest several types of counts. Select some of these types, and add some additional ideas to their lists.

6. Start a file of counting books, songs, and fingerplays for children. Perhaps you can remember some from your childhood. You might also consult anthologies of songs, and the children's section of your library. When examining counting books, ask yourself if the book can be used in various ways. Also, try to think of some activities or questions that might naturally lead out of the book.

7. Examine the booklet *Pictorial Representation* prepared by the Nuffield Project (New York: John Wiley, 1967), and compare the examples given there of graphs with those on pages 79–80. The Nuffield Project is an English curriculum development project that has produced many attractive booklets for teachers, all full of examples of children's work. The project places a strong emphasis on graphing and other forms of pictorial representation.

8. On pages 80–84, you saw a brief introduction to probability through choice devices. Upper elementary school children may enjoy further investigations in this area. You will find sample activities and some more detailed mathematical analysis in *Prediction and Probability* by Johnson et al. This book is part of the series *Applications in Mathematics, Course A* (Glenview, Illinois: Scott, Foresman, 1972), designed for ninth graders, with an emphasis on motivating hands-on activities. You will find many ideas that can be adapted for younger students. Try some of the activities in this book. Which could you modify for use with elementary school children?

9. Special education youngsters often need simple easy-to-handle materials to learn mathematics. Many such materials are illustrated in *Functional Mathematics for the Mentally Retarded* by Daniel Peterson (Columbus, Ohio: Charles E. Merrill, 1973). Such materials are available commercially, but they are often expensive. Examine "Simple Materials for Teaching Early Number

Concepts to Trainable-Level Mentally Retarded Pupils" by Jenny Armstrong and Harold Schmidt (*The Arithmetic Teacher,* 19:2 (February 1972), pp. 149–153). This article describes easily constructed, inexpensive materials to teach counting. In what ways are the materials multisensory? What are some other similar counting materials you could make from everyday objects? Can you think of some which the children could make themselves?

NOTES

1. The book *Workjobs* by Mary Baratta-Lorton (Menlo Park, California: Addison-Wesley, 1972) has many appealing examples of this type of activity, all of which can be made from inexpensive or junk materials.
2. Catherine and Margaret Stern, *Children Discover Arithmetic* (New York: Harper and Row, 1971), pp. 24–76.
3. Jean Piaget, *The Child's Conception of Number* (New York: W. W. Norton, 1965), p. 50. (4;3) means 4 years and 3 months.
4. Piaget, *The Child's Conception of Number,* p. 52.
5. Piaget, *The Child's Conception of Number,* p. 55.
6. The words *eleven* and *twelve* derive from the Teutonic "ein-lif" and "twa-lif," which mean, respectively, "one left over (ten)" and "two left over (ten)."
7. Robert Mager, among others, proposed more stringent types of behavioral objectives: "Given a set of 1–9 objects drawn on a page, the child identifies and writes a numeral for the number of objects in the set, getting 4 of 5 exercises correct to pass." According to Mager in his *Preparing Instructional Objectives* (Palo Alto, California: Fearon Publishers, Inc., 1962), a behavioral objective should include (1) a statement of observable learner behavior, (2) conditions under which learning or evaluation is to occur, and (3) criteria for passing the objective. While such behavioral objectives are appropriate for certain educational purposes (such as detailed evaluation of student performance in a program), you may find that less stringent behavioral objectives will suffice for the purpose of helping you plan and evaluate classroom instruction.

CHAPTER 3

INFORMAL GEOMETRY

INTRODUCTION

Which of the figures drawn below seem to you "geometric"? Which of them would you expect to see as part of the elementary school geometry curriculum?

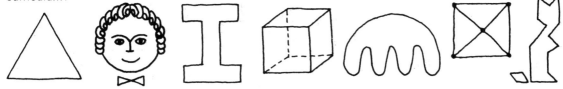

In fact, all of these figures appear in this chapter. The chapter deals with a variety of geometric topics and with techniques and materials suitable for presenting these topics informally to elementary school children.

The elementary school curriculum has traditionally included geometry topics, such as naming shapes and measuring length, area, and volume. However in recent years many geometry materials — activity cards, texts, and other resources — have been developed to encourage children to explore informally a wider range of geometry topics. The teacher may find that these developments present challenges: to understand the new and perhaps unfamiliar concepts, to find suitable manipulative materials, and to adapt the teaching of concepts to various levels of child development and to various classroom situations.

This chapter contains a variety of activities designed to strengthen your intuitive understanding of the geometry concepts involved, and to give examples of activities and materials suitable for children. The activities all use inexpensive easily made materials, and directions for their construction — from paper, cellophane tape, straws, pipe cleaners, cardboard — are included. (For work with children, you may find that the various similar commercial materials described later in the chapter will be easier to manipulate, and more durable and appealing.) The Activities — Solids, Tangrams, and Sticks — introduce three ways of thinking about geometry: as three-dimensional or space-filling, as two-dimensional or dealing with flat regions, and as one-dimensional or made up of line segments. Discussion Questions and Comments concern the role of informal geometry in the mathematics curriculum, geometry concepts arising in the Activities, and modifications of the Activities for use with children. Follow-up Sections — Mirrors and Symmetry, Mazes, and Networks — involve some topics introduced in the elementary school curriculum relatively recently (for example, symmetry and topological properties).

One theme running throughout this book is that mathematics can be useful and relevant to children's surroundings. The Follow-up Section on environmental geometry explores this theme in relation to circles as we see them all around us. A geometry scope and sequence typical of many current text series is included in another section, together with a discussion of why and how the themes introduced in previous activities are incorporated into teaching these topics. Finally, a section discusses various models, meanings, and activities involving points, lines, and planes.

Later chapters (Measurement and the Metric System and Geometry on a Geoboard) concern some aspects of elementary school geometry that have not been developed here, in particular, the measurement of length, area, volume, and angle, and coordinate geometry.

ACTIVITIES

Activity 1.

Materials: Scissors; cellophane tape; copies of page 93
For this activity, work in groups of four to six.

1. *Building.* (**Note:** This may be started before class to save time.) Build a closed solid shape from the given shapes. For example,

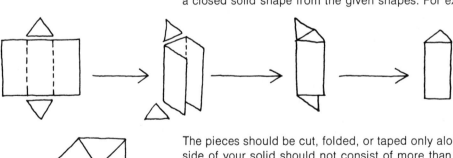

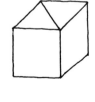

The pieces should be cut, folded, or taped only along the edges. A flat side of your solid should not consist of more than one shape; for example, the two solids drawn to the left are *not* appropriate. Do you see why? (The top of the first is made up of two triangles joined to make a diamond , and the top of the second is made up of a

square and a rectangle joined to make a long rectangle .)

Try to make three different solid shapes — no duplications allowed in your group! Do your constructions remind you of real objects?

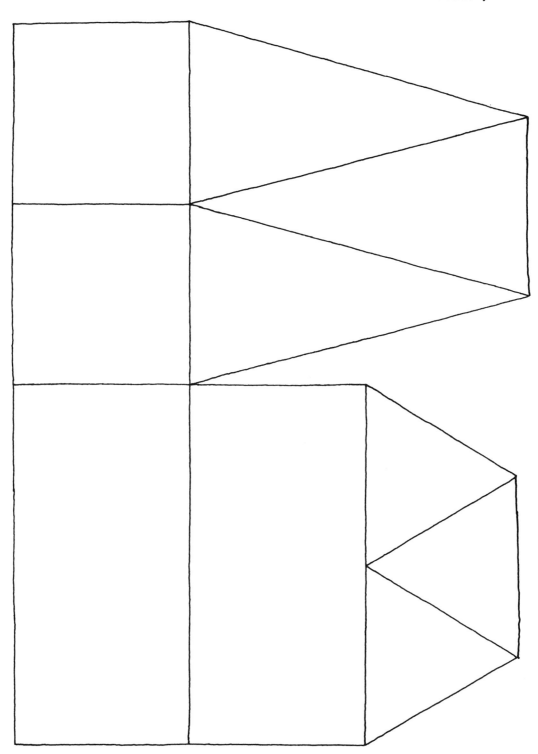

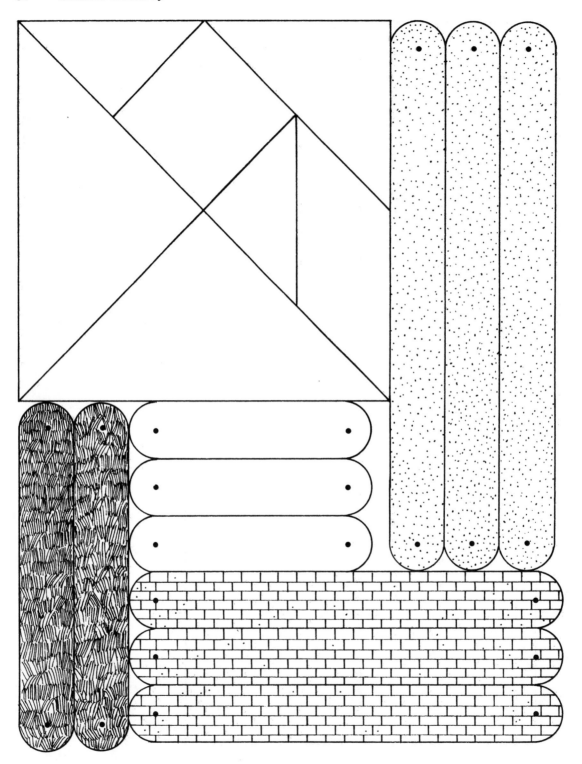

2. *Sorting.* Sort the pieces that your group has made. Describe two possible ways to sort them. _____
Play Guess My Rule: one person thinks of a rule and starts sorting without telling the rule, while the others try to guess where the remaining pieces belong.

3. *Some Questions.* What was the smallest number of shapes you used to build a solid? _____ What was the largest number? _____ Can you imagine using more? less? Did you make, or can you imagine making, a solid using *only* squares? _____ only the smaller triangles? _____ only the larger triangles? _____ only the rectangles? Did you make, or can you imagine making, solids using

just ⬜ 's and △ 's _____   just ⬜ 's and △ 's _____

just ⬜ 's and ▭ 's _____   just △ 's and △ 's _____

just △ 's and ▭ 's _____   just △ 's and ▭ 's _____

4. *Some Names.* The way of sorting solids shown here introduces two special types of solids, prisms and pyramids. Which solids could be made from the shapes you used?

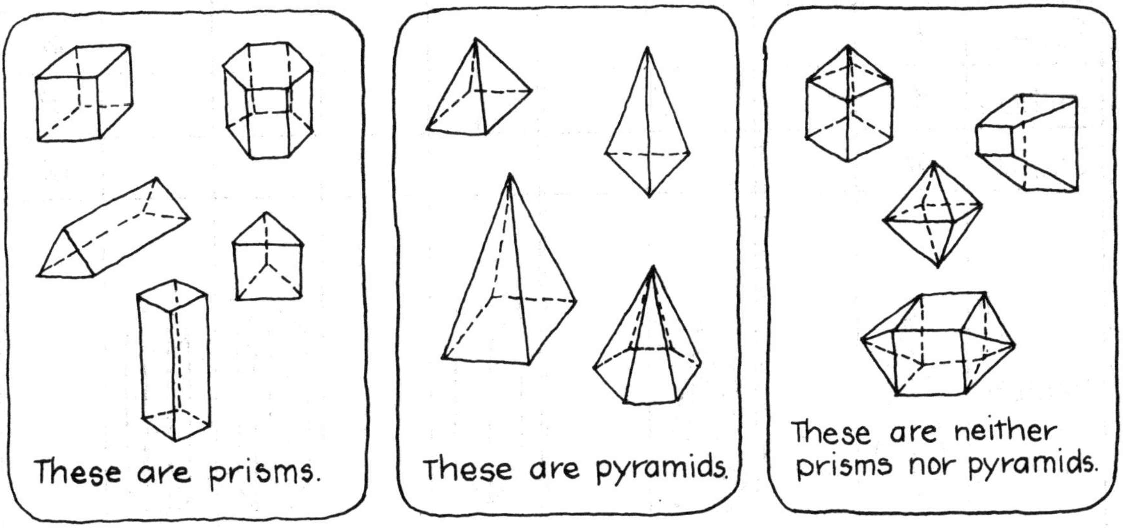

These are prisms.

These are pyramids.

These are neither prisms nor pyramids.

In which loops do your shapes belong? Sort them and compare your results with a neighbor.
List some properties of a prism.

List some properties of a pyramid.

A triangular prism is like an optical prism: it has two triangular faces and the others are rectangles. In the loop above, there are two triangular prisms, a hexagonal prism, and two _____ prisms.

5. *Faces, Vertices, and Edges.* Examples of a cube are dice or sugar cubes. Did you make a cube? Find the picture of a cube in part 4. Describe another everyday example:

A cube has 6 *faces.* What is a face?
A cube has 8 *vertices.* What is a vertex?
A cube has 12 *edges.* What is an edge?
Find the pictures of square pyramids in part 4. A square pyramid has _____ faces, _____ vertices, and _____ edges.
Fill in the chart below. A few of the figures have been sketched. Sketch the missing ones.

	Triangular Pyramid	Square Pyramid	Pentagonal Pyramid	Hexagonal Pyramid	Triangular Prism	Square Prism	Pentagonal Prism	Hexagonal Prism	Cube
Faces	4								6
Vertices	4								8
Edges	6								12
Sketch	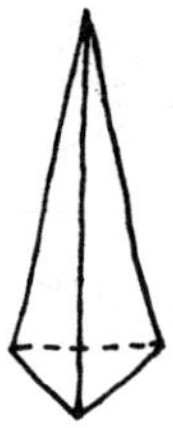		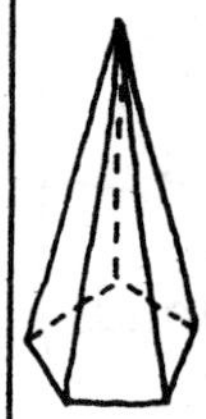		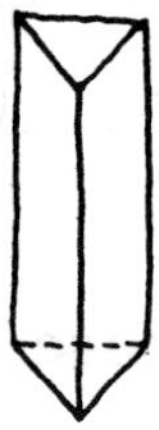			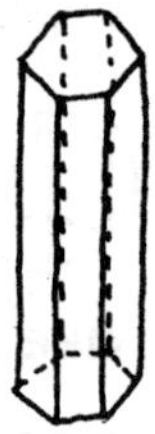	

Do you notice any patterns? You might see some patterns which work just for pyramids, or just for prisms. Describe these patterns below.
    Pattern for pyramids:
    Pattern for prisms:
There is also a pattern that relates the number of faces, the number of edges, and the number of vertices for any of these figures. (**Hint:** To

see it, add the number of faces and vertices and compare the sum to the number of edges.) Describe the pattern below. Use your own pieces to check this pattern for other solids.

Faces			
Vertices			
Edges			
Sketch			

6. *Mobiles.* (Optional) Make a mobile from the shapes you constructed. You might use some method of classifying to design your mobile. Do you see how this mobile is organized?

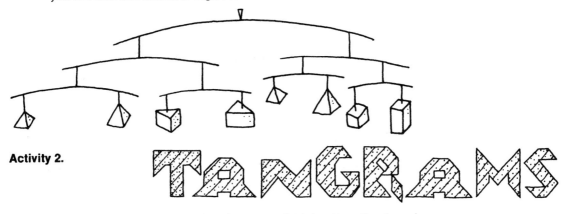

Activity 2.

TANGRAMS

In Activity 1, you explored how flat shapes can be joined together to make three-dimensional forms. In this activity you will again be putting shapes together, but this time to make patterns that lie flat on the page. The particular collection of pieces that you will use for this is a traditional and popular puzzle, known as tangrams, originating in China around 1800.[1]

Materials: Scissors; paste; cardboard; duplicated copy of page 94
Directions: To make a tangram puzzle, cut out the square from the given duplicated sheet and paste it onto a piece of cardboard. Then cut along all of the lines, including the outer edge of the square.

1. a. Do you think that the pieces you cut out can be arranged to make the large cat on page 99? Try it by placing the pieces on top of the large white cat.
   b. Choose one of the small figures — a cat or a letter — and try to make a similar shape using all of the pieces. Each one can be made using all seven pieces.[2] Which was easier, making the large cat or making shapes similar to the small figures? Why?
   c. Make your own puzzle. Puzzles need not use all seven pieces. Pick three pieces, make a shape with them (without overlaps), and outline it.
   Ask your neighbor to solve your puzzle without telling which pieces you used. Did your neighbor use the same pieces and arrange them as you did?
   Can your shape be made with fewer than three pieces? _____ with more than three pieces? _____
   Variation: Try your puzzle on someone else, but this time tell them which pieces you used. Was it easier for them to do?
   d. Puzzles can be given verbally, without a diagram. Try these.

   Make the parallelogram (⟋⟋) with two small triangles.
   Make the largest triangle with a square and some triangles.
   Can you make a square with two pieces? _____ three pieces? _____ four pieces? _____
   Can you make a triangle with two pieces? _____ three pieces? _____ four pieces? _____
   Make a rectangle with three pieces. Can you do it another way?
   (More difficult) Use all seven pieces to make each of the following puzzles:
   a triangle; two squares that are the same size; the original square. (**Note:** It will help if you have an outline of the original four-inch square.)

2. *Sorting.* Sort the seven pieces. Which ones belong together? Why? Perhaps you sorted in one of the ways drawn below. In each case, label the piles.

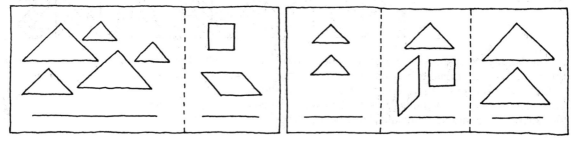

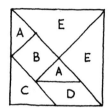

3. *Numbers and the Tangram Pieces.* For convenience, label the tangram pieces as shown here.

a. How many *different* shapes can you make from the two small triangles  ? Draw some.

b. How many copies of the small triangle are needed to cover each of the other pieces?

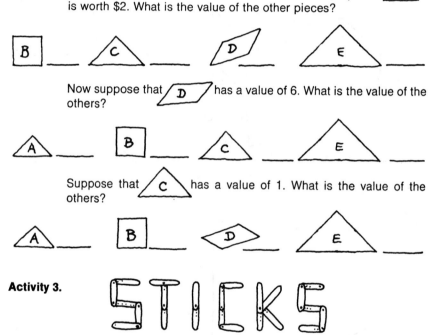

B ___   C ___   D ___   E ___

(Does this have anything to do with the sorting shown in part 2?)

c. Suppose that the puzzle is made of silver, and the piece A is worth $2. What is the value of the other pieces?

B ___   C ___   D ___   E ___

Now suppose that D has a value of 6. What is the value of the others?

A ___   B ___   C ___   E ___

Suppose that C has a value of 1. What is the value of the others?

A ___   B ___   D ___   E ___

Activity 3.   STICKS

In the previous activities you looked at shapes as regions or surfaces. Now instead you will work with the outlines or edges of regions.

Many commercial materials, described further on, can be used for activities like the following. We will use a substitute which has some limitations, but which you or children can make, and which does allow you to experience the potential of the more attractive and easily handled commercial materials.

Materials: (Use either the straws and accompanying materials or the geostrips.) Straws (4 each of white, green, red, and yellow); scissors; ruler; thick pipe cleaners (or little lumps of clay, or heavy thread and paper clips). Duplicated copy of page 94 (for geostrips); paste; scissors; cardboard; paper punch; paper fasteners.

Directions: To use the straws, cut them into lengths as follows: white (W), 2 inches; green (G), 3 inches; red (R), 4 inches; and yellow (Y), 5 inches.

Use some material for joining the straws, such as short segments of thick pipe cleaners, little lumps of clay, or heavy thread and "needles" made from bent paper clips.

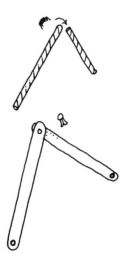

To make the geostrips, paste the duplicated copy of page 94 onto a piece of cardboard, then cut out the strips, using a paper punch to make the holes. The textures are intended to suggest the following colors: green (G, tufts of grass), red (R, brick), yellow (Y, sand), and white (W, smooth). The lengths between holes are in the same proportion as described for straws. Use paper fasteners to join the strips through the holes.

In some activities you may find it easier simply to place the straws so that they just touch, or the geostrips so that the holes are matched, while in others it will be necessary to fasten them.

1. *Triangles*

    a. Make two triangles, and compare them with your neighbors'. Were the triangles alike in any way?

    Triangles can be named by three letters representing the colors of the sides. For example, make W G R. Is G R W the same triangle? Make a triangle with only two colors of sticks. Name it with letters and sketch it.

    Make a triangle with only one color. Name it with letters and sketch it.

    b. List all the possible color combinations that can be made with three sides where

    all sides have the same color _____ _____ _____ _____

    two sides have the same color and the third is different

    _____ _____ _____ _____ _____ _____ _____ _____ _____ _____ _____

    all sides have different colors _____ _____ _____ _____

    Some of the color combinations above will *not* make a triangle. Circle those that do not work. (You should find three.)

    If two sticks together are shorter than a third stick, then one (can, can't) _____ make a triangle.

    In a triangle, the sum of the lengths of any two sides is _____ than the length of the third side.

    c. In part b, triangles are classified into three groups which have special names: *isosceles,* from Greek, *iso-* meaning equal and *skelos* meaning leg; *equilateral,* from Latin, *equi-* meaning equal and *latus* meaning side; and *scalene,* from Greek, *skalenos* meaning limping or uneven.

    From the word origins, match the type of triangle to its name.

        All sides have the same color: _____

        Two sides have the same color, the third is different: _____

        All sides have different colors: _____

            (**Note:** If you described the triangles where all sides have the same color as isosceles, you would in fact be correct; but these triangles are also equilateral. Are all isosceles triangles equilateral? Are all equilateral triangles isosceles?

d. Take two different triangles with all sides the same color, for example, WWW and RRR. Can you hold up one so that its outline

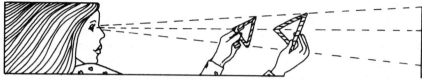

exactly covers the other? _____ (See the picture here.) Try this with two triangles where all sides have different colors, for example, WGR and GRY. Does one triangle exactly cover the other?

If one triangle can be made to cover the other in this way, we say the two triangles are *similar*. This definition of similarity depends on the two shapes being held in parallel planes — that is, both facing in the same direction. (You might experiment with trying to line up two triangles visually which are *not* similar by tilting one of them.) Are *all* triangles with all sides the same color (that is, equilateral triangles) similar? _____ Can you make any pair of triangles with two sides the same color and a third different (that is, isosceles but not equilateral) which are similar?

e. Make a triangle with a white, a green, and a red side. Is your triangle the same as your neighbor's? By "the same" we mean "the same size and the same shape," or *congruent*. Two triangles are congruent if you can place one exactly on top of the other so that it just fits. Notice that if two shapes are congruent, then they are also similar.

Do you think that any two triangles made from W, G, and R sides will be congruent?

If two people take sides of the same three colors and make triangles, will the triangles always be congruent?

2. *Polygons*

a. Take one of each color side: W, G, R, and Y. Make a four-sided figure (a *quadrilateral* from the Latin *quadri-* meaning four and *latus* meaning side). Is your quadrilateral congruent to your neighbor's? _____ If you keep the pieces flat on the table, can you move the sides around (without disconnecting them) so that your shape is congruent to your neighbor's?

Sketch your quadilateral in two different formations — make one convex and the other nonconvex. The concept of *convex* shapes was introduced on page 28. A figure is said to be convex if the line segment joining any two points in the figure lies inside the figure.

b. Make a quadrilateral with four sides of the same color. What sorts of figures can you get by moving the edges around? (Can you make a nonconvex one?) Draw three and name them.

Take 2 G's and 2 Y's, and make a quadrilateral. What sorts of shapes can you make? You should find that there are two ways to join the sticks. Draw some shapes that you can get from each way. What do you observe about the two kinds of shapes? Which can you name?

G's next to each other.

G's opposite each other.

c. Make a flat figure using more than four sides. Draw it. You made a polygon (from Greek, *poly* meaning many and *gon* meaning angle). What sort of a polygon did you make? Prefixes for "-gon" come from the Greek words for numbers: penta- (5), hexa- (6), hepta- (7), octa- (8), nona- (9), deca- (10). Yours is a _____gon. (Triangles and quadrilaterals are also polygons, but of course their names do not fit the same pattern.)

d. (Optional) If you make a triangle from geostrips, it is rigid — that is, you cannot change its shape without bending the cardboard. If, however, you make a quadrilaterial from geostrips, it is flexible. If you want it to stay rigid, you must add one "stiffening strip" on a diagonal.

How many stiffening strips would you need to make a pentagon stay rigid? _____ a hexagon? _____ an "*n*-gon"? _____

3. *Three-dimensional Shapes.* Imagine using straws for this activity.

   a. Suppose a pyramid is made with straws of the same color. How many straws are needed? What kind of triangles are the faces of the pyramid? How many straws would you need to make a cube?

   b. Could you make a shape like a milk carton with our straws? (See figure.) Which colors would you use and how many of each? Could you make a shape like a brick? Which colors would you use and how many of each?

  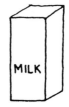 

DISCUSSION QUESTIONS AND COMMENTS

What Is Meant by Informal Geometry?

Do you remember doing geometry activities like the ones in this chapter in school? Perhaps your most recent memories of geometry are from a high school course which stressed the deductive nature of mathematics. Beginning with certain undefined terms (such as point, line, plane) and assumed facts or postulates (such as "Two points determine exactly one line"), one can define other geometric concepts and logically deduce or prove various theorems (such as "The diagonals of a square are perpendicular"). This kind of geometry might be called formal — although high school courses vary considerably in the amount of formality or rigor. Most mathematics educators and teachers agree that formal geometry does not belong in the standard elementary school curriculum. The approach to geometry in grades K–6 should be informal — that is, characterized by exploration, discovery, use of manipulative materials, and relations to the child's environment. Geometry is something children *do*, not something they read about. It is to be experienced.

Teachers sometimes try to use the method by which they last learned geometry to teach geometry to children — that is, they may give a definition for a concept (as is done in a formal development) and expect children to use this definition to identify examples of the concept. However this approach is not appropriate for young children who do not reason in the same way as high school students or adults, and do not really know what definitions are all about. In the same spirit that Piaget has studied the stages in a child's intellectual development, the Dutch professor P.-H. van Hiele has studied and described various levels of geometric thought and their implications for teaching geometry.[3] Van Hiele found that children must proceed through these levels in order, although the ages at which these levels are attained seem to vary widely and depend on the sort of geometry experiences made available to the child. At first, children might deal with geometric concepts just by looking. They may say a shape is a square because it looks like one, without being able to describe why. Later, after various experiences with manipulative materials, they will discover and describe many properties of a square. Eventually they will learn that some properties are dependent on others, and they will see certain logical relations between them. Only then will they understand that to identify and to define a square completely, one needs isolate only a few properties in a definition.

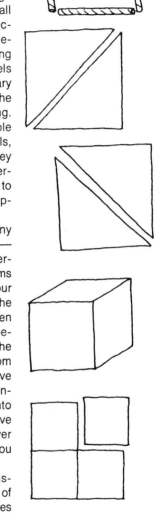

In the initial Activities in this chapter, you experienced a few of the many ways in which children might learn about squares. In each set of Activities — Solids, Tangrams, and Sticks — you may have thought of a square in a different way. The stick model for a square suggests thinking of a square in terms of its sides. Making a square with strips or straws leads us to see that the four sides of a square must have equal length, but that this is not enough — the straws must also be adjusted so that the corners all look the same. When using the tangram pieces to make square regions, the need is seen for a special type of corner (a right angle) to make a shape that looks square. The tangram model also leads children to see that a square can be formed from two congruent triangles in two ways (see diagram) and so the diagonals have the same length. When building solids from squares, you were probably concerned with matching lengths of sides, and also with how the corners fit into an angle between two other sides. You probably noticed that a solid can have three squares meeting at a vertex, in this case at a vertex of a cube. However if you had tried to build a solid with four squares meeting at a vertex, you would have found that it was impossible because the four squares lie flat.

After extended experiences with a variety of materials, children may discover and verbalize some of the following properties of a square. (Some of these properties are also possessed by other figures; for example, rectangles or diamonds.)

    a. It has four sides.
    b. The sides have equal length.
    c. Opposite sides are parallel.
    d. It has four angles.
    e. All the angles are congruent.
    f. All the angles are right angles.

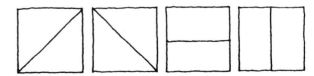

g. The region it bounds can be folded in half in four ways.
h. Square regions can be fitted together to cover the top of a table.
i. You see it on the sides of a cube.
j. The region it bounds can be formed from two congruent triangular regions.
k. The diagonals have the same length.
l. Add another property.

Children will eventually see that the properties listed above are interrelated. For example,
(a) and (d) — Figures which have four sides also have four angles.
(b) and (c) — Figures with four equal sides have opposite sides parallel.
Write a relationship involving properties (d), (e), and (f).

At a later age, possibly in high school, children may attain a more formal level of geometric thought and work with definitions — a collection of properties, without unnecessary ones, which determines a square exactly. Which of the following are definitions of a square? (**Hint:** Only one is *not!*)

A square is a polygon with four right angles and all sides of equal length.
A square is a four-sided polygon whose sides are all of equal length.
A square is a four-sided polygon with all sides of equal length and all angles congruent.
A square is a quadrilateral with sides of equal length whose diagonals are also of equal length.

According to van Hiele, many children have difficulty attaining this formal level of geometric thought because they lack experience at the preceding levels, especially with exploration, discovery, and description of a variety of geometric properties.

Some teachers stress the *naming* of shapes in their geometry work with young children. These teachers might not want to use the tangram puzzle in a kindergarten class because the children do not know the name for piece $\angle\boxed{D}\,$. Some kindergarten children may actually enjoy saying "parallelogram." However their knowing the name does not guarantee their knowledge of any properties of the piece, and is not essential for their enjoyment of play with the pieces (which will lay groundwork for later mathematical concepts). There is no need to pressure children to learn names for shapes or to feel that children should only deal with shapes they can name. It is important that they have opportunities to "get the feel" of a wide range of geometric concepts and to give their own descriptions before attaching the formal names to the concepts. They should have a rich diet of informal geometry using materials, such as solids, tangrams, straws, and those used later in this chapter, or similar commercial materials.

What Mathematical Concepts and Processes Arose in the Activities?

Many of the initial Activities involved classification leading to building up concepts and terminology. For example in Solids, your constructions were classified as prisms, pyramids, or neither; in Tangrams, pieces were classified as triangles, quadrilaterals, or by their size; and in Sticks, triangles were classified as isosceles, equilateral, or scalene, and polygons were classified by their number of sides. These Activities are intended to do more, however, than have you classify shapes and name them.

First, you were asked to describe your classification schemes verbally. But also, in each set of Activities, you experienced some other mathematical processes. For example, in Solids, you collected data about the number of vertices, sides, and edges, looked for patterns relating these numbers, and described these patterns. You also may have exercised your ability to visualize and sketch three-dimensional constructions. In Tangrams, when doing the large cat puzzle, you were estimating lengths when finding the edge that fits, and when doing the small ones, you were recognizing similarity of shapes. When examining how many of one shape fit into another (Activity 2, part 3b) you were measuring area. When you attached numerical values to certain shapes (Activity 2, part 3c) you were applying your knowledge of the operations of multiplication and division of whole numbers and fractions. In Sticks, when listing all possible triangles that could be formed, you probably organized the color combinations in some way. You also examined how shapes made from sticks can be changed by adjusting the angles.

Many geometry activities for children are now available in textbooks or on task cards. As you examine them, think about whether children are being involved in many processes beyond classification and naming of shapes and geometric relationships. Even if a teacher's primary objective is to practice terminology, this can be accomplished in process-oriented activities (as will be seen in the Follow-up Section on points, lines, and planes).

How Can Activities Be Modified for Other Materials?

There are various commercial materials available that resemble those you used in the initial Activities. The Activities can be modified for use with these materials.

Solids

Durable shapes for constructing solids are available commercially. One such set of shapes has notches at the corners, and adjacent sides can be fastened with rubber bands. These are much easier for children to manipulate than the paper models you used, and also they are reusable.

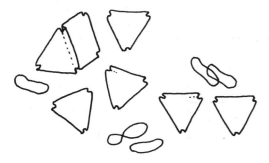

For many classification activities with solids, you can find models in the world around you. In the Activities in this chapter, you dealt only with a particular type of solid shape, a *polyhedron*. Study the creature card below and write a description of a polyhedron.

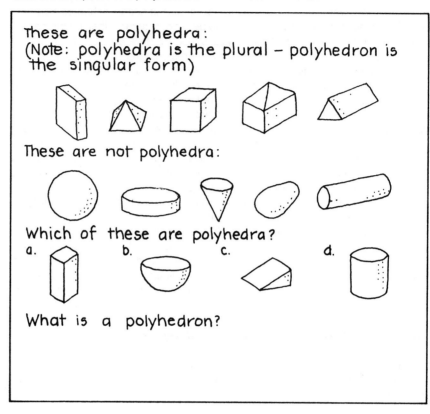

These are polyhedra:
(Note: polyhedra is the plural — polyhedron is the singular form)

These are not polyhedra:

Which of these are polyhedra?
a.   b.   c.   d.

What is a polyhedron?

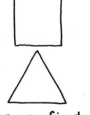

Find the solid whose faces just fit in these outlines.

Can you find more than one?

You may remember (Activity 3, part 2c) that *poly* is Greek for many. What do you think *hedron* comes from?

Do the sketches in the creature card remind you of everyday objects? Write names for such objects next to the figures, if you can. For classification activities with children, you might start a collection of solid shapes. Look for unusual boxes, containers, paper cups, etc.

If you have a collection of polyhedra available, you can make puzzles related to the questions in Activity 1, part 3. The puzzles can be written on activity cards to be kept with the box of solids. See the example provided. Which of the solids drawn below would be solutions to this puzzle?

a.   b.   c.   d.   e.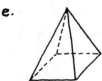

Tangrams

Attractive wooden, plastic, or cardboard tangram sets are available commercially, together with puzzles printed on activity cards. You will also find many puzzles in books.[4] The classic tangram puzzles — for example the cats in Activity 2 — may be too difficult for some children, especially if they lack self-confidence. Here are three ways in which this sort of puzzle can be simplified.

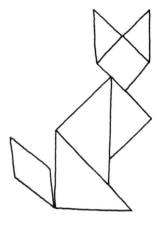

1. Outline the puzzle pieces. The puzzle then becomes an exercise in estimation of size and matching of shapes.
2. Begin with puzzles with fewer pieces. Have children make such simpler puzzles (as you did in Activity 2, part 1c, or as in the puzzles at the top of page 110).
3. Provide a sequence of puzzles of increasing difficulty. The card to the left below is to be used with a sequence of envelopes. The envelopes are numbered and should be used in that order. Each envelope contains a set of color-coded shapes.

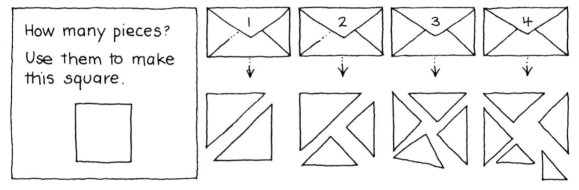

Children's work with tangram puzzles can be motivated and encouraged by displays on a bulletin board. You might want every child to have his own set so that he can work on designing and solving puzzles in his free time, in and out of school. However it is expensive to buy enough commercially made tangram sets for a whole class — and very time-consuming for a teacher to make them. Instead, children can make their own. This might encourage them to look after the set more carefully and also they can learn about the pieces while making their set. You could have children simply cut out a printed outline (such as on page 94, which could be reproduced on oak tag on a spirit duplicating machine), but perhaps a more interesting and informative procedure would be to give each child a square of paper (four inches by four inches is a good size) and give them instructions about how to fold, carefully crease, and then tear or cut the square. For a more durable set, pieces can be pasted or traced onto cardboard.

(Optional) Try this yourself. Take a square of paper and try to divide it precisely into the pieces of the tangram puzzle, as shown here, *only* by folding and cutting or tearing — without rulers! (As an extra challenge, take *any* piece of paper, and just by folding, make yourself a square to begin with.) Can you give verbal directions for this sequence of steps?

Shape puzzles can also be constructed from other classroom materials. Many educational supply companies sell collections of wooden or plastic shapes which children can use to create patterns. Children can do the activities below (resembling tangram puzzles) with any set of shapes that include equilateral triangles and squares (with sides of equal length). Children can invent such tasks themselves and try them on their friends. Here are problems at three levels of difficulty.

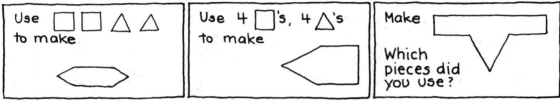

Sticks

Plastic geostrips are available commercially, or children can cut them from colored oak tag. (A paper cutter will help.) The plastic version is more durable and easier to work with; it is also much more expensive. Some commercial sets of colored plastic sticks come with little rubber "joiners" which are quite strong, but still flexible. Some come with small plastic balls with holes to put the sticks in. The sets with rigid balls are not suitable for studying flexibility of polygons (as in Activity 3, part 2), while geostrips are not suitable for building in three dimensions (as in Activity 3, part 3). Some sets are not color-coded by length, as in our Activities. However, you can usually pick out such a color-coded set if the activity requires it. Children can also build two- and three-dimensional constructions from toothpicks stuck into whole dried peas that have been soaked in water for a couple of hours to soften them. (In a day or so they will dry out and harden again.) These toothpick constructions — or ones made with colored straws — make especially nice holiday decorations.

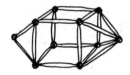

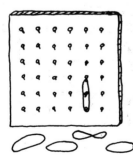

Another Type of Material

With another type of material, children construct squares not primarily from regions of a plane, nor from pieces of a line, but rather from the sets of points that form the corners or vertices. One common example of this type of material is the geoboard, a wooden or plastic board with little nails or pegs at regular intervals. Children make shapes by stretching rubber bands around the pegs. On the picture of a geoboard shown here, determine how a child might make a square with a rubber band. Can you do it in other ways? We will explore geoboards more thoroughly in a later chapter.

FOLLOW-UP SECTIONS

MIRRORS AND SYMMETRY

Reflections are an important part of our perception of the world. We see ourselves in the mirror, use a rear-view mirror in a car, or see trees reflected in a lake. A mirror image is very close to the original, but it is not the same. Mirrors are fascinating to many children — after all, Alice went "through the looking glass" to get to Wonderland. In this section, we will explore how mirrors are related to a type of geometry known as *symmetry*. We will begin with informal activities, and later show how symmetry fits into a broader mathematical structure.

You will need a rectangular pocket mirror, without any edging. (You might feel that a glass mirror is dangerous for use with children. One can buy nonbreakable ones of polished metal or plastic.) Here are examples of two uses of a mirror.

A. Find the hidden WOW in each of the drawings below. Put a mirror on the dotted line in the first two. Where does the mirror go in the third?

1. TOMORROW

2. WCFields

3.

B. Put a mirror on the dotted line in the picture below. What do you see? Can you make time go backwards? Can you make twins?

Pages 112 and 113 present two types of mirror activities.[5] The pages should be photocopied and the squares cut apart so that children can work with them separately and sort them.

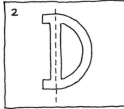

Directions for Pattern Cards. Place the mirror on each of the cards 2–9 to try to make the pattern on pattern card 1. For example, put the mirror on the dotted line indicated on card 2, as shown here, to see the picture on pattern card 1.

Sort the cards into two piles — those from which you *can* make the pattern, and those from which you *cannot.* You should be able to make the pattern with all but four cards. List the four cards: _____ _____ _____ _____

Draw two more pictures from which you *can* make the pattern.

Directions for Mirror Cards: Place the mirror on the mirror card 1 to try to make each pattern on the other cards 2–9. For example, put the mirror on the dotted line indicated on mirror card 1, as shown here, to see the pattern on card 2.

   Sort the cards into two piles — those which *can* be done in one pile, and those which *cannot* be done in another pile. Two of these cards cannot be duplicated. List the two cards: _____ _____ Draw two more patterns that *can* be made from mirror card 1.

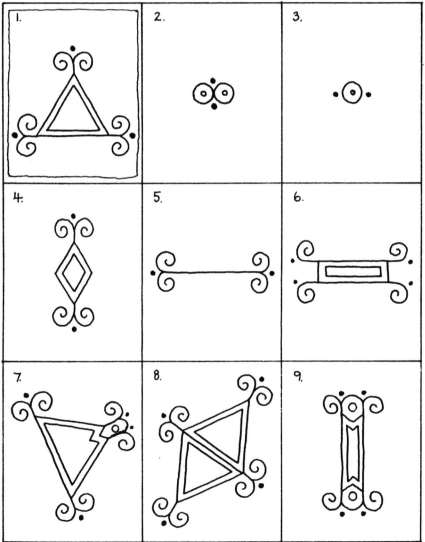

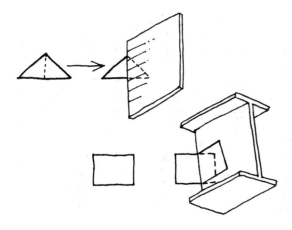

The pattern card and mirror card activities are informal ways to give children experience with a geometry concept (line symmetry) which can be formalized later. A *line of symmetry* (or *axis of symmetry*) for a figure is a line on which you can stand a mirror so that the image that you see in the mirror is just like the part of the figure that the mirror is hiding. This is particularly easy to see with a *Mira*[6] —a commercially produced piece of red plastic which reflects, but through which you can also see the paper behind. Use a mirror or a Mira to find all lines of symmetry for the figures below. Draw the lines of symmetry on each of the figures and indicate how many lines of symmetry each figure has.

Triangles

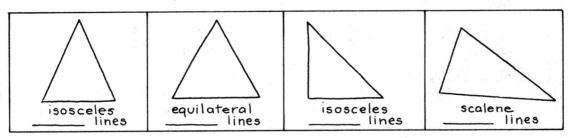

Can you generalize? An equilateral triangle is a triangle that has exactly _____ lines of symmetry; an isosceles triangle (which is not equilateral) has exactly _____ lines of symmetry. (Can you draw a triangle which has exactly *two* lines of symmetry? _____ Why?)

Quadrilaterals

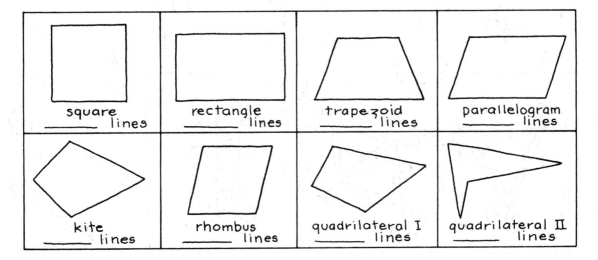

Which have

    four lines of symmetry? _____
    two lines of symmetry? _____ _____
    one line of symmetry? _____ _____
    no lines of symmetry? _____ _____ _____

You should have found two quadrilaterals that have two lines of symmetry. A rhombus has lines of symmetry through its _____; a rectangle has lines of symmetry through its _____.

    Upper elementary school children might use a mirror activity such as this to review definitions learned previously (for example, a square is a four-sided polygon with four right angles and all sides of equal length). Reviewing such definitions can be tedious and boring — but it may be more interesting and challenging if done using symmetry. Children could formulate new definitions of shapes (for example, a square is a four-sided polygon with four lines of symmetry) and then refer back to the old definitions to see how they correspond.

Other Polygons

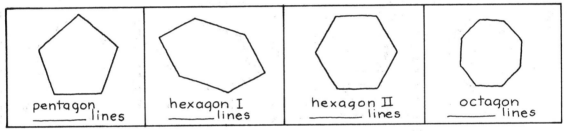

A polygon is *regular* if all of its sides are of equal length, *and* all of the interior angles are congruent. For example, equilateral triangles and squares are regular, and so are the pentagon, hexagon II, and octagon above. (Why aren't nonsquare rectangles and hexagon I above regular?) Fill in the following: A regular polygon with n sides has _____ lines of symmetry.

Other Figures

All of the figures drawn above have between zero and eight lines of symmetry, *except* the circle. Since *any* diameter of a circle is a line of symmetry for it, the circle has an infinite number of lines of symmetry.

Other Activities Involving Line Symmetry

Some text series include problems in which children are expected to identify lines of symmetry on the printed page by eye. These problems may be difficult for children who have had little or no previous experience with symmetry. Children can actively experience symmetry in many ways to build up their ability to recognize it in pictures. Of course, they can use mirrors, as in the activities before, but the materials below are also suitable.

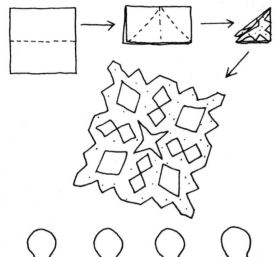

Paperfolding. Children can fold paper, cut out pieces from the folded paper, and unfold. What patterns can you make? How can you fold it to make a "snowflake"? The following are some more difficult variations:

> As you cut, predict how many holes you will have in the final pattern. Check by counting.
> How can you fold paper to make a chain of paper dolls?
> Make a pattern, unfold and make a "shadow painting" by using your pattern as a stencil; have someone tell you where you folded your pattern.

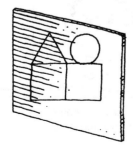

Inkblots. Spill ink or paint on paper, fold, rub, and unfold. What do you see?

Building Games. Use colored blocks of any shapes. One child builds a pattern and another copies the pattern in "mirror image." Check with a mirror.

Symmetry Hunt. Hunt for things that have line symmetry. Check by using a mirror. You might look at letters, people, plants, decorations, and pictures of all sorts.

Other Types of Symmetry

The pinwheel to the right does not have any lines of symmetry — if you don't believe it, try it with a mirror — but it has another type of symmetry or regularity. If you were to cut out the pinwheel, hold the center fixed on a flat surface with a pin, and spin it around, then it would look just the same after a quarter turn. This figure has *rotational symmetry*. A figure is said to have rotational symmetry about a point if it can be rotated or turned about that point (by some amount less than a full circle) so that it fits exactly on top of its previous position. Which of the figures below have rotational symmetry? (If you are not sure, you could trace a figure on tracing paper and then try to turn the tracing paper to fit over the outline in another way.)

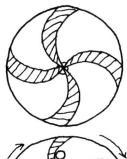

a.  b.  c.  d. 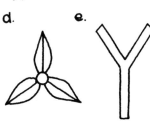 e.

If you examine regular patterns or decorations — on wallpaper, buildings, edges of printed material — you will find many examples of both line symmetry and rotational symmetry. Some patterns may have still another type of symmetry or regularity, as do the strips below.

These patterns are said to have *translational symmetry*. If you move the strip sideways a certain amount, the pattern will fit exactly on top of its original position. On the first pattern above, an arrow indicates how far the pattern must be moved so that it fits. Draw such arrows on the other strips also.

Symmetry and Motions

You have seen how both rotational and translational symmetry can be viewed in terms of motions of the figure or object. You can determine if a figure or pattern has these two types of symmetry by either rotating or turning it about a point, or sliding it along a line. Can you see how line symmetry can also be viewed in terms of motions? The heart-shaped figure to the right has the dotted line as a line of symmetry. Imagine this shape as being cut out of paper. How could you move the piece of paper so that it would again fit over the outline?

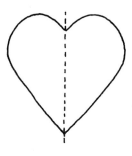

The study of motions is a branch of geometry, called transformational or motion geometry, which has been included in the elementary school curriculum relatively recently. One use of transformational geometry is in the study of symmetry — line, rotational, and translational. In the later chapter (Geometry on a Geoboard), we will see more of the types of motions connected with each type of symmetry: flips, turns, and slides (or as they are called more formally, reflections, rotations, and translations).

Maze activities such as those in this section can serve to introduce certain concepts related to curves, and also to provide an opportunity to discover a pattern.

Cat and Mice

The lines below are walls. The cat would like to capture the mice. Neither cat nor mice can cross the walls. Which mice are not safe?

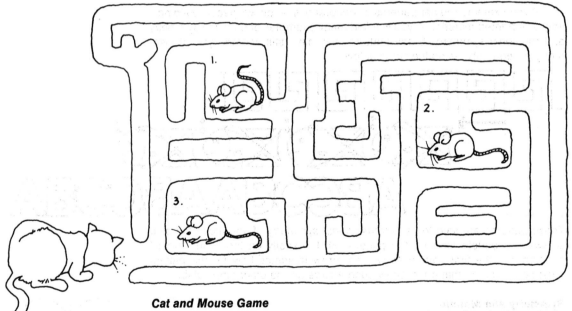

Cat and Mouse Game

Two people can play a game on the maze above. One is the cat, the other the mouse. Each holds a sharp pencil over the maze and with eyes closed, lowers it onto the page. If the "cat" can get from its pencil point to the mouse's pencil point without crossing a wall, the cat gets a point. If the "mouse" is safe, the mouse gets a point. Try this game.

Variation: Color in all of the places where the mouse would *not* be safe from the cat as drawn above. Would this coloring help you to check who has won in the Cat and Mouse Game?

A Pattern to Discover

There is an easy way to tell if the cat can get to the mouse, even without coloring in a complicated maze. Draw a direct path from mouse 1 (who is safe) to the cat. How many times does this path cross the wall? _____ Try this for mouse 2 (who is *not* safe) — the path crosses the wall _____ times. For mouse 3 (who is safe) the path crosses the wall _____ times. Try putting the mouse in various positions. In each case, draw paths from the mouse to the cat, crossing the walls, but avoid having the path just "graze" the wall

like this: ⌐\ . Instead wriggle the path a little so that it either misses the

wall entirely (⌐) or goes through the wall twice (⤙⤚). Try this for eight different positions of the mouse, and fill in this table.

	Number of Intersections
Mouse safe	
Mouse in danger	

When do you think the mouse is safe?

Check your theory with other mouse positions and compare it with someone else's theory.

Tracers

All preceding activities depended on the "wall" or maze being of a certain type. To describe this type of curve, we need some vocabulary. Do the creature cards below.

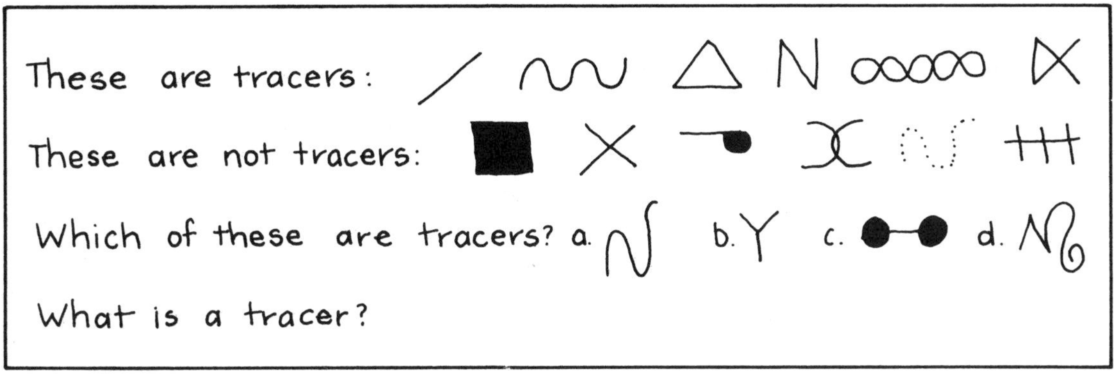

Tracers are more commonly called *curves*. Notice that the mathematical use of the word *curve* is somewhat different from everyday usage. In speech, we distinguish between the straight parts of a road and the curves. However in mathematical language, a straight line segment is a curve. Children can think of a curve as anything that can be traced with a fine pencil, without lifting it from the paper and without doubling back; or as anything that can be made from a fine piece of string laid on a page without cutting.

Closed Curves

The creature cards below introduce the concept and related terminology for some types of curves.

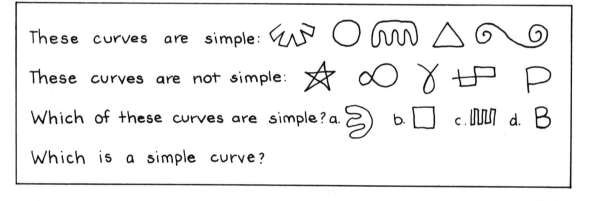

Note: A curve that is not closed is called *open.*

Simple Curves

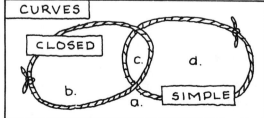

In which of the four regions of the loop diagram shown here does each curve above belong?

The curves in the *intersection* of the two sets (closed curves and simple curves) are *simple closed curves.* The curve that forms the wall in the Cat and Mouse Game is of this type, and we have seen that this curve separated the page into two regions — one where the mice are not safe, and one where they are. In fact any simple closed curve separates a flat surface into an "inside" and an "outside."

What happens if you try to make a maze from a curve that is not simple and closed? Color in the regions where the mouse is safe in these mazes.

NETWORKS

An Old Problem

The map drawn here is of the German town of Konigsberg (in the 18th century). The town was built on an island and on the banks of the river Pregel. Could a person plan a walk in the city so that he will cross each bridge *exactly* once?

The problem above was studied, generalized, and solved by the great mathematician Leonard Euler in 1735. One step in the solution was abstracting the problem. Since we are only interested in the bridges, we can think of the land masses as "blobs" or points.

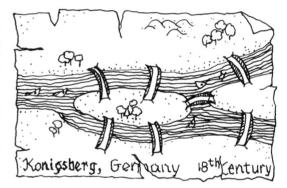

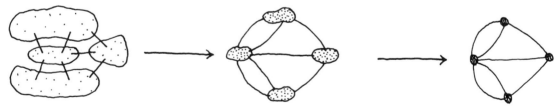

Now try to trace a path around this abstracted plan of the city. Could you plan a route that goes along each "bridge" or curve just once? What would happen if a new bridge was built, so that the abstract plan looked like this diagram? Could you now plan a path that crosses each bridge just once? (**Hint:** Start at the "island" or dot on the left.)

Discovering a Pattern

In this section you will discover a way to tell if a route can be planned to traverse each curve just once on any plan like the one above. First, some terminology will help. Plans like the one above are called *networks.* A network is made up of points (called vertices, or vertex in the singular), and curves connecting them called edges. Some networks can be "traced"; that is, you can place a pencil on one vertex and trace a path over the network that covers each edge exactly once. For example, the modified plan of Konigsberg can be traced. Some networks cannot be traced; for example, the original plan of Konigsberg. Try to trace the following networks. When you can trace them, describe your path by listing in order the vertices passed through. The first network has been done.

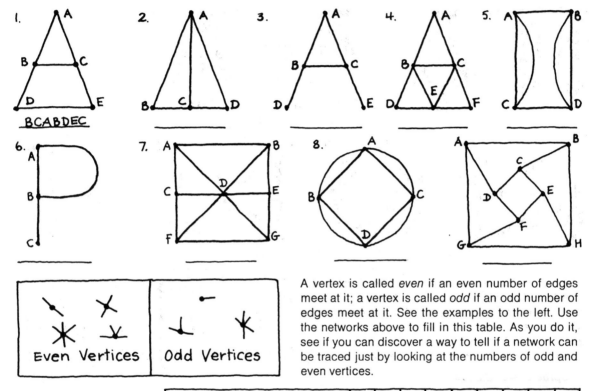

A vertex is called *even* if an even number of edges meet at it; a vertex is called *odd* if an odd number of edges meet at it. See the examples to the left. Use the networks above to fill in this table. As you do it, see if you can discover a way to tell if a network can be traced just by looking at the numbers of odd and even vertices.

Network	1	2	3	4	5	6	7	8	9
Number of Even Vertices	3								
Number of Odd Vertices	2								
Can it be traced?	Yes								

Make a conjecture: A network can be traced if _____.

Hint: You need only look at the number of *odd* vertices.

Try to check your conjecture. Draw some more networks to try it out. Can you make a network that disproves your conjecture? Does your conjecture work for the problem of the Bridges of Konigsberg? Compare your conjecture with someone else's.

When are two networks "the same"?

Can you trace network (1) below? _____ (2)? _____ (3)? _____ (4)? _____

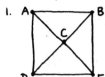 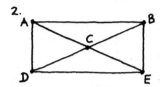 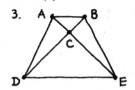 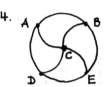

You may have actually tried all four, but you probably recognized that in terms of tracing, they are all the same — for example, (2) is just (1) stretched out sideways. If you could trace (1) (and you cannot) the same path would work for all of the others. Draw and label another network that is also the "same" as the ones above in the space provided.

Networks in the Elementary School Curriculum

Network activities are sometimes introduced to children in the upper elementary grades for several reasons:

1. They are fun and allow a certain choice and creativity for the child.
2. They give children a chance to apply the number concept of odd and even.
3. They provide an opportunity for children to investigate a situation, form a conjecture, check it, and discover something.
4. They provide children with an experience of a different branch of mathematics. What determines whether or not a network can be traced is not length of edges, size of angles, or even straightness of edges, but rather more general spatial relationships. This is characteristic of *topology*, the study of properties of figures that are not altered by stretching, shrinking, or other types of continuous deformation. Examples of such properties are traceability of a network and openness or simpleness of a curve. The game below is another activity where topological properties are of primary importance.

Sprouts — A Game for Two Players[7]

Start with three dots. Each player in turn joins two dots with a curve and puts a new dot on this curve. Each dot can be the endpoint of *no more than three curves;* also curves cannot cross other curves. The last player to be able to draw a curve wins. Steps in a sample game are shown below. Make a possible "next move" on the last diagram.

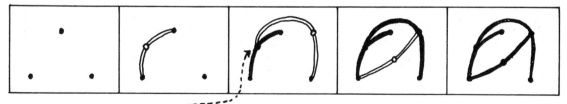

Note: This vertex is now "used up" — it cannot be used again since it has three edges.

Environmental Geometry — or What Are These Pictures About?

You might notice that all of the pictures above have something in common — they all have something "rounded" in them. Here are some questions
that we could ask about these pictures.

1. Some of the pictures look like "true" circles (for example, the _____).
   How many "true" circles do you see above? _____ Other objects (for
   example, the top of the glass held in the hand, or the tennis racket)
   look like ovals or ellipses. How many of these can you find? _____

2. You might say that some of the ovals are really circles since you know that they represent objects which when seen from a certain angle are circles (for example, the wheels of the bicycle). Find another example of a slanted view of a circle. _____ How many ovals can you find which are not of this type, that is, which are not slanted views of circles? _____

3. You probably noticed that the picture of the tennis ball and orange slice are "true" circles. Would a tennis ball look like a circle from any viewpoint? _____ a slice of orange? _____ Would *any* slice from the jelly roll look like a circle? _____

4. Have you ever wondered why some of these common objects are circular in shape? A teacher might ask children questions, such as "Why are wheels round? Why is the earth roughly ball-shaped or spherical? Why are plates round? Why is a tennis ball spherical? Why is a clock-face usually round?" These questions are not easy to answer! However, they can lead to some interesting discussion. (Children's answers might involve rolling — in one direction or in any direction — blowing bubbles, a potter's wheel, and a minute hand.)

These pictures and questions illustrate an environmental approach to geometry. The concern is not only with the construction and naming of shapes presented in a somewhat abstract and "clean" form (as in most activities in this chapter), but also with the recognition of where and why these shapes occur in our environment. Many properties of geometric figures assume new meaning when looked at in this light. For example, childrern learn that a radius of a circle is a line segment from the circle's center to a point on the circle, and that all radii of a given circle have the same length. This concept might be illustrated and brought to life by the movement of the minute hand (a radius) of a clock as the tip sweeps along a circle. Similarly, a compass (as pictured above) might provide a vivid image of a *diameter* — a line segment through the circle's center with endpoints on the circle. Children often experience geometry in their environment; for example, when they play with blocks (as shown here) they will discover many uses of shapes. The blocks that make good ramps have two triangular faces, and the ones that are rounded will roll down them. (Cylinders roll neatly in just one direction, but spheres or marbles may roll anywhere.) An observant teacher can encourage children to verbalize these discoveries involving geometry in the world around them.

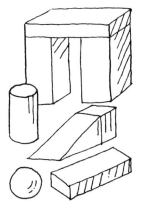

Children may enjoy expressing their discoveries of shapes around them by making their own shape books or shape posters. They might cut out pictures from magazines and sort them by shape, and paste them on a corresponding poster or page of a shape book. This activity may be a challenge — in fact, for some children it will present special problems. First, recognition of a shape might involve various perceptual abilities, such as figure-ground perception (being able to see a shape in spite of distracting background stimuli), or recognition of an object from a "slanted" view. (Would you accept the bicycle wheels to be put on a page of circles in a shape book?) Second, many pictures will contain more than one type of shape, so pictures may appear on different shape pages depending on how the child perceives the shapes. (Should the tennis racket go on a page of ovals or a page of squares?)

Geometry in the Elementary School Curriculum

What Geometry Concepts Appear in the Elementary School Mathematics Curriculum?

Current elementary school mathematics programs vary considerably as to the amount and type of geometry presented. Below are listed the geometry topics (as distinct from measurement) as they appear in a typical K–6 scope and sequence chart. These topics will be reviewed and reinforced in subsequent grades. These geometry concepts will also be reviewed and applied in the treatment of measurement (such as length, perimeter, area, volume). We will discuss these measurement topics in later chapters in this text: Measurement and the Metric System and Geometry on a Geoboard.

Grade	
K	Shapes; shapes with corners; preparation for congruence; mirror pictures
1	Three-dimensional shapes; congruent figures; inside of closed figures; triangle; square; rectangle; circle
2	Open and closed figures; sides and corners of polygons; symmetry; coordinate geometry
3	Pentagon; octagon; segment; diagonal; angle; right angle; congruence of segments; radius; diameter; cube; similar objects
4	Polygon; regular polygon; quadrilateral; parallelogram; point; endpoint; line; ray; parallel lines; intersecting lines; constructions; graphing function rules; finding function rules
5	Scalene, isosceles, and equilateral triangles; perpendicular lines; acute and obtuse angles; congruence of angles; prism; pyramid; faces; vertices; edges; similar figures
6	Central angle; polyhedron; cylinder and sphere; moving and enlarging figures on a grid; four quadrants

Teachers will find that this scope and sequence gives a good overview of the geometry content in grades K–6, but they will need to examine the text and teacher's guide to find out how the geometry topics are presented. Text series vary in their grade placement of various topics. You might compare this geometry scope and sequence with text series from different publishers.

Many geometry topics are developed at various levels of abstraction throughout elementary school. For example, children learn about solids at almost every grade level, beginning with informal activities without much formal terminology, and later developing understanding of properties and accurate terminology. Activity 1, Solids, could be modified to fit several grade levels. Judging from the scope and sequence chart above, at what range of grade levels might you do activities like the following:

Sorting — Activity 1, part 2
Some Questions — Activity 1, part 3
Some Names — Activity 1, part 4
Faces, Vertices, and Edges — Activity 1, part 5

Teachers may discuss geometry topics informally as they arise in children's activities long before they occur in the standard curriculum. For example, kindergarten children's play with blocks provides a fine opportunity for children to verbalize their observations about solids that may include describing the shapes of the faces or "sides," and counting the number of vertices or "corners." Most of the Activities in this chapter can be done at varying levels of formality and at several grade levels. The format of the activity with children will depend on children's prior experiences with geometry.

Why Should Informal Geometry Be Taught in the Elementary School?

As indicated before, current textbook series include much more varied geometry topics now than before the coming of "new math" in the early 1960s. There are several reasons for presenting this material to elementary school children.

1. Geometry as the study of space and spatial relationships is helpful to our functioning in and to our appreciation of our environment. Through informal geometry activities children can be helped to develop everyday vocabulary for and understanding of shape and space concepts (inside, outside, above, below, next to, round, straight).

2. Geometry activities can be aesthetically pleasing. They can give children an opportunity to be creative and also to look more closely and analytically at visual patterns around them.

3. Children need a variety of informal geometry experiences to prepare them for the more formal geometry of high school and later mathematics.

4. Geometry is closely interrelated with other mathematics topics. Many numerical topics depend heavily on spatial relations — for example, an intuitive sense of symmetry is often called for in textbook models for fractions

(such as, shade $\frac{1}{2}$: $\heartsuit$). This chapter has many numerical aspects — in particular, fractions were used in Activity 2, Tangrams, and odd and even numbers came up in mazes (page 118) and networks (page 121). Geometry activities can thus be used to develop and give practice with various number topics in the elementary school curriculum.

5. Different children have different learning styles. Some children have greater ability to deal with spatial concepts than with verbal or numerical concepts. This ability can be used to develop their confidence, and also through geometric models for number, to help them develop numerical concepts. Other children may have relatively undeveloped spatial ability — these children may develop their ability to deal with spatial relations through geometry activities in school. When children do geometry activities, the teacher is given an opportunity to diagnose the children's individual difficulties or strengths in spatial relations, which will perhaps provide clues about adapting other learning materials accordingly.

6. Geometry provides a rich context for discovery learning. This discovery can be carefully guided by a series of questions leading to a particular result, or can be left open to a variety of results. An example of an open discovery situation would be to give children a collection of solids and ask them what they can find out about them. This might lead to classification, or building, or measurement, or constructions. A little more guidance could be pro-

vided by pointing out edges, vertices, and faces of polyhedra and asking children to look for number relationships among them. Further guidance may be needed; children could be given a chart as on page 96. Finally, one could suggest adding the number of vertices to the number of faces and comparing the sum with the number of edges. The amount of guidance necessary depends on how able the children are to see various possibilities for themselves, on how essential a teacher considers the discovery of a given idea, and on how much time is available for exploration. Children should experience all of the stages in an investigation — forming the question, making observations, forming theories, checking them, and comparing their theories with those of others.

In spite of these various justifications for including many geometry activities in elementary school, the geometry experienced by children is often meager and unexciting. Some teachers are tempted to omit the geometry sections of the curriculum. They often feel that these sections are not important, perhaps they do not really understand the geometry themselves, and they feel pressured to stress computational skills and vocabulary in their classes. Teachers sometimes use the geometry pages in a textbook series inappropriately, treating geometry in a formal and unchallenging way. Often teachers teach as they have been taught, so that teachers without genuine informal experiences in geometry may not be able to teach it in an informal activity-oriented manner. We hope that your experiences with geometry activities in this chapter will enable you to see the potential for geometry in the elementary school.

Points, Lines, Planes . . .

You can use the initial Activities in this chapter — Solids, Tangrams, and Sticks — to help children get an intuitive feel for concepts upon which much of later geometry is built; for example, points, line segments, and plane regions. In this section we will discuss how these concepts can be developed, symbolized, and applied, and also some questions involving relationships among these concepts.

Models

The table (page 129) lists some concepts that are usually introduced in the lower elementary grades and then extended and developed more formally in the upper elementary grades. (These concepts provide applications of set topics, and also are fundamental to the formal axiomatic study of geometry in high school.) They should at first be approached in the spirit of environmental geometry. Many everyday objects or actions remind us of concepts such as point, line, or plane. The table includes several such models for each concept. Add another model for each one.

Eventually these ideas are abstracted, and children must learn to recognize diagrams for them on the printed page (such as $\longleftrightarrow$ for line), and also corresponding symbolic notation (such as $\overleftrightarrow{AB}$ for line). We will consider questions concerning teaching notation in a later chapter using geoboards. For now, the diagrams and corresponding notation are included in the left-hand column of the table for your review.

Concept, diagram, symbol	Model

Point
 	
 •P
	Bullseye
	    (center of the target)
	 "X marks the spot"
	    (intersection of lines)
	 Vertex of a cube
	 Tip of an arrow
	 Peg on a pegboard
	 New York City on a map
	 Corner of a page 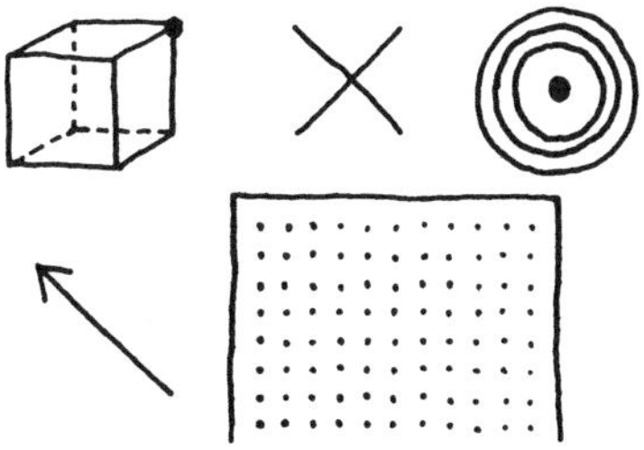

Line segment
 	
 $\overline{PQ}$ 

 P _____ Q
	Shortest distance
	    between two points
	 Edge of a cube
	 Rubber band stretched
	    between two points
	 Straw or geostrip
	 Edge of this page
	 Fold in a piece of paper 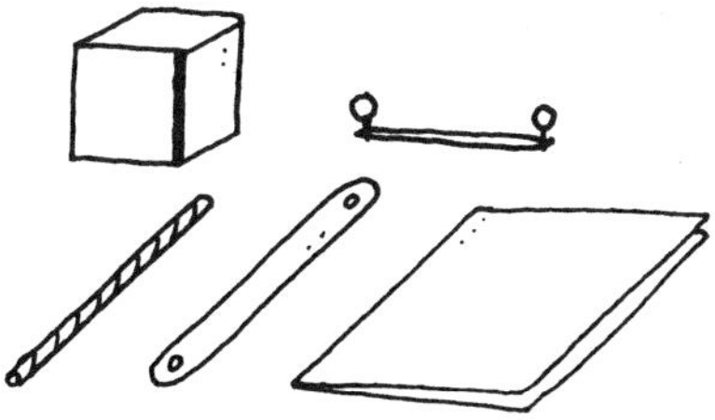

Line $\overleftrightarrow{PQ}$
 P   Q
	Straight road stretching
	    in either direction
	    across a plain 

Ray $\overrightarrow{PQ}$ 
 P   Q
	Light shining from
	    a flashlight
	 Path of a rocket in
	    space (with no gravity)
	 Line of sight 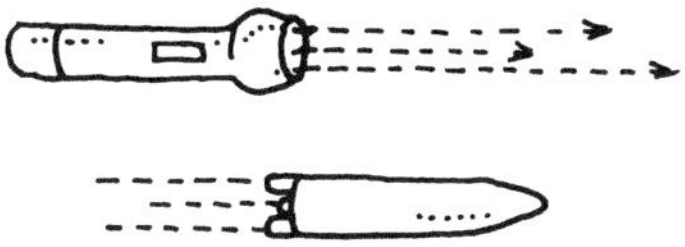

Parallel lines $AB\|\|CD$ 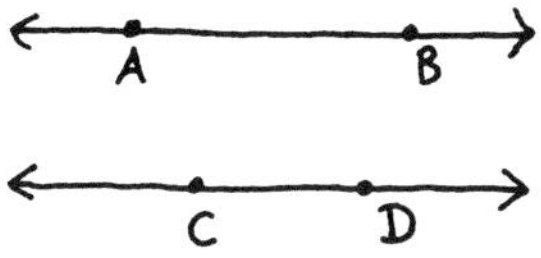
 A   B
 C   D
	Railroad tracks
	 Lined paper
	 Two opposite sides
	    of a window
	 Weaving — warp with warp
	
	 Complete: Two lines are
	    parallel if 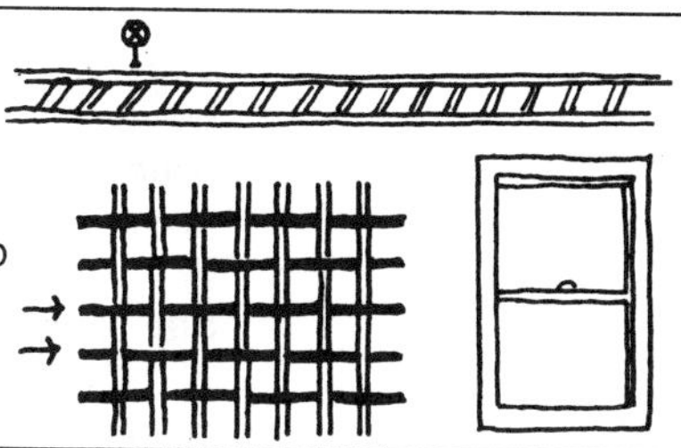

Angle A C B $\angle ABC$ 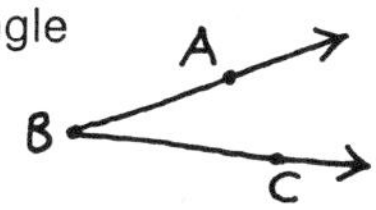	Hands of a clock Turn in a road Two joined geostrips Corner of a shape 
Perpendicular lines $AB\perp CD$ 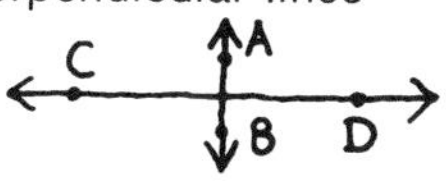 C A B D	Two edges of a door meeting at a corner Legs of table and top Weaving — warp with woof 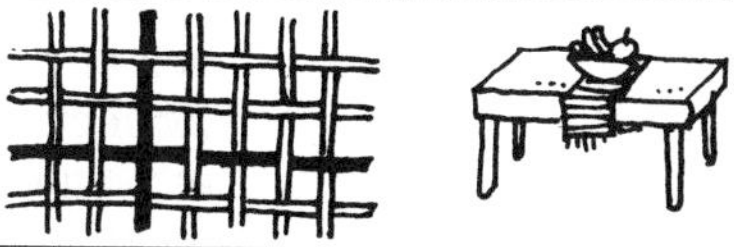
Plane 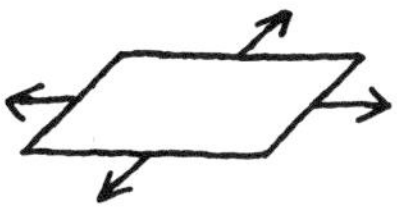	Chalkboard Floor Surface of a lake Face of a cube 

For which concept was it most difficult to find models? _____
Why?

You probably found that most models for "straightness" were in fact models for *line segments* — that is, for the part of a line which lies between two points, because we cannot really experience a *line* (which stretches infinitely in both directions). In the same way, your models for *planes* were probably actually for *plane regions* (as were the examples given). A plane extends infinitely in all directions, a concept for which we cannot find a physical model. You may have found it difficult to find a true model for an *angle*, which is actually made up of two *rays* (extending infinitely) with a common endpoint.

Could you define a line? a point? When the ancient Greeks built geometry from logical foundations, both point and line were taken to be undefined terms. We have intuitive feelings for the meaning of these terms, but probably find it difficult to describe these abstract concepts precisely. It is especially important for children to have many concrete models associated with the terms so that they can abstract the common features. For example, if they hear the term *plane* associated with a variety of flat surfaces, they will come to appreciate intuitively the flat nature of a plane.

One goal of the elementary school geometry curriculum is that children should learn and use mathematics vocabulary and notation such as on the left side of the preceding table. However a more basic and important goal is that children understand how these ideas arise in their environment, as on the right side of the table. The vocabulary and symbolism should be introduced after children have encountered the geometry idea and when children have some use for it. Sometimes models for these geometry concepts arise quite naturally in our environment, as shown by the examples above. But sometimes children can also be helped to abstract these ideas by using specially designed materials, such as solids, sticks (straws or geostrips), or geoboards (as described on page 110). For example, the geoboard gives children very direct experiences with a line segment as being the shortest possible path between two points. Here the pegs stand for points, and since the rubber band tends to contract, it automatically assumes the shortest path between two pegs.

Set Terminology

One reason sometimes cited for introducing set language (for example, union, intersection) in the elementary school curriculum is that these concepts can be used in developing geometry — in particular relationships between points, lines, rays, angles, etc. For example, a line is a *set* of points, an angle is the *union* of two rays with a common endpoint, or two lines can *intersect* in a point. However, the geometry concepts can be developed without symbolism for sets and with less formal language, and teachers should not let children's lack of background in set terminology prevent them from working with these concepts. Just how much set language is used should depend on how easy and natural the children find it. Some geometry ideas expressed in set language may be particularly difficult for children — for example, the notion of a line as a set of points. In fact Piaget's research has shown that young children have considerable trouble with this idea of a line. The language of sets should be used only so long as it helps, rather than hinders, communication.

Patterns

Children can use the concepts listed in the preceding table and practice the notation while gaining experience with other mathematical processes. The examples below involve finding number patterns associated with notation for rays, angles, and line segments.

Rays. One special subset of the line $\overleftrightarrow{AB}$ is the ray $\overrightarrow{AB}$, the set of all points on the line that are on the same side of A as B (including A). That is, start at A, go towards B, and keep going (the thickened part of the diagram to the right). On the other hand, $\overrightarrow{BA}$ means start at B, go towards A, and keep going. Draw the ray $\overrightarrow{BA}$ on the given line. In the table below, consider how many *different* rays you can name using the points marked in each diagram. (Notice that in the second line, $\overrightarrow{AB} = \overrightarrow{AC}$. Do you see why?)

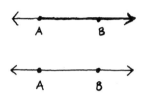

Diagram	Names for Rays	Number of Different Rays
← A • • B →	$\overrightarrow{AB}$, $\overrightarrow{BA}$	2
← A • B • C →		
← A • B • C • D →		
← A • B • C • D • E →		

Do you see the pattern?

Angles. An angle can be defined as the union of two rays that have a common endpoint. Notice that the angle to the right can be named in several ways: as ∠ A O C or ∠ B O C or ∠ _____ or ∠ _____. In the table below, consider how many different angles you can name in each diagram.

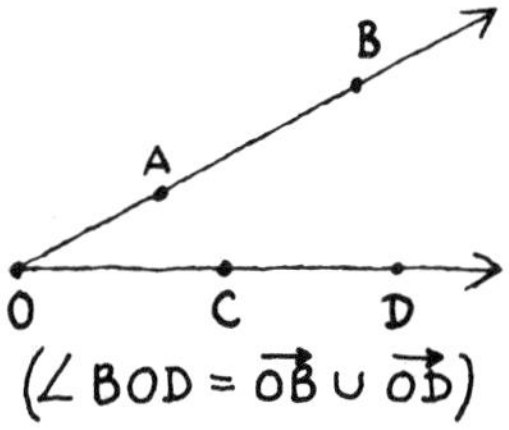

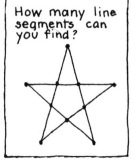

$(\angle BOD = \overrightarrow{OB} \cup \overrightarrow{OD})$

Diagram	Names for Angles	Number of Different Angles
O ← A / B →	∠ AOB	1
O ← A / B / C →		3
O ← A / B / C / D →		
O ← A / B / C / D / E →		

Do you see the pattern? (**Hint:** See p. 84.)

How many line segments can you find?

How many line segments can you find?

Line Segments. This activity basically involves counting, but the counting becomes easier if you notice a pattern, and if you label the points in some way.

Activities Involving Relationships Between Concepts

Children's work with points, lines, rays, line segments, planes, etc. is often unmotivated and primarily a matter of memorizing terminology. Patterns such as those before can allow children to use the concepts and practice notation; however, they may seem a little contrived or artificial. Children may find the concepts more interesting and useful if they consider deeper questions about the relationships between these concepts, such as given below.

Three Dimensions. Is it possible to have two points for which there is *no* line containing them both? Decide if there exist examples as described below. You *may* find this model of a cube useful in formulating your answers and justifying them. Describe the examples if they do exist.

1. Three points that are not all on the same line: _____
2. Three points that are not all on the same plane: _____
3. Four points that are not all on the same plane: _____
4. Two lines that do not lie in the same plane: _____
5. Three lines, each of which is perpendicular to the other two: _____
6. Three lines, all of which are parallel to each other: _____
7. If two lines in a plane do not meet, must they be parallel? _____
8. If two line segments in a plane do not meet, must they be parallel? ___
9. If two lines in space do not meet, must they be parallel? _____

Your answers to examples (6)–(9) will depend on what you mean by *parallel*. A dictionary definition is "continuously equidistant."

Intersections. What types of sets could be expressed as the intersection of two rays? The possibilties are drawn below.

Diagram				
Intersection of $\overleftrightarrow{AB}$ and $\overleftrightarrow{CD}$	The empty set	A point	A ray (in fact $\overrightarrow{CD}$)	A line segment (in fact $\overline{AC}$)

This example involves intersection properties of rays. How line segments, lines, and planes intersect might also be considered. Answer the questions below. Draw a diagram to explain whenever your answer is yes.

1. Can the intersection of two line segments be a point? _____
   a line segment? _____
   a ray? _____
   a line? _____

2. Can the intersection of two lines be a point? _____
   a line segment? _____
   a ray? _____
   a line? _____

3. Can the intersection of a line and a plane be a point? _____

a line segment? _____

a ray? _____

a line? _____

Slicing Shapes. To answer the questions below you should imagine slicing various hollow three-dimensional shapes. For example, suppose that a plane intersects or "slices" a cube. What sets could you get as the intersection?

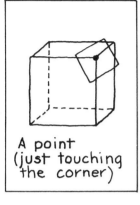

A point
(just touching
the corner)

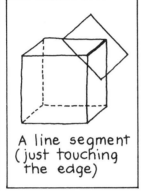

A line segment
(just touching
the edge)

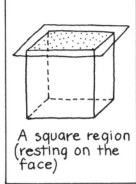

A square region
(resting on the
face)

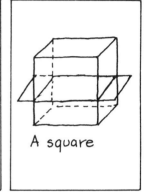

A square

If you have a transparent plastic model of a cube, you can form these intersection sets by putting some water in the cube and tipping it to see what shape is formed by where the surface of the water meets the cube.

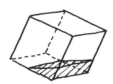

1. What other shapes can you get? Try "turning" the plane (or the cube) in various ways. Draw two more possible intersection sets.

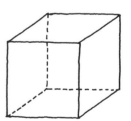

2. Suppose a plane intersects a sphere. What intersection sets could you get? Draw some.

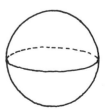

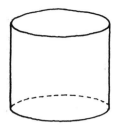

3. Suppose a plane intersects a cylinder. What intersection sets could you get? Draw some.

Which of the questions in these activities involving relationships between concepts above would give children practice with notation or dealing with geometry concepts symbolically?

Which would provide practice with recognizing concepts?

Which did you find more challenging, the patterns involving rays, angles, and line segments, or the questions in this section?

Does Precise Language Matter?

Children and teachers are often careless when using some geometry terms — for example, calling a line segment a line. When the context for the terms is clear, it probably doesn't matter if children misuse the words, but teachers should use correct terminology themselves and gradually correct children's usage. But later on, sloppy use of terms can lead to false statements. Do you see why the statements below are incorrect as they stand? Correct the underlined words.

If two line segments in a plane do not meet, then they are parallel.

The length of the line A B is two centimeters.

An angle is the union of two line segments with a common endpoint.

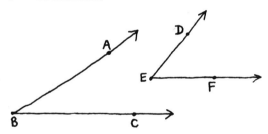

Note: The last statement might lead a child to make the common error of describing angle A B C to the right as being larger than angle D E F. Do you see why?

TEST YOUR UNDERSTANDING

Review of Terminology

In this chapter, we have developed and used a number of geometry terms. The problems below are intended to pull together some of these terms for your reference. Match the terms to their definitions or pictures. Use a dictionary, if necessary. (More than one figure may correspond to each term.)

1. Here are terms referring to *curves.* The mathematical meaning of curve is somewhat different from the everyday meaning. A curve is any path that can be traced, from a beginning point to an endpoint, say with a pencil, that does not double back on itself (although it may cross itself). Match pictures, words, and meanings.

The beginning and endpoints are the same.   Open

The curve does not cross itself (except perhaps the beginning and endpoints, which are the same).   Closed

The beginning and end points are different.   Simple

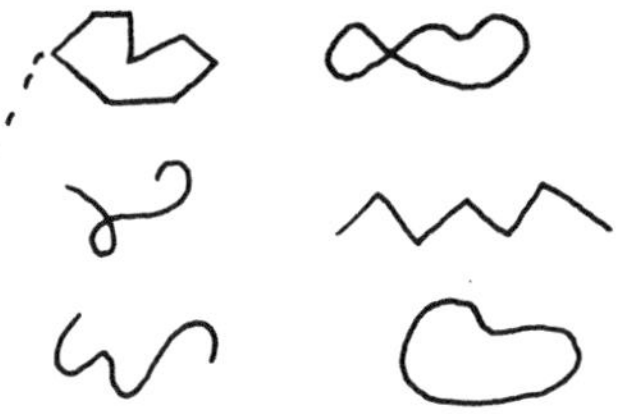

2. A special type of simple closed curve, the polygons, receives a lot of attention in geometry. A polygon is a curve that is made up entirely of line segments (paths that represent the shortest distance between two points), that does not cross itself, and whose beginning and endpoint are the same. Match the type of polygon below to the description and figures.

   a. Terms about *triangles* (polygons with three angles, and thus three sides or line segments):

   All three sides have different lengths.   Equilateral

   All three sides are equal in length.   Isosceles

   Two of the three sides are equal in length.   Scalene

   b. Terms about quadrilaterals (polygons with four sides):

   All four angles are right angles.   Square

   The four sides are equal in length.   Rectangle

   Four sides are equal in length, and four angles are all right angles.   Parallelogram

   One pair of opposite sides is parallel.   Rhombus

   Both pairs of opposite sides are parallel.   Trapezoid

3. The two terms below refer to a relationship between two figures. Match each term to its meaning.

   Congruent   One figure can be moved (without distortion of length) to fit exactly on the other.

   Similar   One figure can be enlarged (if necessary) so that it can be moved to fit exactly on top of the other.

   Which of the figures below are *congruent* to this shape?
   Which of the figures below are *similar* to this shape?

   a. 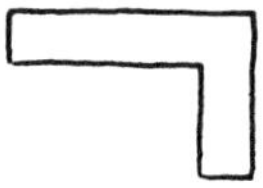   b.    c. 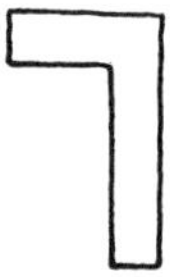   d. 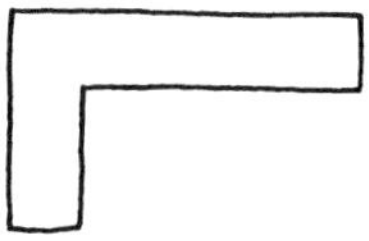   e.

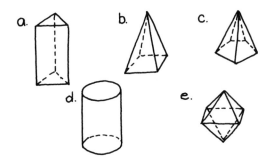

4. Match each sketch to the description of the figure.

_____ A pyramid with five faces.

_____ A prism with nine edges.

_____ A pyramid with six vertices.

_____ A polyhedron that is neither a pyramid nor a prism.

_____ A solid that is not a polyhedron.

Questions Using Terminology

1. About Solids . . .

   a. Name some everyday models for prisms, pyramids, and other polyhedra; and for spheres and cylinders.

   b. Suppose that you want to build models of various prisms and polyhedra from light cardboard. Can you design plans for making them? Two plans are shown here. Many other plans are possible; however, these two are quite easy to construct and adapt for other prisms and pyramids. (Fold on the dotted lines.)

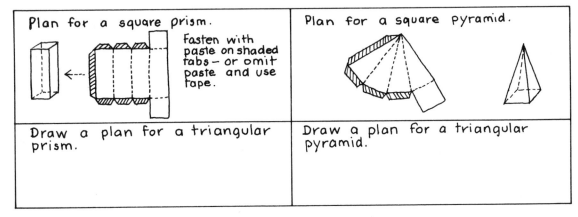

Plan for a square prism. Fasten with paste on shaded tabs – or omit paste and use tape.	Plan for a square pyramid.
Draw a plan for a triangular prism.	Draw a plan for a triangular pyramid.

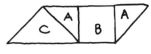

2. Answer the following about tangrams:

   a. Can you make a triangle from some of the tangram pieces that is *not* similar to piece A?

   b. How many different squares can you make using some or all of the pieces?

   c. Why is piece E *not* similar to this parallelogram?

   d. Suppose that the puzzle is made of silver, and that the whole square consisting of seven pieces is worth $4. How much would each of the pieces A–E be worth?

   e. Describe some mathematical processes that can be experienced when using tangrams.

3. Answer the following about polygons:

   a. Draw all lines of symmetry for each of the figures to the right.
   b. How can you use lines of symmetry to classify triangles as isosceles, scalene, or equilateral? Use the figures to explain.
   c. Can you arrange six toothpicks (or straws of equal length) to make *exactly* four triangles? (**Hint:** See Activity 3, part 3a.)

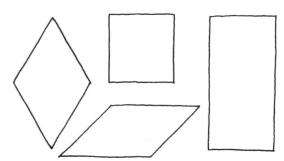

4. Consider the letters of the alphabet.

   A B C D E F G H I J K L M N O P Q R S T U V W X Y Z

   Use them for the following tasks:

a. Sort the letters by symmetry. Indicate lines of symmetry with dotted lines.

Q R | A B | Ø H

No lines of symmetry | One line of symmetry | Two lines of symmetry

b. Provide labels for these loops. Complete the sorting.

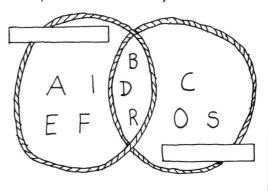

A I   B D R   C
E F   O S

c. Can you guess the rule for this sorting? Complete it.

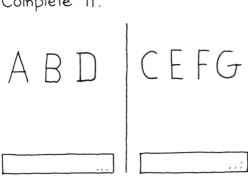

A B D | C E F G

d. Describe another way in which you could sort the letters according to some aspect of their shape.

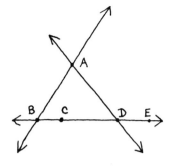

5. Refer to the diagram, which shows some lines, line segments, rays, and angles. Match the symbols in the left column below with the expressions in the right column. You should find two entries in the right column that correspond to each entry in the left column.

$\overleftrightarrow{C\,D}$ _____ the intersection of $\overrightarrow{C\,E}$ and $\overrightarrow{D\,B}$

            _____ the intersection of $\overrightarrow{B\,A}$ and $\overrightarrow{B\,D}$

∡ A B D   _____ the line $\overleftrightarrow{B\,E}$

            _____ the union of $\overrightarrow{B\,A}$ and $\overrightarrow{B\,D}$

$\overline{C\,D}$ _____ the union of $\overrightarrow{C\,E}$ and $\overrightarrow{D\,B}$

            _____ the union of $\overrightarrow{B\,E}$ and $\overrightarrow{B\,A}$

the point B   _____ the intersection of $\overline{B\,D}$ and $\overline{C\,E}$

            _____ the intersection of $\overleftrightarrow{C\,E}$ and $\overrightarrow{A\,B}$

6. What is meant by *informal geometry*? Why should informal geometry experiences be included in the elementary school curriculum?

7. What is meant by *environmental geometry*? Give examples of objects or situations in which children could see models for the following concepts in their everyday environment: circles, a radius, squares, cubes, line segments, parallel lines, and planes.

FURTHER READINGS AND PROJECTS

1. On page 126 there were listed geometry topics as they are introduced by grade level in a typical textbook series. Examine a textbook series and make a similar listing of topics. How are the two listings alike? different?

2. There are several commercial sources for instructional materials related to tangrams. Examine some catalogues from educational supply companies to see what is available. In particular, examine the activity cards and accompanying teachers' guide developed by the Elementary Science Study (St. Louis: Webster Division, McGraw-Hill, 1968). Note how the cards are sequenced according to difficulty. Using these as a model, you might design your own sequence of tangram puzzles and try them with children.

3. Many of the materials you have seen or used in this chapter are sold commercially in more desirable formats (which may be easier for children to handle). Examine catalogues from educational supply companies to look for materials with which children can construct solids, either from regions or from sticks or straws. Also look for symmetry materials. If possible, examine a *Mira* (the plastic device described on page 114), the accompanying activity books, and the Mirror Cards developed by the Elementary Science Study (St. Louis: Webster Division, McGraw-Hill, 1967).

4. In Activity 1, Solids, you constructed three-dimensional shapes, classified them, and explored a relationship between the edges, faces, and vertices of a polyhedron. The study of solids can relate to other areas in mathematics (for example, dice and probability), or in science (for example, classification of crystals). Here are some examples of where solids arise:

    a. Read "Making Crystal Models" (pp. 235–242) in *Creative Sciencing* by Alfred DeVito and Gerald H. Krockover (Boston: Little, Brown, 1976). Make some models for crystals.

    b. Read "Unifying Science and Mathematics in the Elementary School: One Approach" by Leland Webb and David Ost in *The Arithmetic Teacher* 22:1 (January 1975), pp. 67–72. It describes the experiences of children using USMES (Unified Science and Mathematics in the Elementary School) materials on "Design of Dice" and "Design of a Burglar Alarm System." Also examine the USMES booklet "Dice Design: Teacher's Resource Book" (Newton, Massachusetts: Education Development Center, 1973).

    c. Make some interesting solids. *Polyhedron Models for the Classroom* by Magnus J. Wenninger (Reston, Virginia: NCTM, 1966) provides directions for constructing them.

  5. As discussed on page 125, young children in nursery schools, day care centers, and kindergartens can experience geometry through a variety of play situations with materials, such as blocks and everyday objects (coffee cans, boxes). Examine the following references that present ideas about spatial play activities. What are children "learning" through this play? Can you think of other materials for spatial play?

    Elizabeth Shuard and Hilary Williams, "Learning About Space" in *Elementary School Mathematics Today: A Resource for Teachers* (Menlo Park, California: Addison-Wesley, 1970), Chapter 11.

    W. Liedtke, "Experiences with Blocks in Kindergarten,'" *The Arithmetic Teacher* 22:5 (May 1975), pp. 406–412.

    Nancy Hensel, "Back to Basics with Block Play," *Day Care and Early Education* 5:1 (Fall 1977), pp. 36–38, 41.

    Elizabeth S. Hirsch, ed., *The Block Book* (Washington, D.C.: National Association for the Education of Young Children, 1974).

  6. On pages 124–125, we discussed how geometry can be developed in terms of the environment. The Nuffield Project in England has produced many attractive geometry materials. The booklets "Beginnings" (1967), "Shape and Size 2" (1967), and "Shape and Size 3" (1968; all from New York: John Wiley), each contain examples of how geometry concepts can be developed in the classroom. They have also produced the booklet "Environmental Geometry" (1969) that concentrates on how children's geometry experiences can be extended beyond the classroom, into the more complicated environment outside. Examine this booklet. Does it give you ideas for using your environment to develop geometry concepts? You might also examine some books about shapes written for children in your library. Are these books consistent with the environmental approach of the Nuffield Project?

  7. Informal geometry activities can provide children with opportunities to use and develop their visual-perceptual abilities. However, children with perceptual difficulties (for example, the learning disabled, mentally retarded, or those with a developmental lag in abilities) may find such activities frustrating or too difficult and may have trouble with other tasks that draw upon visual-perceptual abilities (such as reading and writing numerals and letters, counting or sorting objects, drawing shapes or copying patterns with shape blocks). Helping such youngsters often requires the cooperative efforts of a specialist, and the classroom teacher should be aware of some of the types of

visual-perceptual problems that children may have — for example, figure-ground, visual memory, perceptual constancy, and spatial relationships. Examine the "Form and Perception" sections of Chapters 3, 4, and 5 of *Mathematics for the Mentally Retarded* by Daniel Peterson (Columbus, Ohio: Charles E. Merrill, 1973). These sections discuss ideas and materials involving visual-perception development.

NOTES

1. For an intriguing history of the puzzle, see Martin Gardner's article, "Mathematical Games, On the fanciful history and the creative challenges of the puzzle game of tangrams," in *Scientific American* 231:2 (August 1974), pp. 98–103 B.

2. For many more attractive pictures, see Ronald C. Read, *Tangrams, 330 Puzzles* (New York: Dover, 1965).

3. See "La Pensee de l'Enfant et la Geometrie," *Bulletin de l'Association des Professeurs de Mathematiques de l'Enseignment Public,* 198 (Mars [March] 1959).

4. See Ronald C. Read, *Tangrams, 330 Puzzles* (New York: Dover, 1965), or the set of *Tangram Cards* designed by the Elementary Science Study (ESS) (St. Louis: Webster Division, McGraw–Hill, 1968).

5. These mirror activities resemble the attractive *Mirror Card* sets from the Elementary Science Study (ESS) (St. Louis: Webster Division, McGraw–Hill, 1967).

6. The *Mira* devices and accompanying instructural materials (*Mira Math Activities for the Elementary School,* 1973) are available from Mira Math Company, PO Box 625, Station B, Willowdale, Ontario MZK 2PQ, Canada.

7. For an analysis and history of this game, invented on February 21, 1967, see the chapter "Sprouts and Brussels Sprouts" in Martin Gardner, *Mathematical Carnival* (New York: Alfred A. Knopf, 1975).

CHAPTER 4

DEVELOPING OPERATIONS ON COUNTING NUMBERS WITH CUISENAIRE RODS

INTRODUCTION

A child asks you, "What does 'plus' mean?" How would you answer? Perhaps you might do some numerical examples, such as $2 + 1 = 3$ and $3 + 5 = 8$ for the child, using your fingers or some coins as illustrated below. Would you think of acting out these examples with a measurement-type material instead of a discrete or counting material — for example, on a number line, or with cardboard number strips placed on a number track as shown below? The addition $3 + 5$ is done by joining a number strip 5 units long to a number strip 3 units long.

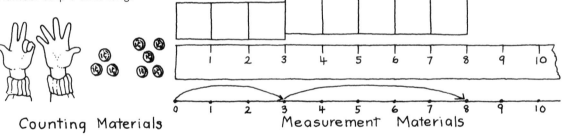

Counting Materials   Measurement Materials

Children can work with many different materials — both the counting type and the measurement type — to learn arithmetic. This chapter focuses on one measurement type material, colored rods, and their use to develop the meaning of the operations of addition, subtraction, multiplication, and division of counting numbers, $\{1, 2, 3, \ldots\}$. The next chapter describes how children can use other materials to develop an understanding of these operations and how they can gain mastery of basic facts.

While many types of colored rods are available, in this chapter you will work with Cuisenaire rods (developed by the Belgian teacher Georges Cuisenaire). These rods have been selected for several reasons.

1. Their use for developing operations can be generalized — for example, the action that shows addition of counting numbers (such as $2 + 3 = 5$) can also show addition of fractions ($2/6 + 3/6 = 5/6$) and decimals ($.2 + .3 = .5$).
2. They (or similar materials) are commonly available in schools in sufficient quantity for use by several children at once.

3. They can be used to develop a wide variety of topics (for example, in geometry) other than those directly related to arithmetic.
4. They are constructed with metric dimensions and are suited for teaching measurement of length in the metric system.
5. This measurement-type material for number is probably less familiar than the discrete type to most adults.
6. The rods have a pleasant feel, attractive colors, and are fun to work with.

The activities in this chapter primarily concern the use of the rods to do addition and multiplication and to solve equations and inequalities, although some suggest how the rods can involve a broad range of mathematical topics, for example, finding number patterns and exploring geometry. Discussion questions and comments deal with the mathematics embodied by the rods and ways to implement rod activities with children at both lower and upper-elementary grade levels. Examples are given of informal rod activities to introduce mathematical concepts to children. Also, other types of rod materials are illustrated along with a more abstract measurement model for number — the number line. The use of these materials to help children do arithmetic problems, such as $3 + 2 = \square$ and $3 \times 2 = \square$ is considered as well as suggestions for extending their use to fractions and decimals. A section discusses children's difficulties with the number line and ways to avoid them.

A Follow-up Section deals with equations in one unknown (for example, $3 + \square = 8$), and in two unknowns (for example, $\square + \triangle = 8$), including representing these solutions as ordered pairs and by a graph. A second Follow-up Section discusses the four operations on counting numbers, their meanings, relationships between them, and some of their properties — as illustrated by the Cuisenaire rods.

ACTIVITIES

Activity 1. Free Play

1. Just play with the rods. Create something. Describe what you made.
2. Take one rod of each color. Now make something. What did you make?
3. What mathematical concepts arose in what you did with the rods?

Activity 2. Guess the Color — A Group Experiment

1. Hold your hands behind your back and have your partner put a rod into them without your seeing it. Try to guess the color. Then have your partner try this. Which rods are easiest to guess?
2. We will try an experiment. First divide your class into three groups I, II, and III, with everyone repeating part 1 *five* times. Group I will guess the color of the rods without looking at any rods. Group II will look at a jumbled pile of rods while guessing. Group III will first build a staircase (one rod of each color) and look at it while guessing.

Form a hypothesis about which of the three groups, I, II, or III, will find it easiest to guess the color of the rods correctly. Hypothesis:
Try this experiment. (Do not pick white or red rods, which are easy to guess.) Record the results for your class below.

	Number of people in the group	Scores (number of rods guessed correctly out of five)	Sum of all scores in the group	Average score
Group 1				
Group 2				
Group 3				

Which group found it easiest to guess correctly? Did the experiment support your hypothesis? Which rods did you find the most difficult to guess? Try to explain why.

Activity 3. Trains for Addition

Use the code shown for the Cuisenaire rods. Can you explain why the code was chosen this way?

w = white	d = dark green
r = red	k = black
g = light green	n = brown
p = purple	e = blue
y = yellow	o = orange

A "three-car train," consisting of a red rod, a white rod, and a purple rod, is as long as a black rod. The diagram shows that a red plus a white plus a purple equals a black, or symbolically: r + w + p = k.

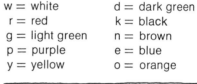

1. A train consisting of a red rod and a purple rod is as long as a _____ rod. Therefore, r + p = ☐.
2. Using the rods, work out answers to the following exercises:
   r + g = ☐   y + y = ☐   w + r + g = ☐
   g + r = ☐   e + w = ☐   g + w + r = ☐
   Write and solve your own exercise.
3. Use the rods. Draw a line to match each exercise with its answer.
   Did you really work out each of the four exercises with the rods? If not, explain.

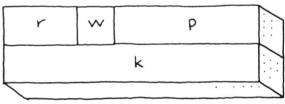

4. Use the rods to determine which statements are true and which are false.
   r + e + d = o + k _____
   k + k + k = o + o + k _____
   w + p + r = r + y + w _____
   r + r + r + r = p + p _____

+	w	r	g	p	y	d	k	n	e
w									
r									
g									
p									
y									
d									
k									
n									
e									

Rod Addition Table

5. Fill in the Rod Addition Table shown. It will make a nice pattern if you use colored pencils. Could the table go further?

6. Use the Rod Addition Table to solve the following:

$w + n = \square$

$w + g + d = \square$

(Do this two different ways — left to right, and right to left.)

Activity 4. Trains of the Same Color

1. Make a train with four red rods. How long is it? $r + r + r + r = \square$

2. Complete.

$r + r = \square$

$r + r + r = \square$

$r + r + r + r = \square$

$r + r + r + r + r = \square$

3. Instead of writing $r + r + r + r = \square$, we could write the shorter expression $4 \times r = \square$ (read "four of the red rods are equal to $\square$"). Use rods to solve the following: $2 \times g = \square$ $3 \times g = \square$ $2 \times y = \square$

4. Use rods to solve the following: $2 \times r + 2 \times g = \square$
   Make $r + g$ and then make another $r + g$. Complete. $2 \times (r + g) = \square$
   Does $2 \times g + 2 \times r = 2 \times (r + g)$?

5. Make a train of red rods as long as a train of light green rods.
   _____ reds = _____ greens   Can you do this another way?
   _____ reds = _____ greens   Can you do this still another way?

Activity 5. Number Sentences

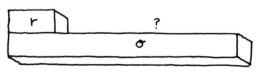

1. An orange rod can be made from a red rod and a _____ rod. We say that n is the solution to $r + \square = o$. Use the rods to complete each addition sentence below.
   $r + \square = e$ $\square + d = o$ $\square + y = n$
   $e = y + \square$ $k + \square = e$

2. Complete these sentences just by referring to the Rod Addition Table in Activity 3. $\square + r = e$ $g + \square = e$

3. Two rods of the same color equal an orange. Find the color of the rods. We can write this as a sentence, $\square + \square = o$.
   The same symbol (here y) must go in each box.
   Use rods to solve the following: $\square + \square = d$ $\square + \square + w = y$
   $\square + \square + \square = e$
4. How many red rods make a brown? _____ We can write this as $\square \times r = n$. (**Note:** A *number* goes in $\square$.)
   Complete: $\square \times p = n$ $\square \times g = d$
5. Complete the sentence $3 \times \square = d$. This sentence means "3 of what rod make a dark green" or "make a train as long as a _____ using _____ rods."
   Complete: $3 \times \square = e$ $2 \times \square + w = e$

Activity 6. Solutions: None? One? Many?

Use the rods to complete each sentence. Write the number of solutions for each sentence in the blank to the left of it.

_____ $g + \square = y$
_____ $g + \square = g$
_____ $y + \square = g$
_____ $r + \square = \square + r$
_____ $2 \times \square = e$
_____ $r + g + \square = \square + g + r$

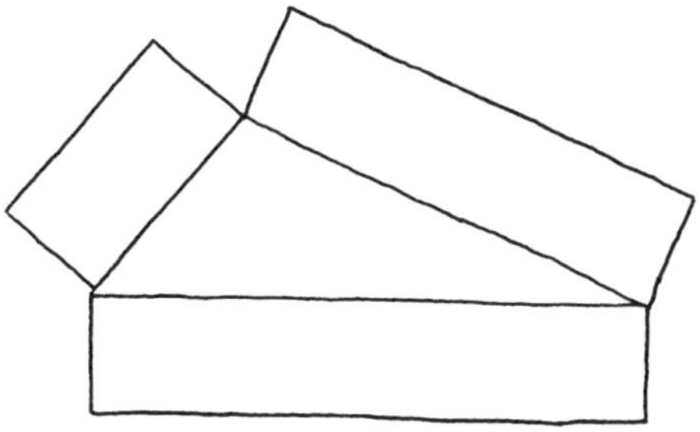

Activity 7. Making Triangles

1. Make a triangle with a red, a yellow, and a purple rod, as shown here. The rods should just fit at each corner, as if hinged. Can you make a triangle with any three rods? _____
2. Take a light green and a yellow rod.
   What rods can you use with them to make a triangle?
   What rods will not work?
3. How can you predict when three rods will make a triangle?
   (**Hint:** See Chapter 3, Activity 3, Sticks, part 1b.)

Activity 8. Inequalities

Make a staircase. 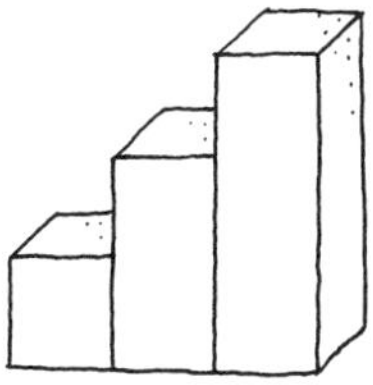
1. Which rods are shorter than a yellow?
   We can write this symbolically as $\square < y$.
   Find all solutions to $\square < n$ _____, $n < \square$ _____.
2. "Which rods are longer than a purple (that is, $\square > p$) and shorter than a blue (that is, $\square < e$)?" can be written symbolically as "Solve $\square > p$ and $\square < e$" or more compactly as "Solve $p < \square < e$." What are the solutions for this inequality?
3. Find all solutions for each inequality.
   $k < \square$ $\square + r < k$ $p < \square$ and $\square < d$ $p < \square < o$

Activity 9. Many Ways to Name a Rod

1. Use two rods to make a purple. Draw your solutions in the space provided. (**Note:** There are three different ways to do this.)

$\square + \triangle = y$

$\square$	$\triangle$
w	p

$\square + \triangle = d$

$\square$	$\triangle$

Rod	Number of Solutions to $\square + \triangle = $ Rod
w	
r	
g	
p	3
y	4
d	
k	
n	
e	
o	

$\square$	$\triangle$
I	o

2. "What two rods make a purple?" can be written symbolically as $\square + \triangle = p$. This is a sentence or equation in two unknowns. The *same* or *different* symbols for the rods can go in the square and the triangle. For example, the same symbol r can be written in both the $\square$ and the $\triangle$, since $\boxed{r} + \triangle = p$. Or, w can go in the $\square$ and g in the $\triangle$, since $\boxed{w} + \triangle = p$. Find all solutions for $\square + \triangle = y$. Record them in the table, where one solution "w and p" has already been written. (**Note:** You should find four solutions.)

3. Refer to the Rod Addition Table in Activity 3 to solve $\square + \triangle = d$. Record the solutions in the table. How many solutions did you find?

4. Results of part 2 indicate that there are three different solutions for $\square + \triangle = p$ and four for $\square + \triangle = y$. This has been recorded in the table. Use the results of part 3 to fill in the table for $\square + \triangle = d$. Do you see a pattern? Complete the table. Check the number of solutions for $\square + \triangle = n$ by referring to the Rod Addition Table in Activity 3.

5. "I am thinking of three rods which make a black" can be written as $\square + \triangle + \bigcirc = k$. List four solutions for this equation. (Are there more solutions?)

6. One solution to $\square \times \triangle = o$ is listed in the table. List other possible solutions. (**Note:** $\square$'s are numbers, and $\triangle$'s are rods.)

7. Find all solutions to this inequality: $\square + \triangle < y$. (**Note:** There are six.)

Activity 10. Making Graphs of Rod Sentences and Inequalities

In Activity 9, part 2, you found that there were four solutions to $\square + \triangle = y$. (The solutions were w and p, r and g, g and r, p and w.) Here a graph has been made for these four solutions.

1. Refer to your answers for Activity 9, part 3. Use the same grid as above and make a graph for the solutions to $\square + \triangle = d$.

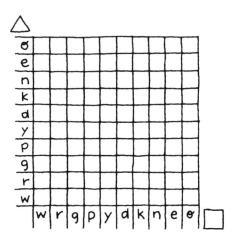

2. Use the results of Activity 9, part 6 to make a graph for the four solutions to $\square \times \triangle = o$. Does the graph form a straight line as in part 1 above?

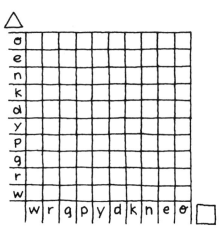

3. Use the results of Activity 9, part 7 to make a graph for all the solutions to the inequality $\square + \triangle < y$.

Number of Solutions to $\square + \triangle <$ Rod	
w	
r	
9	
p	
y	
d	
k	
n	
e	
o	

Activity 11. Counting Solutions (Optional)

1. In Activity 9, part 4, you found a pattern for the number of solutions for equations of the form $\square + \triangle =$ Rod. Is there also a pattern for the number of solutions for inequalities of the form $\square + \triangle <$ Rod? Fill in this table and try to find a pattern. (You might "see" a pattern if you look closely at Activity 10, part 3. Reviewing page 84 on number patterns may also help.)

2. A Challenge Problem: Make a similar chart to show how many solutions there are for equations of the form $\square + \triangle + \bigcirc =$ Rod. Do you see a pattern?

Activity 12. Squares and Rectangles (Optional)

1. What color rod fits exactly in this rectangle? _____ Can you fill in this rectangle with rods of the same color? What color rods did you use? _____ how many? _____ Can you do this another way? What color rods? _____ how many? _____ Still another way? What color rods? _____ how many? _____

2. Can you cover the region at left exactly using rods of only one color? What color would you use? Can you do this with rods of any other one color?

3. Is this a square? _____
   What color rod do you need to cover this region entirely with one color? _____
   How many rods in the square? _____
   Another color? _____
   How many rods? _____
   Another color? _____
   How many rods? _____

Activity 13. Special Squares (Optional)

1. Take three light green and four purple rods. Cover a square below with them. Can you do this three different ways? Draw your results below.

2. Cover the square with yellow rods. How many did you use? Now make a square with three light green rods. Try this with four purple rods. You should now be able to conclude that the area of the yellow square is the same as the total area of the two other squares combined (the light green and the purple one). Now make a triangle (as in Activity 7) with a light green, a purple, and a yellow rod. What kind of triangle did you make? You have illustrated a classical theorem of geometry (which you may have learned in a more numerical context). What is it?

3. Can you make an attractive square (any size) using rods of all the colors?

4. Can you make a square (any size) that can be covered by two rods of each color? Why or why not?

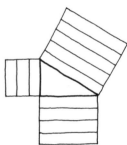

Activity 14. Making Hollow Squares (Optional)

1. You can make a hollow square with a white, two purple, a yellow, and a dark green rod, as shown here. If these rods were placed end to end in a straight line, how many white rods long would the line be? _____ (You might see how long by first placing orange rod(s) below it and then filling in the leftover space with white rods.)

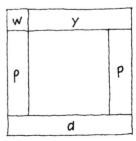

2. Can you make a hollow square with any set of rods? Investigate this by completing the table below. Find the length (in white rods) of a straight line of the rods in each set. Also, try to make a hollow square with the set of rods.

Rods	Length in white rods	Can you make a square?
(a) w, w, w, w, r, r		
(b) r, g, g, g, p		
(c) w, w, w, r, r, p, y		
(d) w, w, r, g, g, p		
(e) r, r, p, p, d, d		
(f) w, w, r, r, p		
(g) r, r, g, g, p, p		
(h) Add a set which yields a square.		

How can you predict whether a set will make a square?

Activity 15. Putting the Rods Away

When you have finished with the rods, make the pattern on page 151. If you cannot do this, you are missing some of the rods. Get the missing ones from your instructor, and then put away just the rods needed to make this pattern. Then with the remaining rods, make the pattern on page 152. Again, if you cannot do this, get the missing rods from your instructor. Now put away these rods. Turn in to your instructor the rods you have left over. If you had a complete set of rods, you should have been able to make these two patterns with no rods left over. Which method for putting away the rods would you as a teacher prefer to do with children when they have finished with the rods: the method above, or one where children simply count the rods of each color (for example, 4 orange rods, 4 blue rods, . . . , 20 white rods)? Why?

DISCUSSION QUESTIONS AND COMMENTS

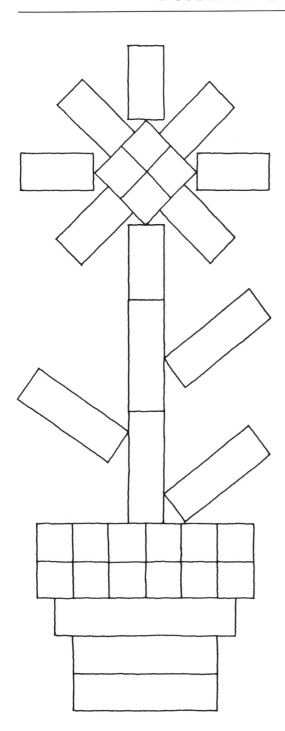

Why Play with the Rods?

The Cuisenaire rods are an example of a structured mathematics material, that is, a material that is designed primarily to help children learn specific mathematical topics (such as addition) or experience specific mathematical processes (such as seriation). Another example of a structured mathematics material is the set of attribute pieces used in Chapter 1 that can be used to teach topics such as intersection of sets and processes such as classification. Structured materials may also be used in other ways — for example, the Cuisenaire rods can be used to explore relationships in geometry (as in Activity 7, Making Triangles) or number patterns (as in Activity 11, Counting Solutions). Playing with the rods gives children an opportunity to discover and describe characteristics of this structured material and so should precede activities (such as Activities 2–14) which focus on specific topics or assume familiarity with the rods. Children might make designs, such as the flower drawn here, when playing with the rods. Making this flower might have helped a child to see that white rods can be used to make squares and rectangles. This could lead to an exploration of making these shapes with other rods. Seeing this flower design, a teacher might ask if the stem could be replaced by just one rod — this, of course, relates to addition of rods.

Did you make a "staircase" in Activity 1? Children often build various kinds of staircases (with rods flat on a table or standing on end) when given a chance to play with the rods. This experience helps the children realize that the rods come in different colors and lengths and that the rods can be arranged from smallest to largest. Staircases (a) and (b) above also show that certain rods are a regular amount longer than the rod before them. Staircases (b) and (d) show symmetry.

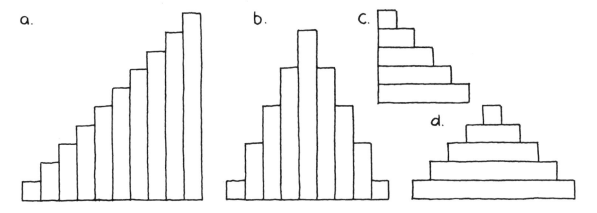

Mark which of the following characteristics of the rods or relationships between rods might a first or second grader discover by playing with the rods.

1. The length of a rod is related to its color.
2. The longest rod is orange.
3. One red rod is as long as two white rods.
4. The symbol for "light green" is "g."
5. Rods joined end to end are as long as some other rod.
6. Squares and rectangles can be made with the rods.
7. There are more red rods than orange rods in a set.

Children should have ample opportunity to play with the rods and share (show, talk about) what they made with other children. One way to provide children with such opportunities is to have children work in pairs or small groups, sharing a box or bag of rods. A teacher can circulate around the class, observe what the children have made, and have them talk about their work. Another way is to offer the rods as an option during free time. Over a period of time, all the children in the class could get a chance to work with the rods. In both of these situations, a teacher may want to focus children's attention on specific aspects of the rods by commenting on or asking questions about what they made or did with the rods. Doing this requires that the teacher recognizes the mathematics embodied in the rod play and also finds the appropriate thing to say to the child, without being overly directive.

Mathematics Embodied by the Rods

Cuisenaire rods can be used in a natural way to teach several whole number concepts — for example, addition, addition sentences, and multiplication as repeated addition, as suggested in Activities 4, 5, and 6. The rods can also be used to teach other topics — for example, geometric shapes, fractions, decimals, and measurement in the metric system, as we shall see in subsequent chapters. To use the rods effectively with children, you need to understand how the rods embody certain mathematical concepts.

Do you think that the following rod activity is an appropriate use of the rods for teaching the concept of addition? Why or why not?

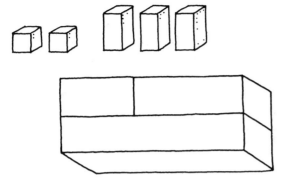

Teacher: Everyone take two white rods. Now take three red rods. How many rods do you have altogether?

It is possible for children to do 2 + 3 with the rods as described above. They could also do this addition with five white rods, or with any discrete set of five objects (such as fingers). However, the rods are designed to embody the measurement concept of number; this means that addition should be interpreted as the joining of two rods end to end, and should look something like the diagram shown here. The development of other related topics (for example, addition sentences, addition of fractions, addition on the number line) depends upon this interpretation of addition.

Mark the arrangement of rods shown that is most appropriate for showing that addition is commutative — that is, r + g = g + r. Why?

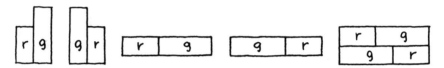

The diagrams below show how rods can be used to illustrate various mathematical topics. Match the diagrams with the topics.

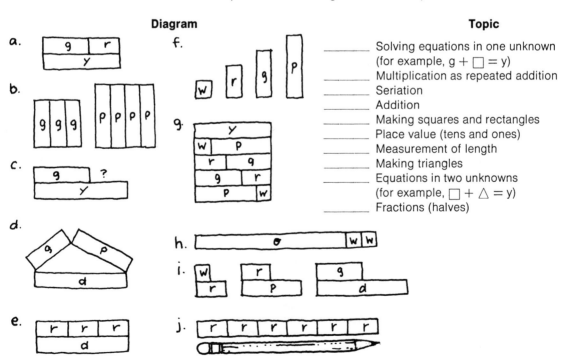

Diagram

a. g | r / y

b. g | g | g   p | p | p | p

c. g | ? / y

d. g / p / d

e. r | r | r / d

f. w r g p

g. y / w | p / r | g / g | r / p | w

h. o | w | w

i. w / r   r / p   g / d

j. r | r | r | r | r | r

Topic

_____ Solving equations in one unknown (for example, g + □ = y)
_____ Multiplication as repeated addition
_____ Seriation
_____ Addition
_____ Making squares and rectangles
_____ Place value (tens and ones)
_____ Measurement of length
_____ Making triangles
_____ Equations in two unknowns (for example, □ + △ = y)
_____ Fractions (halves)

Using Rod Activities with Children

Could elementary school children do rod activities, such as Activity 3, Trains for Addition, or Activity 4, Trains of the Same Color? Perhaps you might answer this question with a qualified yes, thinking that children who can read and who have some facility in dealing with symbolism (for example, r + g = $\square$ or $\square$ + $\triangle$ = y) could handle these Activities. In fact, rod activities similar to Activities 3–7 are used in the upper elementary grades, and also at the junior high school level, to help students understand equations in one and two unknowns and learn to use related symbolism. These experiences precede entirely symbolic work in writing and solving equations, such as $\square$ + 5 = 7 or x + y = 7.

The rod activities you did could be modified in various ways for use with elementary school children. Children will probably need more problems on a particular topic, such as rod addition, than you did. For example, Activity 3, part 1, might be expanded into several activities as suggested by the rod addition activity cards shown below.

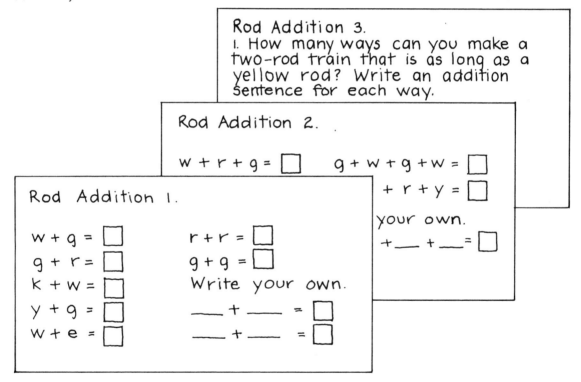

Sets of rod activity cards are available commercially. Of course, you — or perhaps the children you teach — can prepare sets which are tailored to the needs of your class. Activity cards like these are most suitable for individualized or small group work with the rods.

Rod activities can also be done as games. For example, the game Rodringo (with the clues described on page 156) involves rod addition.

Game — Rodringo

This is a Bingo-type game to be played by four people. Each player should take a different "board" below. A caller draws a clue card and shows it to the players, who put the "solution" in a space on their board where it fits exactly (if possible). The first player to fill the board wins. Examples of clues cards are

| $w + g = \square$ | $g + r = \square$ | $w + r + g = \square$ |

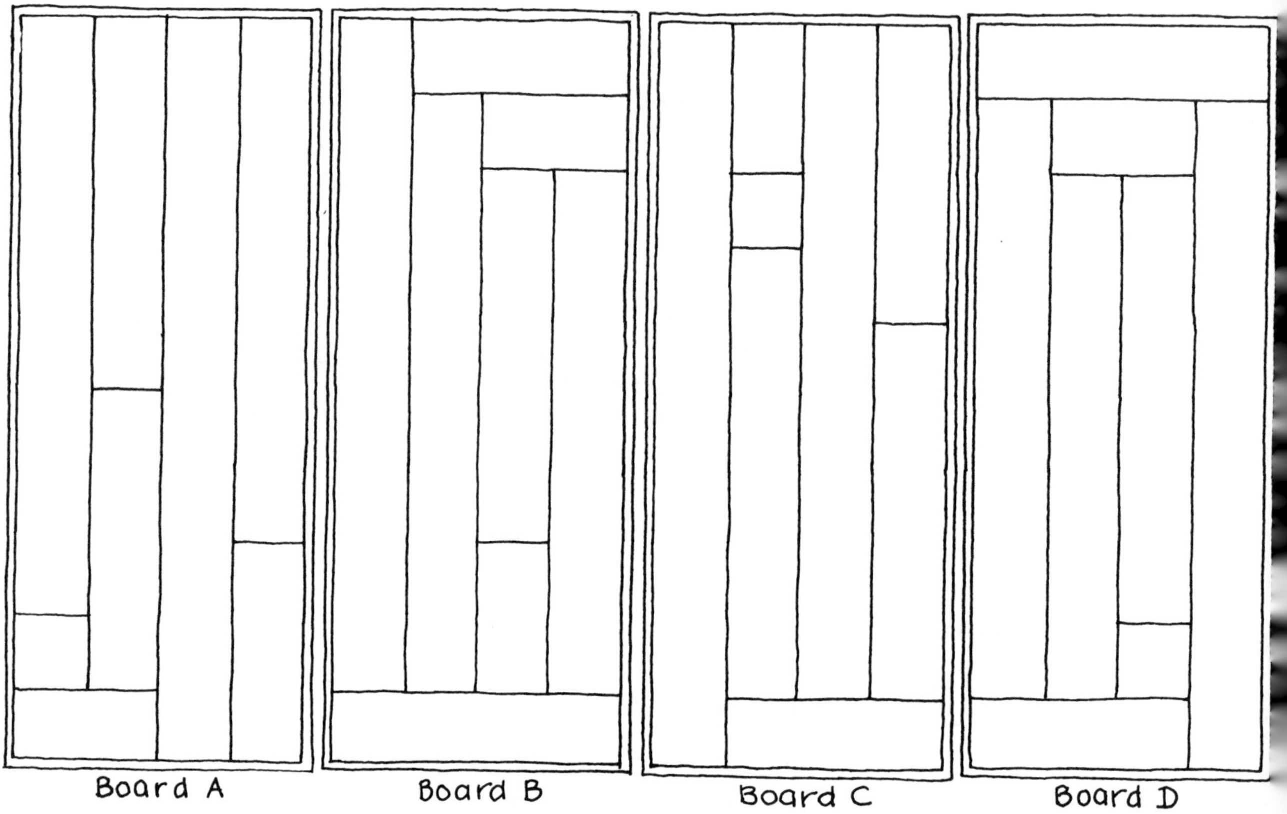

Board A   Board B   Board C   Board D

Clue cards can easily be changed to relate this game to another topic (for example, addition sentences like $r + \square = y$) or to several topics (for example, number sentences with one unknown, inequalities). Can you think of any wild-card clues that would have *any* rod as a solution? Write one. _____ Can you think of any clues that are complete duds — there are *no* solutions? Write one. _____ Can you think of a clue that has several (but not all) of the rods as solutions?

When using rod activities with children, you should consider how to sequence the activities over a period of time. While you did Activities 1–14 in a short amount of time, children will need considerably more time to do a sequence of some similar or modified activities. For example, the three activity cards on rod addition (see page 155) might be done in short sessions over a one-week period with some children, while others may complete them all at once. You should consider previous experience of the children with the rods and their abilities when you plan rod activities.

Informal Rod Activities

Informal rod activities such as those described below can be done with children in lower elementary grades. At this level, activities should focus primarily on building up understanding of the concepts embodied by the rods and secondarily, when appropriate, on using related notation and symbolism. Most important in doing informal rod activities with young children is your ability to give directions — verbally in simple language, or visually by showing the rods.

Behind Your Back

The teacher holds up three rods — perhaps, a purple, a yellow, and a black — and tells children to take these rods. After having children hold these rods behind their backs, the teacher holds up one of the rods and asks them to find the rod of that color just by touch and hold it up. (Having children hold the answer up allows the teacher to check their responses visually.)

The teacher may repeat this for the purple and black rods, and for other sets of rods until the children become successful. Children can also pick the rods (maybe their favorite colors) and play the role of the teacher.

In this activity children may find the rod by seriating the three rods — putting them in order — behind their backs and then picking the smallest, middle size, or largest, as appropriate. The activity helps children associate color with lengths of rods (as in Activity 2, Guess the Color) and also prepares them for later informal activities on order and inequalities.

The following activity indicates how children can solve addition sentences or find the missing addend and also discover a relationship between solutions to this kind of problem.[1]

Which Rod Fits?

The teacher shows the children a "rod sandwich" — a purple rod between two blue rods (see diagram A) — and has them make it. Then, pointing to the space between the two blue rods, the teacher asks what rod fits there. (What sentence or equation are the children solving here?) Children try rods until they find that the yellow rod fits, and hold up their solutions.

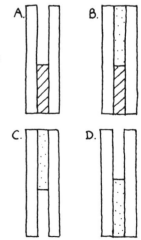

Then the teacher holds the rods at the upper end (see diagram B) and shakes them so that the purple rod falls out (see diagram C). The teacher turns the rods over (see diagram D) and asks what rod now fits there. (What sentence or equation are the children now solving?) Again, the children try this with their own rods, finding that the purple rod fits.

The teacher repeats this procedure until the children immediately see what rod fits. Then this is done for other combinations of rods (for example, light green between two blue) to lead children to discover a relationship between the solutions for the two rod situations. What do they discover?

Once children have learned to make trains from two rods, they can do the following informal activity which involves solving equations in two unknowns.

Many Ways to Make a Train

The teacher has children make a train from a red and a light green rod and then asks what rod is just as long as this train. Children show their answers, maybe by placing the rod (yellow) beside the two rods. Then the teacher asks, "How can trains be made as long as a yellow rod from two rods?" Children show and describe different ways to do this. The teacher may then ask, "How many ways can this be done for a red rod? a light green rod? a purple rod?"

These activities suggest that children can experience mathematical topics, such as ordering a set and solving rod sentences with one and two unknowns at a concrete level, often long before they learn to solve number sentences such as $\Box + 3 = 4$ and $\Box + \triangle = 4$ at a more abstract level. Teachers can provide a spiral development of a topic over a period of time (even over several grades). For example, kindergarten children can solve rod sentences with two unknowns by doing rod activities, such as Activity 9, Many Ways to Name a Rod, which are presented orally to them. Later, perhaps in grade 1, they can do a variation of this activity which requires them to act out solutions to symbolically presented sentences (for example, $\Box + \triangle = y$). Still later they can solve number sentences (for example, $\Box + \triangle = 5$) at a purely symbolic level. This spiral development illustrates what Jerome Bruner meant by his often quoted statement: "the foundations of any subject may be taught to anybody at any age in some form."[2] It is important for the teacher to find the "form" appropriate for particular children.

When doing informal activities with children, it is important to give them directions in language that they understand. For example, rather than saying "Solve $r + y = \Box$" or "What is a red plus a yellow?" to a child, you might say, "What train is made from a red and a yellow?"

Below are verbal directions you might use in informal rod activities with children. Match the verbal directions with an appropriate topic that might be "taught" in the activity.

1. What train can be made from a white, a red, and a dark green rod?

_____ Multiplication sentences such as $\Box \times r = d$

2. How many red rods make a dark green rod?

_____ Inequalities, such as $r < \Box < d$

3. What two rods make a dark green?

_____ Addition sentences with one unknown, such as $r + \Box = d$

4. What rods are between a red and a dark green?

_____ Addition sentences with two unknowns, such as $\Box + \triangle = d$

5. Two rods make a dark green. One rod is red. What color is the other rod?

_____ Multiplication sentences, such as $2 \times \Box = d$

6. Two rods of the same color make a dark green. What color are the rods?

_____ Addition of two or more rods

Learning the Code

A teacher may want children to do rod activities presented in written format (as on the activity cards shown on page 155). However, children may have difficulty remembering the letter code for the colors. The following approach can help them use the code.

The teacher gives each child a duplicated copy of a rod staircase (drawn to size) with the code written on it. Each child places rods where they fit and then colors in the staircase. (It may be difficult to find just the right colors in a regular box of crayons. Special crayon sets with only these colors are available commercially, or could be assembled by the teacher.) In later work, the children use their own color-coded staircase to "translate" from rods to letters and vice versa.

This approach can be used even if children cannot read words for the colors. Children need only recognize letters and colors.

The teacher can also display a large color-coded staircase on a bulletin board. A child who loses his own colored staircase (made as above) could make another one by just referring to the display model. Would the display model suffice instead of individual staircases for each child? One problem with the large display model might be that children cannot easily see the coded letters. Are there any other difficulties?

Children might enjoy coloring pictures such as those drawn on pages 151 and 152. If the symbols (w,r,p, . . . , o) were written in (as shown here), this coloring would provide practice in identifying the color for a given letter.

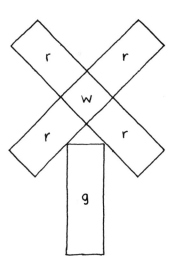

Children can also play games such as the following one to help them become familiar with the letter code. For example, the game Rod Race is appropriate for reviewing the letter code and also for informally introducing trains (sequence of rods "added" together).

Game — Rod Race

Materials: Several sets of rods; sets of 30 small cards with rod code letters on them (three cards for each color); master code chart with rod colors and code letters

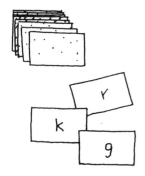

Directions:

1. Mix the cards and place them face down in a pile.
2. On the floor draw a starting line and a finish line about three feet apart.
3. Player A draws a card, checks the master code if necessary, takes the proper rod, and places it on the starting line. (See diagram.) He puts his card on the bottom of the pile face down.
4. Other players repeat step 3.
5. Players continue drawing cards and placing rods end to end until a player reaches the finish line.

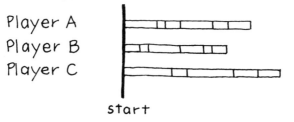

Player A

Player B

Player C

start   Finish

Instead of using the cards described above, actual colors can be used or an outline of the size of the rod can be used, or more than one rod (for example, "k and r") per card can be used. How could you modify the cards for this game so that it could be used as a review for addition of rods? Give an example of what you would put on the cards.

The game above involves the process of putting rods together end to end to form a new length — that is, addition. Another important process is breaking a length into two lengths. To introduce this idea, Rod Race could be modified as described below.

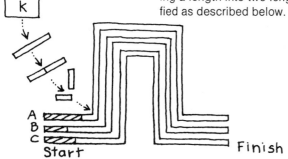

Instead of using a straight track, use a twisted one, as shown here. If a rod doesn't fit exactly within the track, it can be exchanged for two other rods (which joined end to end make the rod) which will fit. The track could be drawn on a piece of cardboard or duplicated. What does this game review? What topic does it introduce? On the track as drawn here, do all players have the same length to cover?

Other Materials Similar to Cuisenaire Rods

As you have seen, Cuisenaire rods can be used to develop the meaning of addition as joining. Do you think that the rods can also help children to solve addition sentences, such as $3 + 2 = \square$, $6 + 6 = \square$, or $9 + 3 = \square$?

The Cuisenaire rods are sometimes recommended for teaching arithmetic — for example, addition facts in grade 1. The sum $2 + 3 = \square$ can be found by joining a red rod (representing 2) and a light green rod (3), yielding a yellow (5), (top of page 161). Here each rod is assigned a numerical value:

white = 1, red = 2, light green = 3, . . . , orange = 10. This assignment of numbers to rods involves measurement of length — here a white rod is taken as the unit of measurement. Once children have associated a number with each rod, they can use the rods to work out sums (such as 2 + 3 = ☐) and solve number sentences (such as 2 + ☐ = 5) just as is done with the letter codes for the rods. (Here r + g = ☐ corresponds to 2 + 3 = ☐.)

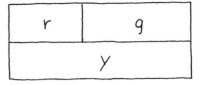

Match each Cuisenaire rod diagram with the appropriate arithmetic exercise.

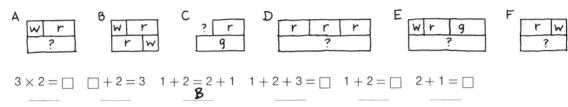

3 × 2 = ☐   ☐ + 2 = 3   1 + 2 = 2 + 1   1 + 2 + 3 = ☐   1 + 2 = ☐   2 + 1 = ☐
_____   _____   ___**B**___   _____   _____   _____

Arithmetic can also be taught with other rod materials that embody the measurement concept of number. Some of these rod materials closely resemble Cuisenaire rods — they are of the same size but may have different colors. Cardboard punch-out versions of the rods are included in some workbooks for children. Other materials are more significantly different from the Cuisenaire rods — they are larger and have notches or markings to show the number of units in a rod (for example, the color-coded wooden Stern rods, named after their developer Catherine Stern). Interlocking plastic cubes (Unifix cubes or Centicubes) can be joined to make colored rods of different lengths. You can use these rod materials as you did Cuisenaire rods in most of the Activities 1–14.

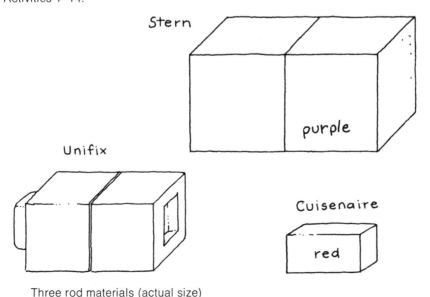

Three rod materials (actual size)

The diagram below shows how you can solve $2 + 3 = \square$ with Cuisenaire rods, Stern rods, and number strips (a teacher-made or student-made cardboard version of Stern rods).

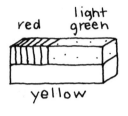

Cuisenaire Rods

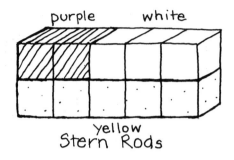

Stern Rods

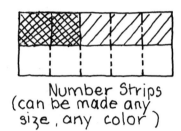

Number Strips (can be made any size, any color)

1. Which material, Cuisenaire rods or Stern rods, more clearly shows you that 2 + 3 equals 5? Why?
2. Why might a child find the solution using Cuisenaire rods less clear than the solution using number strips?
3. Some children may not have developed sufficient fine motor skills to work with Cuisenaire rods easily. The Stern rods are larger and easier to manipulate than Cuisenaire rods. Might young children have trouble manipulating number strips? Why?
4. Could you show that 9 + 3 = 12 with any of these rod materials? Of course, there is no Cuisenaire rod for 9 + 3 (that is, e + g), but you might realize that e + g = o + r, or 9 + 3 = 10 + 2 = 12, as shown below.

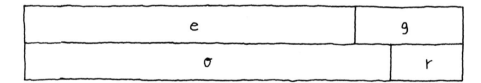

You can use this approach, which depends upon place value (tens and ones), with the rod materials to find sums that are larger than 10 (such as 5 + 6, 5 + 7, ... 9 + 9). Another way to find these sums is by placing rods on a number track and reading off the answer. (See below.) In fact, special number tracks are made for some materials (such as Stern rods, Unifix cubes). These tracks come in sections of ten that can be joined to make a number track from 0 to 100, thereby making it easy to do addition (such as 9 + 3 = 12) and multiplication (such as $3 \times 8 = 8 + 8 + 8 = 24$). The diagram below shows 9 + 3 = 12 on a Stern number track.

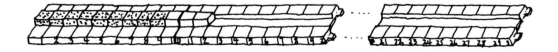

The use of rod materials on a number track leads naturally to work with a more abstract measurement model for number — the number line. A child might have drawn this number-line solution for $9 + 3 = \square$, thinking "I begin

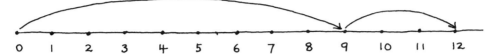

at 0 and first move 9 spaces, and then move another 3 spaces, ending at 12." The child could also relate a number-line story situation to $9 + 3 = \square$. For example, a car begins at 0 Street and goes 9 blocks and then 3 more blocks, ending at 12th Street. The child might move a small toy car on a number-line road to act out this situation.

Draw a solution using Cuisenaire rods for $3 \times 4 = \square$ on the number track below.

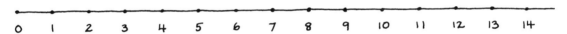

Children can easily make a number track for Cuisenaire rods. (In fact, they can use a ruler marked in centimeters as a track.)

Draw a number-line solution to $3 \times 4 = \square$. Does it correspond to the Cuisenaire rod solution you drew?

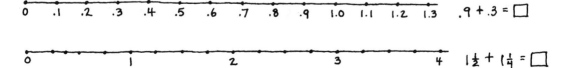

Children can also use rods to develop addition of fractions, decimals, and large numbers. Refer to the diagram and fill in the table showing what the diagram means if we assign numbers to the rods in different ways.

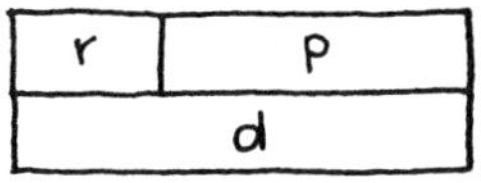

r	p
d	

W = 1	W = ___	σ = 1 ,W = .1	W = 5
r = ___, p = ___	r = ___, p = 1	r = ___, p = ___	r = ___, p = ___
d = ___	d = ___	d = ___	d = ___
The diagram shows	The diagram shows	The diagram shows	The diagram shows
___ + ___ = ___	___ + ___ = ___	___ + ___ = ___	___ + ___ = ___

Number lines can also be used for work with fractions, decimals, and large numbers. Draw a number-line solution for each of these exercises.

$.9 + .3 = \square$

$1\tfrac{1}{2} + 1\tfrac{1}{4} = \square$

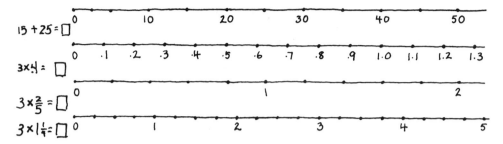

$15 + 25 =$ □

$3 \times 4 =$ □

$3 \times \frac{2}{5} =$ □

$3 \times 1\frac{1}{4} =$ □

Furthermore, the number-line approach to arithmetic is particularly useful for developing operations on the integers, $(\ldots, {}^{-}2, {}^{-}1, 0, {}^{+}1, {}^{+}2, \ldots)$. Complete the exercises.

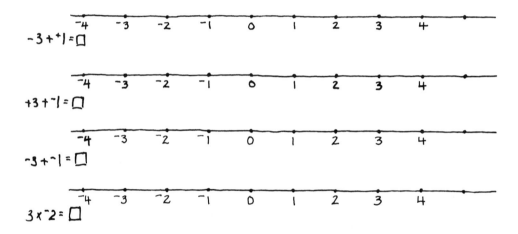

${}^{-}3 + {}^{+}1 =$ □

${}^{+}3 + {}^{-}1 =$ □

${}^{-}3 + {}^{-}1 =$ □

$3 \times {}^{-}2 =$ □

These exercises suggest that procedures for doing whole number exercises with rods on a number track or with a number line can be easily extended to more complex, related exercises involving fractions, decimals, and integers. For this reason, the number line plays an important role in the elementary school mathematics curriculum. The next section concerns ways to introduce the number line to children.

The Number Line

Children's Difficulties with the Number Line

Children sometimes encounter difficulty with the number line. Children in grades 1–2 may not understand the number line as a measurement model for number or how to act out simple whole number exercises on it. Older children may not be able to use it to do exercises involving fractions and decimals because they did not use it to do simpler, related whole number exercises.

Children's solutions to some number-line situations are shown on the next page. Identify the error in each solution and describe the child's difficulty.

Teacher's instructions to child	Child's response	Child's difficulty
1. Write the numbers on this number line.	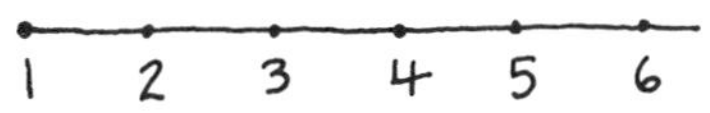 1 2 3 4 5 6	
2. Write the numbers 0-7 on this number line.	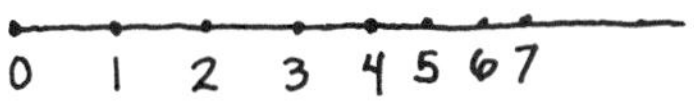 0 1 2 3 4 5 6 7	
3. Draw a number line solution to 3+4=☐.	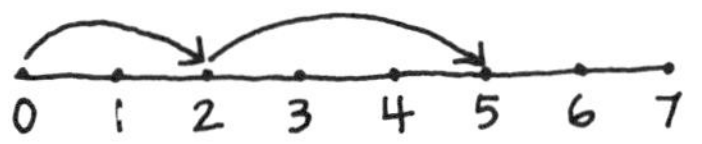 0 1 2 3 4 5 6 7	
4. Draw a number line solution to 2+3=☐.	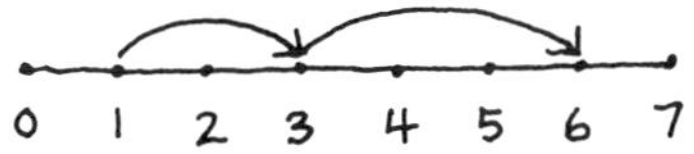 0 1 2 3 4 5 6 7	
5. Draw a number line solution to 2+5=☐.	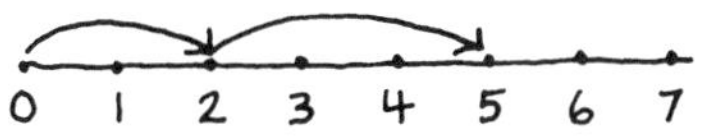 0 1 2 3 4 5 6 7	

There are several reasons why children have the difficulties shown above. For example, difficulties (1) and (2) may arise because children have not had sufficient experience with the measurement concept of number or because they have not had a chance to build up a number line (that is, they were given a number line rather than being asked to construct one). Other difficulties may arise because children do not really understand addition as putting two lengths together — perhaps because they have not done addition with materials such as Cuisenaire rods or number strips or have not dealt with related story problems in a measurement context and acted them out physically on a number line.

Early Experiences Leading to the Number Line

The following activities can help children develop an understanding of the number line and avoid the difficulties discussed above. In particular, these activities show the placement of numerals on a line at regularly spaced intervals and the interpretation of addition as movement on a line or the joining of lengths.

1. *Preschool and Kindergarten Play.* Most day-care centers, nursery schools, and kindergartens have a variety of blocks available for

young children to play with. Children will often spontaneously arrange blocks in a "track," "path," or "road." Such play serves as an important readiness experience for the number line, *especially* if children are encouraged to build tracks with blocks that are all the same size, so that the spacing is uniform. If the blocks are large, children often enjoy walking along their tracks. Many children will also build "towers" — again, if the blocks are uniform, this type of play also gives readiness experiences for number-line activities. Name two materials other than blocks that children could play with in this way.

2. *Unifix Cube Track Race.* Unifix cubes can be used with a number track. Two children, each having their own track, can have "races to 20." Roll a die, take that many cubes and say the total. If a child rolled a "3" and already had the cubes shown below, he should say "_____."

Is the placement of numbers on this track the same as on a number line?

3. *Hop-on Number Line.* Children write the numbers 1–10 on large uniform sheets of paper (or use commercially available rubberized pads with the numbers 1–10). Children then tape the sheets of paper in order on the floor. (Since the paper is of uniform size, the numbers are automatically spaced evenly.) The teacher can then play a game called Hop to the Number, with each child getting a chance to begin at the starting place (labeled *Start*) and hop to the given number, counting the hops as they go.

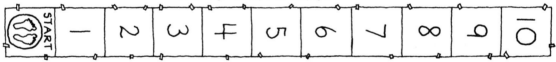

A variation — instead of having children themselves hop on a floor number line, the teacher could have children move small teddy-bear counters or model cars along a number line at their desks. Name another situation that children could use for hopping activities at their desks.

4. *Hanging Up the Numbers.* The numbers 0–20 are written on small index cards. Paper clips can be bent to make hooks to hang up the cards. Children hang the cards on a "line" (such as a string stretched across the room). Straws or cardboard tubes of uniform length can be threaded on the line to help children hang the cards at equally spaced intervals. As they are doing this, children can be asked, "How many straws have you used to get to 5?"

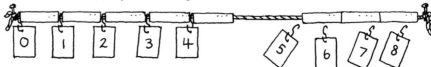

5. *Hop-on Number Line Revisited.* The numbers 0–10 are written on small discs of cardboard. Children arrange the discs in order on a line (a piece of tape on the floor, or on their desks), using a book or a pencil to get them evenly spaced. Children can then play Hop to the Number as described previously.

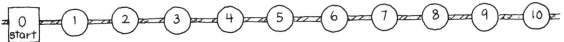

These activities are designed to help children understand how a number line is constructed — that numbers are evenly spaced and represent distance from a "start" or 0. Which activities would most help a child who counts dots rather than spaces (difficulty (3), page 165)? _____ Which would most help a child with difficulty (4) — that is, starting at 1 rather than at 0? _____ with difficulty (5)? _____

FOLLOW-UP SECTIONS

Number Sentences

Equations or number sentences, as they are commonly called in textbooks for grades 1–4, are included throughout the elementary school mathematics curriculum. Solving sentences such as $\Box + 3 = 5$, $\Box + 8 = 14$, and $\triangle - \Box = 5$ provides an interesting format for reinforcing and reviewing basic arithmetic skills[3] as well as readiness for a later more formal algebraic treatment of equations such as $x + y = -3$ and $y = 2x + 4$ in grades 6–9. In the lower elementary grades children often use boxes or frames such as $\Box$, $\triangle$, or $\bigcirc$ rather than letters such as x, y, to represent unknowns because they find it easier to refer to the frames as things to be filled in with numbers than to letters as things to be replaced by numbers.

While writing and solving sentences with frames can be interesting and easy for some children in the primary grades, it may present others with difficulties. Which answer for each addition sentence below might you expect from a first grader who has trouble with mathematics? Why?

1. $1 + 2 = \Box$ 1 2 3 4 5
2. $1 + \Box = 3$ 1 2 3 4 5
3. $1 + 1 + \Box = 3$ 1 2 3 4 5

The first grader might know that $1 + 2 = 3$ and give 3 as the answer for (1) but 4 for (2) and 5 for (3). In fact, this child may generally complete number sentences like (1) correctly but miss those like (2) and (3). One reason for this difficulty might be that the child sees a "+" in $1 + \Box = 3$ and responds by adding 1 and 3. If he has done many sentences of the form $1 + 2 = \Box$, he may respond in the same way to similar looking sentences such as $1 + \Box = 3$ (that is, adding the two numbers he sees). Also, he may not understand the concept of a number sentence or an equation and the related symbolism. Modifications of Activity 5, Number Sentences, and Activity 6, Solutions:

None? One? Many?, can be used to provide children with concrete experiences in solving and writing addition sentences before they work with numerical ones (such as $1 + \square = 3$). Children can also be given activities in which they are asked to use rods to check if a statement, such as $\boxed{p} + w = g$, is true or false (as in Activity 3, part 4).

Number sentences or equations in two unknown (for example, $x + y = 5$ or $\square + \triangle = 5$) may also be difficult for children in grades 6–8. Activities like Activity 9, Many Ways to Name a Rod can help children solve such equations and work with related symbolism. Activity 10, Making Graphs of Number Sentences and Inequalities, can be used to extend this work to graphing solutions of equations in two unknowns.

Number Sentences or Equations in Two Unknowns and Ordered Pairs

Suppose that a white rod is taken as a unit (that is, 1). Then $r = 2$, $g = 3$, $p = 4$, and $y = 5$. The rod sentence or equation $\square + \triangle = y$ can be translated into the number sentence $\square + \triangle = 5$ or $x + y = 5$. The Cuisenaire rod solution $\square = w$ and $\triangle = p$ translates into $x = 1$ and $y = 4$, or in *ordered pair* notation $(1,4)$.

1. What ordered pair corresponds to $\square = p$ and $\square = w$?
2. In Activities 9 and 10, $\square$ and $\triangle$ were filled in with color codes corresponding to the numbers 1, 2, 3, . . . , 10. We can say that the *replacement set* for $\square$ and $\triangle$ was $\{1,2,3, \ldots , 10\}$. Of course, replacement sets can include other numbers such as 0, or fractions. The ordered pair $(0,5)$ is a solution to $x + y = 5$, but it cannot be represented by the rods since there is no analogue for 0. What other ordered pair solutions for $x + y = 5$ cannot be represented by the rods?

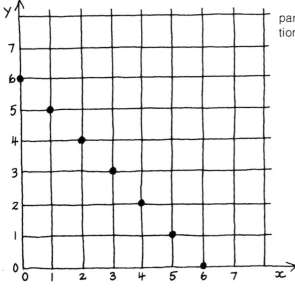

Making a graph of $\square + \triangle = d$ in Activity 10, part 1 corresponds to making a graph of the solutions to $x + y = 6$ on the coordinate plane.

1. What equation corresponds to $\square + \triangle = p$?
   _____

2. List the ordered pairs for the solutions to $x + y = 4$ and then make a graph. The graphs of $x + y = 6$ and $x + y = 4$ lie on lines that are _____

3. What can you say about graphs of equations of the following form:

$$x + y = \boxed{\text{some number}} \ ?$$

$\square \times \triangle = n$ translates into $x \times y = 8$. For $x \times y = 8$, list ordered pairs for all solutions that correspond to Cuisenaire rod solutions. (There are only four.) Make a graph of the solutions to the right. Do the points lie on a straight line as in the graph for $x + y = 4$ above?

Suppose that fractional values are allowed for x and y. Complete this table and then add these solutions to the graph for $x \times y = 8$.

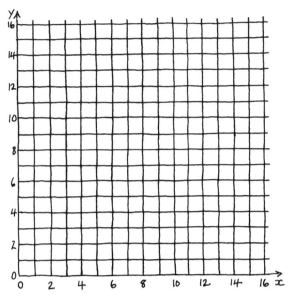

x	y
	$\frac{1}{2}$
$\frac{1}{2}$	
3	$\frac{8}{3}$ or $2\frac{2}{3}$
	3

The inequality $\square + \triangle < p$ corresponds to $x + y < 4$. Let the replacement set for x and y be $\{0,1,2,\ldots\}$. List all ordered pairs for solutions to this inequality. Then make a graph using the ordered pairs.

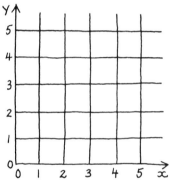

Operations ($+$, $-$, $\times$, $\div$) on Counting Numbers

In what ways are addition, subtraction, multiplication, and division alike? How are these operations related? What are some of their properties? This section deals with these questions and also suggests how some of these relationships and properties can be illustrated by the rods. Chapter 5 will describe how other materials can be used for this purpose and how children can use relationships and properties to learn basic facts.

Binary Operations

Addition, subtraction, multiplication, and division of counting numbers, $\{1, 2, 3, 4, 5, \ldots\}$, are alike in several ways. Each involves taking a pair of numbers (such as 6 and 3) and associating with them another number (such as $6 + 3 = 9$, $6 - 3 = 3$, $6 \times 3 = 18$, $6 \div 3 = 2$). That is, each is an example of a *binary operation* (binary being derived from the Latin, *binarius* meaning two at a time). Two other binary operations are (1) the greatest common divisor (GCD) of two numbers — for example, the GCD of 12 and 18 is 6; (2) the average of two numbers — for example, the average of 10 and 14 is 12.

Does addition of two counting numbers always yield a counting number? _____ does subtraction? _____ does multiplication? _____ division? _____ GCD? _____ average? _____

The operations of addition, multiplication, and GCD are *closed* on the set of counting numbers. The operations of subtraction, division, and average are *not* closed on the set of counting numbers. Write a definition for "An operation is *closed* on the set of counting numbers. . . ."

Addition and Subtraction

In Activity 3, Trains for Addition, you did addition by joining two rods end to end. Do you recall doing any subtraction in the Activities? If you thought of subtraction as "taking away," as you were probably taught in elementary school, then you would find you could not easily act out subtraction with the rods — for example, how could you take a red rod away from a yellow rod to solve $y - r = \square$? However, subtraction can be interpreted in a way other than "take away," as suggested by these two situations:

Betsy lives three blocks from school. If she has walked one block from home, how many more blocks does she have to walk to get to school?
Lauren knitted one foot of a three foot long scarf. How many more feet still have to be knitted?

We can represent these two situations by an addition sentence $1 + \square = 3$, or by a subtraction sentence, $3 - 1 = \square$. In the same way, the rod addition sentence $w + \square = g$ gives rise to a subtraction sentence $g - w = \square$, where to solve $g - w = \square$ we think how much more is to be added to w to get g.

1. Refer to the rod diagrams, fill in the blanks, and solve.

Subtraction Sentence | Related Addition Sentence

$y - r = \square$

$y - p = \square$

_____

$5 - 1 = \square$

_____

$w + \square = y$

$2 + \square = 5$

_____

Circle the subtraction sentences below that cannot be solved with the rods. (Why can't they be solved?)

$y - r = \square$ $y - y = \square$ $w - y = \square$ $w - p = \square$

2. Subtraction can be defined in terms of addition as follows: $a - b$ is that number which when added to b gives a. That is, $a - b = \square$ means that _____ $+ \square =$ _____. This additive approach is sometimes used to develop the concept of subtraction in grades 1–2. However, the take-away notion is usually used at first.

3. Do you see how to solve subtractions by referring to the Rod Addition Table in Activity 3? Refer to the table to solve the following:

$n - r = \square$ $o - d = \square$ $o - (n - r) = \square$ $(o - n) - r = \square$

4. Subtraction sentences such as those below (included in some grade 1–2 textbooks) are often difficult for children. Answers can be obtained by trial and error or by thinking addition. Write and solve an appropriate addition sentence for each subtraction.

$6 - \square = 2$
$\square - 6 = 2$
$\square - 4 = 7$
$7 - \square = 4$

The additive approach to subtraction is often used to develop subtraction of integers in later grades.[4] For example, $^+3 - {}^-5 = \square$ is done by solving a related addition equation $^-5 + \square = {}^+3$.

You can also do subtraction exercises on a number line by thinking addition. For example, to do $5 - 2 = \square$, you can think: how many more spaces must one move if one first moves 2 spaces and wants to end at 5? Draw a similar number-line solution for these two exercises.

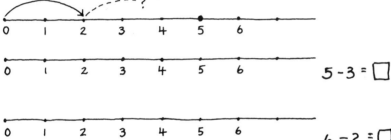

$5 - 3 = \square$

$6 - 2 = \square$

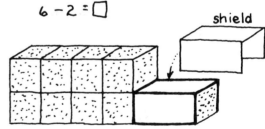

shield

Subtracting with Cuisenaire rods is done via addition. The Stern program[5] uses a method for subtraction that is closer to the take-away method. $6 - 2 = \square$ is solved by covering up two units of a six rod with a cardboard "2-shield" and then finding the rod that shows how much is left. Can this "cover-up-and-find-what's-left" method for subtraction be used with Cuisenaire rods? Why?

The diagram below shows how the subtraction $6 - 2 = \square$ can be interpreted as take away on the number line. Does this diagram correspond to the Stern rod solution?

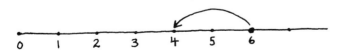

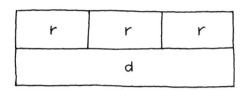

Multiplication and Addition

Multiplication can be thought of as repeated addition — that is, as a train of rods of the same color — for example, $3 \times r = r + r + r = d$, or $3 \times 2 = 2 + 2 + 2 = 6$.

Write each multiplication as a repeated addition and solve.

$2 \times r = \square$
$4 \times 3 = \square$
$3 \times 4 = \square$

Why doesn't $r \times 2$ make sense given the above interpretation of rod multiplication?

Note: This interpretation of multiplication of rods is different from that given in some guides for using Cuisenaire rods. The example below presents another way to interpret rod multiplication. The multiplication $g \times p$ (or 3×4) is represented by a "tower" of a light green rod placed on top of a purple rod to make a cross. This multiplication is then solved by making a rectangle of purple rods that is as wide as a light green rod, and then determining the length of a train of the purple rods used. Here $g \times p$ equals an orange and a red (or 3×4 is 12).

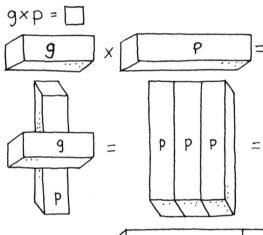

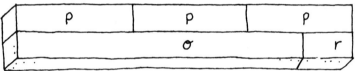

Thus, $g \times p = o + r$

To solve $r \times y$ you would make a "tower" of a _____ rod placed on top of a _____ rod, then form a rectangle of _____ rods that is as wide as a _____ rod, and finally find the length of a train of the _____ rods used. Here $r \times y$ equals _____. Suppose you were to solve $y \times r = \square$. In what way would the solution differ from the way you would have done $r \times y = \square$?

Which interpretation for rod multiplication do you find easier to work with, the one above, or the one you used in the Activities?

Multiplication and Division

How can we solve $6 \div 2 = \square$? One way is to think of $6 \div 2$ as meaning how many 2's are in 6; that is, solve $\square \times 2 = 6$. A rod solution for this sentence is shown to the left, where one thinks how many reds make a dark green; that is, solve $\square \times r = d$.

Another way to solve $6 \div 2 = \square$ is to divide 6 into 2 equal parts; that is, solve $2 \times \square = 6$. A rod solution for this interpretation of $6 \div 2$ is shown to the left.

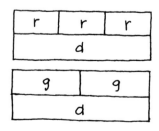

   Thus, the division $6 \div 2 = \square$ can be interpreted two different ways: one way is to relate it to the multiplication $\square \times 2 = 6$, and the other way is to relate it to the multiplication $2 \times \square = 6$. Draw rod diagrams to show how $8 \div 4 = \square$ can be solved two different ways. Write a multiplication that corresponds to each diagram.

   Write two multiplication sentences that correspond to these division sentences:

$12 \div 2 = \square$ _____ _____

$12 \div \square = 3$ _____ _____

   The examples above show that division can be defined in terms of multiplication: $a \div b$ equals that number which when multiplied by b equals a. That is, $a \div b = \square$ means that _____ $\times \square =$ _____ or $\square \times$ _____ =

_____.

Division and Subtraction

   How many times can groups of 3 be taken from 24? You may have answered this question by doing division rather than by doing subtraction several times. Division can be thought of as repeated subtraction; for example, $6 \div 2 = \square$ can mean how many times can 2 be taken away from 6, as shown here. Notice that this interpretation for $6 \div 2$ relates to the multiplication $\square \times 2 = 6$ (that is, how many 2's are in 6).

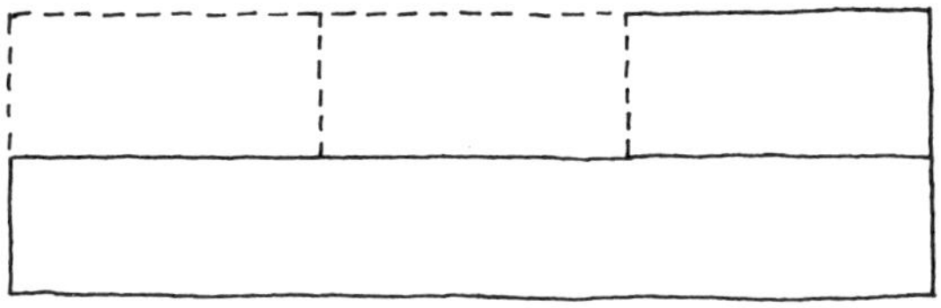

   This diagram corresponds to the division that

asks how many 3's are in 7 or $3 \overline{\smash{)}7}$ $^{2\,R\,1}$. Draw a diagram for how many _____ are in _____ or $2 \overline{\smash{)}7}$.

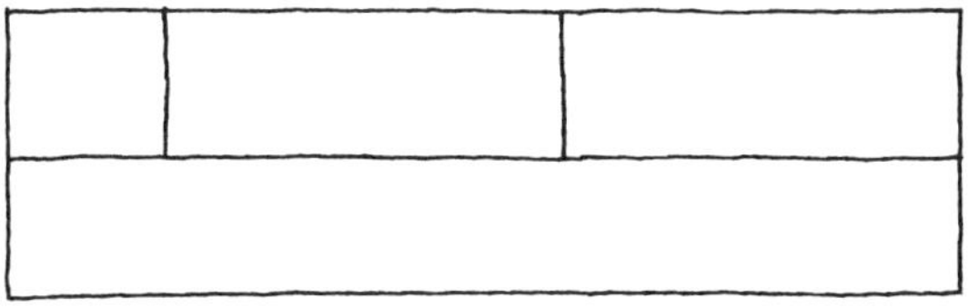

   A number-line solution for $6 \div 2 = \square$ is drawn below. Does it show division as repeated subtraction? Make number line drawings for these division exercises.

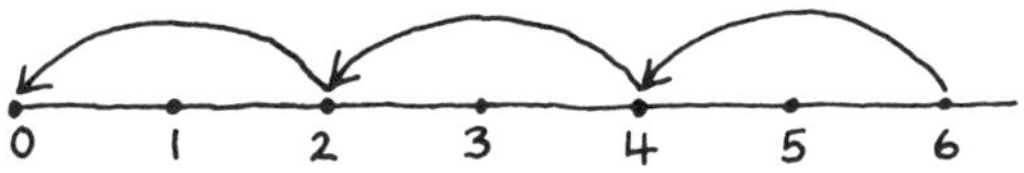

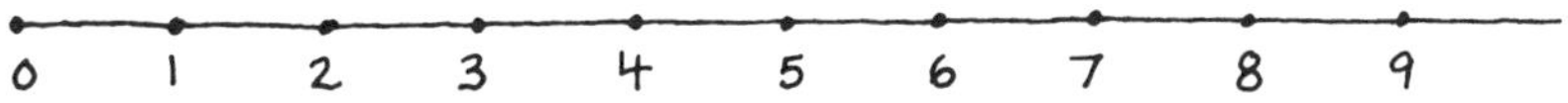

$8 \div 4 = \square$

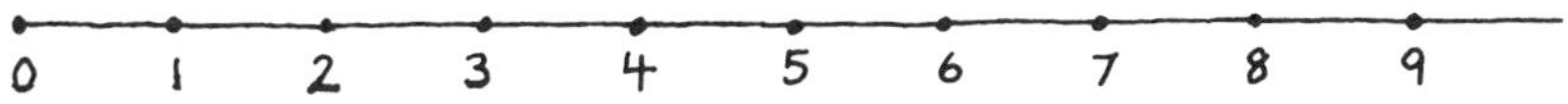

$9 \div 4 = \square$

Properties of Operations

Commutative Property. Operations on the counting numbers have various properties. For example, addition and multiplication both have the commutative property; that is, the order of the two numbers in addition and multiplication can be reversed without changing the answers: $2 + 3 = 3 + 2$, $2 \times 3 = 3 \times 2$. More formally, for any counting numbers a and b, $a + b = b + a$ and $a \times b = b \times a$.

Are any of the operations below commutative? If not, give an example.

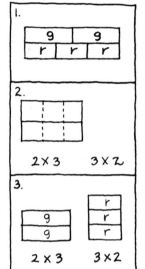

Subtraction
GCD
Division
Average

The rods can illustrate the commutative property of addition (or that addition satisfies the commutative property), but what about multiplication? Does diagram 1 show that $2 \times 3 = 3 \times 2$?

Sometimes the multiplication 2×3 is interpreted as 2 rows with 3 in each row. Diagram 2 shows this interpretation of 2×3 with Stern rods or number strips. 3×2 means _____ rows with _____ in each row. Draw this to the left. Does this pair of diagrams show that $2 \times 3 = 3 \times 2$?

Diagram 3 shows 2×3 and 3×2 with the Cuisenaire rods arranged in rectangles. Does this show you that multiplication is commutative?

Which diagram, 1, 2, or 3, most clearly indicates to you that multiplication is commutative? Why?

Associative Property. Do these two arithmetic exercises:

a. $38 + 17 + 3 =$ _____
b. $9 \times 25 \times 4 =$ _____

We usually add a series of numbers (as in (a) above) from left to right, just as we read. Did you add them from left to right; that is, $38 + 17 = 55$, then $55 + 3 = 58$? Perhaps you saw that it was easier to add from right to left: $17 + 3 = 20$, then $38 + 20 = 58$. Likewise, you may have multiplied in (b) as follows: $25 \times 4 = 100$, then $9 \times 100 = 900$. These solutions to (a) and (b) illustrate that both addition and multiplication are *associative* — that is, for any counting numbers a, b, and c,

$$(a + b) + c = a + (b + c)$$

and $(a \times b) \times c =$ _____.

Are any of these operations associative? If not, give an example.

Subtraction
Division
Average (Optional)

While children may be able to use the associative properties and even state them in terms, such as "I can add the first two numbers and then add the third," or "I can add the second two numbers and then the first," they may find the notation with parentheses very difficult unless they have experiences calling for such notation.

Rods can be used to show the associative property of addition. Complete the diagram below to show right to left addition of the rods.

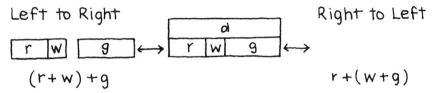

Left to Right   Right to Left

$(r + w) + g$ $r + (w + g)$

Can you use rods to show associativity of multiplication? Explain.

Distributive Properties. How many white rods are needed to cover the arrangement of rods shown on page 151?

Perhaps you solved this problem by noticing that there are 4 groups of rods with 1 white, 1 red . . . , 1 orange in each group. Therefore, the number of white rods in all is four times the number of white rods in each group, or $4 \times (1 + 2 + 3 + \ldots + 10)$, or 4×55. You could also have solved this problem by first noticing that there are 4 white rods, 4 red, etc. Thus, the answer is $(4 \times 1) + (4 \times 2) + (4 \times 3) + \ldots + (4 \times 10)$. Either method works! Which did you use? This problem illustrates that

$$4 \times (1 + 2 + 3 + \ldots + 10) = (4 \times 1) + (4 \times 2) + (4 \times 3) + \ldots + (4 \times 10)$$

This is an example of the distributive property of multiplication over addition. This property states that for any counting numbers a, b, and c,

$$a \times (b + c) = (a \times b) + (a \times c)$$

The example below illustrates how this distributive property can be used to find the answer to 7×12.

$$7 \times 12 = 7 \times (10 + 2) = (7 \times 10) + (7 \times 2) = 70 + 14 = 84$$

The rod diagrams below show that $3 \times (w + r) = \underline{\hspace{1cm}} \times w + \underline{\hspace{1cm}} \times r$.

w	r	w	r	w	r
w	w	w	r	r	r

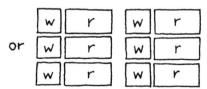

or

Check to see if there is a distributive property of multiplication over subtraction.

$3 \times (100 - 1) = \underline{\hspace{3cm}} = \underline{\hspace{2cm}} = \underline{\hspace{1cm}}$

Do you see how this problem suggests a quick way to compute 3×99 mentally? Use the distributive property of multiplication over subtraction to compute mentally: $5 \times 99 = \underline{\hspace{1cm}}$ and $4 \times 998 = \underline{\hspace{1cm}}$.

Identity Properties. The *identity property* for addition (on the set {0,1,2, 3, . . .}) states that a special number 0, when added to any number, leaves the number unchanged. For example, $0 + 7 = 7$, $99 + 0 = 99$, or more generally, for any whole number a,

$$0 + a = a + 0 = a$$

It can also be said that 0 is the identity for addition. Is there a Cuisenaire rod for 0? Sometimes a little square piece of paper is used as a model for 0 with rods. The diagram to the left shows that $2 + 0 = 2$. What problems can you foresee with this model for 0? (**Hint:** What is 1000×0? How thick is a pile of 1000 sheets of paper?)

Another way to deal with 0 is to have it mean "no rod." For example, when asked, what rod do you add to a red to get a red, children might respond, "add nothing," or "no other rod." Which approach to 0 do you prefer? Do you think the Cuisenaire rods are a suitable material for learning about 0? What else would you suggest? (**Note:** This will be treated in the next chapter.)

Is there an identity property for multiplication? Complete the following: There is a special number _____ which when multiplied by any number gives that number back again. That is, $7 \times$ _____ $= 7$, _____ $\times 99 = 99$, or more generally, for any counting number a,

$$a \times 1 = 1 \times a = a$$

Are the Cuisenaire rods suitable for showing $1 \times a = a$? _____ $a \times 1 = a$? _____

Why do you think that these two properties are called identity properties?

TEST YOUR UNDERSTANDING

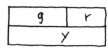

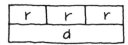

1. Refer to the rod diagrams to solve each of these.
   a. $g + r = \square$ d. $d \div r = \square$
   b. $y - r = \square$ e. $\square + r = y$
   c. $\square \times r = d$ f. $3 \times r = \square$
2. Name some mathematical concepts or topics that can be taught informally with Cuisenaire rods.
3. Give two examples of how children might discover characteristics of the Cuisenaire rods by playing with them.
4. What verbal directions would you give children in informal rod activities related to these sentences?
   a. $3 \times r = \square$
   b. $\square + \triangle + \bigcirc = y$
   c. $p \div r = \square$
5. Describe some ways to help children use the letter code for colors of the rods.
6. Describe how Cuisenaire rods, Stern rods, or number strips can be used to solve each of these.
   $8 + 4 = \square$, $8 - 4 = \square$, $8 \times 4 = \square$, $8 \div 4 = \square$.
   Compare the relative merits of Stern rods and Cuisenaire rods for helping children solve basic arithmetic exercises, such as $2 + 5 = \square$ and $2 \times 5 = \square$.

7. Give examples to show how the same arrangement of rods can illustrate addition sentences involving counting numbers, fractions, and decimals.

8. Illustrate some errors that children make on the number line. Describe ways for introducing the number line to prevent these difficulties.

9. Draw diagrams showing how to do $8 \div 2 = \square$ two different ways. Write a corresponding multiplication sentence for each way. Draw a diagram showing a repeated subtraction solution for $4\overline{)13}$ using the rods.

10. Which statements are true for operations on the set of counting numbers? If a statement is false, give an example of when it is false.
    a. Addition is closed.
    b. Division is closed.
    c. Subtraction is associative.
    d. Division is commutative.
    e. One is the identity for multiplication.
    f. One is the identity for division.
    g. Multiplication is distributive over addition.
    h. Multiplication is distributive over subtraction.

11. a. Refer to the Rod Addition Table on page 144 to find all solutions for $\square + r = \triangle$. List them in this table and make a graph.

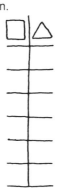 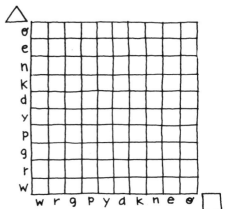

   b. Fill in each table and make a graph of the solutions. Use different colors for each number sentence.

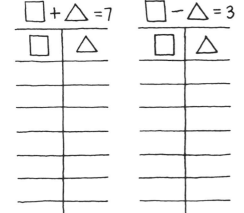 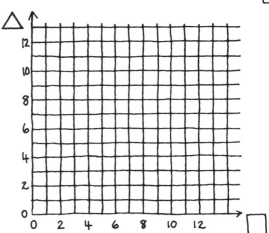

Are there any solutions that are in both tables?

12. The diagram indicates certain relationships between the operations. In what way does the relationship between addition and multiplication resemble the relationship between subtraction and division? In what way does the relationship between addition and subtraction resemble the relationship between multiplication and division?

FURTHER READINGS AND PROJECTS

1. Read "George Cuisenaire and His Rainbow Rods" by Rosemary March (*Learning,* 6:5 (November 1977), pp. 81–86). It traces the development of color rods by Georges Cuisenaire and their worldwide promotion by Caleb Gattegno. Uses of the rods with children, adults, and handicapped youngsters are described. Which of the uses of the rods cited in this article and in "Rods Can Help Children at All Grade Levels" by Patricia Davidson (*Learning,* 6:5 (November 1977), pp. 86–88) have you seen in this chapter?

2. Examine the Preface and Introduction in *Idea Book for Cuisenaire Rods at the Primary Level* by Patricia Davidson (New Rochelle, New York: Cuisenaire Co. of America, 1977) and then look at some of the many rod activities for young children in this book. Activities are accompanied by suggestions for teachers and photographs of children engaged in the activities. If you can, try some of the activities with a child or a group of children.

3. Examine *Using the Cuisenaire Rods — A Photo/Text Guide for Teachers* (Cuisenaire Co. of America, 1969). Check how each of the four operations is to be acted out. Then compare the procedures described in the manual with how you acted out each operation in this chapter. Are there any differences? If so, what, and for what operations?

4. Examine a set of commercial activity cards for the Cuisenaire rods (for example, *Student Activity Cards for Cuisenaire Rods* (New Rochelle, New York: Cuisenaire Co. of America, 1969). Are the activities sequenced from easy to more difficult or more complex? Could they be used with children in grades K–1? If so, how? Do any of the activity cards deal with the *arithmetic* of the rods rather than the *algebra* of the rods?

5. First read parts I ("Strategy") and II ("Fear and Failure") of *How Children Fail* (New York: Dell, 1964) by John Holt. Then read part III ("Real Learning") which describes several children's experiences in doing mathematics with Cuisenaire rods (as mentioned on page 157). In what ways do the rods help children "learn"? How does working with materials such as the rods enable children to demonstrate their potential for learning mathematics, especially slow learners or retarded youngsters?

6. Read Chapters 2 ("The Importance of Structure") and 3 ("Readiness

for Learning") in Jerome Bruner's *The Process of Education* (New York: Random House, 1960). How can activities with Cuisenaire rods help children discover structure in mathematics? How might children's work with the rods support Bruner's contention that "any subject can be taught effectively in some intellectually honest form to children at any stage of development"? (See Chapter 3, p. 33 of Bruner's book.)

7. The film "Mathematics for Five-Year-Olds" shows kindergarten children doing activities in a unique mathematics readiness program for grades K–1, Mason Math. (Information about rental or purchase of the film and Mason Math materials is available from Miss Mason, Miss Mason School, 53 Bayard Lane, Box 456, Princeton, N.J. 08540.) Young children are shown using a number line to act out solutions to number sentences involving whole numbers, for example, $3 + 5 = \square$, $3 \times 5 = \square$, $3 \times 5 + 1 = \square$, $3 + 5 + 1 + 2 + 1 = \square$, $3 + \square = 5$. Also shown is their use of the number line to extend this work to the *integers*. If possible, view the film and describe your reactions to the children's work in the Mason Math program. The teacher's manual for the Mason Math program contains step by step daily lesson plans. Did you find any of the ideas in the film or guide, in particular those involving the number line, especially interesting?

NOTES

1. On pp. 91–95 of *How Children Fail* (New York: Dell, 1964), John Holt gives a vivid and moving description of a similar activity done by Caleb Gattegno (who introduced the Cuisenaire rods in many countries, including the United States) with retarded adolescents.
2. Jerome Bruner, *The Process of Education* (New York: Random House, 1960), p. 52.
3. See the material on frame arithmetic in the Madison Project, which was designed to supplement the usual school programs in arithmetic. For example, see Robert Davis, *Discovery in Mathematics: A Text for Teachers* (Menlo Park, California: Addison-Wesley, 1964).
4. The Madison Project, a curriculum development project in the 1960s, focused on providing children with creative learning experiences in mathematics. See *Explorations in Mathematics* by Robert Davis (Palo Alto, California: Addison-Wesley, 1964) for uses of number lines to develop operations on the integers.
5. See Catherine and Margaret Stern, *Children Discover Arithmetic* (New York: Harper and Row, 1971).

CHAPTER 5

BASIC FACTS AND THEIR
USES – OPERATIONS
ON WHOLE NUMBERS

INTRODUCTION

What does it mean to say that a child has *learned* the basic facts of arithmetic — for example, the multiplication facts? When can children be expected to develop an understanding of addition, subtraction, multiplication, and division of whole numbers, to deal with these operations symbolically (for example, $3 \times 4 = \square$), and to acquire skill with them? What types of activities can help children learn basic facts?

These questions about the learning of basic facts concern a major part of the elementary school mathematics curriculum for grades 1–4. Children can think about an operation such as multiplication in various ways. For example, examine the written work (below) of some children who were asked, "What is three times four?"

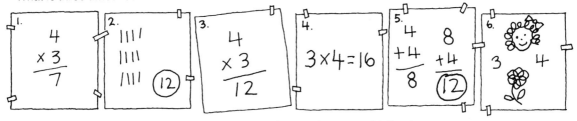

Based on this work, which children seem to understand what multiplication means? _____ Which child probably knows 3×4 from recall? _____ Can you suggest what might be causing the errors in (1) and (4)? The child who drew the "doodle" in (6) might not understand the question, or might simply not be interested. Have you ever reacted this way to a question?

Children should eventually be able to answer a question such as "What is three times four?" instantaneously, but this knowledge is not very useful unless children also know when it is appropriate to use multiplication. Most children find it easier to learn basic facts if they understand what they mean (3 groups of 4), when they are used (3 cookies costing 4¢ each), and how they are related ($3 \times 4 = 2 \times 4 + 4$). However children need more than this understanding to develop the skill they will need, and attention must be given to skill-building practice activities. Some "new math" programs of the 1960s have been criticized for over-reacting to the rote-learning approach to teaching arithmetic and for not devoting appropriate attention to building skills. Now teachers must be wary of an equally unbalanced swing in the other direction as indicated by pressures for "back to basics" by rote methods. A program based on understanding is not an alternative to one that builds skill, but rather a prerequisite.

This chapter is one in a series dealing with operations on whole numbers. Before this, Chapter 4 introduced the operations using one commonly available material for number, Cuisenaire rods. This chapter discusses how children can use other materials to learn these operations and their properties and eventually master basic facts — that is, facts related to addition and multiplication of whole numbers less than 10 (for example, $8 + 7$, $15 - 7$, 8×7, $56 \div 7$). Later, Chapter 9, Whole Number Algorithms and Their Uses, concerns procedures we use to perform operations on larger whole numbers.

The Activities in this chapter involve the use of various materials for solving problems involving basic facts (for example, beans, chips, the balance beam, a beadboard). Some Activities present challenging games that can be played at the concrete level with materials or at the semiconcrete and abstract levels. Others focus on the usefulness of particular materials for acting out basic facts.

The Discussion Questions and Comments concern several aspects of teaching basic facts: when and how basic facts are taught in elementary school; how operations arise in story situations and can be acted out and drawn using various models for number; why several models should be used; and how properties of operations can be shown by different materials.

Follow-up Sections discuss and illustrate how three general principles for teaching skills apply to basic facts: integrate application and problem-solving situations of interest to children into learning of basic facts; have children use the structure of arithmetic to master basic facts; and provide activities (introductory, developmental, review-practice) appropriate to a child's stage of mastery.

This chapter is not intended to give a complete summary of techniques and activities for teaching basic facts. Rather, it touches on some specific methods and general themes. For more detailed sequences of activities for children, you might examine some good elementary school mathematics programs. Several innovative programs are mentioned in the course of the Activities and Discussion Questions and Comments sections. It is hoped that this brief encounter will lead to a deeper study of the fine curriculum materials available.

ACTIVITIES

Activity 1. Poison Apple Games

Play each of the four Poison Apple Games described below. As you play them, try to find a strategy for winning.

Materials: 15 "apples" (chips, beans, or pennies), one of which is designated as a poison apple"

Directions:

1. Game 1: Start with 15 "apples." Two players take turns taking away 1, 2, or 3 apples. The player who takes the poison apple loses.

2. Game 2 is a variation of Game 1 in which players also say how many apples they took away and how many were left after each of their turns.

3. Game 3 is played at the semiconcrete or pictorial level with players crossing off the apples they take away. Also, they keep a written record for each stage of the game (see example below).

Example
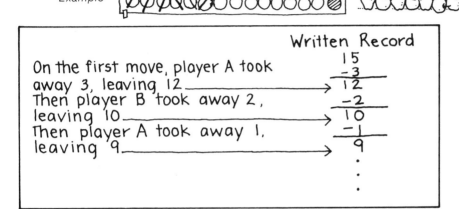

	Written Record
On the first move, player A took away 3, leaving 12	15 −3 12
Then player B took away 2, leaving 10	−2 10
Then player A took away 1, leaving 9	−1 9 . . .

4. Game 4 is played by just crossing out numbers, as shown below for the example in Game 3.

What is the earliest point at which you know who will win?

How can you make sure you win?

Does it make a difference who goes first? Why?

(Optional) Try to discover a strategy for winning, if 1–4 apples can be taken away. What if 1–5 apples could be taken away?

Activity 2. Beans in Circles

1. In the diagrams here, beans have been placed in three circles and numbers have been written in the squares between the circles. Look at examples (a) and (b) to figure out why these numbers have been filled in the squares. Then fill in the empty square in example (b).

2. The sum of the number of beans in two connected circles is written in the square between the circles. Fill in the circle and two squares.

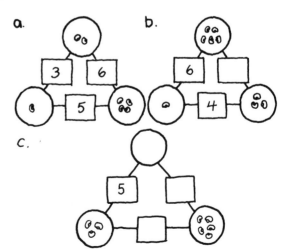

3. Place beans in the circle to solve each puzzle.

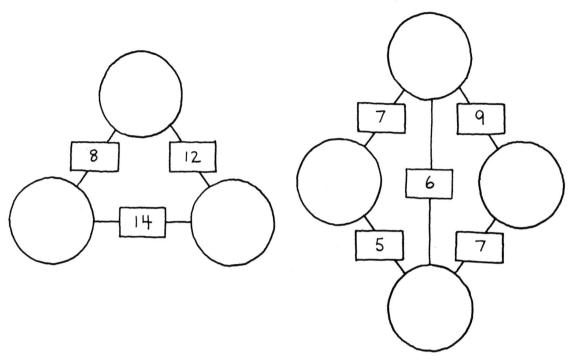

4. Use beans to make your own puzzle. Draw the puzzle outline, put the beans in the circles and fill in the squares. Then remove the beans and try the puzzle on your neighbor.
5. Solve each puzzle. (Optional)

a.

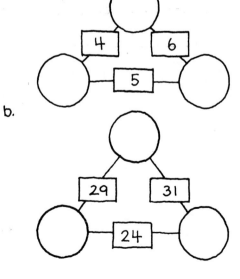

b.

Hint: You can use half beans. Explore: Will any similar puzzle with three consecutive whole numbers in the boxes always require fractional parts of beans?

You probably solved this puzzle at the abstract level without beans. Can you design a similar puzzle involving decimals that is to be solved abstractly?

Activity 3. The Balance Beam

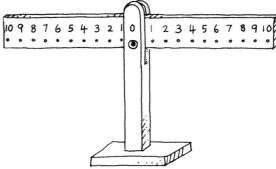

1. On one side of the balance beam place one weight on 4 and one on 5. Now place one more weight to balance this. Draw this on the balance beam.

2. On one side of the balance beam place one weight on 4 and one on 8. Can you balance this by

one weight? ____	If so, where? ____ ·
two weights? ____	If so, where? ____ and ____
three weights? ____	If so, where? ____, ____, ____
five weights? ____	If so, where? ____, ____, ____, ____, ____
eleven weights? ____	If so, describe where you could place them.

3. Place one weight on 6. Where can you place two weights on the other side to balance this? How many ways can this be done? Write an addition sentence for each way. _____

4. On one side place three weights on 2. Balance this with one weight.
   Write an addition sentence for this. _____
   Write a multiplication sentence for this. _____
   Can you illustrate the commutative property of multiplication on the balance beam — for example, $4 \times 3 = 3 \times 4$? If so, demonstrate how. Can you work out 3×13 on the balance beam? If so, demonstrate how.

5. On one side place one weight on 10 and one on 2 to make 12.
   a. Place weights just on 2 to balance this. Draw this to the right. How many weights did you place on 2? _____ weights on 2
   b. Place weights just on 4 to balance 12. _____ weights on 4
   c. On which other numbers can you place several weights to balance 12?
      _____ weights on _____
      _____ weights on _____
   d. Write a division sentence for a.
      _____ ÷ _____ = _____
      Write a related multiplication sentence for a. _____ × _____ = _____

6. On one side place one weight on 10. Now take two weights and place them on the other side to balance this. Two weights on _____
   Write a division sentence. _____ ÷ _____ = _____

7. Use the balance beam to solve $9 \div 2$.
   Which number sentence below corresponds to your solution?
   $$9 = 4 \times 2 + 1 \qquad 9 = 2 \times 4 + 1$$

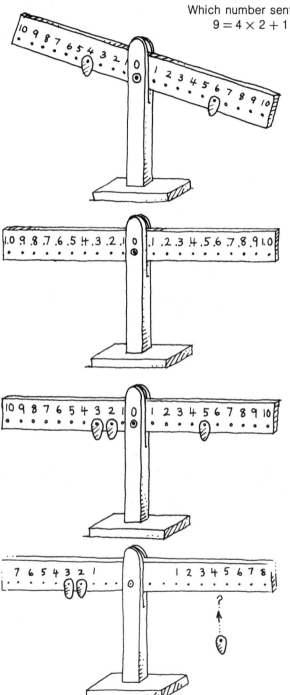

8. Place weights as shown to the left. Now place one weight to make this balance. Write an addition sentence.

9. Can you solve $9 - 5 = \square$ on the balance beam? If so, how are you interpreting subtraction?

10. On one side place one weight each on 1, 4, 7, and 8. Balance this by placing four weights on just one number. Four weights on _____ What have you just found? **Hint:** 5 is the A _ _ _ A _ E of 1, 4, 7, and 8.

11. (Optional) Suppose that a balance beam has been marked in tenths as shown to the left. Which of these number sentences could not easily be acted out on this type of balance beam? Why?

   a. $.9 + .3 = \square$
   b. $3 \times .9 = \square$
   c. $.9 \times .3 = \square$
   d. $.9 \div .3 = \square$

12. Does this picture of a balance beam show you *why* $2 + 3 = 5$? If you think so, try this experiment. Relabel the balance beam as shown below, put one weight on 2 and one weight on 3, and ask anyone who has done a few exercises using a balance beam where to put a weight to balance the beam. Many people will be surprised! This may convince you that while the balance beam can be an enjoyable device to use for practice, it is magic from the child's point of view, and does not show *why* the answer is what it is.

Activity 4. Action for Basic Facts

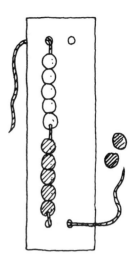

In Activity 3, you used the balance beam to act out solutions to number sentences, such as $4 + 5 = \square$, $3 \times 2 = \square$, $12 \div 2 = \square$, and $9 - 5 = \square$. You may have found the balance beam an interesting and novel material for doing these computations, but also may have felt that other materials would be more effective for helping children learn to do them. In this Activity you can compare two other materials for acting out basic facts: a counting material, such as chips, color cubes, straws, or shells, and a bead board or counting frame. Counting frames (containing two strands for addition facts; ten strands for multiplication facts) are available commercially, or can be inexpensively constructed. Beads or buttons can be threaded on a string or shoelace, and then attached to a cardboard backing, as shown to the right. Holes for threading can be punched in the cardboard. Two colors of beads can be used. As you do the problems below, think about what the advantages are of having two colors.

Work in small groups. Act out each basic fact with *both* of these materials, as if you were demonstrating the solutions to children who are just beginning to learn about that type of fact. Also answer the related questions.

1. Fact: $4 + 5 = \square$
   With which material could you most clearly show a child why $4 + 5 = 9$: the balance beam or either of these two materials?

2. Fact: $9 + 5 = \square$
   Which material leads more naturally to the following solution? Why?
   Solution: $9 + 5$ is the same as $9 + 1$ and 4 more, or $10 + 4$, or 14.

3. Fact: $9 - 5 = \square$
   Which (if any) of the diagrams below show the action of your solution? _____

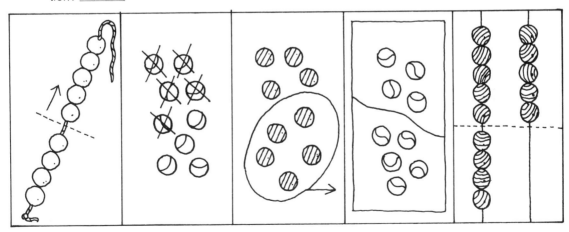

Do any of these diagrams suggest ways to act out $9 - 5 = \square$ that are different from those you did with the two materials?

4. Fact: $4 \times 3 = \square$
    Draw a diagram (to the left) to show how you arranged objects or beads to solve $4 \times 3 = \square$.
    Your solution should show 4×3 as repeated addition — that is, as four groups of 3, or $3 + 3 + 3 + 3$.
    Draw a diagram (similar to the one you drew above) to show 3×4. Do your diagrams for 4×3 and 3×4 show you why multiplication of whole numbers is commutative? If so, how?

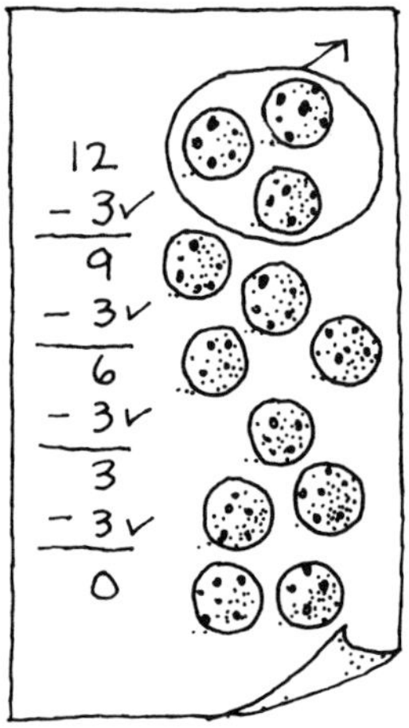

5. Problem: I have a dozen cookies.
    I give them out 3 at a time.
    How many people can I give them to?
    Complete the diagram to the left to show the action of passing out groups of 3 cookies. Note how your diagram shows a repeated subtraction solution for $12 \div 3 = \square$ as presented here.
    Complete the diagram below to show a repeated subtraction solution for $20 \div 6 = \square$.

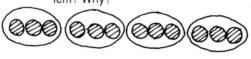

6. Problem: I have 12 cards to deal to 3 people.
    How many cards does each person get?
    Which diagram below shows the action for your solution to this problem? Why?

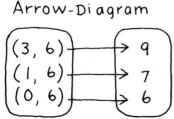 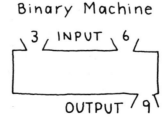 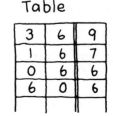

7. (Optional) Problem: What is the average of 1, 4, 7, and 8?

Activity 5. Arrows and Machines

Addition and subtraction are examples of binary operations — that is, rules that associate to any two numbers of a certain type another number. For example, the rule "add" associates to the pair of numbers 3 and 6 the number 9. Three ways to represent addition are given below.

| Arrow-Diagram | Binary Machine | Table |

Determine the rule for each of these diagrams. Can you think of more than one answer for any of them?

a.   b.   c.

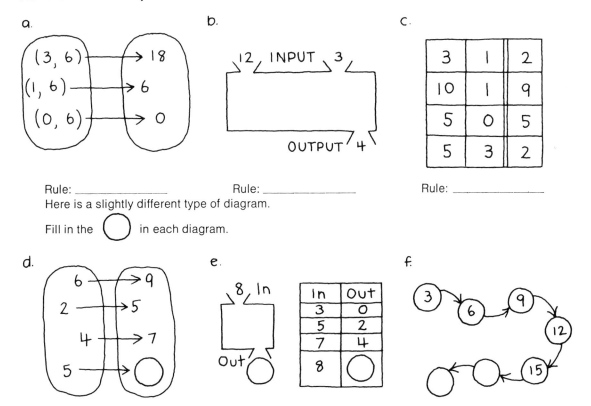

Rule: _____   Rule: _____   Rule: _____

Here is a slightly different type of diagram.

Fill in the ◯ in each diagram.

d.   e.   f.

The arrows in (d) and (f) stand for "addition of 3" rather than addition in general as before. The machine in (e) shows "subtraction of 3" rather than subtraction. Activities 6, 7, and 8 involve these three types of diagrams which can be used to present challenging problems to children.

Activity 6. Story — "A Funny Thing Happened on the Way to the Beanstalk"

1. Read this story and act out each step using beans. Start with 1 to 5 beans.
   How many beans are you starting with?

   As you know, Jack was given some beans in exchange for his old mother's favorite cow. He put them in his pocket and walked home. (Place Jack's beans on the table in front of you.) On his way home, Jack saw 3 more beans on the road — he picked them up and also put them in his pocket. The beans were magic, of course, and when Jack sneezed (as a hay truck went by), this was the signal for each bean to turn into 2 beans! Then Jack tripped over a big stone and 4 beans fell on the ground. He saw a dog and whistled at it, and the magic beans responded — each *pair* of beans became *one* bean! Now it was getting dark and so Jack started running to get home on time — one bean jumped out of his pocket. When he got home, how many beans did Jack have in his pocket?

How many beans did you end with?

2. The diagram below indicates how this story could be acted out. Draw dots to represent the beans in Jack's pocket at each step in the story.

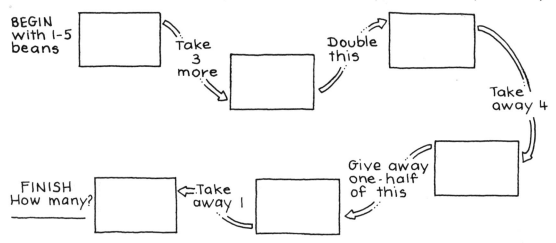

3. Begin with a different amount of beans, and try the story again but using just numbers. What do you notice?

4. (Optional) Label the last two arrows in the diagram so that you end with the same number you began with. Test your answer. Can you fill in the blanks in two different ways?

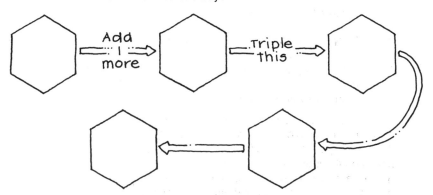

5. (Optional) Make up another bean story and a related diagram that yields the same number of beans you began with.

Activity 7. Arrow Paths[1]

1. Complete each arrow path and describe what the arrow means.

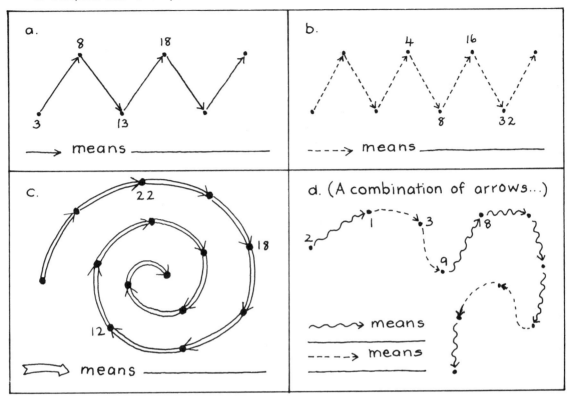

2. Perhaps you chose the following "names" (or some equivalent expressions) for the arrow paths above: (a) is + 5 or add 5; (b) is × 2, times 2, or double; and (c) is − 2, take-away two, or minus two. Name the dots for each arrow path below. ⟶ means +5, − − −⟶ means × 2, and ⟿ means + 3.

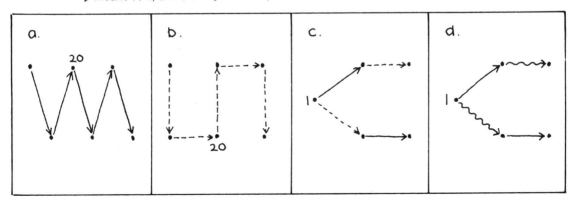

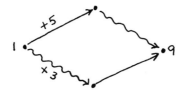 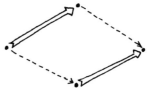

The arrow paths in (d) could be drawn as shown here, since they end at the same number 9. Could the arrow paths in (c) also be drawn this way?

Suppose that the diagram for two arrows ——→ and - - -→ looks like this, whatever number you start with. If ——→ means + 4, find a name for - - -→. (There are several correct answers.)

If ——→ means × 2, then - - -→ could mean _____.

If ——→ means ÷ 1, then - - -→ could mean _____.

Can you make some kind of generalization here?

3. Make an arrow path from 1 to 10 using the arrows $\overset{+4}{\leadsto}$ and $\overset{-3}{\longrightarrow}$. Then do it another way.

•
1   •
                                                                 10

Make paths from 1 to 10 using arrows $\overset{×2}{\dashrightarrow}$ and $\overset{+2}{\longrightarrow}$
Which path uses the most arrows? the fewest?

•
1   •
                                                                 10

4. Use only the numbers in the loop to name the dots.

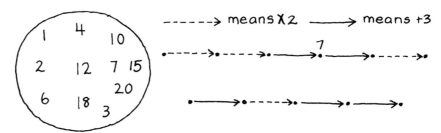

5. Could you create an arrow path with fractions instead of whole numbers? with decimals instead of whole numbers? Draw one, leaving some points or arrows unnamed. Try it on your neighbor. (You might use different colors to distinguish your arrows.)

Activity 8. Machines and Tables[2]

1. The rule for the machine to the right is "triple and then subtract 1," or symbolically $3 \times \square - 1$, or $3 \times n - 1$. Fill in the missing numbers in the table.

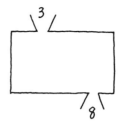

In	Out
3	8
4	11
10	29
5	
	20
20	

2. Find the rule for this machine.
   Rule: _____
   Can you write this rule another way?
   Which is more interesting: "given a rule, fill in the table" or "given a table, find the rule"? Why?

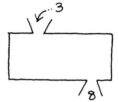

In	Out
3	8
4	10
10	22
6	14
5	12

(Optional) Suppose that the numbers in the Input and Output were switched here — for example, $8 \longrightarrow 3$ rather than $3 \longrightarrow 8$, and $10 \longrightarrow 4$ rather than $4 \longrightarrow 10$. Fill in the table for this reversed situation. What is the rule here?

In	Out
8	3
10	4

3. Two machines can be put together to make a big machine, as shown here. Machine A has the rule "double" and machine B has the rule "add 3." If a 10 goes into the big machine, it first drops into machine A, and 20 comes out and goes into machine B, yielding 23. Thus, if 10 goes into the big machine, 23 comes out. We can show this by using arrows:

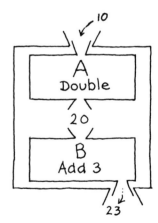

$$10 \xrightarrow{\quad A \quad} 20 \xrightarrow{\quad B \quad} 23$$

a. Fill in each ◯

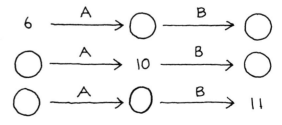

In	Out
10	23
6	
5	
4	
3	

b. Complete this table for the big machine.

c. Mark an X next to each of the following that *could* be a rule for the big machine.

_____ Add 3 and double

_____ Add 1½ and double

_____ Double and add 3

_____ Add 1, double, add 1

d. Suppose that machines A and B were switched — that is, B was on top and A on the bottom. Are the results for A on top and B on the bottom the same as for B on top and A on the bottom? Can you find a rule for this reversed situation?

e. (Optional) For what kinds of rules can machines A and B be switched without changing the results for the big machine? Give some examples of rules for machines A and B.

4. Here is a table for the big machine.

In	Out
1	1
2	2
3	3
4	4

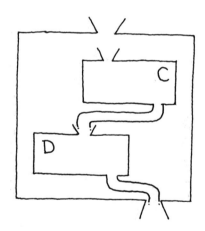

a. What is a rule for this big machine?

b. If machine C has the rule "+5," what is the rule for machine D?

c. Give some rules for other pairs of machines which like C and D, together yield the same number you began with. (These machines or functions are sometimes said to be "inverses of each other," that is, they undo each other.)

_____ and _____;

_____ and _____;

_____ and _____

DISCUSSION QUESTIONS AND COMMENTS

Understanding, Skill, and Application

Suppose you asked children to answer the written subtraction sentence $8 - 3 = \square$. How might they respond?

1. A child might say "5" immediately.
2. A child might read "$8 - 3 = \square$" as "eight take away three" but not remember the answer, although he may be able to find the answer by using some material such as chips or his fingers.
3. A child may be unfamiliar with the symbols $-$, $=$, and $\square$, and hence be unable to answer the written number sentence. However, if the sentence was read aloud as "how much is eight take away three," he might be able to solve it by acting it out.
4. A child may not even know what to do when the problem is read to him. This child may be unfamiliar with the language of subtraction and not understand how to act out "eight take away three."

Response 4 indicates the least knowledge about subtraction. Response 3 indicates that the child understands the concept of subtraction and associates the action of "taking away" with it. However, he may still be unable to solve $8 - 3 = \square$ because reading the number sentence requires familiarity with symbols. The child giving response 2 seems to know what subtraction means. He understands the process of subtraction and can deal with symbols in subtraction sentences; but he has not yet mastered the basic facts of subtraction. Finally, response 1 seems to indicate that the child knows this subtraction fact.

These responses suggest that basic facts are learned in the following sequence:

$$\text{Concept} \longrightarrow \text{Concept and Notation} \longrightarrow \text{Skill}$$

Understanding the concept of subtraction does not imply skill with subtraction facts. Does skill imply understanding? A child who has been taught subtraction facts by rote may be able to answer "$8 - 3 = 5$" quickly but may have little understanding of subtraction, quickly forget subtraction facts, and find it difficult to apply them. (Response 1 does not give enough information to determine if this is the case; one would have to talk further with this child to know.)

The learning sequence above lies at the heart of sound mathematics programs which stress both skill and understanding. In contrast, many mathematics programs developed before the 1950s placed exclusive emphasis on skill, with children learning their basic facts by rote. Some "new math" programs have been justly criticized for placing disproportional emphasis on understanding: "It's not the answer that counts, it's how you get the answer." There must be a balance between understanding and skill, with understanding preceding skill.

In Activity 1, you played Poison Apple in four different formats. Which of the following formats would be appropriate for kindergarten children who can count rationally to 20 but have not yet been formally introduced to the concept, language, and notation of subtraction: Game 1, Game 2, Game 3, or Game 4? _____ Which game is least appropriate for these kindergarten children? _____ Why?

Which of these games involve the process of "taking away" to act out subtraction sentences? _____ Which involve language for subtraction? _____ Which involve written notation for subtraction? _____ Which involve the skill of subtraction, that is, the ability to do subtraction from memory? _____

Is there more to really "knowing" subtraction than understanding the concept, language, and notation, and being able to do subtraction from memory? Sometimes a child who understands subtraction and also knows the subtraction facts may have difficulty in solving verbal problems, such as "I had 8¢ and went to the store to buy a cookie for 3¢. How much money do I have now?" This difficulty can arise because applications or uses of basic facts have followed rather than been integrated into the learning of basic facts. All too often, the teaching of basic facts follows the sequence:

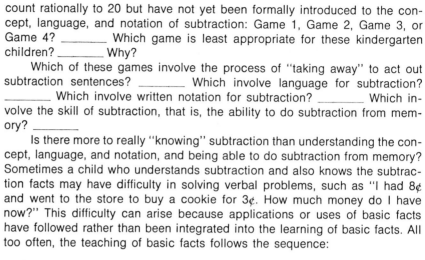

Moreover, the applications may have been limited to routine story problems which had little relevance to children's interests. Rather, both concepts and skills should be developed in the context of meaningful and interesting applications and problem-solving situations, as suggested by the diagram below.

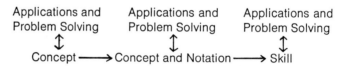

Learning arithmetic skills should not be an end in itself. From the very beginning, children should use what they are learning in ways that interest them — in their everyday lives, in games and puzzles, and in a wide range of problem-solving situations such as those described on pages 214 to 218.

Do you think that children would find the Poison Apple Game an interesting application of subtraction? Do you think it involves problem solving in searching for a strategy? As you saw above, the Poison Apple Game is an example of an activity that can be placed at all steps of the learning sequence and that also incorporates applications or uses of subtraction and problem solving.

Scope and Sequence

At what grade level are children usually introduced to the concept of addition? of multiplication? By what grade should they have acquired skill with the basic facts of addition? Answers to these questions can be found in a scope and sequence chart (often provided by teacher's guides to texts or state and local curriculum guides) that indicates when children are expected to understand and then master basic facts. The table summarizes the part of a scope and sequence chart related to basic facts — that is, facts related to addition and multiplication of numbers 0–9 (for example, $7 + 5 = \square$, $12 - 5 = \square$, $5 \times 6 = \square$, $30 \div 5 = \square$). Basic facts together with arithmetic of multidigit whole numbers (for example, $117 + 238 = \square$, $902 - 344 = \square$, $24 \times 13 = \square$, $126 \div 4 = \square$) make up a large portion of what is sometimes called the whole number strand in a mathematics program. (Chapter 9, Whole Number Algorithms and Their Uses, deals with teaching arithmetic involving larger whole numbers.)

	Introduce Concept	Develop Concept and Notation	Build Skill
Addition	K	1	2
Subtraction	K	1	2
Multiplication	2	2-3	3-4
Division	2	3	3-4

The table indicates that by the end of the first grade, most children can be expected to understand the concept of subtraction and associate the action of subtraction with language and notation. More specifically, children should be able to

1. act out solutions to verbally stated subtraction situations. ("I have eight apples and give away three. How many do I have left?")
2. act out solutions to written subtraction sentences.
3. write a number sentence for a subtraction situation or a diagram depicting subtraction.

However, mastery of subtraction facts is not expected until later, generally during the second grade. Most textbook series also include some review-practice activities in grades 3 through 6 to help children maintain skill with basic facts. Of course, these facts are continually practiced through their use in other computation.

Judging from the preceding table, at what grade level might you expect children to do the following:

___ Play Poison Apple Games 1 and 2 with chips but without notation.
___ Play Poison Apple Game 3 with chips and notation for subtraction.
___ Solve puzzles like Beans in Circles with beans.
___ Use a bead board to do multiplication exercises, such as 4×3, 5×2, and 7×4.
___ Use a balance beam to check answers in an activity involving facts, such as $8 + 6$, $9 + 3$, and $4 + 6$.
___ Use counting materials to act out solutions to division situations, such as $12 \div 3$, $24 \div 8$, and $18 \div 6$.
___ Solve problems involving Arrow Paths (part 2).

While a scope and sequence chart provides some guidance to a teacher for planning instruction, there are several dangers in adhering rigidly to the grade level placement of topics, especially for more capable children or for children who are slow learners of mathematics. For example, a teacher may wrongly interpret the general exclusion of material on multiplication and division before the second grade as ruling out any informal introduction of these concepts to younger children (such as by discussing sharing a plate of cookies among 4 children when such a situation arises). In fact, some mathematics programs include material on multiplication and division in grades 1 and 2. These programs usually provide children with earlier and more extended experiences with the concept and notation for each operation before stressing mastery of facts.

Another danger is that a teacher may think that only topics specified for a grade level should be covered, and so may have children who have already mastered these topics review them again and again. Rather these children should be given further mathematical experiences. For example, first graders who have learned the basic facts of addition and subtraction could begin work on addition of two-digit numbers or on multiplication. (Do you see any difficulty with this type of *acceleration*?) As an alternative, the children could explore related topics in greater depth or solve challenging problems using the skills they have mastered (for example, Activity 2, Beans in Circles; Activity 7, Arrow Paths; Activity 8, Machines and Tables). This is sometimes called *enrichment* of the curriculum. (Do you see any problems with this *enrichment* approach?)

Also, teachers may think that they must cover all the material specified by the scope and sequence chart for their grade, and, as a result, may rush children into studying topics that they are not yet ready to learn. For example, children who have not acquired skill with addition during the second grade may find the development of multiplication at the beginning of the third grade to be tedious and frustrating, especially if addition skills are required to do multiplication (such as $3 \times 4 = 4 + 4 + 4 = \square$). Their third grade teacher should realize that this lack of skill in addition is not normal and that such children need attention in this area. The teacher might postpone work on multiplication until the children review the concepts of addition and subtraction and build up these skills. These students might also require extra remedial instruction in mathematics.

The ultimate guide to planning instruction should be the children, not the scope and sequence. Teachers should use the scope and sequence to form general grade level expectations, at the same time recognizing that children who are behind or beyond these expectations may require special instruction. In most classes children's abilities and achievement vary considerably so that uniform instruction based on a scope and sequence cannot meet the needs of all children. A teacher can group children with similar needs and tailor instruction accordingly — for example, providing review-practice games to build skills for some children and providing enrichment activities for others before going on to a new topic. To provide instruction that meets the needs of all children in a class, a teacher must have knowledge of a variety of activities for remediation and enrichment, and also have the support of school administrators to depart from the scope and sequence, when necessary.

Stories, Action, and Diagrams — The Meanings of Operations

A first step in helping children learn basic facts is to have them understand the concept — what the operation means. An operation can have different meanings, depending upon the material used to illustrate it or on the situation in which it is used. For example, if you used chips to play the Poison Apple games, you would think of subtraction as "take away." However, if you used a balance beam or Cuisenaire rods to do subtraction, you would interpret it in a different way, in terms of addition. For example, $8 - 3 = \square$ means how much more do I need to add to 3 to make 8.

This section presents story problems illustrating different types of application situations for operations together with diagrams (similar to those commonly found in textbooks) showing how the problems could be solved with various materials, such as chips, number strips, or a number line. Read each story problem and imagine what materials you could select to act it out and how you could represent the action by a diagram. Then identitfy the diagram on the right that best matches the solution. As you do this, think about whether the diagrams show the action clearly and whether you could improve any of the diagrams.

Addition

All of the stories and diagrams below concern the addition $3 + 4 = \square$. On the line to the left of each story problem write the letter of the diagram which fits it best.

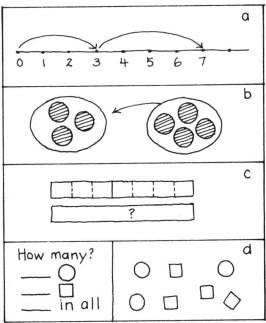

Which Diagram?

_____ There are 3 apples in a bowl. I put in 4 more. How many are there now?

_____ I have 3 dogs and 4 cats. How many pets do I have?

_____ I walk 3 blocks, buy a paper, and then walk another 4 blocks. How far have I walked?

_____ This morning 3 centimeters of snow fell. This afternoon it snowed another 4 centimeters. How much snow fell today?

Sometimes addition is "active" — that is, the two sets of objects or lengths are physically combined or put together — and sometimes "static" — objects are classified or counted. Which problem above seems "static"? _____

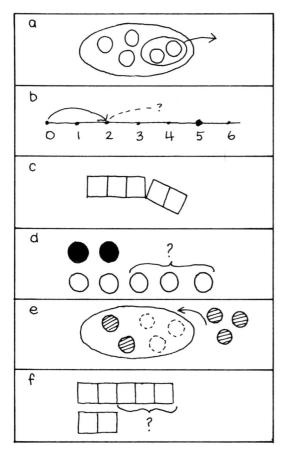

a

b

c

d

e

f

Subtraction

All of the stories and diagrams below concern the subtraction $5 - 2 = \square$. Match the diagrams to the stories and also write your own in the blanks.

Which Diagram?

Take-away Subtraction

_____ I have 5 inches of ribbon, and I cut off 2 inches. How much is left?

a _____

_____

Missing Addend Subtraction

_____ I have 2 cups on a table and there are 5 children. How many more cups must I get?

b _____

_____

Comparison Subtraction

_____ Today 2 centimeters of snow fell and yesterday 5 centimeters fell. How much more did it snow yesterday than today?

d _____

_____

Which type of verbal problem do you usually associate with subtraction — take-away, missing addend, or comparison? For which type is it easiest to represent the action for the solution by a diagram? Which type would you expect to be easiest for children to solve? Which type would be most difficult? Why?

Which of these three types of subtraction situations would you use to develop the concept of subtraction with first graders who are just beginning their study of subtraction? Why?

Children experience all three types of subtraction situations in their everyday life, and hence all can be meaningfully included in their mathematics program. Usually take-away problems are done first in grades 1–2, and the other types are done later, once the concept of subtraction as "take-away" has been established and some skill with subtraction has been acquired.

Children often have difficulty solving missing addend and comparison subtraction problems. One reason is that the words "more" and "greater than" suggest addition to the children, especially if they have associated subtraction only with take-away situations. Children will sometimes find it helpful to read aloud or listen to these problems before doing them, and also to interpret their answers to see that they make sense.

Multiplication
All of the stories and diagrams below involve the multiplication $3 \times 4 = \square$.

Which Diagram?
Grouping

_____ How many wheels do 3 cars have?

_____ Three 4-inch pieces of ribbon will make what length?

Array

_____ Children in a marching band line up in 3 rows with 4 in each row. How many children are in the band?

_____ A table top is covered by 3 rows of tiles with 4 tiles fitting across the table top. How many tiles cover the table top?

Combinations (or *Cartesian Product*)

_____ I am making cookies with 3 flavors: vanilla, chocolate, and raisin. Cookies will be made in 4 shapes. How many different cookies can I make?

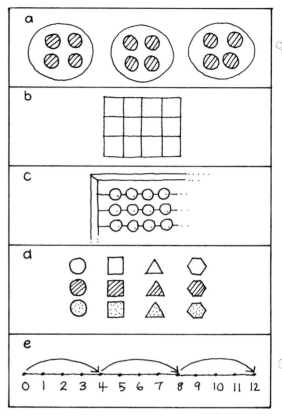

Write stories and draw diagrams of the indicated types of multiplication problems for $4 \times 3 = \square$. Create stories different from those above.

Stories   Diagrams

Grouping   _____

_____

_____

Array   _____

_____

_____

_____

Combinations   _____

_____

_____

_____

Which types of problems would you do with third graders who are just beginning to study multiplication? Which do you think would be the most difficult for them? For which type is the diagram for 3×4 most clearly the same as the diagram for 4×3?

Textbooks usually use diagrams such as those above and photographs or drawings of everyday objects to help children understand the meaning of multiplication. Each of the drawings below illustrates 3 × 4 as 3 groups of 4. Before using these semiconcrete models for multiplication, a teacher may want to have children work with objects — for example, toy racing cars, tables in the room, or squares made from straws connected by pipe cleaners. A child might hold up 2, then 3, then 4 toy cars to show the products 2 × 4, 3 × 4, and 4 × 4, each time saying how many cars, and how many wheels on these cars altogether.

Wheels on 3 racecars   Legs on 3 tables   Sides on 3 squares

Name two models for each of the following numbers that would appeal to children for showing multiplication: 2, 3, 5.

The models drawn above are all of the "grouping" type. Some materials can be used to show both grouping and array interpretations of multiplication, for example, a pegboard — a wooden or plastic board with holes in which colored pegs (or golf tees) can be inserted. Two different pegboard solutions for 3 × 4 are shown here. Which interpretation of multiplication is used in Solution A? _____ in B? _____ Which method, A or B, allows you to more easily read off the answer? _____ Which method do you prefer? Why?

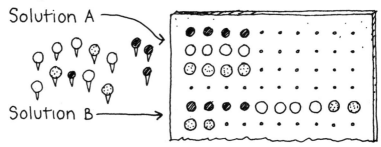

Solution A

Solution B

In this chapter we have been following the convention that 3 × 4 means 3 groups of 4, or 4 + 4 + 4. Informal language for the "×" symbol can help children to remember the meaning. For example, children can read "3 × 4" as "3 of the 4's" or "3 groups of 4." Multiplication is also written vertically meaning 3 times 4. Some mathematics programs use just the opposite convention — that is, 3 × 4 is read as "3 multiplied by 4" and means 3 taken 4 times or 3 + 3 + 3 + 3. Which way were you taught multiplication: was 3 × 4 said to mean 3 groups of 4 or 4 groups of 3? Children who do not yet know that 3 × 4 and 4 × 3 represent the same number may find it confusing if sometimes 3 × 4 means 4 + 4 + 4 and other times 3 + 3 + 3 + 3. Teachers should check which convention is used in their text materials and which their children use. A teacher should adapt to the usage in the text and be consistent. Sometimes textbooks try to avoid this problem by introducing the array model for multiplication from the start, because it is clear from the diagrams that a 3 × 4 array is the same size as a 4 × 3 array.

3 x 4   4 x 3

Division

All of the stories and diagrams below involve the division $10 \div 2 = \square$.

Which Diagram?

Partitive or *Sharing Division*: Find two equal *parts* of 10, or share 10 things between 2.

_____ Ten cards are dealt to 2 children. How many cards does each child get?
_____ Two children want to share a 10-centimeter string of licorice. How much will each one get?

Measurement or *Repeated Subtraction Division*: Measure 10 with units of 2, or ask how many 2's are in 10.

_____ I have 10 slices of bread. How many sandwiches (2 slices each) can I make?
_____ I have a piece of licorice 10 centimeters long. I cut off pieces 2 centimeters long for some friends. How many friends can I give a piece to?

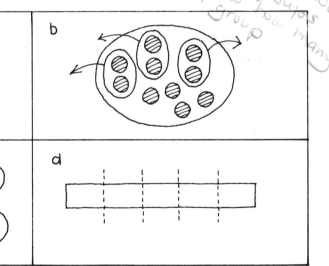

Write stories and draw diagrams of the type indicated to show $10 \div 5 = \square$. Create stories different from those just presented.

	Stories	**Diagrams**

Sharing

_____
_____
_____

Repeated

Subtraction

_____
_____
_____
_____
_____
_____
_____
_____
_____
_____

When you think of division such as $10 \div 2 = \square$, which type of problem do you think of more naturally: sharing or repeated subtraction? Which type of problem do you think children would find more difficult to solve by making a diagram? Why?

Which number line diagram for $10 \div 2$ corresponds to the measurement or repeated subtraction interpretation for division?

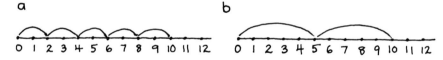

a   b

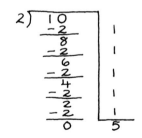

Note how the number line diagram (a) shows the action of repeatedly subtracting 2's from 10, as shown symbolically to the right. Draw a diagram similar to (a) to show a repeated subtraction solution for $12 \div 4 = \square$.

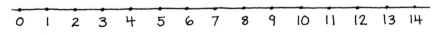

Division sentences can be related to multiplication sentences in two ways — for example, $10 \div 2 = \square$ is related to $2 \times \square = 10$ and $\square \times 2 = 10$. Which multiplication sentence corresponds to each question below?

Sharing: Two groups of how many make 10?

Repeated Subtraction: How many 2's are in 10?

Frequently multiplication sentences like these are included in third and fourth grade textbooks before division is developed. Skill with these sentences can help children later to master division facts.

Different types of situations or materials lead to different types of answers. For example, one answer for $7 \div 2 = \square$ is 3 with a remainder of 1 (3 R 1) where the division sentences is acted out with chips or Unifix cubes. However, in some situations 3 R 1 may be an unnatural answer — for example:

1. I want to make shelves 2 feet long. How many can I make from a piece of wood 7 feet long? (Here the answer to the question would be 3.)
2. Seven people in a group want to rent motor scooters to tour Martha's Vineyard. Two can ride on a scooter. How many scooters must they rent? (Here the answer would be 4.)
3. Two people want to share 7 cookies. How many does each get? (Here the answer would be a fraction, $3\frac{1}{2}$.)

For each story below, indicate sharing or repeated subtraction for the interpretation of division, and write what the answer would be.

	Sharing or Repeated Subtraction?	Answer
I want to share 10 cookies among 3 friends. What do they each get?	_____	_____
I have 10 meters of fabric and I want to make curtains that take 3 meters each. How many curtains can I make?	_____	_____
I want to share 10 marbles among 3 people. What do they each get?	_____	_____
It takes me 3 minutes to read one page. How many pages can I read in 10 minutes?	_____	_____

Ways to Present Story Problems

A teacher can use story problems and diagrams such as those above to help children learn about basic facts. The stories can be presented in ways other than a written format. For example, children who cannot yet read could solve problems told to them by their teacher. A sensitive teacher will recognize that many everyday classroom situations lead naturally to number questions involving basic facts. Below are some questions a teacher could ask about classroom clothing. Identify the number sentence involved in each.

_____ We have 5 aprons for the paint easels. Two children are about to put on aprons. How many children can still work at the easels?
_____ Four children have taken off their boots. How many boots?
_____ John's mother bought him 2 new shirts yesterday. He had 5 shirts before. Now how many does he have?
_____ There are 12 mittens on a table. How many pairs are there?

Provide questions related to some other classroom material or activity that involve the indicated operations. (Use cookies, crayons, lining up for lunch.)

Addition

Subtraction

Multiplication

Division

Children can also make up their own story problems and ask them of classmates who can solve them using materials. Children might make pictures for story problems, show them, and have others tell the story problem and solve it. Pictures such as those below can be used in a similar way. For example, the picture with horses' heads showing over a fence could be shown to children with an appropriate verbal question — "How many legs?" (corresponding to the number sentence $3 \times 4 = \square$) or "How many _____?" (corresponding to the number sentence $3 \times 2 = \square$). Many pictures can be used to provide more than one question. Next to each picture write several number sentences which arise naturally from it.

Everyday situations and picture problems provide children with opportunities to develop and use language for operations. After children have done this, they might begin work with short written problems, perhaps writing and solving their own before doing those in a text or workbook. These informal oral and written experiences may prevent later difficulties that children sometimes have with word problems. (Suggestions for teaching word problems are discussed in Chapter 9.)

In this section you have also been asked to imagine solving story problems with materials and to relate the action to diagrams. When children are learning about basic facts, they need to handle and move materials around rather than just look at diagrams. The questions below involve actions with bean sticks (popsicle sticks with 1, 2, 3, 4, or 5 beans glued on them). Identify the operation involved with each.

_____ Pick up 3 sticks like this  . How many beans?

_____ Here are 8 beans to make some bean sticks with. Put 2 on each stick. How many bean sticks can you make?

_____ Close your eyes; pick up 2 sticks. How many beans do you have?

_____ Here is 1 stick . How many more beans do you need to make it a stick like this ?

A teacher should be able to interpret each of the four operations in terms of actions with available classroom materials. Below, try this with Unifix cubes — colored plastic cubes which can be easily joined together and separated. One example is given.

> **Note:** Children may attach some meaning to the cubes — rockets, or apartment buildings, or candy bars, or trains. Be sure to pick up on children's interests when they are using these materials.

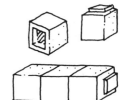

Addition

Subtraction   Make a train as long as this one (8 long). Now leave off 3 cars. How many do you have left?

Multiplication

Division

Multiple Embodiments, or Why So Many Materials?

We have seen that the four operations can be acted out with a variety of materials. For example, $2 + 3 = \square$ might be solved in many ways as shown below. Some of these ways are alike: A, C and E all involve forming two sets and counting the total, while B and F require thinking of number as length and addition as the joining of lengths end to end. The balance beam solution differs from all of the others.

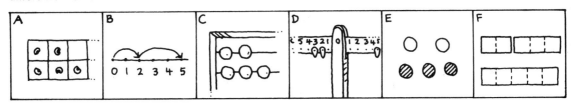

Below are shown ways to solve $4 \times 2 = \square$ with different materials. Which of the ways (if any) resembles the grouping or repeated-addition solution in A? _____ Which resembles the number line solution in B? _____ the array solution in C? _____ the balance beam solution? _____

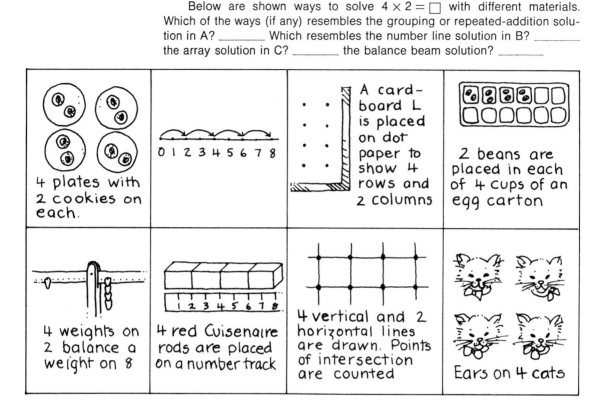

4 plates with 2 cookies on each.	0 1 2 3 4 5 6 7 8	A cardboard L is placed on dot paper to show 4 rows and 2 columns	2 beans are placed in each of 4 cups of an egg carton
4 weights on 2 balance a weight on 8	4 red Cuisenaire rods are placed on a number track	4 vertical and 2 horizontal lines are drawn. Points of intersection are counted	Ears on 4 cats

A teacher may not be able to have children use all of the materials above for learning addition or multiplication but may try to select materials that are available and appropriate to children's preferences. School budget may also be a factor, but many materials can be made inexpensively (such as number strips and bead boards). Would you use different types of materials for teaching addition — for example, chips, number strips, and a balance beam? Or would you stick to one type of material, perhaps a discrete type, such as beans, chips, or cubes?

The use of different types of materials is justified by what Zoltan Dienes[3] calls the *multiple embodiments* principle. Dienes maintains that children are better able to form the abstraction behind an operation if they experience it in various models (or in *multiple embodiments*) and that this broad experience will help children to transfer their learning of the operation from these classroom situations to other new situations. Most commercial textbook series appear to accept this principle, because different types of materials for number and operations on numbers are pictured. However, this principle may not apply to all children. For certain learning-disabled children a variety of embodiments may create confusion that gets in the way of learning the operations. Mathematics programs for such children may concentrate almost exclusively on one material and on one set of procedures for acting out problems involving basic facts.

Properties of Operations

When do you remember first learning about properties of operations, for example the commutative property of addition? Did you use this property before you learned a name for it? Did you ever discover any properties on your own? Properties are included in the elementary school curriculum — both because they can be used to help children learn basic arithmetic and also because they can provide a context for discovery and exploration.

Illustrating Properties with Materials

When children use materials such as chips, a balance beam, or Cuisenaire rods to act out problems, they may also learn in a natural way about properties of the operations involved. For example, when doing rod addition, children may notice that the order of the rods doesn't affect the answer — that is, that addition is commutative. The examples below suggest how certain actions with other materials can illustrate properties.

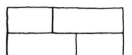

Additive Property of 0

$\square + 0 = \square$ and $0 + \square = \square$

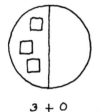

3 + 0   0 + 3

Place cubes on a paper plate with a line drawn across it.

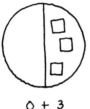

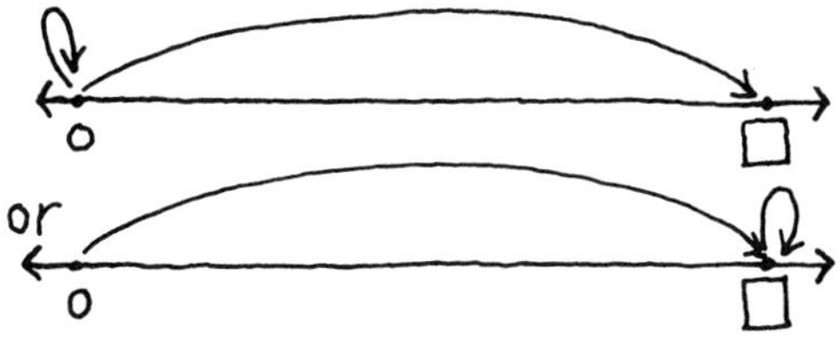

Draw a number line.

Commutative Property of Addition

$\square + \triangle = \triangle + \square$

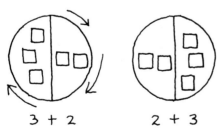

3 + 2   2 + 3

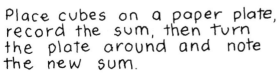

Place cubes on a paper plate, record the sum, then turn the plate around and note the new sum.

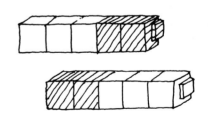

Unifix cubes in two colors.

Associative Property of Addition

$$\square + (\triangle + \bigcirc) = (\square + \triangle) + \bigcirc$$

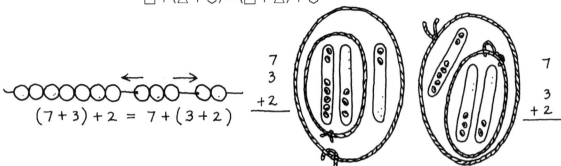

$$
\begin{array}{r}
7 \\
3 \\
+2 \\
\hline
\end{array}
$$

$$
\begin{array}{r}
7 \\
3 \\
+2 \\
\hline
\end{array}
$$

$$(7+3) + 2 = 7 + (3+2)$$

Slide 3 to the right or left on the bead stick.

Place bean sticks in loops.

Multiplicative Property of 1

$$\square \times 1 = \square \text{ and } 1 \times \square = \square$$

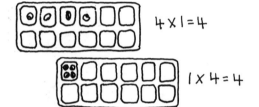

$$4 \times 1 = 4$$

$$1 \times 4 = 4$$

$$4 \times 1 = 4$$

$$1 \times 4 = 4$$

Place beans in egg cartons.

Commutative Property of Multiplication

$$\square \times \triangle = \triangle \times \square$$

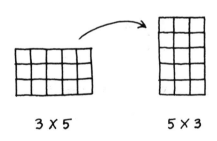

3 X 5   5 X 3

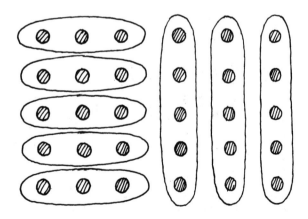

Use arrays to show that the number of squares in the two diagrams is the same if the first diagram is turned sideways.

Draw loops on an array in two different ways.

Associative Property of Multiplication

$\square \times (\triangle \times \bigcirc) = (\square \times \triangle) \times \bigcirc$

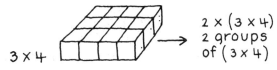

3×4

$2 \times (3 \times 4)$
2 groups
of (3×4)

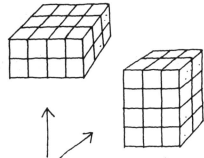

2×3

$(2 \times 3) \times 4$
(2×3) groups
or columns of 4

Use cubes to form a three-dimensional array.

These two constructions have the same number of cubes, as can be seen if one stack is turned.

Distributive Property of Multiplication over Addition

$\square \times (\triangle + \bigcirc) = (\square \times \triangle) + (\square \times \bigcirc)$

Use arrays drawn on paper that is folded on the dotted line.

```
OOOOO OOOOO|OOO
OOOOO OOOOO|OOO
```

```
OOOOO OOOOO:OOO
OOOOO OOOOO:OOO
```

2 rows of 10 and 2 rows of 3
$2 \times 10 + 2 \times 3$

2 rows of (10 and 3)
$2 \times (10 + 3)$

This type of illustration is used later to develop multiplication of a two-digit number by a one-digit number. For example

$2 \times 13 = 2 \times (10 + 3) = (2 \times 10) + (2 \times 3) = 20 + 6 = 26$

Teaching About Properties

Properties of operations on whole numbers are included formally in some mathematics programs during grades 4–8, that is, children learn terminology for properties and represent them symbolically — for example, $a + 0 = a$, or $\square + 0 = \square$ for the *identity property for addition* or the *zero property for addition.* Younger children can learn this property informally and express it in their own language, perhaps as "You get the same number when you add zero," or "Zero doesn't do anything when you add." The important thing is not whether a child knows the exact term for a property or can express it symbolically, but rather that the child understands it and can use it. Sometimes pressures to teach properties cause teachers to have children simply memorize them. Rather properties should be viewed as patterns which children can discover. For example, having children do multiplication exercises such as $2 \times 3 = \square$, $3 \times 2 = \square$, $4 \times 5 = \square$, and $5 \times 4 = \square$, can guide them to make

$$\begin{array}{r} 8 \\ 7 \\ +3 \\ \hline \end{array}$$

a generalization: the answer for multiplication is the same when the numbers are reversed, or $\triangle \times \bigcirc = \bigcirc \times \triangle$.

When children are given opportunities to search for patterns in arithmetic, they may formulate properties other than those illustrated on pages 209–211. For example, when children are adding a column of three one-digit numbers, they can be encouraged to add up or down, leading them to see that the answer is the same either way — a property which could be expressed symbolically as $\square + \triangle + \bigcirc = \bigcirc + \triangle + \square$. (Which way might children find it easier to add these numbers, up or down? Why?) If one child claims to have discovered a new property such as "you can add up or down," others may want to explain why it seems to always work or check this by trying examples.

Is this statement always true? $\square \times (\triangle + 1) = \square \times \triangle + \square$ Try some examples.

Expressions such as $\square + \bigcirc + \triangle = \triangle + \bigcirc + \square$ and $\square + 0 = \square$ are true for all whole numbers that are put in the frames (provided the same number goes in like frames). Such expressions or properties are sometimes called identities.[4] Some expressions are true only for *some* numbers (such as $\square + 2 = 5$) or for *no* numbers (such as $\square \times 0 = 2$). Check whether the expressions below are always true, sometimes true, or never true when the frames are filled in with whole numbers {0, 1, 2, . . . }. If an expression is not always true, give an example when it is true and when it is false.

	Always	Sometimes	Never	
(a)	A	S	N	$\square + 7 = 7 + \square$
(b)	A	S	N	$\square - 3 = 3 - \square$
(c)	A	S	N	$\square \times 3 = 3 \times \square$
(d)	A	S	N	$\square - \hexagon = \hexagon - \square$
(e)	A	S	N	$\square - 0 = \square$
(f)	A	S	N	$\square \times 0 = 0$
(g)	A	S	N	$\square + 1 = \square$
(h)	A	S	N	$\square - (\hexagon - \triangle) = (\square - \hexagon) - \triangle$
(i)	A	S	N	$\square \times (\triangle - \hexagon) = (\square \times \triangle) - (\square \times \hexagon)$
(j)	A	S	N	$(\square + 1) \times (\square + 1) = \square \times \square + (2 \times \square) + 1$

For the expressions below use the replacement set {1, 2, 3 ...}.

	Always	Sometimes	Never	
(k)	A	S	N	$1 \div \square = \square$
(l)	A	S	N	$0 \div \square = 0$
(m)	A	S	N	$\square \div \square = 1$
(n)	A	S	N	$\square \div 1 = \square$
(o)	A	S	N	$\square \div \triangle = \triangle \div \square$
(p)	A	S	N	$\square \div (\triangle \div \hexagon) = (\square \div \triangle) \div \hexagon$

For expressions (k)–(p) the replacement set {1,2,3, . . .} was used rather than {0,1,2,3, . . .} because division by 0 is not defined. Expressions such as $6 \div 0$ and $0 \div 0$ have no meaning. To see why, consider what $6 \div 0$ might mean. $6 \div 0 = \square$ asks how many 0's are in 6, or complete $\square \times 0 = 6$. But any number times 0 is 0 (and not 6) as you saw in (f) above. Therefore, there is no solution for $6 \div 0 = \square$.

On the other hand, consider what $0 \div 0$ might mean. $0 \div 0 = \square$ asks how many 0's are in 0 or $\square \times 0 = 0$. Here *any* number can be put in the $\square$ to make $\square \times 0 = 0$ true. Therefore $0 \div 0$ might stand for any number whatsoever, and thus cannot be defined.

(Optional) Try $6 \div 0$, $0 \div 6$, and $0 \div 0$ on an electronic hand calculator. What answers did you get? Was your calculator correct?

Terminology for Operations

While some children may be able to solve $8 + 7 = \square$ or what is 8 plus 7, they may be unable to solve, what is the sum of 8 and 7. Terminology such as sum, product, commutativity, and distributive property can cause difficulties for children, even those who may understand these ideas and are able to express them in their own words (for example, "you can turn the numbers around" for commutativity). Some textbooks have been criticized for excessive use of terminology and symbolism, especially at the lower elementary levels. Terminology should be used when it clarifies mathematical ideas for children, and not when it confuses them.

The terms listed below are included here so that you can review their meaning. Some of them (for example, sum, product, factor) are usually included in textbooks for children; others (for example, minuend, addend) receive little or no emphasis in children's books but may appear in the teacher's guide or reference material for teachers — for example, in a description of "missing addend" or "missing factor" problems. Use the terms to fill in the blanks. Two terms are used twice. (Refer to a dictionary if necessary.)

FOLLOW-UP SECTIONS

These Follow-up Sections discuss ways to help children understand operations on whole numbers and develop and use basic facts. There are three general themes — each stressed in a separate section — that apply to teaching many other skill-related topics in mathematics. The themes are listed below.

A teacher should have children use the mathematics they are learning in situations which interest them. This motivates their learning and makes it easier for them to apply it later in everyday life.

A teacher should encourage children to look for and use relationships in mathematics. For example, children can use properties of operations and relationships between basic facts to master arithmetic skills more efficiently.

A teacher should be aware of how children develop skills — beginning with their understanding of a concept and progressing through mastery of the skill — and plan appropriate types of activities.

Using Basic Facts: Applications and Problem Solving

As discussed earlier, children should not only develop basic skills but also be able to use them. This reflects a current concern about integrating *applications* and *problem solving* throughout the school mathematics curriculum in order to insure that children will grow up able to appreciate and use mathematics both in their everyday lives and in their occupations. However, there are many possible interpretations of *applications* and *problem solving.* What do you think they mean? Would children's interpretations be the same as yours?

In earlier sections, we saw examples that might be called applications of basic facts — story problems, number situations presented through pictures, and incidental classroom situations (pages 199–207). These applications tend to be less complex than those encountered in real life, which generally require more than one operation, and involve larger numbers or fractional parts. Also, in real life, identifying the problem to be solved is often a difficult first step. Some curriculum materials are designed to expose children to applications in this broader sense — for example, USMES (Unified Science and Mathematics for Elementary School).[5]

The USMES program is an interdisciplinary one intended to help teachers supplement the standard mathematics curriculum by providing children with general challenges about their environment — for example, designing a better playground, examining ways to improve local pedestrian crossings, designing a new soft drink (and selling it). These open-ended applications require that children first identify and formulate problems and then use a variety of skills — both in mathematics and other areas — to solve them. The USMES teacher resource books include logs of children's work on such projects, suggestions on how to get the children involved, and possible questions a teacher might ask to guide children away from time-consuming, unproductive approaches toward more constructive ones, without being dictating. Also included for children are "How To" Cards — for example, how to make different types of graphs; to find the median for a set of data; to use some particular tools to build something, to use measuring devices such as a stop watch. This approach reflects the philosophy that children should develop and review skills when they see the need to use them, rather than before.

While the USMES materials are meant mainly for upper elementary school children and tend to involve a variety of mathematical skills, they can offer teachers ideas and suggestions for planning and implementing similar kinds of applications of basic facts with younger children. For example, the following situation can lead to several uses of addition and subtraction. Answer the questions and the related discussion questions below.

1. Suppose you buy an apple and a container of milk. How much will this cost?
2. What is the cost of 3 oatmeal cookies and 2 cartons of milk?
3. What could you buy by spending exactly 15¢?
4. How much change do you get from 15¢ if you buy a banana and 2 chocolate chip cookies?
5. Suppose that you and 3 friends want to buy snacks to take along on a class field trip. Decide on how much to spend and what you plan to buy.

Which questions above might you describe as a routine application of addition or subtraction? _____ Which give the most practice with arithmetic?

Which would a teacher find easiest to correct? _____ Are these the questions that children would enjoy most? _____

Could you have children solve these problems at the concrete level? If so, how?

Could you adapt these questions to give third or fourth graders practice in multiplication and division facts? If so, how?

Which questions come closest to applications in the USMES sense?

Can you think of some other open-ended question that could be related to this situation?

Incidental classroom situations, current topics in the news, and children's daily experiences can lead to applications of basic facts. Chapter 9 will deal with applications in situations involving arithmetic of larger whole numbers.

Children may also think of puzzles and games as uses or applications of arithmetic. Puzzles are frequently included in textbooks to motivate practice of skills. Although the two examples below may not be challenging to most children, they can nevertheless be fun because children may find their format novel or interesting. Try these.

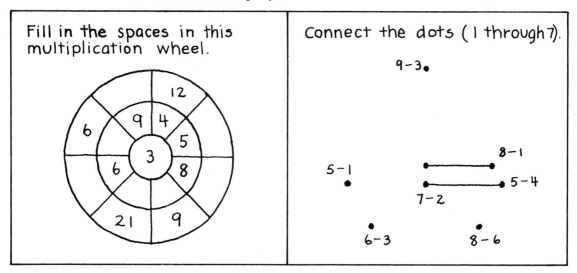

Could these be adapted for other operations?

Everyday situations, picture problems, and the games and puzzles described above as well as most written story problems can be characterized as involving "routine" solving — that is, if a child understands the problem he can go right ahead and find the answer, and the problem is done. The term "problem solving" is sometimes used to describe situations that are more challenging, involve higher-order thought processes (for example, choosing a method of solution, or discovering a pattern), or lead in a natural way to some deeper mathematics. Children can be given questions that they understand and find interesting but that they do not immediately know how to solve. Activity 2, Beans in Circles (pages 183–184), is an example of this type of problem-solving situation — it can challenge children to think, to try different numbers of beans in the circles and perhaps to look for a short cut or strategy to solve problems of this type. Children may well be willing to do a great deal more arithmetic to solve such a problem than routine ones. This kind of problem solving also encourages children to come up with different ways to solve problems, especially if children work together and discuss their solutions.

The bean-stick activity described below indicates how problem solving can lead children to further investigations of mathematics.

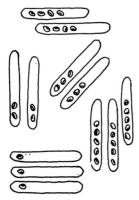

Bean Sticks

Children can be introduced to bean sticks (popsicle sticks with 1, 2, 3, 4, or 5 beans glued on them) and asked to pick up 1 bean, 2 beans, . . . , 5 beans, and then 6 beans. If they respond that 6 beans can't be picked up, it can be suggested that more than one stick can be picked up at a time. After coming up with different ways to pick up 6 beans, they can be asked to pick up 7 beans and then 8 beans.

Once children have had opportunities to solve these types of problems, they may begin to investigate mathematics on their own. They may ask their own questions now and explore. For example, a first grader might speculate about the ways to pick up 6 beans and ask, "How many ways can I do this with two bean sticks?" or "What if I picked up three beansticks?" Now the child is interacting with the problem to be solved and formulating related questions by himself, probably because he finds them interesting. Problem situations that can be solved in different ways often provide a stimulus for these higher order explorations and investigations.

In the investigation above, children were working in the *concrete* or *manipulative* mode, using bean sticks to find how many ways to make 6 beans, 7 beans, etc. This investigation could also be carried out in the *semi-concrete* or *representational* mode by older children who could refer to diagrams of bean sticks, or in the *abstract* mode if they just write addition sentences for sums equal to 6, 7, etc. Children can engage in problem solving and exploration of mathematics if problems are presented to them in a way that is appropriate to their stage of intellectual development — perhaps in a manipulative activity, or through diagrams or pictures, or in a symbolic or abstract format.

This point is stressed by Robert Wirtz whose elementary school mathematics materials provide ways to give children a rich variety of experiences in all three modes.[6] Wirtz uses this diagram to characterize mathematics instruction that can vary in mode of presentation (moving horizontally in the diagram) and in type of thought process involved (moving vertically). Wirtz feels that, regrettably, most mathematics instruction provided for children involves low-level thought processes ("remembering experiences" as he calls them) — for example, recall of basic facts, answering a straightforward story problem, stating a definition. Also, instruction moves too quickly from the manipulative mode to the abstract or symbolic mode. Hence, most of children's mathematical experiences are restricted to the upper-right part of the diagram — to "remembering experiences in an abstract mode." (Were most of your elementary school mathematics experiences of this type?)

Activities you did in this chapter (and also in other chapters) can be categorized according to Wirtz's diagram. In which mode (manipulative, representational, or abstract) do you think most of the Activities have been presented?

In elementary school classrooms it is probably the left-hand column — experiences in the manipulative mode — that is most neglected, especially at the problem-solving and investigations levels. Examples of "remembering experiences in a manipulative mode" include playing the Poison Apple Game without looking for a strategy to win, or doing rod addition (such as r + g =

□, r + w + g = □). Manipulative experiences at the problem-solving level might be Activity 2, Beans in Circles, and finding the number of solutions using Cuisenaire rods for equations of the form □ + △ = Rod (Activity 9, part 4 in Chapter 4). Still in a concrete or manipulative mode, these problems may each lead to further investigations — for example, generalizing strategies for solving puzzles like Beans in Circles, or finding combinations of numbers that will not give solutions, or searching for patterns in the number of rod solutions to equations of the form □ + △ + ○ = Rod.

The Poison Apple Game could, in fact, be done in nine different ways — by mixing modes (with chips, crossing off circles drawn on paper, writing subtraction sentences) and by mixing types of thought processes (just playing the game without looking for a strategy to win; playing and looking for a strategy; exploring changes in rules — what if you took away 1–4 or 1–5 apples, or began with 20).

How would you categorize each of the following activities?

	Level of Thought Process	Mode
A Funny Thing Happened on the Way to the Beanstalk, part 1	_____	_____
A Funny Thing . . . , part 3	_____	_____
Machines and Tables, part 1	_____	_____
Machines and Tables, part 2	_____	_____
Machines and Tables, part 3e	_____	_____

Wirtz urges teachers to provide instruction of all nine types in the diagram, and offers three main principles for teaching mathematics: (1) Introduce basic operations of arithmetic at the manipulative level. For example, use games such as Poison Apple (Game 1 or 2), or materials as in Activity 4, Action for Basic Facts. (2) Provide abundant drill and practice at the problem-solving level. For example, use games such as Poison Apple (Game 3 or 4); Activity 7, Arrow Paths; or Activity 8, Machines and Tables, which allow for more than one method of solution. (3) Encourage children to make independent investigations. For example, the Poison Apple Game may challenge children to find a winning strategy for it and variations of it.

In particular, rather than having children proceed horizontally from "remembered experiences in the manipulative mode" to the abstract mode, as is usually done if one follows a textbook, a teacher could also give children activities that allow for vertical movement.

In a later section we will see how these principles can be applied in sequencing activities to teach basic facts.

Using Structure to Learn Basic Facts

This section discusses how children can use the structure of arithmetic — for example, properties of addition or certain relationships between addition — to learn basic facts in an organized and efficient way.[7]

Addition and Subtraction

By the end of the second grade, most children should have mastered the basic facts of addition and subtraction. The addition facts are sometimes recorded in an addition table as shown here.

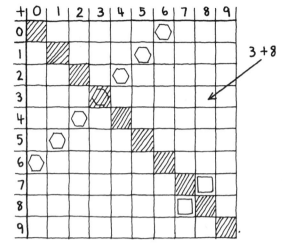

3 + 8

1. Why does the table only go from 0 through 9? Why isn't 12 + 3 a basic fact?

Write some addition facts you think children might find difficult.

How many basic facts are in the table? _____ Did you learn these facts by memorizing them one by one, by learning them in some organized way, or by using some short cuts to remember some of them? If so, describe any short cuts.

2. Fill in the top row of the table. When filling in the top row, you probably did not think about the 10 addition sentences you were doing. Instead, you probably applied a rule: "zero plus a number is that number," or more formally, $0 + n = n$. Children may have convinced themselves that this is always true by working with materials such as cubes placed on paper plates as described on page 209. By using properties, children can reduce the number of facts they must memorize.

3. Fill in 3 + 8 and 8 + 3 in the addition table above.

The sums 3 + 8 and 8 + 3 are equally easy for you to solve from recall. However, children who are just beginning to learn addition may take longer to do 3 + 8 than 8 + 3 because of the way they act out addition. Which method for solving 8 + 3 described below would require more time to solve 3 + 8? I _____ II _____

Method I. Count out 8 chips and count out 3 chips.
Join them and count the total:

⊘ ⊘ ⊘ ⊘ ⊘ ⊘ ⊘ ⊘   ⊘ ⊘ ⊘
"1 2 3 4 5 6 7 8   9 10 11"

Method II. Count out only the chips to be added on (here 3).
Find the total by counting on from 8:

⊘ ⊘ ⊘
"9 10 11"

Children using method II would do 3 + 8 faster if they could recognize that the sum □ + △ is the same as △ + □; that is, if they could apply the commutative property of addition to do 3 + 8 by solving 8 + 3. In general, using the commutative property cuts down the number of basic facts to be learned from 100 to 55 (10 diagonal facts and 45 facts on the side of the diagonal, in the preceding addition table).

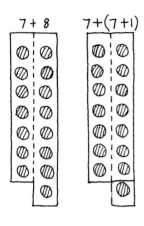

7 + 8   7 + (7 + 1)

4. Fill in the facts in the shaded squares along the diagonal and the squares marked ⬚ in the addition table.

Children typically learn the *double facts* (1 + 1, 2 + 2, 3 + 3, etc.) more easily than others. They can use these double facts to learn *neighbor facts;* for example, 7 + 8. 7 + 8 can be thought of as 7 + (7 + 1) or (7 + 7) + 1, or 14 + 1 which equals 15. What property of addition does this use? Try this method on the neighbor fact

5 + 6 = _____ = _____ = _____ = _____

5. *Bridging facts* are those basic facts whose sum is greater than 10 — for example, 3 + 8, 6 + 8, 8 + 8, and 8 + 7. Some bridging facts are easier to learn than others, for example, doubles (6 + 6, 7 + 7, . . .) and neighbor facts (6 + 7, 7 + 8, . . .) as discussed above. Make a list of some bridging facts which are neither doubles nor neighbor facts. Are the facts that you considered difficult to learn of this type? Children often have difficulty mastering bridging facts, and later find them an obstacle when they have to do multidigit addition with exchanging. However, children can be helped to learn these facts by using materials that show 5's and 10's in a way that enables them to relate these facts to easier ones they might already know, as described below.

Bean Sticks: 6 + 5 = ▢

(Children make and use special bean sticks showing 5's, for example,

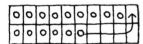 for 3, ⬭ for 6, ⬭ for 8.)

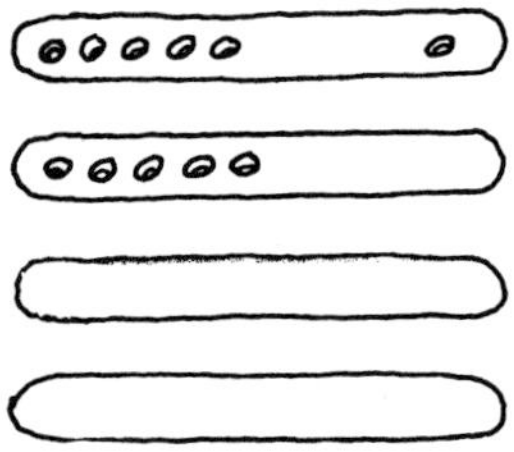

A child took bean sticks for 6 and 5, placed them as shown to the left, and found the total by seeing two groups of 5, or 10 and 1 more, making 11.

Draw a bean stick solution to 9 + 6 = ▢ to the left, and describe how to find the total.

Do you see why the special bean sticks help?

Markers: 9 + 6 = ▢

(Markers are placed in outlines drawn on paper or cardboard.)

A child put 9 markers on top and 6 on the bottom. Moving 1 from the bottom to the top, he found the total: 10 + 5 is 15. Thus, the child is thinking of 9 + 6 as 9 plus 1 plus 5 more.

This method can be extended beyond basic addition facts to other additions, such as 19 + 6, 29 + 6, 39 + 6. For example, to solve 19 + 6, think 19 + 1 and 5 more, or 25. To solve 39 + 6, think _____.

6. Fill in the ◯'s in the addition table.

After introducing the concept and notation for addition, most textbooks develop addition facts by families of sums, for example the 6-family: 0 + 6 = 6, 1 + 5 = 6, 2 + 4 = 6, 3 + 3 = 6, 4 + 2 = 6, 5 + 1 = 6, 6 + 0 = 6. How many of these facts in the 6-family must a child memorize if he can apply the commutative property of addition?

> One family that receives special attention is the 10-family. How does your knowledge of these facts help you do this addition quickly?

> The decomposition of a number into a sum (for example 6 into $2 + 4$ or $3 + 3$) is an important prerequisite skill for the following approach to bridging facts by using tens.

$$\begin{array}{r} 3 \\ 7 \\ 4 \\ 9 \\ 1 \\ +6 \\ \hline \end{array}$$

Example: $7 + 6 = 7 + 3 + 3 = 10 + 3 = 13$
Complete: $8 + 6 =$ _____ $+$ _____ $=$ _____ $+$ _____ $=$ _____

Here the key step is decomposing 6 into an appropriate sum and also knowing addition facts for 10. If children are not skillful in decomposition, they may find this method more difficult than simply counting out 8 things and 6 more and then finding the total. This method can be confusing to children if it is presented simply at the abstract level as is done in some textbooks.

> 7. Children do not usually make a table for subtraction facts. (Can you explain why?) However, subtraction facts can be found by referring to the addition table. How could you answer $15 - 8 = \square$ from the addition table?

> Subtraction facts are usually taught in relation to addition facts — for example, as shown by the set of these exercises. Children sometimes "catch

$$\begin{array}{cccc} 15 & 15 & 8 & 7 \\ -7 & -8 & +7 & +8 \\ \hline \end{array}$$

on" to these exercises and will fill in the facts just from the pattern (that is, write whichever is missing of 7, 8, and 15). Children can, alternatively, be asked to take a sum, for example $5 + 6 = 11$, and write three related sentences.

> Children can use structure to learn subtraction facts in ways similar to those discussed above for addition. Below, complete the subtractions as done in the examples which illustrate how more difficult subtraction facts can be found from easier ones.

Example: $15 - 8 = \square$

> $15 - 8$ equals 15 take away 5 and then another 3, that is, $(15 - 5) - 3 = 10 - 3 = 7$.
> $13 - 9 =$

Example: This method can be extended to subtractions such as $35 - 8$ as follows:

> $35 - 8$ equals 35 take away 5 and then another 3, that is, $(35 - 5) - 3 = 30 - 3 = 27$.
> $46 - 8 =$

Note that here skill in decomposing the number being subtracted into an appropriate sum (for example, 8 into 5 and 3) is a prerequisite for this method.

Example: $17 - 9 = \square$

$17 - 9$ equals 17 take away 10 plus 1, that is, $17 - 9 = (17 - 10) + 1$, or $7 + 1$ which equals 8.

$18 - 9 =$

Multiplication Table

×	0	1	2	3	4	5	6	7	8	9
0		0	0	0	0	0	0	0	0	0
1	0		2	3	4	5	6	7	8	9
2	0	2		6	8	10	12	14	16	18
3	0	3	6		12	15	18	21	24	27
4	0	4	8	12						
5	0	5	10	15						
6	0	6	12	18						
7	0	7	14	21						
8	0	8	16	24						
9	0	9	18	27						

2×8

Multiplication and Division

Refer to the partially completed multiplication table to answer the following questions.

1. Which multiplication facts do you think children would find easy? Why?

Which do you recall as being difficult? Mark them with an X on the table.

Just as the structure of addition can help children learn addition facts, so too can the structure of multiplication help them master multiplication facts. For example, children may learn multiplication facts involving 1 by realizing that 1 group of objects is just that many objects, that is, $1 \times \square = \square$ — the identity property for multiplication. Or a child who knows 3×6 is 18 but does not recall 4×6 might reason: 4×6 is four 6's which is three 6's and one more 6, which would be $18 + 6$, or 24.

2. How could a child use the 3's column to fill in the 6's column? Do it. Children might think of 6×7 as double 3×7 or $21 + 21 = 42$. More formally this method is $6 \times 7 = (2 \times 3) \times 7 = 2 \times (3 \times 7) = 2 \times 21$, which equals 42. What property is being used here? Draw loops in the diagram to the left to show 6×7 as double 3×7.

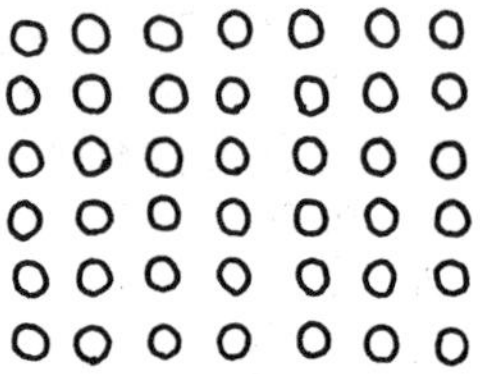

```
O O O O  O O O
O O O O  O O O
O O O O  O O O
O O O O  O O O
O O O O  O O O
O O O O  O O O
```

3. How could a child use the 6's column to fill in the 6's row? Do it.

(**Note:** You probably saw that the 6's column reads just like the 6's row, that is, $0 \times 6, 1 \times 6, 2 \times 6, \ldots$ is just the same as $6 \times 0, 6 \times 1, 6 \times 2, \ldots$. What property of multiplication does this use?)

Fill in the 9's column. Do you see any pattern involving the digits of the answers? Sometimes children learn to multiply 9 as follows: 9×8 is nine 8's, which equals ten 8's minus one 8, or $80 - 8 = 72$. Use this method to find 9×6.

What property does this use?

4. Sometimes children build multiplication facts they do not know by heart from those that they do know. For example, not knowing 7×8, a child might think 7×8 means seven 8's or five 8's plus two 8's — or $40 + 16$, which is 56. Write two different ways to obtain 8×6 from easier facts.

$8 \times 6 =$

$8 \times 6 =$

Draw loops on the diagrams below to show these two different solutions.

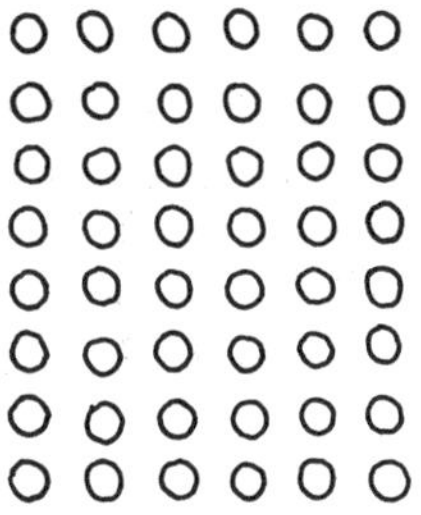

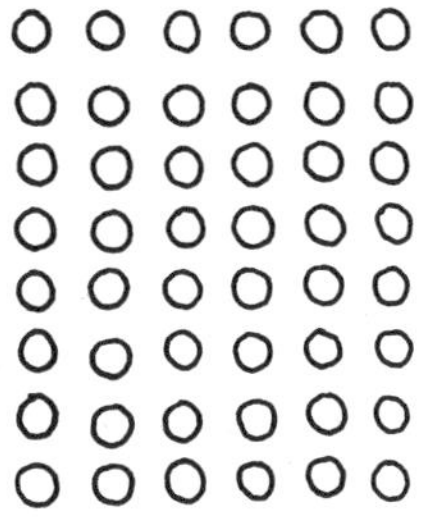

What property is used here? _____ Fill in the facts in the shaded squares in the preceding multiplication table.

Children sometimes learn these facts before others. A child who knows 6 × 6 can find 6 × 7 by the method above: 6 × 7 = 6 × (6 + 1) = 36 + _____ = _____.

5. Children sometimes learn to recite their tables — that is, recite the entries in an entire row or column. Below are described two devices to demonstrate the entries in the 4 row (4 × 0, 4 × 1, 4 × 2, . . .) and the 4 column (0 × 4, 1 × 4, 2 × 4, . . .). Which shows which?

Dots are stuck on a folded piece of paper. The parts can be unfolded bit by bit to show first 1 rectangle, then 2, then 3, . . .

Row or column? _____

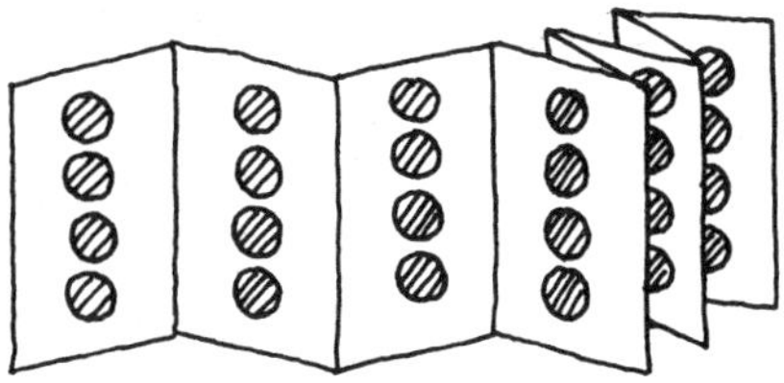

Four rows of dots are stuck on a sheet of paper or cardboard. A large piece of paper is slowly moved across to show first 1 column of dots, then 2, then 3, . . .

Row or column? _____

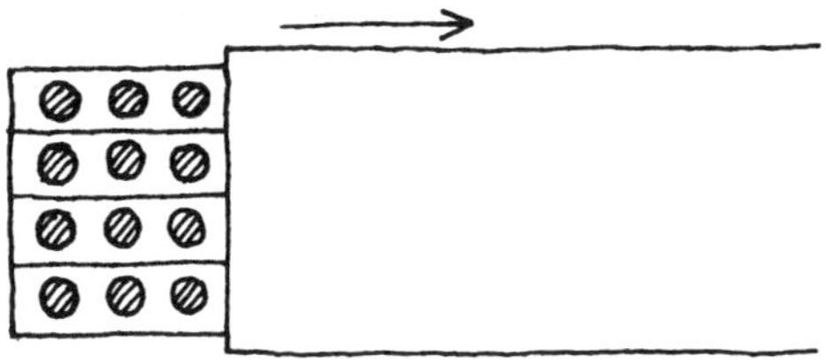

6. How could you solve 24 ÷ 3 = ☐ by referring to the multiplication table? Often the relationship between multiplication and division is developed in textbooks by presenting division sentences (for example, 24 ÷ 3 = ☐) along with a corresponding multiplication sentence (for example, 8 × 3 = ☐). Write two multiplication and two division sentences for this diagram.

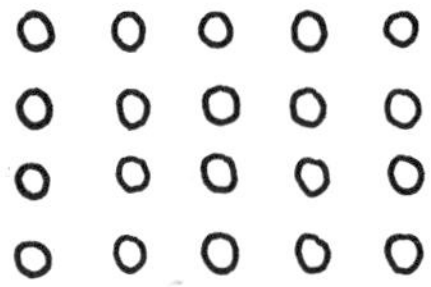

_____ _____ _____ _____

As you saw above, there are a variety of ways in which children can use the structure of arithmetic to learn basic facts. Be careful not to teach these methods by rote, because their usefulness depends on understanding, and without understanding, they can only confuse. Rather try to develop such methods through the use of concrete materials and build on the properties that children already understand.

**Three Types of Activities: Introductory,
Developmental, and Review-Practice**

Teachers in grades 1–4 devote a major part of their mathematics instruction to helping children develop basic skills. In this section we will examine three types of activities which accomplish this task. These types of activities fit into a sequence which reflects how children master basic facts. This sequence applies to children's learning of other skills both in mathematics and in other subject areas.

How Children Gain Mastery of Basic Facts

Do you recall how you learned basic facts, for example, for multiplication? Did you learn them quickly and remember them without doing much practice? The ability to master basic facts varies from child to child, but, in general, children gain mastery gradually over a period of time. The diagram below suggests how children learn basic facts, beginning with their understanding of the operation and progressing toward quick and accurate recall of all the facts.

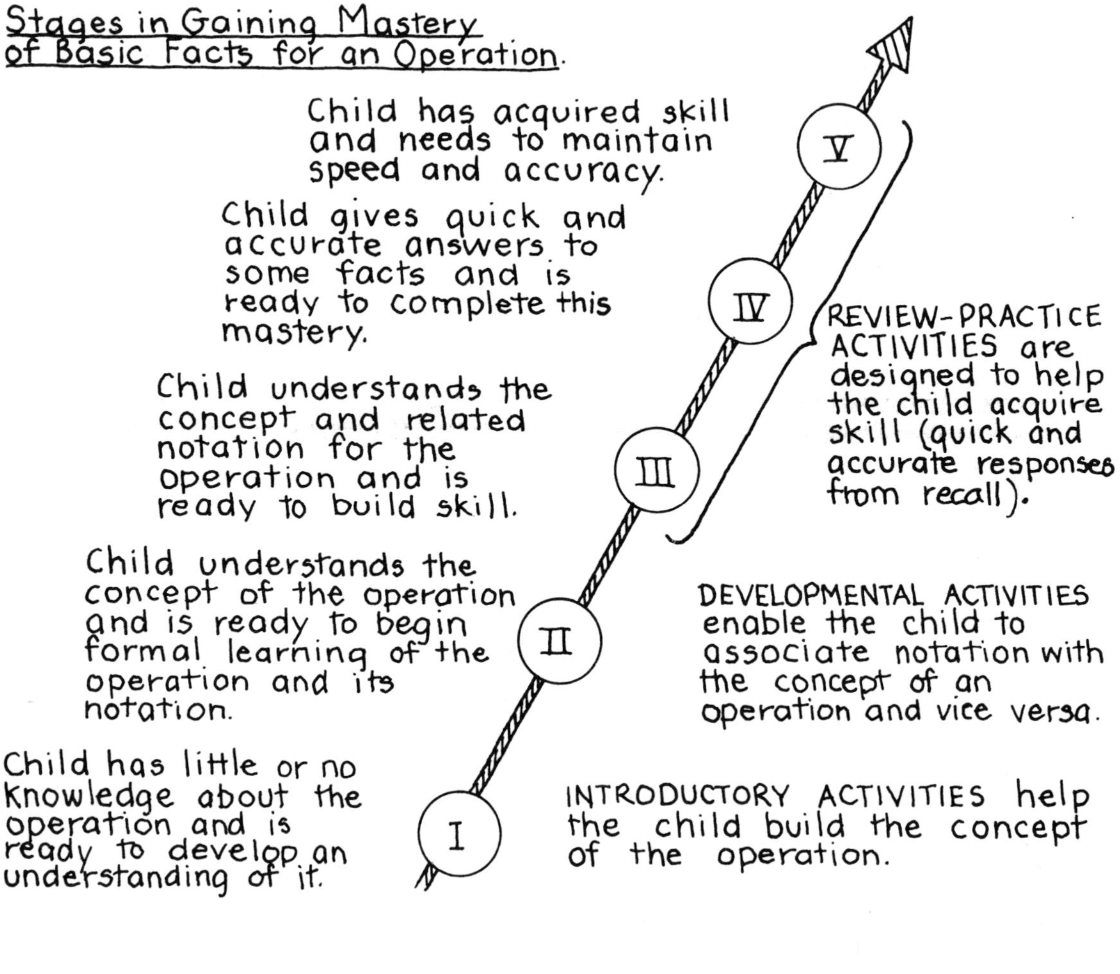

Stages in Gaining Mastery of Basic Facts for an Operation.

Child has acquired skill and needs to maintain speed and accuracy.

Child gives quick and accurate answers to some facts and is ready to complete this mastery.

Child understands the concept and related notation for the operation and is ready to build skill.

Child understands the concept of the operation and is ready to begin formal learning of the operation and its notation.

Child has little or no knowledge about the operation and is ready to develop an understanding of it.

(V)

(IV) REVIEW-PRACTICE ACTIVITIES are designed to help the child acquire skill (quick and accurate responses from recall).

(III)

(II) DEVELOPMENTAL ACTIVITIES enable the child to associate notation with the concept of an operation and vice versa.

(I) INTRODUCTORY ACTIVITIES help the child build the concept of the operation.

At which stage would you place these children?

_____ A kindergarten child can use materials to solve addition situations presented orally but cannot yet read symbolic number sentences such as $1 + 3 = \square$.

_____ A first grader is making Cuisenaire rod trains from directions like $r + g = \square$.

_____ A first grader is using a calculator to check 20 addition facts he did in one minute.

_____ A first grader realizes that he does not need to use his Unifix cubes to solve some easy addition sentences such as $1 + 1 = \square$, $2 + 1 = \square$, and $3 + 2 = \square$.

_____ A second grader is using a number line to solve addition sentences he does not yet know by heart.

The diagram above suggests a time sequence, but not how long each stage will take. A first grade teacher may wonder how much instruction should be devoted to developing the concept and notation for addition before providing children with activities to build skills. A second grade teacher might be concerned about the amount of review-practice activities her students need to reach stage V for addition and subtraction facts. No time rule can be given, because each child is an individual and progresses through the sequence at his own rate according to aptitude and prior learning. A scope and sequence for basic facts provides some perspective on the time sequence for typical children. However, the teacher must consider the particular needs of each child in planning instruction.

Which type of activity (introductory, developmental, review-practice) is each of the following?

Poison Apple Game 2 _____
Poison Apple Game 3 _____
Poison Apple Game 4 _____

Do you remember lessons in elementary school of the introductory type? the developmental type? the review-practice type?

Which of these three types of activities might *not* have been given by a teacher who believed in straight rote memorization of basic facts and who thought that using materials (chips, fingers) was an undesirable crutch?

Which type of lesson might *not* have been done enough by a teacher who thought that "new math" programs stressed understanding and played down memorization of basic facts?

Which type of lesson might be appropriate in this remedial situation? A sixth grader answers incorrectly almost all of the simple multiplications (for example, 4×6, 6×3, 5×4) on a paper-and-pencil quiz.

Introductory Activities

Introductory activities are intended to help children build up understanding of concepts such as the operation of subtraction. Desirable characteristics of this type of activity include (1) active involvement of children, probably with some manipulative material (such as Unifix cubes, Cuisenaire rods) or real world objects; (2) informal language for an operation (for example, make **3** piles of cubes with 5 in each pile) and little or no use of notation for the operation (for example, ×); and (3) application or problem-solving situations that are interesting and meaningful to the children.

The primary objective for an introductory lesson is as follows: given a problem related to an operation, the child solves the problem, at the concrete level with materials, at the semiconcrete level by a drawing, or at the abstract level by using mental imagery for the action involved. This sort of learning objective can be evaluated by observing a child's responses to informal tasks or questions. For example, the teacher asks a child to solve this problem with chips: You have 8 cents and spend 3. How many do you have left? The teacher asks a child how many children will be left at his table when Jim, Jenny, and Jack leave. Add one of your own.

Introductory activities can arise incidentally from everyday situations, from appropriately designed games, as well as in more structured classroom lessons. The sample introductory activities below highlight one or more of the three characteristics of this type of activity. As you read the sketches of these activities, determine which characteristics are emphasized.

Incidental Situations

1. *My Family.* Following a discussion by children about how many children are in their families, they draw pictures of their families. They show their pictures, telling how many big people, how many children, and how many in all.

FIRST	LAST	TOTAL
MAE 3	WEST 4	7
CHARLIE 7	CHAPLIN 7	14

2. *Names.* After reading a story about Rumpelstiltskin, a teacher picks up on the children's fascination with long names. As a follow-up for the whole class, the teacher might have children print their names and related numbers on a chart.

GIRLS ——
BOYS ——
CHILDREN ——

3. *Attendance.* As a daily routine the class, along with a daily attendance-taker, counts the number of boys and records this, then the number of girls and records this. Then the number present is counted and recorded. Characteristics other than sex can be used for grouping children or attendance — for example, blue eyes and others, long sleeves and others.

4. *Milk and Cookies.* The teacher prices milk at 3¢ and cookies at 1¢ each. (Prices are changed each week.) The teacher gives each child 10 "pennies" (chips) which they count out to "pay" for their milk and cookies. Situations that children can act out are

   a. how much do you pay for a milk and a cookie?

   b. how much do you have left after buying a milk?

   c. how much will 3 milks cost?

   d. how many milks can you buy with your money?

Games and Puzzles

1. *Colored Rod Activities.* Children make two-car trains without notation (see Activity 3, page 143), or play Rod Race (see page 159).

2. *Tower Game.*

   Materials: Unifix cubes; six dried lima beans painted red on one side; a shaker; a board (made from one-inch squares)

   Directions: The materials above are needed for each player. Players take turns throwing the beans. On each throw, they get as many Unifix cubes as there are red sides up. They make these into a tower, and stand the tower on a square of their board. There are five rounds, and towers from each round go in corresponding squares. (Leave a blank square if the score is zero.) At the end, the player with the most cubes wins. This is found by having each player make a "giant tower" from all of his towers.

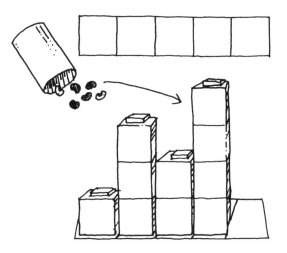

   Variation: Have the player with the fewest cubes be the winner.

3. *Beans in Circles.* Children place beans to make the numbers in the boxes.

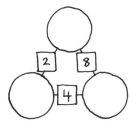

4. *Poison Apple Games 1 and 2* (action with informal language) — see page 182.

Lessons

1. *Chickadee Song.* The children all sing the following song:

"There were five little chickadees, sitting by the door,
One flew away, and then there were four.
There were four little chickadees, sitting in a tree,
One flew away, and then there were three."
(and so forth: ". . . wondering what to do,
. . . having lots of fun,
. . . sitting in the sun.")

The first time, the children themselves act as the chickadees. Later, each child holds up five fingers to represent the chickadees and puts fingers down one by one as they "fly away." Later the teacher can vary the song, for example, "There were five little chickadees, flying round about, *two* flew away, and then there were — ?"

2. *Jack and the Beanstalk Story* (Activity 6). The teacher tells a story (involving only addition and subtraction) and children use chips or beans. The teacher could also begin a story and have some child continue while others act it out. Also, the teacher could show the action and have children create a story line for each action.

3. *Making Triangles.* The teacher has children each take 12 toothpicks and make triangles from them. They repeat this for 6, 9, 15, 18, 21, 24, 27. Children record their results: _____ toothpicks, _____ triangles.

Developmental Activities

When children understand the concept of an operation, they are ready to develop and use formal language and symbolism for the operation through developmental activities that have two main types of learning objectives:

1. Given a situation, action, or diagram for an operation, the child writes and solves a corresponding number sentence.
2. Given a written number sentence, the child solves it with materials or by a drawing.

Questions and tasks such as those below can be used to evaluate children on these two types of objectives.

1. Write a multiplication sentence for this diagram.
2. Solve $4 \times 2 = \square$ with a material and explain how you got your answer.

Four desirable characteristics of developmental activities are that they: (1) associate action or an appropriate diagram with notation; (2) show the relationships between facts (when possible); (3) emphasize applications and problem solving that are of interest to the child; (4) involve each child as actively as possible.

Developmental activities can occur in incidental situations, games and planned lessons, as illustrated below.

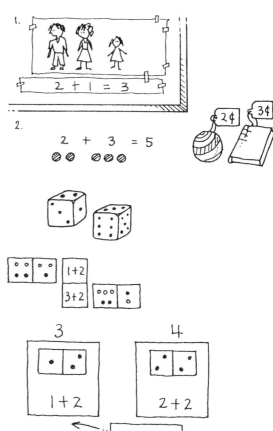

Incidental Situations

1. *Children in a Family.* Children write an addition sentence for the number of boys and girls in their family. Sentences and pictures might be displayed on a bulletin board.
2. *Shopping.* Items in a class store can be conveniently priced (1¢, 2¢, 3¢, . . .). Children can select two things they would like to buy, write a sentence for them, and count out their pennies accordingly.

Games and Puzzles

1. *Poison Apple Game* 3 (with notation).
2. *Any Game That Uses Two Dice.* Children record the addition sentence for their roll before they move.
3. *Addition Dominoes.* Children can play dominoes with a special teacher-made set, where a picture with black and white dots is to be matched to an addition sentence.

Lessons

1. *Dominoes.* Children take turns selecting a domino. For each domino they write numerals on a card (or if writing is inappropriate, they can select the already prepared card), place the domino on the card, and place both the card and the domino under the sum on a chart. Note that numerals should be directly under the dots.

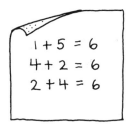

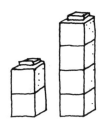

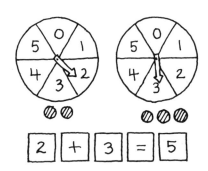

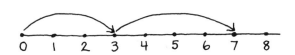

2. *Unifix cubes.* Have each child take his own number of Unifix cubes (4–10) and see how many ways he can arrange them in two piles and write addition sentences for each arrangement. The children will probably notice certain patterns (such as the commutative property of addition, or the number of ways each number can be written as a sum).

3. *Spinners.* Each child has a collection of numeral cards (1–10), one card each for |+| and |=|, and an envelope with 10 chips. One child comes to the front, spins two transparent spinners on an overhead projector to get two numbers between 0 and 5 that are to be added. The teacher draws the appropriate circles on the chalkboard to indicate chips and then writes the number sentence on the board (such as 2 |+| 3 |=| ☐). The children use their own chips and cards in the same way for this spin. Then the children are asked to hold up the numeral card that shows the answer to this sentence ⑤. On subsequent spins, the teacher does not demonstrate the solution first, but rather has the children act it out at their desks and then hold up (not say) the corresponding card for the sum. Afterwards one child shows the completed number sentence on the board. The teacher can observe who is not placing the chips correctly and who is not holding up the appropriate numeral cards. These children can work with the teacher in a small group later.

4. *Number Line.* The teacher writes a number sentence (such as $3 + 4 = ☐$) on the board. Children act it out on their desk number lines. Then one child draws the solution on the board and tells a related story.

Which of the four lessons above showed relationships between basic addition facts? _____ Which has the goal: given an addition situation, write and solve an addition sentence? _____ Which could be done individually by a student rather than in a small group or whole class? _____

Often a teacher will want to follow-up a developmental lesson with some classroom activity or homework assignment which reinforces or extends what was learned that day. The follow-up assignment should be appropriate for the developmental lesson. For example, if the lesson involved acting out addition sentences with some material (for example, chips, Unifix cubes), the children could do a similar assignment using materials at home (for example, toothpicks, pennies, chips, or other things commonly found around the home). Worksheets can be structured to have children solve problems actively such as by actually placing beans in circles or doing something, as in these examples.[8]

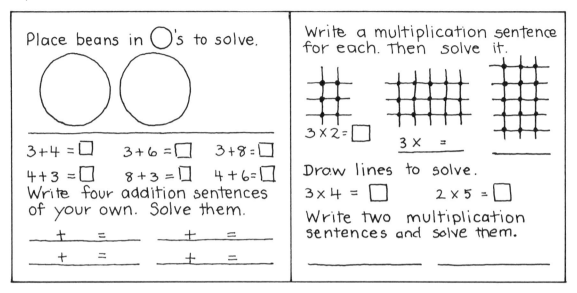

When diagrams of solutions to number sentences are part of a follow-up, make sure that the diagrams correspond to the way in which children solved the number sentences with materials in class. For example, a worksheet with arrays of dots is appropriate for children who used a bead board to do multiplication.

Sometimes the classroom activity must be specifically designed to correspond to diagrams in textbook exercises which are used as a follow-up. For example, a teacher who planned to use diagrams as shown to the right as a follow-up could cut out large cardboard pieces in these shapes and use them as "trays" for chips, showing how to move the arrow so that all of the chips are put together on the square. Children could take turns drawing cards with problems on them, arranging chips to correspond, and joining chips to show the answer.

Review-Practice Activities

Once children have achieved the two goals of developmental activities described above, they are ready to bypass the use of materials or diagrams to solve a number sentence and rely on memory.

Some children make the transition more quickly and easily than others. Children also vary in their ability (and willingness) to memorize the facts rather than work them out by a diagram or with materials. Therefore, teachers must provide children with a variety of skill-building or review-practice activities — some that will encourage them away from the manipulative solution when they are ready and others that will encourage them to give responses quickly.

Here are some general principles for designing and conducting review-practice activities. The principles apply to basic skills and other topics in mathematics, as well as to skills in other subject areas.

1. Since forgetting is inevitable, teachers should make review-practice activities available to *all* children, tailoring the activities to meet the needs of individual students.
2. Children need skill-building activities that require speed as well as accuracy, especially if the responses are to become automatic. Children may also need to practice basic facts even after responses become automatic, in order to maintain speed.
3. Children will remember information such as basic facts longer if they consider it important. Children's attitude toward skills can be improved if a teacher sets appropriate expectations for speed and accuracy and evaluates children on them, plans interesting review-practice activities, and rewards children's performance and effort.
4. Review-practice activities should involve those children who need drill the most. Individualized or small-group activities may be more appropriate for drill than whole-group ones where children who do not need the practice may get bored and those who do may not get enough attention.
5. Drill should emphasize those facts each child needs to practice. The child's confidence can be built up by beginning with a review of facts he knows and then systematically including new facts to be mastered. Both teacher and child should evaluate progress, noting improvement and identifying facts that are still not mastered.
6. Children need direction about what to do when they make a mistake or are stuck on a basic fact. For example, they might first figure out the answer — by using materials, making a diagram, or relating the fact to those they know. Then they might repeat the fact orally or in writing. The child should return to the missed fact periodically until it is learned.
7. Drill is needed, but should not be overdone. Research has shown that short sessions of drill spaced at short intervals over a long period of time are more effective than fewer, longer sessions.

There are many ways to provide review and practice. Often basic facts can be reviewed and practiced incidentally in other mathematics topics or in other curriculum areas. A useful but often overdone approach is to use textbooks and workbooks. There are many other more motivating, interesting, and effective techniques. Several are described below, along with desirable characteristics of drill activities which exemplify them. The most effective way to provide drill is to use a variety of review-practice activities suited to the needs and interests of the children.

Practice examples should be appropriate to the children's level of skill.

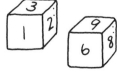

Example: In a practice game using dice, one group of children may need work on facts involving addition of numbers 0–4. These children might play the game with dice marked 0,1,2,2,3,4. For other children, these facts might be too easy — instead they might use dice marked 4,5,6,7,8,9.

Example: Children buy objects at a class store, using mental arithmetic skills in subtraction. They might select an item (costing 8¢), give coins (two nickels), and then state the change they should get back without acting out the subtraction with materials or by a drawing. The amount they have to spend and the prices can change as they learn different subtraction facts.

Practice can lead to some discovery which is intriguing in itself.

Example: In Activity 6, A Funny Thing Happened on the Way to the Beanstalk, you discovered that you always end up with the same number of beans that you began with. This could become a practice activity. Write entirely symbolic directions for this activity.

Practice can be motivated and made exciting by some deeper questions.

Example: Do you know how to win the Poison Apple Games yet? There *is* a winning strategy, and if you go first, you should always be able to win. In fact, if you know the strategy, games of this type can provide practice not only in subtraction but also in division.

Practice is most effective if children receive immediate reinforcement for correct and incorrect answers. This can be provided for individuals by self-checking activity cards (for example, the answer might be on the back). When a small group of children play a game involving skills, they will probably correct each other. Also some materials check themselves, such as the puzzle below.

Example: Add the numbers as indicated by the arrows. The puzzle on the left has been started. Try the one in the middle. Then fill in your own numbers and try the one on the right.

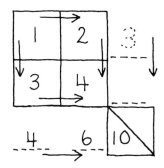
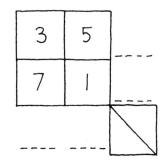
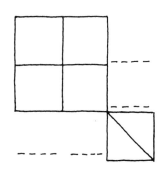

Use activities that are enjoyable and fun for children. Drill need not be dull and tedious, nor restricted to paper-and-pencil. Many interesting media devices are available commercially — children can use special calculators, tape recorders, or a variety of teaching machines. Children are often motivated by the novelty of such devices to practice skills, but sometimes the novelty wears off and a good thing can be overdone. Games, songs, and puzzles can also provide an interesting and novel context for drill. Teachers' guides, books on games for teaching mathematics and professional journals (for example, *The Arithmetic Teacher, The Instructor, Early Years*) contain many excellent games and activities for drill. (See the Bibliography for articles about games and activities for review-practice.)

Songs. A teacher or students can create short singing drills, for example, a multiplication song. Children can sing along, clapping their hands after each problem is sung. Children can also take turns leading the singing, even selecting their own melodies and rhythms. Rhythm can be changed to increase the speed in response.

A difficulty with this drill activity is that children who do not know the basic facts may "hum the melody" but not sing the lyrics of the song. How might a teacher try to make sure that all children sing, not hum, along?

Puzzles. Cross-number puzzles and number hunts (see below) provide an interesting format for drill.

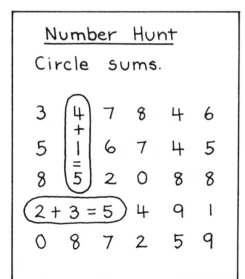

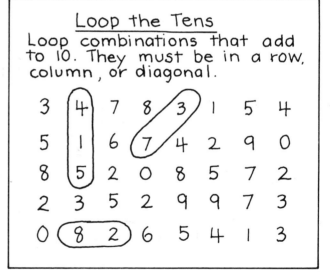

Today's Date. Children write the date in different ways. Second graders might use only addition and subtraction, while fourth graders might use all four operations or combinations of them. (They might write their own number sentence for the date on the board when they come to school in the morning.) An interesting follow-up might be to have children classify the number sentences.

Table Facts. A child draws number squares one by one from a bag and places them where they belong on the multiplication table. If he cannot place the number square, he places it aside to check it later. The child records how many facts he placed in three minutes (subtracting the number squares placed aside from the number placed in the table). Children can repeat this game from time to time, and make a chart of their progress.

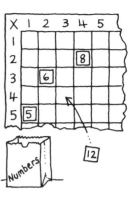

This game can be simplified to deal only with, say, products of numbers less than 5, or made more difficult by including some numbers which do not fit in the table, such as 17 or 26. Could you make a game like this for addition?

Popular Games. Many popular games can be adapted to give practice, and children may enjoy inventing their own rules. Competition should not be overemphasized. It is sometimes desirable to have a combination of chance (no skill in playing the game) and strategy (some choices to be made). Below is an example of a game that is primarily one of chance, but that allows some strategy.

Cover-up

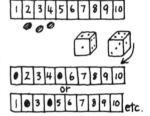

Materials: 2 dice, bingo chips, or other markers; a board with 1–10 spaces for each player

Directions: Players take turns rolling the dice. They can use chips to cover up any two numbers whose sum is the number they rolled, provided neither is already covered. If a player cannot cover a combination on his turn, he does nothing. The first to cover all spaces wins.

TEST YOUR UNDERSTANDING

1. Which material do you think is more appropriate for introducing the topics below to children who are just beginning to learn them? Why?

Topic	Materials
Addition (7 + 3 = ☐)	Bean sticks or Cuisenaire rods
Subtraction (7 − 3 = ☐)	Chips or balance beam
Multiplication (3 × 4 = ☐)	Bead board or dots drawn on paper
Division (14 ÷ 2 = ☐)	Bead board or chips

2. Agree or disagree: Children can only work with applications of an operation after they have developed skill with it.

3. According to the scope and sequence chart on page 197, at what grade level might you find the following textbook problems? Some problems may be appropriate to several grade levels.

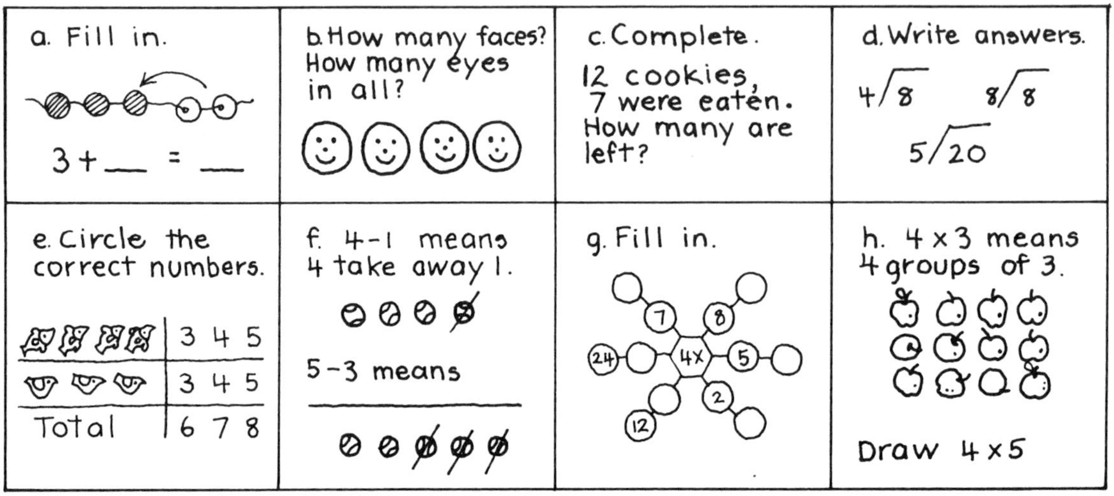

a. Fill in.	b. How many faces? How many eyes in all?	c. Complete. 12 cookies, 7 were eaten. How many are left?	d. Write answers.
3 + __ = __	☺ ☺ ☺ ☺		$4\overline{)8}$ $8\overline{)8}$ $5\overline{)20}$
e. Circle the correct numbers. Total	f. 4−1 means 4 take away 1. 5−3 means ____	g. Fill in.	h. 4 × 3 means 4 groups of 3. Draw 4 × 5

e. Circle the correct numbers.

	3 4 5
	3 4 5
Total	6 7 8

4. Write a story for each type of number sentence below. Draw a diagram showing how to act out the solution with some material. Also draw a picture problem for any two of them.

    a. Addition 7 + 3 = ☐
    b. Take-away subtraction 7 − 3 = ☐
    c. Comparative subtraction 7 − 3 = ☐
    d. Missing-addend subtraction 7 −3 = ☐
    e. Grouping multiplication 2 × 3 = ☐
    f. Array multiplication 2 × 3 = ☐
    g. Combinations multiplication 2 × 3 = ☐
    h. Partitive division 6 ÷ 2 = ☐
    i. Repeated subtraction division 6 ÷ 2 = ☐

5. What is the *multiple embodiments principle*?
Describe three different embodiments a child could use to act out subtraction sentences (such as 6 − 2 = ☐).
Does this principle apply to all children? Explain.

6. Describe (or demonstrate) how materials could be used to illustrate: the commutative property of addition; the zero property for addition; the distributive property of multiplication over addition.

7. Which of the expressions below are always true when the frames are filled in with whole numbers {0, 1, 2, 3, . . .}? If an expression is not always true, give an example when it is true and when it is false.
    a. ○ − (☐ − △) = (○ −☐) − △
    b. ☐ × (△ − ○) = (☐ × △) − (☐ × ○)
    c. ☐ ÷ ☐ = 1
    d. (☐ − 1) × (☐ + 1) = ☐ × ☐ − 1

8. How can children use the structure of arithmetic to learn the *bridging facts* of addition? What difficulties might a child have in using the following decomposition method to find $8 + 6$? $8 + 6 = 8 + 2 + 4 = 10 + 4 = 14$

9. Give an example of how children can learn multiplication facts such as 9×8 and 6×7 from easier facts.

10. Describe an application situation in which children could use basic facts in a variety of ways.

11. What does Wirtz mean by "problem solving"? Give an example of a problem-solving activity in each of three modes — manipulative, representational, and symbolic.

12. Describe some characteristics of introductory activities. How do they differ from developmental activities? Could the activity below be an introductory activity for some operation? If so, which operation? Could it also be a review-practice type activity for another operation? If so, which one?

Children select objects to buy from their class store and figure out the total cost as shown here.

13. Which of the principles for review-practice activities given on pages 231–232 do you think is most important? Why? What would you have a child do when he makes a mistake or does not know a fact in a review-practice activity?

14. Describe an appropriate follow-up homework assignment for a lesson in which children use chips to act out subtractions, such as $7 - 3 = \square$, $8 - 3 = \square$, and $5 - 1 = \square$.

15. Describe an enrichment activity that is appropriate for second graders who have already mastered the basic facts of addition and subtraction.

16. Describe how children progress through stages toward mastery of basic facts for an operation.

17. Different types of evaluation tasks are given below. For which stage of mastery is each most appropriate?

　　a. The teacher says, "Use the Unifix cubes to solve $4 + 5 = \square$."
　　b. (Written test item) Draw a diagram to show 4×5.
　　c. The teacher gives a child a one-minute oral quiz on bridging facts.
　　d. The teacher observes children's participation in the Chickadee Song (see page 228).

e. The teacher observes a child using flash cards to practice more difficult division facts (such as $72 \div 8 = \square$).

f. The teacher checks a child's homework on subtraction facts and has the child explain how several answers were gotten (both correct and incorrect ones).

g. A child tests himself in less than two minutes on 20 multiplication facts presented on a new electronic skill-building device and reports that he got them all correct to the teacher. (The device generates facts and indicates if a child's answer is correct or incorrect.)

FURTHER READINGS AND PROJECTS

1. What does it mean to know basic facts? On pages 195–196 "know" was characterized as meaning "understand," "have skill" and "be able to apply." Read the following two articles and decide whether their interpretations of understanding and skill agree with those presented in this chapter. Also compare the instructional sequence recommended by Ashlock with that discussed on pages 224–235. Robert B. Ashlock, "Teaching Basic Facts: Three Classes of Activities," *The Arithmetic Teacher,* 18:6 (October 1971), pp. 359–364. Charles Thompson and William Dunlop, "Basic Facts: Do Your Children Understand or Do They Memorize?" *The Arithmetic Teacher,* 25:3 (December 1977), pp. 14–16.

2. Examine material on basic facts in a text for grade 1, 2, or 3. Are there any applications? Do they appear before, during, or after development of the operation involved? Would you classify them as involving routine problem solving or some type of higher-order problem solving? Are there any situations that require children to identify and formulate problems on their own? Are the applications interesting and relevant to children at the grade level for which the problems were intended?

3. Activity 7, Arrow Paths is similar to ones found in the Comprehensive School Mathematics Program (CSMP) materials. Read the following article to get an overview of that program, and then examine the sections listed below on arrow paths: Burt Kaufman and Vincent H. Haag, "New Math or Old Math? — The Wrong Question," in *The Arithmetic Teacher,* 24:3 (March 1977).

Examine the following sections on arrow diagrams in "Numerical Relations" in *Teacher's Guide to CSMP Mathematics for the Upper Primary Grades — Part I* (Volume B) (St. Louis: CEMREL, Inc., 1975): 1. Adding and Subtracting Functions; 3. How to Become the Friend of a Number; 5. Roads and Problem Solving; 6. Multiplying Functions; 7. Composition of Functions. Also examine workbook pages on "Which Roads" and "10 is Playing with Some of His Friends" in *Teacher's Guide to CSMP Mathematics for the Upper Primary Grades* — Part II (Volume F) (St. Louis: CEMREL, Inc., 1975). Could you use ideas from the CSMP materials in situations where you were using some other mathematics program with children?

4. The concept of function is an important one which arises in many different areas of mathematics. This chapter dealt with functions involving numbers in Activity 7, Arrow Paths and Activity 8, Machines and Tables. Later in

Chapter 8, Geometry on a Geoboard, we will touch on functions in transformation geometry. For more about functions at the elementary school level, examine the following:

Marvin Karlin, "Machines," *The Arithmetic Teacher* 12:4 (April 1965), pp. 327–334.

David Johnson and Louis Cohen, "Functions," *The Arithmetic Teacher* 17:4 (April 1970), pp. 305–315.

5. How can children master basic facts by knowing and using the structure of arithmetic? This question was dealt with on pages 218–223. For in depth answers, examine *Children Discover Arithmetic* by Catherine and Margaret Stern (New York: Harper and Row, 1971) in which are described specific activities and games involving Stern materials that help children understand the structure of arithmetic and gain mastery of arithmetic skills. Examine how an operation is developed — for example, read the following chapters that focus on addition facts: Chapter 1. Teaching Arithmetic; Chapter 5. Writing Numbers and Addition Stories; Chapter 7. Mastery of Addition; Chapter 9. Problem Solving in Addition and Subtraction; Chapter 13. Structural Techniques to Master Bridging Facts. Give an example of one activity that develops structure of addition and indicate how the structure is embodied in the activity.

6. Examine these articles that describe and illustrate some methods and materials for helping learning disabled and educable mentally retarded children learn basic facts. What is "special" about the methods recommended? "The Learning Disabled Child — Learning Basic Facts" by Ann Myers and Carol Thornton, in *The Arithmetic Teacher* 25:3 (December 1977) pp. 46–50, and "Helping the Special Child Measure Up in Basic Fact Skills" by Carol Thornton, in *Teaching Exceptional Children* (Winter 1977), pp. 54–55, focus on how learning disabled children can learn and use relationships between basic facts. The second article includes mini-lessons that illustrate strategies for helping special children.

The articles below are concerned with the educable mentally retarded child, and are all to be found in the journal *Education and Training of the Mentally Retarded:*

Sharon Metz Kokaska, "A Notation System in Arithmetic Skills," 10:2 (April 1975), pp. 96–101.

Nicholas Radeka, "Manual Manipulation — A Hand-y Way of Multiplying," 10:2 (April 1975), pp. 102–103.

Earl Ogletree and Vilma Ujaki, "A Motoric Approach to Teaching Multiplication to the Mentally Retarded Child," 11:2 (April 1976), pp. 129–134.

7. On Pages 216–218 we discussed briefly Robert Wirtz's matrix for characterizing mathematics instruction. The CDA Elementary School Mathematics program developed by Wirtz contains activities for each cell of the matrix, but especially for the problem-solving level. The CDA program consists of *Individualized Computation* (Levels A-F), and *Patterns and Problems*

(Levels A-F), with supplementary materials including *Drill and Practice at the Problem-Solving Level*. *Individualized Computation* provides children with opportunities to move ahead in learning mathematics at their own rates and in their own ways. It is multi-graded and also self-correcting. *Patterns and Problems* is designed to encourage maximum interaction in heterogeneous groups.

Before examining these materials, look at CDA's *Mathematics for Everyone* which provides an overview of the program. In particular, examine part C, "Learning Theory," which discusses the Wirtz matrix. Then explore the CDA materials (Levels A and B) which involve basic facts. Try some of the activities. Read some "Letters for Parents" and comment on them. How would you like to use these materials in grades 1–2?

8. There are many books available on activities and games to build and maintain skills with basic facts. Five of them are listed below. Examine some of them and describe some activities in them that you think children would particularly enjoy and that would be effective for building skill with basic facts. Also, check whether any activities involve "problem solving" in Wirtz's sense.

"Games: Practice Activities for the Basic Facts," chapter 3 (pp. 39–50) in the 1978 NCTM Yearbook, *Developing Computational Skills* (Reston, Virginia: NCTM, 1978).

Enoch Dumas, *Math Activities for Child Involvement* (Boston: Allyn and Bacon, 1971).

S. Jeanne Kelly, *Learning Mathematics Through Activities* (Cupertino, California: James E. Freel and Associates, 1973).

Leonard M. Kennedy and Ruth L. Michon, *Games for Individualizing Mathematics Learning* (Columbus, Ohio: Charles E. Merrill, 1973).

Edna L. Sykes, *Arithmetic Activities Handbook: An Individualized and Group Approach to Teaching the Basic Skills* (West Nyack, New York: Parker Publishing Company, 1976).

9. One ingredient for effective instruction is the planning and preparation done by the teacher. Write lesson plans for an introductory, a developmental, and a review-practice activity for some operation. Each plan should include a learning objective for the lesson, a clear and sufficiently detailed description of the lesson (imagine that someone else must use your plan and write for them), including questions that you might ask, and some type of evaluation and/or follow-up for the lesson (if appropriate).

NOTES

1. The language of "arrows" is used in many interesting and challenging ways in the Comprehensive School Mathematics Program (CSMP) materials for elementary school (St. Louis: CEMREL, Inc., 1975). Notice how these problems provide opportunities to discover and create patterns while also giving practice with skills.

2. See Marvin Karlin, "Machines," in *The Arithmetic Teacher* 12:4 (April 1965), pp. 327–334.

3. See Chapter 2 of Zoltan P. Dienes, *Building Up Mathematics* (London: Hutchinson Educational Ltd., 1960), for more about the "Multiple Embodiments Principle," or the "Perceptual Variability Principle," as he refers to it there. See also Robert E. Reys

and Thomas N. Post, *The Mathematics Laboratory: Theory to Practice* (Boston: Prindle, Weber & Schmidt, 1973), pp. 45–47.

4. The Madison Project, an innovative mathematics project of the 1960s that emphasized supplementing the elementary school curriculum with informal explorations by children, includes a variety of activities involving properties. Children "collect" expressions that are always true and later organize and classify them. See *Discovery in Mathematics: A Text for Teachers* by Robert Davis (Palo Alto, California: Addison-Wesley, 1964).

5. USMES materials were developed by and are available from Education Development Center, 55 Chapel Street, Newton, Massachusetts 02160.

6. Robert Wirtz's CDA (Curriculum Development Associates, Inc., 1211 Connecticut Avenue NW, Washington, D.C. 20036) materials include a basic program for children (*Individualized Computations, Patterns and Problems*) and teacher resource materials to supplement the mathematics program—*Drill and Practice at the Problem Solving Level,* which stresses the development of skills through problem solving. This resource contains many interesting problems that can be approached in a manipulative mode, including Beans in Circles and activities with bean sticks.

7. For more details for this sort of approach to develop arithmetic skills, see *Children Discover Arithmetic: An Introduction to Structural Arithmetic* by Catherine Stern and Margaret Stern (New York: Harper and Row, Publishers, 1971).

8. These worksheets are adapted from activities in Robert Wirtz's *Individualized Computation* (Washington, D.C.: Curriculum Development Associates, 1974). For more examples, see books a_1 and b_2 in the series.

CHAPTER 6

MEASUREMENT AND
THE METRIC SYSTEM

INTRODUCTION

There are many ways in which we attach numbers to things around us. Complete the following statements about yourself:

I am _____ old.
I am _____ tall.
I weigh about _____.
My waist measures _____.
I drink _____ of water a day.
I travel a distance of about _____ a day.
My temperature is _____.

These questions all involve measurements of some sort. You probably answered the questions with a numeral and some unit; for example, "125 pounds," "28 inches," or "4 cups." Write three more statements about yourself which involve measurement.

If you read a collection of statements about someone else, you might feel that you knew a fair amount about him. But what if his list included:

I am 190 centimeters tall.
I weigh about 90 kilograms.
I drink 1 liter of water a day.
My temperature is 37 degrees.

Would these statements mean anything to you? Such statements would be meaningful to people educated almost anywhere in the world outside the United States — they involve the metric system of measurement. It is important that teachers begin now to prepare themselves and school children to think and work with metric units, for the United States is now committed to a changeover from the English system to the metric system of measurement. Activities in this chapter are designed to help you develop an intuitive understanding of the metric system, and at the same time to gain experience with general types of measurement situations.

Activities 1–10 are designed to build up the concept of measurement of length in a sequence that is also suitable for children: first, direct comparison of length; then, measurement using a nonstandard unit, leading to selection of a standard unit (in this case a metric one); then, constructing and using a ruler; finally, extending this system to measuring both larger and smaller objects. After a brief description of the metric system, Activities 11–18 are presented and involve applications and extensions of these concepts, as well as an introduction to area and volume measurement. Discussion Questions and Comments concern the meaning and uses of measurement, and sequencing instruction in measurement from early experiences through upper elementary school. The sequence you followed in Activities 1–10 will be analyzed and applied to teaching measurement of capacity and weight.

The Follow-up Sections discuss the implications of Piaget's research into how children learn measurement, and where measurement arises in the curriculum. The history and characteristics of the metric system are described, concentrating on building up an intuitive feel for the most important units of length, area, volume, capacity, weight or mass, and for temperature. In addition, special benefits and difficulties with teaching the metric system will be discussed. Finally, there are some examples given of ways to provide further practice in estimating and measuring, with an emphasis on some activities that children can do at home as well as in school.

ACTIVITIES

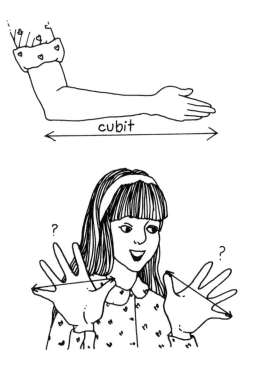

Activity 1. Comparing Lengths

1. Work with a partner. Find out who has the longer cubit (see diagram) and who has the shorter cubit. How did you do it?
2. Stretch your hand as widely as you can, as shown here. This is called a handspan. Are you right- or left-handed? Do you think that your right handspan is longer than, shorter than, or the same as your left handspan? Try it. Which is longer?
3. Look at the pictures on page 246. Which looks longer, the ball-point pen or the fork? How might you check your guess, using *only* your hands?

Activity 2. Hand Measuring

Suppose that you would like to measure your desk or table to see if it will fit into a certain corner, but you do not have any standard measuring equipment (such as a ruler). Use your hand to measure across (the shortest dimension) the top of your desk or table.

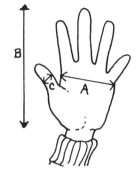

1. Use the width of your hand as a unit. The table is about _____ units across.

2. Use the length of your hand as a unit. The table is about _____ units across.

3. Use the width of your thumb as a unit. The table is about _____ units across.
4. Which unit would you use if you expected the table to be a tight fit?
5. Are your measurements in parts 1, 2, and 3 the same as your neighbor's? _____ Can you tell from the measurements whose thumb is wider?
6. Why would or wouldn't hand widths, hand lengths, and thumb widths be good units for measuring length?
7. Actually a "hand" is a unit of measure, now used only for measuring the height of a horse's shoulder. The hand dates back to the sixteenth century. Which part of the hand — width, length, or span — do you think was used in measuring a horse who is 14 hands tall?

Activity 3. Other Materials

Activity 2 involved using parts of the hand for measuring the table. You might have found your hand undesirable for this, since it is flexible — that is, you can squeeze it and it changes in size. Many everyday things can be used for measuring length; for example, drinking straws.

1. Find two objects you carry around that would make good units for measuring length.
2. List five items shown below that would be suitable for measuring length.

3. What qualities should an object have to be good for measuring length?

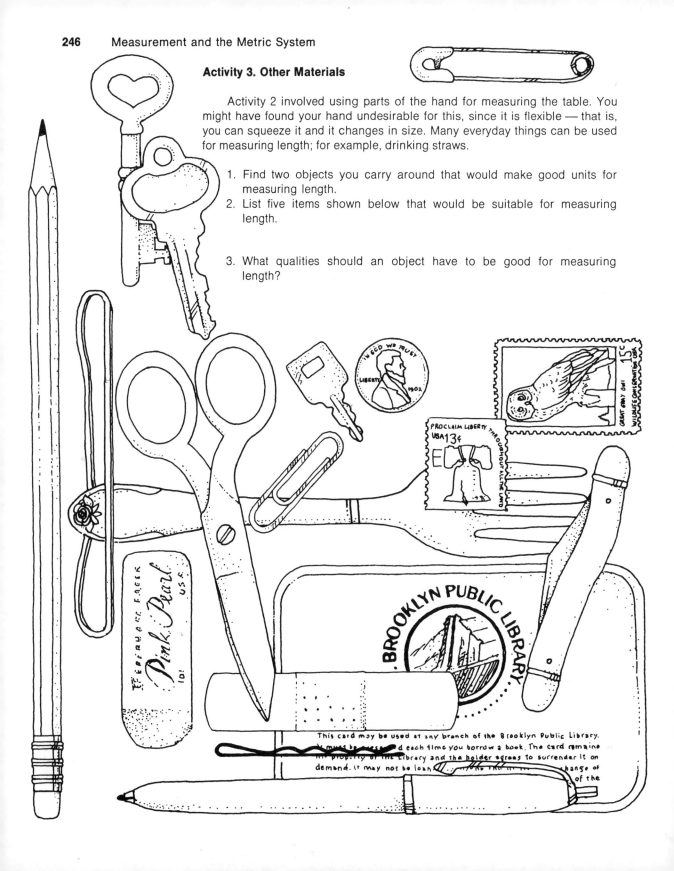

Activity 4. Estimate and Measure with Cuisenaire Rods

1. Use white Cuisenaire rods to measure the length of your little finger and of the orange rod.
    little finger = _____ whites   orange rod = _____ whites
2. First estimate the length of the paper clip in white rods. Then measure it.

Estimate _____

Measure _____

3. Estimate first, then measure. Use the white rods.

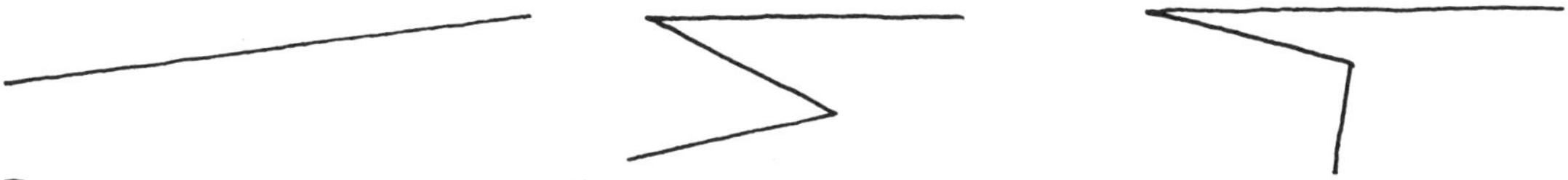

Estimate _____   Estimate _____   Estimate _____

Measure _____   Measure _____   Measure _____

4. Estimate how many white rods fit across the bottom of this page.
    You probably do not have enough white rods to measure this width. Try to use some shortcut procedure (for example, use some longer rods as well). Describe your method.
    The measurement is _____ white rods.

Activity 5. Centimeters

The white Cuisenaire rods were chosen as a unit in Activity 4 for a special reason — they measure one *centimeter* (cm) on each side. Do you see why we can call them "centimeter cubes"?

Test your ability to estimate length in centimeters. Look for objects in the picture in Activity 3 with the approximate lengths or widths given below.

1 cm   width of paper clip,   _____   _____
5 cm   _____,   _____
10 cm _____,   _____

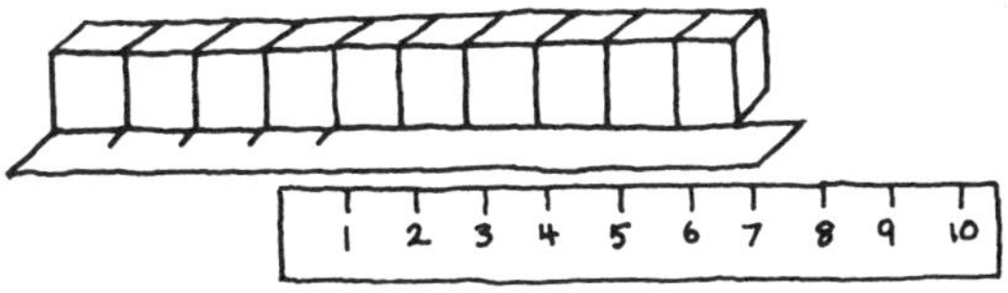

Activity 6. Making a Ruler

Make yourself a centimeter ruler from a strip of paper or a popsicle stick. The ruler is to be 10 centimeters long. First, line up 10 white rods on the edge of a piece of paper. Second, mark off the rods on the strip. Third, write 1, 2, . . . , 10 on the ruler and cut it out so that it looks like the diagram to the right. Compare your ruler to the orange rod. Does it match exactly? If not, did you follow the directions *exactly*? Do you see why your marks might not be accurate?

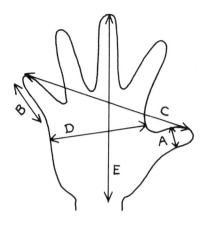

Activity 7. Measuring With Your Centimeter Ruler

Stretch your hand wide, place it on a piece of paper and trace around it. Use your 10-centimeter ruler to measure these parts of your hand (see diagram) in centimeters.

The width of my thumb (A) is _____ cm.
The length of my little finger (B) is _____ cm.
The span of my hand (C) is _____ cm.
The width of my palm (D) is _____ cm.
The length of my hand (E) is _____ cm. (This is from the tip of the middle finger to the wrist.)

Palmists claim that the relative lengths of your ring finger and index finger show whether you are more artistic or philosophical. If your ring finger is longer, then supposedly you are creative and need freedom to let your spirit work. If the index finger is longer, you are a leader with a strong philosophy of understanding. Which are you (or are the fingers of the same length)? If your index finger is very long, approaching the length of the middle finger, your ego is out of proportion and your self-importance can cause problems! How about you?

Just for Fun: How wide is your smile? Have a partner measure your smile. _____ cm How big is your partner's smile? _____ cm How far can you stick your tongue out? _____ cm

Activity 8. Measuring Your Height

How tall are you? Estimate your height in centimeters. _____ cm
Measure your height. Work with a partner. _____ cm
Is your homemade ruler appropriate for this measurement? _____ If not, what would you suggest instead?

Activity 9. Some Other Units

1. The centimeter or white rod is too small to measure large things conveniently. Perhaps in Activity 4, part 4, you used the orange Cuisenaire rods to measure the width of the page. Since 10 white rods make an orange rod, it is easy to say how wide the page is if you know how many oranges and whites it measures. You will see how you might measure the width of this page with orange and white rods.

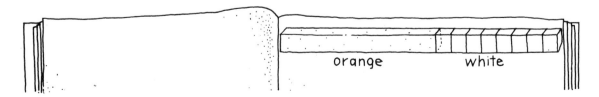

orange   white

It takes a little more than one orange rod and eight white rods, or
_____ white rods. This measurement could be written as 18 cm.

Measure the length of this page with orange rods and white rods.
Write the measurements as follows: _____ oranges and _____
whites, or _____ whites, or _____ cm.

A combination of orange rods and white rods is more convenient
than white rods alone for measuring the length of the page — but still
using just these rods is inconvenient for measuring greater lengths,
such as your height, the width of the room, or the length of the hall.

Just as you made a 10-centimeter ruler from 10 white Cuisenaire
rods (see diagram 1), so you could make a longer ruler from 10
orange rods (see diagram 2). You could make such a ruler from a
long piece of wood or you could make a tape measure by marking
cloth tape.

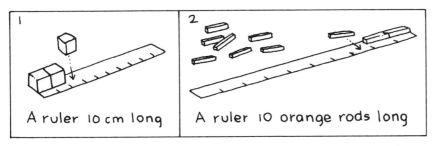

Or you could make five copies of the two strips below, cut them out,
glue them to cardboard, connect them, and mark centimeters as
shown. This ruler would be 100 centimeters long.

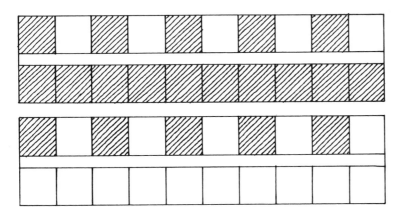

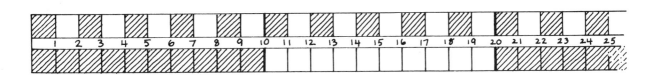

2. The lengths you have been working with — the orange rod and the 100-centimeter ruler — do in fact have their own names. A length of 100 centimeters is called a *meter* (m). The meter is the basic unit of length in the metric system.

   Use a meter stick or tape measure to find out which of these would be about one meter long. Mark each picture "more," "less," or "about a meter."

The length of an orange rod — 10 cm — is called a *decimeter* (dm). Use an orange rod to find which of these is about one decimeter long. Mark each picture "more," "less," or "about a decimeter."

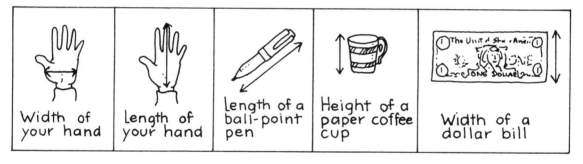

3. You saw that 10 white Cuisenaire rods were the same length as one orange rod, and so 10 centimeters = 1 decimeter, or 10 cm = 1 dm. We can also say

   1 white rod = one-tenth of an orange rod

   $$1 \text{ centimeter} = \frac{1}{10} \text{ decimeter or } .1 \text{ decimeter}$$

   $$1 \text{ cm} = \frac{1}{10} \text{ dm} \quad \text{or} \quad .1 \text{ dm}$$

   Complete the following. Think of the relationships between the various rods and a meter stick. Use either fractions $\left(\frac{1}{10} \text{ or } \frac{1}{100}\right)$ or decimals (.1 or .01) when necessary.

   _____ cm = 1 m; 1 cm = _____ m
   _____ dm = 1 m; 1 dm = _____ m

4. Suppose that you measured your height and found that you were 160 centimeters tall. (See the diagram to the right.) If you had measured yourself with orange rods or decimeters, you would have found that you were 16 decimeters tall. If this length was written in terms of meters, you would be 1 meter and 60 hundredths of a meter, or 1.60 meters.

   Suppose that a child was measured and found to be 90 centimeters tall. Write the height in decimeters and in meters.

   90 cm = _____ dm = _____ m

   How old do you think this child might be?

5. Centimeters and meters will be the most frequently used metric units for length. Determine your measurements, as listed below. Use a meter stick or tape measure. Find the measurements in both centimeters and meters.

   Height _____ cm or _____ m

   Waist _____ cm or _____ m

   Arm span (as far as you can stretch right fingertip from left fingertip)

   _____ cm or _____ m

   Cubit _____ cm or _____ m

   (**Note:** Are two of these measurements very close? Would you have guessed this? Do other people have the same result?)

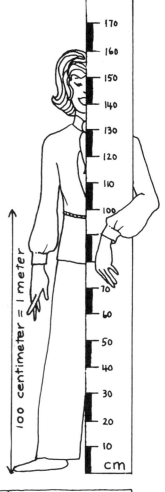

Activity 10. Game — Estimate and Measure

Directions: This game can be played with 2–6 players. Take turns. One player names something in the room that everyone can see, and also a unit (cm, dm, or m). Everyone writes an estimate for the measurement in the stated unit. The person who named the object measures it, and whoever was closest gets one point. (In case of ties, all players with the best guess gets one point.) The first player to get four points wins. Record the choices of objects and your guesses below.

Object	Unit	Estimate	Measurement

Note: No doubt you have noticed that the names of the three units that you have used so far (meter, decimeter, and centimeter) are related. All have the stem word "meter" (sometimes spelled "metre").[1] Compare this with units of the English system — inch, foot, and yard — which have no linguistic relationship. In fact, you saw that

$$100 \ \textit{centi--meters} = 1 \ \text{meter}$$
and so $1 \ \textit{centi--meter} = \text{one-}\textit{hundredth} \text{ of a meter}$

which indicates that *centi* means hundredth. (Think of our word *cent* for one-hundredth of a dollar.) Complete the following:

$$\underline{\hspace{2cm}} \ \textit{deci--meters} = 1 \ \text{meter}$$
and so 1 *deci*--meter $=$ one- $\underline{\hspace{3cm}}$ of a meter

and so *deci* means $\underline{\hspace{3cm}}$.

In the metric system, larger and smaller units are named by adding prefixes (such as centi- and deci-) to a base unit (meter). You probably noticed that the prefixes are based on multiples of 10, as are many things around us (most importantly, place value notation and money). This makes the metric system much easier to work with than the English system (where *12* inches = 1 foot, *3* feet = 1 yard, . . .). There are prefixes corresponding to many powers of 10; however, only a few are in common use. The chart below shows the commonly used metric units for length.

kilometer	hectometer	dekameter	meter	decimeter	centimeter	millimeter
km	hm	dam	m	dm	cm	mm
1000 m	100 m	10 m	1 m	$\frac{1}{10}$ m	$\frac{1}{100}$ m	$\frac{1}{1000}$ m

Hectometer and dekameter are not commonly used. These lengths are usually described in meters, as for example in the Olympic "100-meter dash." Note that a millimeter is one-*tenth* of a centimeter. To see how long a millimeter is, divide this centimeter length into 10 approximately equal parts. How many millimeters are in one decimeter? $\underline{\hspace{1.5cm}}$ in one meter? $\underline{\hspace{1.5cm}}$

Which unit would you use to measure the distance between New York City and Washington D.C.? $\underline{\hspace{1.5cm}}$ The length of a newborn baby? $\underline{\hspace{1.5cm}}$ The length of an ant? $\underline{\hspace{1.5cm}}$ The length of a swimming pool? $\underline{\hspace{1.5cm}}$

Activities 11–18, presented in task-card format, have various goals: to apply what you know already about measuring length in metric units; to introduce new techniques and devices for measuring length (such as a trundle wheel or calipers); and to introduce metric measurement of area and volume. (The main goals for each Activity are listed at the top of the task card.) Each Activity consists of two parts. Part 1 is a relatively direct task that should not take you very long. Part 2 shows how this simple measurement task can be put into a broader context, involving choice of procedures, problem solving, searching for patterns, or creating new problems. Both types of tasks have their place in the classroom — the first as a quick mini-activity for children to do in odd moments of time, and the second as a more sustained project, leading to further investigations. Some Activities require special equipment (11–14, and 15, if you use a map wheel) while others can easily be done at home with everyday material (16–18 and 15, if you use string).

Do at least three of the Activities and read the others.

Activity 11. How Long is Ten Meters?

Goals: To estimate and measure distances in meters (5–50 meters); to use a new measuring device, a trundle wheel.

Materials: Trundle wheel (A plastic or wooden wheel with a circumference of one meter, that is fixed at the end of a handle. It can be pushed along the ground so that the wheel·turns and measures the distance covered.)

1. Work with a partner. Walk away from each other until you think you are about 10 meters apart. Check your estimate with the trundle wheel. Try again — this time for 5 meters, then for 15 meters.
2. a. Is there a hallway outside your room? If so, how many meters long is it? First *estimate*. Think of more than one way that you could make a reasonable estimate without using any formal measuring equipment (such as meter sticks or a trundle wheel). Describe your methods. Then check your estimates with a trundle wheel.
   b. Estimate and measure some other distances: the distance to the nearest water fountain, nearest bathroom, nearest stairway . . . . (In a school, children might make and record these measurements on signs in the hallways.)
   c. Find something that is about 10 meters long, wide, or tall. Can you find something that measures 50 meters?

Activity 12. Walking

Goals: To develop a feeling for a kilometer in terms of walking time and in terms of daily routines and landmarks; to measure meters with a trundle wheel.

Materials: Watch or clock; trundle wheel, meter stick, or meter tape

1. Using a trundle wheel, find out how long it takes you to walk 50 meters at a normal walking pace. _____ seconds. How long will it take you to walk a kilometer? _____ minutes. How many kilometers could you walk in an hour? _____ Compare your results with someone else's.
2. Estimate how many kilometers *you* usually walk in a day. Think of a distance near you of about 1 kilometer. Think of a location that is about 1 kilometer from where you are now.

Activity 13. Around and Across

Goals: To estimate and measure in centimeters; to use new tools (calipers) to measure in a situation where a ruler is inadequate (such as through a solid object); to investigate the relation between circumference and diameter of a circle (in part 2).

Materials: Meter stick; string; calipers; assorted round objects (spheres or cylinders) — lids, cups, tubes, balls, etc.

1. Pull out a piece of string that you think will fit around your head (just above eye level). Estimate the distance around your head in centimeters, then measure your head with string.

   Estimate: _____ cm
   Measure: _____ cm

   Estimate the width across your head in centimeters (just above the ears).

   Estimate: _____ cm

   Could you measure this with a ruler? Try it with calipers.

   Measure _____ cm

2. Take several objects with a circular cross section and repeat the two measurements you made of your head — "around" (circumference) and "across" (diameter). Make a chart.

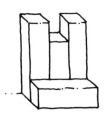

Object	Circumference	Diameter	

In the last column, write the quotient of the circumference divided by the diameter. (Use a calculator if you want to.) The numbers in the last column should be fairly close. What is the average of these numbers? (Is it about 3.14, an approximation to π?)

Divide the measurement around your head by the measurement across your head (from part 1). Is the quotient close to the numbers in the last column in the table? Why or why not?

Activity 14. Cuisenaire Rod Sculptures

Goals: To measure volume and area informally; to investigate a number pattern relating volume to surface area (in part 2).

Materials: Cuisenaire rods; cellophane tape

1. Take two purple and two light green rods, and tape them together to make a sculpture like this.

   How many white rods would it take to build this shape? _____

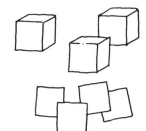

Suppose that you want to cover it with gold leaf which comes in squares just the size of the faces of a white rod. How many such squares would you need? (Cover the bottom as well as the sides.)
_____

2. Use the same rods (two purples and two light greens) to make your own sculpture. How many white rods would it take to build it? _____ How many little squares of gold leaf would you need to cover it? _____ Compare your answers with other people's. What was the same? What was different? Could you build something that uses *less* gold leaf from these rods? Could you build something that uses *more* gold leaf?
    Take one rod of each color. Fill in the table.

Rod	w	r	g	p	y	d	k	n	e	o
Volume, or number of white rods needed to build the rod	1	2								
Surface area, or number of gold-leaf squares needed to cover the rod entirely	6	10								

Do you see a pattern?
The symbols for colors are: w = white, r = red, g = light green, p = purple, y = yellow, d = dark green, k = black, n = brown, e = blue, o = orange.

Activity 15. Maps

Goals: To use a new measuring device (map wheel or a piece of string) to measure distances, possibly along curved paths; to relate kilometers to local surroundings.

Materials: Map wheel or string; centimeter ruler; local map with a scale in kilometers per centimeter (Questions below should be adapted for a local map.)

1. On the map of mid-Manhattan (page 256), the scale is about .8 kilometers to the centimeter. Use the map wheel or string and ruler to find each distance.
    How wide is Manhattan at 34th St.? _____ km How far is it from 14th St. to 34th St.? _____ km How many streets are there in a kilometer?

2. How would you go from the lower tip of Manhattan (Battery Park) to the Coliseum? Find three different routes. Which is longest? Which is shortest? How far is it "as the crow flies"?

    Use a map that shows where you live and where you are now. How far are you from where you live? _____ km Find some other distances to measure on the map.
        Note: You may find that local maps do not yet have scales in kilometers per centimeter. However you

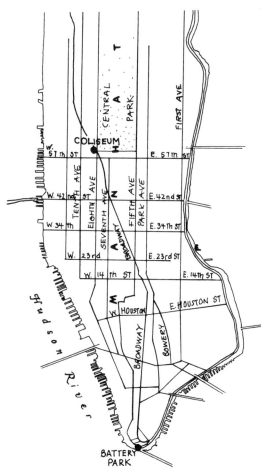

can easily convert the scale. Find the scale in miles per inch, and multiply this number by .6 to find the scale in kilometers per centimeter. The teacher should write the new scale on a piece of paper glued over the original scale before students do this activity.

Activity 16. Pennies for Your Thoughts

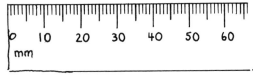

Goals: To measure in millimeters; to discover how small objects can be measured accurately by measuring multiple copies of them.
Materials: Cents; millimeter ruler

1. How thick is a cent? Use this millimeter ruler to find out. About _____ mm

You can measure the thickness of a cent more accurately if you measure a pile of cents, instead of just one. Make a pile of 10 cents and measure it. _____ mm Now, how thick would you say a cent is? _____ mm

How could you get an even more accurate measurement?

2. Which would you rather have, a pile of pennies as tall as your hand-span, or a row of pennies laid side by side as long as your height? (Refer to Activities 7 and 8 for your measurements in centimeters.)

Activity 17. All about Milk Cartons

Goals: To measure in centimeters; to measure area (square centimeters) and volume (cubic centimeters).

Materials: Milk carton (for convenience, the top can be removed so that the carton looks like those in the diagram); centimeter ruler; centimeter grid paper (see page 300); centimeter cubes

1. What can you measure about a milk carton? Try these.
   How tall is it? _____ cm
   How wide is it? _____ cm
   How deep is it? _____ cm
   If you wanted to cover the outside smoothly (with no overlaps) with centimeter grid paper, how many little squares would it take? _____
   Describe how you found your answer.
   How many centimeter cubes will fit inside it if you pack them carefully? _____ Describe how you found your answer.

2. Design some open boxes that will hold 1000 centimeter cubes. For each, find the height, width, depth, and surface area (how many little squares will cover it). Which has the greatest surface area? Which has the least? Could you design a box with greater surface area? with less surface area?

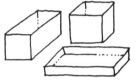

Activity 18. How Big is Your Foot?

Goals: To use a centimeter grid to measure the area of an irregular region; to explore how length, width, and area of footprints change as a person grows (in part 2). .

Materials: Centimeter grid paper (see page 300).

1. To the right is a tracing of the foot of a one-month-old baby on centimeter grid paper.
   How long is the foot (toe to heel)? _____ cm
   How wide is the foot? _____ cm
   How many little squares does the foot cover? _____
   Count them, estimating the total of all the fragments of squares. About _____ squares

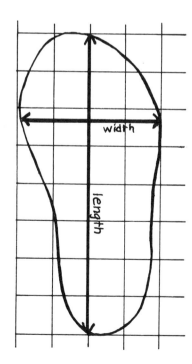

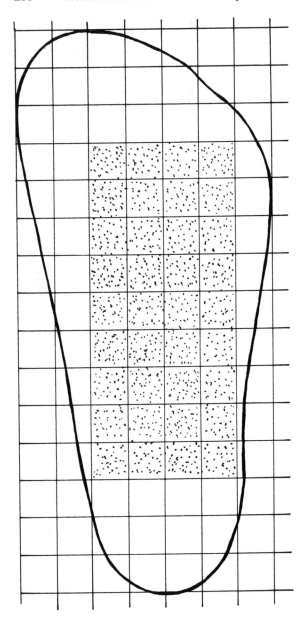

2. a. Here is a tracing of the foot of a four year old.
        How long is the foot? _____ cm
        How wide is the foot? _____ cm
        How many little squares does it cover?

        _____

        Note that the counting of squares can be simplified by looking for "blocks" of squares — an example is shaded. Again, estimate the total of all the fragments of squares. About _____ squares are covered.
    b. Trace your own foot on centimeter grid paper and find the same measurements.
        Length _____ cm
        Width _____ cm
        Number of squares covered _____
    c. How many times longer is the child's foot than the baby's foot? _____
        How many times wider is the child's foot than the baby's foot? _____
        How many times more squares does the child's foot cover than the baby's foot?

        _____

    d. Repeat the comparisons in part (c) using your own foot measurements. How does your foot compare to the baby's foot? Does the number of squares covered grow the same amount as the length or width?

DISCUSSION QUESTIONS AND COMMENTS

What Is Measurement?

The Activities in this chapter are designed to develop the concept of measurement of length, to extend and apply this concept, and to introduce physical measurement of other attributes of objects (area, volume). Measurement of any type and in any system (metric or English) involves certain basic principles. First, measurement is essentially a matter of comparison of the size or quantity (maybe length, or volume, or weight) of an object with some fixed size or quantity. This fixed size or quantity is called a *unit.* The statement that a piece of string is "3 units long" doesn't tell you much unless you know what unit was used to measure the string; it might be 3 centimeters, 3 inches, or 3 meters. Second, the unit we use depends on the size of the object being measured. For example, we use kilometers to measure the distance between cities, and centimeters for the width of this page. Third, measuring an object with a unit involves assigning some number to that object. For example, if a pencil is to be measured in centimeters, the number assigned might be 17. Fourth, measurement is always approximate. It is unlikely that objects you measure will be exactly the size of your unit or some multiple of the unit. For example, when you measured the picture of the paper clip in Activity 4, you probably said that it was 3 white rods, or 3 centimeters long. If you look closely at the picture to the right, you will find that in fact it is a little more. However it is certainly closer to 3 centimeters than to 4 centimeters, and so 3 centimeters was an appropriate answer. This difference between the length of the real object and the measured length (to some unit) is called *error of measurement* and is to be expected in any measurement situation. If a more precise description of the length of the paper clip were needed, it could be measured in millimeters. It is about _____ mm long. The smaller the unit, the smaller the possible error of measurement will be.

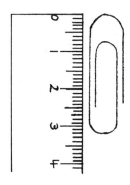

What Attributes of an Object Can You Measure?

As you saw in the Introduction, you can measure many different attributes of yourself — height, weight, age. Activities 1–10 in this chapter concentrated on measurement of length — how long, how tall, how wide, how thick — all of which can be measured with a ruler or tape measure. Appropriate units are centimeter, decimeter, meter, kilometer (or inch, foot, yard, mile). People measure length in many situations. A taxicab driver measures distance traveled on a trip; a carpenter plans the width and length of a bookshelf; a tailor measures the width of a seam or the length of binding needed for a hem.

An interior decorator has a different concern — not just with length, width, or height of a room, but also with wall space or floor space; that is, with *area.* Units for area should be regions that can cover a flat surface completely with no overlaps, such as tiles. Which objects drawn on page 246 could be used as units for area?

One possible nonstandard unit for area is a dollar bill. About how many dollar bills would cover this page? Standard units for area are derived from units for length — for example, square centimeters or square inches. Chapter 8, Geometry on a Geoboard, will discuss finding area of various geometric regions.

A milk salesperson has still another concern about size — with filling space, that is, with *capacity* of a carton (How much milk will fit into the carton?) and with *volume* of a carton (How many cartons will fit inside a crate or on a store refrigerator shelf?). Sometimes the words *capacity* and *volume* are used interchangeably. Which concept is involved (how much contained or how much space occupied) is usually clear from the context. Standard units for volume are also derived from units for length — for example, cubic inches or cubic centimeters. For capacity, we use pints, quarts, and gallons as standard units in the English system, and milliliters and liters in the metric system. You may measure volume or capacity when calculating how large a room is in order to find what size air conditioner is required; or when measuring ingredients for a cake and choosing a large enough pan to bake it in.

Finally, most of the food we eat is sold by *weight*. Standard units for weight are ounces and pounds in the English system, and grams and kilograms in the metric system.

Name some other attributes of things besides length, area, volume, capacity, or weight that we can measure.

Teaching Measurement — A Sequence of Activities

Children learn concepts of measurement gradually. Below are listed six types of measurement activities that should be done more or less in this sequence to help children to understand the process of choosing a unit (such as centimeter and meter), to estimate measurements, and to use devices (such as a ruler) to measure objects in the world around them.

Type of Activity	Activity
I	Compare objects, first directly, then indirectly
II	Measure with non standard units (such as hands, paper clips for length)
III	Select a unit, measure and estimate in this unit, using concrete materials (such as Cuisenaire rods)
IV	Extend measurement to related units (such as orange Cuisenaire rods or meter sticks)
V	Construct a measurement device (such as a ruler)
VI	Use the measurement device in measuring and estimating

(Types I, II, III, V, and VI should occur in that order; however activities of type IV might arise at various points between III and VI.) Complete the matching of Activities 1–10 on length with the six types of measurement activities. (There can be more than one activity matched to each type.)

Activities 1 2 3 4 5 6 7 8 9 10

Types I II III IV V VI

A teacher should try to motivate and give meaning to the measurement process through applications to the child's world. Each of the six types of activities can involve the child himself or objects which are familiar and interesting to him. Examples of measurement activities that are integrated into many aspects of the curriculum are discussed later.

This sequence of activities can serve as a guide for teaching other types of measurement, such as capacity, volume, or weight. While measurement of length is taught formally throughout elementary school, measurement of capacity and weight is often learned by children primarily through incidental measuring situations. Many classroom activities can give experiences with measuring — just how children measure when doing these activities will depend on their grade level and previous experiences with measurement. A sequence is given of ways in which children can measure capacity that corresponds to the sequence given for length. There are also indications of how these ways to measure can be incorporated into various activities — cooking, measuring soil for plants, planning a fish tank.

Materials for measuring capacity or volume can be of several types. Capacities can most easily be compared by pouring water or some other such flowing substance. But in some situations other materials are more appropriate; for example, cubes or blocks of various sizes are convenient for filling boxes and showing how volume can be found from other measurements. Two activities of type I are described below, one concentrating on comparison of liquid containers, and the other considering what materials could be used for measuring volume in other situations — for example, when containers do not hold water.

Type I. Comparison of Capacity

Materials: 2 containers; water
Which holds more? Guess, then check. (Children can check by pouring water or sand from one to the other.)

Materials: Various containers (some boxes, cylinders, irregular shapes, some that hold water, and some that do not); materials for filling (water, sand, rice, beans, marbles, centimeter cubes, larger cubes, styrofoam filling materials, etc.)
Which holds most? least? Arrange them in order. Which materials would be best to use to check your guess? Why? (If children discuss which materials are "better" for measuring, this activity might also concern choice of units for measurement.)

Children gain informal experience with questions like these at an early age, through water and sand play. Of course, children who do not conserve volume may have considerable difficulty with this type of question (as will be discussed in a Follow-up Section). In fact, adults will often be deceived by the shape of a container, and will not accurately predict which of two containers holds more! To reduce the confusion due to irregular shapes, a teacher might use containers that differ in only one way — perhaps have children compare

The goal of this type of activity is to help children learn what it means to be empty or full, to hold more or less, and to see how capacity can be compared directly with water or other materials.

Children might deal with these comparison questions in deciding which bowl will hold more and should be used for mixing a cake; which cage is larger and should be used for the rabbit in the class; which bucket holds more and should be used for fetching soil for planting.

Type II. Measuring Capacity with Nonstandard Units

Materials: Various containers (some boxes and some irregular shapes); small and large cups; rice; small and large cubes

How many small cupfuls of rice fit in the jar? How many large cupfuls? How many small cubes fit in the box? How many large cubes?

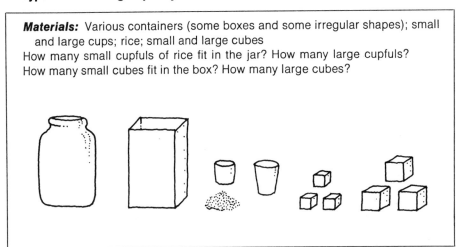

This type of measurement might arise when children are making modeling clay. A recipe might read "4 🥄cornstarch, 8 🥄baking soda, 5 🥄water. Cook over medium heat 4 minutes and cool." It does not matter what container is chosen as the "🥄" so long as it is used consistently throughout. This type of measurement might also arise when children are making pudding to serve in little paper cups. They have to ask themselves, how many servings can be made from one recipe that makes 1 quart? Children can check by filling up an empty quart carton with paper cupfuls of water.

Type III. Selecting a Unit, Estimating and Measuring Capacity with the Unit

Materials: Several containers; small plastic cup; rice or water
How many cups will it take to fill this container? Guess, then try it. Put your
  results in this table. Try it with other containers.

	Estimate	Measure
Jug		
Milk carton		

When children follow standard recipes using cups or milliliters, they will
need to do this type of measurement. It may also arise if the class gets a new
fish tank. Children may find that the type of fish they plan to get (guppies)
requires 6 cups of water for each fish (approximately 1 centimeter long). To
see how many fish can live in their tank, children will need to find the capacity
of the tank in terms of the standard unit, a cup.

Type IV. Extending Measurement to Related Units

Materials: 1 large jar; 1 large plastic cup and 1 small one; rice or water
How many small cupfuls will it take to fill the jar? Do you have a short-cut
  method to get the answer? (How many small cupfuls does it take to fill the
  large cup?)

This extension to other units will be suggested by any situation where a
large capacity is to be measured. In the example above involving the fish tank,
children will probably find that it is easier to see how many cups fill a quart
and then measure the fish tank in terms of quarts. Or when fetching soil in a
large bucket, they may measure the bucket to see if it will hold enough soil
for each child to plant a pot by first seeing how many potfuls of water will fill
a large can, and then measuring the bucket with the can. Another situation
where children might do this type of measurement is when making a rough
count of the number of beans in a jar. (See Chapter 2, Activity 4, Beans).
They might first count the number of beans in a spoonful, then see how many
spoonfuls fill a cup, and finally how many cupfuls fill the jar.

Type V. Construct a Measuring Device

Materials: Translucent container (plastic milk jug or bleach bottle); water colored with food coloring; small cup; marking pen
Use your small cup to fill the container, one cup at a time. Mark the level after each addition.

It may be particularly useful for children to make measures for metric capacity themselves if their school has only a few commercial ones. These student-made devices can be used for a variety of classroom measuring situations, especially for cooking from metric recipes.

Type VI. Using the Measurement Device

Materials: Graduated measure; water; various kitchen containers
Find some containers and estimate how many small cups of water will fill them. Then measure with your graduated measure. Fill in the table.

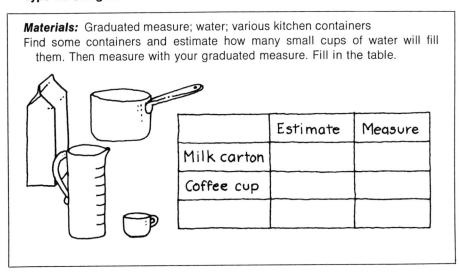

	Estimate	Measure
Milk carton		
Coffee cup		

Children can find many things to measure that fit into a broader pattern or scheme. They might use homemade graduated measures to find out how fast a bowl of water evaporates in their classroom — leaving a bowl of water undisturbed on the radiator, measuring the contents each day, and graphing it. Or they might measure how much water is wasted daily from a leaking faucet.

A teacher might want children to find the volume of something that is not a container. Children can use their experience with measuring capacity to measure the volume of other types of objects.

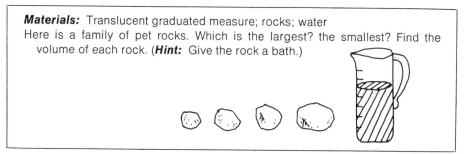

Materials: Translucent graduated measure; rocks; water
Here is a family of pet rocks. Which is the largest? the smallest? Find the volume of each rock. (**Hint:** Give the rock a bath.)

Children fill the container to a certain level with water, place the rock in the container, and note how much the water rises. (This approach is very useful for measuring, say, ¼ cup of butter for cooking. Fill a cup ½ full with water, and then add lumps of cold butter until the water level has risen sufficiently — that is, to ¾ — then drain the butter.) The same task can be done by filling a container to the top with water, placing the rock in the water, and measuring the overflow.

Six "measurement of weight" activities follow, but they are not listed in a sequence for children. Read them and then arrange them in the appropriate order for children to do them.

| (Type I) | (Type II) | (Type III) | (Type IV) | (Type V) | (Type VI) |

(**Note:** For these activities children can use a two-pan balance, as shown here, and a variety of objects including some standardized weights. The following activities use "cubeograms" — plastic cubes the size of white Cuisenaire rods that weigh 1 gram (g), the unit of weight in the metric system, and commercial weights in the sizes indicated.)

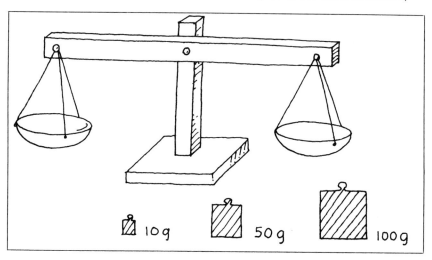

1. **Materials:** Weights (, ,); cubeograms; book; various small objects; two-pan balance

   How many cubeograms balance ? _____ ? _____ ? _____

   Use this information to find out how many cubeograms would balance your book. Make a table.

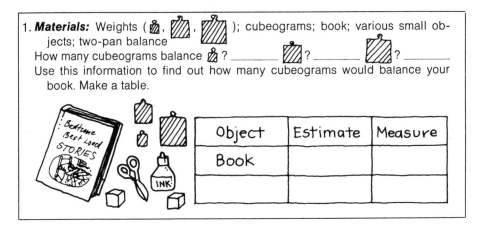

Object	Estimate	Measure
Book		

2. **Materials:** Apples, pennies, wooden cubes, washers, and other small objects; two-pan balance

   How many pennies balance the apple? How many wooden cubes balance the apple? What else could you use to balance the apple?

3. **Materials:** Plastic bags; colored rubber bands; sand; weights; two-pan balance

   Fill a bag with sand so that it and a rubber band *just* balance 10 cubeograms. Fasten it with a red rubber band and label it "10 g." Make four like this. Then fill a bag with sand so that it and a rubber band *just* balance 50 cubeograms. Fasten it with a blue rubber band and label it "50 g."

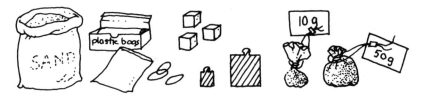

4. **Materials:** Apples and bananas; two-pan balance

   Which is heavier, an apple or a banana? Which apple is heaviest? lightest?

5. ***Materials:*** Pencils and other small objects; cubeograms; two-pan balance
How many cubeograms balance the pencil? Estimate, then measure. Fill in the table.

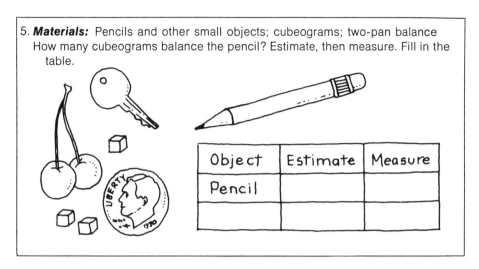

Object	Estimate	Measure
Pencil		

6. ***Materials:*** Plastic cup; water; weights; two-pan balance
Hold the plastic cup in your hand and fill it with water until you think it weighs as much as 50 grams. Then check your guess by weighing. Dump out the water and try the next one. Record your results in a table.

Weight You Were Trying to Make	Weight You Actually Made
50 grams	
150 grams	
80 grams	
20 grams	

What Difficulties Do Children Have Using a Ruler?

Even at the upper elementary and junior high levels, teachers often find that their students cannot use a ruler (either metric or English system) to measure length. Students tend to make several kinds of errors. Examine each "error pattern" below and on page 268. Use your 10 centimeter ruler. Work out the last exercise in each case as the child might have.

1. Grade 2 (child used a 10-centimeter ruler.)

Length __6__ cm   Length __5__ cm   Length ___ cm

Possible difficulty: _____

2. Grade 3 (Child used a 10-centimeter ruler.)

_____   _____   _____

Length _6_ cm   Length _8_ cm   Length ___ cm

Possible difficulty: _____

3. Grade 7 (Child used a ruler marked in millimeters.)

_____   _____   _____

Length _40_ mm   Length _20_ mm   Length ___ cm

Possible difficulty: _____

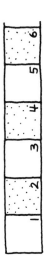

One cause for these types of difficulties is that the child does not understand the process of measurement as repeated placement of a unit. Such children may need activities of types II and III to help build this concept. Other children may have been given rulers without really understanding how they were made and what is their purpose: to provide an easy way to do repeated measurement without placing copies of the units. Difficulty (1), where children line up the end of the object to be measured with "1" on the ruler, may result from a lack of understanding that the "1" means that one unit lies to the left. (Instead they think of counting, and hence measuring, as starting at 1.) In measuring with concrete units (Cuisenaire rods) and *then* making a ruler, children build up a feeling for how to use the ruler. Thus an activity of type V is crucial in the sequence leading to skill with measurement devices. Some children may not be capable of progressing from use of repeated units to a ruler. Intermediary rulers made by pasting units on a strip of paper may help these children (see the diagram to the left). There are several reasons why children should construct their own measuring devices. First, they gain insight into what the measurement device is and how it is used. Second, it is less expensive. Also, if children have their own rulers, they can measure at home where measurement is particularly relevant. Finally, it is their own measurement device and they can take pride in making it themselves.

FOLLOW-UP SECTIONS

How Children Develop the Ability to Measure

Children develop the ability to deal with number and to measure length and weight gradually over a period of time. According to Piaget, children progress through an invariant age-related sequence of stages in developing these abilities. Piaget created many interview situations to discover just what children understand about measurement and the attributes that we measure (such as length, area, volume). In one situation, children were shown a tower built of blocks on a table, and were asked to build another tower — just as tall — on another table that was in fact lower than the first table. Children may first try to do this just by eye. Later they may try to check that the heights are the same by laying a stick across the tops (diagram A), and still later they might use the stick as a measuring device *vertically* to check that the two towers are the same height. (See diagram B.)

Piaget found that in many situations involving measurement, preoperational children (usually ages two through seven) were unable to think of more than one feature of a situation at a time — that is, they will consider only the *tops* of the towers (diagram A) and will not coordinate this aspect with the *bottoms* of the towers. This phenomenon is also seen in Piagetian experiments dealing with conservation of length and volume. For example, a test for conservation of length goes as follows: the interviewer shows a child two sticks that are arranged as in diagram C, and makes sure that the child agrees that the two sticks have the same length. Then the interviewer moves one stick as shown in diagram D. Some young children in the preoperational stage will say that the stick moved to the right is now longer. Such a child does not conserve length — that is, does not conceive of length as a property of an object that does not change when the position of the object is changed.

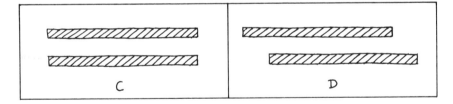

In another experiment, the interviewer arranges toothpicks as in diagram E, and describes these as two roads for an ant to crawl along. Preoperational children may agree that the ant has just as far to go on these two roads, but when one road is rearranged to be jagged, as in diagram F, they will say that now the ant has further to go if he takes the top road.

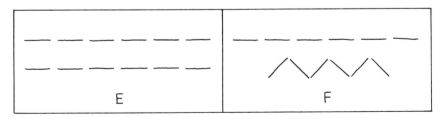

Children as old as nine or ten years may be unable to conserve volume. They might agree that containers A and B hold the same amount (diagram G), but then say that container C has more than A, after the interviewer has poured the water from B into C. These children center on one aspect of this situation — the height of the water in the container — and ignore the width of the container. Also, in the conservation tasks above, nonconservers are unable to reverse mentally the action involved (for example, pouring the liquid from B to C) and hence do not see what has remained invariant or been conserved (for example, the amount of water has not changed).

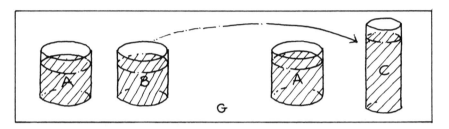

These findings should caution teachers not to take too much for granted about how well children understand measurement. Some educators feel that Piagetian research implies that children should not be taught a topic such as measurement of length until they are ready to learn it; that is, can conserve length. Others feel that children should be exposed to situations where their perceptions seem to mislead them. Teachers should encourage children to act out measurement situations and to talk about them. Teachers cannot *teach* children to conserve, but they can encourage children to experiment, talk about it, and add to their experience of the attributes being measured. Piaget's research also indicates that children's formal learning of measurement should begin with experiences of *comparison* (that is, type I) so that a teacher can observe whether children conserve the attribute being measured.

Piaget has also found that the concepts of length (of an object) and distance (between things, through space) are not equivalent in difficulty for young children; the latter seems to be much more difficult. Teachers can first give children many experiences with measuring lengths of objects before introducing distance — and, if necessary, introduce an object (such as a piece of string) to represent the distance physically.

Teachers should be encouraged to try Piagetian-type tasks informally to see for themselves just how children approach these tasks. Observation of children's performance can help teachers to plan appropriate readiness activities for measurement. Children in kindergarten and first grade can and should have a rich and varied experience of comparison and concrete measurement of various types — for examples, of placing concrete objects (blocks) end to end next to some object and counting them — but teachers should not be surprised if some children do not expect the same result when the object being measured is in a new position. In a sense these children are not measuring length (since "length" does not really mean much to them); however, these counting activities lay the foundation for later understanding of measurement concepts.

Young children may find it difficult to measure a length by using one unit repeatedly. Children at this level should be allowed to use multiple copies of the unit as long as they need. For example, if measuring across their class-room with their own feet, children could first stand on newspaper, trace their foot, then cut through several layers to have many copies at once. These can be laid end to end so children can *see* and count each footprint, rather than having to remember and imagine footsteps as they pace them out. Similarly, they might measure across a piece of paper by pasting on a row of uniform squares of colored paper, or by stamping out squares with a rubber stamp.

Where Does Measurement Arise in the Curriculum?

Very young children who play with blocks, at a water table, or in a sand box are experiencing and learning something about measuring length, area, volume, and weight — however, children do not have formal experience with units for area, volume, and weight until many years later. In general, children in the primary grades should experience plenty of measurement of types I, II, and III (comparison, measurement with nonstandard concrete units, and mea-surement with concrete standard units) and some activities of type IV in a very concrete way (measuring things with orange and white Cuisenaire rods) *be-fore* they work with a ruler. The emphasis is on measurement of length. In the upper elementary grades, children do activities of types V–VI for length, con-structing and using measuring devices in a variety of situations, and also activities of all types for area, volume, and weight. If these older children have not had measurement experiences of types I–IV, it will probably be necessary to provide such activities.

Mathematics programs may include separate units on measurement. However, measurement should not be taught *only* in these units, for measure-ment may be related to other topics in mathematics and also easily integrated into other parts of the curriculum. Integration of mathematics topics into other areas is desirable for several reasons: (1) A teacher may be able to use a child's interests to motivate learning and practice of mathematics skills. (2) Children learn more when practice of skills occurs frequently throughout the day and is not restricted to a mathematics lesson. (3) Mathematics will be useful to children only if they learn how and where it can arise in investigating the world around them.

Here are some classroom situations in which measurement activities (of *all* types, I–VI) are incorporated into other subject areas. As you read them, decide which involve measurement of length, area, volume, and weight.

> *Seesaws.* The kindergarten children were playing on a seesaw in the playground, and discovered that some of them seemed to have a dif-ficult time getting off the ground. The teacher had children come to the seesaw in pairs, each sit at just the same place, and decide which of the two was heavier, or were they just about the same weight?

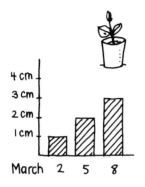

Growing Beans. A first grade class wanted to plant bean seeds in little paper cups, one for each child. The soil was to be donated by a friendly neighborhood garden store. How much soil should be gotten? The children had a big bucket. They measured with paper cups filled with water to see how far up the bucket should be filled so that they would all have enough soil to plant their seeds. They later kept a chart of how tall the beans had grown every few days by cutting pieces of ribbon to match the heights of their plants, and pasting them to grid paper marked in centimeters.

Swimming. Joanne, a second grader, came to school one day very pleased about her two new badges that showed she had been able to swim first 20, then 50 meters. Her teacher suggested that she take the class trundle wheel and use it to mark off the lengths in the hallway so that the class could see what she had done. It turned out that the hall was shorter than 50 meters, and so during playtime Joanne marked off her 50 meters in the playground.

Throwing a Ball. Some third grade children were very interested in baseball, and they wanted to see how far they could throw a ball. They organized a contest. The playground was measured with a long rope that was knotted at every meter. Some children wanted to see if their throw improved, and so they measured their throws every few weeks and kept a chart to see their progress.

Designing a Banner. A fourth grade class wanted to make a banner to cover a large stretch of wall. It was decided that each child should make one rectangular piece of felt and glue or sew a pattern on it. A few rectangles could be used for a title on the banner. How can they determine how big a piece each child should have? How should the the pieces be organized? The children measured the wall in decimeters and drew a scale drawing on square-centimeter paper. With the help of the scale drawing, they decided how to design their banner.

Social Studies. A fifth grade class was studying the neighborhood of the school. They first made a map and then a cardboard model of the four blocks surrounding the school. This project involved several field trips with meter sticks, trundle wheel, and a long rope that was marked (by knots) in meters. The construction of buildings from cardboard was done to scale using grid paper marked in centimeters.

Building Shelves. A sixth grade class built some shelves for their classroom (a project which in itself involved a lot of measuring). Then they wanted to paint their shelves. The paint catalogue said that 1 liter of paint covered 9 square meters. How much paint did they need?

Write three of your own ideas for integrating measurement into other areas of the curriculum. Try to vary age level, subject area, and type of activity involved.

1. Grade Level _____ Measurement of _____ (length, area, etc.) Type of activity (as on page 260) _____

2. Grade Level _____ Measurement of _____ Type of activity _____

3. Grade Level _____ Measurement of _____ Type of activity _____

Measurement can also be related to various other topics in mathematics. One important topic is the number line, which can be developed naturally from measurement of length; in particular, placing nonstandard units in a line to measure length and then constructing and using a related ruler. Early work in measuring length leads to the use of a number line for whole numbers, while later work suggests the location of fractions and decimals on a number line.

Another topic is place value, which can be related to measuring in the metric system where the units centimeter, decimeter, and meter provide concrete models for ones, tens, and hundreds (or for hundredths, tenths, and ones, depending on what one takes as the unit). This will be discussed further on.

Measurement is naturally woven into the study of geometry; for example, the study of patterns in and techniques for finding perimeter, area, and volume (which we will discuss in Chapter 8, Geometry on a Geoboard).

Applications of measurement can also provide practice of skills; for example, fourth grade children are reviewing addition of several three-digit numbers. The teacher poses the problem: How long a line would we form if we lay down end to end, one after the other? Children measure themselves (for example, 125 cm) and then decide on an efficient way to do this calculation.

The Metric System

The Activities in this chapter involved measurement either with nonstandard units, or with metric units. However the Activities could just as well be done with units of the English system. Up to this point, discussion has concerned the teaching of *measurement* rather than the teaching of the metric system. In this section, we will examine the history of the metric system, reasons for the imminent changeover from the English to metric system in the United States, and the special concerns of the elementary school teacher during and after this change.

The first Activities in this chapter involved using parts of the body as units of measure (hand, cubit, thumb). This type of measurement is ancient — it was used by the early Babylonians and Egyptians. The English system of measurement evolved from many such measures in a variety of earlier cultures. For example, it is said that one inch was the length of three barley corns laid end to end; a yard was a standard pace; a mile was the distance marched by a Roman army in one hour. As a result, these units were not intentionally related to one another. As commerce became more distant and sophisticated, measures became standardized, sometimes in arbitrary ways. Legend says that King Henry I of England (early twelfth century) decreed that a yard should be the distance from the tip of his nose to the end of his thumb. The English system was standardized by the eighteenth century and was adopted in many parts of the world, in particular in English colonies (including America). However the system has drawbacks arising from its unplanned and somewhat accidental development. For example, there are many numbers to remember — *12* inches = 1 foot, *3* feet = 1 yard, _____ yards = 1 mile, _____ ounces = 1 pound, _____ quarts = 1 gallon. This can lead to complicated arithmetic when you convert from one unit to another.

The metric system of measurement had a quite different sort of history. Several individuals, especially scientists, saw the advantages of a carefully planned system of measurement. Such a system was not fully developed until 1790, during the French Revolution, when the French Academy of Sciences appointed a commission to "deduce an invariable standard for all the measures and all the weights." The meter, the fundamental unit of length, was defined to be one ten-millionth of the distance from North Pole to equator, along a longitude passing through Paris — an enduring standard, as opposed to a king's arm span. To make the system of measurement coincide with the way numbers are written (that is, base 10), other units for length were created by multiplying or dividing the meter by 10 and its multiples (and addition of prefixes to indicate these multiples — for example, kilo-, centi-). Units for volume and weight (or mass) were defined in terms of the units for length, as we shall see below. Thus the entire system of measurement was designed to be easy to handle computationally (since it is based on powers of 10) and logically interrelated, thus much more appropriate for scientific and technological use than the English system.

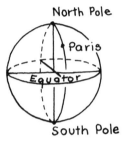

The metric system became compulsory in France in 1840, and its use spread rapidly throughout the world as technology advanced.[2] In the United States, metric units have been recognized legally since 1866. In 1875, the United States and sixteen other countries signed an international treaty, the Metric Convention, that established agreement about procedures for adopting further refinements of the system. Since 1893, even in the United States, metric standards have been used to define English units for weights and measures.

By 1975, the United States was the only major industrial nation not committed to conversion to the metric system. This isolation is a disadvantage in international trade and scientific communication (for example, the Common Market countries will now import products measured only in metric units), and also because our current system is much harder to work with than need be. In December, 1975, Congress passed and the president signed into law the Metric Conversion Act ensuring that the United States will convert to the metric system of measurement. Many products are already sold in metric containers (for example, 2-liter bottles of soft drinks) and if you look around you, you will see metric equivalents on many items that are sold by English units.

Teachers in the coming years will find themselves responsible for teaching children who will live their adult lives in a metric world. This presents special challenges to teachers who themselves find the metric system unfamiliar and hence perhaps a bit frightening. Activities in this chapter were designed to give you an intuitive feel for the metric units of length. Adults may want to estimate a length in centimeters by thinking inches, then converting to metric by a formula. This approach, however, is much more difficult, even for adults, than taking the time to learn the new language and to think in the metric units. "Think Metric!" is a slogan adopted by the National Council of Teachers of Mathematics. You will probably find it helpful to associate some common object or part of your body with each commonly used metric unit.

The Prefix System

You have seen the prefixes kilo-, centi-, deci-, and milli- applied to the metric unit *meter* to name new units for measuring length. In the same way, these prefixes and other rarer ones can be affixed to the other metric units, *gram* (for weight), or *liter* (for capacity). That is,

$$1 \text{ kilometer } = 1000 \text{ meters}$$
$$1 \text{ kilogram } = 1000 \text{ grams}$$
$$1 \text{ millimeter } = \frac{1}{1000} \text{ meter}$$
$$1 \text{ milliliter } = \frac{1}{1000} \text{ liter}$$

The complete range of prefixes is written below — but, as we discuss the various units, we shall see that only some of the terms are in common use.

Kilo-	Hecta-	Deka-	—	Deci-	Centi-	Milli-
1000	100	10	1	$\frac{1}{10}$	$\frac{1}{100}$	$\frac{1}{1000}$
⌞——— (Greek origin)———⌟				⌞———(Latin origin)———⌟		

There are other words in our language that have the same origins as these prefixes. For example, you might look up the origins of the words decimate, centipede, and millennium. Can you think of other words with these stems? There are other prefixes for even smaller and larger quantities: *micro-* means one-millionth or .000001, and *mega-* means one million or 1,000,000. However scientists usually will modify one unit, say a meter, by using exponential notation, (for example, 10^6 meters instead of 1 megameter).

Measurement of Length

As we have seen, the *meter* is the basic unit of length. Do you now have a "feel" for how long it is? A meter is

a little longer than a yard.
about the height of a doorknob.
about as far as you can stretch your finger tips from your nose.
about the length of a baseball bat.

Write two more.

Meters are or will be used to measure such things as athletic fields, swimming pools, and the distance to a stop sign. Write two more.

For larger distances, we use 1000 meters, or 1 *kilometer.* It is difficult to visualize this distance — perhaps it helps to know that a kilometer is four long city blocks. Most people walk a kilometer in about 10–15 minutes. New national highway speed limits will be about 90 kilometers per hour. Name something which is about 1 kilometer from where you are now.

For smaller measurements, we can use decimeters. Actually these are rarely used as units for measuring in real life. However activities involving orange rods (together with meter sticks and white rods) help children to learn the relationships between the units decimeter, centimeter, and meter. A decimeter is

the length of an orange Cuisenaire rod;
about the width of a piece of packaged bread.

Write one more.

More commonly *centimeters* are used for everyday measurement. A centimeter is

the length of a white Cuisenaire rod;
about the width of the iris of your eye.
a little more than the width of a standard paper clip.

Write two more.

Centimeters are or will be used to measure such things as width of fabric for sewing, sizes of paper (this is about 19 cm by 23.5 cm), and lengths of ribbon. Write two more.

Millimeters are used for even more precise measurements. A millimeter is

about the thickness of a dime;
about the thickness of wire in a paper clip.

Write two more.

Millimeters are or will be used to measure such things as camera film (35 millimeters), cigarettes (the new 100's and 120's), and nuts and bolts. Write two more.

Measurement of Area

Area is measured by units derived from the units for length. Small areas might be measured by square centimeters, the area of this square. The fingernail of your little finger may have an area of approximately one square centimeter (or 1 cm²). A slice of toast has an area of about one square decimeter. The tops of some tables have an area of about one square meter. For larger measurements of area — for example, for measuring a field — the metric unit is a *hectare,* the area of a square 100 meters on a side, or 10,000 square meters. (Hectare is actually the prefix *hecta-* or 100 affixed to the rarely used unit *are,* which is the area of a square 10 meters on a side, or 100 square meters.)

About how many square decimeters (pieces of toast) would fit on this page? _____ About how many white Cuisenaire rods would fit on a square decimeter? _____ on this page? _____ This page measures about _____ square decimeters or _____ square centimeters.

Which unit, square centimeters, square decimeters, square meters, or hectares would be most reasonably used to measure each of the following:

Land that belongs to a farm _____
Area of a footprint _____
Land used for a flower garden _____
Paper used to wrap this book as a present _____
Amount of silver sheet that is needed to make a bangle bracelet _____
Area of shelves in a classroom so that the amount of paint needed can
    be calculated _____

Area measurement is defined in terms of covering a region with units. Most often area is *not* found by measuring directly with a unit but rather by computation from formulas involving length measurement. (For example, you probably remember formulas for measuring the area of rectangles, triangles, or circles.) Such formulas will be discussed in Chapter 8, Geometry on a Geoboard. However children should experience direct measurement of area with concrete units *first* to see why the formulas are just shortcut ways to do the direct measurement.

Measurement of Volume

As with area, volume is measured in units derived from the metric units for length. Most commonly used is the *cubic centimeter* (often symbolized *cc*), which is the volume of a white Cuisenaire rod. Medicine bottles sometimes use this unit.

Similarly, we can measure with a *cubic meter.* Children can build a "skeleton" of a cubic meter from meter sticks, and see how many of them could fit inside. Could you sit inside a cubic meter? _____ Could someone else join you there?

Imagine three amounts of liquid — a cubic centimeter, a cubic decimeter, and a cubic meter. Which of these amounts do you think you would be most likely to use for measuring in everyday life?

For liquid capacity, the most commonly used unit is a *liter* (L). This is defined to be the capacity of a cubic decimeter.
Note: The unit *liter* is commonly symbolized with a capital "L" because a lowercase "l" can easily be confused with the numeral "1." Sometimes the symbol ℓ (script "l") is also used, but this is less convenient since it does not appear on most typewriters.

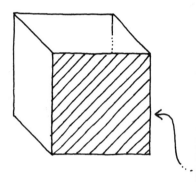

You can build a cardboard cubic decimeter. Each face should be the size of the square around these words. Tape five squares together, leaving the top open. It will hold a liter.

You can use it to measure water if you construct it from heavy cardboard and line it with a plastic bag.

A liter is a little more than a quart, and we can expect to see liter bottles of milk on grocery shelves.

How many white Cuisenaire rods would fit in this box?

(Hint: How many would fit in a layer on the bottom? How many layers would there be?)

Using metric prefixes, we can derive other units for capacity from a liter. The most commonly used one is a *milliliter* (mL), one-thousandth of a liter — the capacity or volume of a white Cuisenaire rod or a cubic centimeter.

Match each object on the left below with its approximate measurement of volume or capacity on the right. Some measurements will remain unmatched.

Chestnut	2 cubic centimeters
	8 cubic centimeters
Marble	10 cubic centimeters
Coffee cup	20 cubic centimeters
Quart bottle	175 milliliters
	500 milliliters
Orange Cuisenaire rod	946 milliliters
Gas tank of a Volkswagen	38 liters
	100 liters

Occasionally two other units for capacity are used: A *centiliter* (cL) is

one-hundredth of a liter, or _____ milliliters;
the volume of _____ white Cuisenaire rods.

A *deciliter* (dL) is
    one-tenth of a liter, or _____ milliliters;
    the volume of _____ white Cuisenaire rods.

Which unit — liter, deciliter, centiliter, or milliliter — would you use to measure each of the following:

    Amount of milk a cow produces in a month
    Amount of milk in a cake recipe
    Amount of liquid to be given in a dose of cough syrup
    Bottle of wine
    Amount of liquid in a perfume bottle

> **Note:** Several answers are acceptable for some of these. For example, bottles or carafes of wine in Europe are sometimes marked .75 L (Portugal), sometimes 7.5 dL (Switzerland), and sometimes 75 cL (France). The most common units, however, are milliliters and liters.

If children graduate a jar to make their own device for measuring capacity (see page 264, type V activity), they will probably find it convenient to use a unit of one deciliter, or 100 milliliters. One can find small plastic containers that hold a little more than 100 milliliters. Using a standard measure children can mark 100 mL on these cups and use them to make other measures.

If children want to measure the volume of smaller things, they might use a tall thin pill bottle and graduate it in steps of 10 mL.

Measurement of Weight

One elegant aspect of the metric system is that the unit of weight (or, more correctly, mass)[3] is defined in terms of volume measurement. A *gram* is the weight of one cubic centimeter of water at a temperature just above freezing. (The temperature is 4° Celsius, at which water has its maximum density.) If you were to make a little box the size of a white Cuisenaire rod, the amount of ice cold water it held would weigh one gram. A gram is

    the weight of a cubeogram;
    about the weight of a paper clip (although this is variable).

Write two more.

It is difficult for most people to have a "feel" for weights as small as these. A more accessible unit is the *kilogram,* which is 1000 grams. As you saw above, there are 1000 cubic centimeters or white Cuisenaire rods in a liter, and so a liter of ice cold water weighs 1000 grams or 1 kilogram. Since a liter is a little more than a quart, a kilogram is a little more than the weight of a quart carton of milk. (In fact a kilogram is about 2.2 pounds.) In the future we will probably buy meat and vegetables by the kilogram. Meat that now costs about $2 a pound can be expected to cost about $_____ a kilogram.

Grams and kilograms are the most common units for everyday measurement. Which unit, gram or kilogram, would you expect to use in each of the following situations:

Weighing flour for a batch of cookies
Buying herbs or spices
Weighing yourself
Weighing gold for a ring

For much larger weights, one uses the metric ton, which is 1000 kilograms. This is the weight of one cubic meter of cold water, and is a little more than an English ton. Grain and coal, for example, are sold in large quantity by the metric ton.

Measurement of Temperature

You may have heard radio announcements that say it is 10° Celsius — how should you dress? At present Celsius temperatures are usually given at the same time as Fahrenheit temperatures, and if you have a good memory for numbers, you may learn to associate Celsius measurements with various types of weather.

C°
120°
100° Water boils (212° Fahrenheit)
80°
60°
37° Normal body temperature
20° Average room temperature
0° Water freezes (32° Fahrenheit)
-20°

The Celsius scale is conveniently designed so that water freezes at 0° Celsius and boils at 100° Celsius. Unlike many other attributes that we measure directly (such as length, width, volume), we cannot describe a *unit* of temperature with which we measure by repeated placement of the unit. Rather we measure temperature only indirectly through reading a scale on a thermometer. Before learning to read a scale, children should have many physical experiences with the attribute of temperature, such as describing and ordering hot, warm, cold, and icy water, or discussing how the weather affects what we wear.

To build up a feel for the metric measurement of temperature, you should measure, record, and arrange many different temperatures. For example, you — or school children — might make a bulletin board. Each child should use a Celsius thermometer to measure several different things, places, and times. Then they might draw pictures of the things on small file cards and note the temperatures. These cards can then be collected and fastened to a bulletin board as shown here.

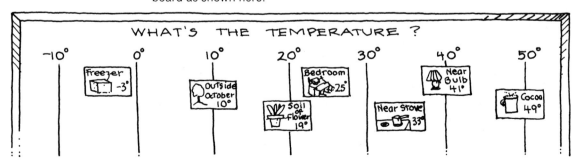

Children might also measure temperature in a more methodical way. They might keep a daily record of the outdoor temperature at 10 A.M. and make a graph over several months. Or they might boil some water, put it in a coffee cup, measure the temperature every five minutes as it cools to room temperature, and make a graph. They might also start with a glass of ice water and record how fast it warms to room temperature. They might try various experiments — what happens if the water is in a styrofoam cup? in a paper cup? in a china cup?

Introducing Metric Units for Length

In Activities 1–10, the first standard unit introduced was the white Cuisenaire rod or centimeter (Activity 5). Later this unit was used to introduce related units — decimeter and meter — needed to measure larger objects. Since *meter* is the root word, it might seem more logical to you to present this unit to children first, and then use it to define centimeter and decimeter. However, there are reasons for children to begin with the smaller units.

1. It is desirable for children to have a great deal of hands-on experience measuring. It is usually not very practical to have every child in a class measuring lengths of several meters, but it is quite feasible to have each child measure objects that are 1 to 50 centimeters long; that is, things that will easily fit on a desk. Also, children can easily make and carry around their own centimeter rulers.
2. In grades 1–2 children do not yet understand the notion of tenth and hundredth, which is usually developed later in grades 3–5 when fractions and decimals are studied. However they can describe a meter in terms of centimeters (as 100 centimeters). In these grades, building up decimeters and meters from centimeters can reinforce children's understand of counting 1–100 and of place-value notation.

In the upper grades (4–8) you might want to begin with the meter when introducing metric units to children who understand the meaning of measurement, but who have not yet been exposed to the metric system.

The Metric System and Place-Value Topics

Problem-solving situations involving measurement can provide both practical and intriguing ways to develop and practice basic computation skills (see page 273). The metric system is a base-10 system for measurement, and hence will be particularly valuable for developing and reinforcing many place-value topics in a way that was not possible in the English system.

Place-value topics at the lower elementary school level mainly concern whole numbers 1–999. The metric system provides a convenient model for these numbers, where the unit is the centimeter (white Cuisenaire rod), the ten is the decimeter (orange rod) and the hundred is a meter (meter stick). Using this model, 123 can be represented by one meter stick, two orange rods, and three white rods, which also shows 123 as 1 hundred + 2 tens + 3 ones, or 100 + 20 + 3. This metric model for place value can also be inter-related with another place-value model, money. Children could "shop" for lengths of wood (white and orange Cuisenaire rods and meter sticks) where the wood costs 1¢ for 1 cm, 10¢ for 10 cm or 1 dm, and 100¢ for 100 cm or

1 m. They might want to buy as much wood as their height (say 123 cm). They would find that they could buy it by paying for 1 meter stick, 2 orange rods, and 3 white rods, that is, 100¢ + 20¢ + 3¢. On the other hand, they could also buy it by choosing 12 orange rods and 3 white rods. Another type of problem might be: what pieces of wood could you buy if you have 36¢?

At the upper elementary level, place-value topics are extended to larger whole numbers (1–1,000,000) and decimal fractions (such as, 1.04, .375). Here the metric system provides a natural model for decimal fractions: the meter is 1, a decimeter (orange rod) is $\frac{1}{10}$ or .1, a centimeter (white rod) is $\frac{1}{100}$ or .01, and a millimeter is _____ or _____. Using this model, the following can be illustrated: the meaning of decimal fractions (for example, .05 as 5 cm, .002 as 2 mm); equivalence of decimal fractions (for example, .20 = .2 because 20 cm = 2 dm); expanded numerals (.15 = .1 + .05 because 15 cm = 1 dm + 5 cm). Measuring and finding the perimeter of a rectangle provides practice in adding decimals. Division of decimals can even be acted out; for example, .36 ÷ .06 = ☐ means how many 6 cm lengths are in 36 cm? This place-value model can also be related to money, with 1 m, 1 dm, and 1 cm costing $1, $.10, and $.01, respectively.

Methods of conversion from one metric unit to another one are related to place-value and decimal notation. The diagram below can be used to strengthen children's understanding of this relationship.

decimeters

centimeters

millimeters

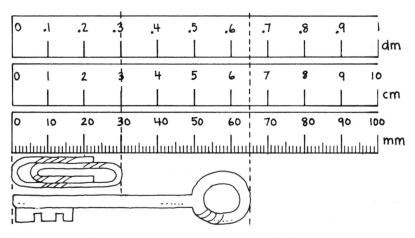

Children can use this chart to see that, for example, .3 dm = 3 cm = 30 mm (see the paper clip) or that .65 dm = 6.5 cm = 65 mm (see the key).

Draw in the dotted lines that would show other ways to write the measurements below, and complete.

.8 dm = _____ cm = _____ mm
_____ dm = 4.5 cm = _____ mm
_____ dm = _____ cm = 6 mm

Do you see how children could use this approach to convert meters to decimeters, centimeters or millimeters? For example, complete the following, and imagine using a diagram like the one on page 282:

.6 m = _____ dm = _____ cm = _____ mm

_____ m =   12 dm = _____ cm = _____ mm

_____ m = _____ dm =   12 cm = _____ mm

_____ m = _____ dm = _____ cm =   132 mm

Could you use this approach on a graduated capacity measure (see pages 259–260) to show the relationship between liters and milliliters? For example, complete the following:

2.2 L = _____ mL   750 mL = _____ L

Already there is agreement that the coming conversion to the metric system of measurement (and also the widespread availability of inexpensive hand-held calculators) will soon influence the elementary school curriculum. In particular, the close connection between the metric system and decimal notation may lead to an earlier introduction of decimal fractions in elementary school, and also to a deemphasis of fractions which in everyday life arise most often when measuring in the English system (for example, 3/8-inch buttons, 1/16-inch wire, 1/4 cup of milk).

Some Challenges and Difficulties in Teaching the Metric System

Why Not Learn Metric by Conversions?

People tend to hang on to what is familiar to them. Since most of us were raised "thinking English" about measurement, we may approach a metric estimation of length by first estimating in inches, and then converting by a formula. Such an approach is for adults only, and probably then only for a few in technical fields where exact conversions are important. It is certainly not appropriate for children who do not yet have a firm notion of what the English units represent. It may take a great many years before English units disappear from everyday use, and it is expected that mathematics programs will have children measuring in both systems. If children have sufficient experiences with nonstandard units, it should not be difficult for them to accept that sometimes one uses one unit, and sometimes another. But before long, metric measurements will be dominant in our society, and it will be inefficient to think of these units in terms of the receding English ones. Many activities in this chapter have involved estimation and hunting for objects of certain measurements. Through activities of these types children will form more and more accurate "internal rulers," and the use of metric units in measurement will become as natural to them as any other meaningful everyday vocabulary.

For upper elementary school children who do already have a solid basis in the English system, activities such as the following might help them to discover the relationship between the English system and the metric system, and thus to see where a conversion formula comes from.

Estimate How Long

Materials: 3 lengths of dowel, marked A, B, and C; meter stick or tape
Directions:

1. Guess how long each stick is. Check with a meter stick. Make a table like the one below.

	Estimate	Measure
Stick A		
Stick B		
Stick C		

2. These three lengths have other names. Do you know them? They are inch, foot, and yard. Measure each to the nearest millimeter, and make a table like this one.

	English	Metric
Stick A	1 inch	_____ mm or _____ cm
Stick B	1 foot	_____ mm or _____ cm
Stick C	1 yard	_____ mm or _____ cm

A Note about Converting Sensibly. If you *do* find yourself in a position where it is necessary to convert an English measurement to a metric measurement, at least do it sensibly. For example, you might be "translating" an old knitting pattern that tells you to knit 3 inches of ribbing. Some people might look at a table and find that 1 inch is 2.54 cm, and so 3 inches is 3×2.54 cm, and translate this direction as "knit 7.62 cm of ribbing." This accuracy of measurement is quite inappropriate for the situation. It would be more sensible to say "knit 8 cm of ribbing," or possibly "knit 7.5 cm of ribbing." It is hoped that legislators are sensible when it comes to changing highway speed signs. The national highway speed limit of 55 miles per hour translates (by the formula 1 mi = 1.6093 km) to 88.5115 kilometers per hour. We hope that this will be rounded off to the easily read figure of 90 kilometers per hour, rather than to 88 kilometers per hour which by the letter of the law is now the speed limit in terms of kilometers per hour.

What Is the Teacher's Role in Metric Conversion?

While the United States is gradually changing to the metric system, teachers will find themselves assuming a major part of the responsibility for educating the next generation, and possibly the present generation, in the metric system. Parents of today's school children may be alarmed and confused by the work their children are doing in school if they do not understand it. Teachers can help to "spread the metric word" to parents and to the community in several ways. First, teachers can give children assignments to do at home that will help to explain the metric system to parents. For example, if children have made centimeter rulers, they might take them home and measure certain things about people in their family — handspans, width of smile, etc. Second, teachers can plan bulletin boards for the school that focus on building concepts of metric measurements. These may be seen by school personnel, other teachers, children, and also visiting parents. Children can also make signs with metric distances (as described in Activity 11, part 2). Third, teachers might have their children prepare metric displays for local places of business — for example, in a grocery store to explain what is meant by the metric markings on food packages. Finally, teachers might find that parents of their students would appreciate a metric workshop, in which adults can begin to build some feeling for the metric units and learn about why the country is going metric, and why their children should not be taught by a direct "conversion" method.

Watch Your Tongue! No Four-Letter Words, Please! (~~Foot, Inch, Yard, Mile~~)

Children hear units of measurement mentioned by adults long before they begin to use them formally. Of course, children will hear their parents talk about how many miles to drive, how many yards of fabric, how many quarts of milk. But teachers can help children to accept metric units as equally natural by using them whenever they might arise in speech and writing. In physical education class, ask a child to move over a few centimeters, rather than to move over a few inches. Describe how you walked for kilometers and kilometers, not miles and miles! It may be difficult to change your everyday speech in this way, but hearing metric units informally in this way will be of help to school children.

What Can You Do About Equipment?

Each child learning about measurement needs hands-on experiences with measuring equipment. Some teachers may feel that it is difficult or impossible to start teaching metric measurement because their school does not have sufficient quantity of metric measuring devices, and school budgets will not allow purchase of new equipment at this time. Of course, a school should have at least one set of standard measuring devices (for example, centimeter cubes, weights, capacity measures), but, from them, teachers and children can construct other sets for classroom use. When children construct their own measuring devices, there are other benefits besides saving money. First, children will learn more about the meaning of measurement through making measuring tools themselves. Second, they may feel more personally involved, and will be likely to use the measuring equipment carefully. Finally, if children have their own very inexpensive measuring materials, they can be asked to take them home to measure all sorts of things around them, thus developing an appreciation of how measurements relate to everyday situations.

If they have centimeter cubes or white Cuisenaire rods, children can easily make their own 10-centimeter rulers as outlined in Activity 6, Making a Ruler. They can also make meter tapes or sticks from the plan in Activity 9, Some Other Units.

For measurement of volume, one set of standard measures can be used

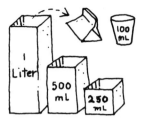

to supply each child with a little cup marked to hold 100 mL, and children can use these to graduate their own liter measures. Also it is useful to know that if you cut a one quart milk carton along the fold, the resulting open container will hold just about one liter. (The milk companies must leave a little extra room.) Children could cover these cut-off cartons with self-adhesive plastic and mark them "1 LITER." They could also cut cartons to one-half of the height and one-quarter of the height to get measures for 500 mL and 250 mL. These containers could be used in metric cooking activities.

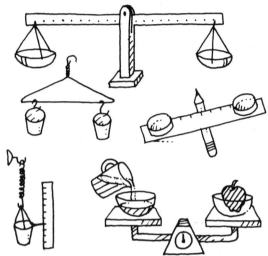

As for measuring weight, a two-pan balance is not an especially metric device — many schools have had them for years. One can also adapt a "mathematical balance beam" (see diagram) by suspending paper cups or plastic bowls at each end. Simple balances can be made from a piece of wood (possibly a ruler balanced on a pencil), or from a coat hanger, paper clips, and paper cups. Children can also design their own spring scales, using a metal spring or a piece of sewing elastic. From one set of standard metric weights children can make many other sets, as described on page 266, Activity 3. (In fact, a nickel can be used as a standard weight since it weighs about 5 grams.) Children can also measure weights of objects with water, if they have accurate capacity measures. That is, balance the object with water, and then measure how much water was required. (For example, 250 mL of water weighs 250 g.)

Some measuring equipment for the English system can be adapted for the metric system. One can put tape over the scale on a thermometer and relabel it, and similarly one can relabel spring scales.

A great deal of metric measuring equipment is on the market today. Teachers should examine this material carefully to get ideas for homemade substitutes and ways to adapt other equipment, and to request purchase of supplies that are really necessary.

Providing Further Practice of Estimation and Measurement

How Well Do You Estimate in Centimeters?

Estimation is an important aspect of measurement. For this activity, use the pictures of objects on page 246 (although you could also use any collection of objects).

First, for each object listed, *estimate* the described length in centimeters, and enter your estimate in the appropriate column in the table.

Then, when you have estimated *all* of the lengths, use your ruler to measure them, and enter the measurements in the appropriate column in the table.

Do you think that you can estimate lengths in centimeters well? You can see how well you estimate by making a graph of your results on a piece of graph paper like the one shown on page 287.

Notice that on this piece of graph paper, the horizontal axis is marked "Measurement" and the vertical axis is marked "Estimate." This means that if, for example, the actual measurement was 6 cm and you estimated 5 cm, you would start at the lower left corner, go *over* 6 spaces and *up* 5 spaces, and put a dot at this point.

Do this for each object that you estimated and measured.

Notice that if you estimated perfectly, you would place a dot on the diagonal line.

What does it mean if you placed a dot *above* the line?

Do you consistently overestimate or underestimate? Are you better on short things than on long ones?

Note: A graph of this type could be made to show estimates versus measurements of volume or weight. It could also show other relationships between two sets of numbers (for example, children's age versus height, or height versus weight).

Object	Esti-mate	Mea-sure
Length of ball-point pen		
Length of safety pin		
Width of paper clip		
Perimeter of small stamp		
Length of library card		
Length of pencil		
Diagonal of library card		
Length of bigger stamp		
Length of pocket knife		
Width of eraser		
Length of fork		
Length of rubber band (if cut and opened up)		
Length of longest key		

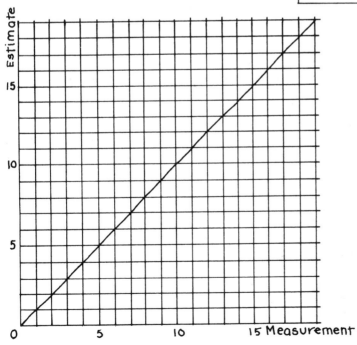

Metric Hunts

Children can go on "metric hunts" such as those described below in their classrooms, or at home, if they have their own homemade measuring equipment. You can adapt the choice of objects to the children's level and interests.

Length and Area. Try these yourself, using your homemade centimeter ruler or meter tape (see Activity 9, Some Other Units).

Find and Measure. . .

	Estimate	Measure
The length of your toothbrush.	_____	_____
The height of your dining table.	_____	_____
The length of your bed.	_____	_____
The area of your bathroom mirror.	_____	_____
The area of the top of your dining table.	_____	_____

Can You Find? ? ?

An object measuring 8 cm.	_____
An object measuring 4 dm.	_____
A distance of 3 m.	_____
A surface with area 1 square meter.	_____

Which of these two metric hunts do you think children would enjoy more? Why?

Capacity. Children can do activities such as the two above for capacity instead of length or area, but, of course, they must have appropriate measuring devices. Some homes already have metric capacity measures (because many everyday cooking implements are now being sold with markings for both cups and milliliters) — however many children may not have access to this equipment. Children can make their own very inexpensive capacity measures, earlier, and use them to do homework assignments such as the one below. Try them, if you have the appropriate measuring device.

Find and Measure. . .

	Estimate	Measure
The capacity of a glass you would use for juice.	_____	_____
The capacity of the most commonly used cooking pot in your kitchen.	_____	_____
The capacity of your bathroom sink.	_____	_____
Another.	_____	_____

Can You Find? ? ?

A container that holds 50 mL.	_____
A container that holds 200 mL.	_____
A container that holds 500 mL.	_____
A container that holds 1 L.	_____

Weight. It is a bit more complicated to provide children with equipment so that they can go on metric hunts for weight at home. It is not difficult to provide children with their own standard weights — they can make them as described on page 266 or use common objects (a nickel weighs about 5 g and a quart of milk in a cardboard carton weighs about 1 kg). The difficulty is for children to find or make a scale or balance. It is a nice challenge for them to rig up equipment with everyday materials, as illustrated on page 286. However, if this seems too difficult or time consuming an assignment, you could have children bring to school objects from home that they *estimate* to be appropriate, and check them on the school's measuring equipment. A sample might be as follows:

Find and Measure. . .

	Estimate	Measure
The weight of your toothbrush.	_____	_____
The weight of a can of soup (compare the measurement with the label.)	_____	_____
Another.	_____	_____

Can You Find? ? ?

An object weighing 10 g.	_____
An object weighing 100 g.	_____
An object weighing 500 g.	_____
An object weighing 1 kg.	_____

Make a Weighing Device

As mentioned above, it can be complicated for children to have and use their own metric devices. Here are instructions for an easily portable gadget that children could make, suitable for measuring weights less than 100 grams or so.

Materials: cardboard; carbon paper; 2 paper clips; paper fastener; paste; scissors; paper punch; something heavy (washer or rock); standard weights (nickels are appropriate — they weigh about 5 grams)

Directions:

1. Trace the three pieces on page 290 onto cardboard (use carbon paper) and cut out. Punch holes as shown. Cut a small square of thick cardboard (about 2 cm by 2 cm) to paste between the "arms" B and C, to keep them apart.

2. Assemble your weighing device. Paste the square between arms B and C, and fasten the arms on either side of the wheel A with a paper fastener through the holes marked "x." Use a paper clip to fasten something heavy at the bottom of the wheel (hole "y") and use a paper clip on the longer extension of the wheel (to hole "z") to hold the things you are going to weigh. (You can put things in a small plastic bag if convenient.)

3. Use a set of standard weights (5 or 10 grams) to graduate your weighing device. First, mark the position of the arrow when nothing is hanging. Then, hang weights and mark where the arrow points.

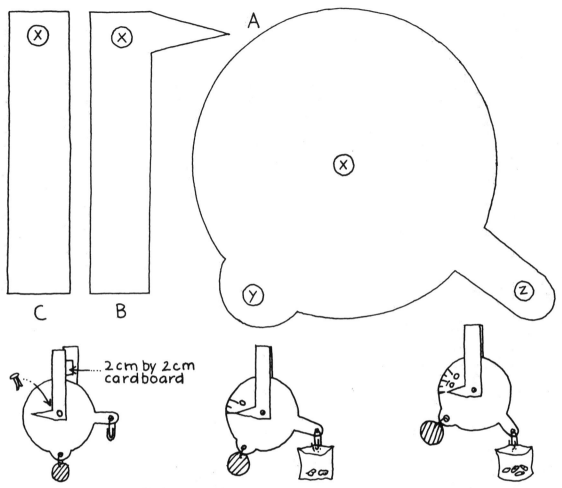

C   **B**

2 cm by 2 cm cardboard

Variations: The weighing device can be modified to be either more or less sensitive, either by fastening a heavier weight at hole y, or by making the extension to hole z longer. In either case, the device must be regraduated after these changes have been made.

TEST YOUR UNDERSTANDING

1. Imagine an ordinary wooden pencil about this size. Choose the most suitable measurements described from the list.

_____ a. its weight
_____ b. its length
_____ c. thickness of
             unsharpened lead
_____ d. its width
_____ e. its volume

a. 1 cm
b. 6 cm
c. 12 cm
d. 2 mm
e. ½ mm
f. 9 cubic centimeters
g. 1 cubic decimeter
h. 1 g
i. 8 g
j. 250 g

2. Complete the following vital statistics: your height: _____ cm or _____ m; your waist: _____ cm; your weight: _____ kg
   Name some part of your body that has each of these measures:

   1 cm _____   5 cm _____
   1 dm _____   1 m _____

3. Write the letters where they belong on the ruler below. Use the following code:

A: .3 dm
E: 17 mm, 4.3 cm, 1.45 dm,
   81 mm, .88 dm
I: 137 mm
L: 13.5 cm
M: 7.5 cm
O: 63 mm, 1.13 dm

P: .5 cm, 23 mm
R: .01 m, 3.6 cm, 1.5 dm, 123 mm
T: 14 cm, 57 mm, .95 dm
U: 1.19 dm
Y: .11 m

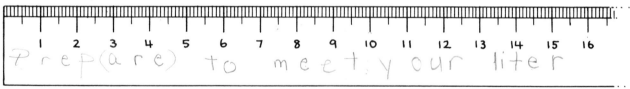

4. Draw lines to match the columns:

   12 L   12 g
   12 cc   12 mg
   12 cL   of cold water weighs   12 kg
   1.2 L   .12 kg
   .012 L   1200 g

5. Look on your bathroom and kitchen shelves and in newspapers and magazines to find some metric labels and uses of metric measurements. List some. Can you find m, mm, g, mg, L, mL, cc?

6. Suppose that you are doing the following activities with school children. For each, list the ways measurement could arise. What type of

measurement and what type of activity (comparison, nonstandard units, etc.) is involved?

> Baking cookies with first graders
> Physical education class with third graders
> Study of plants with fifth graders

Add one more activity.

7. Describe a sequence of six types of activities for teaching measurement (for example, of length). Why should children have experiences with nonstandard units before using standard ones? Why should children construct their own measurement devices?

8. What is meant by "conservation of length"? Should children who do not yet conserve length be expected to do measurement activities?

9. How can study of the metric system help children to build the concept of place value in both lower and upper elementary school grades?

10. A child was seen to measure 3 centimeters from the edge of the paper by placing a ruler as shown in the diagram. What could you do to help this child understand the concept of linear measurement?

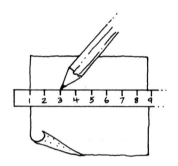

11. a. A class was making costumes for a school play. Each of the 25 children needed a piece of ribbon 38 centimeters. How many meters of ribbon did the class need?

  b. A class was making costumes for a school play. Each of the 25 children needed a piece of ribbon 1 foot 3 inches long. How many yards of ribbon did the class need?

  c. Did you realize that these two problems represented the same situation? Which problem was more difficult to work out? Why?

12. Explain how the metric units for length, capacity, and weight are interrelated.

13. How could you explain to children how the metric units for length (mm, cm, dm, m) are related — that is, how to complete examples like the ones below?

> My height is _____ cm or _____ dm or _____ m.
> This pencil has length _____ mm or _____ cm or _____ m.

FURTHER READINGS AND PROJECTS

1. Examine the teacher's guide to a textbook series. Does the development of measurement of length correspond to the sequence outlined on pages 260–261? If it varies, how does it vary? Are the variations pedagogically sound?

2. *The Arithmetic Teacher* has a regular feature, "Let's Do It," that provides teachers with practical teaching ideas. Read the two articles from this section, "Developing the Concept of Linear Measurement" (November 1974) and "An Introduction to Weight Measurement" (January 1976), both by James V. Bruni and Helene Silverman. Is the sequence of activities suggested consistent with the sequence outlined on pages 260–261?

3. Make yourself a complete "mini-metric lab." Using materials in this chapter or common household objects, you can make the following: centimeter ruler, millimeter ruler (page 291), meter tape, or meter stick; liter measure (perhaps a cardboard cubic decimeter), graduated liter bottle; weights (use nickels for small weights, a liter of water for larger ones); a balance scale, and also a spring scale, or the measuring device on pages 289–290 for smaller weights; a thermometer (use an old one, and make a strip to go over it). See pages 285–286 for some hints.

4. *Notes on Mathematics in the Primary Schools* by Members of the Association of Teachers of Mathematics (New York: Cambridge University Press, 1968) is a collection of reports from teachers of mathematical thoughts and interesting investigations of their students. Read the section on Measurement at the beginning of Chapter 6, which illustrates varied understandings — and misunderstandings — about measurement. Do you think that you could help some of these children avoid the mistakes they made by following the sequence of measurement activities in this chapter? Do you see how satisfying it is for children to respond to some challenging question, where the method of solution is not immediately apparent? (Note that this was written *before* English schools completely switched to the metric system. Do you see how the metric system makes measuring much easier?)

5. *The Arithmetic Teacher* is a good source of ideas about teaching measurement and the metric system. In recent years, this journal has devoted part of the section "Reviewing and Viewing" to evaluating new metric materials: books for both teachers and children, activity cards, games, and filmstrips. Examine some of these reviews. Do you agree with the criteria by which materials seem to be evaluated? Most issues of this journal will also carry some articles about teaching or using metric measurement. In particular, you might look at the issue of April 1973, which was entirely devoted to metric measurement.

6. Many of the activities in this chapter suggested the importance of estimation in learning about measurement. Read Chapter 5, "Estimation as Part of Learning to Measure," by George W. Bright, pp. 87–104 of the 1976 Yearbook of the National Council of Teachers of Mathematics, *Measuring in School Mathematics* (Reston, Virginia: NCTM, 1976). This article provides an analysis of types of estimation activities, and suggests ways in which estimation skills can be taught and evaluated.

7. As this country is converting to the metric system, you will see a variety of messages designed to help the public learn about the new system of measurement. There are special television programs for school children and adults, spot announcements on radio and television, special brochures available free from various government agencies, as well as metric promotional materials distributed by businesses. Examine some of these. Do any stress conversion? Could you improve on any of these materials?

NOTES

1. It is not yet clear which spelling, metre or meter, will be adopted in this country. "Metre" conforms to international usage, but "meter" continues to be used by many American publishers.

2. In fact, the metric system of meaturement is commonly known throughout the world as SI, which stands for the French term *Système International d'Unités*.

3. Scientists draw a distinction between *weight* and *mass*. The weight of an object depends on gravitational force. For example, you may have seen films of astronauts jumping on the moon, where they weigh much less than on earth. However, mass is a quality of an object that is the same on earth, the moon, or anywhere else. Since gravity is roughly constant on the earth's surface, the words *mass* and *weight* are used interchangeably for everyday measuring purposes. Most elementary school materials will refer to gram and kilogram as units of weight when, in fact, they are units of mass.

CHAPTER 7

PLACE VALUE

INTRODUCTION

How do children learn about our system for writing numbers, especially numbers greater than 10? It is sometimes difficult for adults to approach this problem, since we take our numeration system (or way of writing numbers) for granted. Try for a moment to forget all that you know about written or spoken names for numbers. Read the activity below.

Arranging Beans

Two people each take a spoonful of beans (or a handful of pennies, or any collection of small objects whose quantity is too great to be recognized "by eye" but not too large to be counted easily). Without writing, talking, drawing symbols in the air, mouthing words, or any other verbal or symbolic means, determine who has more beans. Then try to communicate how many beans each person has. You *are* allowed to move your beans around to make groups or patterns. (Don't arrange them in the shape of numerals!) Describe what you did.

How would you do this activity?

Four diagrams on page 296 show different ways that students could have approached this problem. Look at each diagram and fill in the blanks. Then decide which diagram is the clearest for quickly telling who has more. _____ In which diagram is it easiest to tell exactly *how many* objects there are? _____

If you devised some convenient method for communicating in the above activity, you probably used some form of grouping. A straightforward one-to-one correspondence can be used (as in diagram 1), but this does not give much feel for how many objects there are. Grouping them (as in diagrams 2, 3, and 4) in some way does give such a feel, and also leads to an easy way to describe the quantity. Grouping is fundamental to all systems of writing numbers — and there have been several different systems in the course of history such as roman numerals. Our own system is based on grouping by 10 which is an especially convenient number for us since we have 10 fingers. Some ways of grouping show 10 more easily than other. For example, you may feel that you should count all of the groups in diagram 3, but in diagram 4, having counted one row you can be sure that the other rows all have the same number. For another example of a systematic grouping procedure, look to the right. How many small squares are there?

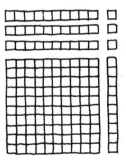

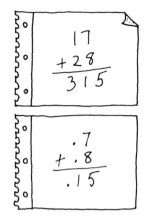

When we write numerals, we need only use ten symbols (0,1,2,3,4,5,6,7, 8,9), and each symbol can have different values. Our system is called a *place-value* system because the value of a digit in a numeral is determined by its "place." For example, when we write 123, the digit 2 means 2 *tens* or *twenty* because the 2 is in the tens' place. Children are usually able to count by rote up to 23, or even to count objects meaningfully up to 23, and to read 23 as "twenty-three," without realizing how this notation relates to tens and ones. It is important that children have a solid understanding of place value, for many of the standard procedures of arithmetic depend on it. For example, children who do not understand place value may easily make the common mistake shown to the left. Similarly, since notation for decimals is just an extension of place value for whole numbers, many errors with decimal computation can also be traced to poor understanding of place value. One example of such an error is shown to the left.

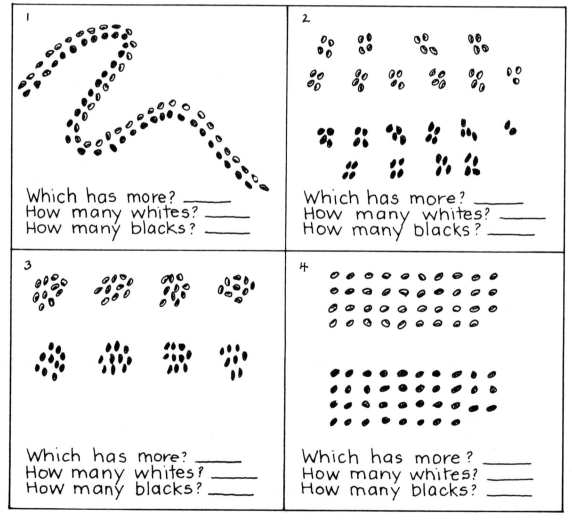

Chapter 2, Number and Its Uses, provided examples of materials that children can use to count large numbers by grouping into tens and hundreds. This chapter concerns ways in which different types of concrete materials can be used to build understanding of our place-value system of numeration, and how place value is used in procedures for addition and subtraction. Since you already know a great deal about grouping by 10 and about our numeration system, the type and sequence of the place-value activities in this chapter will not be identical to those followed by children — in particular, you will do many activities involving notation in bases other than base ten (which usually is taught in elementary school only as an enrichment topic in upper grades) so that you will see what is involved in learning a new numeration system.

The first set of Activities uses colored chips as a model for place value, and the second set uses a different model, multibase blocks or a homemade substitute. Discussion Questions and Comments concern the use of these Activities with children at various grade levels, and a comparison of the types of place-value models with which children can do the Activities. The Follow-up Sections concern the development of notation as a progression from concrete to semiconcrete to symbolic. This progression is examined in detail for addition and subtraction of two- and three-digit numbers. Extensions and applications of place value are also discussed — in particular, place-value models for decimal fractions, and the role of bases other than base ten in the curriculum. To demonstrate that the two place-value models used in the Activities in this chapter — colored chips and multibase blocks — are not especially new, a section looks briefly at Montessori mathematics materials for numeration.

Many of the Activities involve games with dice. A section discusses probability in the context of throwing two dice, and the effect of changes in the dice on the expected length of the games. Finally, there is a description of some ancient numeration systems which do not depend on place value.

ACTIVITIES WITH COLORED CHIPS

Activity 1. Collect and Exchange Game

The goal of the game described below is to give children experiences of exchanging and to develop their concept of place value. Play the game in groups of 2–4.

Materials: 2 dice; colored chips or markers in white, red, and blue (poker chips are ideal, but you can also use squares of oak tag which are easily cut on a paper cutter); Exchange Game Sheet (see page 299) for each player

Directions: Imagine that you live in a distant country called Fiveton. The money system in Fiveton is somewhat different from ours. Fiveton people have three types of coins: a white chip (worth 1¢ of our money); a red chip that equals 5 white chips; and a blue chip that equals 5 red chips.

Players take turns. They roll two dice, pick up as many white chips as the sum of what is rolled, and place them on the Exchange Game Sheet in the appropriate columns. Players should exchange whenever possible —

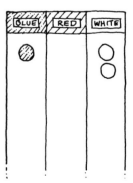

1 red for 5 whites, 1 blue for 5 reds. The winner is the first person to get 1 blue chip.

As you place your chips on the sheet, *read off* your score aloud. For example, this Exchange Game Sheet shows that a player has 1 blue and 2 white chips. This player would say, "One blue, no reds and two whites."

Activity 2. Collect and Exchange Game with Recording

Play the Exchange Game again, with the following changes:

1. Place chips on the Exchange Game Sheet and at the same time keep a written record of your total score after each round.

   For example, on the first round, a player rolled a 3, picked up 3 white chips, and recorded his score, as shown here. On the second round, he rolled a 2, picked up 2 whites, exchanged his 5 whites for a red, and recorded his score of 1 red and 0 whites.

   Suppose he rolls a 4 in the next round. Fill in his score for the third round.

2. The winner is the first player to get *2* blue chips. Stop playing when there is a winner. (To be fair, you should finish up the whole round, in case there is a tie.)

   Use a blank table like the one at left to keep a record of your total score after each round of the game.

   How many rounds did your game take?

Round	I Rolled	My Score		
		B	R	W
1	3			3
2	2		1	0
3				

Round	I Rolled	My Score		
		B	R	W
1				
2				
3				
4				
5				
6				
7				
8				
9				
10				
11				

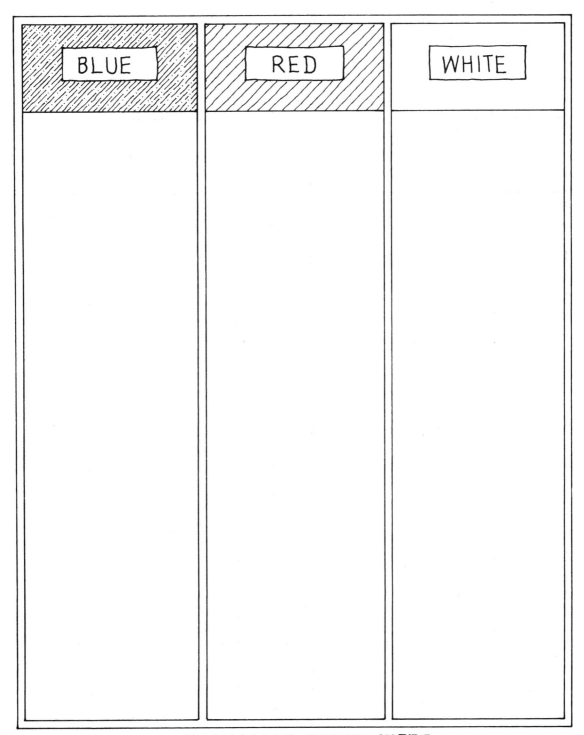

EXCHANGE GAME SHEET

Centimeter Grid Paper

Activity 3. Chips and Numerals

1. Take 1 red and 3 white chips — that is, 1r 3w. Trade in or exchange the red for whites. How many whites does this yield? 1r 3w = _____ whites. Without actually trading in red chips, determine how many whites 3r 1w equals. 3r 1w = _____ whites. (Could you explain your answer with chips?)

2. Diagram 1 shows that 2r 3w equals 13 whites. The arrows show that 2 reds have been exchanged for whites.
   Complete diagram 2 to show that 1b 1r 2w equal 32 whites.

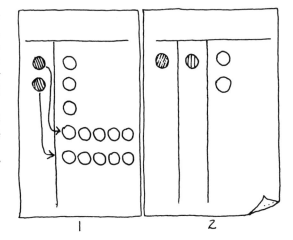

1   2

3. How many whites does each of the following equal?
   2r 3w = _____ whites   1b 0r 0w = _____ whites
   2b 3r 4w = _____ whites

4. When describing the price of something in Fiveton, you might decide that instead of writing 2b 3r 4w you would write a shorter more compact expression, 234_F, where the F means a *Fiveton* numeral. You might say this numeral is "two-three-four in the Fiveton's system," or "two-three-four base five." How many whites are the following worth?
   31_F = _____ 101_F = _____ 311_F = _____

5. Diagram 3 shows how grouping by fives and exchanging yields 101_F for 26 whites.
   Complete diagram 4 to show how exchanging yields 113_F for 33 whites.

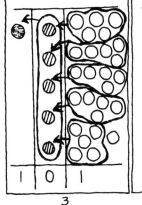

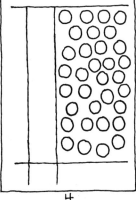

3   4

6. A player had 24_F in the Collect and Exchange Game and rolled 3. What was his new total? _____
   Diagram 5 shows this situation. What does the arrow mean? _____

5

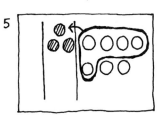

This action could be recorded as follows:

$$
\begin{array}{ll}
& 1 \nwarrow \\
\text{Had} & 24_F \\
\text{Rolled} & +\ 3_F \\
\hline
\text{New Total} & 32_F
\end{array}
$$

What does the 1 mean? _____

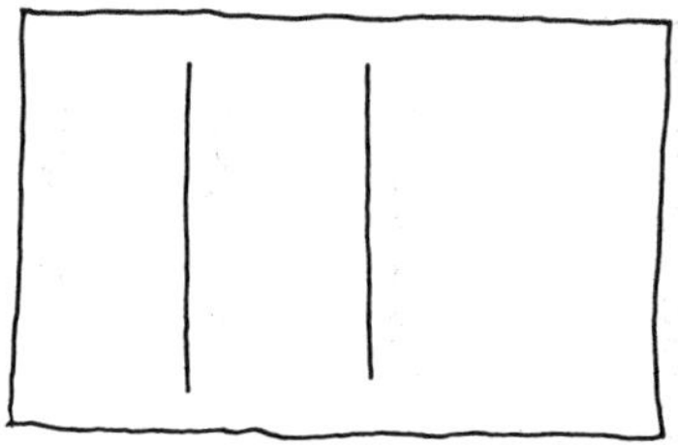

Draw a diagram similar to diagram 2 to show the solution to

$$
\begin{array}{ll}
\text{Had} & 143_F \\
\text{Rolled} & +\ 12_F \\
\hline
\text{New Total} &
\end{array}
$$

7. Recall that 1 white is worth one of our cents. Therefore, a Fiveton numeral for the number of cents in a nickel is 10_F. (Do you see why?) Write Fiveton numerals for the number of cents in each of the following:

   two nickels _____
   twenty-three cents _____
   a quarter _____
   a dollar _____
   a quarter and three nickels _____
   seventy-nine cents _____

Activity 4. Comparison

1. At one point in their Collect and Exchange Game, two players had the chips drawn below.

   Player 1: ⬤⬤◯◯   Player 2: ⬤◯◯◯◯

   Who was ahead? _____ Demonstrate to your neighbor why this is so.
2. Circle the greater of each pair.

   44_F or 100_F 210_F or 134_F 120_F or 102_F

Activity 5. Counting

Take 27 chips. A Fiveton person would count the chips as written below, saying "one, two, three, four, one-zero, one-one, . . ." Continue the counting below. Have one person put down the chips one by one, and another person exchange them and say the numeral in Fiveton.

1_F	2_F	3_F	4_F	10_F	11_F	
_____	_____	_____	_____	_____	_____	_____
_____	_____	_____	_____	42_F	_____	_____
_____	_____	_____	_____	_____	_____	_____
_____	_____	_____				

Write the next five Fiveton numerals. 342_F _____ _____ _____

_____ _____

Activity 6. Threeton — A New Country

You recently met some inhabitants of a country called *Threeton.*

1. Threeton's system for writing numbers resembles that in Fiveton, and Threeton people also use colored chips for money. In Threeton, 1 red = _____ whites, 1 blue = _____ reds, and 1 blue = _____ whites.

2. Suppose your score in a Threeton Collect and Exchange Game was 1r 2w. How many white chips does this equal? 12_T = _____ whites (Read this as "one-two base three.")

3. Make a drawing similar to diagram 3, Activity 3, to show how grouping by threes and exchanging yields 122_T for the 17 chips drawn to the right. This shows that
$$17 = 122_T.$$

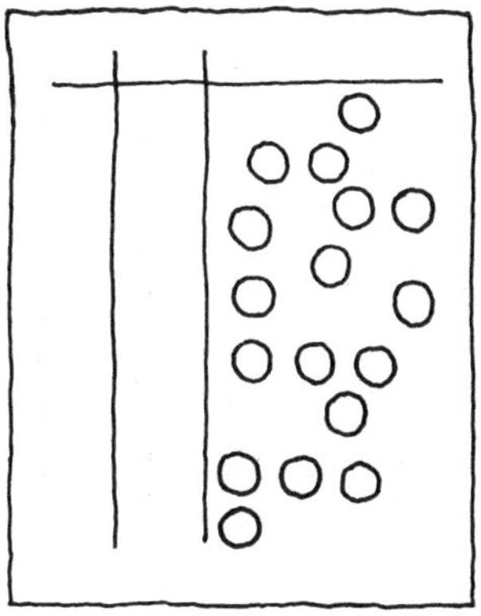

4. Complete: $12 =$ _____$_T$ $26 =$ _____$_T$

5. Write the next four Threeton numerals.

1_T 2_T 10_T 11_T

_____ _____ _____ _____

_____ _____ _____ _____

Activity 7. Exchange and Give-Away Game

Materials: See Activity 1
Directions: This game resembles the Collect and Exchange Game, but instead of accumulating chips, the aim is to get rid of them.

1. Again the exchange rate is 5 to 1. Begin with 2 blues. Roll 2 dice, and *discard* that many whites. Work with the chips, placing them on your Exchange Game Sheet and exchanging as needed. The winner is the first to discard all chips (but to be fair, finish the round when someone wins). Use this blank chart to record your score after each round.

   Which was more fun, the Collect and Exchange Game of Activities 1 and 2, or the Exchange and Give-Away Game?   Why?

Round	You Rolled	Your Score		
		B	R	W
Begin	——	2	O	O
1				
2				
3				
4				
5				
6				
7				
8				
9				
10				

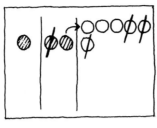

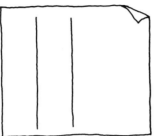

2. A player had 121_F and rolled 13_F. What was his new score? _____ The diagram to the left shows this situation. What does the arrow mean? What do the lines through the chips mean? The action could be recorded like this:

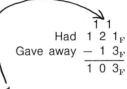

$$
\begin{array}{r}
\overset{1}{}\overset{1}{} \\
\text{Had} \quad 1\ 2\ 1_F \\
\text{Gave away} \quad -\ 1\ 3_F \\
\hline
1\ 0\ 3_F
\end{array}
$$

$$\overset{1}{}$$

What does the 1 stand for?
(Could you read it as 11_F?)
Draw a diagram showing the solution to

$$
\begin{array}{r}
\text{Had} \quad 3\ 1\ 4_F \\
\text{Gave away} \quad -\ 2\ 1_F \\
\hline
\end{array}
$$

Activity 8. More Colors of Chips

1. Suppose the Fiveton exchange games were played with five colors of chips: yellow, green, blue, red, white.
   Fill in the following:

   1 red = _____ white
   1 blue = _____ red = _____ white
   1 green = _____ blue = _____ red = _____ white
   1 yellow = _____ green = _____ blue = _____ red = _____ white

2. Complete the place-value chart below which shows the values (in whites) of the various colors of chips in base five.

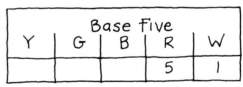

Base Five				
Y	G	B	R	W
			5	1

3. How many white chips would 2341_F equal?   (a) 221   (b) 721   (c) 346
4. What is the greatest number you can write with five digits in base five? _____$_F$
5. Suppose that you played the exchange games in *Tenton;* that is, you might think of the white chips as being worth 1¢, reds worth 10¢, and blues worth 100¢ (or a dollar). Fill in the place-value chart below.

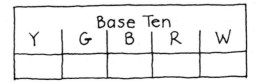

Base Ten				
Y	G	B	R	W

What is the greatest number you can write with five digits in base ten? _____

6. In Activity 6 you worked with the monetary system in Threeton. Fill in the place-value chart showing values of chips in base three.

Base Three				
Y	G	B	R	W

What is the greatest number you can write with five digits in base three? _____T

DISCUSSION QUESTIONS AND COMMENTS — ACTIVITIES WITH COLORED CHIPS

Are Exchange Games Appropriate in Grades 1 and 2?

Do you think that the exchange games — Activities 1, 2, and 7 — could be played by children in grades 1 and 2? If so, what would they learn from the games? What difficulties might they have?

You have probably realized that these games concern the concept of place value or positional notation for numbers; in fact the games you played concerned the base-five system for writing numbers. Some teachers feel that exchange games are not appropriate for introducing place value to children in grades 1–2, but that the games are fine for reinforcing the concept of place value with upper elementary school children in grades 5–6.

Others disagree. They feel that first and second graders should play exchange games in several bases, including base ten, to gain badly needed concrete experiences with the significance of position *before* children begin formal work with two- and three-digit base-ten numerals in their textbooks. In addition, these games can provide valuable practice with other early mathematics skills; for example, counting, grouping, exchanging, basic addition facts (especially if the dice are labeled with numerals 1, 2, 3, 4, 5, 6) as well as preparation for addition and subtraction of two-digit numbers.

What do you think?

Young children may have difficulty playing the game in Activity 1. Here are three difficulties that children might have.

1. One child rolled the dice and got [⚅] [⚄] . The dice were of standard size and the child had difficulty counting the dots with his finger — he did not yet know the fact "6 + 5" from recall — and so he said he had 9. What modifications could you make in the game to avoid this sort of difficulty?

Some teachers suggest using just one die, preferably large (maybe made from a foam cube). However, with this modification it will take twice as long to get

two blue chips and complete the game. How could you modify the game to avoid an overly long game using just one die?

First graders often enjoy a modified exchange game in which they use one die, and only *two* colors of chips (red and white). The winner is the first person to get four red chips. A teacher might modify the game in this way partly to shorten the game, but also because first graders do not yet need experiences with three-digit numbers (which will be studied in grade 2). Second grade teachers would be more likely to use three colors of chips in the exchange games.

2. One child had collected six white chips but was reluctant to trade them in; six white chips *looked* like much more than one red and one white chip! One possible way to help with this difficulty would be to make the red chips bigger than the white ones, and the blue still bigger. (This is sometimes but not always done with coinage systems. How do a penny and a nickel compare in size? a nickel and a dime?) Another would be to have children collect little red "cups" (painted sections of an egg carton) instead of red chips, with the rule that you can have a cup only if you have five white chips to put in it. Can you think of another way to help young children with this difficulty?

3. If children are excited when they play the exchange games, they may inadvertently move their Exchange Game Sheets, knock off some chips, and lose track of their score. This difficulty can be avoided if you make more elaborate playing boards by pasting small boxes to a cardboard backing as shown.

Should Exchange Games Be Played in Various Bases?

Some teachers agree that first graders may find it helpful to play a modified exchange game (two colors only) in Tenton, but question the use of games in other bases. There are two reasons for using various base exchange games with young children.

Children sometimes find that the game in Tenton is actually a little more difficult than in Threeton or Fiveton because it is more difficult for them to count to 10 than to 3 or 5. They cannot "see" groups of 10, often have to recount, and sometimes make mistakes. Look at these pictures. Put a circle around the pictures that you are *sure* of the number without counting.

Most adults find that they are not sure of numbers over 5 without counting (unless the groups are arranged in some special pattern, as on playing cards). Children could be expected to have an even greater problem. If children play exchange games in Threeton and Fiveton, they can experience exchanging without the difficulties of quickly and accurately counting to higher numbers.

Also the game will be more exciting than in Tenton because it takes fewer whites to make an exchange, and so the game goes faster. It may be easier to introduce exchange games to children in Fiveton; then play games in Threeton, Fourton, and Sixton before eventually playing many games in Tenton.

In addition to this reason for playing exchange games with exchange "rates" less than 10, there is a broader theoretical justification. Mathematics educator Zoltan Dienes has found that children are better able to generalize and abstract the concepts of place value and exchanging by doing activities with several bases rather than just base ten.[1] He feels that this abstraction leads to better understanding of the role of place value in our everyday base-ten arithmetic. Do you agree with Dienes?

Where Should Symbolic Work in Other Bases Occur in the Mathematics Curriculum?

In the Activities with colored chips, you developed and used notation in base five (Activities 2–5) and in base three (Activity 6). (You could equally well use these Activities to develop notation in base four, six, etc.) These activities in different bases were included here for you — adults who already know much about base ten — to help you get a feel for what it is like to learn the system for the first time. There is some controversy about developing *notation* in bases other than ten with children. Such notation was included in some innovative programs of the 1960s (in "new math" programs) mainly in grades 5–8. One motivation for the inclusion of other bases in the curriculum was that base-two (binary) numerals and sometimes base-eight (octal) numerals are used with computers. A second motivation was to reinforce children's understanding of place value and its use in arithmetic.

However in the early 1970s there was some reaction against the inclusion of symbolic material on bases other than ten and against the formal and mechanical way in which it was sometimes presented. Current trends seem to be to provide children with concrete multibase experiences (such as through exchange games) in lower grades for several reasons. Check the reasons stated below that seem to you to be valid for including exchange games in various bases in grades 1–3.

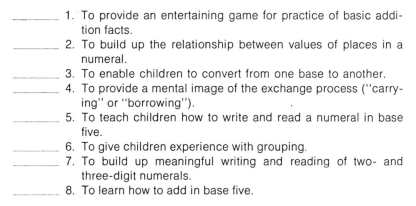

_____ 1. To provide an entertaining game for practice of basic addition facts.
_____ 2. To build up the relationship between values of places in a numeral.
_____ 3. To enable children to convert from one base to another.
_____ 4. To provide a mental image of the exchange process ("carrying" or "borrowing").
_____ 5. To teach children how to write and read a numeral in base five.
_____ 6. To give children experience with grouping.
_____ 7. To build up meaningful writing and reading of two- and three-digit numerals.
_____ 8. To learn how to add in base five.

Formal notation (such as 312_F) and arithmetic (such as $312_F - 142_F$) in bases other than ten are seldom taught in the early grades, but may be introduced as enrichment activities for children in the upper grades. Children often find it fun to work with a new code for numbers, and these symbolic activities can provide a lot of informal practice with arithmetic, as well as a context for discovering patterns.

Different Models for Place Value (in Base Ten)

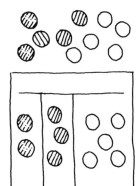

Materials Similar to Colored Chips

A child who has had many experiences playing exchange games with colored chips in base ten might "see" two hundred and thirty-five as a collection of 2 blue chips, 3 red chips, and 5 white chips. If he has always played the game on an Exchange Game Sheet, he may also "see" this number in terms of position. When working with the chips, did you *always* use the Exchange Game Sheet? If you want children to develop an understanding of positional notation (that the value of a digit depends on position) you will want to make sure that children do "see" numbers in terms of positions, yet if children can rely on color, they may be tempted to ignore the place-value chart. Some teachers use the following trick to make sure that children use position: After children have played many exchange games and thoroughly understand the rules of exchange and placement of chips, the red and blue chips suddenly "disappear." The children are asked if they can figure out a way to play the game anyway, using just white chips and the Exchange Game Sheet. Can you?

Children sometimes use other materials for place value which closely resemble the colored chips — either in the use of color (or some other symbol), or position, or both color and position to represent value. Three examples are drawn below.

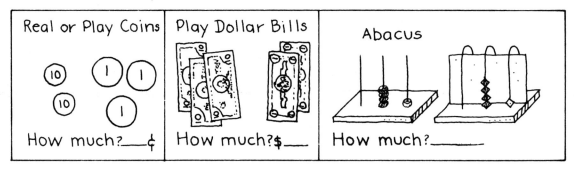

Note: Two types of abacus are shown. Both have beads which slip on the wires. (On each type, beads are sometimes of different colors on the different wires, and sometimes all the same color.) Beads can be removed from the one on the left, while on the one on the right, beads slip over the wires behind a "screen" so that unused beads are hidden and cannot be removed from the wires. Do you see how the simpler abacus on the left very closely resembles the Exchange Game Sheet in principle?

Some types of abacus, like the one on the right, are made with 20 beads on a wire. What advantages does this have?

As we mentioned, children sometimes have difficulty with exchange games when they do not understand the relationship between red and white chips. Do you think that a child might have a similar difficulty with an abacus? _____ with coins? _____ with dollar bills? _____

In all materials similar to colored chips, a child must somehow *remember* the relationship between the colors, coins, symbols, or positions. There is no way to tell from the material itself (if one does not *know* what "10" means) that the piece for 10 is worth 10 of the pieces for 1. Two visual clues were suggested: red cups to hold white chips, or varying sizes of chips. These modifications suggest two other types of place-value models.

Grouping Materials

Children can represent numbers with materials that they themselves actually count, group into tens, fasten together, and unfasten. (Examples of this type were given in Chapter 2, Number and Its Uses.) Which modification just suggested does this type of material resemble? _____ Here are two examples.

Pebbles in Bags	Bundles of Sticks	
How many? _____ (Children put 10 pebbles into little plastic bags.)	How many? _____ (Children fasten together bundles of 10 popsicle sticks with rubber bands.)	

Some teachers recommend using bundles of plastic spoons or forks, because they can be stacked and fastened neatly so that children can see all 10 in a bundle on an overhead projector. Can you think of another material of this sort; that is, some objects that children can actually group and fasten together to make tens? Draw "13" with your model in the space provided.

Structured Materials

A third type of place-value model is midway between these two types. Children do not actually fasten groups of 10 together, but they do not have to rely on memory for the relationship between the pieces. Instead, the material is structured in such a way that the pieces for 100 *show* that they are worth 10 of the pieces of 10, or 100 of the pieces of 1. One such material is the multibase arithmetic blocks.

ACTIVITIES WITH MULTIBASE ARITHMETIC BLOCKS AND SQUARED MATERIAL

Note: The next Activities deal with multibase arithmetic blocks, commonly associated with Zoltan Dienes, who used them to teach place value and arithmetic in various bases. These multibase arithmetic blocks are often made from wood, and lines are scored into the surface of the wood. Some educational supply companies make similar blocks from colored plastic. For the following Activities you will need a selection of pieces from the base four, base five, base ten, and one other base sets.

Most of the Activities can also be done with pieces cut from squared paper pasted onto cardboard — however it is preferable to have the wooden blocks available, at least for demonstration in Activities 9, 10, and 16.

Activity 1. Getting Acquainted

Build something with the pieces.
How can you sort the pieces?
Can you make any of the pieces out of other pieces?
The pieces are commonly named as follows:

This is a base-five set.

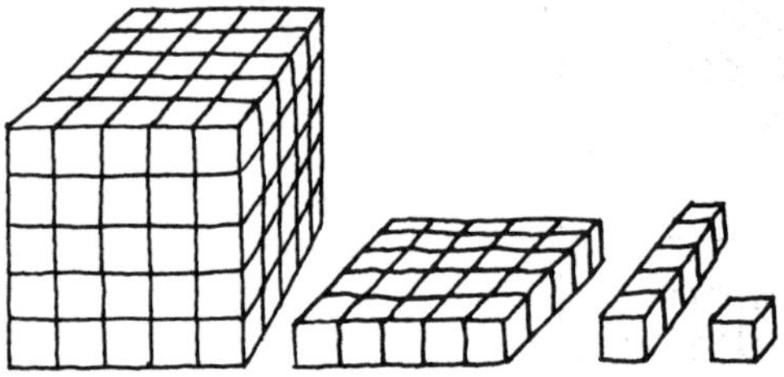

Block   Flat   Long   Unit

Use the space below to draw pictures of the pieces from a base-four set.

Block   Flat   Long   Unit

An inexpensive substitute for the wooden flats, longs, and units can be made from squared paper or cardboard.

This is a base-five set.

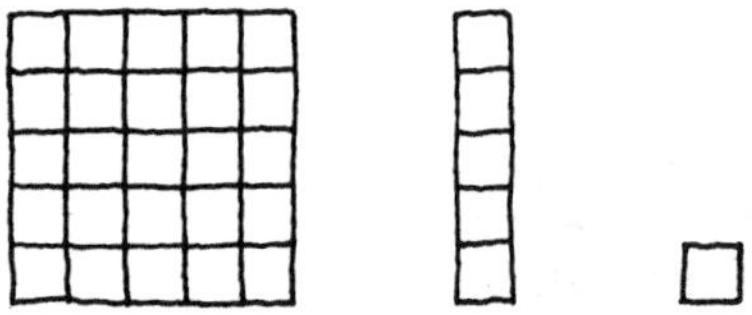

Flat   Long   Unit

Use this space to draw a base-four set.

Flat   Long   Unit

Activity 2. Number Patterns

Fill in this table.
Do you see any patterns?
Describe them.

	Base Four	Base Five	Base ▢	Base Ten
Number of units needed to make one long				
Number of units needed to make one flat				
Number of units needed to make one block				

Activity 3. Ways to Write Numbers

1. Use pieces from the base-four set. Count out 26 units. If you trade some of the units in for longs or flats, what might you end up with? One possibility is shown below.

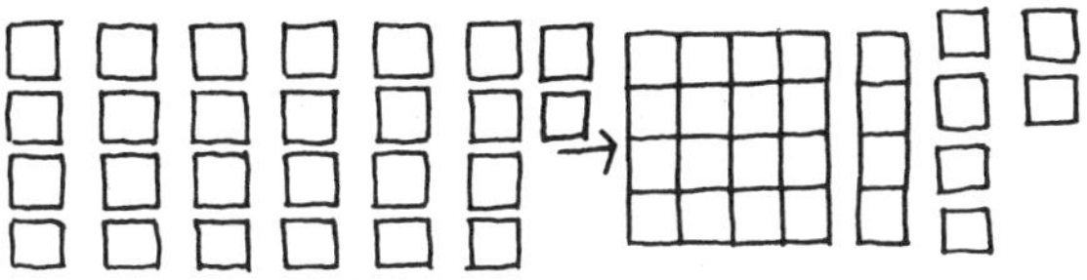

The result is 1 flat, 1 long, and 6 units, which is recorded in the first row of this table. In what other ways could you trade in 26 units? Complete the examples shown in the second and third rows, and provide two more. The first row in the table represents $1 + 1 + 6 = 8$ pieces. Which row in the table represents the *least* number of separate pieces? What is the *greatest* number of rate pieces? _____ What is the *greatest* number of separate pieces you could use? _____ Could you use exactly 11 pieces to represent 26? How? _____ You could have a row with 5 pieces — do you see how? How would you write the number 26 in base four? 26 = _____ Four

2. Imagine using base-ten pieces, and suppose that you had 273 units. Fill in the missing numbers in this table. Which row represents the least number of pieces? _____

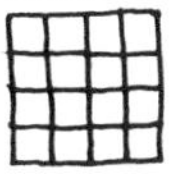

Base Four

1	1	6
	6	
	2	

Base Ten

1		3
2	6	
1		13
	7	3

```
┌─────────────────────────────────────┐
│            Base Five                 │
├──────────┬──────────┬────────┬───────┤
│   ▞▀▀▞   │   ▭      │   ▯    │   ▫   │
│  ▞  ▞    │          │        │       │
├──────────┼──────────┼────────┼───────┤
│          │          │        │       │
│          │          │        │       │
├──────────┼──────────┼────────┼───────┤
│          │          │        │       │
│          │          │        │       │
└──────────┴──────────┴────────┴───────┘
```

Do you see how you could use the base-ten pieces to demonstrate to children that all of these entries correspond to 273 units? Do you see why it is necessary to be able to write 273 in different ways? (**Hint:** Complete these subtractions.)

$$\begin{array}{ccc} 273 & 273 & 273 \\ -91 & -19 & -89 \end{array}$$

3. Try to write a given number in various ways in Base Five abstractly. *Imagine* using a base-five set, and counting out 206 units. Fill in some rows in this table.
   Complete: 206 = _____ₑFive

Activity 4. Comparisons

Have one person take the pieces for 211_{Five}, and another take pieces for 133_{Five}. Who would have the most units if all of the pieces were traded in for units? Describe a way to show why this is so *without* trading, using the materials.

Fill in all of the circles below with <, >, or =. Can you demonstrate why your answer is correct using the materials?

44_{Five} ◯ 100_{Five} 321_{Five} ◯ 312_{Five} 12344_{Five} ◯ 21000_{Five}

Children sometimes have difficulty deciding which is the greater of two three-digit numbers. Do you see how to use the base-ten materials to show that 210 > 199?

Activity 5. Expanded Notation

□□□|..

Use a base-five set of pieces. Take 3 flats, 1 long, and 2 units. How can we write this in base five? _____ₑFive. How many units does this represent? The procedure given below might describe how you would answer.

= 3 flats   and 1 long   and 2 units   = 312_{Five}
= 3 × _____ units + 1 × _____ units + 2 × _____ units
= _____ units   + _____ units   + _____ units   = _____ units

Now try this again. Take the pieces indicated, draw them, and fill in the steps to find out how many units.

243_{Five} □□|||... ≅   _____ units

1203_{Five} _____ units

312_{Six} _____ units

What happens in base ten?

$312_{Ten} = 3 \times$ _____ units $+ 1 \times$ _____ units $+ 2 \times$ _____ units

Activity 6. Return of the Exchange Game

Children could play the exchange games (like those in Activities 1, 2, and 7) with multibase materials just as you did with colored chips. Which material do you think children would find easier for these games, chips, wooden blocks, or cardboard squared materials? Which do you think they would find more enjoyable? As you have seen in the Activities with colored chips, the basic format of an exchange game can be varied — you can change the goal (such as 1 or 2 blue chips), the dice (such as one or two), and whether you collect or give away pieces. This time, you will play a game that shows how the format can be modified to give experience with addition of two-digit numbers.

Play *either* of the games, Make a Cube or Break a Cube, and read the other one.

Materials: Both games require multibase materials (preferably wooden) in base five (or some other base) — and a chance device consisting of six dried lima beans with one side marked "•" for *unit,* and the other side marked "▬" for *long.* You could also use six coins, chips, or bottle caps with stuck-on dots that are marked in this way on each side. If you want the game to go more quickly, use more beans or coins, chips, bottle caps. Each player will need an Exchange Game Sheet marked with flats on the left, longs in the middle, and units on the right; and a score sheet, as shown below.

Make a Cube

Directions: The objective of the game is to build a cube with the wooden blocks (or to make a stack of 5 flats, if you are playing with cardboard pieces).

Toss the beans and pick up as many *units* as you toss "•"s and as many *longs* as you toss "▬"s. Exchange whenever possible. Place your pieces in columns on an Exchange Game Sheet. Keep your score as shown below.

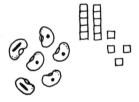

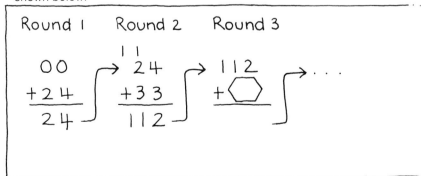

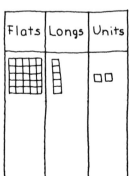

This player's score sheet shows that he rolled 2 longs and 4 units on round 1. On round 2 he got 3 longs and 3 units. Combining these pieces with those he

already had and exchanging yielded 1 flat, 1 long, and 2 units. Note how the exchange is indicated symbolically in the addition for round 2. He would enter

his roll on round 3 in the .

Play the game in a group of 2–4 players and record your score below. Play until one player can make a cube, then complete the round. The winner is the person with the highest score.

(**Note:** If you toss, for example, the beans

then you should record your score as 20_F, and not 15_F. Do you see why?)

Score Sheet for Make a Cube

Round 1	Round 2	Round 3	Round 4	Round 5	Round 6	Round 7
00 +	+	+	+	+	+	+

Break a Cube

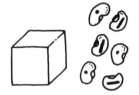

Directions: Begin with a block (or a stack of 5 flats, if you are playing with cardboard pieces). The objective of the game is to discard everything. The first person to discard all of his pieces is the winner.

Toss the beans and discard as many *units* as you toss "•"s, and as many *longs* as you toss " ▬ "s: Exchange whenever necessary. Place your pieces in columns on an Exchange Game Sheet. Keep your score as shown below.

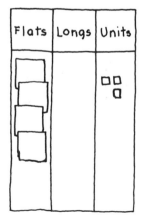

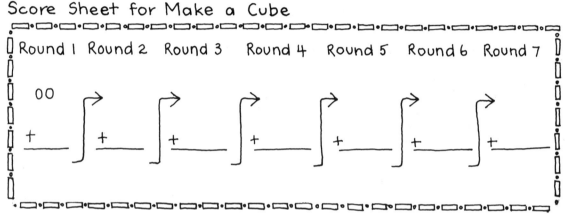

This player's score sheet shows that he rolled 4 longs and 2 units on round 1. He exchanged the block for 5 flats, and then a flat for 5 longs, and then a long for 5 units (and so had 4 flats, and 5 or 10_F units). He then discarded 4 longs and 2 units, and was left with 4 flats and 3 units, or 403_F. On round 2 he rolled 3 longs and 3 units. Do you see how he exchanged and discarded pieces to

be left with 320_F? He would enter his roll on round 3 in the ⬡.

Play the game in a group of 2–4 players, and record your score below.

Score Sheet for Break a Cube

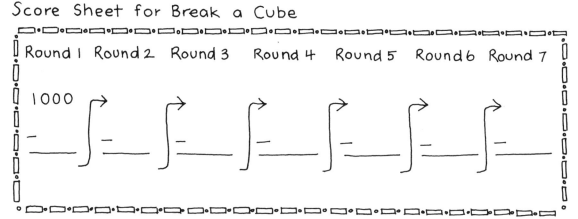

Round 1   Round 2   Round 3   Round 4   Round 5   Round 6   Round 7

1000 →   →   →   →   →   →   →

Could these two games be modified to give experience with addition and subtraction of two *three*-digit numbers? How?

Could you play these two games with the colored-chip model for place value?

Activity 7. Some Situations

The exchange games that you have played all involved addition and subtraction, collecting and giving away chips or multibase arithmetic blocks. This activity concerns some other types of situations, which require you to think of the multibase arithmetic blocks as money (in the same way that you thought of the colored chips as money).

Act out each situation with materials, and then match each with a corresponding base-five number sentence.

1. You want to take enough pieces from the bank in Fiveton so that you can give each of your four friends 1 long and 2 units for a present. How would you write the amount you must withdraw (in Fiveton)?

_____F

2. Your account in the bank has 4 flats, 2 longs, and 2 units. If you withdraw 103_F (the amount you need for the presents for your friends), how much will you have left? _____F

3. You are about to leave Fiveton for good, and you want to share your wealth among your four friends. Your bank account now has 314_F. How much will each friend get? _____F

Number Sentences

$12_F \div 4 = \square$

$422_F - 103_F = \square$

$314_F \div 4 = \square$

$4 \times 314_F = \square$

$4 \times 12_F = \square$

$422_F + 103_F = \square$

$314_F - 4 = \square$

Activity 8. More Patterns (Optional)

1. Suppose we cut a unit from one corner of a flat. Build something that has this leftover shape from longs and units (using as few pieces as possible). Do this for each base below. Do you see a pattern?

   Base four: _____ longs, _____ units
   Base five: _____ longs, _____ units
   Base six: _____ longs, _____ units
   Base ten: _____ longs, _____ units
   Base *n*: _____ longs, _____ units

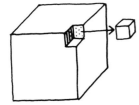

2. Suppose we cut a unit from one corner of a block. Build something that has this leftover shape from flats, longs, and units (using as few pieces as possible). Do this for each base below. Do you see a pattern?

   Base four: _____ flats, _____ longs, _____ units
   Base five: _____ flats, _____ longs, _____ units
   Base six: _____ flats, _____ longs, _____ units
   Base ten: _____ flats, _____ longs, _____ units
   Base *n*: _____ flats, _____ longs, _____ units

3. Now look again at Activity 8, More Colors of Chips. Do you see how the question about the greatest number you can write with a certain number of digits in a certain base relates to the patterns above?

DISCUSSION QUESTIONS AND COMMENTS — ACTIVITIES WITH MULTIBASE BLOCKS

What Is the "Structure" of the Multibase Blocks?

Relationships

Playing with the multibase blocks (for example, the base-five pieces) may help children to discover relationships between types of pieces — that is, the structure of the material. What relationships might children discover if the teacher asks them to "make pieces out of other pieces"?

Which relationship is relatively difficult to formulate by simply looking at the base-five pieces (or a picture of them)?

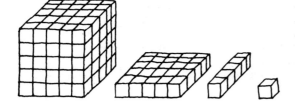

_____ A long equals 5 units.
_____ A flat equals 25 units.
_____ A block equals 125 units.

Suppose a fourth grader claims that a block equals 150 units because 6 × 25 equals 150. Look closely at the base-five block on page 316. Why might a child make this error? [2]

Names for the Pieces

What other name might a child give to a "flat"? The flat has 5 rows with 5 units in each row. Therefore it has 5 × 5 (or 25) units. 5 × 5 can also be written as 5^2 and read as "five squared." Why is "five squared" a reasonable term for 5 × 5?

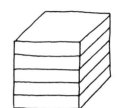

Children might refer to the block as a "_____." (**Hint:** Think of a sugar "_____.") The block has 5 levels with 5 × 5 units in each level. Thus the block has _____ × _____ × _____ (or _____) units. 5 × 5 × 5 can be written as 5^3 which is read as "five _____ed." Why is this a reasonable term for 5 × 5 × 5?

The multibase blocks are useful for helping children to develop the concept and terminology for *squared* and *cubed*. 5^2 is also read as "five to the second power." *Powers,* or *exponential notation* (5 is the base, 2 is the exponent) are included in most mathematics programs in grades 5–8. Do the multibase materials provide a model for 5 × 5 × 5 × 5 or 5^4? _____ Is there a term like *squared* or *cubed* that we can logically use for 5^4, instead of five to the fourth power? _____ Why not?

The expanded exponential form for 1346 is $1 \times 10^3 + 3 \times 10^2 + 4 \times 10^1 + 6 \times 1$. You might think that the pattern $10^3, 10^2, 10^1, \ldots$ should be followed by 10^0. In fact the symbol 10^0 means 1, and so the expanded form for 1346 is sometimes written $1 \times 10^3 + 3 \times 10^2 + 4 \times 10^1 + 6 \times 10^0$. Write the number 12,403 in this form. _____

Materials Similar to Multibase Blocks

Multibase arithmetic blocks are available from many commercial sources, in wood or plastic. Many schools find them quite expensive, especially if they are purchased in quantity sufficient for whole class use. "Squared material" is an example of a very inexpensive teacher-made substitute. A teacher could reproduce squared paper — for greater durability, glue the paper onto light cardboard — then cut it up. Printed cardboard squares divided into 100 small squares are also inexpensively available.

Here are two other structured materials of the same type as multibase blocks.

Bean sticks can be made by gluing dried beans to popsicle sticks — black or red beans provide a nice color contrast. Sticks are then glued to a cardboard backing to make a "raft." Here is a picture of some base-ten bean sticks.

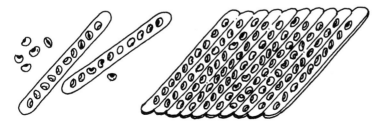

How many beans?

Brightly colored strings of plastic *beads* can be purchased that are permanently fastened to a central thread. (These strings are often used for bead curtains.) The strings can be cut into lengths of 10 beads, and single beads. Ten of the little strings can be packaged in a plastic bag, or else fastened at one end by a twisted piece of wire to make a "tassel."

How many beads?

Which material could children make themselves?

Wooden blocks _____   Squared material _____   Bean sticks _____
Beads _____

Suppose that you teach second grade. You would like each child to keep materials with which to illustrate numbers up to 200 in a box. Which material(s) would be suitable? (You have a limited budget.)

Wooden blocks _____   Squared material _____   Bean sticks _____
Beads _____

With which material can you conveniently "show" 1000?

Wooden blocks _____   Squared material _____   Bean sticks _____
Beads _____

Which material do you think children would enjoy most?

Wooden blocks _____   Squared material _____   Bean sticks _____
Beads _____

Three Types of Place-Value Models — A Comparison

Here are three commonly used models for place value. Of which "type," colored-chip, grouping, or structured, is each model? (See pages 308–309 for the meaning of these terms.)

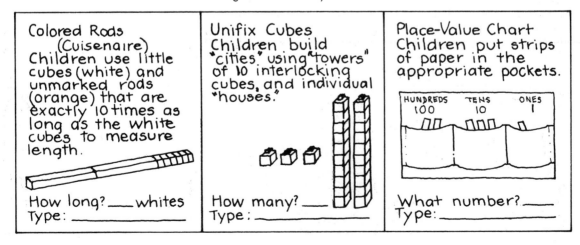

Colored Rods
  (Cuisenaire)
Children use little cubes (white) and unmarked rods (orange) that are exactly 10 times as long as the white cubes to measure length.

How long? ___ whites
Type: _____

Unifix Cubes
Children build "cities" using "towers" of 10 interlocking cubes, and individual "houses."

How many? ___
Type: _____

Place-Value Chart
Children put strips of paper in the appropriate pockets.

HUNDREDS	TENS	ONES
100	10	1

What number? ___
Type: _____

You have seen that there are many available materials with which children can illustrate numbers. (The following are examples: chips, coins and dollar bills, abacus, pebbles in bags, bundles of sticks, wooden multibase blocks, squared material, bean sticks, beans, and the three on page 318.) Which type of material do you think that children should use first?

In the Activities in this chapter, you began by using colored chips as a model for place value, and then later used structured materials (multibase blocks or squared material). However, other sequences may be better for children. They may find it easier to begin with some material that they themselves can form into groups (such as a grouping material), then go on to a material that is already formed, but that *shows* the relationship between pieces (such as a structured material), and finally use the more abstract place-value models, such as color chips, an abacus, or a place-value chart.

Could you play exchange games (in base ten) with all of the materials listed above? If not, which materials would not be suitable?

Some models are much less convenient for exchange games with three places because the model for 100 is unwieldy (for example, pebbles in bags) but we certainly *could* play the two-place game with any of these models, provided that each child has sufficient materials. Is it desirable or even feasible to use all 13 of these models with a second grade class? Is it desirable to use one model exclusively? Many teachers give their students experience with several different models, chosen carefully to suit the children's preferences, the class budget, and available storage space. A teacher might keep materials for exchange games in separate boxes — with directions inside each one — where each box uses different materials, perhaps chips, or coins, or play money, or Cuisenaire rods, or bean sticks. Then children could choose the game they prefer or be directed to a new box if they need more experience with the corrsponding model for place value.

There are, however, more fundamental reasons for offering a variety of models for place value, or multiple embodiments.

1. Individual Differences in Learning Style. One child may find a given material useful for learning a topic, while another may not. One second grader might attach meaning to two-digit numerals through multibase blocks, while another might find it easier to use a grouping material such as bundles of sticks (perhaps because he has not had enough experience grouping). Thus, using several different types of materials for a topic enables the teacher to reach all of the pupils in the class more effectively.

2. Transfer of Learning. *Transfer* means the ability to apply some knowledge or process in a new situation. The use of multiple embodiments facilitates transfer of learning. For example, experiences with colored chips may help children to understand coinage, while multibase blocks may help them to understand the relation between metric units (centimeter and decimeter).

3. Extension to Other Mathematical Topics. Which material, multibase blocks or an abacus, is more suitable for showing the number 12,542? _____
It is very difficult to use the multibase blocks to show large numbers, while an abacus provides a convenient model. However, decimals such as 1.32 can be represented easily with multibase blocks, while children find an abacus a more difficult model for this concept. A fifth grade teacher who was teaching decimals and large numbers might wish that his students had used both em-

bodiments in earlier grades, because he could then build on this prior experience.

Developing Notation

We have now seen a variety of materials with which children can illustrate numbers, using ones, tens, and hundreds. How do we teach children to associate a written symbol with these physical models; in particular, how do we help children to develop place-value notation? The way we write numbers may have little meaning for some children in grades 1–2. A child may see the symbol "23" just as a "2" placed next to a "3." Even if a child reads "23" as "twenty-three," he may not realize that this means 2 tens and 3 ones, or have any feel about how great is the quantity represented. Thus children regard numerals as mysterious, and they may think of arithmetic as a matter of memorizing ways to manipulate meaningless symbols.

Children need special activities designed to help them build up concepts and notation for a topic such as place value. First, children need activities that involve the concept of place value but do not involve written notation. Activity 1, Collect and Exchange Game, is of this type; it introduces children to the concepts of exchanging (such as the relationships between red and white chips, blue and red chips), and place value (such as chips of certain values go in certain places). Children could play the game *without* placing chips in the appropriate columns in the Exchange Game Sheet, by simply collecting chips; however this less structured activity may not help them to build the concept of place value.

Second, activities without notation should then be followed by those in which the action is accompanied by written notation. In Activity 2, Collect and Exchange Game with Recording, the action is the placement of chips in columns on the Exchange Game Sheet, and the associated notation is the recording of the number of chips in the columns of the table. Both the placement of chips and the writing of the tally are needed so that the child associates physical action with the written notation — thus acquiring mental imagery of exchanging chips to help give meaning to later symbolic procedures. Such activities should be repeated several times before shorter notation, such as "2r 1w" or "21" is introduced. This progression from the concrete activity to the symbolic can be represented in a diagram. (Assume that we are in Tenton, or base ten.)

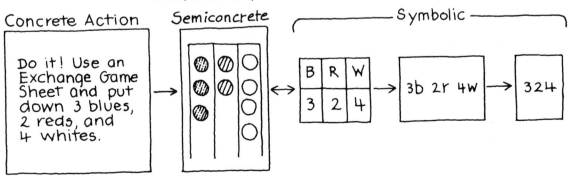

Notice that "3b 2r 4w" is a bridge in helping children build up abstract place-value notation for the concrete materials. The same sequence of steps can be followed with other materials, for example, multibase blocks. Fill in the boxes below.

What mental imagery do *you* associate with 123_{Five}? Draw it. (Did you use chips or multibase blocks? Could you?)

Are the recommendations of Dienes consistent with Piaget's learning theory; that is, the analysis of ways in which children think at different stages of intellectual development?

Once children have learned about the standard notation for numbers and are working on written exercises involving these symbols, it is desirable to have them refer back occasionally to some physical action or a picture of it. This helps to reinforce the mental imagery developed from earlier experiences with colored chips or multibase blocks.

FOLLOW-UP SECTIONS

Representing Actions for Operations

In this section we will discuss ways in which to act out arithmetic problems with concrete materials (squared materials in this case), and how to record the actions symbolically. The examples are all worked out in base five. Since you probably have not had a lot of arithmetic practice in this system, working in base five will help you to see what is really going in base ten, and how children feel when they are taught the base ten procedures for the first time.

Actions for Addition

In the exchange games with colored chips (Activities 1–2) and with multibase blocks (Activity 6) you acted out base five addition such as $24_F + 13_F$. You could do this in several different ways. Three procedures are described on pages 322–323 for solving the situation with multibase materials or squared materials (base five).

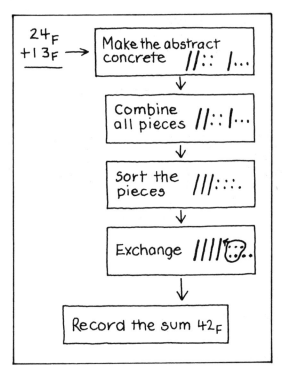

Method 1:

Make two piles, one with 2 longs and 4 units, the other with 1 long and 3 units. Push the piles together, sort the pieces, and exchange 5 units for 1 long. The result is 4 longs and 2 units, which is recorded 42_F.

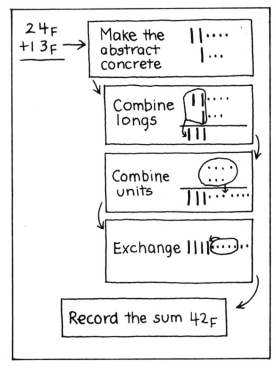

Method 2:

Take 2 longs and 4 units, placing the 4 units to the right of the longs. Under these pieces, place 1 long and 3 units. Combine the longs, giving 3 longs. Combine the units, giving 7 units. Exchange 5 units for 1 long, now getting 4 longs and 2 units. The answer is 42_F.

Method 3:

Arrange 2 longs and 4 units, and 1 long and 3 units as in method 2. Combine the units; exchange 5 units for 1 long that is placed on top of the other longs. Now combine longs, yielding 4 longs. The answer is recorded as 42_F.

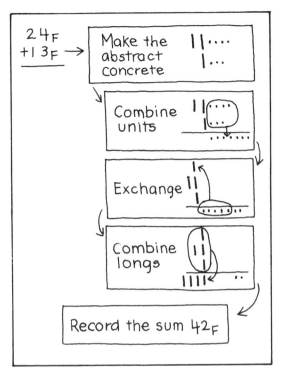

Which of these three methods for solving $24_F + 13_F$ concretely seems most natural to you? _____ Is any method more difficult than the others? _____ less difficult? _____ If children are learning to solve two-digit addition (with base-ten blocks or squared materials), does it matter which method they use? Do you think any one of these methods is preferable? Why?

Recording the Action for Addition Symbolically

All three of the methods for two-digit addition yield the correct result, and are efficient for doing addition at the *concrete* level. However, important differences emerge when we try to record these methods symbolically. How would you record the action with numerals in each case? Below is one possible way to record the action in method 1. Complete the other two additions in a way which corresponds to the action.

Method 1   Method 2   Method 3

$$2\ 4_F \qquad 2\ 4_F \qquad 2\ 4_F$$
$$+\ 1\ 3_F \qquad +\ 1\ 3_F \qquad +\ 1\ 3_F$$

Method 1:
$$\overline{{}^1 3\ 7}$$
$$4\ 2_F$$

Which method corresponds most clearly to the way you learned to do multidigit addition in school? _____ Which method might children try to use if they transfer their left-to-right orientation from reading to doing addition?

While all three methods for acting out additions with materials can relate to valid symbolic procedures (or algorithms), it is desirable that children learn the most efficient and common procedure; namely, that corresponding to method 3. If children are encouraged to act out additions with concrete materials in a methodical way, from right to left (starting with units, then longs, then flats), they will be able to learn the standard symbolic procedure for addition as a natural way to record a familiar action, rather than as a jumble of memorized rules.

The left-hand column of the diagram below shows steps in a three-digit addition, worked by method 3. On the right-hand side, draw the action and record the corresponding steps in the symbolic procedure for $242_F + 133_F$.

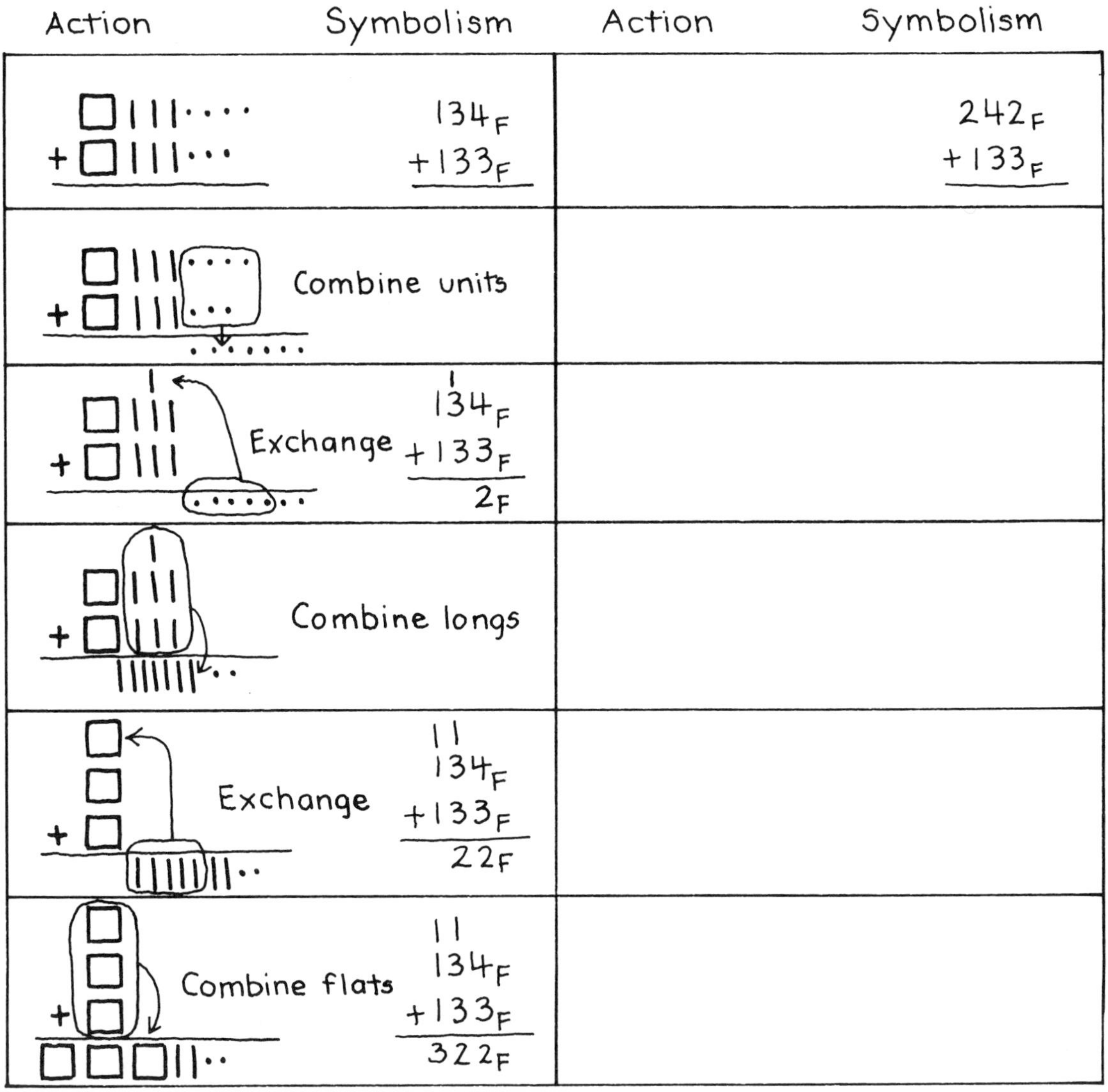

Action	Symbolism	Action	Symbolism
☐ | | | · · · · + ☐ | | | · · ·	134_F $+133_F$		242_F $+133_F$
☐ | | | [· · · ·] + ☐ | | | [· ·] · · · · · ·	Combine units		
☐ | | | + ☐ | | | (· · · · ·) · ·	Exchange	$\overset{1}{134_F}$ $+133_F$ 2_F		
☐ | | | + ☐ | | | | | | | | | · ·	Combine longs		
☐ ☐ + ☐ | | | | | | | | · ·	Exchange	$\overset{1\,1}{134_F}$ $+133_F$ 22_F		
☐ ☐ ☐ + ☐ ☐ ☐ ☐ | | · ·	Combine flats	$\overset{1\,1}{134_F}$ $+133_F$ 322_F		

Try the additions below at the symbolic level *alone*. As you do them, imagine acting them out with materials.

$$1\ 0\ 3\ 1_F \qquad 1\ 2\ 0\ 4_F \qquad 1\ 0\ 4\ 4_F \qquad 1\ 2\ 3\ 0_F$$
$$\underline{+\ 1\ 0\ 1\ 2_F} \qquad \underline{+\quad 3\ 3\ 4_F} \qquad \underline{+\quad 4\ 4\ 4_F} \qquad \underline{+\quad 3\ 1\ 3_F}$$

(You can check yourself on these additions — they should all have the same answer.)

Actions for Subtraction

In Activity 7 with colored chips and Break a Cube of Activity 6 with blocks, you acted out base-five subtraction exercises. As with addition, you probably found that you could act them out in several ways. For example, imagine doing the subtraction $32_F - 13_F$ with multibase blocks or squared materials. Below there are drawn steps in the action corresponding to this subtraction using two different methods. Can you explain what is being done at each stage?

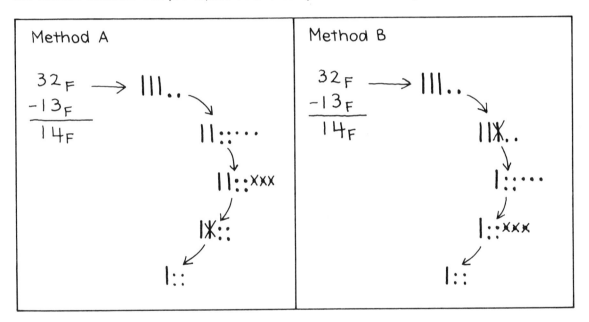

Which method above corresponds to doing the subtraction from left to right (such as first longs, then units)? _____ from right to left? _____ Which method corresponds to the way you learned to do subtraction in school? _____ Do you see any difficulties with trying to record the other method?

Recording the Action for Subtraction

Study the left-hand column of the diagram on page 326, which shows the three-digit subtraction $241_F - 114_F$. The action is indicated by drawings done in a different format than the one above, and the symbolism corresponds to this action. (Which method, A or B, is being used? _____) Then in the right-hand column, draw the action and record the corresponding steps in the symbolic procedure for $321_F - 123_F$.

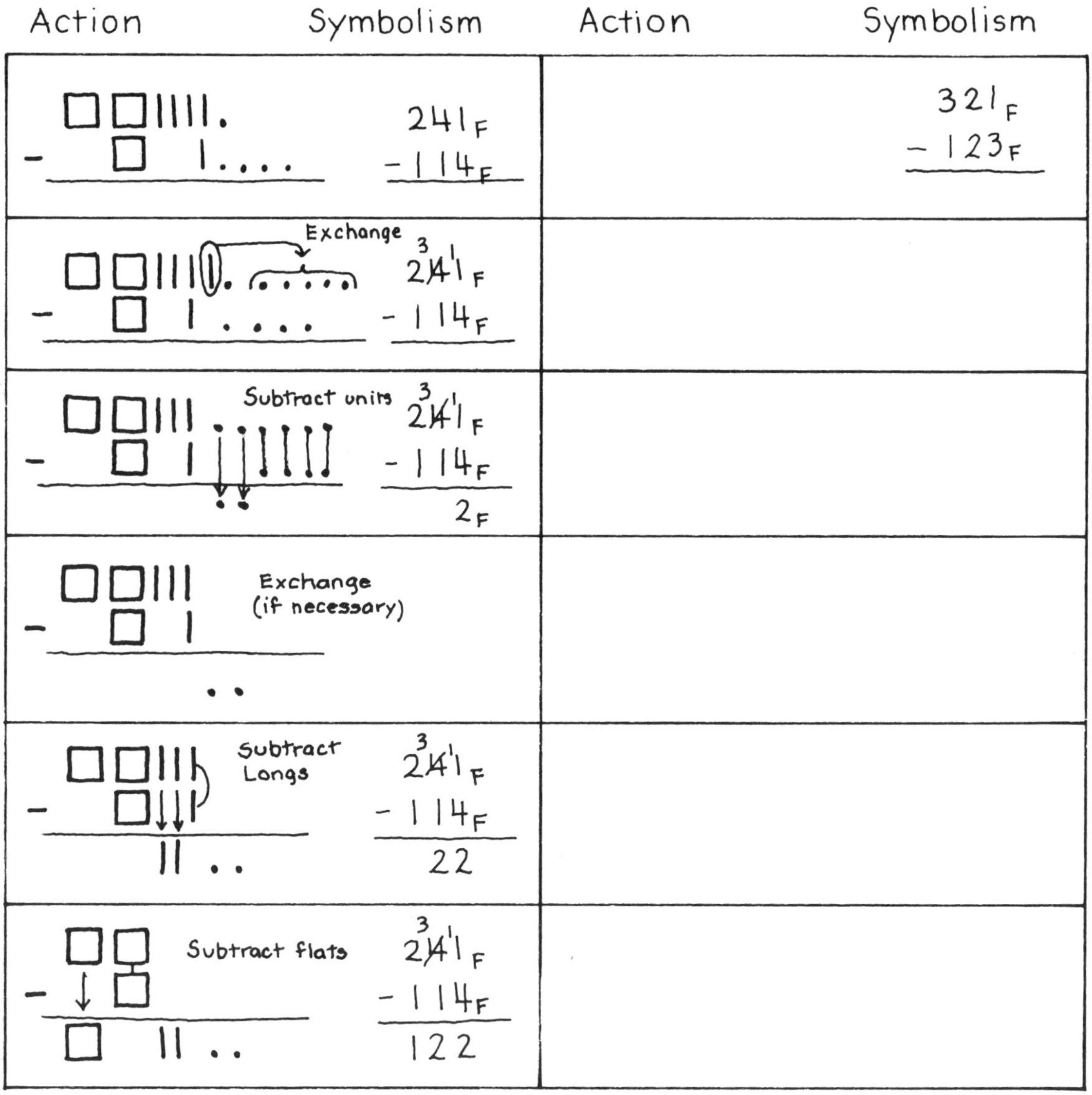

Action	Symbolism	Action	Symbolism

It is not much more difficult to act out subtraction than to act out addition. However, you may have noticed that it is more difficult to make drawings that show subtraction (because if you draw both the whole and the part taken away, there is duplication). Do you think that the drawing given above shows subtraction clearly? If not, can you think of a better way to represent this action?

Try the subtractions below at the symbolic level alone. As you do them, imagine acting them out with materials.

$$\begin{array}{r} 2\ 0\ 4\ 3\ _F \\ -\ 1\ 0\ 3\ 1\ _F \\ \hline \end{array} \qquad \begin{array}{r} 2\ 0\ 4\ 3\ _F \\ -\ 1\ 2\ 0\ 4\ _F \\ \hline \end{array} \qquad \begin{array}{r} 2\ 0\ 4\ 3\ _F \\ -\ \ \ 4\ 4\ 4\ _F \\ \hline \end{array} \qquad \begin{array}{r} 2\ 0\ 4\ 3\ _F \\ -\ 1\ 2\ 3\ 0\ _F \\ \hline \end{array}$$

(You can check yourself on these subtractions — look back on page 325.)

Actions for Multiplication and Division

The previous sections have concerned acting out addition and subtraction of two- and three-digit numbers with materials in such a way as to correspond to the usual symbolic format, or algorithm. This is relatively easy to do with addition and subtraction, using any place-value model (abacus, colored chips, bean sticks — although we have used multibase materials). The situation for multiplication and division is somewhat more complicated; certain examples (such as 3×123, $462 \div 4$, or those in Activity 7 for base five) can be acted out just as easily as additions and subtractions, but other examples with larger numbers (such as 123×436 or $4631 \div 123$) are difficult to handle concretely, and depend on a thorough understanding at the symbolic level. (Teaching the procedures for these more complicated examples will be discussed in Chapter 9, Whole Number Algorithms and Their Uses.)

Imagine using multibase materials (base five). For three exercises following, diagrams suggest solutions with base-five materials together with a corresponding symbolic format. *Draw* how you would act out the remaining three exercises, and write them in a suitable symbolic format. Does your action correspond to the symbolic format?

	Action	Symbolic Format
1. $4 \times 132_F$	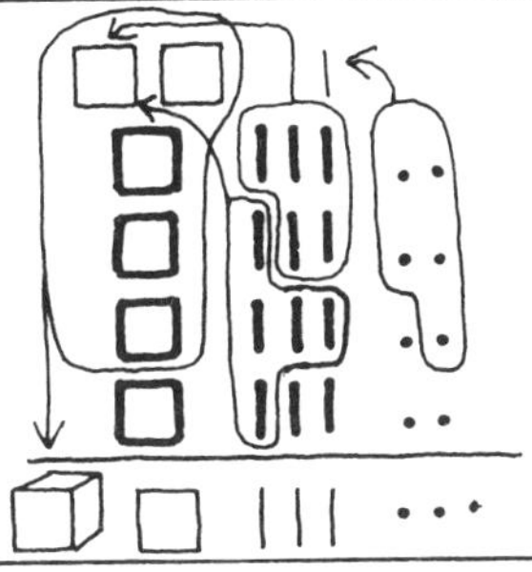	$$\begin{array}{r} 2\ 1 \\ 1\ 3\ 2\ _F \\ \times\ \ 4 \\ \hline 1\ 1\ 3\ 3\ _F \end{array}$$
2. $3 \times 123_F$		

	Action	Symbolic Format
3. $424_F \div 123_F$	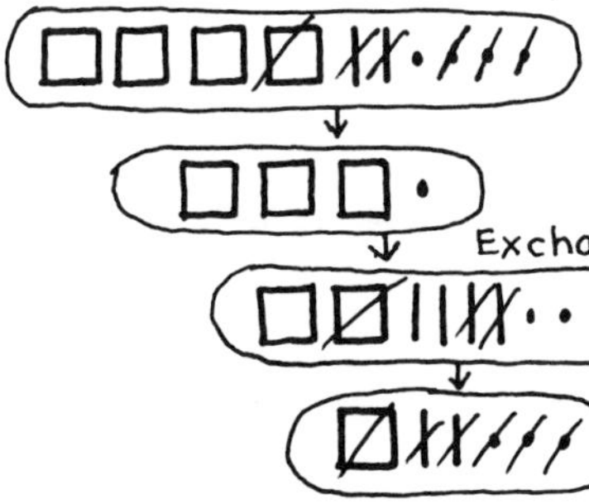	$123\overline{)424}$ $\underline{-123}$ 1 $\not{3}\,\not{0}\,1$ $\underline{-123}$ 1 123 $\underline{-123}$ 1 0 Ans. 3
4. $233_F \div 32_F$		
5. $431_F \div 2$	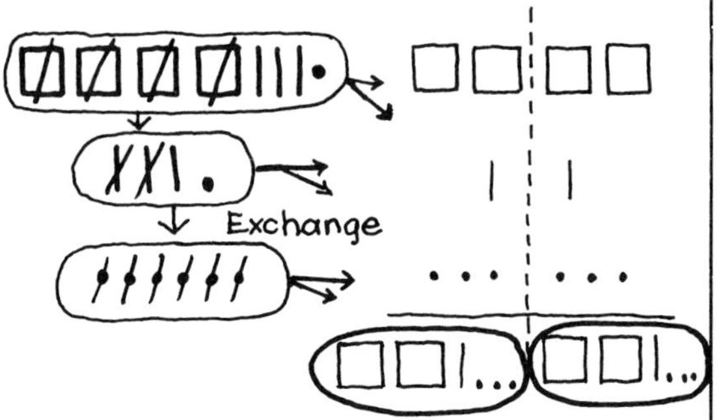	$2\overline{)431}$ $-400 = 2 \times 200_F$ 31 $-20 = 2 \times 10_F$ 11 $-11 = 2 \times 3_F$ 0 213_F
6. $233_F \div 2$		

Note: Which of the divisions (3) or (5) used the *partitive* or *sharing* interpretation of division? _____ Which used the *measurement* or *repeated subtraction* interpretation? _____ Could you easily do either one with the other approach?

Extending Place-Value Notation to Decimal Fractions

Chips and Money

Activities 1–8 involving colored chips suggested that a monetary system (such as chips in Fiveton) could serve as a model for place value. Of course, if we select just certain coins from our own coinage system, we also have a model for base-ten numeration. For example,

74¢ is represented by _____ dimes + _____ cents;

174¢ is represented by _____ dollars + _____ dimes + _____ cents

In everyday life we do not write 174¢ — rather we express this value in dollars, as $1.74. This alternate way of writing money suggests that the chip-trading model of numeration can easily be extended to decimal fractions. In this notation, a dollar is chosen to be the unit. When we write the amount $213.98, the value of each digit is determined by its place. Using the model of coins and bills, we could "see" this amount, as shown here.

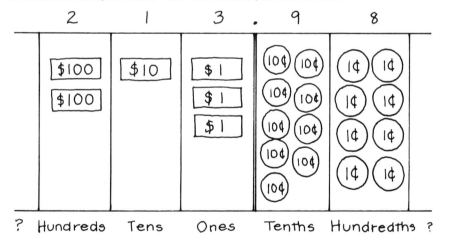

This chart could be extended in both directions. The next column to the *left* would stand for _____; the next column to the *right* would stand for _____. (In fact there *is* a monetary value for this column to the right. A *mill* is worth one-tenth of a cent or one-thousandth of a dollar. The cash value of store coupons is often expressed in mills.)

Children could play a Collect and Exchange Game with play money and at the same time develop decimal notation and addition such as 1.27 + .14. (For this game children might use two dice, and take the *product* of the two numbers showing. This will make the game go faster, and give practice with multiplication facts, which is probably more appropriate at the grade level where children are learning addition of decimal fractions.)

Structured Materials

While money does provide us with a natural model for decimal notation, it has the same drawbacks that colored chips have as a model for whole number notation — one cannot see the value relationships between pieces. One must remember that 10 cents are worth 1 dime and that 10 dimes are worth 1 dollar. As you saw earlier, structured materials such as multibase blocks avoid this difficulty. In fact, the blocks can provide an effective model for place-value notation for decimal fractions.

Imagine using a base-ten set of multibase blocks. (Notation for fractional numbers could also be developed in this way in any other base.) Suppose that the *flat* (☐) is chosen to be equal to 1. Since 10 longs (|) make a flat, the long represents one-tenth or .1. Likewise, since _____ small cubes (•) make a flat, a small cube represents one-_____ (or _____). Fill in the blanks below.

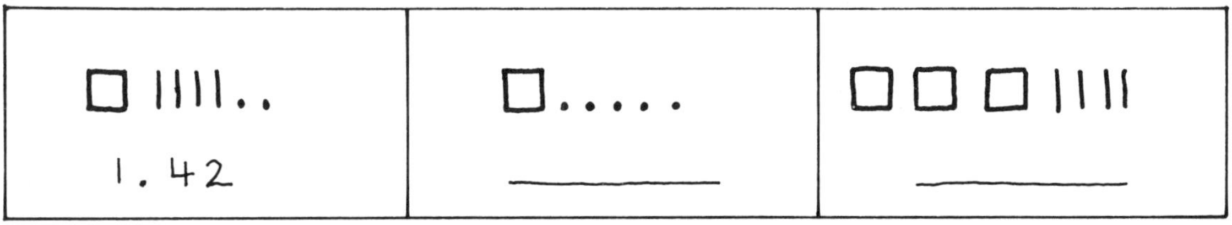

☐ ‖‖..	☐.....	☐ ☐ ☐ ‖‖
1.42	_____	_____

Did you write 3.4 or 3.40 for the drawing to the right? Either is correct. The first means 3 ones and 4 tenths, while the second means 3 units and 4 tenths and 0 hundredths. It does not matter whether or not we include the information that there are no hundredths. The expression 3.40 is sometimes read as "three and forty-hundredths," which simply expresses the fact that the 4 longs could be exchanged for 40 small cubes, that is, four-tenths is the same as forty-hundredths.

Decimals can be written in an expanded form that brings attention to the value of each position. Complete the examples below.

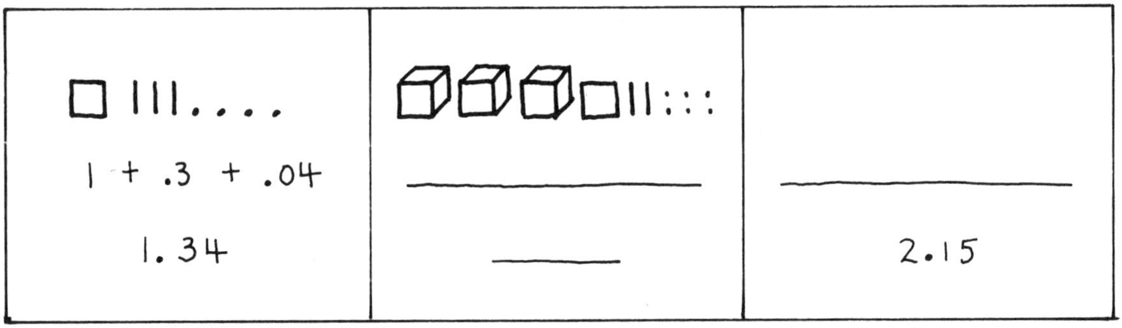

☐ ‖‖.,..	▱▱▱☐‖:::	
1 + .3 + .04	_____	_____
1.34	_____	2.15

In the examples above, multibase blocks were used as models for decimal fractions no greater than 99.99, and with no more than two decimal places. Could you use these materials to show the number 1.213? 123.4? 123.45? If so, how? If not, why not? (**Hint:** A block other than the flat might be taken as "1.")

Acting Out Operations on Decimal Fractions

It is relatively easy to act out decimal additions and subtractions with place-value materials in just the same way that whole-number situations are done. Two examples of such actions are drawn below. Write the corresponding symbolic formats. Here again, ☐ = 1.

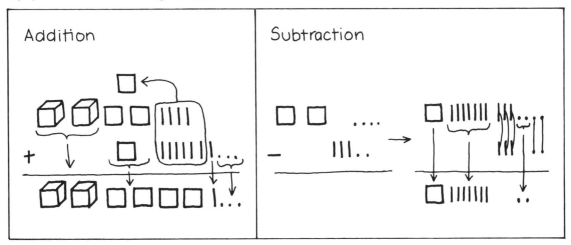

Notice that the first example above, 22.4 + 1.73, is of a type that frequently causes children difficulty. Children might write this as $\begin{array}{r} 2\,2.4 \\ +\ 1.7\,3 \end{array}$ and then add. However if they represent both numbers in terms of a place-value model such as the multibase blocks, they will see that it makes no sense to add 3 small cubes to 4 longs, and that instead this should be written as $\begin{array}{r} 2\,2.4 \\ +\ \ 1.7\,3 \end{array}$ or $\begin{array}{r} 2\,2.4\,0 \\ +\ \ 1.7\,3 \end{array}$.

The action shown in the diagram for the addition above can actually be interpreted in several ways. If you took the small cube to be the unit (as you did in the earlier activities with these materials), the diagram would show 2240 + 173. However if the *long* (|) was chosen to be 1, then the small cube (•) would be one-tenth or .1, and the flat (☐) would be 10. The diagram would then correspond to 224 + _____. On the other hand, if the *block* (⬛) was chosen to be 1, the diagram would show the addition _____ + _____.

As is the case with multiplication and division of multidigit whole numbers, some simple situations with decimals can be acted out easily with place-value materials. Can you imagine how to act out 4 × 21.23 or 12.56 ÷ 4? However more complicated multiplications and divisions involving decimals depend on a thorough understanding of the algorithms for multidigit whole number computation, and an understanding of fractions. Teaching these more complicated procedures will be considered in Chapter 11, Rational Numbers.

Place Value in Bases Other than Ten

This section, containing more materials and activities related to place-value notation in bases other than ten, is intended to show you some of the potential of multibase arithmetic as a source of enrichment in the upper elementary grades.

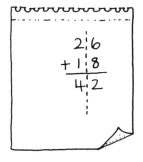

Multibase Arithmetic in Everyday Life

Do you think the addition to the left is correct? Perhaps it would seem correct if you related it to this story problem: I have 2 feet 6 inches of ribbon on one spool, and 1 foot 8 inches on another spool. How much do I have in all?

Although you may not think of this situation as arithmetic in base twelve, it does involve the fundamental concepts of grouping and exchanging (such as 12 inches for 1 foot). Can you label the columns in the following additions (for example, as "feet" and "inches")? All involve common measurement situations.

$$
\begin{array}{cccccccccc}
1 & 2 & & 4 & 9 & & 1 & 3 & & 1 & 50 & & 2 & 5 \\
 & 2 & & +3 & 7 & & +1 & 2 & & +2 & 15 & & +3 & 6 \\
+ & 1 & & \overline{8 \;\; 4} & & & \overline{3 \;\; 1} & & & \overline{4 \;\; 5} & & & \overline{6 \;\; 4} \\
\overline{2 \;\; 2} & & & & & & & & & & &
\end{array}
$$

(**Note:** You might have used — not in this order — yards/feet, feet/inches, quarts/cups, weeks/days, hours/minutes.)

Experiences with grouping and exchanging in connection with common measurements can strengthen children's understanding of the processes involved in arithmetic of various bases. Of course as was seen in Chapter 6, Measurement and the Metric System, the metric system provides an especially convenient model for base ten.

Colored Chips and Other Bases

In Activities 1–8 you used chips as a model for place value in base five, and also in base three. You could play the exchange games with any "exchange rate" that you choose. If you played in Fourton, or base four, then 4 whites would be worth 1 red, 4 reds worth 1 blue, and so forth. Fill in the place-value chart in base four for some more colors of chips. (See Activity 8.)

Base Four				
Y	G	B	R	W
			4	1

Suppose that you played the games in base ⬡ (where the ⬡ could be filled in with any number,

2,3,4,5, . . .). Use your results from page 332 and from Activity 8 to fill in the place-value chart for base ⬡. (**Hint:** The blue chip should be worth ⬡ × ⬡ or ⬡².)

Base ⬡				
Y	G	B	R	W
				1

If you want to find out the value of a handful of white chips in terms of blue, red, and white chips, you might do it by physically grouping the chips. (Many people will count a jarful of pennies in this way, by making little piles of 5 or 10.) but if the chips are just drawn on paper, you may find it easier to find how many by drawing loops to indicate the grouping and exchanging. In fact if you use colored loops, you might build on the colored-chip image. For example, the chips to the right have been counted in Fiveton or base five. The *dotted* line (- - - - -) indicates *red* loops, and the *solid* line (———) indicates *blue* loops. How many chips are there in base five? _____Five

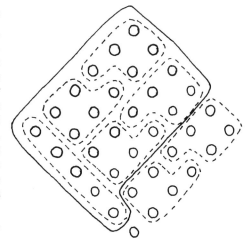

Count this same array by "looping" (in color, if possible) in the indicated bases.

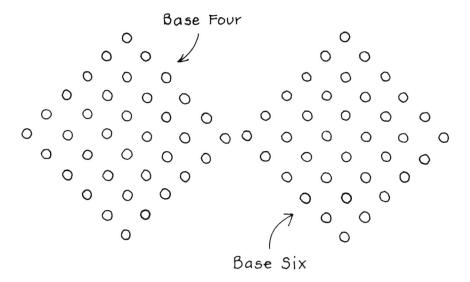

Base Four

Base Six

Base-Two Multibase Blocks — Units, Longs, Flats, Blocks, and More

If you can examine a commercial set of the rectangular base-two multibase blocks, you will find that the pieces are somewhat different from those described for other bases. There are units, longs, flats, and blocks as expected, but also there are bigger pieces. Write how many units it would take to make each piece below.

Block-Block

Flat Block

Long Block

Block

Flat

Long   Unit

Can you imagine what piece would go next, on the left?

It is often easier to read numerals in any base if you group the digits in threes by commas. Thus in base two we might write the numeral 1101110_{Two} as $1,101,110_{Two}$. Do you see how this grouping by threes corresponds to a pattern in the pieces? That is, the three positions to the right stand for the pieces , while the next three positions to the left stand for larger versions of these pieces. (Could this pattern continue to the left?)

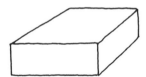

Could you expand the base-ten materials in the same way, to make a long-block, a flat-block, and a block-block? (Remember that blocks in base-ten sets are usually 10 centimeters or a little less on a side. How big would the block-block be? Approximately how much would it weigh?) While it is not feasible to *see* the base-ten model for the larger pieces, you may be able to imagine it by looking at the base-two materials.

More on Base Two

Binary numerals (base two) are used with computers, because in base two, only two digits are required, 0 and 1. These digits are readily communicated to a machine by having a switch "off" or "on." (This has been one reason for including base-two arithmetic in the curriculum.) Fill in the place-value chart for base two.

$1,000,000_{Two}$	$100,000_{Two}$	$10,000_{Two}$	$1,000_{Two}$	100_{Two}	10_{Two}	1_{Two}
				4	2	1

As you can see, it takes a large number of digits to write numbers that in base ten require only two digits. For example $99 = 64 + 32 + 2 + 1$ and so we write 99 as $1,100,011_{Two}$.

There is a close connection between how numbers are written in base two and in base eight, the discovery of which may provide children with a challenge involving considerable practice with arithmetic. Fill in this place-value chart for base eight.

$1,000$ Eight	100 Eight	10 Eight	1 Eight
			1

Now fill in the table below, in which several numbers are expressed in base ten (top row) and also in both base two and base eight.

Base Ten	1	2	3	4	5	6	7	8	12	25	35	99
Base Two	1	10	11	100				1,000	1,100			1,100,011
Base Eight	1	2	3	4	5	6	7	10			43	

Do you see a relationship between how numbers are written in base two and in base eight? (**Hint:** It is important to group the base-two digits by threes, and look at the numerals for the numbers 1–7.) If you do not see it, try some more numbers.

This relationship between base-two and base-eight numerals can be useful in work with computers — while it is difficult to copy and read a large number in base two, one can easily convert it to base eight and thus have a much more convenient numeral to work with.

Other Bases in the Elementary School Curriculum

Do you remember enjoying work with bases other than ten in elementary or high school? Do you think that children might enjoy some of the multibase activities in this chapter?

The arithmetic of bases other than ten, introduced in the upper elementary school curriculum in the 1960s, has met with opposition partly because it was often taught by rote with little or no motivation or understanding, and was perceived as busy work, unrelated to real-life problems, by both teachers and students. However, as you have seen, this topic need not be taught at an entirely symbolic level, and it can provide a context for some thought-provoking questions and explorations. Children often enjoy the novelty of a new "code," and the challenges that the materials can provide. Multibase arithmetic can serve a useful role in the upper elementary school curriculum as an enrichment topic — a chance to practice basic computational skills while engaging in new mathematical investigations.

Montessori Materials for Numeration

Maria Montessori was an Italian doctor who devoted much of her life to developing a system of educating children, largely through the use of concrete materials and very structured activities with them. Although her school (founded in 1907) was originally designed to aid poor Italian children, there are now Montessori schools (with varying degrees of adherence to original methods) throughout the world.[3] Some of the Montessori materials for numeration will no doubt appear familiar to you from your experience in this chapter.

Beads
Children work with small beads strung on wire. There are different colors for the numbers one to ten. The "ten" beads are "golden." Children see that a string of ten tens can be folded up to make a square, which they call a "hundred"; and that ten of the "hundreds" can be fastened to make a "thousand."

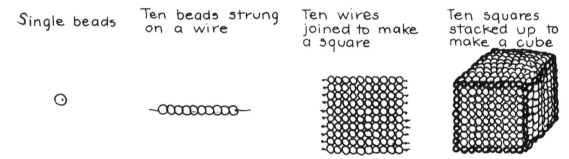

The materials also include similar sets of pieces for each number 2–10. For example, for the "fours," the pieces look like this.

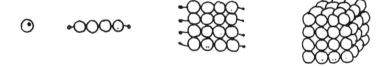

What does this remind you of?

Teen Board and Ten Board
Children make numerals on these boards by inserting pieces of wood in the unit's place. They match the numerals with the appropriate collection of beads.

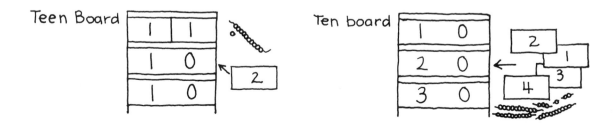

Chips

Children use colored chips which they accumulate to show larger numbers. These stand for the "golden-bead" pieces.

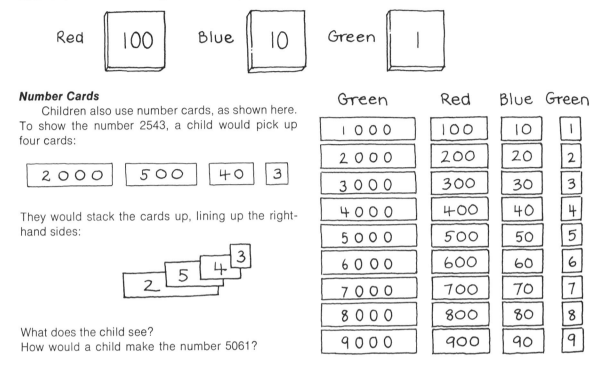

Number Cards

Children also use number cards, as shown here. To show the number 2543, a child would pick up four cards:

They would stack the cards up, lining up the right-hand sides:

What does the child see?

How would a child make the number 5061?

Green	Red	Blue	Green
1 0 0 0	1 0 0	1 0	1
2 0 0 0	2 0 0	2 0	2
3 0 0 0	3 0 0	3 0	3
4 0 0 0	4 0 0	4 0	4
5 0 0 0	5 0 0	5 0	5
6 0 0 0	6 0 0	6 0	6
7 0 0 0	7 0 0	7 0	7
8 0 0 0	8 0 0	8 0	8
9 0 0 0	9 0 0	9 0	9

Exchange Games Again — Dice, Probability, and the Rules

In the Activities in this chapter you have seen several modifications of exchange games. If you plan to modify the game to play it with children, you should know the effects of changing the rules on the length of the game. To examine these effects, we will first examine what happened in the games that you played. Refer to Activity 1 with chips, Collect and Exchange Game, and Activity 7, Exchange and Give-Away Game. Look at the entries in the column showing what you rolled in each round. To get a wider range of rolls, also look at someone else's score chart. Fill in the table below. All entries will be between 2 and 12. (Do you see why?)

Rolls	2	3	4	5	6	7	8	9	10	11	12
Your rolls in Activity 2											
Your rolls in Activity 7											
Someone else's rolls in Activity 2											
Someone else's rolls in Activity 7											

1. How many rounds did your games take? _____ _____ Compare your answer with that of other groups. How many rounds would you guess the game would take in general? _____

2. How many white chips must you collect (or give away) to win the exchange games on pages 297–298 and 301? _____

3. What is the average of all rolls recorded in the table on page 337? _____ (How did you get the answer? Compare your method with that of someone else. Did they do it the same way?)

4. Using the information in 2 and 3, how long do you think an average game would take? _____ rounds

When you look at the rolls recorded in your table, do any numbers seem to be especially common? _____ Are any especially rare? _____ To see how your impressions compare with class results, complete the following table.

Rolls	2	3	4	5	6	7	8	9	10	11	12
Number of times you obtained each roll (top two rows above)											
Total number of times each roll was obtained in the class											

How many times was a pair of dice thrown in the whole class? _____ How can you tell from the table above?

Which sum would you predict would come up *most* often if this game was played repeatedly? _____ Which sum would come up *least* often? _____

Figure out how to make a graph of the information in the table above on this piece of graph paper.

In Chapter 2, Number and Its Uses, a distinction was made between an *experimental* and a *theoretical* approach to chance, or probability. An experimental approach involves performing an experiment a large number of times, and observing the outcomes, as you did above. You probably found that some numbers are much more common than others as the sum of two dice. A theoretical approach involves trying to explain why the outcomes should be this way. Can you explain why your graph above looks the way it does?

To be more precise, in a theoretical approach we can list all of the possible outcomes that can occur when you perform an experiment (in this case, rolling two dice) and also determine exactly what the probability of each outcome is. When you roll two dice, you get a pair of numbers, both in the set {1,2,3,4,5,6}. We assume that all of these pairs or outcomes are equally likely.

The possible sums are 2, 3, 4, . . . , 12. You can get a sum of 2 in just *one* way: 1 + 1, or as a 1 on both dice. You can get a score of 3 in *two* ways: 1 + 2 and 2 + 1 (since the 2 could be on either of the dice). Below list all of the ways that you can get each number as a sum when you roll two dice.

Number	Ways to get the number as a sum of two dice	Number of ways
2	1 + 1	1
3	1 + 2 , 2 + 1	2
4		
5		
6		
7		
8		
9		
10		
11		
12		

Remember that the theoretical probability of an event is the number of ways in which that event can occur divided by the total number of possible outcomes. How many possible outcomes are there in this case? _____ To find the probability of the event, "rolling a sum of 2," we divide the number of ways to get a sum of 2 (that is, 1) by the total number of ways two dice can land (that is, 36). Does this theoretical probability of $\frac{1}{36}$ correspond to the actual number of times that you and your classmates rolled a 2? That is, did you get a 2 approximately one time out of 36?

Suppose that you wanted to use this game to give children practice of addition facts. Do you think that children would be likely to get much practice with the bridging facts; that is, sums of over 10? _____ Why?

To provide practice with these more difficult facts, you could change the dice; perhaps label them {4,5,6,7,8,9}. If you did this, what would the *average* sum rolled be? _____ Which sums do you think would arise most often? _____ If children used these dice to play an exchange game where the goal was two blue chips, or 50 white chips, about how many rounds would you expect the game to take? _____

We have investigated the results of throwing two dice and finding the sum through data collected in the exchange games, because that data was readily available. Children may enjoy investigating this question on its own in the activity on page 340, which also provides considerable practice with basic addition facts.

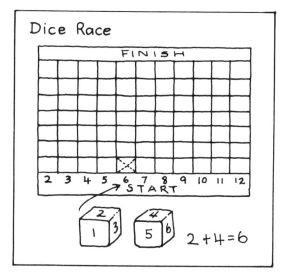

Children work cooperatively, in small groups. Each group has a copy of the "race track," as shown here. Children each roll two dice, and make an X in the column above the sum of the numbers rolled. (They can either take turns, or do it simultaneously.) They continue making such marks until one number wins; that is, the spaces above it are marked with X's all the way to the top. Children can speculate on which number will probably win each time. When several groups have completed their races, the results can be compared.

What numbers do you think will win most often in the Dice Race? _____
Could you design a Dice Race that would give children practice with subtraction instead of addition?

A Little History

There are alternatives to our place-value system of numeration, and if children are left to play the exchange games without an Exchange Game Sheet (which encourages a certain type of placement of chips), they may develop numeration systems similar to some developed by ancient cultures. These ancient numeration systems are sometimes included in the elementary school curriculum for practical reasons (such as reading roman numerals on a clockface), and also for cultural enrichment. Perhaps their study could add to social studies units on the corresponding ancient civilizations.

Most cultures have grouped things by tens, although five (one hand) and twenty (hands and feet) have also been used. Twelve and sixty are also fairly common grouping numbers. Where do we still find 12 used as a grouping number? _____ 60? _____

Suppose that we are in Tenton. Can you think of a convenient way to describe this collection of chips?   ⊘⊘⊘⊘◯

One possibility might be b b r r r w. This idea rather resembles the ancient Egyptian system in which there was a symbol for 1 (|), for 10(∩), for 100 (℃), for 1000 (ℱ), and so forth for powers of 10. Symbols were repeated as many times as necessary. Our numeral 1 3 4 2 corresponds to ℱ℃℃℃∩∩∩∩||. Fill in the blanks below.

Egyptian system	℃℃∩∩∩∩		ℱℱℱ∩∩||||	
Our system		369		1976

What disadvantages does this system have? (**Hint:** Write 9999 in Egyptian numerals.)

Another system which is in some ways like the Egyptian is the Roman system. Again there are symbols for 1 (I), 10 (X), 100 (C), 1000 (M), and so forth for powers of 10. However the Roman system had some refinements. Instead of writing 8 as IIIIIIII, the Romans introduced other grouping units; for 5 (V), 50 (L), and 500 (D). Thus 7 8 6 was written as DCCLXXXVI. A further (and much later) refinement was the "subtractive principle"; to make it easier to write a number such as 9 (VIIII in early times), subtraction could be indicated by putting a symbol for a smaller number to the left of the symbol for a larger number. (Since $9 = 10 - 1$, 9 could be written as IX.) Fill in the blanks below.

Roman system	DCCVIII		CCXCIX	
Our system		369		1976

What disadvantages does the Roman system have as compared to our system? (**Hint:** If the credits to a movie say that it was made in MCMXLIV, can you tell easily how old it is? Also, try to multiply 369 by 479 in Roman numerals.)

Another possible way to record ⊗⊗⊗⊘⊘○ was suggested in the course of the chip-trading activities: 2 b 3 r 1 w. The Chinese developed a system much like this in the third century B.C. They used symbols for 1–9, 10, 100, 1000, etc. as shown below.

1	2	3	4	5	6	7	8	9	10	100	1000
一	二	三	四	五	六	七	八	九	十	百	千

Numerals could be written from the top downward or from right to left. Two hundred and thirty-one would be written as follows:

二　　百　　三　　十　　一

or　2　hundreds　3　tens　one

which resembles　2　　b　　3　r　1 w

In this system, 3 0 0 0 would be written as 三千 . There was no *need* for a 0 as a place holder here, since 千 conveys "thousands." Fill in the blanks below.

Chinese system	七百二十六		八百五十	
Our system		369		1976

What disadvantages can you see to this system? (**Hint:** Using the information above, can you write 98,153 in the Chinese system?) There is also a symbol indicating a gap, 零 . Thus 3204 is written as 三千二百零四 (or 3 thousand 2 hundred (gap) 4) and 3004 is written as 三千零四 (or 3 thousand (gap) 4). This symbol is used in a different way from our zero. Do you see why? Sometimes we use "and" informally in the same way. If you ask someone to read "2001" aloud, many will say "two thousand *and* one." However, many teachers would say this is incorrect; that is, 2001 should be read "two thousand one," and the word "and" should be reserved to indicate a decimal point, as in "one hundred twenty-three *and* five-tenths" for 123.5.

> **Note:** Our *spoken* description of numbers is of the same type as the Chinese written numeration system. However there have been contractions — we no longer say "four tens," but rather "forty." The suffix *-ty* comes from the Old English *-tig,* meaning tens.

One disadvantage in common to all three of these ancient numeration systems is that to write larger and larger numbers, more and more new symbols must be invented. However, since there was relatively little need for very large numbers, these numeration systems worked reasonably well. How many different symbols do we need (that is, how many different numeral keys on a typewriter) to describe any number whatever, however large it may be?[4]

TEST YOUR UNDERSTANDING

1. How many white chips are there? Suppose they were traded in for red and blue chips according to the rules of Activity 1, Collect and Exchange Game. What chips would result? (Draw loops to indicate the exchanges.)

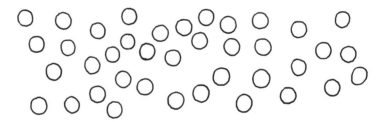

2. Suppose you are playing the Collect and Exchange Game (in Activity 1), and you have 1 blue, 2 reds, and 4 whites.

   a. How many more whites do you need to win?
   b. Could you win on the next roll?
   c. Suppose that on your next turn you roll ⚁ ⚁ . What will your new score be? Write the corresponding addition sentence in base five. _____ + _____ = _____

3. In what base is this collection of squared material? How many units does this picture represent? Write an expanded numeral for this picture.

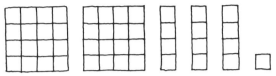

4. Draw a picture to show 123_Five using squared materials, and use it to show how many units (base ten) there are in 123_Five.

5. Solve these in base five. Draw diagrams for (a) and (c) showing how you would use multibase blocks or squared material to act out the solutions.

   a. $\begin{array}{r} 342_F \\ +133_F \end{array}$ b. $\begin{array}{r} 1234_F \\ +\ \ 444_F \end{array}$ c. $\begin{array}{r} 342_F \\ -133_F \end{array}$ d. $\begin{array}{r} 1000_F \\ -\ \ 324_F \end{array}$

6. Here is a diagram representing some base-five squared material.

   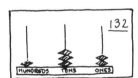

   a. If the pieces were combined, how would you write the total amount in base five? (Draw loops to indicate the exchanges.)
   b. Write a related addition sentence in base five.
      _____ + _____ + _____ = _____
   c. Write a related multiplication sentence in base five.
      _____ × _____ = _____

7. Two common computational errors related to place value were described in the Introduction. How would you use the concrete materials described in this chapter to help children avoid these errors?

8. Name three types of models for place value (base ten) and give examples of each. For each example, draw a picture showing "one hundred thirty-five." Why might it be desirable for children to use more than one type of model?

9. This picture shows an "open abacus." Would you use an abacus before, after, or instead of a chip-trading activity? Fill in numerals or beads.

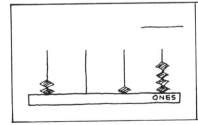
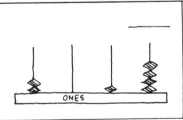
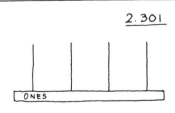

10. What are the arguments for and against having first graders (a) do informal activities such as exchange games (without notation) in bases other than ten; and (b) write notation for numbers in bases other than ten? Where do you stand?

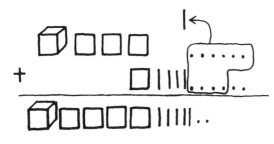

11. The diagram to the left shows an addition situation acted out with multibase materials. Write a symbolic expression for this situation, if

    a. the small cube (•) is 1.
    b. the long (❘) is 1.
    c. the flat (☐) is 1.
    d. the block (⬚) is 1.

12. A fourth grade teacher realizes that the children enjoy playing the exchange game and wants to adapt it to provide practice with multiplication skills. This teacher has the children play the game in base ten, and has two possible rules: (a) Children roll *one* die, and must multiply their score by some given number (2, 3, etc., depending on where practice is needed); (b) Children roll *two* dice, and a player's score is the product of the numbers showing. Can you think of some other rules that could be used in an exchange game to practice basic skills?

13. Self-checking "poke-through cards" (see page 63) can be an enjoyable way for children to practice skills. Teachers can also use them to evaluate children's understanding of place value: Design cards of this type which relate to the following problems:

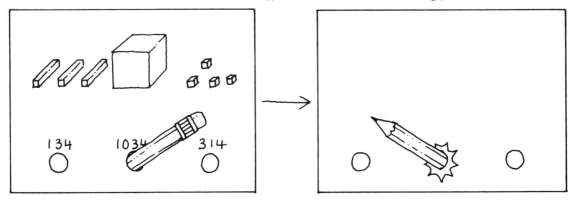

    a. Given a bean-stick drawing, choose the correct numeral.
    b. Given a numeral, choose the correct drawing of multibase blocks.
    c. Given numerals and a diagram with multibase blocks of an addition situation, choose the numeral for the answer.
    d. Given a number written in expanded form, choose the numeral.
    e. Given a collection of dimes and pennies, choose the correct numeral.

Which of the semiconcrete or pictorial questions above could you ask with concrete materials? Why might it be preferable to ask some questions in the concrete mode?

14. What do you take from S I X to make nine? (**Hint:** See page 341.)

15. *An Amusement.* This is a Hundred's Chart. Cut a square corner from a piece of paper and place it so that a square array of the numbers shows in the left-hand corner.

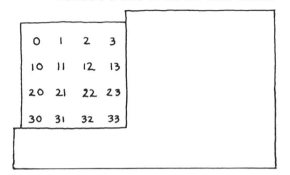

0	1	2	3	4	5	6	7	8	9
10	11	12	13	14	15	16	17	18	19
20	21	22	23	24	25	26	27	28	29
30	31	32	33	34	35	36	37	38	39
40	41	42	43	44	45	46	47	48	49
50	51	52	53	54	55	56	57	58	59
60	61	62	63	64	65	66	67	68	69
70	71	72	73	74	75	76	77	78	79
80	81	82	83	84	85	86	87	88	89
90	91	92	93	94	95	96	97	98	99

What do you notice about the numbers showing? (**Hint:** See Activity 5 with chips.) Try it for different sized squares.

FURTHER READINGS AND PROJECTS

1. You have seen a variety of types of materials suitable for teaching children about place value. Examine some catalogues from educational supply companies to see what materials are available commercially. You will probably find commercial versions of homemade materials we have used (such as chip-trading materials), ways in which other materials can be modified to deal with place value (such as special "joiners" so that Unifix cubes can be put together to make multibase blocks), and also some useful supplementary materials (such as rubber stamps with pictures of units, longs, flats, and blocks so that you can easily make pictorial task cards). Which of the commercial materials that you found could be made by a teacher? Did you find materials of each of the three types, colored chips, grouping, and structured?

2. It is sometimes difficult for adults to understand just what difficulties children have with place value. For an anecdotal account of two young children's discovery of how our numbers are written, read "Lorena and Molly and Maths and Me" by Rose Grossman (*Mathematics Teaching* 68 (September 1974), pp. 4–6). *Mathematics Teaching* is an English journal which quite often publishes this type of anecdotal article. It has some useful regular features including comparison of several varieties of apparatus of some particular type, and reviews of new materials. Another article describing children's difficulties learning about place value is "Teaching Tens to Timmy, or A Caution in Teaching with Physical Models" by Esther R. Steinberg and Bonnie Anderson, in *The Arithmetic Teacher* 20:8 (December 1973), pp. 620–625.

3. On pages 305–307, we discussed how exchange games can be played with young children, in particular in bases other than ten (without notation, of course). The book *Let's Play Maths* by Michael Holt and Zoltan Dienes (New York: Walker, 1973; Harmondsworth, Eng.: Penguin, 1973) provides another

format for this sort of game. Examine Set 9, "Number Games," in particular the games "Sesame," "Arapanza," "Sesame Dice," and "Swops and Shops." Try some of these with children, if you can.

4. Examine Chapter 11, "Place Value," in *Mathematics Their Way* by Mary Barrata-Lorton (Menlo Park, Cal.: Addison-Wesley, 1976). You will find a very attractive presentation of activities for young children which resemble those in this chapter. A record of teacher-child dialogue is accompanied by photographs of children working with various materials (Unifix, beans, buttons, . . .). Do you think that the sequence of activities is consistent with the sequence described on page 320? Look at the "Questions for Teachers" at the end of this chapter in *Mathematics Their Way*. Do you agree with the responses?

5. In the section A Little History, pages 342–344, a few samples of ways in which other civilizations have written numerals were given. For more details on the history of both our own words and symbols for numbers, and those of other peoples, consult the booklet *Numbers and Numerals* by David Eugene Smith and Jekuthiel Ginsburg (Reston, Va.: NCTM, 1937). Another good source is the Thirty-first Yearbook of the National Council of Teachers of Mathematics, *Historical Topics for the Mathematics Classroom*. These historical mathematical topics can provide interesting sidelights on other curriculum areas. One such example is given in the article "Multidisciplinary: Kids Dig Egypt" by Dorothy Needham, in *Teacher* 95:4 (April 1978), pp. 82–86.

6. Examine the book *Teaching Montessori in the Home* (*The School Years*) by Elizabeth Hainstock (New York: Random House, 1971). This book describes some of the Montessori mathematics materials, how to make substitutes, and how the materials can be used by parents in a Montessori mathematics program at home with young children. You will find the materials described on pages 336–337 of this chapter under the headings "The Golden Bead Material," "The Seguin Boards," "The Number Symbol Cards," and (for a modified form of the colored chips) "The Short Division Board." Read some of the exercises suggested for these materials. Do you think these would be effective lessons? Could you modify them for use with groups of children in school?

7. In *Building Up Mathematics* (London: Hutchinson Educational Ltd. 1960), Zoltan P. Dienes describes several principles for helping children learn mathematics — in particular arithmetical concepts of place value and algorithms for whole numbers. Read Chapter 2, "A Theory of Mathematical Learning," which concerns Dienes's notion of mathematics, what it means to learn mathematics, and principles for teaching it. Then read Chapter 3, "Arithmetical Concepts," and note how multibase activities lead to a general understanding of place value and algorithms. How are the following principles applied in these activities: Dynamic Principle, Constructivity Principle, Mathematical Variability Principle?

8. Examine a textbook series for the upper elementary grades. Is notation for numerals in bases other than ten included? If so, are any concrete materials used as models? Do children learn to do arithmetic in other bases? Are there interesting challenges and applications? Do you think children would enjoy this topic?

NOTES

1. Zoltan P. Dienes, ''Arithmetical Concepts,'' *Building Up Mathematics* (London: Hutchinson Educational Ltd., 1960), pp. 37–62.

2. The child was counting the squares on the faces of the cube — that is, he reasoned that there were 6 faces and 25 squares on each. What was the child finding, volume or surface area? Having this child build a block from flats would lead him to discover the correct answer.

3. For further reading, see E. M. Standing, *The Montessori Revolution in Education* (New York: Schocken Books, 1966).

4. Further details about these numeration systems (and others) can be found in *Historical Topics for the Mathematics Classroom,* the Thirty-first Yearbook of the National Council of Teachers of Mathematics (Washington, D.C.: NCTM, 1969) pp. 18–49.

CHAPTER 8

GEOMETRY ON A GEOBOARD

INTRODUCTION

What do you remember of your own high school or elementary school geometry course? Some people remember a few formulas — perhaps $A = b \times h$ or $A = \pi r^2$ or $a^2 + b^2 = c^2$ — or perhaps some isolated facts, such as "A line is determined by two points," or "The sum of the angles of a triangle is a straight angle." Many of these memories involve measurement of length, area, or angle.

Examine the drawings below and write two questions about the measurement aspects of each drawing.

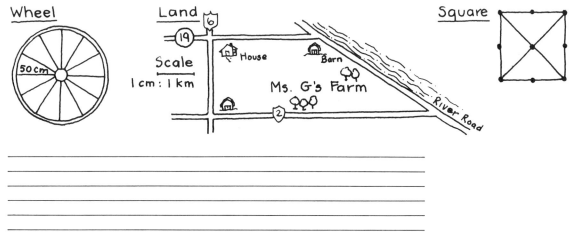

_____

_____

_____

_____

_____

_____

Here are some measurement questions that could be raised about the drawings.

How high is the wheel?
How far does the wheel roll if it is turned a complete revolution?
What is the angle between the spokes?
How much land does Ms. G. own?
Which barn is farther from Ms. G's house?
How long is the fence around her estate?
How long is the diagonal of the square?
What is the area of each triangle?
How many right angles are there?

Did you write questions similar to any of these? Which of the questions do you think you could answer?

In Chapter 3, Informal Geometry, we explored many aspects of geometry which can be considered by elementary school children, none of which involved measurement directly (for example, classification of polygons, symmetry, networks, solids, types of curves). In Chapter 6, Measurement and the Metric System, we concentrated on building up the concept of direct physical measurement. In this chapter we will look more closely at some aspects of geometry that rely on measurement and that make up a large part of the upper elementary school geometry curriculum — in particular, patterns and relationships between measurements (for example, how the area of a rectangle is related to the lengths of its sides).

The Activities in this chapter all involve a commonly available and very versatile mathematics material, a geoboard. This is a plastic or wooden board with a regular pattern of pegs or nails around which rubber bands can be stretched to make patterns and shapes. The Activities are designed to develop aspects of geometry that arise naturally from the material. The regular placement of nails or pegs suggests a system of notation for points, line segments, and polygons made by rubber bands. Activities 1–7 develop this idea. The structure of the geoboard also leads to measurement. Activities 8–13 concern development of the concepts and techniques for measuring perimeter and area. Finally, in Activities 14–16, you are asked to discover patterns involving area measurement.

Discussion Questions and Comments concern why, how, and when geoboards can be used with children and how geoboards compare with other materials for teaching certain topics. The chapter contains many pattern-finding activities, in some cases leading to formulas. Inductive and deductive reasoning approaches to these patterns are compared.

Follow-up Sections concern various approaches to teaching measurement of area, angle, and length. In particular, intuitive explanations are given for some measurement formulas. A brief section provides an introduction to transformation geometry. Finally, some measurement techniques and concepts developed on the geoboard are applied to measuring circles, in particular developing formulas for circumference and area in terms of the radius.

ACTIVITIES

Activity 1. Play

Use rubber bands to make something on your geoboard. Show it to a neighbor. What mathematical question could you ask about what you or your neighbor made? Do these questions involve any of these ideas: triangle, parallel, perpendicular, corners, lines, overlap, larger, angle?

Activity 2. Shape Copying

These shape-copying activities are best done either in a small group, or in a whole class setting where shapes to be copied are made on a transparent geoboard and displayed on an overhead projector. As you do the shape-copying tasks below, think about what methods you used to copy the shapes.

1. *Duplicate a Shape.* One person makes a shape with one rubber band on a geoboard and holds it up for the others to see. Others make the shape on their own geoboards.
2. *Upside Down.* One person makes a shape and shows it to the others who copy the shape as it would look upside down.

   As a variation, others could copy the shape as it would look if rotated 90° clockwise, or as it would look in a mirror. If the shape is made on a transparent geoboard on an overhead projector, you can check on the mirror image by flipping the geoboard over.
3. *Out of Sight, Out of Mind?* One person makes a shape and shows it for only 10 seconds. The others cannot begin to copy the shape until it is out of sight.

Did you find it easier to copy the shapes that you could name? What methods did you use to copy the shapes?

Activity 3. Line Segments: A Geoboard Game for Two Players

Materials: Geoboard; rubber bands

Directions: Two players take turns making line segments with rubber bands on a geoboard. The first player makes a line segment between any two pegs (see line segment 1). The second player makes a line segment from either end (peg A or peg B) of the first player's line segment. In the example, the second player made one from peg B (see line segment 2). Now the first player moves again, making another line segment according to the following rules:

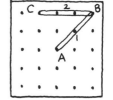

1. Players must begin at one of the two endpoints that are available at any given time. (In example (a), line segments must begin at A or C.)
2. Line segments cannot cross each other. (In example (b), this move is *not* allowed!)
3. New line segments cannot *end* at a peg that is already on a line segment. (In example (c), this move is *not* allowed!)

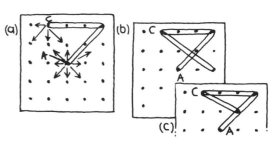

Here are some moves (dotted lines) that the first player *could* make in the example given. Find two more possible moves.

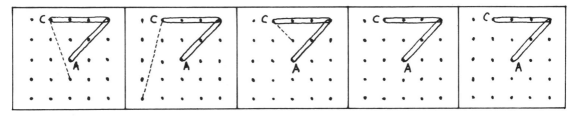

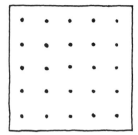

The loser is the first person who cannot make another line segment.

1. Play the game with another person on one geoboard.
2. Play the game again with this person, but now share a geoboard dot diagram, as shown here. Draw the line segments. Use a straightedge, if necessary.
3. Suppose that you wanted to play the dot-diagram game again with this person tonight, by telephone. How might you communicate your construction of line segments?

Activity 4. Line Segments — But Don't Peek

Did you find a way to play the line-segment game by telephone? One way would be to devise some way to name the pegs on the geoboard and then use these names to describe line segments. Let us agree to use the lettered geoboard, as shown here.

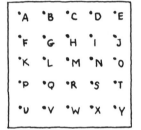

1. Play the line-segment game again, but pretend that you and your partner are on the telephone and you cannot see each other or each other's diagrams. Perhaps you might sit back to back. Each of you should record all of the moves on your own lettered geoboard dot diagram. Call off your moves by naming the endpoints of the line segments you want to make.
2. Which of the three ways of playing the line-segment game did you like best? on a geoboard? on dot-paper? by naming line segments?

Activity 5. Notation: Words and Polygons

Activity 4 was designed to motivate the use of letters to name line segments. In this Activity, letter notation is used to name shapes or polygons.

1. On your geoboard, stretch a rubber band around pegs G, E, and O. Draw this triangle, named G E O on this dot diagram.

SIT

JOG

HOP

RUN

TALK (T to A to L to K, back to T)

SLIP

LISP

(<u>Note</u>: These two should be different.)

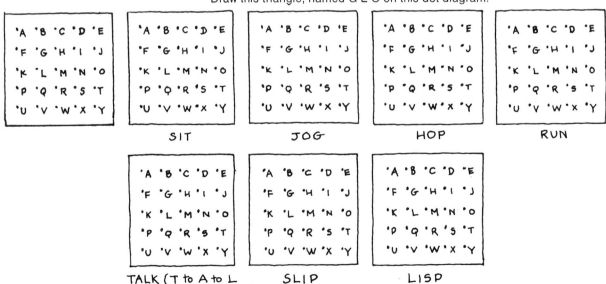

2. What are your initials? _____ Do they form a triangle?
3. Draw the shapes indicated on each of these dot diagrams.

Which shape is not a polygon? _____ Why not?
Which shapes are right triangles? _____ scalene triangles? _____
Will any three letters form a triangle? Explain.

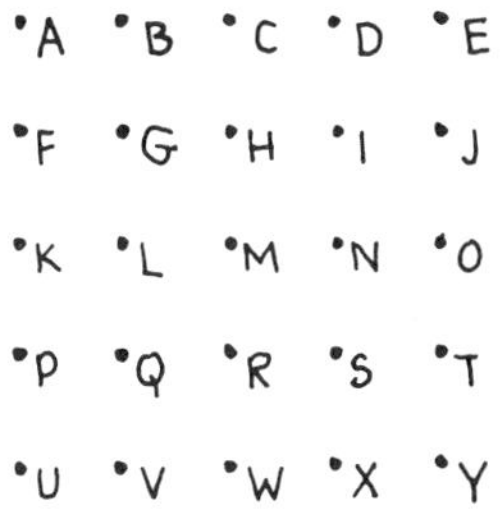

Activity 6. Stretch a Polygon

•A •B •C •D •E

•F •G •H •I •J

•K •L •M •N •O

•P •Q •R •S •T

•U •V •W •X •Y

1. Use only one rubber band (preferably one that stretches quite a bit) and make a polygon with seven sides on your geoboard.
2. Extend the seven-sided polygon. Try to make a polygon with the largest number of sides possible on your geoboard. Draw the polygon to the right. Name it.

_____

How many sides does your polygon have?
How many vertices (corners) does it have?
3. (Optional) You might try making the polygon with the largest number of sides on 2 × 2, 3 × 3, 4 × 4, etc. geoboards. Is there a pattern to the largest number of sides possible?

Activity 7. Guess My Rule

Geoboards can be used for a whole class sorting activity, as follows: Everyone should make a shape from one rubber band on their geoboard. One person decides on a rule, and sorts the geoboard into two collections: those with shapes obeying the rule in one collection, and all the others in another collection. The rest of the class tries to guess the rule; they try to decide in advance where their shape belongs. Here is a possible rule. Can you guess it?

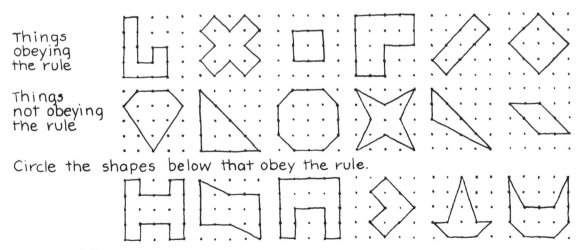

Things obeying the rule

Things not obeying the rule

Circle the shapes below that obey the rule.

What is the rule?

List some different rules that you might use for sorting shapes on a geoboard.

Activity 8. Measurement on a Geoboard — Introduction

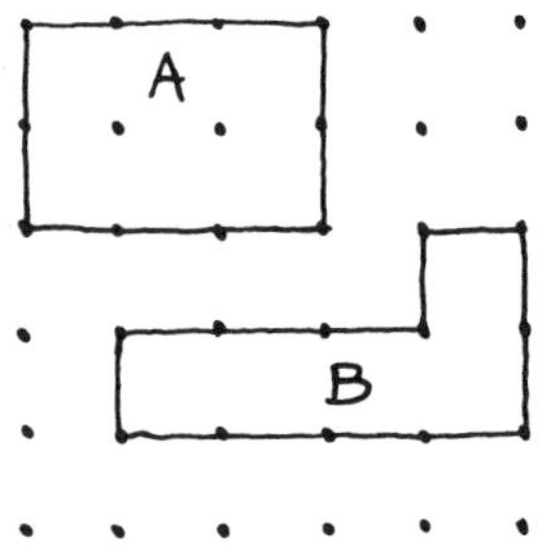

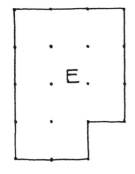

Suppose that the shapes to the left represent pens for animals in a zoo. Which pen is larger? The answer depends on your perception of the situation. If you are interested in grass in the pen for the animals to graze on, then pen _____ is larger. However if you are concerned about how much fencing is needed for the pens, then pen _____ would take more. The next Activities will consider these two questions: How much space is in the pen, the *area*? How much fencing is needed, the *perimeter*?

Activity 9. Perimeter — The Distance Around

To answer the question of which pen, A or B, needed more fencing, you may have measured the perimeter of the two pens by counting how many units (distance between pegs, •——•) made up each outline.

1. Look at each of the figures drawn below and *guess* which has the largest perimeter and the smallest perimeter. Largest? Smallest?

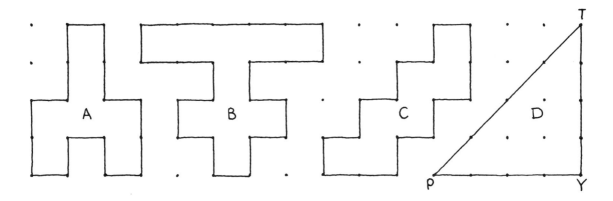

2. The figures are drawn on centimeter-dot paper (where the distance between two dots, horizontally or vertically, is one centimeter). Find the perimeter of each of these figures:

   A: _____ cm   B: _____ cm   C: _____ cm   D: _____ cm
   E: _____ cm

   Did you guess which had the largest perimeter? Do figures A and C look like they have the same perimeter?

3. Did you say that the perimeter of figure D (triangle P Y T) was 12 cm? If you did, you might have said that segment $\overline{TY}$ measures 4 cm, $\overline{PY}$ measures 4 cm, and $\overline{PT}$ measures 4 cm. Look closely at $\overline{PY}$ and $\overline{PT}$. Do they look like they have the same length? $\overline{PY}$ is 4 cm long, but $\overline{PT}$ is surely longer. Measure $\overline{PT}$ with a centimeter ruler. _____ cm Can you explain why $\overline{PT}$ is not 4 cm long, and why someone might think that it *is* 4 cm long?

   (The exact measurement of $\overline{PT}$ can be found by the Pythagorean theorem, which will be discussed later in the chapter.)

Activity 10. Area

1. What is the area of this shape? This question asks how many *units* of area it will take to cover it, and the answer depends on the region selected as a unit. Imagine that you had cut out several copies of each of the shapes below. How many copies of each would it take to cover the shape without overlapping?

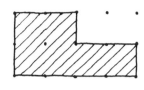

a.   b.   c.

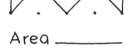

Which of the shapes above do you think would be most natural to take as a unit of area? _____ Why?

2. For this and all subsequent Activities, let ●——● (the horizontal distance between nails) be the unit of length, and let the square region (b above) be the unit of area. Square units can be cut from colored paper to fit exactly between the nails of your geoboard. Children can find the area of many shapes by covering them with these units and pieces of them. (See the figure to the right.)

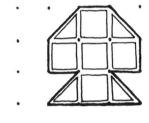

What is the area of ◺ ? _____ What is the area of the shape here?

3. Draw how you could place the square and triangular pieces on the shapes below to find their area.

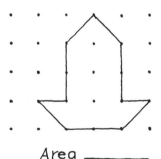
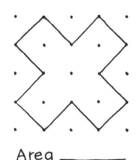

Area _____   Area _____   Area _____

Make your own
Area _____

Activity 11. Growing and Shrinking

Make this shape on your geoboard. Try to change the shape in the ways described on page 356. (**Hint:** It is possible to do all of these with shapes made up entirely of squares. You may find it difficult to calculate perimeters if you allow diagonal edges.) Use a solid line to outline the new shape. The first one has been done.

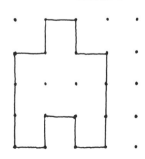

Keep perimeter the same and make area smaller. Keep perimeter the same and make area larger. Keep area the same and make perimeter smaller. Keep area the same and make perimeter larger.

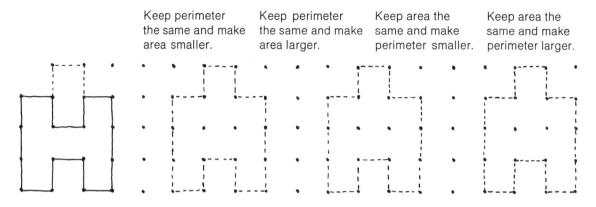

Activity 12. Right Triangles

Perhaps in Activity 10 you made a shape that could not be covered exactly by the paper squares and triangles. For example, your shape might have been a right triangle like some of those below.

1. Find the areas of the rectangles and right triangles below.

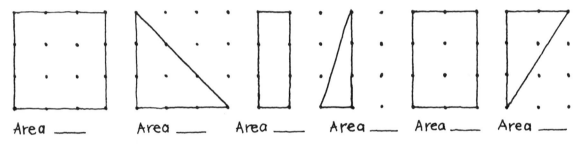

Area ___   Area ___   Area ___   Area ___   Area ___   Area ___

2. Draw an appropriate rectangle around each triangle to find its area.
   Area of X _____
   Area of Y _____
   Area of Z _____

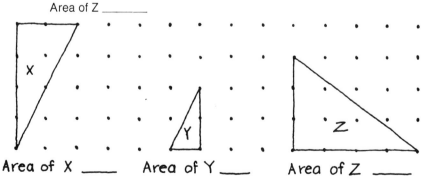

Area of X ___   Area of Y ___   Area of Z ___

3. The area of a right triangle equals _____ the area of _____.

4. The shape to the right has been divided into triangles and rectangles whose areas you can now determine very easily. Find the area of this shape. Area _____ Similarly subdivide the other shapes below, and find their areas. One of the shapes cannot be subdivided in this way — which one is it?

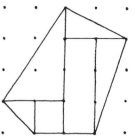

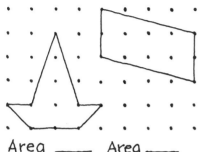

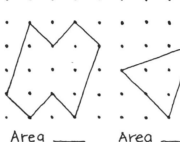

Area ____   Area ____   Area ____   Area ____

Activity 13. Another Approach to Area

In Activity 12, part 4, you probably found the area of the parallelogram by cutting it up into two right triangles and a rectangle. (See diagram.) There are shapes that cannot be cut up in this way — for such shapes you can find another method. Think of finding a *bigger* rectangle, and cutting pieces away to get the parallelogram. Follow this procedure:

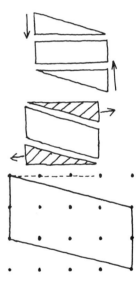

1. Draw the large rectangle. Complete this rectangle to the right — its area is 12 units.
2. Find the area of the parts of the large rectangle that you want to cut away. Here there are two right triangles each with area 2.
3. Subtract from the area of the rectangle the areas of the cut-away parts, leaving the area of the original shape, $12 - 2 - 2 = 8$.

Use this procedure to find the areas of the two shapes below.

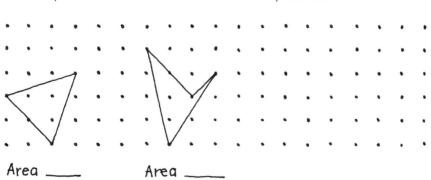

Area ____   Area ____

Using this procedure, you can find the area of *any* shape you can make on the geoboard. Draw a shape in the space above to the right, and find its area using this procedure.

You can check your answers in Activities 12 and 13 on page 359.

Activity 14. A Pattern

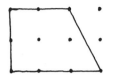

There are many patterns that you can find involving area on a geoboard. This one involves a relationship between the pegs inside, the pegs touching the rubber band, and the area of a polygon. Consider this polygon. We call a nail an *interior* nail if it is inside the polygon but does *not* touch the rubber band. This polygon has two interior nails. A nail is called a *boundary* nail if it does in fact touch the rubber band. This polygon has 8 boundary nails.

In this Activity, make figures on your geoboard that *all* have *one* interior nail, but different numbers of boundary nails, and find their areas. When you have made the figures on your geoboard, copy them in the appropriate spaces below. One has been done. You might start with the shape drawn with 4 boundary nails, and make it grow by adding one boundary nail at a time.

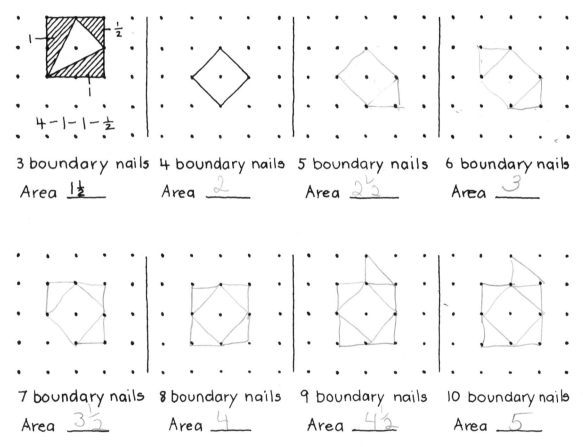

3 boundary nails
Area 1½

4 boundary nails
Area 2

5 boundary nails
Area 2½

6 boundary nails
Area 3

7 boundary nails
Area 3½

8 boundary nails
Area 4

9 boundary nails
Area 4½

10 boundary nails
Area 5

Compare your results with your neighbor's. What do you notice?

What is the relationship between the number of boundary nails and the area?

nails × 2 = area

This pattern can be extended. A formula, Pick's theorem, gives the area of any polygon on a geoboard in terms of the number of interior nails and the number of boundary nails. We will discuss this formula in the Follow-up Sections.

Activity 15. Squares in Squares in Squares . . .

Find the areas of the squares drawn to the right. Fill in the table.

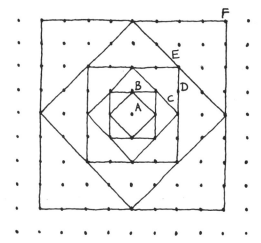

Square	A	B	C	D	E	F
Area	2	4	8	16	32	64

Do you see a pattern?

Activity 16. Parallelograms

Imagine making the rectangle ABQP on your geoboard, and then moving the top (AB) sideways to the right, first to BC, then to CD, and so forth. The steps are drawn below. Find the area of each of these parallelograms.

What remains the same? length of base? length of sides? height? area?

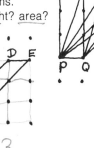

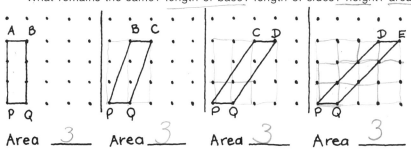

Area ___3___   Area ___3___   Area ___3___   Area ___3___

What do you notice?

Check your answers: Activity 12, part 4: Areas are 10, 6, 8, 10, 4. Activity 13: Areas are 4, 3½.

DISCUSSION QUESTIONS AND COMMENTS

Why Use Geoboards?

Did you find the geoboard an attractive material to work with? Do you think children will?

Many young children find that working on a geoboard is more fun than doing pencil and paper work with the same concepts. Perhaps it is the multi-sensory nature of the material that appeals — the color of the rubber bands, the pleasing "twang," or the springy feel of a taut band — or perhaps the neatness of the results. If a geoboard is made available to children, they will usually start to play with it without any special instructions, creating interesting designs.

In addition to being fun to use, geoboards can allow young children to express their thoughts about geometry by making shapes with rubber bands long before they are able to draw them accurately. For example, children in kindergarten and first grade who are still learning to write numerals and letters may not be able to draw a square, but on a geoboard they may be able to demonstrate that they know how to make a square. It is simply easier to make a square or rectangle with a rubber band on a geoboard than it is to draw it or construct it (as from straws or toothpicks). For this reason, geoboards are sometimes used to help diagnose young children's perceptual problems (for example, ability to make shapes or to copy shapes). Through copying activities, children can develop perceptual abilities that are prerequisite to writing or reading letters. Finally, the geoboard allows children to undo an error easily or to change their minds about a design — whereas, redoing a shape or design made with crayon on paper is often difficult or frustrating. This perhaps leads to more courageous and open investigations of geometry.

Older children can also benefit from work on a geoboard, which can be used as a means of presenting challenging questions (such as finding the patterns in Activities 14 and 15). Children can experiment, collect data, and form generalizations about these questions.

Geoboards are an example of a *structured* mathematics material — that is, their use leads quite naturally to certain mathematical concepts. (Other examples of structured materials are attribute pieces, leading to classification, and multibase blocks, leading to place-value numeration.) Even when children use geoboards informally, certain mathematical concepts are likely to arise; in more directed activities, geoboards can easily be used to develop and review many geometry topics. Which of the concepts listed below do *not* arise naturally through work on the geoboard? Underline them.

Square	Isosceles triangle	Polygon
Rectangle	Line symmetry	Polyhedron (such as a cube)
Circle	Rotational symmetry	Closed and open curves
Area	Congruence	Coordinates
Perimeter	Similarity	Parallelograms
Trapezoid	Perpendicular	Line segment
Angle	Diagonal	Line

Do you think the geoboard is a good material for developing the concept of area? Compare these three tasks. Which activity is most appropriate for children just beginning the study of area?

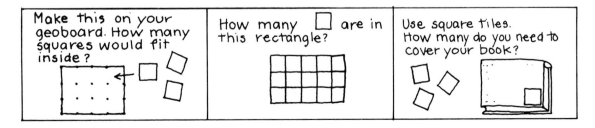

The geoboard does have certain drawbacks for early work with area; squares do not fit around the nails very well, and it is not easy to experience the "covering" aspect of area measurement. However once children have formed this concept of area (through manipulation of tiling materials or work with squared paper) the geoboard can offer them exciting opportunities for review, practice, and extension.

Is the geoboard a good material for the study of perimeter? Which of the activities below is most appropriate for children just beginning the study of perimeter?

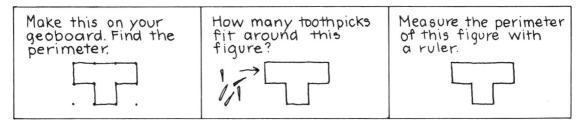

It is reasonable to expect many upper elementary school children to be able to find the area of any polygon they can make on a geoboard with one rubber band (by the technique in Activity 13). However it can be very difficult to find the *perimeter* of most shapes in terms of the geoboard unit of length. (One needs to know the Pythagorean theorem and how to approximate square roots, topics not usually covered until grades 7–8.) Perhaps it is more sensible for children at all grade levels to approach the measurement of perimeter first with concrete units of length (such as toothpicks) and then with rulers marked in standard units (such as centimeters), than to use a geoboard.

At approximately what grade level would you expect children to be able to do each of these tasks? What are the prerequisites for each?

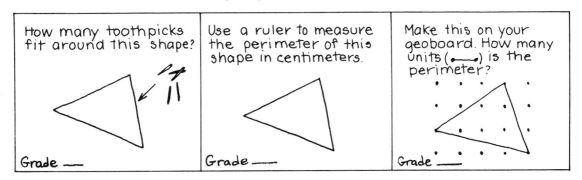

Using Geoboards with Children

Types of Geoboards

In the Activities in this chapter, you worked with a 5 × 5 geoboard because that is the type most commonly available commercially. However most of the Activities can easily be done on other types of geoboards. Geoboards with different peg patterns (page 362) are available commercially, or can

a.

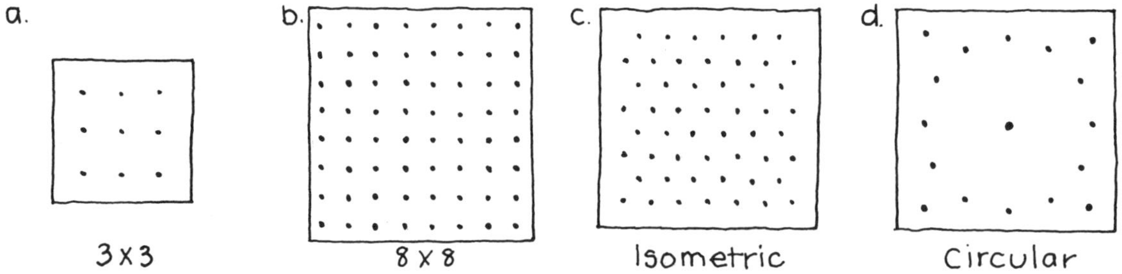

3×3

b.

8 × 8

c.

Isometric

d.

Circular

be made by teachers or children. (Sometimes several 5 × 5 geoboards can easily be fastened together to make a larger working area.) These geoboard variations lead to slightly different activities and mathematical topics.

Could you do Activity 5, Words and Polygons, on board (a)? _____ on board (b)? _____

Could you construct an equilateral triangle on board (a)? _____ on board (c)? _____ on board (d)? _____

Could you do activities with area where a square is the unit of area on board (a)? _____ on board (b)? _____ on board (c)? _____ on board (d)? _____

What would be the natural unit of area on geoboard (c)? _____

Geoboards with fewer, larger, and more widely spaced pegs might be provided for young children who might have trouble manipulating rubber bands over smaller pegs, and for whom too many pegs might be confusing.

If you wish to make a geoboard yourself, try using a piece of graph paper to determine the exact location of the pegs. Lay the graph paper on top of a board and hammer nails through the paper; then pull the paper off. You can also hammer golf tees into a pegboard (but make sure that they are in so firmly that a rubber band will not pull them out).

Using Geoboards in Different Class Groupings

Do you think that every child in a class could be working on a geoboard at one time? Why or why not?

If every child in a class does have a geoboard, then geoboard activities can lead to lively whole group discussion. For example in Activity 7, Guess My Rule, each child could make a shape and the boards could be sorted by the teacher or by one child, possibly into two piles (as shown in the Activity), or possibly into more than two piles. What rule might a child have been thinking of if he sorted the class shapes like this?

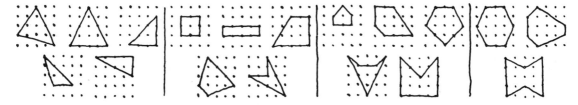

If a whole class is working together on geoboard activities, it is desirable to use a transparent geoboard on an overhead projector to show examples and display children's work to the whole class. Also, in copying games children can check their work by placing the transparent geoboard on top of their own shapes to see if the rubber-band constructions match.

If only a few geoboards are available in a classroom, a teacher can still use them, with children working in a small group or individually. It may be time consuming and disruptive, in terms of classroom management, for a teacher to direct these small group activities. In this situation, task cards can be an effective way to help children do geoboard activities. It is easy to design task cards which involve making or copying specific shapes, and there are various possible ways to present directions. For example, the ones below all involve the same task.

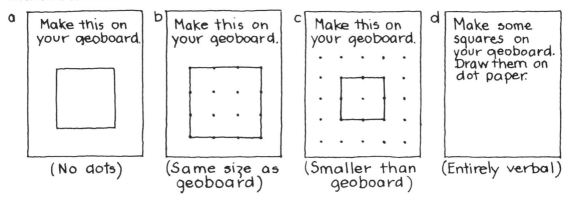

Which task card is most appropriate for kindergarten children?
Why might card (c) be more difficult than card (b)?
Which cards allow more than one solution?
Which might a first or second grader find most interesting?

Activity cards for geoboards are available commercially. The written directions might be too difficult for children to read. Teachers might examine these cards to get ideas for further geoboard activities in which directions can be read to children or presented on teacher-made task cards in simpler language.

How Should a Teacher Sequence Activities With a Geoboard?

Zoltan P. Dienes[1] recommends that the following sequence of activities should be followed in work with structured mathematics material, such as a geoboard: First, preliminary exploration with the material so that children can become aware of the structure of the material, and so that some language associated with the material might arise naturally. Second, structured games or activities designed to help children learn specific concepts or develop and use notation. Third, practice games or activities that reinforce concepts and use of notation previously learned in structured situations.

Most of the Activities in this chapter fit into the second or third type of activity (just which depends on the child — what is development for one child might be review or practice for another). While directions can easily be given to a teacher for conducting structured games and activities, it is more difficult to give directions for a teacher's role in exploratory activities, because the form of interaction depends on what the children choose to do.

When children have a period of exploration on a geoboard, they may produce patterns which contain considerable mathematical potential. The teacher might direct children's attention to certain aspects of their patterns. Suppose a child has made this pattern. Here are some questions that a teacher might ask:

1. How many rubber bands did you use?
2. How many pegs are inside this rubber band?
3. Is this a triangle?
4. How many triangles do you see? How are they alike? How are they different?
5. What will it look like if you turn it upside down? a quarter turn?

Which of these questions seem more interesting to you? While questions (1), (2), and (3) are closed questions involving simple counting and shape recognition, questions (4) and (5) are more open and touch on some more sophisticated mathematical concepts — congruence and similarity, and symmetry. Even if children have not yet learned these concepts formally, a teacher can recognize when they arise and direct children's attention towards examples of them by raising questions as above. It is desirable to avoid asking only questions with one word answers. Try to form questions that give children an opportunity to express themselves and a choice of method of answering.

Here is another pattern that a child might have made during an exploratory activity. Write three questions you might ask about it.

Developing Notation

Activities 3–5 were designed to give children experiences with line segments and to build up notation such as $\overline{AB}$. One criticism of some recent mathematics programs is that too much emphasis is put on notation and symbolism. Notation is sometimes taught as an end in itself — a teacher might plan a lesson just on how to name something. For example, he might say, in essence, "This is how we will name a line segment. Now do the examples on the worksheet." The examples on the worksheet may well be without any real point. Such an approach can be improved by providing children with motivation for learning notation. For example, in Activities 3–4, notation helped in playing line-segment games over the telephone. (Also, in Chapter 3, Informal Geometry, you saw examples of how notation for line segments, rays, lines, and angles can be practiced while searching for patterns or investigating challenging problems.) Notation should only be introduced when its need and use are appreciated. Otherwise, learning notation can be like learning a foreign language which you have no desire or opportunity to speak.

In Activities 4–6 you used a particular type of notation for points; each point was labeled with a letter of the alphabet. This leads quite naturally to the notation AB for a line segment. Was this the sort of notation you thought of for playing the line-segment game without looking (in Activity 3)?

Often children will come up with alternative notations. To describe the line segment here, they might say, "Start in the top row, second peg from the left, and then go to the last column in the middle." Children should be encouraged to be more systematic and to conform to the standard coordinate notation — maybe by always starting at the lower-left corner and saying, "Move 1 space to the right and 4 spaces up" or "Move 4 spaces over and 2 spaces up," to locate the end-points of this line segment. This sort of description leads quite naturally to coordinate (or ordered-pair) notation, a topic usually introduced in the second grade. However children should be allowed as much time as necessary with their own descriptions of this verbal sort or some abbreviated written symbolism (maybe "Over 1, Up 4" or "O 1, U 4," or whatever they invent), before introducing the more abstract ordered pairs such as (1,4). Notation should be seen as a convenient shorthand for some already experienced description.

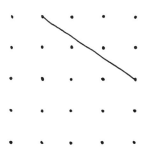

Geoboards can be used in many interesting ways to provide practice of coordinate notation once the idea has been formalized. Children might fasten a strip of paper or tape along the edges of the geoboard to remind them of the numbers associated with the rows and columns. To agree with standard notation, the rows and columns should be marked with numbers as shown below. Sometimes geoboards are used with small circles or squares of paper or cardboard that fit over the pegs to mark points. Such markers can be made from punch-hole reinforcements glued together. An activity such as the one below can give children practice with coordinate notation for points and addition skills, while at the same time it leads to another topic, graphing number sentences or equations.

Put (o)'s on all points where the two coordinates add up to 5. (For example, on (4,1), since $4 + 1 = 5$.)

Put [o]'s on all the pegs where the second coordinate is one more than the first. (For example (0,1), since 1 is one more than 0.)

Are there any pegs with both (o) and [o] on them?

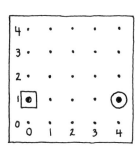

Do you think that second graders could do this activity?

This activity is a simple version of the more abstract exercise below, which you might have first experienced in ninth grade.[2]

Find the solution to the equations

$$x + y = 5$$
$$\text{and} \quad y = x + 1$$

by making a graph of the solution sets and finding the intersection.

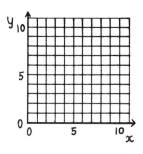

Children will be much better prepared for this work if they have had earlier experiences with the same topics, interpreted of course in an informal concrete way.

The next example is a game which also provides practice in naming points.

Four in a Row

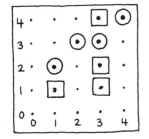

Two players take turns placing markers on pegs.

One uses (○) and the other uses [○]. The markers can be put anywhere on the geoboard. The first player to get four in a row (vertically, horizontally, or diagonally) is the winner.

To practice ordered-pair notation, players name the points as they place their markers; if a point is incorrectly named, they lose a turn.

This game could be played by a whole class divided into two teams. Members of each team take turns calling out their team's moves in coordinate notation. Another team member records the moves on a drawing on the chalkboard.

Discovering Patterns — An Approach to Learning Formulas

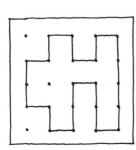

In Activity 14 you probably noticed that when you make *any* figure on a geoboard with exactly one interior nail, the area turns out to be one-half the number of boundary nails. Does this work for this figure that has 22 boundary nails? Do you have any idea why it works?

Looking for patterns provides children with an opportunity to practice skills (in this case finding area) in a self-checking way; once children have established the pattern (perhaps through some comparatively easy situations), they will be able to correct their own errors in more complicated situations. Children often learn formulas by finding patterns. They look at many examples and notice that something works, and so they generalize that it works for any situation. This type of thinking is called *inductive.*

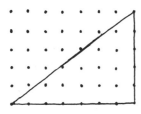

In Activity 12 you also probably discovered a pattern relating the area of a right triangle to the area of the rectangle surrounding it — the area of the right triangle is one-half the area of the rectangle, or one-half the product of the lengths of the two perpendicular sides of the right triangle. Do you think this holds for this triangle? Could you explain why it works for any right triangle?

Reasoning inductively you probably discovered the pattern relating area to the number of boundary pegs in Activity 14, but you probably could not explain why the pattern works or if it will hold for any shape on a geoboard. In Activity 12 you also may have reasoned inductively to find a relationship between the area of the right triangle and of the surrounding rectangle, but in this case you are probably able to explain or informally prove why it will work for any right triangle. This is an example of another type of reasoning, *deductive.* Your explanation may be convincing, even though it is not stated formally and rigorously (that is, based upon certain known and assumed facts or axioms, and organized in a logical fashion). For example, you might say, "If I make the rectangle around the triangle, the other half will be congruent to the original triangle because the sides will all be the same. So the two triangles must have the same area, and the rectangle has twice the area of the triangle."

Patterns arise in relation to most topics in the elementary school curriculum, providing children with many opportunities for inductive reasoning and discovery. In some discovery situations, it is not really possible that children can explain or prove what they have discovered; they simply notice a pattern and trust that it is always true (as for example in Activity 14, with the relation between area and boundary nails). In other discovery situations, however, children are able to give informal but convincing explanations of "why it works" (as for example in Activity 12 with the area of a triangle). A later section illustrates concrete ways in which children can show why the formulas for finding area of various shapes hold. Children enjoy the challenges of thinking mathematically, both inductively and deductively, and should be encouraged to do so whenever possible.

In Activity 15, you may not have actually counted or calculated the area of square F. Rather, since the areas of previous squares were 2, 4, 8, 16, and 32, you might have reasoned that the area of square F was 64, or double 32. If you reasoned just by the pattern, you were reasoning *inductively*. Could you explain *why* this pattern arises, that is, reason *deductively* about this problem?

In Activity 16, if you correctly found the area of the first three parallelograms to be 3 square units, you might have reasoned inductively that parallelogram PQDE must also have area 3 square units. Could you reason deductively to explain why this is so?

FOLLOW-UP SECTIONS

Measuring the Area of Polygons

What is the area of this region on the geoboard? Most people would probably say 12, but 24 would not be an incorrect answer. Do you see why? (If not, see Activity 10, part 1.)

The natural unit of area seems to be ⌐⌐ , however we *might* take other regions as units of area. If someone said the area of this region is 24, what unit might they be using? ⌐⌐ What if they said 6?

Suppose that it is agreed that ⌐⌐ is the unit for area. How might children respond to the question "What is the area of this rectangle?" when shown a drawing of a rectangle on dot paper? A young child might cover the the shape with squares and count them. (Here we would need to phrase the question differently, maybe "How many squares would it take to cover the rectangle?") A third grader might draw in lines and note that there are 3 rows and 4 squares in each, and hence $3 \times 4 = 12$ squares. A fifth grader might quickly respond "12" because he knows that area can be found by multiplying length by width, and in this case the length is 4 and the width 3 units. One hopes that the fifth grader would be able to explain or show (in his own way) why the area can be found in this way.

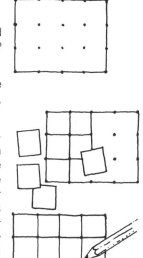

These examples indicate that children's approaches to finding area change as they go through school. In this section, we will discuss how activities should be sequenced to help children understand and gain skill in finding area.

Early Experiences with Area

Children can learn to measure area by the same sequence of types of activities as for measurement of length, capacity, and weight. (See Chapter 6, Measurement and the Metric System.) First, children must understand what attribute of a region is being measured, and what it means for one region to have greater area than another. According to Piaget, young children in the preoperational stage do not yet conserve area — that is, they do not yet recognize that when a region is cut apart and rearranged, the area remains the same. Children may be helped to gain this understanding through concrete experiences of covering different regions with the same pieces. Examples of such activities were given in Chapter 2 using tangrams or other shape puzzles. Children might be made more explicitly aware of the fact that many different regions can have the same area by an activity such as the following, where a given collection of tiles is arranged in various ways. The shapes that children make might be displayed on a class bulletin board. Children might also try this activity with five or six squares.

Materials: ▢ pieces; squared paper to fit the ▢ pieces

Directions: Take 4 ▢ 's.

How many different shapes can you make with them? Color in the shapes on squared paper.

For older children, the question below can be presented. These children might also be encouraged to use ◺ 's to get, for example, a shape like the one to the left.

Materials: Geoboard; dotted paper
Directions: How many different shapes can you make that have area 6? Color them in on dotted paper.

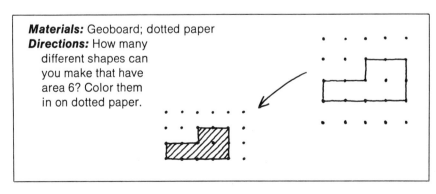

Once children understand the meaning of area and how areas can be compared, they should have many opportunities (such as the example below) to use nonstandard units for area. Many shapes could be used as units of area to cover a flat surface — for example, triangles, rectangles, diamonds, and hexagons. Tiles of these shapes are often used for decorative purposes.

Materials: Several pieces
like △
Directions: Which of
these shapes is larger?

Use △ 's to cover them.

Which takes more?

At some point children will probably decide that, for many things we measure (floors, books, walls), squares are a convenient unit because they fit neatly into rectangular regions. Children are then ready to work with the standard units for area, which are derived from the standard units for length (for example, square centimeter, square inch). Children should measure a wide variety of regions — for example, pieces of paper, table tops, and the blackboard. They can also measure less regular shapes by approximating; for example, they might trace the outline of their foot on squared paper and count the squares and pieces of squares inside. (See How Big Is Your Foot on page 257.) They might also measure area by placing a transparent plastic grid over a region. As with all types of measurement, it is important that children have experience with estimating and measuring so that they realize just what the numbers mean in terms of real objects.

Later Experiences with Area — Developing Formulas

In the upper grades, once children have had the types of experiences just described, they can begin to look for patterns or shortcuts for finding the area of certain basic shapes. Formulas can be presented in a discovery format. Children can fill in tables and search for patterns, as in this activity.

Children's description of the shortcut should at first be in their own language — symbolic notation should come later.

How well children can explain the formula they discover, $A = l \times w$, depends on how much they have been exposed to an array model for multiplication. (See page 201.) If children have often seen multiplication associated with an array of dots or

RECTANGLES
Find the area of each rectangle by counting the little squares. Fill in the table.

Length	Width	Area

Describe a shortcut for finding the area of a rectangle.

squares, then they will easily associate the area of a rectangle with the product of the lengths of two adjacent sides.

Sometimes the formula is given as "base times height" instead of "length times width." Which expression seems more natural depends on the situation. Which would you associate with measurements of these objects?

Area of a wall
Area of a floor
Area of a table top
Area of a television screen

When children are taught area by rote memorization of a formula, they may be totally confused when they are asked for the first time to find "base times height" when they have learned "length times width." However if children learn the formula in a meaningful way, understanding that the two numbers correspond to measurements of the sides of a rectangle, they probably will not be disturbed by the terminology.

Children can use their knowledge of how to measure the area of a rectangle to find the areas of several other regions. The geoboard can be a useful model for the computational techniques; however, children can also use another model — shapes cut from paper that are folded and cut, as in the following description. Sometimes the paper illustrations are more dynamic since we can see the pieces move, but they are also more abstract, because we cannot *see* the units of length and area as we can on a geoboard.

Area of a Right Triangle

Make this triangle on your geoboard.

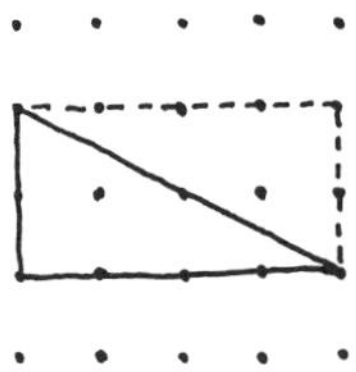

Make a rectangle around it (dotted line).
What is the area of the rectangle? _____
What is the area of the triangle? _____

Cut out a right triangle. 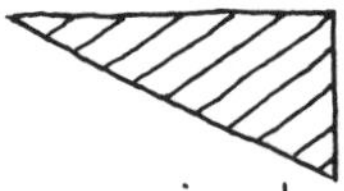
Cut out another one just like it.

Put them together to make a rectangle.

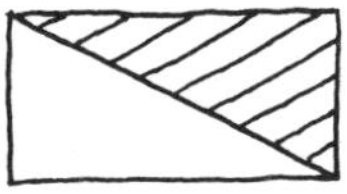

What is the area? _____
What is the area of the triangle? _____

(See also Activity 12, Right Triangles.)
What formula do these activities suggest?

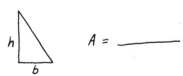

$A =$ _____

Area of a Parallelogram

Find the area of these parallelograms.

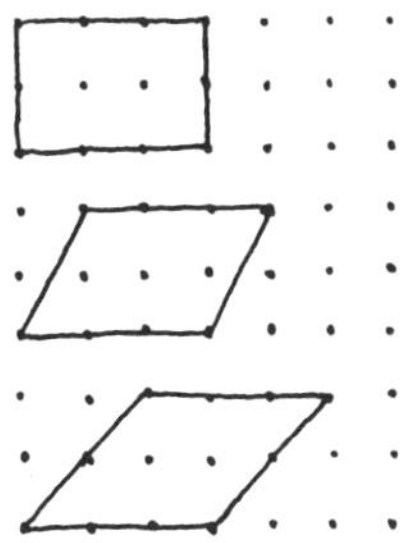

What do you notice?
Try it again. Start with a rectangle and move the top sideways.

Cut out a parallelogram.

Fold it on the dotted line. Cut along the fold and put the cut-off piece as shown.

What is the area of the rectangle? _____
What was the area of the parallelogram? _____

(See also Activity 16, Parallelograms.)
What formula do these activities suggest?
Which method do you prefer? Sometimes children who have learned this formula through a method such as these may forget the formula but be able to reconstruct it by remembering the method. Which method do you think would be easier for a child to remember?

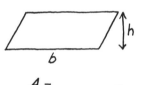

$A =$ _____

Area of Other Triangles

Make this triangle.
Make the double line with another rubber band.
Find the area of the original triangle.
Make a rectangle around it (dotted line) and find its area.

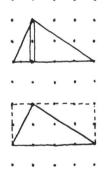

What do you notice?
The area of the triangle is _____ the area of the rectangle.

Cut out a triangle. 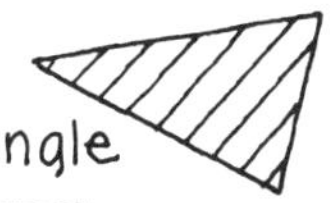
Cut out another triangle just like it.

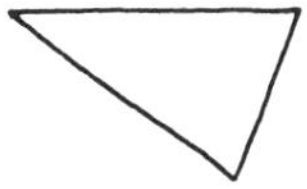

Arrange them like this.

What shape do you get?
What is its area? _____
What is the area of the triangle? _____

Try this method on the triangle drawn below.

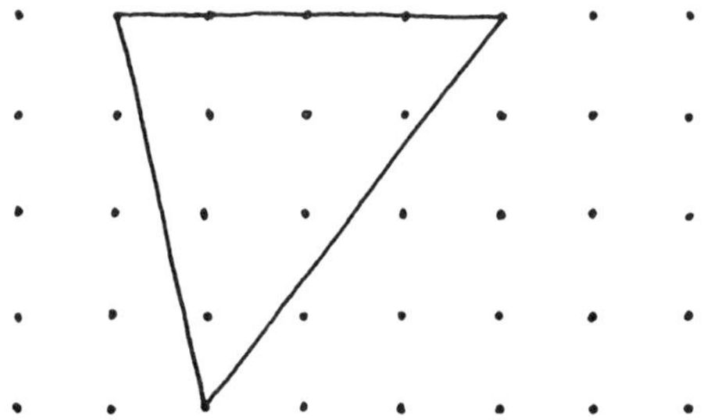

What is the area of the triangle? _____

Try this method on the triangle drawn below. Draw the outline of another triangle just the same size next to this one so that the two make a parallelogram.

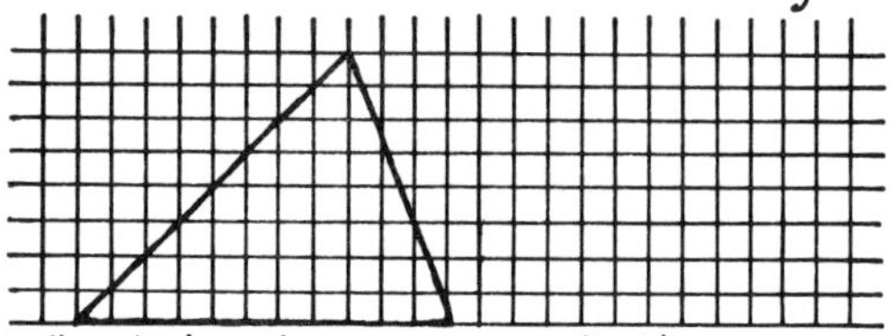

What is the area of the parallelogram? _____
What is the area of the triangle? _____

What formula do these activities suggest?

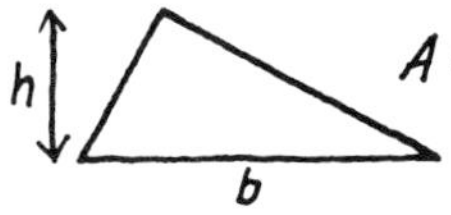

$A =$ _____

Area of a Trapezoid

Make this trapezoid.
Make a parallelogram (dotted line).

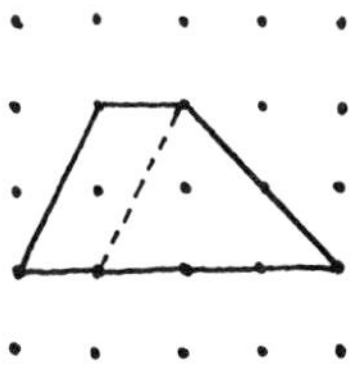

What is the area of the parallelogram? _____
What is the area of the triangle? _____
What is the area of the trapezoid? _____

Cut out a trapezoid.
Cut out another trapezoid just like it. 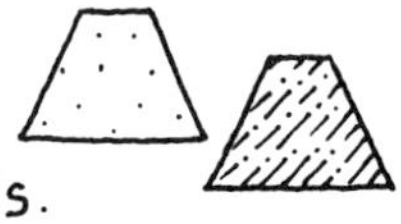
Arrange them like this.

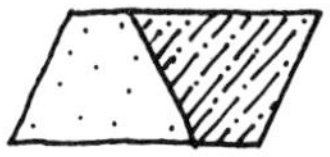

What shape do you get?
What is the length of the top?
of the bottom?
What is the area of the parallelogram?
What is the area of the trapezoid?

Try this method on the trapezoid below.

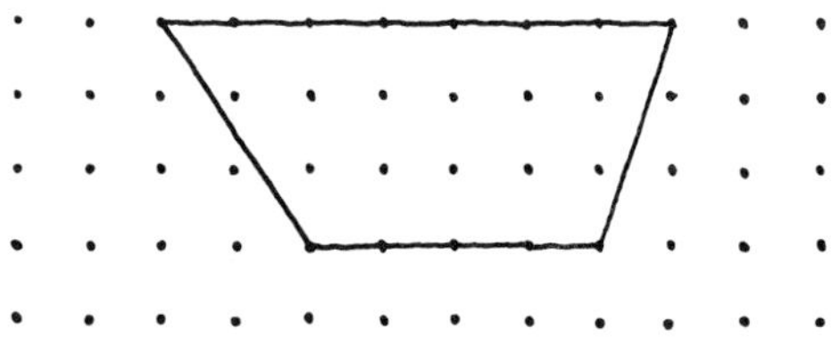

What is the area of the trapezoid? _____

Try this method on the trapezoid drawn below. Draw another one next to it that is just the same size so that together they form a parallelogram.

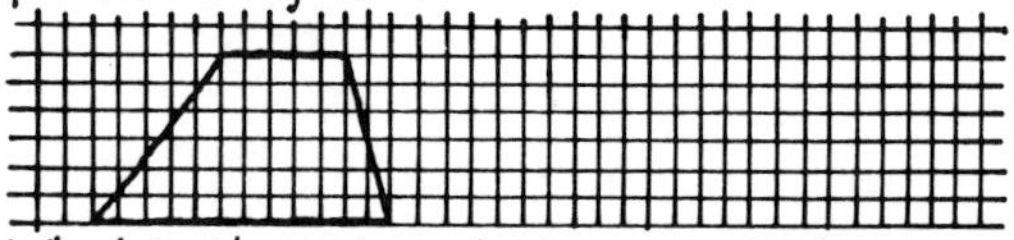

What is the area of the parallelogram?
What is the area of the trapezoid?

Do either of these methods suggest a formula?
If so, what?

$A =$ _____

(You may find it easier to write an expression for the area of a trapezoid using the second method. Write an expression for one-half of the area of this parallelogram.)

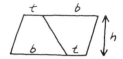

Using Formulas for Area

Children should be shown varied and interesting situations where they can apply their knowledge of methods for finding area. Try to answer these questions. Perhaps you can think of others.

1. *Doorstops.* You want to give a gold-plated doorstop to your uncle (who has everything) as a birthday present. The shape of the doorstop is shown here. You will glue on a thin sheet of gold, with no overlaps, so that each surface is covered. How many square centimeters of gold sheet will it take?

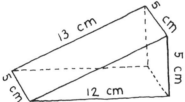

2. *Quilts.* You want to make the top of a patchwork quilt out of three colors of fabric. The quilt is made up from squares, 24 centimeters on a side, as shown below.[3] (There are two possible designs — which do you prefer?) In each, which color will require the most cloth? the least? How many square centimeters of each color will you need for each square? (You might find it helpful to draw the squares of the correct size — 24 cm by 24 cm — and use a ruler to measure the appropriate dimensions.)

Spider's Web

Storm at Sea

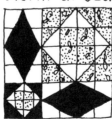

Notice how this square fits into a larger pattern.

3. *Farms.* Ms. G wants to retire to the city. She gives her farm to two nieces, who wish to split the land fairly. One wants the barn by the river and the other wants the house. Suppose they divide the land as shown below. Is this division fair? Who gets more land, and how much more? Draw a boundary line that gives each niece the same amount of land. Can you find another way to do it?

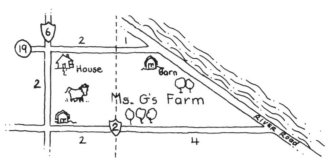

Measuring Angle

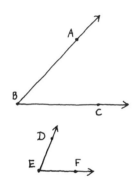

Which of these two angles is greater?

Children sometimes have difficulty answering this question because they do not really understand what is being compared. They may say that ∠ A B C is greater, because they are comparing the lengths of the pieces of line drawn. Perhaps they are unsure about what an angle is. (See pages 129 and 131 for some intuitive ways to suggest the idea of an angle as the union of two rays with a common endpoint.) Teaching measurement of an angle can follow the same sequence of steps described for teaching measurement of other attributes. (See Chapter 6, Measurement and the Metric System.)

Early Experiences with Angles

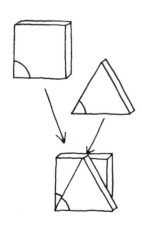

Children's early experiences with angles should involve the action of turning and comparison of how much one turns. Many everyday things involve turning (for example, the hot water tap, hands of a clock, or a television channel selector) and often it makes a considerable difference how much we turn. If children think of a whole turn as making a full circle, returning to the starting point, then they can act out a half-turn or a quarter-turn with their bodies. In physical education activities a teacher can point out how the arm is related to the body as children swing their arms upward. Starting with arms by their sides and moving slowly, they can see first a little gap, then a square corner as their arms are straight out sideways, and then larger and larger angles until their arms are pointing straight up. They can compare how far they have to move their arms to get to certain positions. Later they can compare the angle made by the corners of various shapes (by placing one shape on top of the other) to see that some angles are larger than others.

Do you think that children could be helped to answer the question above (which of the two angles is greater) by a turning approach? by comparing cut-out corners of paper?

One particularly common angle is a *right angle,* which children might recognize in many situations around them, such as the corners of this page or the corners of a table. If you take a piece of paper and first fold it in half, then in half again, you can demonstrate that four right angles make up a full turn.

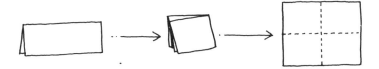

Children can compare other angles to a right angle. Is it greater (obtuse)? Is it smaller (acute)? In your environment, what is the most common type of angle, right, obtuse, or acute?

On a circular geoboard, children can make various angles at the center peg. Do you see how you can make an acute angle? a right angle? an obtuse angle?

Measuring an angle involves choosing one angle as a unit, and seeing how many of these fit into a given angle. Children can measure angles using nonstandard units; for example, if this

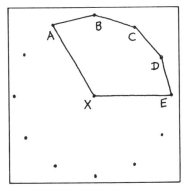

is the unit, what is the measure of angle A X E? _____ units. (Draw lines in the geoboard diagram to show how angle A X E can be broken up into these units.)

Children can also measure angles with wooden blocks representing nonstandard units. A block like the one drawn in the activity below (found in a set of Pattern Blocks) is especially appropriate.

Materials: ╱╱ pieces

Directions: How many ╱╱ fit in each of these

angles? Guess, then measure by placing the pieces.

Eventually children should learn to use the standard unit for measuring angles, a *degree* (symbolized "°"). One degree is a very small angle. There are 360 degrees in a full turn. Thus since four right angles make up a full turn, there are _____ degrees in a right angle. How many degrees are

in a "straight angle"? ⟵⌒⟶   How many degrees are in the acute angle of the diamond-

shaped block in the activity? (╱╱)

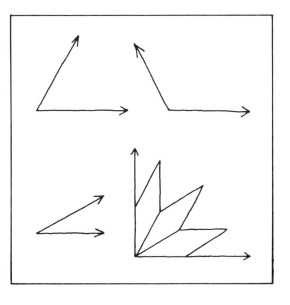

Draw an angle of about 10°.

This angle is fairly small, and so you can see that it would be very difficult to do direct measurement of angles by placing units of 1°. Angles are usually measured with a protractor, which represents degrees arranged around a common vertex. Do you think children could make their own protractors? Why?

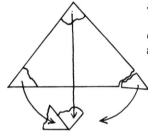

Some Patterns Involving Measurement of Angles

The activity described here would lead children to discover that the sum of the measures of the angles of a triangle is _____. (Try it yourself, if you are unsure.)

Draw a triangle carefully with a ruler.
Cut it out.
Tear off the corners, and place them with the vertices all at one point.
What do you notice? Try it with another triangle.

What would happen if you did this activity for a quadrilateral? Try it: draw and cut out a quadrilateral, tear off its corners, and arrange them with all vertices at one point. You should have shown that the sum of the angles of a quadrilateral is _____.

Another way to show this is to draw a quadrilateral, and then draw a diagonal. What is the sum of the angles in each triangle? _____ in the whole quadrilateral? _____ (What happens if the quadrilateral is not convex? Try it.)

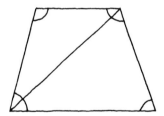
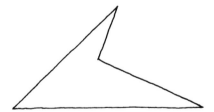

The following approach to these patterns also gives children practice with addition of two- and three-digit numbers. (Of course the answers in this activity may not all be identical, owing to error of measurement, but we hope that children will notice that the sums are always fairly close.)

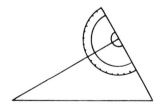

Materials: Protractor; ruler
Directions: Draw a triangle with a ruler. Measure the angles, and add the measures. What do you get? _____ Try it for three more triangles. What do you notice?
Variation: Try it for quadrilaterals.

Squares and Length on a Geoboard

We have already discussed (in Chapter 6, Measurement and the Metric System) how to teach direct measurement of length. This section concerns a pattern relating the lengths of the sides of a right triangle, and how this pattern can be applied to finding the lengths of line segments on a geoboard (such as the diagonal in figure D, Activity 9, part 1).

1. On your geoboard, assume that 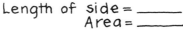 is the unit of length, and

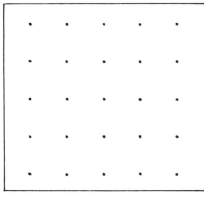 is the unit of area. The dot diagrams in this section are spaced by centimeters, and so you can use a ruler marked in centimeters to measure lengths. Make squares on the geoboard, all of different sizes.

Length of side = _____
Area = _____

Length of side = _____
Area = _____

Length of side = _____
Area = _____

Length of side = _____
Area = _____

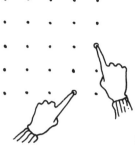

2. Do you think that you have found all possible sizes of squares? If you think so, here is a game. Have someone put fingers on two nails of your geoboard, then see if you can put fingers on two more nails so that a square is formed. Try it with the nails indicated in the diagram to the left. Draw the square. Now try to find other squares. You should fill all of the spaces below with new squares of different areas. For each, find the area. Also, using a centimeter ruler, measure the lengths of the sides of the squares. (Your measurements will be approximate; for example, 2.2 cm.)

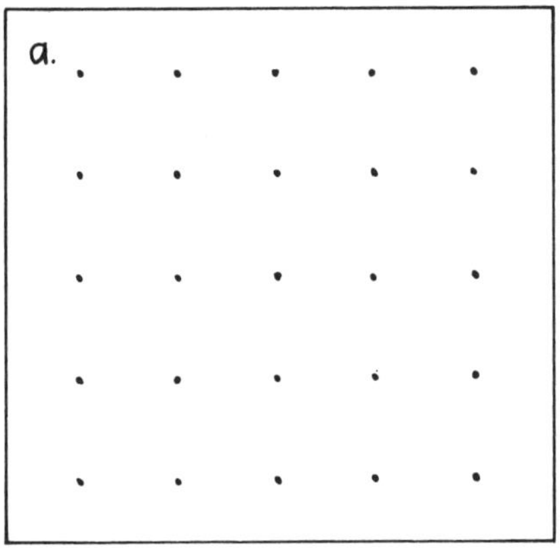

a.

Length of side = _____
Area = _____

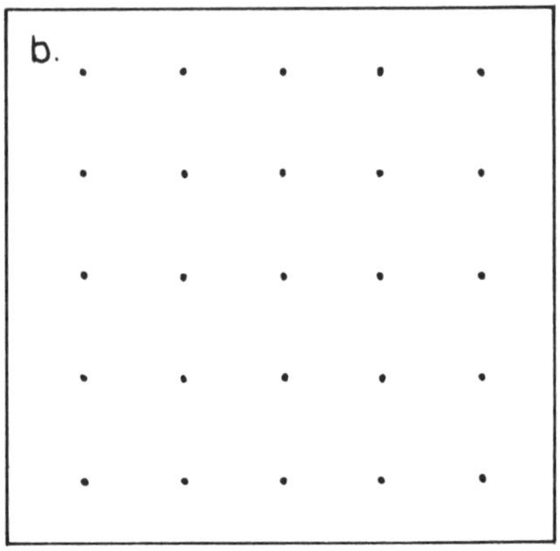

b.

Length of side = _____
Area = _____

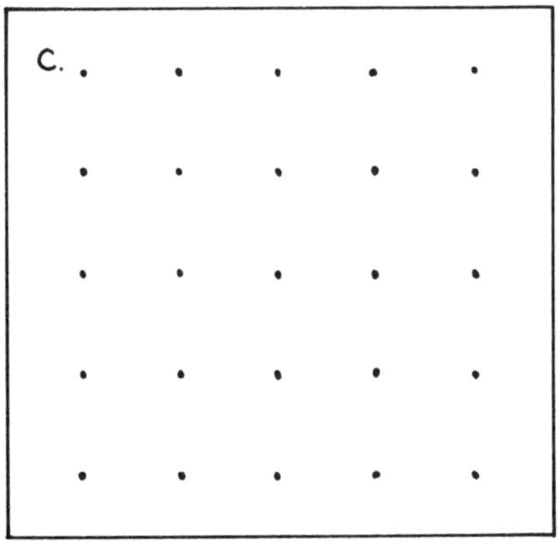

c.

Length of side = _____
Area = _____

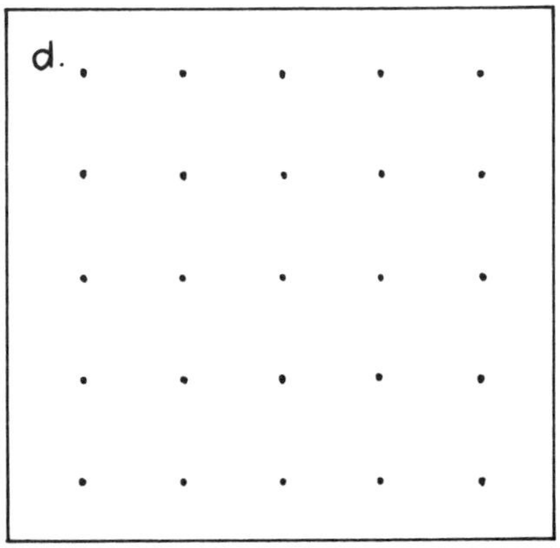

d.

Length of side = _____
Area = _____

a. $s \times s$ = _____
b. $s \times s$ = _____
c. $s \times s$ = _____
d. $s \times s$ = _____

3. In general, if a square has side s, then its area is $s \times s$, or s^2. We can also say that if a square has area a, then its side has length $s = \sqrt{a}$, the square root of a. Check your measurements in part 2 to see how

close you came. For each square, let *s* be the length of the side and find $s \times s$.

4. Do you see how you could predict the area of the square which has the line segment drawn to the right as one side — *without* measuring it? A famous theorem would help: the Pythagorean theorem (after the Greek mathematician Pythagoras who lived in the sixth century B.C.). Here is how it would apply to this problem.

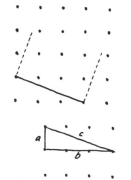

Construct the right triangle shown to the right. The Pythagorean theorem states that

$$a^2 + b^2 = c^2.$$

Here the length *a* is 1 and the length *b* is 3, and so by the theorem,
$$1^2 + 3^2 = c^2, \text{ or } 1 + 9 = c^2, \text{ or } c^2 = 10.$$

This means that a square with a side measuring *c* has an area of 10. *c* is the square root of 10 (that is, $\sqrt{10}$, which is about 3.2). Did you find this square in part 2?

The Pythagorean theorem states that for *any* triangle that has one right angle, $a^2 + b^2 = c^2$, where *a* and *b* are the lengths of the sides adjacent to the right angle, and *c* is the length of the side opposite (sometimes called the *hypotenuse*).

5. You can use the Pythagorean theorem to find the length of *any* line segment on the geoboard by finding a right triangle that has that segment as its hypotenuse. Use the Pythagorean theorem to find each of the lengths marked below and on page 380. Check your answers by measuring. (Unlike the one that has been worked out, the ones to be completed have the length *c* equal to a whole number.)

Line segment I:
$$a = 2, a^2 = 4; b = 5, b^2 = 25;$$
$$a^2 + b^2 = c^2 = 29.$$
Check by measuring: *c* is about 5.4 cm, which is close to $\sqrt{29}$, since $(5.4)^2 = 29.16$

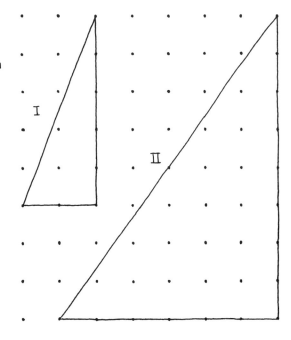

Line segment II:
$$a = \underline{\quad}, a^2 = \underline{\quad}; b = \underline{\quad}, b^2 = \underline{\quad};$$
$$a^2 + b^2 = c^2 = \underline{\quad\quad},$$
and so $c = \underline{\quad\quad}$. (Check by measuring.)

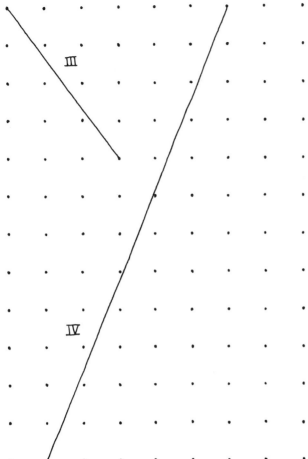

Draw the right triangle for each of these.

Line segment III:
$a =$ ___, $a^2 =$ ___; $b =$ ___, $b^2 =$ ___;
$a^2 + b^2 = c^2 =$ _____,
and so $c =$ _____. (Check by measuring.)

Line segment IV:
$a =$ ___, $a^2 =$ ___; $b =$ ___, $b^2 =$ ___;
$a^2 + b^2 = c^2 =$ _____,
and so $c =$ _____. (Check by measuring.)

Draw your own line segment, and use the Pythagorean theorem to find its length.

Your line segment:
$a =$ ___, $a^2 =$ ___; $b =$ ___, $b^2 =$ ___;
$a^2 + b^2 = c^2 =$ _____,
and so $c =$ _____. (You might use a calculator with a button that finds square root for this, or approximate it.) Check by measuring.

6. It is not difficult to give a geometrical "proof" of the Pythagorean theorem; that is, to show that for any right triangle where the sides adjacent to the right angle have lengths a and b, and where the side opposite the right angle has length c, it is true that $a^2 + b^2 = c^2$.

Take two sides (whose side measure $a + b$) and cut them as indicated to the left.

Notice that each square has four triangular regions, and all of them are congruent to the right triangle drawn below.

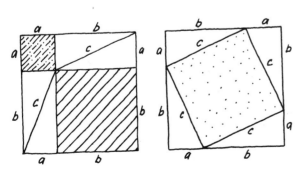

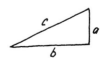

If we "take away" four of these triangles from each of the cut-up squares, the remaining area must be the same, and so we are left with the following:

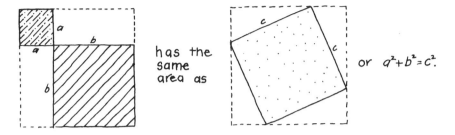

has the same area as

or $a^2 + b^2 = c^2$.

Notice that this will work for *any* numbers *a* and *b*.

A Formula for Area on a Geoboard

The Pythagorean theorem is true for any right triangle, not just for those made on a geoboard. The formula for area, which will be developed in this section, refers just to shapes made on a geoboard or on a similar regular array of dots.

In Activity 14, you probably discovered that for polygons with exactly one interior nail, the area and the number of boundary nails are related by a simple formula. This formula can in fact be modified and extended to apply to other shapes. A more general formula, known as Pick's theorem, tells you the area of a figure made with one rubber band on a geoboard (no crossings) if you know the number of nails in the *interior* and the number of nails that the rubber band touches, the *boundary* nails.

To find this formula, fill in the charts on the next page. First look for a formula for each horizontal row, and then try to find a formula that ties them all together.

This is easiest as a class project. On the chalkboard make spaces for each case (that is, stretch out each of the four charts horizontally along the chalk tray, as shown in the diagram). Each student must make a shape that belongs somewhere, find the area, and put the actual geoboard in the appropriate space.

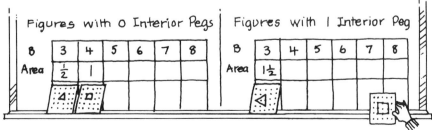

Notice that when doing this activity, children are practicing the skill of finding the area of a polygon at the same time as being involved in a deeper challenge — the search for number patterns and their symbolic description.

Let B = the number of boundary nails, and I = the number of interior nails. (**Note:** The formula is easiest to find in the second chart, where I = 1.)

NO INTERIOR NAILS (I = 0)

B	3	4	5	6	7	
Area	$\frac{1}{2}$	1	$1\frac{1}{2}$	2	$2\frac{1}{2}$	
Picture of the figure	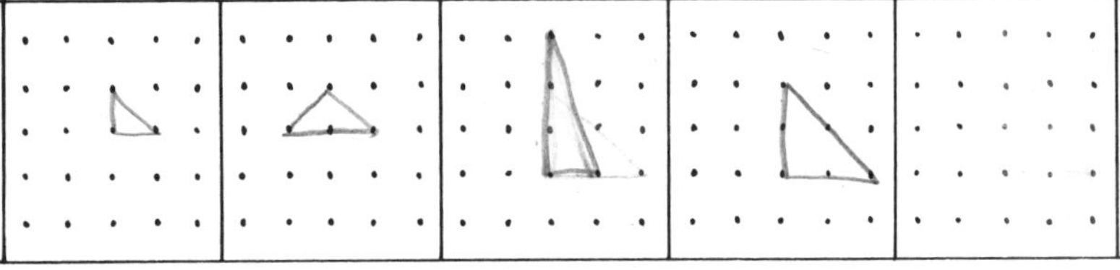					$A = \frac{1}{2}B - 1$

ONE INTERIOR NAIL (I = 1)

B	3	4	5	6	7	
Area	$1\frac{1}{2}$	2	$2\frac{1}{2}$	3	$3\frac{1}{2}$	
Picture of the figure	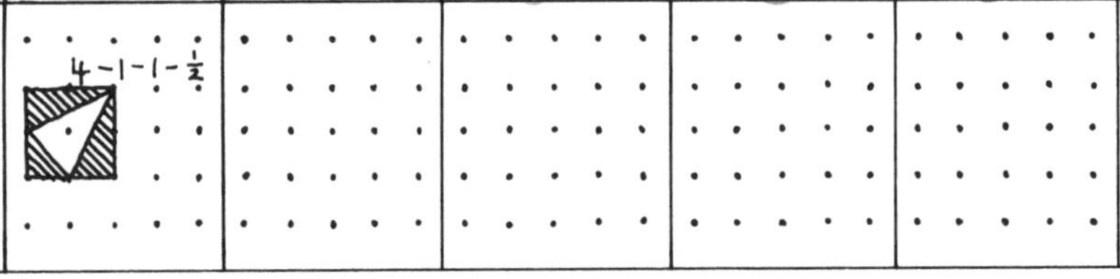 4 - 1 - 1 - $\frac{1}{2}$					$A = \frac{1}{2}B$

TWO INTERIOR NAILS (I = 2)

B	3	4	5	6	7	
Area	$2\frac{1}{2}$	3	$3\frac{1}{2}$	4	$4\frac{1}{2}$	
Picture of the figure	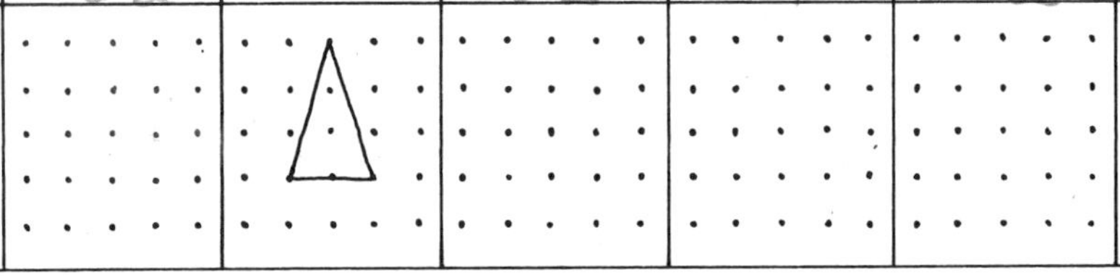					$A = \frac{1}{2}B + 1$

THREE INTERIOR NAILS (I = 3)

B	3	4	5	6	7	
Area	$3\frac{1}{2}$	4	$4\frac{1}{2}$	5	$5\frac{1}{2}$	
Picture of the figure	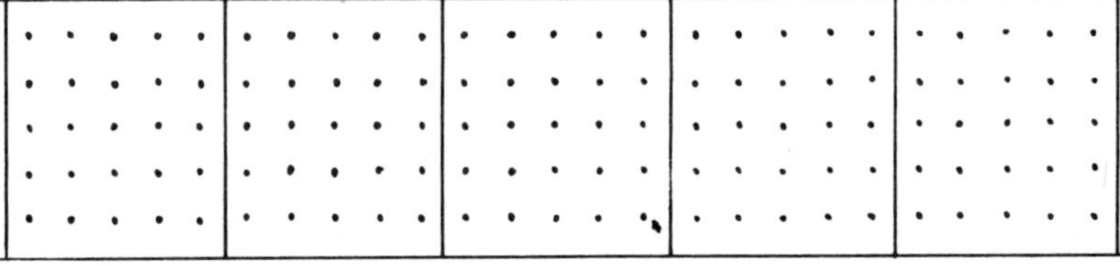					$A = \frac{1}{2}B + 2$

Do you see the pattern that relates these patterns? Write the formula.

Area = _____

(If you give up, the formula is $A = \frac{1}{2}B + I - 1$.)

Check this formula on the figures below. Find the area both by the formula *and* by one of the other methods we have been using.

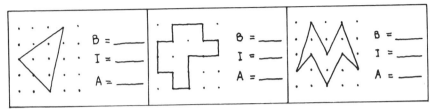

Transformation Geometry

In Activity 2, you copied some shapes upside down on your geoboard. You might have checked the shape you made by rotating or turning your whole geoboard and then comparing the turned copy with the shape you were asked to make. Which of the diagrams below could represent the same geoboard construction as the one drawn to the right? (You might copy the one to the right and try moving it around.)

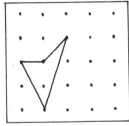

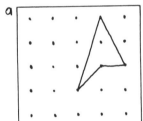 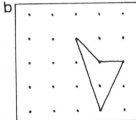 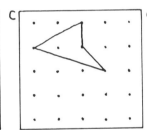 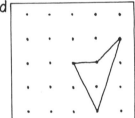

These shapes clearly have something in common — in fact, they are all *congruent*. If you cut out a piece of paper of the original shape, it could be moved to just fit on top of each shape (although for diagram (b) you would have to turn it over). Two of the diagrams, (a) and (c), could be obtained by turning the geoboard, either a quarter turn to the right (diagram _____) or a half-turn (diagram _____). Diagram (d) shows the same shape exactly, but it has been slid two spaces to the right on the geoboard (and so it could not be a picture of the same geoboard). Diagram (b) could be obtained by turning the geoboard over and looking through it.

This discussion of *motion geometry* or *transformation geometry* concerns a branch of geometry that has been entering both the high school and elementary school curriculum — the study of how shapes change when transformed in ways such as those described above. When a shape is turned, slid, or flipped, basic properties of the shape (measure of the sides, angles, and area) remain unchanged. In the elementary school, the study of transformations is very intuitive, both in language and concept. (You have seen how these concepts arise informally in the study of symmetry. See Chapter 3, Informal Geometry.) Later, transformations can be more precisely described in terms of coordinates.

Geoboards suggest the use of a regular array of dots to record shapes. Since their size is limited, geoboards are not suitable for extensive work with transformations; however, dot paper is convenient for recording shapes and the results of transformations of them. Some basic types of transformations which can be performed on shapes on dot paper follow. Two examples of each type are given. In each case, the *solid* figure represents the original figure, and the *dotted* figure represents the figure after the transformation. Fill in the other two examples of each type.

You may find it helpful to use an acetate sheet or tracing paper on top of these diagrams. Trace the original figure on the acetate, move the acetate appropriately, and then see where the tracing lies. This is particularly easy to demonstrate on an overhead projector — use different colors for the original shape and the tracing.

1. *Slides.* The arrow indicates the direction and length of the slide. (If you use a clear plastic sheet, slide it in this way.) Complete the last two examples.

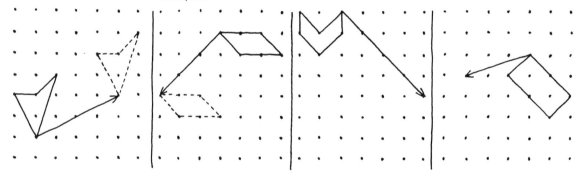

2. *Flips.* Flip the shape *over* the dotted line. Think of the mirror image. (If you use a clear plastic sheet, trace both shape and line, then turn the sheet over so that the line is under its tracing.) Complete the last two examples.

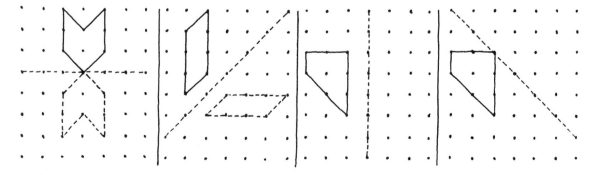

3. *Turns.* Turn the shape about the point marked. The arrow indicates how much to turn. (If you use a clear plastic sheet, put a pin through the sheet at the point indicated after tracing the figure, and turn the sheet the indicated amount.) Complete the last two examples.

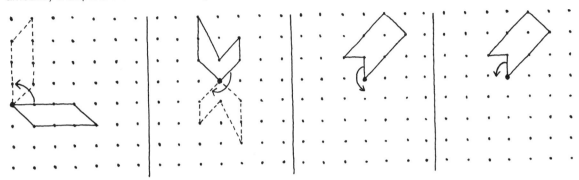

Upper elementary school children who can perform these transformations easily may be challenged to describe them in terms of coordinates. To do this, they might work with shapes drawn on coordinate paper and a particular transformation. They can make a table showing the coordinates of particular points before and after the transformation (similar to the tables for "function machines" on pages 193–194). For example, if they are working with the slide transformation shown below, the table might be as shown.

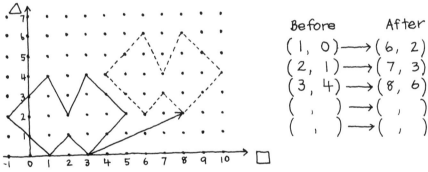

Before	After
$(1, 0) \longrightarrow (6, 2)$	
$(2, 1) \longrightarrow (7, 3)$	
$(3, 4) \longrightarrow (8, 6)$	
$(\quad , \quad) \longrightarrow (\quad , \quad)$	
$(\quad , \quad) \longrightarrow (\quad , \quad)$	

Fill in two more. Do you see the number pattern?
Can you describe the pattern symbolically, $(\square, \triangle) \longrightarrow (\underline{\quad}, \underline{\quad})$?

4. Here is another geometric transformation that changed (a) into (b). (In terms of coordinates, it could be described by specifying that every point in the original shape — say (1,2) — goes to the point obtained by doubling both coordinates — say to (2,4).) What would be a good name for this type of transformation? Does this transformation change the lengths of sides of a figure? the size of angles? the area? This type of transformation is commonly called an *enlargement* or a *similarity*.

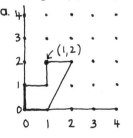

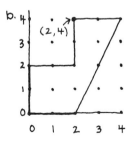

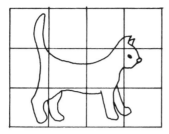

Children can get a feeling for this type of transformation by copying figures from small geoboards onto larger ones, or vice versa. These activities can provide practice with ratio and proportion (for example, the sides of (b) are twice as long as the corresponding sides of (a)). The skill of drawing larger or smaller copies of an original figure is vital to making maps and to copying designs from a geoboard onto a different size of dot paper.

Try to enlarge this drawing.

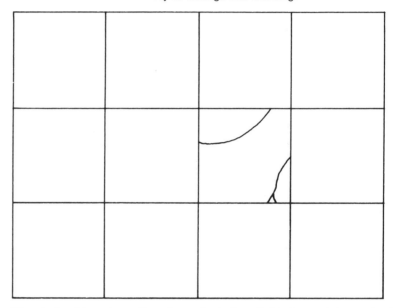

The study of transformations is particularly suitable for enrichment in the upper elementary grades. It can provide both opportunities to practice and apply concepts and skills such as functions and coordinate notation, and also many possibilities for children to engage in their own independent investigations. For example, children might make up their own functions (such as ($\square$, $\triangle$) → ($3 \times \square$, $\triangle + 3$)), and see what they "do" to various shapes. In what ways do the transformed shapes resemble the original? In what ways are they different? What happens to the perimeter? area? angles?

All About Circles

The Activities, Discussion Questions and Comments, and Follow-up Sections of this chapter have, for the most part, involved the measurement of length of line segments or perimeter and area of polygons, all of which can be illustrated quite naturally on a geoboard. Many of the same measurement concepts also apply to shapes other than polygons, for example circles.

Circles are a common shape in our environment. They arise in many everyday situations — in wheels, bubbles, plates, phonograph records, etc.

Very young children learn to recognize them. Try these circle activities which concern aspects of a circle and measurement of a circle.

1. Play with a compass. Make a pattern. Children often like to make this one. Try it.

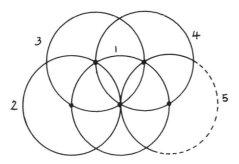

2. Take a glass or cup and trace around it on a piece of paper to make a circle. Can you find its center? First guess — mark what you think is the center with a pencil dot. Then cut it out and check your guess by folding the paper. Describe how you can find the center by folding.

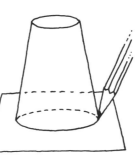

3. This time, take a glass and trace the outline, but try to find the center *without* folding, using only a ruler and a compass. (You can check your guess by using a compass.) What if the circle is too big to be drawn with an ordinary compass? Describe how you might find the center of the top of a circular table that is about two meters across.

4. Suppose you were putting a decorative edging around a table cloth for a circular table. How much edging would you need? Or, in other words, what is the *perimeter* of the circle? Children can make a graph, as shown to the right, to discover the relationship between the diameter of a circle and its perimeter or *circumference*. (For a related activity, see Around and Across, page 254.)

   Materials: Several cylinders of various sizes; bottle caps, tubes, etc.; string

   Directions: For each size circle, stretch a piece of string around the circumference and cut it exactly to this size. Trace the circles as shown on a graph, and paste the string to the graph. Mark the top of the string with a dot. What do you notice?

   In this graph, children can observe that the dots are all on a straight

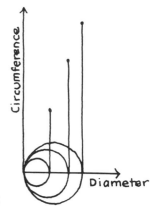

line. Also, if they measure the circumference and diameter of each circle and compute the quotient $\frac{\text{circumference}}{\text{diameter}}$, this number should be fairly close for all circles. (Variations will result from error of measurement and stretchiness of the string.) This number is in fact an approximation for the number π, defined to be the ratio $\frac{\text{circumference}}{\text{diameter}}$. This ratio is the same for all circles. (π is an irrational number that cannot be written as a terminating decimal fraction. One can only approximate it. One approximation is 3.14159. For most purposes, the approximation 3.14 is sufficient.)

Observing that $\frac{\text{circumference}}{\text{diameter}} = \pi$, children can see that the circumference is π times the diameter, or $C = \pi \times d$. Since the diameter is twice as long as the radius, this means that $C = \pi \times 2r$ or $C = 2\pi r$, or the circumference is a bit more than six times the radius of the circle.

5. Suppose you are a farmer watering a field with a rotating sprinkler, and you want to find out how much of your farmland is being irrigated; in other words, what is the *area* of a circular region? Three different approaches to this question are described. Which do you prefer?

First approach. Cut out a circle from paper. Put it in a square whose side is the diameter of the circle. Remove one-quarter of the circle, and try to cut this piece to fit into the corners which are shaded. You will probably have a few small scraps left over. If you can do this, you have shown that the area of a circle is a little more than 3 times the area of the square whose side is the radius of the circle — or the area of a circle is a little more than $3r^2$.

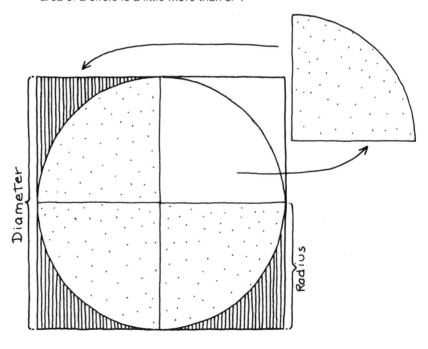

Second approach. A circle with a radius of 1 decimeter (10 centimeters) can be drawn on square-centimeter paper. You can find the area by counting squares. Below there is drawn just one-quarter of such a circle (to scale). Find the area by counting square centimeters.

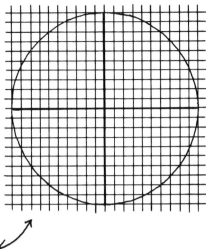

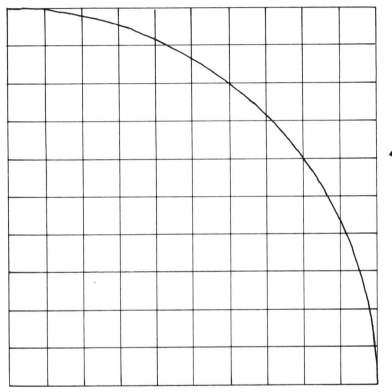

The area of one-quarter of a circle with a radius of 10 centimeters is _____ square centimeters.

A circle with a radius of 10 centimeters has an area of about _____ square centimeters.

Remember that there are 100 square centimeters in 1 square decimeter, so the area of a circle with a radius of 1 decimeter is about _____ square decimeters. (Your answer should be fairly close to π.)

Third approach. Children can cut out a circle with a radius of 1 decimeter, cut it into 16 wedge-shaped pieces, and arrange them as shown into a shape that looks somewhat like a parallelogram. (It will look even more like a parallelogram if you cut the circle into more than 16 wedges.) Children can measure (in decimeters) the height (*h*) and the base (*b*) of the parallelogram, and then find the approximate area of the circle by finding the area of the parallelogram ($h \times b$).

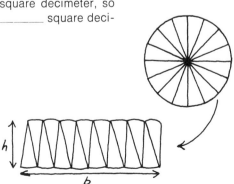

Actually without doing this, you might notice that the height of the parallelogram is approximately the radius of the circle. Also the entire circumference ($2\pi r$) of the circle has been broken up to form the top and base of the parallelogram, and so the base is about one-half of the circumference of the circle, or about πr. This means that the area of the circle is approximately the base of the parallelogram times the height of the parallelogram or $\pi r \times r$, or πr^2.

Which of the three approaches to finding the area of the circle do you think would give you the most accurate measurement of the area of a circle?

Which most convinced you that the area of a circle is a little more than three times the square of the radius?

Which explained why in fact the area of a circle with radius r is πr^2?

TEST YOUR UNDERSTANDING

1. Here are drawn some polygons resembling letters.

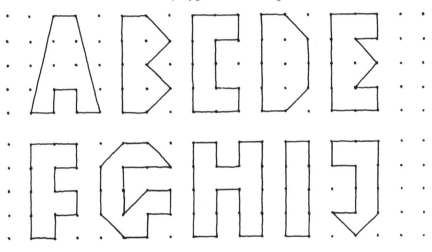

   a. Find the perimeters of letters C, F, H, and I.
   b. Which has the greatest perimeter, C or E?
   c. Find the areas of all the letters. Which has the greatest area? the least?

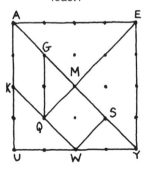

2. Refer to the pattern on the geoboard to the right. Let ⊔ be the unit of area. Find the areas of triangles GMQ, UKW, AEM, and AUY. Does this pattern look familiar?

3. Why should children's early experiences with measurement of area and angles include nonstandard units for area and angles? Give examples of such experiences.

4. Describe limitations of the geoboard for teaching area or perimeter. What materials would you prefer? Why?

5. Suppose that you asked a child to find the area and perimeter of the shape shown here, which is a rectangle with a square cut out from one side. Below are given some *wrong* answers which a child might give. For each, explain how the child might have arrived at this wrong answer, and describe how you would help him to correct the mistake. (Of course you can only *guess* at the reason for the wrong answer. The only way to know for sure is to talk to the child!) Wrong answers for perimeter: 28, 30; wrong answers for area: 48, 32.

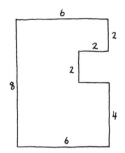

6. Give two reasons why a child might enjoy using a geoboard, and list concepts that might arise through play.

7. a. How many triangles can you make on a geoboard which have UY as one side? _____ (Did you actually *list* the triangles, or did you find a quick way to count them?)
   b. Of these triangles, how many are right triangles?
   c. How many are isosceles?
   d. How many are equilateral?
   e. How many are obtuse?

8. Distinguish between inductive and deductive reasoning, and give examples of each.

9. Describe how you can use geoboards, dot paper, or squared paper (by folding or cutting) to explain these area formulas.

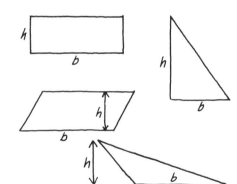

Rectangle: $A = b \times h$

Right triangle: $A = \frac{1}{2} b \times h$

Parallelogram: $A = b \times h$

Any triangle: $A = \frac{1}{2} b \times h$

Describe an activity that would lead a child to discover the formula $A = \frac{1}{2} b \times h$ for the area of a triangle.

10. a. Describe some situations involving motion with angles.
    b. Draw an angle of 120° on the circular geoboard.
    c. A Challenge: How many different sized angles can you make on this geoboard?

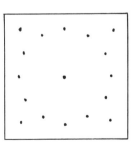

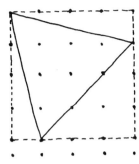

11. Is this triangle equilateral? Test it by two methods. First, trace it on paper. Second, move the tracing to check lengths and angles. Finally, find the lengths of each side using the Pythagorean theorem. Find the area.

12. Explain how children could discover that the circumference of any circle is about three times as long as its diameter. Describe two different approaches to finding the area of a circle.

13. Check that you can now answer all of the measurement questions on page 349.

14. A Challenge: Make a rectangle with an area of four units that is twice as long as it is wide. (Use the diagram to the right.)

15. A Challenge: Investigate: Is it possible to make a polygon on the geoboard whose perimeter is an *odd* whole number?

FURTHER READINGS AND PROJECTS

1. In the Activities in this chapter, you saw several number patterns arising from geometric constructions. Such patterns can provide interesting challenges to upper elementary school children, while they are practicing skills such as finding area or length. Through playing around on a geoboard, try to find some other patterns such as those in Activities 14–16. You will find some ideas in *Patterns and Systems of Elementary Mathematics* by Jonathan Knaupp, Lehi Smith, Paul Shoecraft, and Gary Warkentin (Boston: Houghton Mifflin, 1977).

2. Several sets of geoboard activity cards are available commercially. Examine some. Do you think the activities would interest children? Could the language be modified so that the cards could be used with younger children than intended? Do the activities invite children to discover patterns?

3. Many types of geoboards are available commercially; however, you may wish to make your own, perhaps to get a particular size and arrangement of nails or to give children the experience of making some materials for themselves. As suggested on page 362, it helps to establish your pattern of nails on a piece of graph paper, and then hammer nails right through the paper. Some teachers might feel that sharp nail heads could be dangerous for young children. In the article "Build a Better Geoboard," in *The Arithmetic Teacher* 24:1 (January 1977), pp. 85–86, Judith S. Klein suggests using plastic-headed pushpins instead of nails. Can you think of any disadvantage of this material for activities with geoboards such as copying shapes? for measuring area and perimeter? Design and make yourself a geoboard, and make some activity cards to go with it.

4. On pages 364–366 you saw how geoboards can be used to build coordinate notation, and also to lead to early experiences of graphing. These

topics, and many others, are more formally developed in the Madison Project materials. In particular, examine *Discovery in Mathematics, A Text for Teachers* by Robert B. Davis (Menlo Park, Cal.: Addison-Wesley, 1964). Read the description of the project and the approach to learn what the Madison Project aimed to do. Then to see some particular lessons, which you could in fact adapt to do on a geoboard, read Chapter 7, "The Point Set Game," and Chapter 11, "Graphs."

5. On pages 383–386 there was a brief discussion of transformation geometry. Examine *Geoboards and Motion Geometry for Elementary Teachers* by John J. DelGrande (Glenview, Ill.: Scott Foresman, 1972). Read Chapter 1 which gives ideas for early intuitive experiences children might have with transformations. Later sections develop transformations more formally, in particular the relationship between transformations and coordinate notation. Read Section 3.3 of DelGrande's book and try some of the exercises relating slides, flips, and turns to coordinate notation (for example, numbers 3, 5, 11, 12, 19, 20 of the Exercises 3.3). This book also provides a development and extension of Pick's theorem, which we discussed on pages 381–383.

The formula for Pick's theorem is $A = \frac{1}{2}B + I - 1$.

NOTES

1. See Zoltan P. Dienes, *Building Up Mathematics* (London: Hutchinson Educational Ltd., 1960), pp. 27–28, 32. Dienes refers to this sequencing of preliminary, structured, and practice activities as the Dynamic Principle.

2. You will find more examples of making graphs of number sentences or equations in Chapters 4 and 10.

3. These and many other quilt patterns can be found in *The Perfect Patchwork Primer* by Beth Gutcheon (Baltimore: Penguin, 1973).

CHAPTER 9

WHOLE NUMBER ALGORITHMS AND THEIR USES

INTRODUCTION

Do you think that everyone does arithmetic exercises and verbal problems in the same way? Try these — then give them to someone else to try, preferably someone of a different age or background from yourself. Did you both do them the same way?

a. 6/795

b. 432
   − 1 7 5

c. How old is someone who was born on June 30, 1942?

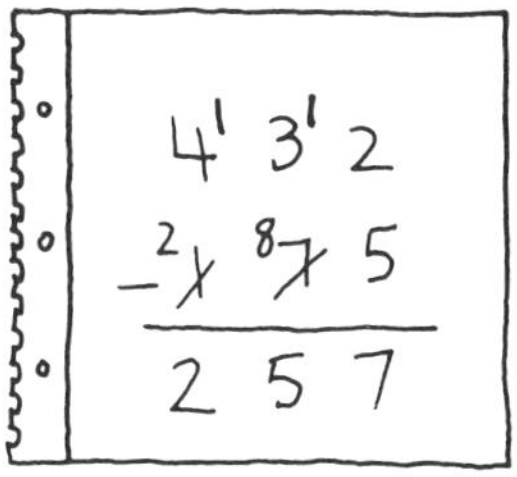

You may have found that there are several ways to do each of these. For example, a child might have done the division (a) by a longer expanded form than an adult, but you could probably figure out how the child's method corresponds to your own. Children are often taught a longer but more easily understood method for an operation before a shortcut standard method. The subtraction can also be done in different ways. You may have found that someone did the subtraction in a manner completely different from your own — perhaps their method looked like the one shown to the right. Is this answer the same as yours? Do you see how the method works? (Subtract 5 from 12, 8 from 13, 2 from 4.) Do you think this method or *algorithm* always gives the correct answer? Try it on these subtractions.

```
 4¹ 3¹ 2
−²₁ ⁸₇ 5
 2 5 7
```

```
  636      730     1234
− 1 4 2   − 2 5 9   −  4 3 5
```

This algorithm for subtraction (sometimes known as the *compensation, equal addends,* or *Austrian* method) has been taught in schools. You may find that some adults or children raised in another country do subtraction this way.

In the verbal problem, there is a real choice about what method to use. Many people would subtract 1942 from the present year; some might add on from 1942 to the present year; while others might think in terms of when they were born and figure out how much older or younger this person is. This problem concerns an application of arithmetic that allows for a choice of methods.

Finally, if you presented these exercises and verbal problems to someone with a calculator easily available, they would probably use it to do them. The widespread availability of calculators has far-reaching implications for teaching algorithms and using them in many new and challenging situations.

This chapter deals with algorithms for operations on whole numbers — that is, ways to do arithmetic with multidigit whole numbers. This chapter extends Chapter 5, Basic Facts and Their Uses — Operations on Whole Numbers, that concerned the meanings of the operations of addition, subtraction, multiplication, and division on whole numbers, and how to help children gain mastery of basic facts and use them in various kinds of application and problem-solving situations. While knowledge of basic facts enables a child to do arithmetic with relatively small numbers (for example, $9 + 4$, 9×4), working with large numbers requires some sort of grouping (for example, by tens and ones) and related place-value notation. This was explored in Chapter 7, Place Value, that also dealt with procedures for operations on multidigit numbers in base five and base ten. Building on these two chapters, this chapter focuses on procedures or algorithms for arithmetic on larger whole numbers.

The Activities concern the notion of algorithm, uses of algorithms in everyday situations, and types of errors children make with algorithms. Also included are games, puzzles, and application situations, some of which indicate ways to use a calculator for learning about algorithms.

Discussion Questions and Comments focus on types of difficulties children have in learning algorithms and some strategies to help prevent these difficulties or to remedy them.

Follow-up Sections concern how concrete activities can be used to introduce algorithms to children and how symbolic procedures for algorithms can be developed from this work with manipulative materials. Specific concrete and semiconcrete approaches for teaching algorithms are discussed as well as some symbolic ones. The scope and sequence of operations on whole numbers (basic facts through algorithms) in the elementary school are discussed and related to the diagnosis of errors and planning of instruction.

One major theme of this book is that mathematics should be useful — a section describes some of the many ways in which children can use algorithms. Finally, a section deals with word problems and ways to help children solve them.

ACTIVITIES

Activity 1. Telling Tales

1. Which operation do *you* use most often: addition, subtraction, multiplication, or division? Describe two situations in which you use this operation.

   a. _____.
   b. _____.

2. Which of these three situations for $3\overline{)69}$ do you find most interesting? _____ useful? _____ realistic? _____

a. Carol, Jennifer, and Andrew chipped in to buy a lottery ticket, #3017. They agreed to share the prize evenly if they won. Their ticket was a winner! (See the table to the right.) How much did each person win?
b. How many yards of rope are in 69 feet?
c. Once upon a time, Jack traded in his only cow for a handful of beans. There were 69. In order to pacify his mother who was furious about the trade, Jack planted the beans very neatly, equally in 3 rows. How many beans did he plant in each row?

> FRIDAY'S DAILY LOTTERY
> # 1917
> Payoff— digits must be in exact order.
>
> | | |
> |---|---|
> | All 4 digits | $2816 |
> | 1st or last 3 | 492 |
> | Any 2 in place | 69 |
> | Any 1 in place | 4 |

3. Describe an interesting situation for $5\overline{)1\ 2\ 5}$.

Compare your situation with one your neighbor has described.

4. Describe a situation for 17 × 152.

Show this situation to your neighbor. Did your neighbor find it interesting? _____ realistic? _____ useful? _____

Activity 2. Many Ways to Do It

Work with a partner or in a small group.

1. Is this addition done correctly? Does this method for adding two two-digit numbers always work? Would you have done the addition this way?
   Does this method work for three-digit numbers? Try it.

$$\begin{array}{r} 28 \\ +14 \\ \hline 12 \\ 30 \\ \hline 42 \end{array}$$

2. Addition can be done in many different ways at the abstract or symbolic level — for example, as shown at the right and below.

   a. $\begin{array}{r} 1 \\ 28 \\ +14 \\ \hline 42 \end{array}$

   b. $\begin{array}{r} 20 + 8 \\ + 10 + 4 \\ \hline 30 + 12 \\ 42 \end{array}$

   c. Done mentally as follows: 28 + 14 equals 28 plus 2 plus 12 more, or 30 plus 12, which equals 42.

d. Done mentally where we think of it in terms of coins: 28 + 14 is a quarter and 3 cents plus a dime and 4 cents, or 35 cents plus 7 cents, which is 42 cents.

You could also do this at the concrete level in ways such as the following: by counting out 28 beans, 14 beans, and then counting the total; with real coins; with squared materials; or with an abacus.

Describe different ways to do the following multiplication and division at the concrete level and at the symbolic level. Try to think of at least three different ways at each level.

Concrete Level	*Symbolic Level*

$$\begin{array}{r} 1\,9 \\ \times\,3 \\ \hline \end{array}$$

$$5\overline{)6\,5}$$

3. Think of different ways (if possible) to do the following exercises at the concrete level. Imagine that you are demonstrating the solutions to children. Are any of these too complex to solve with materials?

$$\begin{array}{r} 1\,9\,2 \\ \times\ \ 3 \\ \hline \end{array} \qquad 2\overline{)6\,5\,3} \qquad 1\,5\,0\overline{)6\,5\,3}$$

Activity 3. Some Unusual Ways to Do Multiplication

There are several different methods for adding, subtracting, multiplying, and dividing whole numbers. This Activity concerns two nonstandard methods for multiplication, *Russian Peasant* method and *Lattice* multiplication. These methods can be used with children in enrichment or remedial situations at the upper elementary level.

1. Lattice multiplication. This method for multiplication was widely used throughout Western Europe and India as early as 1600 A.D. Study the samples and figure out how this method works. Then do the other multiplications using this method.

a. $\begin{array}{r} 1\,5 \\ \times\,5 \\ \hline 7\,5 \end{array}$ 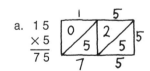   b. $\begin{array}{r} 4\,8 \\ \times\,7 \\ \hline 3\,3\,6 \end{array}$ 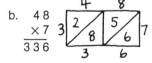   c. $\begin{array}{r} 1\,5\,3 \\ \times\,4 \\ \hline 6\,1\,2 \end{array}$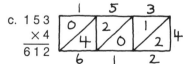

d. $\begin{array}{r} 1\,1\,9 \\ \times\,8 \\ \hline \end{array}$ 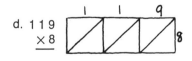   e. $\begin{array}{r} 1\,3 \\ \times\,5\,4 \\ \hline 7\,0\,2 \end{array}$ 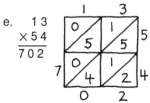   f. $\begin{array}{r} 5\,9 \\ \times\,2\,5 \\ \hline \end{array}$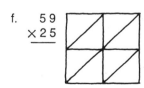

g. What is this multiplication? _____ × _____ = 425 -- -

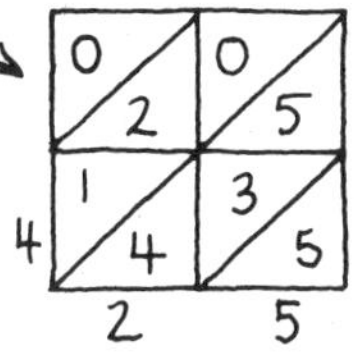

h. Extend this method to multiply 24 × 123.

2. Russian Peasant Multiplication.[1] Lattice multiplication and our stan-
    dard algorithm require knowledge of basic facts of multiplication. The
    Russian Peasant method requires only multiplication by two. Study
    the samples to discover how the method works. Then fill in the blanks
    to describe it.

24 × 36 = 864	Column I	Column II
	~~24~~	~~36~~
	~~12~~	~~72~~
	~~6~~	~~144~~
	3	288
	1	576
		864

35 × 42 = 1470	Column I	Column II
	35	42
	17	84
	~~8~~	~~168~~
	~~4~~	~~336~~
	~~2~~	~~672~~
	1	1344
		1470

16 × 31 = 496	Column I	Column II
	~~16~~	~~31~~
	~~8~~	~~62~~
	~~4~~	~~124~~
	~~2~~	~~248~~
	1	496
		496

31 × 33 = 1023	Column I	Column II
	31	33
	15	66
	7	132
	3	264
	1	528
		1023

Try using the Russian Peasant method for (a) and (b).

a.

	Column I	Column II
14 × 11	14	11
	7	22
	3	44

b.   Column I   Column II
  20 × 36

Description of the Russian Peasant method:

    To multiply two numbers, put the first at the top of Column I and the second at the top of Column II. Then write rows of numbers below the two original numbers, using the following rules:

Column I is formed by _____

_____.

Column II is formed by _____.

Continue to make these rows until _____.

Some rows are then crossed out. These are the rows that _____

_____.

Some numbers are then added. These are the numbers that _____

_____.

3. Which method, Lattice or Russian Peasant, did you find easier to use? By which method is it easier to multiply large numbers? For example, 1234 × 5078?

    While you can do multiplication by both of these methods, can you explain why either of them works?

Activity 4. Error Patterns

    Children get wrong answers for arithmetic exercises such as 78 + 14 or 69 ÷ 3 for many reasons. They may not know basic facts, may make a careless error (as when being distracted), or make errors in a procedure because they do not understand it. Sometimes they repeat the same kind of error in the procedure. To help these children become skillful with algorithms, a teacher should try to find out exactly what type of error the child is making.

1. *Error Patterns.* Examine the samples and work out the last two exercises as the child might have.

a.   3 3   3 8   5 4   4 2   4 7
      +4 4   +4 4   +1 6   +2 4   +2 8
       ———   ———   ———   ———   ———
       7 7   7 1 2   6 1 0

b.
$$
\begin{array}{r} {}^{2}3\,4 \\ \times\,6 \\ \hline 3\,0\,4 \end{array}
\qquad
\begin{array}{r} {}^{4}1\,8 \\ \times\,6 \\ \hline 3\,0\,8 \end{array}
\qquad
\begin{array}{r} 4\,2 \\ \times\,3 \\ \hline 1\,2\,6 \end{array}
\qquad
\begin{array}{r} 2\,4 \\ \times\,3 \\ \hline \end{array}
\qquad
\begin{array}{r} 4\,2 \\ \times\,5 \\ \hline \end{array}
$$

c.
$$
\begin{array}{r} 1\,4\,4 \\ 3\,\overline{)4\,3\,2} \\ 3 \\ \hline 1\,3 \\ 1\,2 \\ \hline 1\,2 \\ 1\,2 \\ \hline 0 \end{array}
\qquad
\begin{array}{r} 1\ 2 \\ 3\,\overline{)3\,0\,6} \\ 3 \\ \hline 0\ 6 \\ -\ 6 \\ \hline 0 \end{array}
\qquad
\begin{array}{r} 1\ 2 \\ 4\,\overline{)4\,0\,8} \\ -\,4 \\ \hline 0\ 8 \\ -\ 8 \\ \hline 0 \end{array}
\qquad
2\,\overline{)6\,0\,4}
\qquad
2\,\overline{)3\,0\,6}
$$

2. *Diagnose the Difficulty.* One person plays the role of a student who makes some kind of systematic error (such as those preceding). The other person plays the role of a teacher who tries to diagnose the difficulty.

   The "student" thinks of an error pattern and tells the "teacher" the general area of difficulty (such as "I seem to have difficulty adding two-digit numbers"). The teacher makes up a written exercise (such as 34 + 17) and has the student work it out in order to diagnose the specific difficulty.

   Try this. See if you can diagnose the difficulty with fewer than five exercises. Then switch roles and try this again. Write your samples in the margin.

Activity 5. Activities Using Algorithms

Children can find algorithms interesting and challenging if they are given good reason to use them. Games, recreational mathematical topics, computational patterns, open-ended problems, as well as conventional verbal problems can motivate the learning and application of algorithms. Work with a partner or in a small group and try the following activities. You will find a calculator a useful tool for speeding computation and helping you solve some of these problems.

1. *Make the Most of It*
   Materials: Choice device, such as cards numbered 1–9, a spinner marked 1–9, or a die labeled with 1–6 or with some other numbers, such as 1, 2, 3, 5, 7, 9; paper
   Directions: Each player first draws the format on page 402 on a sheet of paper. One person using a choice device obtains a digit and calls it out. As each digit is called out, each player writes it in one of the boxes. Numbers cannot be erased or changed once they are written.
   When all the boxes are filled, players compute the sum and the product, and then add these to obtain their scores for the game. The winner is the player to "make the most."

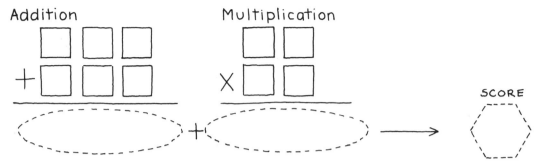

a. Did you get the best possible score, given the numbers that were selected? (You might check with a calculator.)

b. What strategies could you use to get a high score? Where would you put a "9"? a "1"?

c. (Optional) Copy the format above and play Make the Least of It which is one variation of this game. Here the winner is the player who gets the *least* total score.

2. *Water, Water, Everywhere? ? ?*
   Materials: Eyedropper; water; container or graduated cylinder showing milliliters; calculator
   Directions: Use the measurement devices to answer the questions below. There are several approaches you can use, some being faster and more direct than others.

   a. A person uses about 125 liters of water to take a bath. About how many drops of water is this? a million drops? a billion? Take a rough guess.

   b. Now determine how many drops of water are in one liter. Describe your method.

   c. Use your results from (b) to find how many drops of water are in a 125-liter bath. First estimate the amount (without pencil and paper).
   Estimated amount: _____ Calculated amount: _____
   How far off was your estimate?

   d. Water is one of the natural resources that we take for granted. In parts of the United States the 1977 drought led to the rationing of water. People are conserving water by using less water (such as for washing clothes or flushing toilets) and by eliminating wasteful consumption of water (such as dripping faucets). How many liters of water could be conserved in one month by fixing a faucet that drips at the rate of one drop per second? _____ L

   e. Make up another problem related to conservation of water.

   f. (Optional) Approximately how much water is saved each time a toilet is flushed by putting a brick (4 cm by 10 cm by 20 cm) in the tank of the toilet? _____ cc or _____ mL

About how much water could be saved in your house per day if you put a brick in the tank of the toilets in your house? _____ Is this enough for one bath?

3. *An Estimation Game for Two*
   Materials: Calculator
   Directions: Two persons play the game. One person says a two-digit number. Then the other player says a two-digit number. Then both players silently *write* an estimate of the product of the two numbers. Allow only five seconds to make this estimate. The product is then found using a calculator. The player with the closer estimate gets one point. The first player to get five points is the winner.

   a. Did your estimate improve as you played the game?
   b. How could you modify this game for division?

4. *Two Hundred — A Game for Two Players*
   Materials: Paper; pencil (This game could also be played on a calculator.)
   Directions: Two persons play the game. The first player selects any number, 1–99. The other player again selects any number, 1–99, and adds it to the first player's number. The two players continue to take turns selecting numbers 1–99 and adding them to the total score. The one to make a total score of 200 wins.
   Play the game a few times.
   Would you rather go first or second? Why?
   Variations:
   Try one of the variations below.

   a. Aim for 500. Would you rather go first or second?
   b. Aim for 222. Would you rather go first or second?
   c. Start with 200 and take turns *subtracting* numbers 1–99. Would you rather go first or second?
   > (**Note:** This game may be familiar to you from Chapter 5. A similar game there was called Poison Apple. Do you see how the winning strategy for Poison Apple resembles the one for this game?)

5. *Counting Squares*
   Suppose that you put tiles on a counter top, as shown here. Pretend that you do *not* know how to multiply two-digit numbers. Find how many tiles there are on the counter top. (**Hint:** You might try to break up the rectangle into smaller pieces and possibly use your understanding of place value.)

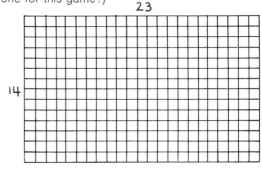

6. *Your Favorite Digit*

a. What is your favorite digit 1–9? Enter this digit below and complete the multiplication.

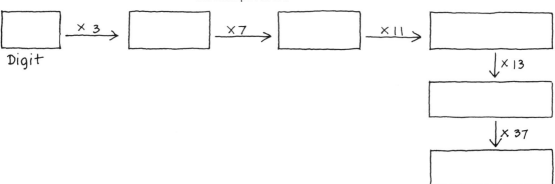

If you did not notice something about your final answer, check your multiplication. Compare your results with your neighbor's.

b. Write your favorite three-digit number and then repeat it (such as 384,384 if you chose 384). Complete the division.

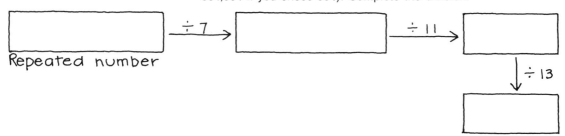

Compare your result with your neighbor's.

c. Do you know why these patterns occur?
   (**Hint:** For part (a), find $3 \times 7 \times 11 \times 13 \times 37 = $ _____.
   Now do you see why part (a) works?)

d. (Optional) Suppose you wanted the outcome of part (a) to be your digit repeated only three times. What two numbers would you multiply the digit by to obtain this result?

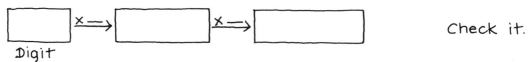

e. (Optional) Pick your favorite two-digit number and complete the multiplication below.

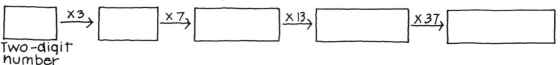

DISCUSSION QUESTIONS AND COMMENTS

What Is an Algorithm?

In Activity 2 you saw that there are many ways to do certain arithmetic exercises. For example, to find the product 14 × 23, we could make 14 piles of counters, each containing 23, and then count up the total; but this would be tedious. Perhaps you found a quicker method to count 14 × 23 in Activity 5, Counting Squares. Or we could add up a column of fourteen 23's. This repeated-addition method is how the multiplication might have been done on an old mechanical calculator. A solution could be obtained quickly by other methods such as Lattice multiplication, Russian Peasant multiplication (Activity 3), or our standard procedure for multiplication.

When we do arithmetic dealing with fairly small numbers — less than 10 — we can experience the action of the operation quite directly by using materials such as chips or a bead board and eventually we commit a certain number of facts to memory — the so-called basic facts. However, when dealing with an operation on larger numbers, such as 14 × 23, we find it more difficult to experience the action directly, and impossible to commit all such multiplications to memory. Thus we feel a need for some convenient procedures which build on what we already know — about basic facts and about place-value notation for larger numbers — to perform such calculations. These procedures are called *algorithms* (or sometimes *algorisms*). The word "algorithm" is derived from the name of a ninth-century Arab mathematician, al-Kwarimzi, who recorded many methods for computation. The power of an algorithm lies in the fact that it will work in the same way for any example of a given type that you may encounter. Many algorithms are possible — for example, you now know at least three algorithms for multiplication (Lattice, Russian Peasant, and the standard one). In the past, when computation was done mostly by hand, it was desirable to teach only the fastest and most efficient algorithms. However, since inexpensive hand-held calculators are now widely available, speed and efficiency seem less important goals. Time-consuming calculations by hand can be done in seconds on a calculator. In later sections of this chapter you will work with several algorithms that are slower to do but more easily understood than the standard ones for multiplication and division. Such "nonstandard" algorithms are taught in elementary school to help children become more secure in their ability to do these computations accurately in *some* way, and to help them understand how the standard algorithms work.

What Difficulties Do Children Have with Algorithms?

Did you ever have an difficulty learning an algorithm for whole numbers — for example, long division? If you did, write an exercise you had difficulty with and try to describe the difficulty.

Children encounter various difficulties in mastering algorithms. As we saw in Activity 4, Error Patterns, some difficulties involve types of errors made consistently in similar exercises.[2] Errors also arise from carelessness, weakness in prerequisite skills (such as basic facts), and poor writing and sloppy placement of numbers in written computations. In this section we examine more closely some types of difficulties children have with algorithms. This look at what children cannot do should provide some insight into what children should learn about algorithms.

Examine the samples of children's work below and describe what (if anything) is done incorrectly.

Child's work   Description of Errors

1.
```
   342      342      495      689
 - 121    - 138    - 139    - 592
 ─────    ─────    ─────    ─────
   221      216      353      116
```

2. Three boys share a prize of 69 marbles. How many does each boy get?
```
    ²69
  x  3
  ─────
    207
```

3.
```
    212        23         17
 4/848      4/812      4/428
  - 8        - 8        -4
 ─────      ─────      ─────
   04        012        028
  - 4        - 12       - 28
 ─────      ─────      ─────
   08          0          0
  - 8
 ─────
    0
```

4. When given this type of exercise, the child responds "I can't do it that way."

Complete.
```
      2
 3/642
  - 6
 ─────
   04
```

Two types of errors occur in sample (1). Errors related to basic facts of subtraction suggest that this child has not mastered the facts that are a prerequisite for multidigit subtraction. Second, errors in the procedure for subtraction suggest that the child may not understand the meaning of subtraction of three-digit numbers. That is, the child thinks of 342 − 138 as three unrelated subtractions: "8 minus 2 is 6, 4 minus 3 is 1, 3 minus 1 is 2," rather than as "three hundred and forty-two minus one hundred and thirty-eight." This inability to grasp the meaning of subtraction of large numbers might reflect a difficulty related to the meaning of numbers in general. Although it is difficult to tell from this written work sample alone, it is possible that this child in fact knows how to subtract some three-digit numbers (no exchanging) but not others (requiring exchanging). Some children cope with difficulties like this by adopting some plausible method and writing some answer (although incorrect) — a procedure they think is better than not answering at all. This type of coping often leads to error patterns in computation, especially when the error pattern yields some correct answers as in this case. Perhaps asking this child to explain (verbally or with materials) how he did simpler prerequisite subtractions (42 − 38) would shed some light on the real nature of the child's difficulty — that is, understanding the "exchange" or "regrouping" process in subtraction.

The error in sample (2) might be classified as "wrong operation." But why did the child multiply rather than divide? Perhaps this difficulty goes back to the child's inability to apply multiplication and division with basic facts. Or the child's recent study of algorithms could have been skill and drill oriented, with little or no application in practical situations. Another cause for this difficulty might be an inability to do division. Again, children may cope with the situation by doing what they can (multiplication) so as not to fail (division). Still another possibility is that the child has difficulty reading the problem. To pinpoint the causes for this type of error, a teacher might have the child read the problem aloud and explain what it means and how to solve it.

The child described in sample (3) may get correct answers in all exercises except for one type of division — those where 0's are required in the quotient. This error may lead you to suspect that the child does division mechanically and really does not understand the meaning of division. Then again, he may be able to act out 408 ÷ 4 (4 flats, 0 longs, 8 units shared in 4 piles gives 1 flat and 2 units in each pile) but may not associate the abstract written solution with the manipulative one. Do you think this child has been taught to check a division answer by estimating the quotient?

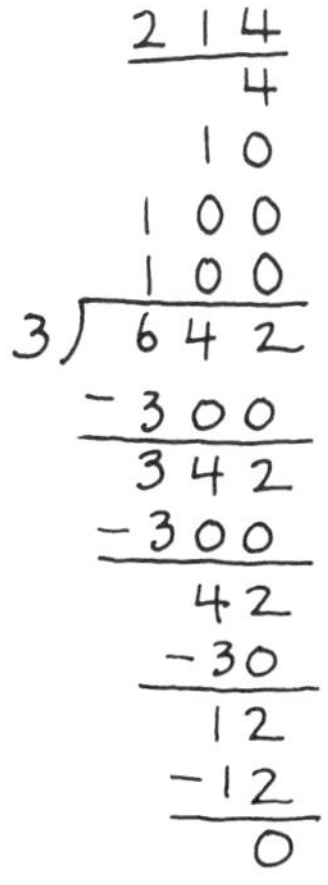

The child described in sample (4), although thinking he "can't" do the exercise, may be able to. Perhaps upon further questioning, the child will reveal that he can do the division, as shown here, but that he has not yet learned the shorter standard algorithm. Or maybe the "I can't" response could really mean "I am not interested in this dumb exercise." An interesting application situation or challenge problem about 642 ÷ 3 might motivate the child to try it.

In summary, the various difficulties indicated by the children's work above can be classified into six general categories:

1. Lack of prerequisites for an algorithm, such as, for the addition of three-digit numbers shown in the example: (a) understanding the meaning of place-value notation; (b) knowledge of basic facts (accurate and quick recall of addition facts), (c) other related skills (addition of three one-digit numbers); (d) skill with simpler forms of the algorithm (addition of two-digit numbers).
2. Lack of techniques of the algorithm, and indirectly lack of understanding why the algorithm is done in a particular way.
3. Inability to apply the algorithm — to recognize which operation to use on which numbers in a given problem situation.
4. Poor number sense — inability to estimate answers and to judge reasonableness of results.

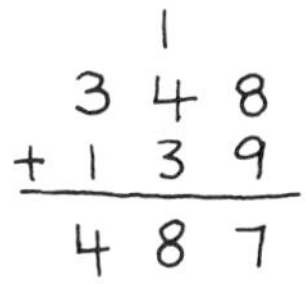

$$
\begin{array}{r}
2\ 1\ 4 \\
4 \\
1\ 0 \\
1\ 0\ 0 \\
1\ 0\ 0 \\
3\overline{)6\ 4\ 2} \\
-3\ 0\ 0 \\
\hline
3\ 4\ 2 \\
-3\ 0\ 0 \\
\hline
4\ 2 \\
-3\ 0 \\
\hline
1\ 2 \\
-1\ 2 \\
\hline
0
\end{array}
$$

$$
\begin{array}{r}
1 \\
3\ 4\ 8 \\
+\ 1\ 3\ 9 \\
\hline
4\ 8\ 7
\end{array}
$$

5. Lack of self-confidence and motivation to accept new challenges and practice new techniques.
6. Carelessness in doing computations or writing numbers.

The Activities in this chapter provide examples of ways to prevent or remedy these types of difficulties. Place a check next to each Activity under the difficulties with which the Activity might help. There may be more than one check for some Activities.

Activity Number	Activity	(1)	(2)	(3)	(4)	(5)	(6)
1	Telling Tales						
2	Many Ways to Do It						
3 – 1	Lattice Multiplication						
5 – 1	Make the Most of It						
5 – 2	Water, Water, Everywhere???						
5 – 3	An Estimation Game for Two						
5 – 4	Two Hundred, A Game for Two Players						
5 – 5	Counting Squares						
5 – 6	Your Favorite Digit						

Does each difficulty have at least one check under it?

How Can We Help Children Learn Algorithms?

Helping children learn algorithms for whole numbers is no easy task. As suggested in the preceding section, children can encounter many difficulties in learning algorithms, especially if their instruction has been primarily rote or at the abstract level. Many of these difficulties can be prevented by appropriate instruction at the concrete, semiconcrete, and abstract levels. The five general suggestions for teaching algorithms that follow may sound familiar, and for good reason. First, Activities 1–5 provided you with some experiences related to these suggestions. Second, some of the suggestions are derived from those discussed in Chapter 5, Basic Facts and Their Uses, since both of these chapters concern operations on whole numbers — but here in situations where the numbers are larger and more difficult to deal with directly through manipulative materials.

Proceed From Concrete to Abstract

In helping children understand the procedures (such as exchange in addition) and related symbolism of an algorithm, proceed from the concrete to the abstract, especially when an algorithm is being introduced to children for the first time. For example, introductory lessons involving chip trading (as in Chapter 7, Place Value) can help children to learn the concept of exchanging. Chip-trading games with notation for addition and other developmental activities can help children relate the symbolism in the algorithm to the action, and vice versa. These experiences help children understand why the addition is performed the way it is.

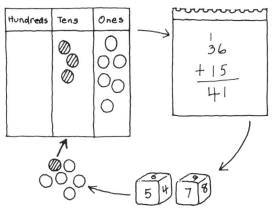

However, often only relatively simple exercises involving algorithms can be done with materials. Algorithms with large numbers are developed naturally and most easily at the abstract level, once understanding and skill have been acquired with simpler exercises. Thus a careful initial development of each algorithm with smaller numbers is critical for later extension of the algorithm to larger numbers. For example, addition of four- and five-digit numbers can be taught at the abstract level (grades 3–4) once children have developed, in a meaningful way, the addition algorithm for two-digit numbers (grades 1–2) and three-digit numbers (grades 2–3).

Use Meaningful Applications

Applications can motivate the learning of a new algorithm. For example, daily attendance could be an introductory activity on addition of two-digit numbers in grades 1 or 2. Also, realistic problem situations can provide children with insight into how the problem can be solved at the concrete level. For example, the following addition situation arising from the children's class store (stocked with empty containers) could be solved with play money — dimes and pennies — illustrating, in a natural way, an action that parallels the method of solving the problem symbolically (such as trade in 10 pennies for a dime).

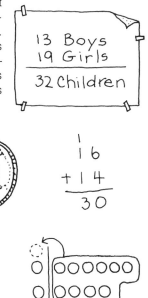

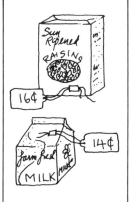

Identify and Evaluate Prerequisites

When teaching an algorithm, identify and evaluate the knowledge and skills that are required. For example, addition of three-digit numbers has several prerequisites. Evaluating children on prerequisites is an important part of planning instruction on algorithms, especially at the upper elementary grades. This can be done by written tests, or by having children act out an exercise or explain in other ways how they did it.

Provide a Variety of Practice Activities

The general principles relating to review and practice of basic facts, outlined in Chapter 5, apply for more advanced computation with whole numbers as well. In particular, practice can be provided by a variety of interesting challenges that involve problem solving and can lead to a further investigation of mathematics. For example, when playing the game Two Hundred from Activity 5, children can practice two- and three-digit addition while at the same time trying to find a winning strategy, and later go on to invent their own variations on the game. Practice can also be self-checking, such as in Your Favorite Digit from Activity 5.

Anticipate the Widespread Use of Hand-held Calculators

Many curriculum changes can be expected from technological innovations such as inexpensive hand-held calculators. Fast, efficient execution of complicated algorithms may no longer be required of most students. Rather, knowing which operation to apply and estimating answers to check for gross errors will be important skills. Controversy exists about the precise role of the calculator in elementary school. Still, a calculator can be a very powerful tool that will open up many fascinating opportunities for problem solving and investigation for children. It can also help children to check their answers quickly and individually so that they get maximum benefit from computational practice. (The Appendix contains some activities with the calculator and provides suggestions about and examples of uses of calculators in elementary school.)

The five suggestions for teaching algorithms also apply to remedial situations. Identifying and evaluating prerequisites is particularly important, where diagnosing a child's difficulties is the first step in effective remedial instruction.[3] The goal of diagnosis should not only be just to identify the type of error the child makes but also to uncover causes for the error. As we discussed, an error pattern may have many possible causes — the real ones can be determined only if the teacher has the child explain how he does the exercises. When diagnosing a child's difficulties, a teacher must let him know that she is genuinely interested in helping him and that she is willing to accept all answers and explanations, even incorrect ones. Also, stress need not be on what the child cannot do but rather on what the child can do in order to build self-confidence. For example, when diagnosing difficulties, begin with exercises the child is likely to get correct and give no more exercises that he cannot do than necessary.

FOLLOW-UP SECTIONS

Action for Algorithms

Children should begin learning arithmetic by manipulating materials and relating symbolic procedures to these actions. This section gives examples of how children could act out algorithms for each operation. As you saw in Chapter 7, Place Value, children can use different place-value materials as models for whole numbers and operations on them. Some materials show the relative value of ones, tens, and hundreds (squared materials, bean sticks, bundles of sticks), while others rely on a more abstract notion of value (abacus, chips for chip trading, and play money). Squared materials and an abacus are used in these examples, but other materials could easily be substituted.

Addition

Children should have informal introductory experiences with multidigit addition such as the exchange games in Chapter 7, Place Value. They should first have experiences without notation and later with some sort of recording before learning how to do algorithms symbolically. These experiences should be followed by activities in which children do addition step by step with materials and record their actions in some appropriate symbolic way. This is illustrated below for the addition 156 + 237. The squares, dashes, and dots represent flats, longs, and units, respectively; and the horizontal lines on the abacus represent small clips to hold the beads up when appropriate. Imagine acting out 156 + 237 with the materials. Do the diagrams convey the action clearly to you?

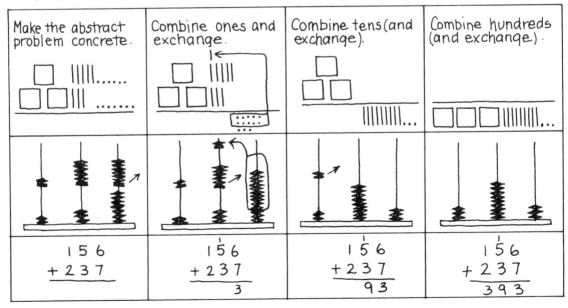

Could you draw a similar sequence of steps for 3,274 + 1,624 with squared material? _____ with an abacus? _____ What about 42,137 + 1,324 with squared material? _____ with an abacus? _____

Subtraction

As with addition, children should have informal experiences with multi-digit subtraction (for example, Activity 7, Exchange and Give-Away Game, Chapter 7) before doing subtraction symbolically.

Imagine acting out 352 − 167 = ☐, and fill in the gaps below in the diagram of the action, again using squared material and an abacus.

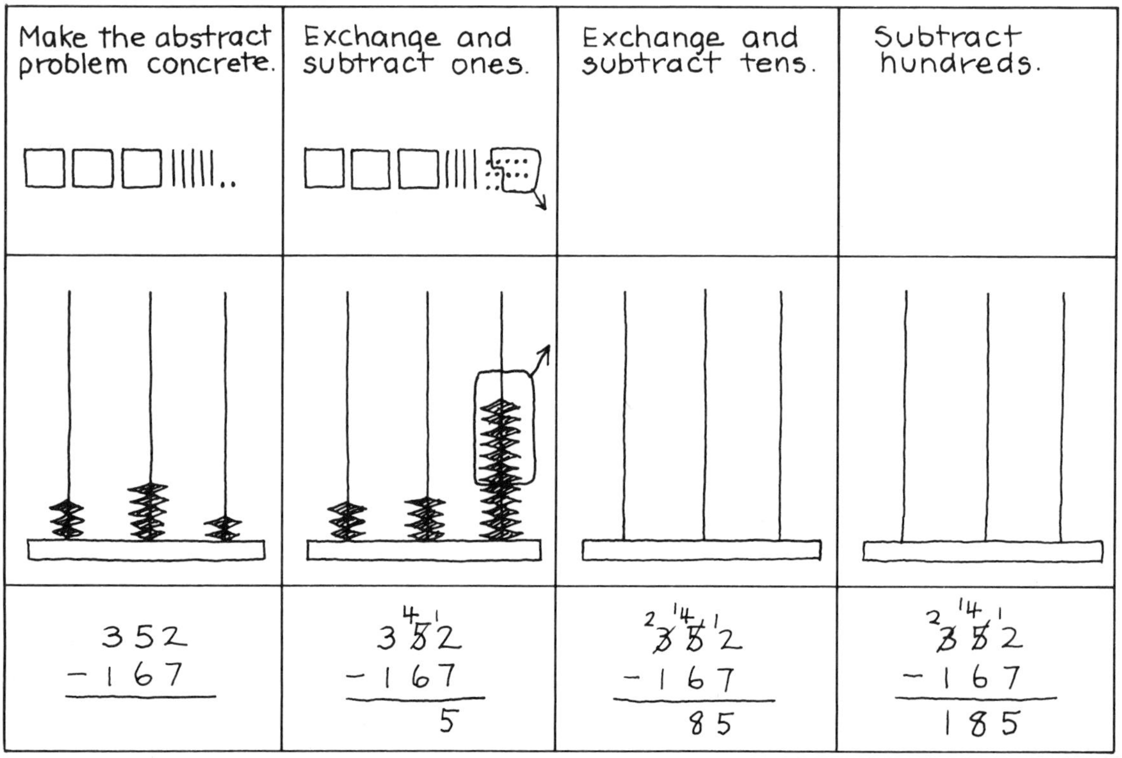

Make the abstract problem concrete.	Exchange and subtract ones.	Exchange and subtract tens.	Subtract hundreds.
☐ ☐ ☐ |||||..	☐ ☐ ☐ |||||⌔		
352 −167	3 ⁴⁄₈ 2 −1 6 7 ⎯⎯ 5	²⁄₃ ¹⁴⁄₈ ¹⁄2 −1 6 7 ⎯⎯ 8 5	²⁄₃ ¹⁴⁄₈ ¹⁄2 −1 6 7 ⎯⎯ 1 8 5

Could you draw a similar sequence of steps for 3,274 − 1,624 with squared material? _____ with an abacus? _____ What about 42,137 − 1,324 with squared material? _____ with an abacus? _____

Which is more difficult to draw, addition or subtraction? Why?

Do children need materials to learn to do exercises such as 42,137 + 1,324 or 42,137 − 1,324? This question is not answered by a simple Yes or No, for the response must take into account the ability and previous learning of the child involved. If a third grader thoroughly understands the algorithm for two- and three-digit numbers and is skillful in using it, then the child may very well be able to generalize the algorithmic procedure for larger numbers at the abstract level. Other children may need to work with materials (for example, an abacus or play money) initially to extend and build up their understanding of the algorithm for exercises involving four- and five-digit numbers.

Since it is somewhat cumbersome and tedious to act out additions and subtractions involving four- and five-digit numbers, it is important to use appropriate materials to teach addition and subtraction of two- and three-digit numbers when the materials can be used easily and efficiently. Such activity, extended over time, will help children gain understanding and skill needed for work with algorithms for larger numbers.

Multiplication and Division — Informal Experiences

Can you imagine informal manipulative activities that might give children experience with multiplication and division of multidigit numbers before they begin symbolic work with algorithms? While such activities are desirable, they are not so easily provided as for addition and subtraction. The two games below, which may remind you of the exchange games in Chapter 7, can provide experiences with relatively simple types of multiplications and divisions — for example, 3×16, 4×125, $64 \div 4$, $166 \div 3$.

Piling It Up

Materials: Squared materials (or another place-value material for ones, tens, hundreds); die marked 1, 2, 2, 3, 3, 4

Directions: This game can be played by 2–4 players. Each player begins with 2 units. Players take turns rolling the die and multiplying the amount they have by the number they roll (1, 2, 3, or 4) as follows:

If you roll a 1, just keep the amount you have;

if you roll a 2, make another group like the one you have, yielding 2 groups of that amount;

if you roll a 3, make 2 more groups like the one you have, yielding 3 groups of that amount (as in the example below);

if you roll a 4, make 3 more groups like the one you have, yielding 4 groups of that amount.

Once you have done this, arranging the groups as illustrated below, combine units, longs, and flats, and exchange as necessary to form a new group which you will multiply on the next round. The first person to get 5 flats is the winner.

Example: Suppose that at some point in the game you have 16: ———...... and that you roll a 3. You would make 2 more piles of 16, giving you 3 groups of 16. Then combine and exchange, yielding 48.

Suppose that on the next round you rolled a 4. You would form _____ more groups of _____, giving you _____ groups of _____. Then combine and exchange, yielding _____.

Variation: After playing this game informally without notation, children can keep a record of their score by filling in the score sheet below.

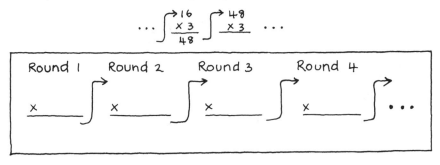

Divide and Conquer

Materials: Squared materials (or another place-value material for ones, tens, and hundreds); die marked 1, 2, 2, 3, 3, 4

Directions: This game can be played by 2–4 players. Each player starts with 5 flats. Players take turns rolling the die and sharing (or dividing) the amount they have into as many groups as the number they roll (1, 2, 3, or 4). Keep only the materials in one of the groups for the next round; discard the other materials (as shown below). The first player to get 2 or fewer units is the winner.

Example: Suppose that at some point you have 166 and you roll a 3. You would exchange the flat and longs as shown below, dividing this amount into 3 groups (5 longs and 5 units) with 1 unit left over.

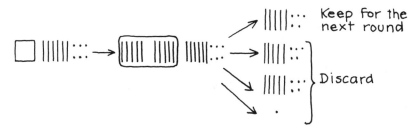

Suppose that on the next round you rolled a 4. You would divide 55 into _____ groups (_____ longs and _____ units) with _____ left over.

Variation: After playing this game informally without notation, children can keep a record of their score by filling in the score sheet below.

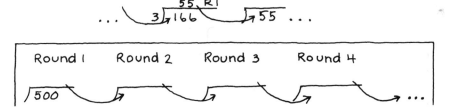

Children who have already learned the concepts of multiplication as repeated addition and division as sharing could play these games (without notation) to lay the groundwork for subsequent study of algorithms. Later, these activities (with notation) can be used to develop the algorithms. These games give informal experience with multiplication and division of one-, two-, and three-digit numbers by 1, 2, 3, and 4, which are relatively easy to act out. Could you modify the games to provide experience with other types of multiplications or divisions? How?

Some multidigit multiplications and divisions cannot be acted out so easily. Imagine acting out the following exercises with squared materials as if you were demonstrating the solutions to children. Circle those exercises that you think *cannot* be easily acted out.

a. $\begin{array}{r} 2\,4 \\ \times\,5 \\ \hline \end{array}$ b. $\begin{array}{r} 2\,4 \\ \times\,1\,2 \\ \hline \end{array}$ c. $\begin{array}{r} 4\,1\,3 \\ \times\,3 \\ \hline \end{array}$ d. $3\,\overline{)\,3\,9}$ e. $13\,\overline{)\,3\,9}$

f. $13\,\overline{)\,4\,1\,3}$ g. $132\,\overline{)\,4\,1\,3}$

You might have thought that (b) could not be acted out easily because the placement of 24 (2 longs and 4 units) in 12 rows would be unwieldy. Both (d) and (e) can be done easily, but by different approaches to division: (d) by sharing 39 in 3 groups and (e) by repeatedly taking away 13 from 39. Perhaps you thought that (f) was not easy to do, since it is tedious to share 413 (4 flats, 1 long, 3 units) in 13 groups or repeatedly subtract 13 from 413. On the other hand, exercise (g), although it looks more difficult than (f), can be done easily by repeated subtraction.

As is the case with addition and subtraction, it is especially important that children gain sufficient experiences at the concrete level with multiplications and divisions that can be acted out easily before proceeding to those that cannot. This concrete experience has many benefits: it can build children's confidence in their ability to do the exercises; it provides a way for children to reconstruct the algorithm if they subsequently forget it; and it can develop a sense for how the numbers can symbolize real-life situations.

In the next two sections we will examine how this basic experience can be provided for multiplication and division.

Developing Multidigit Multiplication

To do the multiplication to the right by the *standard algorithm,* children need many skills. They must be able to identify the products 7×123, 5×123, and 1×123, and know where to place these products. They must also be able to perform these multiplications in their heads and add a column of three digits, possibly with regrouping. The first skill — that is, being able to perform the procedure or algorithm in terms of knowing what to multiply and where to place the product — is usually not difficult for children who have mastered multiplication of two two-digit numbers (as shown to the right). These children can extend their understanding of the algorithm from the simpler case to the more complex. Thus careful development of the standard algorithm for multiplying two-digit numbers (typically in grades 4–5) is especially important. Usually the standard algorithm is preceded by work with algorithms in *ex-*

$$\begin{array}{r} 1\,2\,3 \\ \times\,1\,5\,7 \\ \hline {}^{1}8\,6\,1 \\ {}^{1}6\,1\,5 \\ {}^{1}1\,5\,7 \\ \hline 2\,2\,7\,1\,1 \end{array}$$

$$\begin{array}{r} 2\,7 \\ \times\,1\,2 \\ \hline {}^{1}5\,4 \\ 2\,7 \\ \hline 3\,2\,4 \end{array}$$

panded form in grades 3–4; for example, the three multiplications shown below involve the calculation of partial products.

a.
```
    2 7
  × 1 2
    5 4    2 × 27
  2 7 0   10 × 27
  3 2 4
```

b.
```
    2 7
  × 1 2
    1 4    2 × 7
    4 0    2 × 20
    7 0   10 × 7
  2 0 0   10 × 20
  3 2 4
```

c.
$$12 \times 27 = 12 \times (20 + 7)$$
$$= (12 \times 20) + (12 \times 7)$$
$$= (10 \times 20) + (2 \times 20)$$
$$+ (10 \times 7) + (2 \times 7)$$
$$= 200 + 40 + 70 + 14$$
$$= 324$$

These algorithms in turn depend on the ability to multiply a two-digit number by a one-digit number or by a multiple of 10, 20, 30, etc. Which of the three alternative algorithms above most closely resembles the standard algorithm? _____ Which seems easiest to explain? _____ Why?

Two reasons for teaching one of the algorithms in expanded form above before the shorter standard algorithm are (1) children find the algorithms in expanded form easier to understand than the standard algorithm; and (2) children who understand and have mastered one of the algorithms in expanded form will find it easier to learn the standard algorithm. While these reasons are sound, the question still remains: How do we teach an algorithm using partial products to children? Several approaches will be described.

An Abstract, Formal Approach

Teachers (and some textbooks) may use a purely symbolic and often rote approach to present multidigit multiplication. For example, a teacher might do a few multiplications involving two two-digit numbers on the chalkboard, and then have students complete similar multiplications as shown below.

Study the examples. Then do exercises 1–6.

Examples
```
      1 3              1 2
    × 1 2            × 1 4
      2 6   2 × 13     4 8   4 × 12
    1 3 0  10 × 13   1 2 0  10 × 12
    1 5 6            1 6 8
```

1.
```
    1 4
  × 1 2
  _____    2 × 14
  _____   10 × 14
```

2.
```
    1 5
  × 1 2
  _____    2 × _____
  _____   10 × _____
```

3.
```
    1 4
  × 1 3
```

4.
```
    1 4
  × 1 5
```

5. $15 \times 16 =$ _____

6. $17 \times 19 =$ _____

If the question "Why do we multiply 10 × 13 in the second step of example 1?" arises, the teacher may note that "12 × 13 is really the same as (10 + 2)

× 13, therefore we multiply 10 times 13, and 2 times 13." While this explanation involving the distributive property of multiplication over addition is mathematically correct, it may be too abstract for many youngsters. As a result, these children may not really understand why the multiplication is being performed the way it is, although they may master the procedure by rote and acquire skill in multiplication. Without understanding, children may forget the algorithm and may have difficulty extending the algorithm to larger numbers.

Several concrete and semiconcrete approaches show why an algorithm is done a certain way. Children should use these methods as long as they need to in order to understand them fully.

A Concrete Approach

Place-value models (squared material, bean sticks, chips) can easily be used to act out 2 × 13 in a way that allows us to relate the written algorithm using partial products to the action.

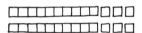

or

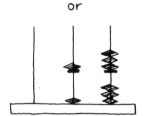

2 × 13 = ☐   Think: 2 × 13 means 2 groups of 13.

```
1 3          Act out: Make 2 groups of 13, (10 + 3).
× 2          Find the total: 2 groups of 3 is 6.
───                           2 groups of 10 is 20.
  6   2 × 3                   The total is 6 + 20 = 26.
2 0   2 × 10
───
2 6
```

The concrete approach with squared materials can be extended to 12 × 13, or 12 groups of 13. The pieces can be laid out, as shown to the right. There are two ways to count the total in this arrangement, corresponding to two different algorithms using partial products. In each arrangement below, draw a loop and label the squared material that corresponds to each partial product (as has been started).

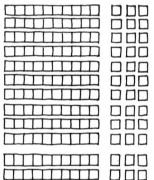

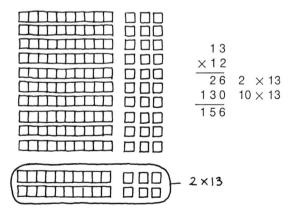

```
  1 3
× 1 2
─────
  2 6   2 × 13
1 3 0   10 × 13
─────
1 5 6
```

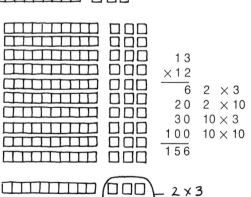

```
  1 3
× 1 2
─────
    6   2 × 3
  2 0   2 × 10
  3 0   10 × 3
1 0 0   10 × 10
─────
1 5 6
```

Complete this diagram to show the action for 25 × 13. Are there any difficulties in making such a drawing?

Can an abacus be used to act out 12 × 13? Why or why not?

There are two obvious drawbacks to doing multiplication using squared materials. First, it is really only convenient for products with factors in the teens; for example, 13 × 14 or 18 × 12. Multiplications such as 25 × 19 or 36 × 68 are unmanageable with materials. Second, the placement of materials can be very time consuming. The next approach, a semiconcrete one, partly avoids these drawbacks.

A Semiconcrete Approach

Doing multiplication exercises such as 2 × 13 or 12 × 13 with squared materials (or similar place-value models) helps children build mental imagery for doing similar exercises at the semiconcrete level on graph paper. Children can use different colors to show the partial products. The multiplication below has been started. Follow the directions to complete the diagram for 12 × 14.

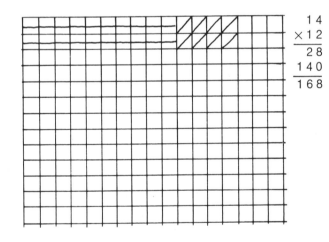

```
    1 4
  × 1 2
  -----
    2 8
  1 4 0
  -----
  1 6 8
```

Think: 12 × 14 means 12 groups of 14.
Act out: Draw one row of 14 ⎫
         Draw a second row of 14 ⎭ (as shown).

Draw the tenth row of 14, and draw a line across the diagram (or change colors, if you are using two different colored pencils) to indicate that you have done 10 groups of 14.
Continue drawing an eleventh row, and a twelfth row.
Find the total: Above the line we have 10 rows of 14, or 100 + 40; below the line we have 2 rows of 14, or 20 + 8, or 28. The total is 140 + 28, or 168.

Do you see any drawbacks to this semiconcrete procedure?

You may have found the drawing in this method time consuming. Some text materials use a ready-made diagram as shown on page 419. This is more abstract since children are not so actively involved with counting, and the method depends on children's understanding of area as a model for multiplication. (You may recognize this approach from Counting Squares in Activity 5 in which you were challenged to count the squares in a 14 by 23 rectangle without using the multiplication algorithm. You may have come up with a diagram like the one below.)

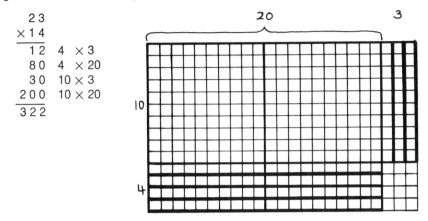

```
  2 3
× 1 4
─────
  1 2    4 × 3
  8 0    4 × 20
  3 0   10 × 3
2 0 0   10 × 20
─────
3 2 2
```

Using this graph paper, outline a rectangle corresponding to the example below, subdivide it into appropriate parts, and then complete the multiplication.

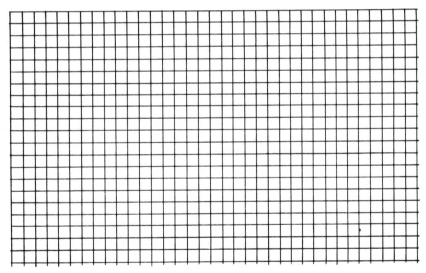

```
  3 2
× 1 6
─────
  1 2   6 × 2
```

Perhaps the best way to help children develop an algorithm using partial products for two-digit numbers is to combine the methods. For example, after children have done multiplication of two-digit numbers by one-digit numbers with materials and related symbolism, they could do a few multiplications of two-digit numbers by two-digit numbers with materials and then a few more by drawing a grid diagram or outlining an appropriate rectangle on graph paper (again with related symbolism). Then they might practice the algorithm at the abstract level, perhaps using approaches described in the next section. Of course, they should periodically review the procedures at the concrete and semiconcrete levels.

Building and Using Tables

The computation of partial products in two-digit multiplications (for example, 4 × 34 and 20 × 34 in this multiplication) sometimes creates difficulties for children. This is especially true for those who are just learning the

```
   34
 × 24
 ────
  136   4 × 34
  680  20 × 34
 ────
  816
```

algorithm, those who have not mastered all of the basic facts of multiplication, or those who have difficulty regrouping in their heads (for example, in 4 × 34). The following approach[4] avoids this difficulty and allows children to focus on the process of the algorithm, having done most of the computation earlier. Complete the activity below.

1. Find these products	34 × 1	34 × 2	34 × 3 ───── 102	34 × 4	34 × 5
	34 × 10	34 × 20 ───── 680	34 × 30	34 × 40	34 × 50
2. Use the results of part 1 to solve each of these. Use these as is done in the example.		34 × 23 ───── 102 680 ───── 782	34 × 13	34 × 42	34 × 35

Note: The table in part 1 might include the products 1 × 34, 2 × 34, . . . , 9 × 34 and 10 × 34, . . . , 90 × 34. Here the table is abbreviated for convenience.

Make up two more exercises that could also be solved by referring to the results of part 1 above. _____ _____
Could this activity be modified easily for doing multiplication of three-digit numbers by two-digit numbers (for example, 23 × 342)? _____ How?

How is the structure of arithmetic used in completing part 1 — that is, what properties can be used to simplify the work?

How is the structure of arithmetic used in completing part 2 on the basis of the results from part 1 — that is, what property is used?

The eventual goal of this type of activity is to have children do a multiplication such as 45 × 34 without reference to part 1 — that is, by computing only the partial products needed to obtain the answer (5 × 34 and 40 × 34).

Some children are confused by the mass of numbers and the exchanging in the approach (a) below for 45 × 34. Using approach (b), these children could do the multiplication for the partial products separately and then find their total. While this requires more writing, the method may help some children to obtain the correct answer easily and consistently.

```
a.  1                        b.
    2
    34                           34        2          1
   ×45                          ×45        34        34
   '170    5 × 34              '170       × 5       ×40
   1360   40 × 34              1360        170      1360
   1,530                       1,530
```

Developing Multidigit Division

Children often find it difficult to understand and become skillful with the standard algorithm for long division. One cause for this difficulty is that the algorithm has several prerequisites which children may not have mastered: skill in multiplication and subtraction algorithms, which of course involves skill in basic facts of multiplication and subtraction, and ability to estimate products. A second cause is the somewhat mystical nature of the division procedure. Why do we begin the division (to the right) by asking how many 14's are there in 35? Why write the 2 over the 5 and not over the 3? Can you explain why?

```
      25
14 / 352
   − 28
      72
   − 70
       2
```

The standard long division algorithm is usually developed in elementary school much like the standard multiplication algorithm — that is, algorithms using expanded form showing partial quotients are presented, leading up to the standard algorithm.

Standard Algorithm   Scaffolding or "Along-the-Side" Algorithm   Stacking Algorithm

```
        34              14 / 476                        34
14 / 476               − 280   20                        4
   − 42                  196                             10
     56                − 140   10                        20
   − 56                   56                         14 / 476
      0                − 56    4                        − 280
                         0     34                         196
                                                       − 140
                                                          56
                                                       − 56
                                                          0
```

Which forms of the division algorithm did you learn in elementary school? _____ Which of the algorithms using expanded form, scaffolding or stacking, more closely resembles the standard algorithm? _____ Which seems easier to explain? _____

The "why" of the division process is more clearly shown by the algorithms using partial quotients. But again, the problem remains: How can we teach these algorithms? In the approach described below, children learn an easier algorithm using partial quotients at the concrete level and then extend the procedure to more complex divisions that are most readily done at the abstract level. After children have mastered an algorithm using partial quotients (usually in grades 4–5), they can proceed to the standard algorithm for division.

The two algorithms using partial quotients — scaffolding and stacking — can be developed with children at the concrete level. These algorithms using partial quotients should be acted out in such a way that the action corresponds exactly to what is written when the algorithm is done at the abstract level.

Children in grades 3–4 may have used chips or beans to act out simple divisions (two-digit numbers divided by one-digit numbers) in different ways and recorded their solutions as shown below. Fill in the blanks and also complete the diagram to show the action that corresponds to the symbolic solution.

Example: 3 $\overline{)\,28}$

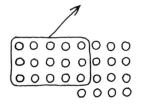

Symbols

$$
\begin{array}{r}
3\,\overline{)\,28} \\
-15 \quad 5 \\
\hline
13 \\
-12 \quad 4 \\
\hline
1 \quad 9 \ R \ 1
\end{array}
$$

Action

1. Lay out 28 chips.
2. Take away 5 groups of 3, or 15.
3. Take away _____ groups of _____, or _____.
4. Find the answer: _____ groups of _____ and _____ left over.

Or children might have solved this by a sharing approach to division:

1. Lay out 28 chips.
2. Place 5 in each of 3 piles.
3. Place 4 in each of 3 piles.
4. Find the answer: _____ in each of _____ piles and _____ left over.

Of course, once children know their multiplication facts, they might do this kind of division more directly:

$$
\begin{array}{r}
9 \\
3\,\overline{)\,28} \\
-27 \\
\hline
1
\end{array}
$$

These experiences relating symbolic procedures to actions for simple divisions provide a basis for division with larger numbers (such as $3\overline{\smash{)}46}$, $3\overline{\smash{)}465}$, $124\overline{\smash{)}427}$) where place value can be used in the division process, as shown below.

Example: $3\overline{\smash{)}46}$

     Symbols

$$
\begin{array}{r}
1\,5 \text{ R } 1 \\
\hline
5 \\
1\,0 \\
3\,\overline{\smash{)}4\,6} \\
-\,3\,0 \\
\hline
1\,6 \\
-\,1\,5 \\
\hline
1
\end{array}
$$

                    Action

1. Take 4 longs and 6 units.
2. Place 1 long in each of 3 groups, leaving 1 long and 6 units.
3. Exchange the 1 remaining long for 10 units.
4. Place 5 units in each of 3 groups, leaving 1 unit.

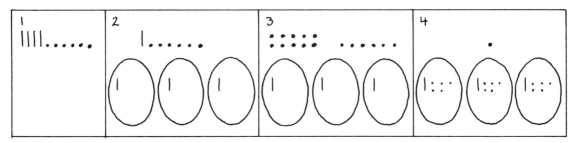

The division $3\overline{\smash{)}46}$ could also have been done using 46 chips. Which approach would be easier: using chips or using squared materials? _____
Why?

    Describe the action for solving $3\overline{\smash{)}465}$ with squared materials.

Example: $3\overline{\smash{)}465}$

     Symbols

$$
\begin{array}{r}
1\,5\,5 \\
\hline
5 \\
5\,0 \\
1\,0\,0 \\
3\,\overline{\smash{)}4\,6\,5} \\
-\,3\,0\,0 \\
\hline
1\,6\,5 \\
-\,1\,5\,0 \\
\hline
1\,5 \\
-\,1\,5 \\
\hline
0
\end{array}
$$

1. Take _____ flats, _____ longs, and _____ units.

2. Place

3.

4.

5.

The division $3\overline{)465}$ is relatively easy to do with squared materials if you interpret the division as sharing. Is it easy if you interpret the division as repeated subtraction? _____ Why or why not?

Some divisions such as $124\overline{)427}$ are very difficult to do by sharing but easy by repeated subtraction.

Example: $124\overline{)427}$

Symbols

```
124 / 427 |
    -124 | 1
   ─────
     303 |
    -124 | 1
   ─────
     179 |
    -124 | 1
   ─────
      55 | 3 R 55
```

Action

1. Lay out 4 flats, 2 longs, 7 units.
2. Take away 1 × 124, or 1 flat, 2 longs, 4 units.
3. Take away 1 × 124, or 1 flat, 2 longs, 4 units.
4. Take away 1 × 124, or 1 flat, 2 longs, 4 units.
5. Total: 3 × 124 was taken away, and 55 was left over.

The division $23\overline{)485}$ is not easy to act out using either approach to division. However, once children understand the algorithm for simpler divisions, they might be able to *imagine* the action in solving this as follows: (Fill in the blanks.)

Example: $23\overline{)485}$

Symbols

```
23 / 485 |
  -230 | 10
  ─────
    255 |
  -230 | 10
  ─────
     25 | 1
    -23 |
  ─────
      2 | 21 R 2
```

Imagined Action

1. Lay out 4 8 5.
2. Take away _____ groups of _____, or _____.
3. Take away _____ groups of _____, or _____.
4. Take away _____ groups of _____
5. Find the answer: _____ groups of _____ were taken away and _____ were left over.

The methods described can be used to help children develop an algorithm using partial quotients. They can also be used with children who have learned an incorrect algorithm or have partly learned one. These children can first do a division with materials and compare this answer to the one they obtained by paper and pencil. Then a teacher can help them redo the division, step by step, using materials and recording the action with appropriate symbolism.

Refer to error pattern (3) on page 406. What material would you give to a child making this error to act out the division? Once the child saw that some of his answers were incorrect, how would you demonstrate the step-by-step solution to those divisions, relating symbolism to action?

Once children understand why an algorithm using partial quotients is done in a particular way, they can begin to acquire skill with it. However, some children may have difficulty writing out a complete solution. Doing partially completed divisions can help these students. Which type of exercise below would you give such children first? _____ second? _____ third? _____ finally? _____

a.
```
 5 / 6 5 |
 - 5 0 |  ?
 ─────
   1 5
 - 1 5 |  ?
 ─────
     0 |  ?
```

b.
```
 3 / 7 2 |
 - 3 0 |  ?
 ─────
   4 2
     ? |  ?
 ─────
   1 2
     ? |  ?
 ─────
     0 |  ?
```

c.
```
 3 / 7 8 |
 - 3 0 | 10
 ─────
   4 8
 - 3 0 |  ?
 ─────
   1 8
 - 1 8 |  6
 ─────
     0 |  ?
```

d.
```
 4 / 7 6 |
```

The approach shown on pages 420–421 for multidigit multiplication can also be applied to division. Complete the divisions below using partial quotients by referring to the multiplications given at the top of the activity. (The multiplications at the top are abbreviated here for convenience; they should include the following multiples of 13: 1×13, 2×13, ..., 9×13 and 10×13, 20×13, ..., 90×13.)

13	13	13	13	13	13	13	13
$\times 1$	$\times 2$	$\times 3$	$\times 4$	$\times 10$	$\times 20$	$\times 30$	$\times 40$
13	26	39	52	130	260	390	520

```
13 / 1 5 6 |
  - 1 3 0 | 10
  ───────
```

```
13 / 4 4 9 |
```

This approach reduces the complexity of the division in two ways. First, it separates the needed multiplication from the process of division. Second, it enables children to focus directly on the selection of partial quotients without estimation. This second feature is especially helpful for many children who have difficulty estimating multiples of the divisor. The eventual goal of this activity is to have children do divisions such as $13 \overline{/ 156}$ without finding all the products — that is, by finding only the partial quotients needed for the division.

Why Teach the Standard Long Division Algorithm?

Children could solve all divisions involving whole numbers by either of the algorithms that show partial quotients. Why then should they be asked to master the standard long division algorithm? One obvious reason is that the standard algorithm requires less time to use, in particular for complex divisions such as $64{,}762 \div 135$. A second reason is that division of decimals is done conventionally by the standard algorithm.

1. $4.24 \div .8$

Standard

```
       5 3
  .8 / 4.2 4
       4 0
      ———
       2 4
       2 4
      ———
         0
```

Partial Quotients

```
  .8 / 4.2 4 |
       4 0 0 | 5
      ——————
         .2 4 |
         .2 4 | .3
        ———————
           0 | 5.3
```

2. Convert 3/8 to a decimal

Standard

```
      .3 7 5
  8 / 3.0 0 0
      2 4
     ———
       6 0
       5 6
      ———
         4 0
         4 0
        ———
           0
```

Partial Quotients

```
  8 / 3.0 0 0 |
      2.4      | .3
     ———
      .6 0 0 |
      .5 6   | .07
     ———
      .0 4 0 |
      .0 4 0 |
     ———     ———
```

Complete problem (2) by the algorithm using partial quotients. Can you foresee any difficulties in using such an algorithm for problems of this type? (**Hint:** Try to convert 3/7 or 1/3 to decimals.)

A third reason for teaching the standard division algorithm is, in some sense, tradition. Prior to the development of "new math" curricula which stressed understanding of algorithms, most children learned only the standard algorithm. Do you remember how you learned to do divisions such as $13\overline{/725}$?

On the other hand, arguments can be given for not teaching the standard algorithm but rather only an algorithm using partial quotients to most children. First, teaching the standard algorithm takes a lot of time, and even then many children (including some who are good at an algorithm using partial quotients) will find the standard algorithm difficult. The standard algorithm requires that children make the best estimate of partial quotients on the first try, and if they guess wrong, they may be frustrated by having to erase. However, when working with one of the two algorithms using expanded form, it does not matter if partial quotients are less than they could be — children can just keep going. Also children are often taught the standard algorithms by rote and are unable to give any reasons (other than "teacher said to") for doing the algorithm in a certain way, and as a result may forget it quickly. Or to remember it, they must practice it over and over, usually leading them to dislike division because the drill was dull and excessive.

Today the calculator enables children to work out even complex long division of whole numbers and decimals quickly and effortlessly. In the past, before calculators became so inexpensively available, there was reason to emphasize the standard algorithms for both multiplication and division as there were no alternatives to paper-and-pencil computation. In the years ahead, the elementary school curriculum may place less emphasis on the standard algorithms and greater emphasis on algorithms using partial products or partial quotients that help children understand the processes and still enable them to gain sufficient skills to do multiplication and division with paper and pencil. This change should be accompanied by instruction at the concrete and semiconcrete levels (to help children build an understanding of the algorithms using expanded form), and by more practice with these algorithms over a longer period of time. Also, it is likely that more attention will be given to problem solving involving the use of algorithms, both by way of paper and pencil and by way of calculators.

Teaching the Standard Algorithm

While there is controversy about the standard long division algorithm, it is still being taught to most children in upper elementary grades. A teacher will of course find that the mathematics text series provides an outline for teaching the algorithm. Some suggestions follow for making the algorithm easier and more meaningful for children.

1. Children who are familiar with some algorithm using partial quotients can build on this knowledge. They might do exercises in different formats at the same time — for example, any two neighboring ones below — to identify common features. Formats could be selected from the sequence below, depending on what is familiar to the children.

2. Some children have difficulty with the multiplication in long division simply because multiplications are presented in an unfamiliar or distracting form; that is, $27\overline{)6308}$ rather than $\times 2$ (with 2 above, 27 below). These children may find it helpful to write out the multiplication on the side — perhaps after having built and used tables (see the format on page 425).
3. Another common difficulty that children have with the standard long division algorithm is in estimating the best multiple of the divisor. This difficulty can be avoided by having children build and use a table of multiples (1 through 9) of the divisor.

4. Children may have difficulty with divisions that involve 0's in the quotient and may make an error as in example (a) below (also see error pattern (3) on page 406). This error may be prevented by having children use an algorithm using partial quotients (see example (b)). Do you see why?

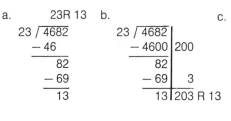

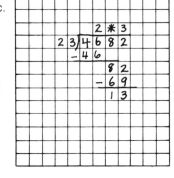

a.
```
      23R 13
23 / 4682
   - 46
   ____
      82
   - 69
   ____
      13
```

b.
```
23 / 4682 |
   - 4600 | 200
   ____
      82 |
   - 69 |   3
   ____
      13 | 203 R 13
```

c.

When doing such divisions with the standard algorithm, it may help children to work on squared paper, so that they are made aware of the gap marked ✱ as in example (c) above.

5. Another way to help children avoid the error described in (4) above is to stress estimation throughout the study of algorithms. If children are encouraged to round off the numbers — for example, to round $23 \overline{)4682}$ to either $23 \overline{)4600}$ or $20 \overline{)5000}$, they will see that the answer must be in the range of 200 or 250, and that the answer 23 is clearly wrong.

6. Finally, all instruction on division — from the first introduction — should involve the meaning of division (either as sharing or as repeated subtraction) and should be related to multiplication. Children should be encouraged to verbalize the corresponding multiplication for any division — for example, "26 ÷ 13 = 2 because two thirteens are twenty-six," or "3 $\overset{19\,R\,1}{\overline{)58}}$ means that there are nineteen threes in fifty-eight with one left over." This leads naturally to the standard method for checking — that is, to check the division 23 $\overset{219\,R\,10}{\overline{)5047}}$ we can check that (23 × 219) + 10 equals 5047. Even if children do not perform this calculation for each division, they can estimate the product and see if their answer is approximately correct.

Algorithms in a Scope and Sequence

This section discusses the scope of the topics related to operations on whole numbers, the grade placement of these topics, and the sequence in which they can occur in the curriculum. The use of the scope and sequence for planning instruction (in regular and in remedial situations) is also considered.

Addition

The eight addition exercises below are usually learned by children during grades 1–4. Which of them do you think is learned first? second? Fill in the letter of the exercise.

First	Second	Third	Fourth	Fifth	Sixth	Seventh	Eighth

a. $\begin{array}{r} 6 \\ +8 \\ \hline \end{array}$ b. $\begin{array}{r} 20 \\ +30 \\ \hline \end{array}$ c. $\begin{array}{r} 23 \\ +36 \\ \hline \end{array}$ d. $\begin{array}{r} 376 \\ +108 \\ \hline \end{array}$ e. $\begin{array}{r} 1 \\ 9 \\ +3 \\ \hline \end{array}$ f. $\begin{array}{r} 36 \\ +48 \\ \hline \end{array}$ g. $\begin{array}{r} 200 \\ +500 \\ \hline \end{array}$ h. $\begin{array}{r} 1984 \\ +1492 \\ \hline \end{array}$

Check whether your sequence for the eight exercises matches that indicated by the scope and sequence chart for addition given below. If your sequence does not agree, can you defend your sequence?

Sample Scope and Sequence: Addition

Topic	Approximate Grade Level
A1 Basic facts	
A2 Multiples of 10	Grade 1
A3 Three or more one-digit numbers	
A4 A two-digit and a one-digit number	
A5 Two two-digit numbers (without exchanging, and then with exchanging)	
A6 Several one- and two-digit numbers	Grade 2
A7 Multiples of 100	
A8 Two three digit numbers (without exchanging, and then with exchanging of ones, tens, and ones and tens)	
	Grade 3
A9 Several one-, two-, and three-digit numbers	
A10 Multiples of 1000	
A11 Four-digit numbers	Grade 4
A12 Five- and six-digit numbers	

Commercial textbook series and local or state curriculum guides tend to vary somewhat, although not radically, in scope and grade level placement of these topics as well as in their sequence. If possible, you might compare this sample scope and sequence for addition (or the ones for multiplication and division that follow) with those for a textbook or curriculum guide. In particular, note any significant differences in scope and sequence of topics.

For most teachers, the scope and sequence are determined by the material in the children's textbook or by the school's curriculum guide for that grade. As has been discussed in Chapter 5, the ability and achievement of the children should guide classroom instruction rather than just the scope and sequence. Situations arise in which the teacher may vary from the scope and sequence of topics for a grade level. For example, introductory activities (such as chip trading) on two- and three-digit addition can be done with first graders who are ready for informal instruction on that topic. Another example arises when children use an individualized instruction program, progressing through it at their own rate. Often some children will be working on material one or two grades levels ahead of other children in their class.

While the sample scope and sequence for addition provides a general overview of addition topics, it may not have sufficient detail to help you plan individual lessons or to guide your diagnosis of specific difficulties a child has with a topic such as two-digit addition. Some scope and sequence charts contain detailed listings of general topics and numerous subtopics. For example, addition of two-digit numbers might be divided into these subtopics.

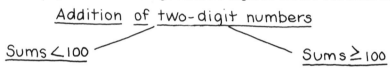

Addition of two-digit numbers

Sums < 100

No exchange
$$\begin{array}{r} 24 \\ +13 \\ \hline \end{array}$$

Exchange ones
$$\begin{array}{r} 24 \\ +18 \\ \hline \end{array}$$

Sums ≥ 100

Exchange tens only
$$\begin{array}{r} 84 \\ +51 \\ \hline \end{array}$$

Exchange ones and tens
$$\begin{array}{r} 84 \\ +57 \\ \hline \end{array}$$

While detailed listings of topics and subtopics (and even sub-subtopics) can be a bit overwhelming and may seem to suggest that every topic should be taught subtopic by subtopic, they can be useful. Teachers should examine such listings critically, with an eye towards using this information to anticipate difficult types of exercises (for example, sums ≥ 100 above), to aid in making up exercises to diagnose a child's difficulties, and to structure remedial instruction in small steps rather than in a large task which can be overwhelming to a child.

$$\begin{array}{r} 18 \\ + \ 6 \\ \hline \end{array} \quad \begin{array}{r} 9 \\ 9 \\ +6 \\ \hline \end{array}$$

One important subskill in doing exercises such as those to the left is "higher-decade addition." Try the exercises. Can you figure out what is meant by "higher-decade addition"? Approaches for helping children gain skill with these exercises (which all involve addition of numbers less than 10 to a number greater than 10, for example, 6 + 18) include using a structured sequence of exercises that show a pattern (as illustrated here) or giving explanations such as the following for 38 + 6 : 8 + 6 is 14 which is more than 10 so the total will be in the 40's (that is, the next or higher decade after the 30's) and the answer will be 44. Try this with 34 + 8. _____

$$\begin{array}{r} 27 \\ \times \ 9 \\ \hline \end{array}$$

$$\begin{array}{r} 28 \\ + \ 6 \\ \hline \end{array} \quad \begin{array}{r} 38 \\ + \ 6 \\ \hline \end{array}$$

$$\begin{array}{r} 8 \\ +6 \\ \hline \end{array} \quad \begin{array}{r} 18 \\ + \ 6 \\ \hline \end{array}$$

Refer to the scope and sequence chart for addition and determine at what grade levels higher decade addition is taught. _____ Although higher decade addition is taught in the lower elementary grades, upper elementary grade teachers may want to give their students review-practice activities on this topic because in later computation it must be done mentally, and not just with paper and pencil.

Subtraction

Usually the scope and sequence of topics for subtraction closely parallel those for addition. Also subtraction topics are often presented after the corresponding addition topics — for example, subtraction of two-digit numbers (without and then with exchanging) would follow addition of two-digit numbers. Checking subtractions provides practice of the corresponding addition topic. Write two different types of subtractions related to addition topic A4 (a two-digit and a one-digit number).

A common error in subtraction that may be due to a certain sequencing of subtraction topics is illustrated here. Complete the last subtraction according to the error pattern.

$$\begin{array}{r} 39 \\ -15 \\ \hline 24 \end{array} \qquad \begin{array}{r} 34 \\ -19 \\ \hline 25 \end{array} \qquad \begin{array}{r} 349 \\ -123 \\ \hline 226 \end{array} \qquad \begin{array}{r} 349 \\ -182 \\ \hline 247 \end{array} \qquad \begin{array}{r} 349 \\ -161 \\ \hline \end{array}$$

Children may make this error because usually subtraction without exchanging is taught and practiced before subtraction with exchanging. Children may think of the method for subtraction without exchanging as "taking the smaller number from the larger." They may then apply this method incorrectly to subtractions that require exchanging, especially if instruction was only at the abstract level. This may suggest that the initial development of subtraction of two-digit numbers treats subtractions without and with exchanging at the same time. (Of course children should use materials in this development, with appropriate recording of the action of subtraction.) Another reason to do this is that situations that motivate subtraction of two-digit numbers naturally involve both types. If children are asked to make up and solve subtraction problems which interest them, no doubt both types will arise.

Multiplication

Examine the topics in the scope and sequence chart for multiplication and match the multiplication exercises (a)–(i) on page 432 with an appropriate topic.

Sample Scope and Sequence: Multiplication		
Topic		Approximate Grade Level
M1 Concept of multiplication and basic facts	a	
M2 One-digit × multiple of 10	___	Grades 2-3
M3 One-digit × two-digit	___	
M4 One-digit × multiple of 100	___	
M5 One-digit × three-digit	___	Grades 3-4
M6 Multiple of 10 × multiple of 10	___	
M7 Two-digit × two-digit	___	
M8 Two-digit × three- and four-digit	___	Grades 4-6
M9 Other multidigit multiplication	___	

a.   3   b.   40   c.   30   d. 215   e. 200   f.   42   g. 1234   h.   13   i.   1234
     × 2   × 2   × 20   × 6   × 7   × 23   × 56   × 4   × 1234

```
  3463
  × 45
 ─────
 17315
 13852
 ─────
 31167
```

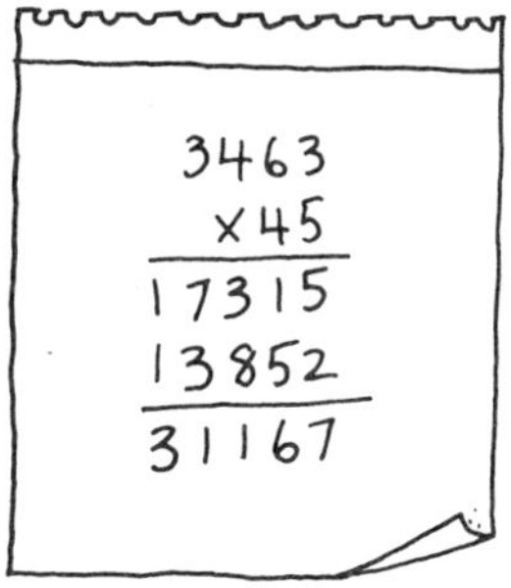

Is the sequence described below appropriate for helping a sixth grader who is having difficulty with the multiplication?

M 2 → M 4 → (one-digit × multiple of 1000) → M 3 →
M 5 → (one-digit × four-digit) → M 6 → M 7 → M 8

Why might this sequence help such a child gain self-confidence better than the sequence M 2 → M 3 → M 4 → . . . → M 8 indicated by the scope and sequence above?

Division

Just as the scope and sequence for subtraction parallels that for addition (the inverse operation), the scope and sequence for division parallels that for multiplication. However, division topics are usually developed somewhat later than the corresponding multiplication topics.

Sample Scope and Sequence: Division

Topic	Approximate Grade Level
D1 Concept of division and basic facts	Grades 3-4
Algorithm Using Partial Quotients	
D2 Division of a two-digit number by a one-digit number (no remainder)	
D3 Division of a two-digit number by a one-digit number (with remainder)	Grades 3-4
D4 Division of a three-digit number by a one-digit number	
D5 Division of two- and three-digit numbers by a two-digit number	Grades 4-5
Standard Algorithm	
D6 Standard division algorithm for D2-D5	
D7 Short division for D2-D4	Grades 4-6
D8 Other multidigit division	

---

1. Refer to the scope and sequence for division above and write a sample division exercise for each of these topics: D2, D3, D6, and D7.

D2   D3   D6   D7

2. Topics for division of whole numbers are often prerequisites for other topics. What division topic, D1–D8, relates to each of the following:

  a. Changing 47/3 to a mixed numeral.
  b. Finding the average (in kg) of the weights of 27 students in a fifth-grade class.
  c. Reducing 7/154 to lowest terms.
  d. Factoring 780 into the product of prime numbers.

3. The division $32 \div 2$ has been done in four different ways below. According to the scope and sequence chart, at what levels would each division most likely have been taught?

a. 32 buttons in 2 piles

Grade _____

b.
$$\frac{16}{6}$$
$$\begin{array}{r} 10 \\ 2 \overline{\smash)32} \\ -20 \\ \hline 12 \\ -12 \\ \hline 0 \end{array}$$

Grade _____

c.
$$\begin{array}{r} 16 \\ 2 \overline{\smash)32} \\ -2 \\ \hline 12 \\ -12 \\ \hline 0 \end{array}$$

Grade _____

d.
$$\begin{array}{r} 16 \\ 2 \overline{\smash)32} \end{array}$$

Grade _____

You probably said that (c), the standard algorithm solution for $32 \div 2$, was done in grades 4 or 5. Different textbook series may introduce the standard algorithm at different grades. One series might introduce it in grade 5 after an algorithm using partial quotients has been used for a couple of years. Another series might introduce it much earlier, shortly after an algorithm using partial quotients has been developed for division of two-digit numbers by one-digit numbers. These differences can cause difficulties for a teacher and students when different text series are used in grades 3–5 or when students change schools.

Because division is usually viewed as an upper grade topic, lower grade teachers may feel somewhat hesitant about teaching division. However introductory activities like the game Divide and Conquer and those below can and should be done when appropriate in grades 2–3 to provide informal groundwork for later development of division. In the activities below, imagine that children are using materials to act out the division situation.

1. *Sharing Cookies* — grade 2. $100 \div 21 = \square$
   A child brought a bag of 100 cookies to class on his birthday. How many cookies did each of the 21 second graders get?
2. *Toothpick Construction* — grade 3. $750 \div 26 = \square$
   Third graders are making designs with toothpicks pasted onto construction paper. The teacher has one box of toothpicks that contains 750 toothpicks. The 26 children want to know how many toothpicks they each get.
3. Add an activity of your own.

Using Algorithms

Sets of symbolic exercises on operations involving multidigit numbers may appear to children to have no relevance to life beyond the mathematics class. Where do you use arithmetic, in particular algorithms on whole numbers? What types of uses of algorithms can a teacher provide for children? This section and the next one on "word problems" concern these two questions, presenting examples of uses of algorithms together with ways to incorporate them into introductory, developmental, and review-practice activities. Ideas and suggestions made in this section for using algorithms build upon those made in Chapter 5, and are also applicable, with appropriate modifications, to other arithmetic topics such as operations on fractions and decimals, and percents.

Types of Situations in Which We Use Algorithms

The Activities at the beginning of this chapter were intended to show you a variety of situations in which algorithms are used. For example, Make the Most of It from Activity 5 was designed to give practice in multiplication, but you also made *incidental* use of the addition algorithm in finding your total score. Checking a bill in a restaurant and balancing a checkbook are everyday situations in which addition and subtraction are used.

You used several algorithms in Water, Water, Everywhere from Activity 5. In fact, this activity was *structured* to require specific algorithms — for example, multidigit multiplication to find the number of drops of water in a bath. Since the numbers were large in this activity, you may have relied on estimation or a calculator for the computation.

A third type of situation in which algorithms are used is in *other mathematics* topics. For example, to find the area of a rectangle measuring 14 centimeters by 23 centimeters, we must multiply 14 by 23. Finding an average involves algorithms for addition and division. There are many mathematics topics in which algorithms are used. In fact, the multiplication and division algorithms themselves require addition and subtraction skills, respectively.

The game Two Hundred from Activity 5 and Your Favorite Digit from Activity 5 are two examples of a *game or puzzle situation* involving specific algorithms. Considerable motivation for drill and practice of algorithms can be provided by games and puzzles which have a self-correcting feature, are presented in a novel format, or lead to deeper problem-solving investigations (for example, finding a winning strategy, or making up and playing variations of the game).

In Activity 1, Telling Tales, you encountered a fifth type of application situation, *word problems.* No doubt this is the type of situation that you most commonly associate with using algorithms in school. A teacher should develop and use a repertoire of application situations in teaching, especially those that grow out of the interests and needs of the children.

Why Emphasize Using Algorithms?

The teaching of mathematics should emphasize its uses. Learning theory supports this principle — material that is meaningful to children is learned better and retained longer than meaningless material. Thus, situations in which children can use mathematics and relate it to themselves and their interests can provide a base for durable learning. Such situations as well as interesting games and puzzles can get children's attention and involve them in a mathematical activity, thereby providing motivation for learning a new topic or practicing a skill. However, it may be hoped that children are not dependent on these external stimuli (that is, provided and structured by the teacher) and that they are themselves motivated to learn. Children may lose any such internal motivation to learn mathematics if their experiences consist primarily of pages of exercises, unrelated to their lives. Such experiences tell a child that "math is dull, useless, irrelevant . . . tune it out . . . you'll never really use this, so why bother." Telling a child that the addition algorithm is useful, even describing its application, will have little lasting effect. However, by discovering a number pattern, playing a game, figuring out a puzzle, or solving a problem — all of which can involve the use of an algorithm — children can experience first hand the usefulness and relevance of mathematics. Children need and want reasons to learn, beyond winning the approval of a teacher or parents, or passing a test.

The sample activities that follow show various ways in which algorithms can be used. These may stimulate you to identify similar situations and then put your good ideas to work in the classroom.

Incidental Situations

Many classroom activities have potential for mathematical thinking even though the main objective is not mathematical. A sensitive teacher can recognize this potential, and can use these incidental situations to underscore the usefulness of the algorithms children are learning. As described in the first example below, an activity (here planting seeds) can stimulate a readiness or introductory activity, or can provide an opportunity to practice an algorithm.

1. *Planting Seeds.* A teacher tells children that he wants to give each child 3 beans to plant. Children ask "Are there enough beans in that little packet?" In a third-grade class the teacher might use this situation as a division challenge for a class of 23 students. The children have studied basic division, but have not yet studied this type of division ($80 \div 23$). The teacher encourages children to suggest ways to answer the question via materials: "80 seeds, 23 children, 3 seeds for each?" In a fifth-grade class, children might answer this question by doing the division algorithm. Some might realize that the remainder in this division means that several children could plant 4 seeds.

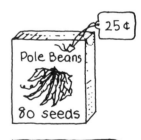

2. *How Many Days Until Christmas?* or until your birthday? or until the summer vacation? Children can answer these questions by counting days on a calendar, but they can also be challenged to answer them by computation.

SOCIAL STUDIES
pages 154 – 168

3. *How Many Pages Did You Read?* One third grader says that the reading assignment is 14 pages long. Some other children counting the pages say "No, 15 pages." Children can discuss how to use subtraction to figure out how many pages are in reading assignments in general.

4. *Speed Reading.* Sixth graders wonder how long their reading assignments will take them. As an experiment, children read for five minutes, count the words read, and then compute the number of words read per minute. They then see how long their assignment will take them.

5. *Bus Rides.* Fifth graders are discussing riding on the bus to and from school each day. Children wonder how much time they spend on the bus in one day, in one week, and then in one year.

6. Add an activity of your own.

Structured Situations

The incidental uses of algorithms are unlikely to provide sustained practice — rather they can motivate children and convince them of the many uses for mathematics. A teacher can structure situations to provide motivation for learning specific skills. Such planned situations can be generated by anticipating incidental situations or by picking up on current interests of children in the class. These planned situations can also be structured to encourage children to formulate their own problems and to offer alternative methods for their solution.

1. *Grocery Shopping.* Grocery flyers and newspaper ads can be useful resources for many types of activities — to introduce a new topic or to provide review-practice.

For example, a teacher might have children discuss the kinds of food their parents bought for their family each week. They could refer to flyers from two local supermarkets to total the cost of the 10 most important items on their weekly shopping lists. Total costs at the two supermarkets can be compared. As a follow-up, children might find the total cost in the store where their parents shop and report these costs to the class.

As a variation of this activity to practice addition and subtraction of one-, two-, and three-digit numbers, a teacher could make a copy of an ad in a newspaper 25 years old and have children compare the cost of feeding a family now and then. Thus, they could see how much their parents' parents may have paid to feed a family and compare it with today's costs.

Another variation is to collect various prices for the same item and display them on a chart, with children asking and answering questions about the prices. For example, below are given prices for sweet corn (collected from newspaper ads over a two week period in late July), together with some questions children might ask:

Which corn is most expensive? least expensive?

How much would it cost at the various prices to buy enough corn so that each person in your family could have 3 ears?

Which is more expensive: corn at 3 for 39¢, 6 for 69¢, or 8 for $1.00?

What arithmetic skills are being practiced in this situation? Do you see how this situation can motivate the study of ratio?

Some children may not be interested in shopping for family groceries and may prefer other situations — for example, shopping for materials for something they will make themselves, or shopping by mail order catalogue or at a school rummage sale.

Add another situation.

2. *Calories.* Fourth graders referred to calorie charts to determine their calorie intake. This activity was part of a health science unit on nutrition. Write two questions that could be raised here. What arithmetic skills did your questions involve?

CALORIE CHART

* cup   ** tablespoon

	Calories/ average serving		Calories/ average serving
Beverages		Orange, medium	70
Coffee or tea, clear	0	Peach, large	50
Cola, 8 oz.	105	Pear, medium	60
Milk, skim, 1 c*	88	**Meat, Poultry, and Fish**	
Milk, whole, 1 c	166	Bacon, 2 strips	95
Bread and Cereals		Beef, sirloin steak, 9 oz.	375
Cornflakes, 3/4 c	62	Chicken, fried, drumstick	64
White bread, 1 slice	65	Frankfurter	125
Wholewheat bread, 1 slice	55	Lamb chop, 3 oz.	450
Dairy		Tuna fish, 1/2 c	170
Butter, 1 T**	100	**Miscellaneous**	
Cheese, American, 1″ cube	79	Cheese sandwich	333
Cheese, Cheddar, 1 oz.	115	French fries, 10 pieces	155
Cheese, cottage, 1 c	240	Hamburger on a bun	492
Egg, boiled or poached	75	Hot dog on a bun	300
Desserts		Peanut butter sandwich	220
Brownie	295	Potato chips, 8-10 large	100
Cake, chocolate, 2″ sq.	356	**Vegetables**	
Doughnut	135	Beets, 1/2 c	40
Ice cream, plain, 1/2 c	150	Carrots, 1/2 c	30
Pie, apple, 4 in. wedge	330	Corn, medium ear	92
Fruits		Peas, 1/2 c	56
Apple, medium	70	Potatoes, mashed, 1 c	145
Banana	85	Tomato, medium	25

---

3. *Bottles and Cans.* Since their state recently passed a law about deposits for beverage bottles and cans, fifth graders decided to collect littered bottles and cans as a class project. Cans were worth 2¢ and small and large bottles were worth 5¢ and 12¢, respectively. Just before the children turned in their collection, the teacher devoted class time to a discussion of related questions. For example, how much were they worth? How long did it take to collect them? How much did the class collect? How much might they collect in one year? How long would it take to collect enough money to buy a pair of gerbils for the class?

Using Algorithms in Other Mathematics Topics

The elementary school mathematics curriculum has been expanded in recent years to include much more than straightforward arithmetic of whole numbers, fractions, and decimals. Teachers may be tempted to postpone or skip the new topics because of pressure to stick to computational skills. But by doing this, teachers deprive children of opportunities to learn new topics which themselves give considerable practice with computation, especially basic facts and algorithms. Some examples of the way algorithms are used in other mathematics topics are given below.

1. *Perimeter.* Third graders use their homemade meter rulers to measure a room in the school or at home in centimeters and find the perimeter of the floor. This activity involves the addition of two- and three-digit numbers. The same kind of activity can be done in grades 5–6 to provide practice with addition of decimals if measurements are expressed in meters (for example, 487 cm = 4.87 m).

2. *Approximating* π. Children can use centimeter tape measures to measure the circumference and diameter of many circular objects — the wastepaper basket, bicycle wheels, lamp shades. They can then divide circumference by diameter (a two- or three-digit number by a two-digit number, usually) and discover that the quotient is always close to 3 (that is, 3 with a remainder), thus finding an approximation for the number π. (See Around and Across in Chapter 6.)

3. *Probability.* As a class project, children perform the experiment of tossing two dice and noting the sum. Each child does this 100 times and notes the results. Children compare their results, and find, for example, the average number of times that a sum of 12 will occur if the dice are rolled 100 times.

Games and Puzzles

Games and puzzles provide alternatives to dull, routine, and unmotivated sets of exercises which typically provide children with little or no immediate feedback about the correctness of their answers. The first four activities below indicate how drill and practice can be made self-checking. The last three activities illustrate types of games that can provide practice with algorithms on whole numbers as well as on fractions and decimals.

1. *Self-checking Methods.* There are several ways to make a routine set of exercises self-checking. Four simple ways are shown below.
   Exercises

   1. $31\,\overline{\smash{)}496}$ 2. $25\,\overline{\smash{)}425}$ 3. $23\,\overline{\smash{)}332}$ 4. $28\,\overline{\smash{)}644}$

   a. Answers are listed on the bottom (perhaps upside down) or on the back of the page: (1) 16; (2) 17; (3) 13; (4) 23.
   b. Answers are listed but not matched to a given problem: 13, 16, 17, 23.
   c. Answers are listed along with some incorrect answers: 13, 14, 15, 16, 20, 23.
   d. Answers are checked by a clue: Sum of (1) and (2) is 33. Sum of (3) and (4) is 36.

   You can also design more varied and motivating self-checking formats than those above. Note how the set of divisions above is made self-checking in Order the Letters.

2. *Order the Letters.* First do the divisions. Then arrange the answers in order, smallest to largest. Write the letters of the divisions below the answer. Do you get the message?

G. $31\overline{\smash{)}496}$ H. $25\overline{\smash{)}425}$ I. $23\overline{\smash{)}322}$ N. $28\overline{\smash{)}644}$

O. $32\overline{\smash{)}704}$ R. $27\overline{\smash{)}351}$ T. $27\overline{\smash{)}567}$

Answers: _____, _____, _____, _____, _____, _____, _____

Letters: _____, _____, _____, _____, _____, _____, _____

3. *Cross-number Puzzles.* (Children can make their own.)

Across	Down
1. 26×59	1. 3×57
4. $432 \div 16$	2. $1304 \div 4$
5. 42^2	3. 79×6

4. *Hidden Number Sentences.* One hidden number sentence has been marked. Can you find more?

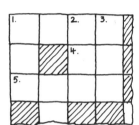

Games which can be played by pairs of students, in small groups, or by a teacher with a whole class provide an enjoyable form of review and practice.

5. An *Estimation Game for Two.* (See Activity 5.) This game can be adapted to provide practice with other operations.
6. *Board Games, Bingo, Card Games.* These activities can easily be adapted to provide practice with algorithms for whole numbers, fractions, and decimals.
7. *Number Race.* Sometimes it is desirable to play games that encourage speed in calculation. Such games must be used with caution so that undue pressure is not put on children who might not yet be able to give quick responses. You might try the following game with children who are evenly matched and enjoy competition. Teams with an equal number of players are formed. A two-digit number is selected. The first player on each team adds the number to itself, then passes the addition to the next team member who adds the number to the sum, and so on. The team to finish first wins. Is this game self-checking? How could this game be modified for subtraction?

Problem-solving Activities

The puzzles and games just described are done by straightforward calculation and do not involve pattern finding, strategies, discovery, or problem solving, as do the activities that follow.

1. *Magic Squares.* Fill in the spaces so that rows, columns, and diagonals all give the same sum.
Could this square be modified for three-digit addition? for addition of fractions or decimals?

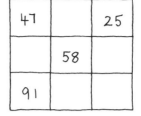

2. *Number Circles.* Remove a number from one circle and put it in another so that each circle will have the same sum.

3. *Matching Circles.* Arrange these numbers in pairs so that all pairs have the same sum.

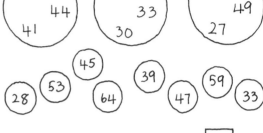

Can children create activities like Number Circles and Matching Circles above?

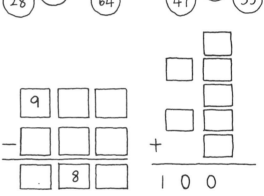

4. *Numbers in Boxes.* Place 1, 2, 3, 4, 5, 6, and 7 in the boxes to the right so that the sum is correct.

Fill in the boxes with the digits 1, 2, 3, 4, 5, 6, and 7 so that the subtraction is correct.

5. *Number Patterns.* Try these multiplications.

$3 \times 37 =$ _____	$13 \times 77 =$ _____
$6 \times 37 =$ _____	$26 \times 77 =$ _____
$9 \times 37 =$ _____	$39 \times 77 =$ ___ __
___ $\times 37 =$ _____	___ $\times 77 =$ _____

The games from Activity 5, Make the Most of It and Two Hundred, can be played on many levels. Children may play them just for fun, as games of chance, without thinking about strategies. After playing Two Hundred a few times, however, they may sense that there is some way to win. When they begin to think this way they are engaging in problem solving. At a later stage, once they understand the strategy for this game, they can try modifying the rules to invent new games and then investigate strategies for them.

Textbook series sometimes include puzzles and games such as those above as "brain teasers" or "challenge problems." Unfortunately, while these problems may challenge the better students, less capable students may feel unsure about even attempting them. A teacher might offer hints to selected challenge problems or devise a sequence which begins with easier examples and leads up to more difficult ones. All children in the class should feel that they can be successful on some level.

Challenge problems can be displayed on a section of the mathematics bulletin board called Problem of the Week. However just providing such problems for children is not sufficient to foster the spirit of problem solving in the classroom. A teacher should encourage children to share and discuss their solutions to problems and praise them for their problem-solving efforts.

Word Problems

Perhaps you recall solving word problems. Did you find them interesting? Were they difficult? Did you see them as situations in which you used mathematics? If you were teaching children now, how would you like them to answer these questions?

Solve the word problem below.

Roberto has collected 113 different United States stamps. Luis has 88. How many more stamps does Roberto have than Luis?

To solve this word problem, you probably (1) read the problem, (2) interpreted what is given and what is to be found, (3) decided on a method for solution (here subtraction) and wrote an appropriate number sentence, such as $113 - 88 = \square$; and (4) computed the answer. Perhaps you also checked your computation or thought about the meaningfulness of the answer.

Children can encounter difficulties with one or more of these four steps. One way to minimize or avoid these difficulties is to give children word problems other than the standard type above. Many current textbooks do just that by including a variety of types of word problems. Solve these sample word problems and determine which would most help children who are having difficulties: reading the problem _____; interpreting it _____; translating it into mathematical language _____; and computing the answer _____.

1. 16 cats
   25 dogs
   How many animals?

2. Use the division example to solve each of these.

$$22 \overline{)838}$$
$$\begin{array}{r} -660 \quad 30 \\ \hline 178 \\ -176 \quad 8 \\ \hline 2 \end{array}$$

a. If 22 pirates equally shared 838 gold coins, how many will each pirate get?
   How many will be left over?

b. The 838 gold coins are to be stored in small boxes that hold 22 coins. How many boxes are needed to store the coins?

3. Postcards take 10-cent stamps and letters, 15-cent stamps. How much does it cost to mail 5 letters and 9 postcards?

4. Make up a problem about each of these pictures. Then solve it.

a.
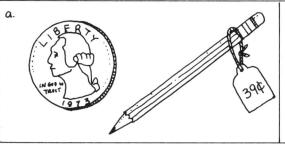

b.
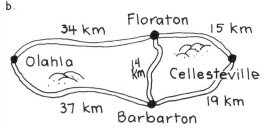

5. Refer to the calorie chart to answer these questions.

a. How many calories are in a lunch of a hamburger on a bun and an apple?
b. How many more calories does a hamburger have than a cheese sandwich?
c. How many calories are in 3 bananas?
d. How many calories are in one-half of an apple?

Calorie Chart	
Hamburger on a bun	492
Hotdog on a bun	300
Peanut butter sandwich	220
Cheese sandwich	333
Apple	70
Banana	85

6. When Jack's 69 beans started to sprout, it turned out that 37 of them were duds. Four rabbits came by and each nibbled the tops of two sprouted beans, and these beans then died. As the beans were growing (rather more quickly than expected), Jack decided to build a fence to protect them. Being a bit clumsy, he trampled one-half of them and these beans did not survive. When the beans were three meters tall, there was a heat wave — it hit 40° C and Jack was so prostrated that he forgot to water them. Nine died. When he finally saw the wilted survivors drooping over the house, he dashed out to water them, and killed two more by overwatering. How many were left? Will Jack find the giant and his goose? Stay tuned!

Difficulties related to reading and interpreting word problems are often attributed to general reading difficulties — poor vocabulary, inability to decode unfamiliar words, poor reading comprehension. Comprehension is particularly important for solving word problems that contain extraneous information (5 and 6 above), or involve long or complex sentences (for example, "If . . . then . . ." sentence structure).

Modification of the standard word problem can help children who have reading difficulties — for example, short verbal problems like (1), nonverbal picture problems like (5), diagram problems like (4); tape-recorded verbal problems; or standard problems where the vocabulary and sentence structure are kept within the capabilities of the child. These modifications strengthen the child's ability to attack word problems and build self-confidence. Some texts also include long problems like (6) to help children improve their reading in quantitative situations. A teacher should remind children that verbal problems often require more careful reading than regular situations, and so children should be given adequate time to read the problems.

Children may find it easier to understand word problems if they read them aloud and restate them in their own words. This approach also helps a teacher to identify specific reading difficulties. Another approach is to have children first say problems and solve them, later say and write them, and finally read and solve word problems. This approach builds up their ability to deal with number situations orally and in writing. Also, by working in small groups to make up and solve problems, children can gain valuable experience in communicating with each other about quantitative situations. This type of small group work can give the teacher an opportunity to observe children's approaches to word problems and to note difficulties they have and also the successful strategies they use.

Sometimes children are taught to look for "key words" (for example, less, lost, take away) which indicate what operation should be used. While this may help some children, it can hinder others who only look for key words and neglect to read and understand the whole problem. Also, some key words have more than one interpretation. For example, *more* can indicate addition (I have 11 stamps. I get 88 *more*. Now I have _____.) and subtraction (Roberto has 113 stamps. Luis has 88. How many *more* does Roberto have than Luis?).

Another cause for the "wrong operation" syndrome is that the child does not understand the number operation involved. This can be prevented by the integration of word problems and applications into learning basic facts and algorithms. In remedial situations, help can be provided by asking the child to imagine the situation in the word problem and to act it out or draw a picture for it. Once a verbal or active solution has been given, the child can write the symbolic solution. Children should also be encouraged to say their answer in a complete sentence and check whether it makes sense. If a wrong operation is used, an incorrect answer can usually be detected in this way. Formulating word problems for given number sentences (as you did in Activity 1, Telling Tales) can also help.

Word problems with completed computations (like 2 on page 442) can help children with difficulties related to translating the problem into mathematics and computing the answer. This type of problem still involves reading and requires interpretation of the computation. Self-checking approaches, the use of a calculator, and estimation of answers can help children with computation difficulties.

These types of difficulties seldom occur in isolation from one another. Moreover, they may be compounded by the child's lack of motivation and self-confidence to solve word problems. A teacher can begin to help children learn to solve word problems by giving them frequent opportunities to make them up and solve them, by providing various types of problems that interest the children and are appropriate to their reading and mathematics background, and by fostering a nonthreatening classroom atmosphere to support the efforts of the children.

Word Problems for the Classroom

In some textbooks, word problems are presented at the end of a chapter on a topic. This organization, which seems to suggest that understanding and skill are prerequisites for applications, might cause a teacher using the book to discuss word problems and applications only at the end of the chapter. As you have seen in the previous sections, application situations (such as word problems, games, puzzles) should be integrated into all instruction to motivate learning of new topics as well as review and practice. Since this may not be done by a textbook, the teacher assumes a key role in helping children experience the usefulness of the mathematics they are learning.

One source for word problems is naturally the teacher's textbook or other textbooks. Current textbook series contain many attractively presented and interesting word problems concerning a host of topics of potential interest to children, from fairy tales to space flights, from grocery shopping to bones in your body. Unfortunately, problem situations do not hold universal appeal for all children. Age level, geographic location, setting (rural versus urban), and cultural background all affect children's interpretation of and identification with problem situations. Thus a teacher needs to supplement problem situations given in a text — that is, to tailor problem situations to the particular interests of the children in the class.

The best source for these problems is the children themselves. Children enjoy writing and solving word problems, especially those with their names in them. Somehow personalizing word problems, even relatively routine ones, seems to generate enthusiasm and interest. Local newspapers, advertisements, and magazines are other sources. A collection of teacher-made and student-made word problems is a valuable teaching aid.

TEST YOUR UNDERSTANDING

1. Give your own definition for "algorithm."
2. Do 134×25 by lattice multiplication and a method using partial products.
3. Write an application situation which interests you for each problem.

$$\begin{array}{r} 125 \\ \times\ 20 \\ \hline \end{array} \qquad 25\,\overline{)\,6700}$$

4. Complete these error patterns. Then name one or two materials you could use to help children correct these errors.

$$\begin{array}{ccccc} \overset{\text{\scriptsize I}}{13} & \overset{2}{14} & \overset{\text{\scriptsize I}}{38} & 34 & 62 \\ \times\ 4 & \times\ 5 & \times\ 2 & \times\ 3 & \times\ 4 \\ \hline 52 & 110 & 56 & & \end{array}$$

$$3\overline{)72}$$
$$\underline{-6}\,|2$$
$$\underline{12}$$
$$\underline{-12}\,|4$$
$$0$$
$$|\overline{6}$$

$$4\overline{)64}$$
$$\underline{-4}\,|1$$
$$\underline{24}$$
$$\underline{-24}\,|6$$
$$0$$
$$|\overline{7}$$

$$5\overline{)75}$$

5. Describe the action for solving $4\overline{)568}$ with squared materials.

Symbols

$$\begin{array}{r} 142 \\ \hline 2 \\ 40 \\ 100 \\ 4\overline{)568} \\ -400 \\ \hline 168 \\ -160 \\ \hline 8 \\ -8 \\ \hline 0 \end{array}$$

Action

1. Take _____ flats, _____ longs, _____ units.

2. Place _____

3. _____

4. _____

5. _____

Do you think that doing this stacking algorithm with materials would help children learn the standard algorithm? Explain.

6. Why is it desirable to have children use materials to learn two- and three-digit addition? Should they use materials to learn addition of four- and five-digit numbers? Circle the exercises that *cannot* be easily acted out with squared materials.

$$\begin{array}{cc} 24 & 124 \\ \times 18 & \times 3 \end{array} \quad 124\overline{)388} \quad 24\overline{)388} \quad 2\overline{)388}$$

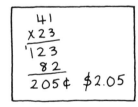

$$\begin{array}{r} 41 \\ \times 23 \\ \hline {}^{1}23 \\ 82 \\ \hline 205¢ \quad \$2.05 \end{array}$$

7. Six types of errors children make with algorithms are discussed on pages 407–408. Which types of errors are illustrated by the exercises below?

a.
$$\begin{array}{r} 438 \\ -172 \\ \hline 345 \end{array}$$

b. A pen costs 41¢.
How much do 23 pens cost?

8. How would you help a child who finds it difficult to compute and place partial products for multiplications such as $\begin{array}{r}34 \\ \times 26\end{array}$ $\begin{array}{r}34 \\ \times 65\end{array}$?

How would you help a child who has difficulty in estimating partial quotients in divisions such as $34\overline{)985}$?

9. Why might a child who cannot do higher-decade addition (see page 430) have difficulty doing exercises such as these?

$$
\begin{array}{r}
377 \\
\times\,7 \\
\hline
\end{array}
\qquad
\begin{array}{r}
398 \\
159 \\
+\,196 \\
\hline
\end{array}
$$

   Describe an approach for helping this child learn higher decade addition.

10. Describe examples of ways in which children can use algorithms in an incidental classroom situation, another mathematics topic, a structured lesson, a game or puzzle.

11. Describe four kinds of difficulties children have in solving word problems. Describe two types of word problems that may help children who have reading difficulties.

12. Activities like (a)–(c) below can be used to evaluate children's understanding of algorithms while they are learning them or to diagnose difficulties in remedial situations. Activities (d)–(j) are types of exercises that you could include on written tests or homework assignments, at appropriate grade levels, to help you and the children evaluate their understanding and ability to apply algorithms. Activities (b) and (c) focus on the relationship between the action for a solution and the way the solution is written symbolically.

    a. Have children use squared materials to act out $121\overline{)485}$. How would you want a child to act this out?

    b. Have children use squared materials to do the multiplication this way and explain where the partial products come from. How would you want a child to act out this multiplication? What kind of explanation would you want given?

    c. Ask children to watch as you do $21\overline{)89}$ with squared materials. Have them write down the numbers to show how you are doing it. (Teacher first takes 2 groups of 21, then 1 group of 21, then 1 more group of 21.) What would you want a child to write down?

$$
\begin{array}{r}
23 \\
\times\,4 \\
\hline
12 \quad 4\times 3 \\
80 \quad 4\times 20 \\
\hline
92
\end{array}
$$

    Complete exercises (d)–(j).

    d. Correct these.

$$
\begin{array}{r}
\overset{3}{}{}_{\scriptscriptstyle 1\,1} \\
\cancel{4}0\,0\,0 \\
-\,1\,5\,6\,0 \\
\hline
2\,5\,4\,0
\end{array}
\qquad
\begin{array}{r}
3\,\overline{)7\,8} \\
-\,6 \quad| \quad 2 \\
\hline
1\,8 \quad| \\
-\,1\,8 \quad| \quad 6 \\
\hline
0\,8
\end{array}
$$

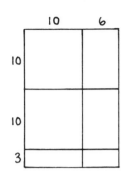

e. What multiplication is shown here?

(1)   33
    × 26

(2)   16
    × 13

(3)   16
    × 23

(4)   60
    × 300

f. Use the multiplication to write answers for the divisions.

    15
  × 12
   ___
    30
   150
   ___
   180

12 /‾180‾   15 /‾182‾

g. Complete the drawing for   25 .
                             + 17

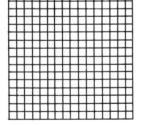

h. Write a word problem for this multiplication.

   134
   × 3
   ___
    12
    90
   300
   ___
   402

i. Draw a solution showing all partial products.

    14
  × 13
   ___
    12
    30
    40
   100
   ___
   182

j. Fill in the blanks.

FURTHER READINGS AND PROJECTS

1. Read Chapter 1, "Diagnosing and Correcting Errors in Computation," in Robert Ashlock's book *Error Patterns in Computation* (Columbus, Ohio: Charles E. Merrill, 1976). Compare his suggestions for preventing patterns of errors (pages 15–18) with the suggestions for teaching algorithms made on pages 408–410 of this chapter. Then examine some of the error patterns involving whole number computations in his book and read his related discussions about sources for the error patterns and ways to help children correct them. You might compare his suggestions with those made in "Helping the Child Who Cannot Do Math" by Persis Herald in *Teacher* 91:7 (March 1974), pp. 46–47, 89. This article concerns helping children with learning disabilities in mathematics.

2. In "Low-Stress Algorithms" in *Measurement in School Mathematics, 1976 Yearbook*, National Council of Teachers of Mathematics (Reston, Va.: NCTM, 1976), pp. 218–239, Barton Hutchings describes algorithms that are particularly useful for upper elementary and junior high school students with "severe needs" in mathematics. Read this article which describes and illustrates low-stress algorithms for all four operations on whole numbers, and try the practice exercises for the reader in the article. How do these algorithms reduce the demands on memory and the need to do mental computation required in the standard algorithms? Why are they called low-stress algorithms? Why might these algorithms be appropriate for a student who never caught on to the standard algorithm for an operation?

3. Refer to a mathematics text or teacher's guide for grades 3, 4, or 5 and examine it to see how an algorithm is developed.
   a. Describe the sequence for developing the algorithm by giving sample exercises. Was the sequence the same as the one described in this chapter? If not, describe differences in scope and sequence.
   b. Was the development of the algorithm done primarily at the abstract level, or were semiconcrete diagrams and concrete materials used? Draw sample diagrams and describe how materials were used, if appropriate.
   c. Did the text give both alternative algorithms (such as partial products) and the standard algorithm? If so, illustrate how an exercise was done with both algorithms. What kind of transition (if any) was made from the expanded algorithm to the standard one?
   d. How were applications of the algorithm incorporated into the text? Were they only at the end of the chapters on the algorithm?
   e. Did the chapter tests involve primarily computation, or did they also test understanding of the algorithm? If understanding was not tested, describe an activity or write a test question to do this.

4. Examine the sections of *Individualized Computation* by Robert Wirtz (Washington, D.C.: Curriculum Development Associates, 1974) that deal with whole number algorithms. For example, you might look at pages 18–38 in Level B2 which concern addition and subtraction of two-digit numbers or pages 21–24, 26–31, and 38–47 in Level D2 which concern multidigit multiplication. How are materials (such as bean sticks, money, and squared material) used? How is the transition from the manipulative level to the representational level and then to the abstract level made? You might also examine

corresponding worksheets in *Drill and Practice at the Problem-Solving Level,* also published by CDA.

5. An important theme in this and other chapters is that children should use the mathematics they are learning. As discussed on pages 434–442, opportunities to do this can be provided in many ways: through incidental situations, games and puzzles, planned lessons, and as suggested in "Math Skills for Survival in the Real World" by Ann Wilderman, in *Teacher* (February 1977), pp. 68–70, through math-application units. Six units are outlined in this article: banking, transportation, taxes, budgeting, shopping, pricing, and advertising. Which would you like to try with children? Why? In what ways would children be using arithmetic, in particular whole number algorithms? Can you think of other topics for the type of units described in her article?

6. Examine the following articles which concern reading and mathematics, in particular as applied to solving verbal problems. Compare suggestions made in the articles to those given in this chapter (pages 442–445) and on pages 205–207. Which suggestions do you think are most useful for children who are just beginning to read (grades K–2) and for older children who have reading difficulties?

N. Wesley Earp, "Procedures of Teaching Reading in Mathematics," *The Arithmetic Teacher,* 17:7 (November 1970), pp. 575–579.

Marilyn Suydam and J. Fred Weaver, "Research on Problem-Solving: Implications for Elementary School Classrooms," *The Arithmetic Teacher,* 25:2 (November 1977), pp. 40–42.

Lloyd Richardson, "The Role of Strategies for Teaching Children to Solve Verbal Problems," *The Arithmetic Teacher,* 22:5 (May 1975), pp. 414–421.

7. Children with learning disabilities often encounter severe difficulties in learning whole-number algorithms. They find the written algorithms perceptually complex. They also have difficulty applying the subskills which must be used in an interrelated manner to do algorithms. Suggestions for helping learning-disabled children acquire skills with whole numbers are provided by John C. Moyer and Margaret Bannochie Moyer, "Computation Implications for Learning-Disabled Children," in *Developing Computational Skills,* 1978 Yearbook of the National Council of Teachers of Mathematics (Reston, Va.: NCTM, 1978), pp. 78–95. Which of the suggestions offered seem most relevant to teaching algorithms?

NOTES

1. This method is a variation of one developed by the early Egyptians. It was common in medieval Europe and has been called the Russian Peasant method since it was supposedly used by Russian peasants until the time of World War I. Children who have not learned standard algorithms may find that nonstandard ones such as those in Activity 3 give them a fresh start.

2. For more about error patterns and ways to prevent or remedy them, see Robert Ashlock, *Error Patterns in Computation* (Columbus, Ohio: Charles E. Merrill, 1976).

3. See Carl A. Backman, "Analyzing Children's Work Procedures," in *Developing Computational Skills,* 1978 Yearbook of the National Council of Teachers of Mathematics (Reston, Va.: NCTM, 1978), pp. 177–195.

4. This approach is used in Robert Wirtz, *Individualized Computation* (Washington, D.C.: Curriculum Development Associates, 1974).

CHAPTER 10

NUMBER PATTERNS

INTRODUCTION

Do you enjoy looking for patterns? Do you get satisfaction from solving problems which at first glance seem very difficult but which you eventually solve using a clever shortcut? Try the problem below. How long do you think it would take you to solve it?

1. What is the sum of the first 100 odd numbers?

If you think that it will take you longer than five minutes to solve this problem, try the questions below which will help you answer it.

2. Find these sums: $1 + 3 =$ _____, $1 + 3 + 5 =$ _____, $1 + 3 + 5 + 7 =$ _____, $1 + 3 + 5 + 7 + 9 =$ _____ What is the sum of the first *five* odd numbers? of the first *six* odd numbers? _____
3. Now can you answer question 1? What is the sum of the first 100 odd numbers? _____
4. Can you explain *why* this is the answer? Look at these diagrams. How many in each?

Put them together.
Now do you see why the pattern works?

These questions give the flavor of a very ancient branch of mathematics, *number theory,* that builds on the basic operations of whole numbers and involves patterns and relationships between numbers. Ancient Greek mathematicians knew of numbers patterns such as the one above, and often related the numbers to geometric patterns. Surprisingly, many questions posed by the ancient Greeks about number patterns have not yet been answered, although many mathematicians have tried to solve them. Today, number theory is an active field of mathematical research.

It is useful for teachers to be aware of such patterns for several reasons. First, activities such as the one above can be used to give children an opportunity to practice computational skills in a self-checking way (because once they see the pattern, they will catch their own mistakes) and also to gain experience in discovery and in reasoning why the pattern works. Also, when number patterns are presented in terms of visual patterns, and vice versa, children can strengthen their ability to see and use relationships between number and geometry. Finally, number patterns and number theory deal with concepts (for example, prime factorization, least common multiple) that are related to other elementary school mathematics topics (for example, writing fractions in simplest form, or adding fractions).

The Activities in this chapter require only colored pencils as materials. They are designed to give you experiences in finding and interrelating numerical and geometric patterns. The Activities can be easily modified to provide children at different age levels with opportunities to be involved creatively with mathematics in a paper-and-pencil context. In Activity 1, Crickets, patterns on a number line lead to the concept of prime number. (A later discussion section deals with another approach to prime numbers using arrays of objects.) In Activity 2, Patterns on a Grid, writing letters and numbers in a rectangular array leads to a search for patterns involving multiples. Patterns on a number chart are used for the Sieve of Eratosthenes, a method for finding prime numbers. The results of the Sieve are related to other topics and questions in number theory — factor trees, unique factorization, a rule for divisibility by three, and a famous conjecture about prime numbers that has challenged mathematicians for over two centuries.

The Discussion Questions and Comments concern the following: how number theory arises in real life and its role in the elementary school curriculum; the use of visual patterns to develop numerical ideas; suggestions for implementing discovery activities; and a closer look at some mathematics underlying the Activities in this chapter.

Follow-up Sections give several uses of the Hundred Chart and some more examples of classical number patterns that fit into even larger patterns. Divisibility rules are presented along with some related methods that children can use to check computations with whole numbers. The use of prime numbers to find the greatest common factor and the least common multiple of two numbers is discussed, and these two ideas (GCF and LCM) are related to earlier topics — for example, loops for classification and properties of binary operations.

ACTIVITIES

Activity 1. Crickets

This Activity is about crickets that jump along a number line. A 2-hopper is a cricket that can only make jumps to the right of 2 spaces each. Suppose that all crickets start jumping at 0.

Would a 1-hopper land on 6? _____ a 2-hopper? _____ a 3-hopper? _____ a 4-hopper? _____ What other type of cricket could land on 6? a _____-hopper.

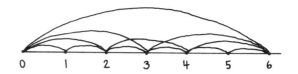

The diagram on page 452 shows that there are four different crickets that can land on 6 (starting at 0 and taking equal-sided jumps). Numbers that divide 6 evenly are called (positive) *divisors* or *factors* of 6. For example, 2 is a divisor of 6, 4 and 12 are not. List the divisors of 6. _____, _____, _____,

_____

Use these number lines to show tracks for all of the crickets that land on each number. In the table below, enter the names and the number of crickets that land on each number (that is, the divisors and the number of divisors of each number).

List the numbers that have exactly two divisors. (There should be six of them in the table.) _____,

_____, _____, _____, _____, _____.

These are called *prime numbers*. Fill in: A number is a *prime* if it has exactly _____ divisors, _____ and itself. Circle the numbers below that are prime: 19, 25, 51, 73, 101, 4036 (**Note:** Three of them are prime.)

You should have found one number that has exactly one divisor. It is _____. Do you think that there are any other numbers that have exactly one divisor? _____ Why?

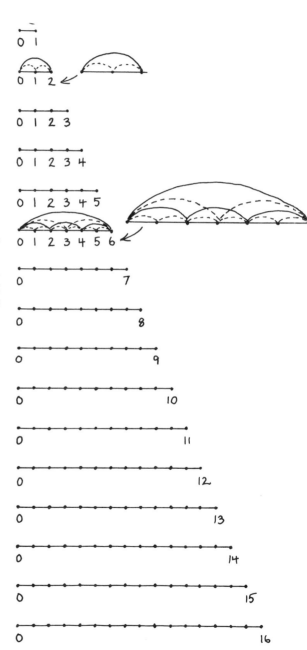

Number	List of Divisors	Number of Divisors
1		
2	1, 2	2
3		
4		
5		
6	1, 2, 3, 6	4
7		
8		
9		
10		
11		
12		
13		
14		
15		
16		

(Optional)   You should have found one number that has six divisors. (It is
_____.) Can you find a number which has *more* than six di-
visors? (It may not be on the table.) Write the number and list
its divisors.

(Optional)   You should have found two numbers in the table that have exactly three divisors (_____ and _____). Can you find two
more numbers that have exactly three divisors? (They are not
in the table.) _____, _____, _____

A

Activity 2. Patterns on a Grid

1. *Your Name.* Write the letters of your first
name in grid A, beginning in the top left
corner and repeating your name as often as
necessary. Shade in all of the spaces that
have the first letter of your name. Do you
see a pattern?
Now try this again in grid B. Is the pattern
different?
Compare your pattern with those of other
people.

B

S	M	T	W	T	F	S
		1	2	3	4	5
6	7	8	9	10	11	12
13	14	15	16	17	18	19
20	21	22	23	24	25	26
27	28	29	30	31		

2. *A Calendar and Multiples.* Here are some
pages from a calendar and some rules for coloring
them. In the first, color all spaces with *even* numbers red. In the second, color all numbers that are
multiples of 3 green, and all multiples of 4 yellow.

S	M	T	W	T	F	S
		1	2	3	4	5
6	7	8	9	10	11	12
13	14	15	16	17	18	19
20	21	22	23	24	25	26
27	28	29	30	31		

S	M	T	W	T	F	S
					1	2	3
4	5	6	7	8	9	10
11	12	13	14	15	16	17
18	19	20	21	22	23	24
25	26	27	28	29	30	31

Make up your own coloring rules for this calendar page. Describe them.

(Optional) In the calendar that is started here, can you tell what number will go in the marked space *without* filling in or counting spaces? How do you do it? Again without counting, can you tell what day of the week the 23rd will be in this month? What arithmetic procedures might you use to solve this?

S	M	T	W	T	F	S
					I	2
			▭			

3. *More Patterns.* Look for patterns of multiples on these charts, and color in the patterns (a different color for each). Below each chart, write the numbers and the patterns they give (for example, vertical or diagonal).

Five in a Row

1	2	3	4	5
6	7	8	9	10
11	12	13	14	15
16	17	18	19	20
21	22	23	24	25

_____
_____

Look at each chart and note which multiples give *vertical* patterns.

Five in a row _____
Six in a Row _____ _____ _____
Ten in a Row _____ _____ _____

Can you guess which multiples will give vertical patterns for Twelve in a Row? (There are five of them.) _____, _____, _____, _____,
_____

What do you notice about multiples that give diagonal (↘ or ↙) patterns? Can you predict which numbers will give diagonal patterns?
(**Note:** In Ten in a Row, you should find that multiples of 2, 3, and 5 all give very vivid patterns. Do you see how you could easily cross off all multiples of 3? of 2? of 5?)

Six in a Row

1	2	3	4	5	6
7	8	9	10	11	12
13	14	15	16	17	18
19	20	21	22	23	24
25	26	27	28	29	30
31	32	33	34	35	36

Ten in a Row

1	2	3	4	5	6	7	8	9	10
11	12	13	14	15	16	17	18	19	20
21	22	23	24	25	26	27	28	29	30
31	32	33	34	35	36	37	38	39	40
41	42	43	44	45	46	47	48	49	50
51	52	53	54	55	56	57	58	59	60
61	62	63	64	65	66	67	68	69	70
71	72	73	74	75	76	77	78	79	80
81	82	83	84	85	86	87	88	89	90
91	92	93	94	95	96	97	98	99	100

_____
_____
_____

Activity 3. The Sieve of Eratosthenes

Do you know offhand if 179 is a prime number? (Is it divisible only by itself and 1?) Do you know how many primes there are between 160 and 170? The ancient Greeks knew of a method to find all prime numbers up to a given number. This method is named after the mathematician Eratosthenes, who lived in Alexandria, Egypt from 276 B.C. to 196 B.C. Use colored pencils and the number chart on page 457 to find all prime numbers that are less than 200. Follow the steps below.

1. Put a circle around the first prime, 2, in *red,* and then cross out all of the other multiples of 2 in *red.* The first number that you cross out will be 4. Remember that in Activity 2, part 2 you found a very easy method for crossing out these numbers, using diagonal lines. Why are these crossed-out numbers not primes?
2. Circle the first number remaining after 2 (which is 3) in *green,* and then cross out all of the remaining multiples of three, in *green.* (6, for example, should be crossed out with both red and green.)
   Why are the numbers crossed off in green not primes?
   What is the first number that you crossed out in green that had not already been marked in red? Enter it in the table, under "3."

Number whose multiples are being crossed out.	2	3							
First number to be crossed out that had not been marked before.	4								

3. Circle the first *unmarked* number after 3 (which is _____) in *black* and then cross out all of the remaining multiples of this number in black. You should find that there is a pattern that makes it easy to cross out these numbers. In the table write the first number that you crossed out in black that was not already crossed out in another color. You should find at this point that 30 has been marked with red, green, and black. List four other numbers that are marked with all three colors. _____ _____ _____ _____
4. Continue this procedure. Each time circle the first unmarked number in a new color and then cross out all multiples of that number in the same color. As you go, fill in the table above.

After a certain number of steps, you should find that you will not need to cross off any more of the remaining unmarked numbers in order to be left only with primes. How many different colors do you need to use before you get to this point?

Put a circle in some new color around all of the remaining unmarked numbers when you are sure that no more will be crossed off. You should have exactly 46 numbers circled. The last number is 199. How do you know that it is divisible only by itself and one?

Number Chart for the Sieve of Eratosthenes

1	2	3	4	5	6	7	8	9	10
11	12	13	14	15	16	17	18	19	20
21	22	23	24	25	26	27	28	29	30
31	32	33	34	35	36	37	38	39	40
41	42	43	44	45	46	47	48	49	50
51	52	53	54	55	56	57	58	59	60
61	62	63	64	65	66	67	68	69	70
71	72	73	74	75	76	77	78	79	80
81	82	83	84	85	86	87	88	89	90
91	92	93	94	95	96	97	98	99	100
101	102	103	104	105	106	107	108	109	110
111	112	113	114	115	116	117	118	119	120
121	122	123	124	125	126	127	128	129	130
131	132	133	134	135	136	137	138	139	140
141	142	143	144	145	146	147	148	149	150
151	152	153	154	155	156	157	158	159	160
161	162	163	164	165	166	167	168	169	170
171	172	173	174	175	176	177	178	179	180
181	182	183	184	185	186	187	188	189	190
191	192	193	194	195	196	197	198	199	200

In Activities 4–7 you can use the information about numbers contained in your completed Number Chart for the Sieve of Eratosthenes.

Activity 4. Factor Trees

1. The colors of your chart tell you a lot about the numbers. For example, you should find that 189 is marked in green and in the color you selected for 7, and so both 3 and 7 are *factors* of 189. 189 can be written as a product:

$$189 = 3 \times 63 = 3 \times 7 \times 9 = 3 \times 7 \times 3 \times 3$$

You can write this as a *factor tree.*

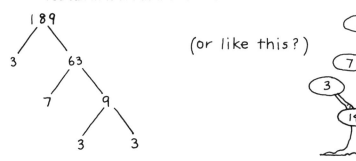

(or like this?)

The factor tree could be "grown" in other ways. One way is shown below on the left. In the other two spaces, draw two more factor trees for 189. Be sure to continue until only primes remain at the "ends."

How are these factor trees alike? How are they different?

2.

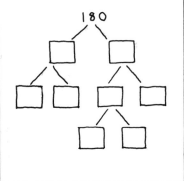

| Draw a factor tree for a number marked <u>only</u> in red, green, and black. | Draw a factor tree for a number marked <u>only</u> with your color for 11. | Fill in the missing parts of this factor tree. |

3. Do the colors give you *all* of the prime factors of a number? (Try making a factor tree for 95, which should be marked only in black. Is 5 the *only* factor of 95 that is a prime? _____)

Activity 5. Game — Subtract a Factor

Directions: Two people play. The first player picks a number (greater than 50). Players take turns. The first must subtract a factor of the number from the number chosen, the second must then subtract a factor of the *difference* from the difference, and so forth. The player who leaves a difference of 0 loses. Use the colors on your Sieve of Eratosthenes to help you play. For example,

168 is the starting number.
First player, subtract 21 from 168, because 21 is a factor of 168 (168 = 21 × 8) leaving 168 − 21 = 147.
Second player, subtract 49 from 147 because 49 is a factor of 147 (147 = 49 × 3), leaving 147 − 49 = 98.
First player, subtract 1 since 1 is a factor of 98, leaving 98 − 1 = 97.
What can the second player subtract now?
(Remember that you lose if you leave zero!)
Can a player be stuck at some point with no possible move? _____ Why?

Activity 6. A Pattern with Threes

Look at the numbers marked with green on your chart; that is, the multiples of 3. Try adding up the digits of some of them. For example, 123 is marked with green. 123 would give 1 + 2 + 3 = 6 as the sum of its digits. What do you notice about the sum of the digits?

Try some numbers that are *not* multiples of 3. What do you notice about the sums of the digits of these numbers? Do you see how to tell if a number is divisible by 3 *without* actually dividing the original number, but just by adding up the digits and then dividing the sum?

Activity 7. Conjectures

1. If you play around with numbers you may notice all sorts of patterns, and you may guess or *conjecture* that some of these patterns will always hold for any choice of numbers. Experimentation with many examples may back up a conjecture — but it may be very difficult to be completely sure that the conjectured pattern or fact will always be true. In fact, disproving conjectures by finding an example which does not work (that is, a *counterexample*) is often easier than proving that conjectures are always true.

   Examine these conjectures. Try to disprove them by providing a counterexample; or try to convince yourself that they are true, either by reasoning, or by trying a sufficient number of examples.

   (***Note:*** A number greater than 1 that is not a prime number is called a *composite number*. A composite number can be written as ☐ × △, where ☐ and △ are whole numbers, neither of which is 1. For example, 8 is composite because 8 = 4 × 2.)

a. The sum of two prime numbers is always prime.
b. The sum of two prime numbers is always even.
c. The product of two prime numbers is always composite.
d. The sum of two composite numbers is always composite.

Are your answers consistent with these facts? 3 + 5 = 8, 2 + 5 = 7, 2 × 3 = 6, 4 + 9 = 13

2. The following question has interested mathematicians for many years:

   Which numbers can be written as a sum of two primes?

   Try to write each number below as a sum of primes and then form your own conjecture. Work with a partner, if possible, to check your answers. Try more numbers to further test your conjectures.

2 __NO__	18 _____	3 _____	19 _____
4 __2 + 2__	20 _____	5 _____	21 _____
6 _____	22 _____	7 _____	23 _____
8 _____	24 _____	9 _____	25 _____
10 _____	26 _____	11 _____	27 _____
12 _____	28 _____	13 _____	29 _____
14 _____	30 _____	15 _____	31 _____
16 _____	32 _____	17 _____	33 _____

   Your conjectures: _____

3. Did you think of any of the statements below as a conjecture? Which of them is *not* true?

a. Any even number can be written as a sum of primes.
b. If an odd number can be written as a sum of two primes, one of the primes must be 2.
c. Any even number greater than 2 can be written as the sum of two primes.

The first statement is false, because 2 cannot be written as the sum of two primes. (Remember that 1 is not a prime number!)

The second statement is true, as you can see if you realize that if two numbers added together give an *odd* number, then one must be even and the other odd. 2 is the only even prime number.

The third statement is a famous conjecture made by the Russian mathematician Christian Goldbach in 1742. No one has yet been able to prove or disprove this conjecture. While no even number has yet been found that *cannot* be written as a sum of two prime numbers (and computers have been able to check very large numbers), mathematicians have not been able to show that no such number will *ever* be found.

Test Goldbach's conjecture on the even numbers 100 and 200, using your Sieve of Eratosthenes to find primes.

$$100 = \underline{\hspace{1cm}} + \underline{\hspace{1cm}} \qquad 200 = \underline{\hspace{1cm}} + \underline{\hspace{1cm}}$$

DISCUSSION QUESTIONS AND COMMENTS

Number Theory Concepts in Everyday Life

In Activity 1, Crickets, you developed the concepts of multiples and primes using a number-line model. While cricket stories may appear quite real to children, they are not situations that arise naturally in everyday life. However multiples and primes do have natural applications.

1. When children go on a field trip from school, they may notice house numbers as they walk down the street. On most streets, something about the house number tells you which side of the street the house is on. What is it?
2. In the game Buzz, children all count in turn, starting at one, *but* every third child must say "buzz" instead of their number. (That is, "one," "two," "buzz," "four," "five," "buzz," . . .) If a child says the wrong thing, he drops out. To make the game more difficult, children must say "buzz" on all multiples of three and on all multiples of four. (For example, "one," "two," "buzz, "buzz," five, "buzz," seven, . . .)
3. Children might try to design rectangular tiled table tops or quilts from a given number of squares. For example, how could you design an alphabet quilt which has one square for each letter of the alphabet? (See how one nineteenth-century American quiltmaker solved this problem.)

A	B	C	D	E
F	G	H	I	J
K	L	M	N	O
P	Q	R	S	T
U	V	W	X	Y
				Z

4. Perhaps you have seen a commercial drawing toy, a Spirograph, based on gears, with which children can make attractive patterns. The edges of various sizes of wheels are indented to make a certain number of cogs. One wheel rolls around inside a larger ring. A pencil point is inserted in a hole in the moving wheel and the pencil makes a pattern as the wheel moves. The nature of the pattern depends on the numerical relation between the number of cogs on the moving wheel and the number of cogs on the stationary wheel. Older children can investigate the relationship — it is related to the greatest common factor.

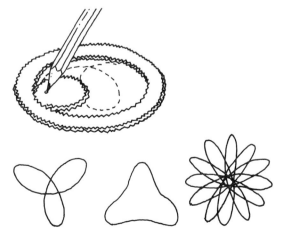

Number Theory in the Elementary School Curriculum

Number theory in a formal sense does not play a prominent role in the elementary school curriculum. First graders generally learn the terms *even* and *odd,* third and fourth graders may learn about *multiples* and *divisors,* and fifth and sixth graders learn about *prime* and *composite numbers.* In some text series, little or no use is made of these concepts once they have been introduced to children who are expected to learn a definition for them and then do a few related exercises. When presented like this, the concepts are soon forgotten, and children see little reason for learning them.

However, the search for patterns with number can and should be an important part of the elementary school curriculum. Pattern-seeking activities can serve several functions — they can provide children with useful and motivated practice of basic number skills and also opportunity to explore and work creatively with mathematics. These activities can often be done on many levels. For example, Activity 2, Patterns on a Grid, dealt with finding patterns in an array of letters or numbers. For this Activity, at what grade level might you expect children to do Your Name? _____ A Calendar and Multiples? _____ More Patterns? _____

Children may not be able to reason about why certain patterns exist in the same way that adults can. However, they can certainly investigate number questions, collect data, make guesses, check them with other data, and compare their results with those of others. In this less formal sense, number theory is and should be included throughout the elementary school curriculum.

Multiples and Primes Developed by an Array Model

In Activity 1 the number-line model for multiplication was used to develop multiples and primes. Children can learn about these concepts using another model for multiplication, an *array.* For example, they might do the next two activities. Read them and complete the table in the second one.

Materials: Square tiles, squared paper
Directions: Take 6 tiles. Arrange them in a rectangle. Can you do it another way? Color in all of the ways you find on the squared paper.
Try it for 5 tiles. Then try it for 9 tiles.

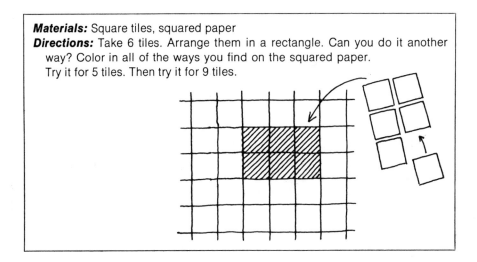

Materials: Square tiles; squared paper
Directions: Take some tiles. Make as many rectangles as you can and record them on the squared paper. Record the rectangles made and how many in the table.

With some numbers of tiles, you should be able to make only two rectangles. List some of these:

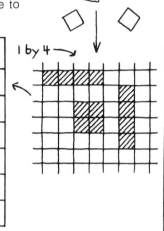

1 by 4 →

Number of tiles	Rectangles made	Number of rectangles
4	1 by 4, 2 by 2, 4 by 1	3
5		
6		
7		
8		

By placing tiles on a strip of paper with two rows (as shown here for the number 6), children can discover that some numbers make a pattern like

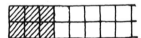

[⎯⎯⎯]   and other numbers make a pattern like [⎾⎯⎯] . This can reinforce children's understanding of *even* and *odd* which they may have been first taught by rote when doing skip counting by twos, perhaps on a number line. This can also lead older children to see why an even number can be expressed as $2 \times \square$ and an odd number as $2 \times \square + 1$, where $\square$ can be replaced by 0, 1, 2, ... Do you see why? Using this geometric interpretation for even and odd, children can show that the sum of two odd numbers is an even number (as shown here). Draw similar diagrams to show that (1) the sum of two even numbers is even, (2) the sum of an odd and an even is _____, and (3) the sum of three odd numbers is _____.

Using Visual Patterns

In this book you have seen many examples of how number concepts can be visualized, often in a pattern of some sort. The Activities in this chapter provide more examples. Some numbers leave "cricket tracks" that look like this, while some are more complicated. (See Activity 1.) Some numbers of dots can be arranged in geometric patterns. (See page 473.) Some types of numbers lie in visually striking patterns when numbers are arranged in an array. (See Activity 2.) Children should be exposed to such visual interpretations of numerical ideas for several reasons.

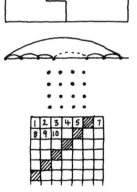

1. Some children seem to like and learn more easily from visual patterns.

   They may "see" $3 + 5$ as  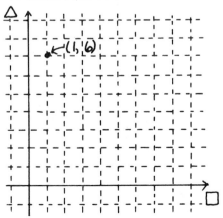, or a prime number as a special sort of pattern. They may be able to learn how to add nine quickly if they think "down one and back one," relating addition to movement on a Hundred Chart. Sometimes children with this sort of spatial inclination are not given sufficient chance to develop it, use it, and relate it to work with numbers.

2. In some cases, visual patterns can serve as an immediate self-check for work with numbers. For example, in Activity 2, children who have recently learned the "Nine Times Table" can probably catch an error once a few squares have been colored in.

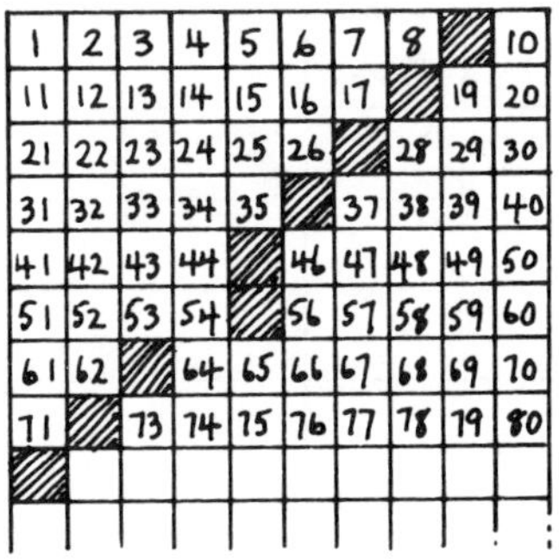

1	2	3	4	5	6	7	8	▨	10
11	12	13	14	15	16	17	▨	19	20
21	22	23	24	25	26	▨	28	29	30
31	32	33	34	35	▨	37	38	39	40
41	42	43	44	▨	46	47	48	49	50
51	52	53	54	▨	56	57	58	59	60
61	62	▨	64	65	66	67	68	69	70
71	▨	73	74	75	76	77	78	79	80
▨									

Examples of the use of visual self-checks are given in some materials from the Madison Project.[1] One enrichment activity for fifth or sixth graders leads to their investigating patterns made by making graphs for solutions to sentences in two variables. Try this sentence.

$$\triangle = 8 - 2 \times \square$$

One solution is (1,6) because $\triangle = 8 - 2 \times \boxed{1}$. (Notice that the $\square$ corresponds to the first position in the ordered pair, and the $\triangle$ corresponds to the second position.) The graph of the solution (1,6) is shown below. Find other solutions ($\square$, $\triangle$) and make a graph of them. (Optional) If $\square = 5$, then $\triangle =$ _____. Does the graph suggest what $8 - 10$ should equal here?

Guiding Discovery

> Betraying a secret that could be discovered by
> the child itself is bad pedagogics; it is even a
> crime. Who has not yet observed six year olds
> discovering and inventing, and who does not
> know how angry they can be if the secret is
> discovered too early? [2]

In Activity 6, A Pattern with Threes, you may have formulated the following rule that tells you when a number is divisible by 3: A number is divisible by 3 if and only if the sum of its digits is divisible by 3. (Check this rule on the number 1,020,304,050. First use the rule to see if 3 will divide this number evenly and then actually divide to check the answer.)

Did you formulate the rule this way? Do you think you would have found the rule if the Activity had been phrased, "Find how to tell if a number is divisible by 3," without suggesting adding the digits?

In Activity 6 you were expected to discover a divisibility rule for 3. In what other Activities in this chapter were you led to discover a rule or a pattern? Do you think that you discovered the patterns intended?

Many mathematics educators today call for "discovery teaching" of mathematics — exposing children to some general question or situation and letting them discover solutions or patterns. Mathematics textbooks often have special segments of discovery activities. Many people enjoy discovering things for themselves more than being told. Also, you probably remember things that you have discovered longer than things learned by rote. However, teaching by discovery is not easy!

First, discovery takes time. Children need much more time to experiment, form ideas, and check them than to copy a rule from the board and apply it as shown by the teacher. Teachers may find themselves pressured to cover other material and unable to make the necessary amount of time available. They may also feel nervous about spending a large amount of time on mathematics that is not directly related to possible test questions. Children may *enjoy* discovery activities, but does this enjoyment guarantee their learning necessary techniques and skills in mathematics? Sometimes children who are allowed free range will make wild guesses and try long unproductive false leads. On the other hand, some children may become frustrated and give up — they may learn that someone else will eventually discover what is meant to be discovered, so why not just wait? Children who have made the discovery may blurt it out and spoil the discovery for others. Finally, a teacher conducting a discovery lesson must have a much more solid understanding of the mathematical ideas behind a question or situation than is required for a traditional expository lesson, because we can never predict just what possibilities children will investigate, and it helps children if the teacher knows more or less where these unexpected possibilities can lead.

In justifying a discovery approach to teaching, perhaps we should reexamine just why we are teaching mathematics. Of course, our goals should include the children's development of computational skills and their application in routine situations. We should also be concerned that children develop and use their curiosity and creative talents; that they learn to apply their skills in new and unexpected situations; that they develop their abilities to analyze, abstract, and reason about their experiences; and that they become self-confident and able to communicate with their peers. Many discovery activities can accomplish a wide range of goals such as those listed above and, at the same time, develop skills in computation.

Discovery situations and activities must be presented with appropriate structure or guidance. Here are a few suggestions for implementing discovery lessons.

1. Make sure that the situation or challenge is understood by all of the children involved. It is desirable to have a situation that can be solved on various levels. For example, A Calendar and Multiples in Activity 2 could be done by counting off every third space; or by thinking mentally "$1 \times 3 = 3$, $2 \times 3 = 6$, $3 \times 3 = 9 \ldots$"; or perhaps by noticing that there is a broader pattern (multiples of 3 lie on a diagonal because on a calendar going down one space and to the left one space corresponds to adding 6, or 2×3). If children can work on this variety of levels, they may avoid the frustration of not knowing where to start and the boredom of having finished before their classmates.

2. Encourage group interaction. Children should learn to express their ideas and to listen to the ideas of their peers. They should also learn that there are usually alternative ways of making a discovery or explaining it. An activity might require that everyone contribute some piece of information. However, it is important not to let discoveries be verbalized too soon. To prevent some children from blurting out a discovery before others have had sufficient opportunity to discover it, a teacher can have children raise their hands if they think they have the answer and go over and check it. This provides recognition and reinforcement needed by the children. Also children should be encouraged to test their rules or theories before they verbalize them.

3. Be prepared to guide discussion with appropriate questions to get children to see for themselves that some investigations will be unproductive, to encourage good starts, and to help children clarify their ideas. Appropriate questioning by the teacher can help children benefit both from discovery learning and from their teacher's knowledge of the mathematics involved.

4. Summarize and help children state conclusions. Discovery lessons can end in an atmosphere of confusion if patterns developed are not clearly stated and agreed upon. Also, it is interesting for children to see that the same situation can lead to different patterns or different ways of describing the same pattern.

A Closer Look at the Mathematics Behind the Activities

In the Activities in this chapter you may have noticed certain patterns, but you may not have been quite sure about how these patterns fit into mathematics. Now we will examine how certain mathematical topics were embodied in the Activities and could be developed further.

Number of Factors
In Activity 1, you filled out a table for the number of factors of a number from 1 to 16. Were crickets helpful in finding and "seeing" the factors of 8? _____ of 16? _____ You may have found it easier to *think* what are the

factors of 16 than to act it out on a number line (but of course you *do* know your multiplication facts — some children might need to make the crickets "jump" to check their basic facts).

For children who are confident about multiplication facts, Activity 1 could be extended. This works well as an activity for the whole class, because while it is tedious for one person to fill in *all* the spaces, it goes quickly if each person contributes one or two entries. For example, each student in a fourth grade class could provide two answers in the table below, which could be written on the chalkboard or on an overhead projector. Fill in the missing entries. When you are looking for factors, check carefully. You might use the method shown here for some factors of 24. Do you see how they are paired? What factor is missing? _____ As you complete the table, look for patterns.

{ 1, 2, 3, 4, 6, 8, 24 }

Number	1	2	3	4	5	6	7	8	9	10	11	12	13	14	15	16	17	18
Number of factors	1	2	2	3	2	4	2	4	3	4	2	6	2	4	4	5	2	8

Number	19	20	21	22	23	24	25	26	27	28	29	30	31	32	33	34	35	36
Number of factors	2																	

Did you notice any patterns in the table?

1. Which numbers have 3 factors? _____ Write the next three numbers that have *exactly* 3 factors. What kind of numbers are these?

2. Which numbers have 4 factors? _____ Predict and check three more numbers that have exactly 4 factors. _____ _____ What do you notice about these numbers?

3. Which numbers have an *odd* number of factors? _____ What do these numbers have in common?

A Challenge: A formula can tell you how many factors a number will have if you know its prime factorization. Can you find the formula? (**Hint:** First look at numbers of the form $p \times p \times p \times \ldots \times p$ or p^n, where p is a prime number. Then try numbers of the form $q \times p^n$ where p and q are different primes.)

Unique Factorization Theorem

In Activity 4, Factor Trees, you were asked to describe what factor trees for the number 189 have in common. Perhaps you noticed that they all "ended" with three 3's and one 7, in some order. The trick described below is related to this observation.

Guess the Color Trick

This trick calls for a set of colored cubes. The class agrees that red stands for 2, green for 3, and blue for 5. Each child picks some cubes of these colors and multiplies their values together. For example, if a green and two blues were picked, the result would be $3 \times 5 \times 5 = 75$. The child then tells the class *only* the answer — 75, in this case.

Could you tell *just* from the answer what colors were picked? What would 2 reds, 1 green, and 2 blues yield as an answer? _____ What cubes would give 4? _____ 6? _____ 12? _____ _____ Can *you* tell what cubes are used if someone tells you only the final product? Describe your method.

This trick may seem startling at first — just tell the number that is the product and you are told how many cubes of each color you have! What makes it work is a theorem that mathematicians call *The Fundamental Theorem of Arithmetic,* or *The Unique Factorization Theorem.* This states that any number can be factored into primes in *just one way* (except for order). That is, 189 could be factored to give $7 \times 3 \times 3 \times 3$, or $3 \times 7 \times 3 \times 3$, or _____, or _____, but whatever the form of the factorization, it must contain exactly three 3's and one 7 and no other primes. This means that in Guess the Color Trick, only one color combination is possible for a given number so long as only *prime* numbers are used for the colors. To find the colors, simply make a factor tree. (It is more dramatic if you can do it in your head!)

Try this trick on someone and see if your ability to guess the colors surprises them. (**Warning:** The trick may not work if the colors do not all represent prime numbers. For example, suppose red stood for 2, green for 3, and blue for 4. A child picks a certain collection of cubes, multiplies, and gets 48. List three *different* collections of cubes he might have.)

The Sieve Again

In Activity 3, you used the Sieve of Eratosthenes to find all prime numbers less than 200. You may have used more, but in fact you only *needed* to use six steps or colors (one for each of the primes 2, 3, 5, 7, 11, and 13). One way to see why this is so is to examine the chart on page 457. At each step in the sieve process, the first *new* number to be crossed out is the square of the prime number whose multiples are being "sieved." Thus for 11, the first new number to be crossed out is 11^2 or 121, for 13 it is 13^2 or 169, and for 17 it would be 17^2 or 289. Since 289 is greater than 200, sieving out the multiples of 17 will remove no new numbers from your charts. All the remaining numbers are prime.

How would you determine whether or not 323 is a prime number?

Of course you *could* extend the number chart up to 323, and continue the sieving process with colored pencils, but this would be tedious. However you can use the principle of the sieve method to quickly determine if 323 is prime. Imagine that you were doing the sieve process. Would 323 be crossed off as a multiple of 2? _____ That is, does 2 divide 323? _____ does 3? _____ Why *don't* you need to check to see if 4 divides 323? _____ does 5? _____ does 7? _____ does 11? _____

You might wonder at this point how many prime numbers you must check as possible divisors of 323. Again use the idea in the chart on page 457: $13^2 = 169$, $17^2 = 289$, and $19^2 = 361$, which is greater than 323. Thus if 323 is not a prime, it must be crossed off as a multiple of 17 at the latest, and so you need only check the prime numbers up to 17 as possible divisors.

Does 13 divide 323? _____ Does 17 divide 323? _____ Is 323 a prime?

In general, to see if a number is prime, find the greatest prime number whose square is less than the given number, and check all primes less than or equal to that prime as possible divisors.

(Optional) Use a calculator to see if the following numbers are prime. This would be a tedious task to undertake without a calculator. With a calculator, you should be able to do it in a few minutes if you follow the procedure outlined above. 437 _____ 937 _____ 1073 _____

How Many Primes Are There?

At each stage in the sieve, more numbers get crossed out as composites. Will we eventually get to the point beyond which *all* numbers will be crossed out? That is, will we eventually run out of primes?

This question can be answered in much the same way as a child's questions, "What is the greatest (whole) number?" or "How many numbers are there?" You can show that there can be no greatest number because however great a number is, you can always add 1 to get an even greater number — there are infinitely many whole numbers.

In much the same way the ancient Greek mathematicians were able to show that there is no greatest prime number. The following elegant trick was recorded by Euclid. Using it, you can show that however many primes you have, you can always find one more *new* one, and so there are infinitely many primes.

Suppose you know of n different primes. Call them $p_1, p_2, \ldots, p_n$. We will show how to find a new prime *not* on this list. Multiply all of the primes together to get $p_1 \times p_2 \times p_3 \times \ldots \times p_n$. Call this product N. This number N is certainly not prime. (Why?) If we add 1 to it, we will get a new number, $N + 1 = (p_1 \times p_2 \times \ldots \times p_n) + 1$. Notice that $N + 1$ cannot be evenly divisible by any of the primes on the list $p_1, p_2, p_3, \ldots p_n$ (because the remainder would always be 1). The Unique Factorization Theorem says that *any* number can be factored uniquely into primes, yet none of the prime factors of $N + 1$ can be on the list $p_1, p_2, \ldots, p_n$. And so either $N + 1$ or one of its factors is a *new* prime. For example, suppose that the only primes you know of are 2, 3, 5, and 7.

Then we would let $p_1 = 2$, $p_2 = 3$, $p_3 = 5$, and $p_4 = 7$.
Then, $N = p_1 \times p_2 \times p_3 \times p_4 = 2 \times 3 \times 5 \times 7 = 210$;
and $N + 1 = 211$. Is 211 a prime number? _____ If not, find its prime factorization.

Mathematicians have thus known for many centuries that there are infinitely many primes, but there are still many mysteries about exactly how they are distributed, and there is no formula known to guarantee a prime number. The use of computers has managed to extend the known list of primes enormously, since a computer can perform in moments calculations that would take an impossible amount of time for human beings. In 1963, a computer at the University of Illinois found a new prime — the largest yet known — $2^{11213} - 1$. This number has well over 4000 digits!

FOLLOW-UP SECTIONS

More Uses of the Hundred Chart

Activities 2 and 3 involved a rectangular array of numbers with "ten in a row." Such an array with 10 rows is called a *Hundred Chart* and can be used for many pattern-finding activities other than those suggested in Activities 2 and 3.

Arrows

The following activity can give children experience with learning a new symbolic language and looking for patterns. It can be used to reinforce certain mathematical topics, while at the same time introducing other topics. As you do the activity, try to identify the mathematical topics involved.

Hundred Chart

1	2	3	4	5	6	7	8	9	10
11	12	13	14	15	16	17	18	19	20
21	22	23	24	25	26	27	28	29	30
31	32	33	34	35	36	37	38	39	40
41	42	43	44	45	46	47	48	49	50
51	52	53	54	55	56	57	58	59	60
61	62	63	64	65	66	67	68	69	70
71	72	73	74	75	76	77	78	79	80
81	82	83	84	85	86	87	88	89	90
91	92	93	94	95	96	97	98	99	100

Travels on the Hundred Chart

Imagine yourself following directions and moving about on the Hundred Chart. Here is a code for movements: ↑ means move one square *up* on the number chart and → means move one space to the *right*. For example, 45 ↑ ↑ → means start at 45 and do the indicated moves: first two spaces up, then one to the right, ending up at 26. 45↑ → → ends at _____. What would ↓ mean? _____ What does 45 ↓ ↓ ← equal? _____ What would be meant by 60→? Many interpretations are possible. For example, some children might say, "You get stuck at the edge and stay at 60," while others might say, "You bounce back to 59." Let us agree that you should go on to the next line, so you would end up at 61. Find 38 ↓→ → →↓.

1. Find: 13 ↑→ →↓← = _____. 78 ↑↑↓→←↓ = _____.
   33 ↑→ →↓→↑→↓= _____.

2. Fill in: 12 ↓ = _____, 23↓ = _____, 46↓ = _____. Can you describe the arrow ↓ with addition? ↓ is the same as adding _____.

   12 ⟶ = _____, 23 ⟶ = _____, 46 ⟶ = _____; and so ⟶ is the same as adding _____. How would you write "add 42" in arrows? _____ subtract 10? _____ subtract 1? _____ subtract 21? _____

3. Write add 9 with arrows (using less than nine arrows). (**Hint:** You might include a↓.) _____ How could you write "subtract 9"? _____

4. What do you think 25 ↗ means? _____ Write ↗ as a combination of *two arrows.* ↗ = _____ What does ↗ mean in arithmetic? (Add or subtract what number?) _____ What about ↘ ? In arrows, ↘ = _____. In arithmetic, ↘ means _____.

5. Fill in the blanks. 65 ↑↑→↗↓↙←↓↑ ↑↑ ⟶↗ = _____ Find a simpler combination of arrows that gives the same result: 65 _____.
   Try this one. 43 ↓↓↘←←←↓↖↖↑↑⟶↘↓↓←←↗↓↑→↓↑= _____

6. Make up another complicated string of arrows (at least 10 arrows) and then make it simpler. Record it.

7. Have you noticed any short cuts when you are trying to simplify a long string of arrows? Describe a shortcut.

8. Try to do these problems *without* using the chart, and then use the chart to check.

   23↑↓↑↓→= _____   23↑↓→↓↑= _____   23→↑↑↓↓= _____
   23↓→←↗↓→↑↓↖ = _____   23↓↑→←↗↙ ↘↖ = _____   23 ↗↓← = _____

9. Does it matter in what order you do the arrows?
   Do you see any combinations that "cancel out"?

This activity perhaps gives an indication of how children can use the Hundred Chart to increase their experience with and understanding of place value, and of adding two-digit numbers. Also in parts (8) and (9) they are gaining experience with an early form of algebraic manipulation of symbols which may help them later when learning algebra more formally.[3]

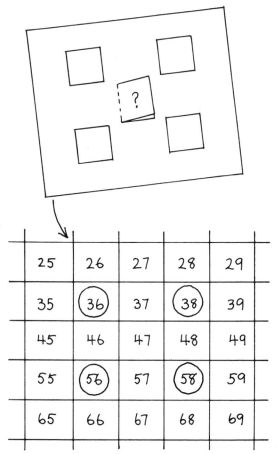

A Trick with Windows

The Hundred Chart can also be used to provide computational practice with two-digit numbers in an amusing self-checking way. You could make a "frame" to fit the Hundred Chart like the one drawn. It has four windows and a door (marked "?") that will open. Children can put this frame anywhere on the Hundred Chart so that four numbers show in the windows. Have children add up the four numbers that they see and then divide the sum by 4. (Try this. The numbers seen in the windows have been circled. Their sum is _____. Divide the sum by 4 to get _____.) Now have children open up the door. What do they see? Try this trick by placing the frame in another position. Does it work in any position? Would the trick work for a larger frame? Try it for 25, 29, 69 and 65.

25	26	27	28	29
35	⟨36⟩	37	⟨38⟩	39
45	46	47	48	49
55	⟨56⟩	57	⟨58⟩	59
65	66	67	68	69

A Challenge: Can you explain why this trick works? (You might explain it using arrows. What happens when you add 36, 36 ↓↓ , 36 → → , and 36 ↓↓ → →, and then divide by 4?) Does it work on other number charts? Try it on the number charts in Activity 2.

Another Trick

Use the Hundred Chart. Circle *any* five neighboring numbers in a row or in a column or in a diagonal. (For example, you might choose 1,2,3,4,5, or 1,11,21,31,41, or 1,12,23,34,35.) Your numbers are _____, _____, _____, _____, _____. Add them up. The sum of your number is _____. Double the sum. The result is _____. If you picked the row across starting at 21, you would have found $(21 + 22 + 23 + 24 + 25) \times 2 = 230$.

Do you notice anything? Try some more examples. You should be able to predict your result very easily just by looking at the middle number chosen. *A Challenge:* Does this trick work on any number chart? Can you see why it works?

There are many more such computational tricks you can do on the Hundred Chart.[4] Perhaps you can find some of your own.

More Patterns

In Chapter 2, Number and Its Uses, you saw two classical number patterns which arise in many places. These patterns had mystical significance to the followers of the Greek mathematician Pythagoras (ca. 580–500 B.C.).[5] Complete these patterns of "figurate" numbers.

Triangular numbers

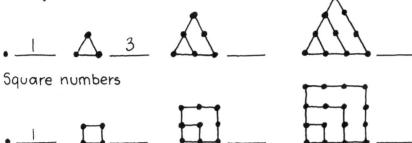

Square numbers

These two patterns fit into even larger patterns in several different ways.

Pentagonal Numbers

(Fill in and draw one more.)

Can you guess what the number pattern will be for *hexagonal* numbers? **Hint:** Examine the numbers arranged to the right; what patterns do you see? (Try taking differences of rows and columns.) Check your guess by drawing and counting some hexagonal numbers. (The grid pattern below might help you to draw them.)

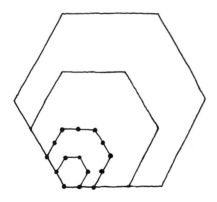

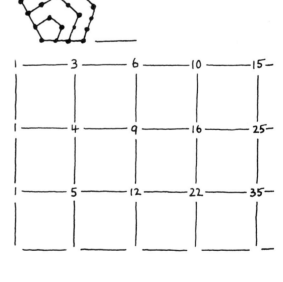

Triangles and Squares

For convenience, let us call the nth triangular number T_n, and the nth square number S_n. That is, T_1 is 1, T_2 is the number of dots $\therefore$ and so $T_2 = 3$. Fill in the blanks.

$T_1 = 1$ $T_2 = 3$ $T_3 =$ _____ $T_4 =$ _____ $T_5 =$ _____

$S_1 = 1$ $S_2 = 4$ $S_3 =$ _____ $S_4 =$ _____ $S_5 =$ _____

Try these calculations. What patterns do you see?

$T_1 + T_2 =$ _____ $T_2 + T_3 =$ _____

$T_3 + T_4 =$ _____ $T_4 + T_5 =$ _____

This pattern can be stated as a general rule: Complete: $T_n + T_{n+1} = S\ \square$. (If you do not see the pattern, check your calculations carefully.) Do you see why the pattern works? Perhaps the diagram below helps.

Pyramidal Numbers

Here is another number pattern. You may find it helpful to build these pyramids from cubes (of wood or sugar). Do you see how this number pattern relates to one of those above? (**Hint:** Take differences between successive terms.)

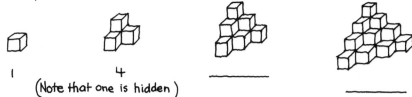

1   4   _____   _____

(Note that one is hidden)

Patterns in Tables of 1–100

A 10 by 10 square grid can be filled in with numbers 1–100 in many ways. A few are shown on page 475. What patterns do you see?

Do you see patterns or rules that allow you to fill in the spaces marked "?" without actually counting or filling in the other spaces?

A *Challenge:* Describe the patterns or rules for finding the numbers in the spaces marked "?":

Grid 1: _____

Grid 2: _____

Grid 3: _____

Grid 4: _____

Grid 1

1	2	3	4	5	6	7	8	9	10
11	12	13	14	15	16	17	18	19	20
21	22	23	24	25	26	27	28	29	30
31	32	33	34	35	36→				
						?			
					?				
				?					

Grid 2

1	3	6	10	15	21	28	36	?	?
2	5	9	14	20	27	35			
4	8	13	19	26	34				
7	12	18	25	33					
11	17	24	32						
16	23	31							
22	30		?						
29									
↗									

Grid 3

								?
							?	
	21	22	23	24	25	26		
	20	7	8	9	10	27		
	19	6	1	2	11	28		
	18	5	4	3	12	29		
	17	16	15	14	13	30		
←36	35	34	33	32	31			
?								
?								

Grid 4

28	27	26	25	24	23	22	21	20	19
29									18
30									17
31									16
32									15
33			?						14
34		?							13
35	?								12
36→									11
1	2	3	4	5	6	7	8	9	10

Do you see where the triangular numbers appear in a neat pattern in one of the grids? _____ the square numbers?

GCF, LCM, and Other Mathematical Topics

Try these two exercises. 1. Express $\frac{16}{24}$ in lowest terms.

2. Add $\frac{1}{12} + \frac{1}{8}$.

There are various ways in which you might have done these exercises. Perhaps in the first one, you realized that 8 is the largest possible divisor of both 16 and 24, and so you thought $\frac{16}{24} = \frac{16 \div 8}{24 \div 8} = \frac{2}{3}$. However you *might* have instead used several steps, for example, $\frac{16}{24} = \frac{16 \div 2}{24 \div 2} = \frac{8}{12} = \frac{8 \div 4}{12 \div 4} = \frac{2}{3}$. In the second exercise, you may have realized that 24 is the smallest number that is a multiple of both 8 and 12, and so you selected 24 as the common denominator and wrote $\frac{1}{12} + \frac{1}{8} = \frac{2}{24} + \frac{3}{24} = \frac{5}{24}$. However you might have used another number as a common denominator, perhaps $8 \times 12 = 96$. Then you would have written $\frac{1}{12} + \frac{1}{8} = \frac{8}{96} + \frac{12}{96} = \frac{20}{96}$ or $\frac{5}{24}$.

Exercises of these two types with fractions provide applications of *Greatest Common Factor* (GCF) and *Least Common Multiple* (LCM). In both cases, their use is not *necessary,* but rather only convenient for performing the operation. Thus these applications do not seem to justify the inclusion of GCF and LCM in the elementary school curriculum. However children might study these two topics to enrich their background in other areas of mathematics — for example, sets, binary operations, and prime factorization as illustrated by the activities below. As you do these activities, think about what kinds of mathematical thinking you are using — for example, finding a pattern, reasoning logically, forming and checking a hypothesis.

(**Note:** In these examples, similar exercises involving GCF and LCM are presented together because they have the same sort of structure. However many children get GCF and LCM confused, perhaps because they are so often treated together. Some educators recommend teaching them at different times to avoid this confusion.)

Loops

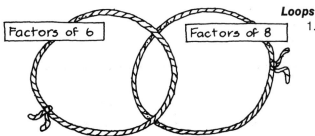

1. Fill in the loops with as many whole numbers as possible.

(**Note:** Your placement should like like).

What is the greatest number in the intersection of the two sets? What is the GCF of 6 and 8?

2. In these examples, the labels are incomplete. What could they be? No more numbers belong in the loops, and each dot stands for a different number. Some have several possible answers. Which are impossible?

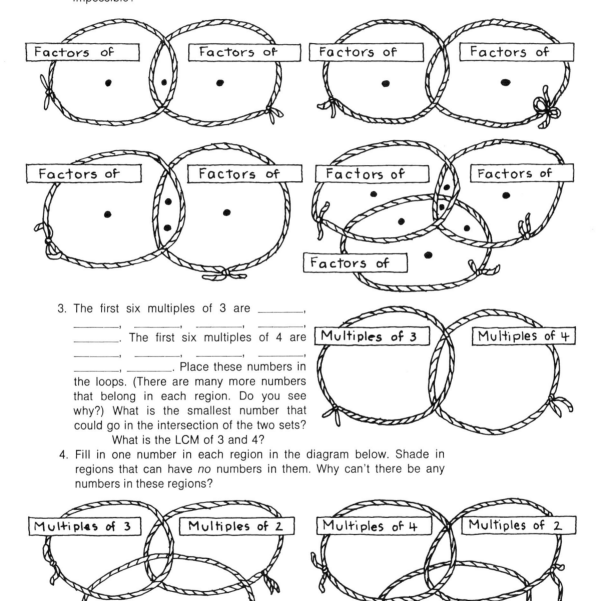

3. The first six multiples of 3 are _____, _____, _____, _____, _____, _____. The first six multiples of 4 are _____, _____, _____, _____, _____, _____. Place these numbers in the loops. (There are many more numbers that belong in each region. Do you see why?) What is the smallest number that could go in the intersection of the two sets?
    What is the LCM of 3 and 4?

4. Fill in one number in each region in the diagram below. Shade in regions that can have *no* numbers in them. Why can't there be any numbers in these regions?

Arrow Diagrams Revisited

In Activity 5, Arrows and Machines, in Chapter 5, you were asked to guess the rules for various arrow diagrams and machines which related to operations on whole numbers. Try these three examples. Fill in the missing spaces in each and guess the rule for each.

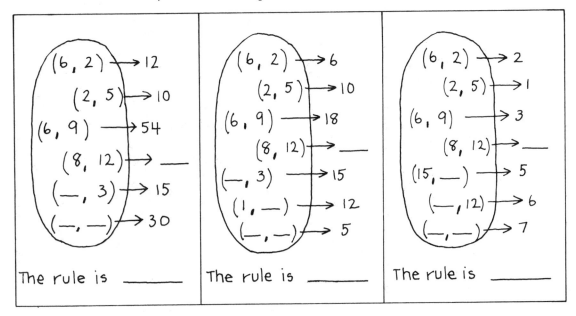

The rule is _____   The rule is _____   The rule is _____

Do you think that these diagrams would provide a suitable context for introducing the ideas of GCF and LCM to children? for reviewing these ideas?

Tables

The examples above indicate that GCF and LCM resemble multiplication in that to any given pair of numbers, each associates another number. That is, they are all *binary operations*.

The operation of GCF might be written in a simpler form. Instead of the GCF of 2 and 6, we might write 2 * 6, which is equal to 2. Fill in the blanks.

$$6 * 4 = _____ \quad 1 * 12 = _____ \quad 3 * 6 = _____$$

Consider just the set of factors of 12 — {1, 2, 3, 4, 6, 12}. Complete this table for GCF on this set. Note how 2 * 3 = 1 has been entered in the table — in the *row* labeled "2" and in the *column* labeled "3." Use your completed table to answer these questions.

*	1	2	3	4	6	12
1						
2			1			
3						
4						
6						
12						

1. If you take any two numbers in this set, is their GCF also in this set? _____ (You should find that this is easy to check — all entries in the table should be 1's, 2's, 3's, 4's, 6's, or 12's.)

This says that the operation GCF is *closed* on the set {1,2,3,4,6,12}, or that the binary operation of GCF satisfies the closure property on the set {1,2,3,4,6,12}.
Is the operation of GCF closed on the set {1,2,4,6,15}? Explain.

2. Is there an identity for this operation; that is, is there some number N such that N * ☐ = ☐ * N = ☐ whatever you choose ☐ to be? _____ How can you tell from the table?

3. Is this operation commutative? _____ How can you tell easily from the table?

4. Is this operation associative? (**Note:** This is difficult to check thoroughly — test a few examples.) Does (3 * 4) * 6 equal 3 * (4 * 6)? Try two more examples.

5. Do you notice anything else special about this operation? If so, can you detect this as some pattern in the table?

In the same way, the LCM is a binary operation on whole numbers. Again, consider the set {1,2,3,4,6,12} and complete the table. We might write 2 o 3 for the LCM of 2 and 3 which is 6. Note how this has been entered in the table. Use the table to answer these questions.

Is "o" closed on this set?
Is there an identity for "o"?
Is "o" commutative?
Is "o" associative?
Do you notice anything else special about this operation?

o	1	2	3	4	6	12
1						
2			6			
3						
4						
6						
12						

Shortcuts

You have probably been finding the GCF and the LCM by testing various factors and multiples of each number. For example, to find the GCF of 4 and 6 you might run through the factors of 4 (1, 2, and 4) and select the largest one which is also a factor of 6 (2). To find the LCM of 4 and 6 you might run through the multiples of 4 in your head (4, 8, 12, . . .) until you find one that is also a multiple of 6 (12). This method may not be practical for finding the GCF and the LCM of larger numbers, for example 144 and 96. However it is easy to find these if you use the prime factorization of each number.

Examine the table on page 480, in which is given the prime factorization of some pairs of numbers, and of their GCF and LCM. Some prime factors have been circled to help you find the GCF. Why were they circled?

Fill in the blanks in the table and try to formulate the rule.

A	B	GCF of A and B	LCM of A and B
12 = ②×2×③	90 = ②×③× 3 × 5	6 = 2 × 3	180 = 2×2 × 3× 3 × 5
8 = ②×②×2	20 = ②×② × 5	4 = 2 × 2	40 = 2×2 × 2 × 5
9 = 3 × 3	40 = 2 × 2 × 2 × 5	1	360 = 2× 2 ×2×3×3×5
15 = ③× 5	12 = 2 × 2 × ③	3	60 = 2×2× 3 × 5
20 = ②×②×5	36 = ②×②× 3 × 3		
30 =	40 =		
100 =	45 =		

Complete the following:

To find the GCF of two numbers, look at their prime factorizations and
_____ .

To find the LCM of two numbers, look at their prime factorizations and
_____ .

Divisibility Rules

Is the number 521,368 a prime number? _____ Is 29,345 a prime number? _____ Probably you answered these two questions very quickly, because it is in general very easy to tell if a number is divisible by 2 (or *even*) or by 5 without actually dividing. Complete the following:

A number is divisible by 2 if and only if its last digit is _____
A number is divisible by 5 if and only if its last digit is _____

These are examples of *divisibility rules* — ways in which you can tell easily if a number is divisible by a certain number just by looking at the digits. You found another example of a divisibility rule in Activity 6, A Pattern with Threes; namely, that a number is divisible by 3 if and only if the sum of its digits is divisible by 3.

To see why these (and other) divisibility rules hold, it is helpful to know a few facts about divisibility. Examine the conjectures in the left-hand column (page 481). Some are always true, while some are not. In the right-hand column, provide examples and decide whether the conjecture is true or false. Two have been done.

(Optional) Try to prove that the true ones are true.

Note: Here *divides* means divides evenly. *a* divides *b* means that $b = a \times x$ for some whole number *x*. Thus 2 divides 4 is true, but 3 divides 4 is false and 4 divides 2 is false.

Conjectures	Examples
1. If *a* divides *b* and *a* divides *c*, then *a* divides $b + c$.	2 divides 4 and 2 divides 6, 2 also divides $4 + 6 = 10$. This is always true: *a* divides *b* means $b = a \times x$; *a* divides *c* means $c = a \times y$; for some whole numbers *x* and *y*. $b + c = (a \times x) + (a \times y)$ $= a \times (x + y)$ and so *a* divides $b + c$.
2. If *a* divides $b + c$, then *a* divides *b* and *a* divides *c*.	This is *not* always true, because 2 divides $5 + 3$, but 2 does not divide either 5 or 3.
3. If *a* divides *b* and *a* divides *c*, then *a* divides $b - c$.	
4. If *a* divides *b*, then *a* divides $b \times c$.	
5. If *a* divides $b \times c$, then *a* divides *b* or *a* divides *c*.	

You should have found that only conjectures 1, 3, and 4 are true. Now we will use them to explain why some of the divisibility rules work. For example, one rule states that if the last digit of a number is even, then 2 divides the number.

To show that 2 divides 34,678, you can write $34,678 = 34,670 + 8$. Now 2 divides 10, and $34,670 = 10 \times 3467$, and so 2 divides 34,670 (by conjecture). Also, 2 divides the last digit 8 since $8 = 2 \times 4$, and so by conjecture (1) we can conclude that 2 divides $34,670 + 8 = 34,678$.

Use this procedure to show that 5 divides 12,345.

Another rule says that if 2 divides a number, then its last digit must be even.

Suppose you know that 2 divides 742○. (The last digit is smudged.) How can we be sure that ○ is even? Notice that $742○ - 7420 = ○$. We know that 2 divides 742 ○ and also 2 divides 7240. (Why?) By conjecture (3) it follows that 2 divides $742 ○ - 7420 = ○$, and so ○ is even.

You probably knew these rules for 2 and 5 before. Do you know a rule for 4? or for 9? Look at the examples below and try to formulate divisibility rules for 4 and 9.

Consider the number 35,412. We can write $35,412 = 35,400 + 12$. 4 divides 100, and so 4 divides $100 \times 354 = 35,400$. Also, 4 divides 12, and so 4 divides the sum $35,400 + 12 = 35,412$.

Rule: 4 divides a number if _____.

Consider the number 3213. We can write it as
$$3 \times 1000 + 2 \times 100 + 1 \times 10 + 3 \text{ or as}$$
$$3 \times (999 + 1) + 2 \times (99 + 1) + 1 \times (9 + 1) + 3.$$
If you apply the distributive property of multiplication over addition and rearrange terms, you see that
$$3213 = [(3 \times 999 + (2 \times 99) + (1 \times 9)] + (3 + 2 + 1 + 3)$$
Now 9 divides $(3 \times 999) + (2 \times 99) + (1 \times 9)$. (Why?) Also, 9 divides the sum $3 + 2 + 1 + 3 = 9$. So 9 divides 3213.

Rule: 9 divides a number if _____.

(**Hint:** This resembles the divisibility rule for 3.)

Using Divisibility to Check Computations

1. Pick a column (top to bottom) in the number chart to the right. For each number in your column, find the sum of the digits. (If the sum of the digits is greater than 10, find the sum of the digits again, for example,
$$93 \to 9 + 3 = 12 \to 1 + 2 = 3.)$$
What do you notice?

Now divide each number in your column by 9. What remainder do you get? _____ Try it for another column. Is your result the same? [6]

A	B	C	D	E	F	G	H	I
1	2	3	4	5	6	7	8	9
10	11	12	13	14	15	16	17	18
19	20	21	22	23	24	25	26	27
28	29	30	31	32	33	34	35	36
37	38	39	40	41	42	43	44	45
46	47	48	49	50	51	52	53	54
55	56	57	58	59	60	61	62	63
64	65	66	67	68	69	70	71	72
73	74	75	76	77	78	79	80	81
82	83	84	85	86	87	88	89	90
91	92	93	94	95	96	97	98	99
100	101	102	103	104	.	.	.	.

2. Now suppose that we pick two different columns — for example, columns C and E. Pick a number from each of these columns and add them — for example, $12 + 23 = 35$. In what column is the result? _____ (Record this in the table.) Try this for 3 more pairs of numbers from columns C and E, and record your results.

In what column were the answers? [7]

Number from Column C	Number from Column E	Column of Sum
12	23	

Try this idea for subtraction. Pick two columns _____ and _____. Now pick a number from each column, and find the difference. In what column is the difference? _____ Record this result. Try it for three more pairs of numbers from the two columns you chose and record your results in the chart to the right.

Is the difference always in the same column? _____ Does it depend on which column you select the larger number from?

Number from Column __	Number from Column __	Column of Difference

Try this idea for multiplication also. Does the same trick work?

A Challenge: Does this trick work on *any* number chart? You can try it on the three charts on page 455. If you take any number from the first column and add it to any number in the third column, will the answer always be in the fourth column? Does it work for difference and product? Do you see why these tricks work?

3. Two main ideas have just been presented: (a) the sum of the digits tells you in what column a number will appear in a chart of nine in a row; and (b) if you know what columns two numbers appear in, you know where their sum, difference, and product will appear. These two ideas can be put together to provide a simple check for many arithmetic computations with whole numbers. This check makes use of what is sometimes called casting out nines. This is how it works for multiplication.

```
  3 7
× 4 3
─────
  1 1 1
1 4 8
─────
1 5 9 1
```

Suppose that you wanted to check this multiplication. Find the sum of the digits of the two numbers being multiplied:

$$37 \rightarrow 3 + 7 = 10 \longrightarrow 1 + 0 = 1$$
$$43 \rightarrow 4 + 3 = 7$$

Do the operation (multiplication) on the sums of the digits: $1 \times 7 = ⑦$. Check by finding the sum of the digits of the answer, 1591:

$$1591 \rightarrow 1 + 5 + 9 + 1 = 16 \rightarrow 1 + 6 = ⑦. \text{ It agrees.}$$

This does not guarantee that the answer is correct, but it does provide a partial check.

Here is a simpler way to write the check.

```
  3 7  ────────→ 10 ──────────→ 1
× 4 3  ──────────────────────→ × 7
─────                            ───
  1 1 1                          ⑦
1 4 8                            ↕
─────                            ⑦
1 5 9 1 ──────→ 16 ──────→ ⑦
```

It agrees.

This procedure can be used to check addition, subtraction, and multiplication easily. Try it with these.

```
  1 3 9      1 2 7 8      3 4 9 0 1
× 5 7      + 6 7 9 2     −   7 8 9 2
```

TEST YOUR UNDERSTANDING

1. Show by a number-line drawing and by an array that 8 is not a prime.
2. Is 437 a prime number? Exactly which primes must you check as possible divisors if you use the Sieve of Eratosthenes?
3. Fill in the blanks in the factor tree on the next page for 240.
   Make a different factor tree for 240.
   What do factor trees for primes look like?

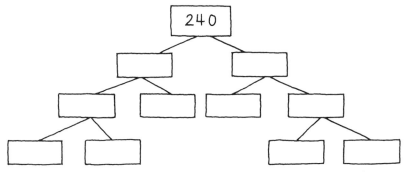

4. Investigate: When is the *difference* of two primes a prime?
5. Below are some numbers written in a code. Can you crack the code and figure out how to write the next few numbers in code? (**Hint:** This code is related to the discussion on page 468.)

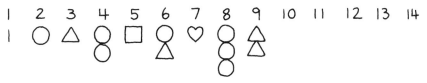

6. Describe some everyday uses of number theory concepts, such as odd, even, prime, multiple, and divisor.
7. Describe two uses of number patterns to provide drill or practice with basic number skills.
8. Fill in the loops with as many whole numbers as possible.
   Fill in the labels on this loop diagram. Each dot stands for a different number, and no more numbers belong in the loops.

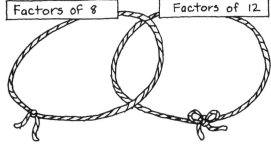

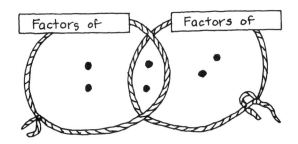

9. The LCM of two numbers is 120, and their GCF is 6. What are the two numbers? Is there more than one pair of numbers that work here? If so, give a second pair.

10. Use the computational check involving nines (see page 484) to check these exercises.

$$476 \quad\quad 476$$
$$+189 \quad \times189$$
$$\overline{665} \quad \overline{89{,}994}$$

11. Suppose that the number 3 6 4,1 2 ⟳ is divisible by 3. (The last digit is smudged.) What could the last digit be? What could the last digit be if the number is also divisible by 2?

A	B	GCF of A and B	LCM of A and B	A×B
4	6			
3	5			
20	30			

12. Here is another pattern relating GCF, LCM, and the product of two numbers. Fill in the table. Try some more.

13. Make a table for the operation GCF on the set of all factors of 30. (There should be 8 factors.) Then answer questions 1–4 on pages 478–479 about this situation. Repeat for the operation LCM on the set of all factors of 30.

14. Can you find a way to relate triangular and square numbers to pentagonal numbers (see pp. 473–474)? **Hint:** Fill in the blanks below.
$$T_1 + S_2 = \text{_____} \quad\quad T_3 + S_4 = \text{_____}$$
$$T_2 + S_3 = \text{_____} \quad\quad T_4 + S_5 = \text{_____}$$
Can you generalize? $T_n + S_{n+1} = \text{_____}$.
Can you make a geometric pattern that shows why this is so? (**Hint:** Look at the arrangement of dots shown here.)

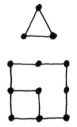 

FURTHER READINGS AND PROJECTS

1. Many mathematical topics and problems have interesting historical origins. Children may be interested in hearing about these origins or in researching them themselves. One good source is *Historical Topics for the Mathematics Classroom,* the Thirty-first Yearbook of the National Council of

Teachers of Mathematics (Washington, D.C.: NCTM, 1969). Read some of the following articles on number theory and describe how you might use ideas in the articles when teaching number theory topics.

"Number Beliefs of the Pythagoreans" (pp. 51–52)
"Figurate Numbers" (pp. 53–58)
"Amicable Numbers" (pp. 58–59)
"Perfect, Deficient, and Abundant Numbers" (pp. 59–61)
"The Infinitude of Primes" (pp. 62–63)
"Eratosthenes" (pp. 72–76)
"Numerology and Gematria" (pp. 74–76)

2. The "Ideas for Teachers" section (pp. 28–32) of *The Arithmetic Teacher,* 25:5 (February 1978) contains two classroom posters and a description of accompanying activities involving pattern recognition and problem solving on a Hundred Chart. Try some of the problems in this section. You might also try problems in Wallace Judd's *Patterns to Play on a Hundred Chart* (Palo Alto, California: Creative Publications, 1975), or read "A New Look for the Hundred's Chart" by Winfred Randolph and Verne Jeffers (*The Arithmetic Teacher,* 21:3 (March 1974), pp. 203–208), which describes uses of the chart for counting, money, and operations on whole numbers and patterns.

3. Read Chapter 3, "Organizing for Individualization: A Classroom Model," in *Organizing for Mathematics Instruction,* the 1977 Yearbook of the National Council of Teachers of Mathematics. Ways are discussed for individualizing inexpensively within a classroom. Examples are drawn from the upper elementary grades and related to number theory topics. Comment on the "types" of learning situations made available to the students.

4. Read "Gus' Magic Numbers: A Key to the Divisibility Tests for Primes" by Charlene Oliver (*The Arithmetic Teacher,* 19:3 (March 1972), pp. 183–189), which presents an interesting account of how a student developed some tests himself. Then read and try the sample problems in "On Divisibility Rules" by Harold Tinnappel, pp. 227–233 of *Enrichment Mathematics for the Grades,* the 1963 Yearbook of the National Council of Teachers of Mathematics.

5. Examine "Number Theory and Patterns," Section 6 in Seaton E. Smith and Carl A. Backman, eds., *Games and Puzzles for Elementary and Middle School Mathematics — Readings from The Arithmetic Teacher* (Reston, Virginia: NCTM, 1975). Which articles did you find most interesting?

6. The Introduction to *Notes on Mathematics in Primary Schools* (London: Cambridge University Press, 1967) notes the importance of enriching the mathematical experiences of young children. The book contains many examples of ways to do this. Section 5, "Visual Representations," provides examples of how numerical relationships can be explored by looking for visual patterns, reflecting a theme discussed on page 464 of this chapter, as well as in other chapters of this book. Which of the ideas in Section 5 have you seen so far in this book? Which do you find most interesting?

7. The discovery of number patterns is sometimes included in textbook materials as an enrichment activity. Examine a text series and see if you can find examples of situations where children are encouraged to find and describe patterns of numbers. If you do not find such examples, do you see how

you could supplement the text materials with interesting challenges involving number patterns?

NOTES

1. See, for example, Robert Davis, *Discovery in Mathematics: A Text for Teachers* (Palo Alto, California: Addison-Wesley, 1965).

2. H. Freudenthal, *Mathematics as an Educational Task* (Boston: Reidel, 1973), p. 417.

3. The potential of this approach is described more thoroughly by David A. Page in *Maneuvers on Lattices, An Example of "Intermediate Invention"* (Watertown, Mass.: Educational Services Inc., 1965).

4. For more examples, see Wallace Judd, *Patterns to Play on a Hundred Chart* (Palo Alto, California: Creative Publications, Inc., 1975).

5. See "Figurate Numbers" (pp. 53–58) and "Numerology and Gematria" (pp. 74–76), in the 1969 NCTM Yearbook, *Historical Topics for the Mathematics Classroom* (Washington, D.C.: NCTM, 1969).

6. You should have found that if you divided a number by 9, the remainder is the same as the sum of the digits of the original number (assuming that you found the sum of the digits again if the original sum was over 10).

7. It is not difficult to see why this trick works. Numbers in Column C are of the form $9n + 3$ (where $n = 0,1,2, \ldots$) and in Column E they are of the form $9m + 5$ (where $m = 0,1,2, \ldots$). If you add numbers of these forms, you get $(9n + 3) + (9m + 5) = (9n + 9m) + (3 + 5) = 9 \times (n + m) + 8$. Numbers of this form ($9s + 8$) are all in Column H. Try this rationale on the other examples.

CHAPTER 11

RATIONAL NUMBERS

INTRODUCTION

When do you use fractions? List as many situations as you can where you have used fractions recently.

You may have mentioned some examples with measurement (of volume, length, time) and possibly some involving counting (for example, if 3 people share a box of 12 cookies then each gets 1/3 of 12). Children must learn to recognize fractions in many different situations. Try this creature card.

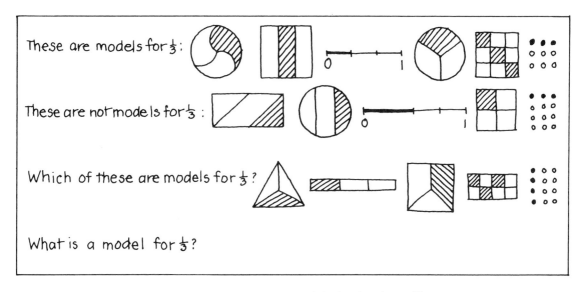

This creature card illustrates three types of models for fractions. The word *fraction* is derived from the Latin word for *break* (as in fracture) and the concept concerns parts of a whole. The whole can be either discrete — a *set,* (as in the black and white dots) — or continuous, usually a *region* (as in the square or circle), or a *length* (as in the number line). In each model, children must learn that finding 1/3 involves dividing a whole into three parts which are the "same" in some way (same number, same area, or same length). Most of the Activities in this unit involve the two continuous or measurement models for fractions, through which children are commonly introduced to fractions in elementary school. The Activities use two commercial materials: Pattern Blocks and Cuisenaire rods. Both materials have a wide range of uses for developing other concepts in both geometry and arithmetic.

The Activities (some with pattern blocks, others with Cuisenaire rods) provide an example of *parallel activities* — they involve different materials but are designed to develop the same concepts. In fact, the Activities correspond exactly — Activity 3 with pattern blocks is essentially the same as Activity 3 with Cuisenaire rods. Using one of the materials, work through Activities 1–9. Then with the other material, work through Activities 1, 3, 6 and 8, and read the remaining Activities.

The Discussion Questions and Comments concern the reason for having children do such parallel activities to develop a concept. Then the concept of rational number is discussed in more detail: what it means, how it arises in real life and in the elementary school curriculum, and how the present study of fractions is likely to change with the advent of the metric system and inexpensive hand-held calculators.

Follow-up Sections look more closely at the various models for fractions appearing in the creature card, and at techniques for motivating and teaching algorithms for fractions. An important first step is to recognize situations in which operations on fractions arise in the real world. Some common error patterns for operations on fractions are presented, which may underline children's need for appropriate manipulative experiences when they are learning algorithms. Addition, subtraction, and multiplication algorithms for fractions are explained using various models for fractions.

Decimals are just another way of writing rational numbers. Algorithms for addition and subtraction of decimals have been developed in Chapter 7. In this chapter, multiplication and division algorithms for decimals are examined. There are also some new ideas for review and practice activities, as well as some adaptations of practice activities illustrated in previous chapters. Finally, the relationship between fractions, decimals (terminating and nonterminating), and the concepts of rational, irrational, and real number are discussed.

> **Note:** The information which follows concerns materials used in this chapter.

Pattern Blocks

The set of pattern blocks used in the Activities includes color-coded pieces of the following shapes:

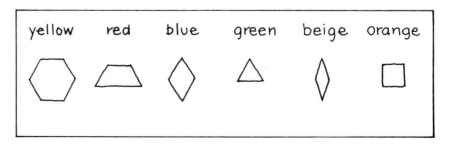

(All sides of these pieces measure one inch, except for the long side of the red trapezoid, which measures two inches.) These pieces can provide children with a rich source of informal geometry experiences, and their uses for mathematical topics other than fractions should not be ignored.

If children are allowed free play with these blocks, they usually produce elaborate tiling patterns. The blocks can also be used in more structured pattern activities for young children. Teachers can draw and color patterns on cards which are to be copied by children (either by placing pieces directly on top of the outline, or by copying to the side of the card).

In previous chapters you have seen some other activities that children could do with the pattern blocks. For example, in Chapter 3, Informal Geometry, the blocks would be suitable for the shape puzzles or explorations of symmetry (Building Games, page 116). Also, in Chapter 8, Geometry on a Geoboard, they could be used as nonstandard units for measurement of area or for measurement of angles.

In the Activities in this chapter, designed to develop fractions through area, you will use only the yellow, red, blue, and green pieces. Similar pieces could be cut from colored cardboard as a substitute for the commercial wooden blocks.

Bean-toss Device

Activities 5 and 7 with pattern blocks and Cuisenaire rods all use a similar choice device to select a color or fraction. (This bean-toss device was used in Chapter 2, Activity 8.) On page 557 you will find four squares labeled by the Activity for which they should be used. When these are cut out, they will just fit in the bottom of a one quart milk carton, cut to form an open box about six centimeters in height. To choose a color or fraction, drop a dried bean into the box from a height of at least 30 centimeters. For work with children, you can make such inserts to fit in the bottom of any convenient box.

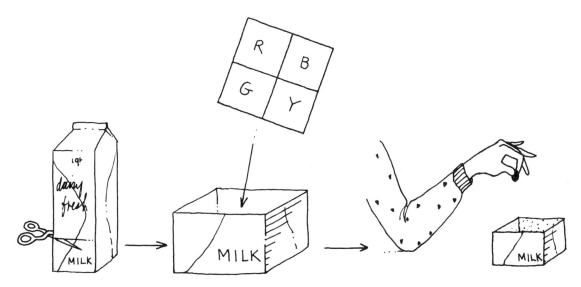

ACTIVITIES WITH PATTERN BLOCKS

Activity 1. Puzzle Games — Some Structured Play

Cover each puzzle with pattern blocks. Try to do each puzzle in two or three different ways.

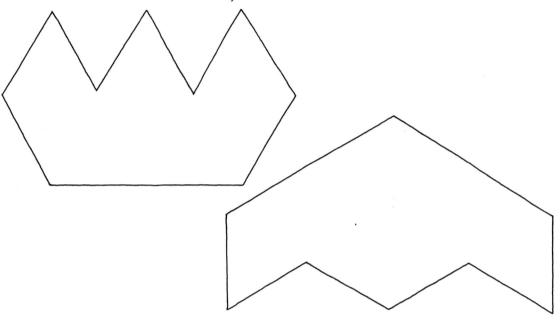

Make up your own puzzle and outline it. Try it on a friend. Did your friend use the same pattern blocks that you did to make the puzzle?

Activity 2. Developing the Concept of One-half

1. Which puzzles can be covered exactly with two blue pieces?

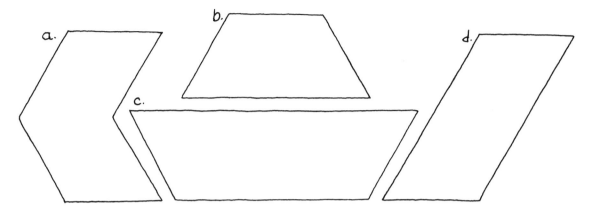

2. A blue piece is half of which shapes above?
3. Use the pattern blocks to determine which blocks have halves. Fill in the table below.

Block	Yellow	Red	Blue	Green
Its Half				

Activity 3. Fractions: Concept and Notation

1. Can you cover this puzzle with red pieces? _____ If so, how many? _____

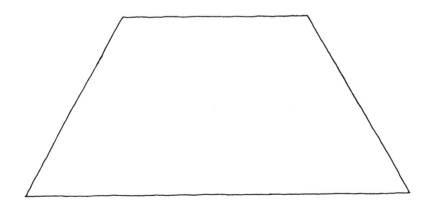

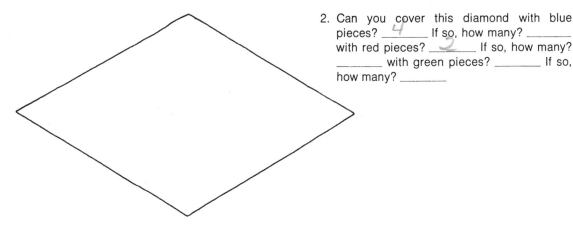

2. Can you cover this diamond with blue pieces? __4__ If so, how many? _____ with red pieces? __2__ If so, how many? _____ with green pieces? _____ If so, how many? _____

3. Cover the hexagon with pieces of the *same color*. Record your results in the table below.

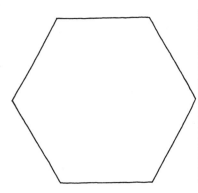

Color of Piece	Red	Blue	Green	Yellow
Number of pieces needed to cover the hexagon	2			
Fraction of the hexagon	$\frac{1}{2}$			

Notice that the 6 in $\frac{1}{6}$ indicates how many pieces (which are all the same) cover the hexagon. What does the 1 mean?

4. The fraction $\frac{2}{6}$ means 2 of the $\frac{1}{6}$'s, as shown below. Write names for the others.

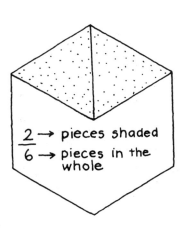

$\frac{2}{6}$ → pieces shaded
pieces in the whole

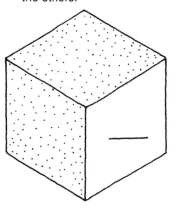

_____

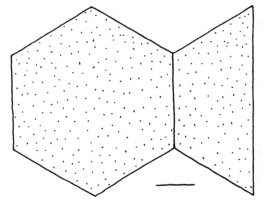

_____

Note: From now on, when numbers are assigned to the pattern blocks, the yellow piece will be 1, the red piece will be $\frac{1}{2}$, the blue $\frac{1}{3}$, and the green $\frac{1}{6}$.

Activity 4. Different Names for the Same Amount

1. Suppose that the pattern blocks were made of solid gold and then painted. Which would you rather have, one blue or three green

   pieces? _____ Which is greater, $\frac{1}{3}$ or $\frac{3}{6}$? _____

2. Shade in $\frac{2}{3}$ of the left-hand hexagon and $\frac{5}{6}$ of the right-hand one.

   Which is greater, $\frac{2}{3}$ or $\frac{5}{6}$?

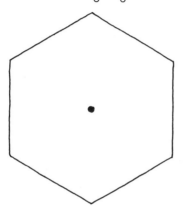 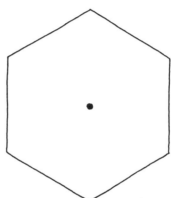

3. The shaded part of this hexagon can be covered with _____ red or with _____ green pieces. Thus $\frac{1}{2}$ and $\frac{3}{6}$ represent the same amount of the whole. We say that $\frac{1}{2}$ is *equivalent* to $\frac{3}{6}$, and we write $\frac{1}{2} = \frac{3}{6}$.

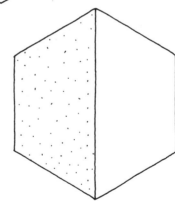

4. Use pieces to show that $\frac{1}{3}$ and $\frac{2}{6}$ cover the same amount of a whole hexagon — that $\frac{1}{3}$ and $\frac{2}{6}$ are equivalent.

5. Take five red pieces. How many halves is this? _____ Write a fraction for it. _____
   Trade in as many reds as you can for hexagons.
   Five red pieces can be traded for _____ hexagons and _____ red.

   The improper fraction $\frac{5}{2}$ names the same amount as the mixed number $2\frac{1}{2}$.

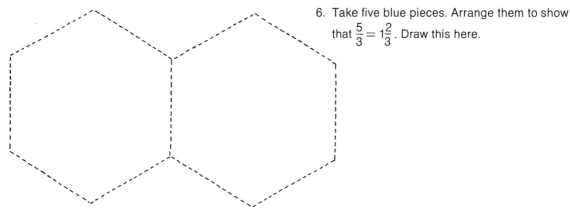

6. Take five blue pieces. Arrange them to show that $\frac{5}{3} = 1\frac{2}{3}$. Draw this here.

Activity 5. Game — Fraction Cover-up

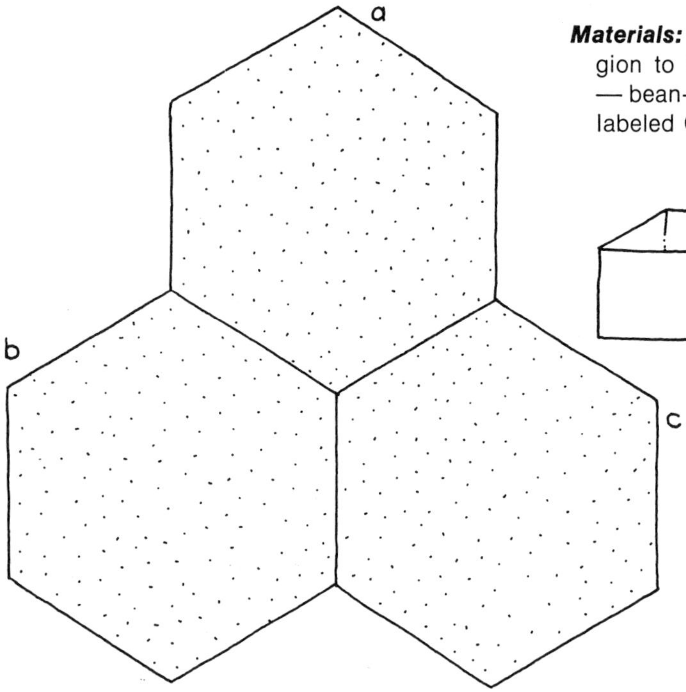

Materials: Pattern blocks; game board (shaded region to the left) for each player; choice device — bean-toss device as shown below, or a die labeled G,G,B,B,R,Y, or a spinner

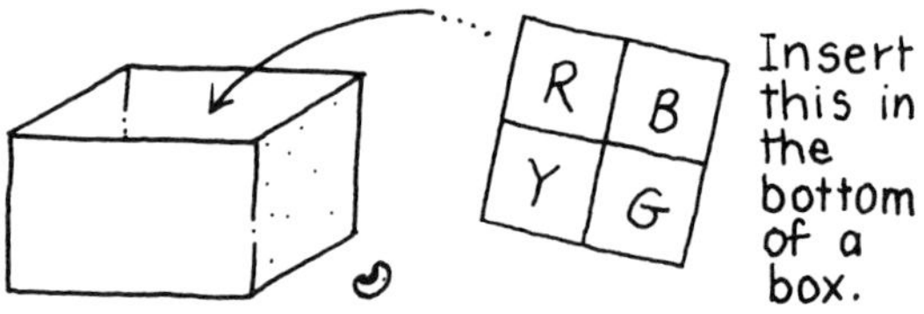

R	B
Y	G

Insert this in the bottom of a box.

Directions: This game can be played with 2–5 players.
  1. Players take turns. Drop a bean in the box and take one piece of the color it lands on. Place the piece in one of the hexagons on your game board. You cannot place a piece so that it covers some of the outline of a hexagon. On each turn, you will collect an additional piece to place on your game board.

2. Once a piece is placed, you may not move it.
3. When you have filled in each hexagon completely, write an addition
   sentence below that describes which pieces are in the hexagon. (For
   example, if you had two reds in one of the hexagons, you would write
   $\frac{1}{2} + \frac{1}{2} = 1$.)

   a. _____   b. _____
   c. _____

4. Once you have covered one hexagon completely, you may trade in
   pieces during the rest of the game. For example, if you toss a "blue,"
   you may pick up one blue and trade it in for two greens.
5. The winner is the first person to cover his game board exactly.

Activity 6. Addition of Fractions

1. Cover the shaded part of the hexagon with two pieces. Do it in two
   different ways. Record the related addition sentences.

2. Cover the shaded part with three pieces. Record the sum.

3. Cover the shaded part with four pieces. Record the sum.
   Can you cover the shaded part with five pieces?

4. Use pattern blocks to show why $\frac{1}{6} + \frac{2}{6} = \frac{3}{6}$
   or $\frac{1}{2}$.

5. Use pattern blocks to combine one red and
   two blues. Write the related addition sentence.

6. Did you act out part 5 above as shown in this diagram? Fill in the
   missing fractions in the diagram

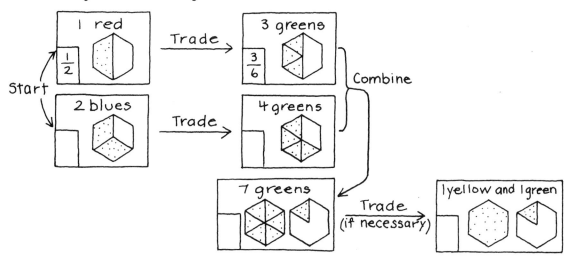

$$\frac{1}{2} = \frac{3}{6}$$
$$+\frac{2}{3} = \frac{4}{6}$$
$$\frac{7}{6} = 1\frac{1}{6}$$

7. Note how the action shown in the preceding diagram parallels the steps you take in doing the addition algorithm as shown to the left.
8. Complete the diagram below and fill in the blanks — both the missing pattern pieces and the missing fractions.

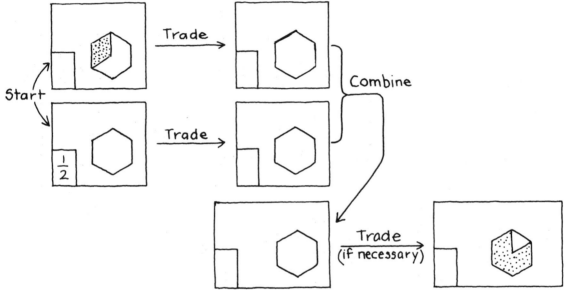

9. Write the addition sentence shown in part 8 in the form shown in part 7.

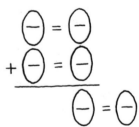

Activity 7. Game — Fraction Subtraction

Materials: Pattern blocks; game board (as shown on page 499) for each player; choice device to pick fractions $\frac{1}{6}, \frac{1}{3}, \frac{1}{2}, \frac{2}{3}$ — bean-toss device as shown below or a die, or a spinner

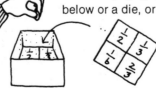

Directions: Play the Fraction Subtraction Game in a group of 2–5 players. Record your score during the game, as indicated in step (3).

1. Place three yellow hexagons on your game board.

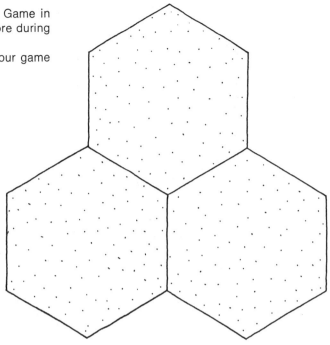

2. Players take turns. Drop a bean in the box to choose a fraction. Take pieces corresponding to this fraction *away* from those on your game board. Exchange pieces as needed. The winner is the first person to get rid of all the pieces.

3. After each toss and the related action with the blocks, write a corresponding subtraction sentence in the table. For example, suppose that on the first toss your bean landed on $\frac{1}{2}$. Then you would exchange a yellow hexagon for two red pieces and take away one red, leaving two yellows and one red; and you would write $3 - \frac{1}{2} = 2\frac{1}{2}$.

   Suppose that on your second toss you got $\frac{1}{2}$ again. Then you would take away the one red piece and be left with two yellows, and you would write (fill in) $2\frac{1}{2} - $ _____

   $= $ _____

Round	My Subtraction Sentence
1	$3 - \frac{1}{6} = 2\frac{5}{6}$
2	$2\frac{5}{6} - \frac{1}{3} = 2\frac{1}{2}$
3	$2\frac{3}{6} - \frac{4}{6} = 1\frac{5}{6}$
4	$1\frac{5}{6} - \frac{1}{6} = 1\frac{4}{6}$
5	$1\frac{4}{6} - \frac{2}{6} = 1\frac{2}{6}$
6	$1\frac{2}{6} - \frac{1}{6} = 1\frac{1}{6}$
7	$1\frac{1}{6} - \frac{1}{6} = 1$
8	$1 - \frac{1}{3} = 2/3$
9	$\frac{2}{3} - \frac{2}{3} = 0$

Activity 8. Multiplication and Division — Some Introductory Activities

1. Use pattern blocks to act out solutions to the problems in the left-hand column. Write the solution for each problem, and then match the problem with the related multiplication or division sentence in the right-hand column.

Problems with Pattern Blocks   *Number Sentence*

a. How many greens are in one blue? _2_   _a_ $\frac{1}{3} \div \frac{1}{6} = 2$

b. Make three piles with two blues in each. How much in all? _6_   _h_ $\frac{1}{2} \div \frac{1}{3} =$

c. How many greens are in two blues? _4_   _d_ $\frac{1}{2} \div 3 =$

d. One red is to be shared among three people. Each person gets a _1/3_ piece, or _gn_.   _e_ $\frac{1}{2} \times \frac{1}{3} =$

e. Half of a blue is a _gn_ piece, or _1/6_.   _c_ $\frac{2}{3} \div \frac{1}{6} =$

f. Three piles with two green in each are the same as a _yellow_ piece, or ___.   _g_ $\frac{1}{6} \div \frac{1}{3} =$

g. How much blue in one green piece? _1/2_   _i_ $2 \times 1\frac{1}{2} =$

h. How much blue in one red piece? _1/2_   _b_ $3 \times \frac{2}{3} =$

i. Two piles with one yellow and one red in each equals ___, or ___.   _f_ $3 \times \frac{2}{6} =$

2. Which example below cannot be acted out with the yellow, red, blue, and green pattern blocks? Why not?

$\frac{1}{2} \times 2\frac{1}{3} =$ _____ $\frac{1}{2} \times \frac{1}{4} =$ _____ $3 \times \frac{1}{6} =$ _____

Activity 9. Handful of Fractions

1. Take a handful of pattern blocks with each of your hands. Place them in two separate piles.

2. Write fractions for the amounts. Left hand _____ Right hand _____

3. If you traded in all of the pieces for greens, how many green pieces would you get for all of the pieces in your right hand? __ in your left hand? _____

4. Which hand held more? __ How much more did it hold? __ Write the related subtraction sentence. _____

5. How much did you have in both hands combined? _____ Write the related addition sentence. _____

ACTIVITIES WITH CUISENAIRE RODS

Activity 1. Puzzle Games — Some Structured Play

Cover each puzzle with Cuisenaire rods of *one* color. Try to do it in several ways.

Which colors can you use to cover (a)?

a.

c.

Which colors can you use to cover (b)?

In how many different ways can (c) be covered with rods of the same color?

b.

Activity 2. Developing the Concept of One-half

1. Which puzzles can be covered exactly by two Cuisenaire rods of the same color?

a.   b.   c.   d.

2. What color rod is half of a purple rod?
3. Do all of the rods have halves? Check which ones do and record your results in the table below.

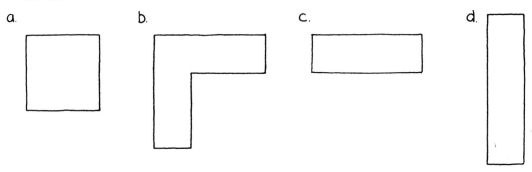

Color of the rod	white w	red r	light green g	purple p	yellow y	dark green d	black k	brown n	blue e	orange o
Color of its half										

Activity 3. Fractions: Concepts and Notation

1. Suppose the length of the box is one unit. Cover the box with rods of the same color in as many ways as possible, and complete the table.

Color of the rod	g			
Number of rods to cover the box	2			
Fraction of the whole box	$\frac{1}{2}$			

What fraction of the box is two white rods? ___3___ three whites? ___2___ two reds? ___3___

2. Fill in the blanks below, if possible. (Some cannot be filled in.) Use the rods to check your answers.

a. A red is $\frac{1}{2}$ of a _____ rod.

b. A red is $\frac{1}{3}$ of a __Dk. g.__ rod.

c. A red is $\frac{1}{4}$ of a __brown__ rod.

d. A red is $\frac{1}{5}$ of a __orange__ rod.

e. __yellow__ is $\frac{1}{2}$ of an orange rod.

f. __purple__ is $\frac{1}{3}$ of an orange rod.

g. _____ is $\frac{1}{4}$ of an orange rod.

h. __red__ is $\frac{1}{5}$ of an orange rod.

Activity 4. Different Names for the Same Amount

In this Activity the length of the box below is taken to be one unit.

1. What colors fill in this box exactly?
   10 white, __5__ red, __2__ __yellow__, and 1 __orange__.
2. Write fractions for the following:
   white __10__ red __5__ yellow __2__ 3 whites __3/10__
   3 reds __3/5__

3. Suppose that the rods were made of solid gold and painted. Which would you rather have, three reds or five whites? Which is greater, $\frac{3}{5}$ or $\frac{5}{10}$?

4. You can cover the shaded part of the box to the right with ___/___ yellow or __5__ white rods. Thus $\frac{1}{2}$ and $\frac{5}{10}$ represent the same amount of the whole; that is, $\frac{1}{2}$ and $\frac{5}{10}$ are *equivalent* fractions.

5. Take rods for $\frac{2}{5}$ and $\frac{4}{10}$. Show that these two fractions are equivalent.

6. Use the rods to help you complete the drawing to the right for a whole, halves, fifths, and tenths. Then use the results from the diagram to make a number line (below) showing halves, fifths, and tenths.

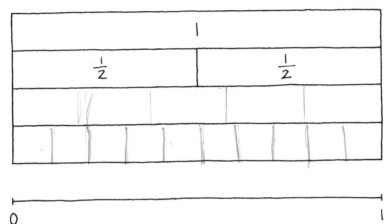

0   1

7. Refer to the diagram or number line to answer, true or false.

$\frac{1}{5} < \frac{1}{10}$ __F__ $\frac{2}{5} = \frac{4}{10}$ __T__ $\frac{1}{2} > \frac{6}{10}$ __F__

8. Take five yellow rods. How many halves is this? _____ Trade them in.

5 yellow = __2__ oranges and __1__ yellow, or $2\frac{1}{2}$

The improper fraction 5/2 names the same amount as does the mixed number $2\frac{1}{2}$.

Take eight red rods. Trade them in and fill in the blank. 8/5 = __1 $\frac{3}{5}$__

Activity 5. Game — Fraction Cover-up

Materials: Cuisenaire rods (w, r, y, o); game board (see shaded region on page 504) for each player; choice device — bean-toss device as shown here or a die labeled w,w,r,r,y,o, or a spinner

a.

Directions: This game can be played with 2–5 players.

1. Players take turns. Drop a bean in the box and take one rod of the color it lands on. Place the rod in one of the boxes on your game board.
2. Once a piece is placed, you may not move it.
3. When you have filled in each box completely, write an addition sentence that describes which pieces are in the box. (For example, if you had two yellows in a box, you would write $1/2 + 1/2 = 1$.)

   a. $\frac{1}{10} + \frac{1}{10} + \frac{4}{10} + \frac{4}{10} = 1$
   b. $4/10 + 6/10 = 1$
   c. $7/10 + 3/10 = 1$

4. You may exchange pieces on any toss. For example, if you toss a yellow, you could pick up a yellow rod or five white rods.
5. The winner is the first person to cover the game board exactly.

b.

c.

Activity 6. Addition of Fractions

Use white, red, yellow and orange rods, and suppose that the orange is 1, and so white $= \frac{1}{10}$, red $= \frac{1}{5}$, and yellow $= \frac{1}{2}$.

1. Make a train of three whites and one red. This train is as long as a _____ rod. This can be written as $\frac{3}{10} +$ _____ $=$ _____.
2. Use rods to show how to act out solutions to the addition sentences below. Draw diagrams similar to the one in the example to show how you acted out the sentence, and write a corresponding symbolic format.

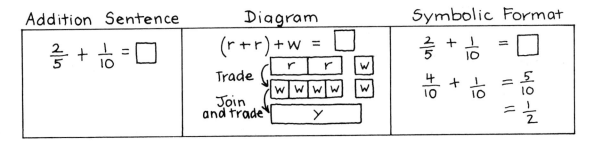

Addition Sentence	Diagram	Symbolic Format
$\frac{2}{5} + \frac{1}{10} = \square$	$(r + r) + w = \square$ Trade Join and trade	$\frac{2}{5} + \frac{1}{10} = \square$ $\frac{4}{10} + \frac{1}{10} = \frac{5}{10}$ $= \frac{1}{2}$

Addition Sentence	Diagram	Symbolic Format
$\frac{1}{2} + \frac{1}{5} = \square$		$\frac{1}{2} + \frac{1}{5} = \square$ $\left(-\right) + \left(-\right) = \left(-\right)$
$\frac{1}{2} + \frac{1}{5} + \frac{1}{10} = \square$		$\frac{1}{2} + \frac{1}{5} + \frac{1}{10} = \square$ $\left(-\right) + \left(-\right) + \left(-\right) = \left(-\right)$ $= \left(-\right)$
$1\frac{1}{10} + \frac{1}{2} = \square$		

Activity 7. Game — Fraction Subtraction

Materials: Cuisenaire rods (w,r,y,o); game board (as drawn to the right) for each player; choice device to pick fractions $\frac{1}{2}, \frac{3}{10}, \frac{1}{5}, \frac{1}{10}$ — a bean-toss device as shown to the right below, a die, or a spinner

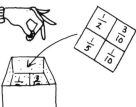

Directions: Play the Fraction Subtraction game in a group of 2–5 players. Record your score during the game as indicated in step (3).

1. Begin by placing two orange rods on your game board.
2. Players take turns. Drop a bean in the box to choose a fraction. Take rods corresponding to this fraction *away* from those on your game board. Take away from top to bottom. Exchange rods as needed. The winner is the first person to get rid of all the rods.
3. Record your score by writing the fraction for your remaining rods after each toss next to your game board. For example, if you tossed ½ on your first turn, you would trade in the top orange rod for two yellows, remove one of the yellows, and write 1½ at the top end of the remaining orange and yellow rod train (at the point marked *).

Activity 8. Multiplication and Division — Some Introductory Activities

Use Cuisenaire rods (w, r, y, o) to act out solutions to the problems in the left-hand column below. Write the solution for each problem, and then match the problem with the related multiplication or division sentence in the right-hand column.

Number Sentence

a. Make two piles with three red rods in each. How much in all? _6/5_

g $\dfrac{1}{2} \div \dfrac{1}{10} =$

b. Share one red and one orange between two people. How much does each get? _6/10_

c $\dfrac{1}{2} \times \dfrac{1}{5} =$

c. Half of a red rod is a _wht_ rod.

d $1 \div \dfrac{1}{5} =$

d. How many red in one orange? _5_

a $2 \times \dfrac{3}{5} = \dfrac{6}{5}$

e. Make two piles with one orange and one red in each. How much in all? _2 x_

f $\dfrac{3}{5} \div 6 =$

f. Share three red rods among six people. Each person gets a _wht_ rod.

b $1\dfrac{1}{5} \div 2 =$

g. How many whites in one yellow? _5_

e $2 \times 1\dfrac{1}{5} =$

Activity 9. Handful of Fractions

1. Take a handful of Cuisenaire rods. Try to divide them into two piles that are about the same. Do this by the "feel" of the weight.
2. Line up each pile and measure them with orange rods. Write a mixed number for each pile. Left pile _____ Right pile _____
3. Which was bigger? How close were you? Write a related subtraction sentence for the difference.
4. How much did you have in your original handful? Write a related addition sentence.

DISCUSSION QUESTIONS AND COMMENTS

Using Pattern Blocks and Cuisenaire Rods in Parallel Activities

The Activities in this chapter were designed to develop fraction concepts: first the meaning of and notation for fractional parts (including the idea that two different fractions can represent the same amount); informal interpretations of the operations addition, subtraction, multiplication, and division of fractions; and the relationship between the action of addition and a symbolic format or algorithm. You saw that these concepts could be developed in parallel activities with two different materials, an area or region model, and a length model for fractions. However, the corresponding activities were not *identical,* because each of the two materials brings out special aspects of the concept of a fraction, and also because each material has certain limitations. In this section, we will look more closely at the special features of these two materials, at other similar materials of the same types, and at why a teacher might want to use both types in parallel activities.

Which of the two materials (pattern blocks or Cuisenaire rods) do you most enjoy working with? Why?

Some fractions can be easily represented by pattern blocks (such as $\frac{1}{2}, \frac{1}{3}$)

and some cannot (such as $\frac{1}{4}$). Check ($\checkmark$) which fractions *cannot* be easily represented by pattern blocks and Cuisenaire rods. (Any rod could be taken as the unit.)

	$\frac{1}{2}$	$\frac{1}{3}$	$\frac{1}{4}$	$\frac{1}{5}$	$\frac{1}{6}$	$\frac{1}{7}$	$\frac{1}{8}$	$\frac{1}{9}$	$\frac{1}{10}$
Pattern Blocks			$\checkmark$						
Cuisenaire Rods									

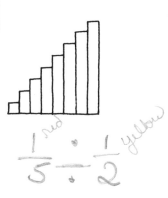

Can pattern blocks or Cuisenaire rods be used to act out the decimal addition sentence $.4 + .1 = .5$?

You may have noticed that it is not easy to use pattern blocks to represent fractions other than halves, thirds, and sixths (because the yellow hexagon seems to be the natural unit, and it does not split up nicely into other parts). However, some other fraction models based on area do not have this limitation. For example, the set of circle pieces is commonly available, either magnetized to stick to a metallic chalkboard (for demonstration), or cut from cardboard or paper (for individual use). Draw lines in the last two circles to show how this material can easily represent fourths and eighths.

Would these circle pieces be as good as pattern blocks for Activities such as those listed below? Why or why not?

Puzzle Games — Some Structured Play (Activity 1)
Different Names for the Same Amount (Activity 4)
Fraction Cover-up (Activity 5)
Addition of Fractions (Activity 6)

Which area model, pattern blocks or circle pieces, would you rather use for developing fraction concepts? Why?

Children may have difficulty using Cuisenaire rods as a model for fractions if they have used the rods intensively for developing whole numbers in grades K–2, always associating the white rod with 1, the red with 2, etc. For such children, many activities involving renaming the rods may be necessary before the rods will be helpful for developing fractions. One such activity is given below. Fill in the blanks.

Suppose the white rod is worth 5¢.
How much are the other rods worth?
w = 5¢, r = _____, g = _____, p = _____

Suppose the purple rod is worth 8¢.
How much are the other rods worth?
w = _____, r = _____, g = _____, p = 8¢

Children sometimes have difficulty using Cuisenaire rods for fractions because they forget what the whole is. One solution is to have children use an outline of unit length in which they place the rods, or a number line marked with units.

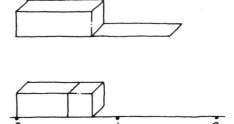

Another fraction material based on length, *fraction rods,* avoids this difficulty.[1] You can make fraction rods: Cut uniform strips of cardboard (about 2 cm by 15 cm) in various colors. Mark all strips of each color with uniform subdivisions. For example, yellow might be halves, blue might be thirds, red might be fourths, and green might be sixths. Now shade in various parts to represent fractions. Make several of each type. (You can use different fractional parts as well.)

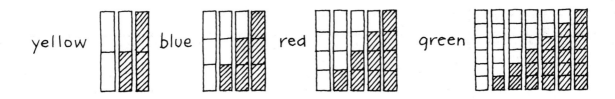

yellow   blue   red   green

These strips can be used in much the same way as Cuisenaire rods; however, they have the advantage that each piece shows both the unit and the fractional parts.

Here are some exercises done with the strips.

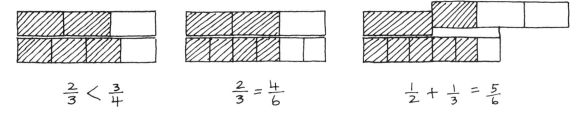

$$\frac{2}{3} < \frac{3}{4} \qquad \frac{2}{3} = \frac{4}{6} \qquad \frac{1}{2} + \frac{1}{3} = \frac{5}{6}$$

In what ways are these materials preferable to Cuisenaire rods for developing fractions?

In what ways are the Cuisenaire rods preferable?

In Chapter 5, you saw several other examples of *multiple embodiments,* such as the two types of fraction models, and why their use is recommended. Perhaps the Activities have suggested to you why it is especially desirable to have children use more than one type of model for fractions. In particular, (1) certain applications of fractions in real life may resemble one model more than another. For example, measuring with a ruler resembles the Cuisenaire rod or length model, while sharing a pizza resembles the model using pattern blocks. (2) Different models bring out different mathematical concepts more forcefully. For example, pattern blocks have a natural unit, the yellow piece, and so are effective for teaching relationships between improper fractions and mixed numbers (such as $\frac{8}{3} = 2\frac{2}{3}$), and Cuisenaire rods can be used to teach decimals (when the orange rod is taken to be the unit). (3) Some teachers may have just one barrel of pattern blocks, and perhaps four boxes of Cuisenaire rods in their classroom. If the entire class is to use *one* of these materials to develop fractions, the material will have to be carefully scheduled and shared. However, if small groups of children do parallel activities with different materials, more children can be working on these concepts at the same time.

How Do Fractional Numbers Arise in Everyday Life?

We often hear in commercials that a certain product is recommended by "3 out of 4 doctors surveyed." (This does not mean, of course, that only 4 doctors were surveyed — perhaps 20 were, in which case 15 recommended the product.) There are many other ways to say this numerically: perhaps the product was recommended by $\frac{3}{4}$ of the doctors, or by $\frac{15}{20}$ of them, or by $\frac{75}{100}$ or .75 or 75% of them. This example indicates that not only are fractional numbers commonly used, but also that a given situation can be described in different ways: by different fractions, by decimals, or by percents.

In the Introduction you listed some places where you use fractions. Where did you last use the fraction

$\dfrac{1}{2}$? $\dfrac{3}{4}$?

$\dfrac{5}{8}$? $\dfrac{7}{11}$?

Many people use fractions most often in measurement. When you measure things in the English system, you probably use certain fractions frequently: $\dfrac{1}{2}$ teaspoon of salt, $\dfrac{3}{4}$ pound of meat in recipes, and sewing patterns usually call for $\dfrac{5}{8}$ inch seams. However few people have much use for a fraction such as $\dfrac{7}{11}$. Commonly, measurement in the English system occurs with fractions whose denominators are 2, 4, 8, and 16. When this country does switch to metric measurements, it will be more natural to measure in tenths and hence to record measurements in decimal notation: 1.3 centimeters, .5 liters, and .4 kilograms.

When it comes to doing arithmetic with fractional quantities, calculators will be used more and more, influencing how we write fractional numbers. To enter the fraction $\dfrac{3}{4}$ on a calculator, you push buttons for 3, ÷, and 4, and of course the display will show .75. The addition $\dfrac{3}{4} + \dfrac{1}{2}$ would be replaced by .75 + .5. As another example, think of what answer you would write for 27 ÷ 4. You might say, "6 with remainder 3," or possibly "$6\dfrac{3}{4}$" but if you do this on a calculator, the answer will read "6.75."

Thus two major influences will affect our everyday use of fractional numbers: the metric system and the hand-held calculator. Both suggest more reliance on decimal notation. However, there will always be some use for fractions in daily life. The words *half* and *quarter* are natural to us and will certainly be used in many situations; for example, time (half-past two). Any family with three children will know the importance of the idea of $\dfrac{1}{3}$ as sharing something among three. Certain ratios cannot easily be expressed in decimals, yet such ratios arise very naturally: if 1 out of 3 doctors surveyed recommend a product, in describing odds or probability (the chances are 3 out of 7), or in scaling diagrams (a drawing might be 1 cm to 6 cm, or 1 : 6). Also, understanding of operations on fractions is essential for later work in mathematics (such as algebra); hence for students planning to enter any field requiring such mathematics. Fractions will continue to be an important tool for describing many real-world situations and so will continue to be taught in school.

What Is a Rational Number?

What number would you attach to the yellow rod?

It could of course be 5, if the *white* rod is 1, or $\frac{5}{6}$ if the _____

rod is 1, or $\frac{1}{2}$ if the _____ rod is 1.

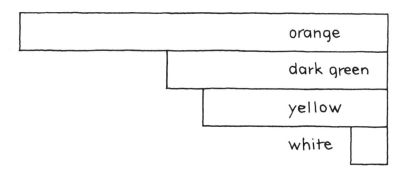

Even if we settle on a unit, say the orange rod, the length of the yellow rod can have several names, for example $\frac{1}{2}$ or $\frac{5}{10}$ or .5 of the orange rod. These symbols $\left(\frac{1}{2}, \frac{5}{10}, .5\right)$ all represent the same *rational number*. The word *rational* indicates that we are concerned with the *ratio* or relationship between one rod (yellow) and another (the orange rod or unit). The number five (the common property of sets with five elements) is represented by many numerals (5 or V or ‖‖‖). In the same way, rational numbers can be represented in many ways; by fractions $\left(\frac{1}{2}\text{ or }\frac{2}{4}\text{ or }\frac{5}{10}\text{ or }\frac{50}{100}\right)$ and by decimals or decimal fractions (.5 or .50). The fractions $\frac{1}{2}$ and $\frac{2}{4}$ are not the *same* because they have different *numerators* (the numerals on top) and different *denominators* (the numerals on the bottom). The fraction $\frac{1}{2}$ indicates one of two equal parts of the whole, while $\frac{2}{4}$ indicates two of four equal parts of the whole. However both fractions represent the same amount or rational number, and so we say that $\frac{1}{2}$ and $\frac{2}{4}$ are *equivalent* fractions and we write $\frac{1}{2} = \frac{2}{4}$. In a later section we will discuss ways to tell if two fractions are equivalent; that is, represent the same number.

Notice that 0 is a rational number, and can be represented by the fractions $\frac{0}{1}, \frac{0}{3}, \frac{0}{2}$ etc. (Think of dividing a whole into 3 parts and taking 0 of them — you have 0.) While 0 can appear as the *numerator* of a fraction, it makes no sense to write a fraction with 0 in the *denominator*. How can we break something into 0 parts? Remember that division by zero makes no sense. (See page 213.)

Do the following activity which involves interpretation of the idea of a rational number.

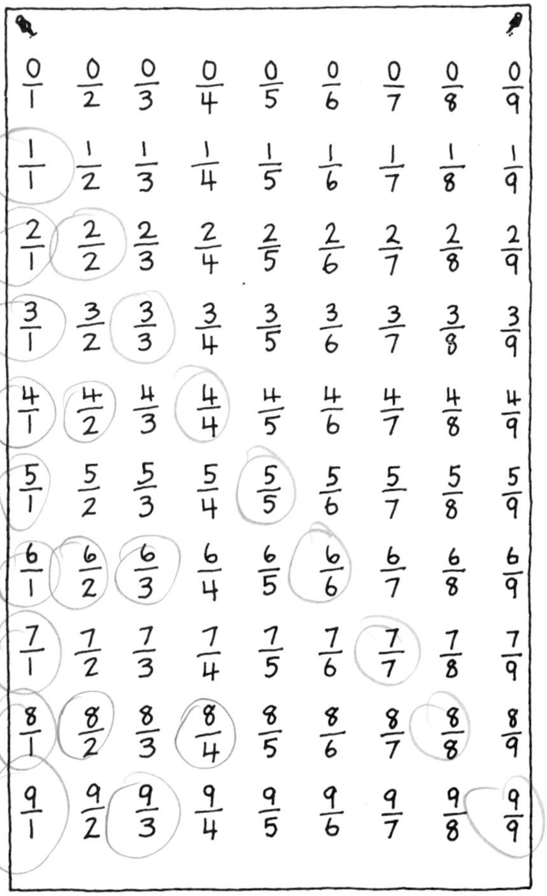

How many fractions are written here?
How many different rational numbers are represented?
Use some method to cross out the duplicates. Did you notice any patterns as you crossed out fractions?

The set of rational numbers also includes negatives (−1/2, −.5). Since rational numbers arise most commonly in real life as measurements (and hence as positive numbers) this chapter concentrates on developing operations on *positive* rational numbers. The operations can easily be extended to negative rational numbers in the same way that operations on whole numbers are extended to integers.

How Do Rational Numbers Appear in the Elementary School Curriculum?

The table on the next page describes the new work with fractions introduced at each grade level in a textbook series. Notice that in grades 1–3, the emphasis is on developing meaning and notation for fractions, while in grades 4–6 children learn about operations on fractions, first addition and subtraction, then later multiplication and division.

Grade

1: Readiness for fractions: symmetry and recognizing two congruent parts.

Area model (with congruent parts) and the words one-half, one-third, one-fourth (no symbols).

2: Introducing names and notation for 1/2, 1/3, 1/4, 2/3, 3/4, 2/2, 3/3, 4/4, using both regions (area model) and sets, in terms of sharing.

3: Fractions in measurement: measuring to 1/4 of an inch on a ruler, finding the area of 1/2 of a rectangle (using 1/2 units).

Folding paper shapes to show 1/2, 1/4, 1/8.

Notation for eighths, ninths, etc.

4: Cuisenaire rods for fractions, changing the unit.

Measuring area with 1/3 and 1/4 of a unit, volume with 1/2 unit.

Formal introduction to concept and terminology for *equivalent* fractions in terms of area and sets; area of a rectangle divided to show equivalent fractions; cross-product method of determining equivalence of fractions.

Fractions as lengths on a number line.

Whole numbers as fraction; mixed numbers.

Equality and inequality of fractional numbers.

Informal addition using Cuisenaire rods on the number line.

5: Ratio and map scales.

Introduction to addition and subtraction of fractional numbers.

Flow charts for algorithms.

Developing skill with addition and subtraction of fractional numbers.

Decimal notation introduced (building on work with fractions). Expanded notation.

Addition and subtraction of decimals.

Relationship between decimals and the metric system.

6: Review of addition and subtraction of fractional numbers, using properties of operations.

Introduction of multiplication and division of fractions.

Addition, subtraction, multiplication, and division of decimals.

Relationship between fractions and decimals.

Several principles concerning the teaching of fractions can be illustrated by this outlined scope and sequence. (These should be familiar to you from earlier discussion of teaching basic facts and whole number algorithms.)

1. Fractions are introduced via various models (or *multiple embodiments*): regions or areas, length, and sets. Which model is used first? ___
_____ Which would you expect to be most difficult? _____ Why?

2. Symbolic notation is introduced only after children have had concrete and semiconcrete experience with a given concept. For example, children do informal work with coloring and verbally naming halves, thirds, and fourths of shapes in the first grade before symbolizing these concepts (1/2, 1/3, 1/4) in the second grade.

3. Children experience operations on fractions first with either a concrete model (rods) or with semiconcrete representations of these models before learning purely symbolic algorithms. For example, addition is treated informally in grade 4 using rods on a number line; in grade 5 addition is introduced by tying symbolism to this concrete experience; then gradually children move away from the representation to develop skill at the symbolic level. (This corresponds to the sequence of introductory, developmental, and review or practice types of lessons described in Chapter 5, Basic Facts and Their Uses.)

If you examine a teacher's guide for a good modern text series, you will see these principles at work in more detail. These guides often contain helpful suggestions for incidental introduction to the concept involved (for example, cutting sandwiches in half during snack time, or breaking the class up into three teams) and for preliminary or supplementary manipulative experiences.

The Activities in this chapter could be used together with a text series using the scope and sequence just described. At what grade level might you expect to use each of these Activities? (Assume that the verbal directions are simplified as necessary to suit the grade level.)

Pattern blocks:
Activity 2 _____ 3 _____ 4 _____ 5 _____ 6 _____ 7 _____ 8 _____

Cuisenaire rods:
Activity 2 _____ 3 _____ 4 _____ 5 _____ 6 _____ 7 _____ 8 _____

(Were there any differences in your grade placements of parallel activities using pattern blocks and Cuisenaire rods? If so, why?)

You might feel that some of the Activities could be used appropriately at several grade levels, if they are slightly modified. For example, Activity 7, Fraction Subtraction, could first be played in grades 1 or 2 if no notation is involved (that is, the choice device uses only colors of pieces), and in grades 2 or 3 if children pick pieces by their fraction names but omit the recording of the subtraction sentence (part 4 of that Activity). As described, with written subtraction sentences, the game should probably be included early in grade 5, since that is when subtraction of fractions is introduced, although it could provide an enrichment activity for some children in grade 4.

The Activities in this chapter all used a concrete or semiconcrete model for fractions, and focused on the first two parts of the learning sequence for developing skill with operations on fractions:

Concept ⎯⎯⎯⎯⎯⟶ Concept and Notation ⎯⎯⎯⎯⎯⟶ Skill

Only in Activity 6, Addition of Fractions, were the actions with materials tied to the algorithm or symbolic procedure. We will examine the later parts of the sequence in more detail in the Follow-up Sections: associating action or drawing to symbolism for all operations on both fractions and decimals and providing review or practice activities to build skill at the symbolic level.

Fractions are a major stumbling block for many upper elementary school students. The fraction curriculum in grades 4–6 is often misunderstood and poorly learned (as will be seen in the next section). One suggested change from this fairly typical curriculum is to spend still more time on introductory manipulative experiences concerning equivalence, addition, subtraction, multiplication, and division of fractions, and perhaps wait until later grades (6–8) to teach purely symbolic algorithms for fractions. It is also possible that children will be introduced to decimals at an earlier age (once we feel the full impact of hand-held calculators and the metric system) and will build skill with operations on decimals as a natural extension of work with place value.

FOLLOW-UP SECTIONS

In the following sections we will consider various aspects of how children develop skills with operations on fractional numbers. This will involve the following considerations: what these operations mean in terms of problem situations; special aspects of each type of model used to represent fractions (area, length, and sets); developing algorithms and relating them to semiconcrete models; and designing appropriate review and practice activities. To see why all of these aspects must be incorporated into effective teaching of fractions, it is perhaps helpful to look at the types of difficulties that children in upper elementary school have with algorithms. For this reason, the first section starts at the end of the learning sequence.

Error Patterns

When children cannot answer a fraction situation correctly, it is often informative to see what wrong answers they do provide. Some mistakes are due to carelessness — miscopying a number, missing a basic fact, or misreading an operation symbol. Other mistakes are much more systematic, when an incorrect procedure has been learned. In each row, some common error pattern is shown. Two examples of each wrong procedure, or error pattern, are given. Complete the remaining example using the error pattern.

Error Pattern		Example
1. $\dfrac{5}{2} = 5\dfrac{1}{2}$	$\dfrac{4}{3} = 4\dfrac{1}{3}$	$\dfrac{10}{2} =$
2. $\dfrac{1}{2} + \dfrac{1}{3} = \dfrac{2}{5}$	$\dfrac{2}{3} + \dfrac{4}{5} = \dfrac{6}{8}$	$\dfrac{1}{4} + \dfrac{2}{3} =$
3. $\dfrac{3}{4} - \dfrac{1}{3} = \dfrac{2}{12}$	$\dfrac{4}{5} - \dfrac{1}{4} = \dfrac{3}{20}$	$\dfrac{2}{3} - \dfrac{1}{4} =$

$\frac{3}{4}$ $3 \div \frac{3}{4}$ $\frac{4}{3}$

Error Pattern		Example
4. $2\frac{1}{2} = \frac{2}{4}$ $+ 3\frac{3}{4} = \frac{3}{4}$ $\frac{5}{4} = 1\frac{1}{4}$	$1\frac{5}{8} = \frac{5}{8}$ $+ 5\frac{1}{2} = \frac{4}{8}$ $\frac{9}{8} = 1\frac{1}{8}$	$3\frac{1}{4}$ $+ 2\frac{2}{3}$
5. $\frac{2}{3} \times \frac{4}{3} = \frac{8}{3}$	$\frac{1}{2} \times \frac{5}{2} = \frac{5}{2}$	$\frac{1}{4} \times \frac{3}{4} =$
6. $\frac{2}{3} \times \frac{1}{4} = \frac{8}{12} \times \frac{3}{12} = \frac{24}{12}$	$\frac{1}{5} \times \frac{3}{4} = \frac{4}{20} \times \frac{15}{20} = \frac{60}{20}$	$\frac{1}{2} \times \frac{3}{5} =$
7. $\frac{2}{3} \times \frac{1}{4} = \frac{8}{3}$	$\frac{1}{5} \times \frac{3}{4} = \frac{4}{15}$	$\frac{1}{2} \times \frac{3}{5} =$
8. $4 \times 3\frac{1}{2} = 12\frac{1}{2}$	$5 \times 1\frac{1}{2} = 5\frac{1}{2}$	$2 \times 6\frac{1}{4} =$
9. $\frac{9}{10} \div \frac{3}{10} = \frac{3}{10}$	$\frac{4}{6} \div \frac{2}{6} = \frac{2}{6}$	$\frac{8}{3} \div \frac{2}{3} =$
10. $\frac{2}{3} \div \frac{2}{5} = \frac{3}{2} \times \frac{2}{5} = \frac{6}{10}$	$\frac{3}{4} \div \frac{1}{8} = \frac{4}{3} \times \frac{1}{8} = \frac{4}{24}$	$\frac{1}{2} \div \frac{2}{3} =$

These errors suggest two questions: Why do children make them? and What can we do to help them avoid such errors? There are probably many reasons for these systematic mistakes. Usually you can only find the real reason for an error by talking to the child who made it.

If children think of arithmetic as a process of moving symbols around according to certain fixed rules, without any connection to reality, then one complicated procedure is as good as another. The child who made error (10) may have learned division of fractions as a memorized slogan, "Invert and multiply." This erroneous procedure of inverting the *first* fraction makes just as much sense as the correct procedure, if it is learned by rote. This is why children should be taught *why* algorithms are done the way they are.

Sometimes teachers unwittingly train children to make certain errors. For example, if children begin their work with addition of fractions with many number sentences like $\frac{1}{3} + \frac{2}{3} = \square$, $\frac{2}{5} + \frac{1}{5} = \square$, and $\frac{3}{4} + \frac{2}{4} = \square$ (all having like denominators), then they will learn to associate addition of fractions just with addition of the numerators, and error (2) is quite likely to develop. (They might also extend this error to (5) for multiplication.) Children often learn by patterns, and we must be careful not to establish misleading ones. Some teachers in early grades teach that "multiplying makes things larger" and "division makes things smaller." These statements are not true for some fractions, and children may be misled by their earlier learning about whole numbers. For this reason, it is important that teachers at all levels understand the school curriculum of later grades.

It is possible to think that common sense might help children catch some of the errors above. In error (5), how could $\frac{2}{3}$ of $\frac{4}{3}$ be greater than $\frac{4}{3}$? Or, in error (4), how could a number greater than 2 and a number greater than 3 together make a number only just greater than 1? The child who made error (1) would probably know quite well that five half dollars are worth two and one-half dollars, but may not think in these terms when doing symbolic problems. Many children do not have a reservoir of common sense to tap, and they have not been encouraged to think of approximations and real-life models for fractions. From their earliest contact with fractions, children should keep in touch with the meaning of fractions and operations on them in terms of real objects and problem situations. The next sections involve relating number sentences to real-world situations, and also to various more abstract models for fractions.

Relating Operations on Fractions to Story Problems and Diagrams

Children should be encouraged to think about operations on fractions informally, in terms of concrete materials (as you did in Activity 8 with pattern blocks and Cuisenaire rods), and in terms of real problem situations and sensible approximations. For each one of the problems below, three possible answers are given. Do not use pencil and paper to solve the problems, but for each one circle the answer that is *closest* to the correct one. You should be able to eliminate some answers as unreasonable for the situation.

1. A flute teacher who gives $\frac{3}{4}$ hour lessons wants to schedule 3 students in one day. How many hours will this take?

2. A fifth-grade class is making aprons for the art room. Each apron requires $\frac{3}{4}$ meter of fabic. How many can the students make from 3 meters of fabric?

3. You want to make two different recipes of cookies. One requires $\frac{3}{4}$ cup of chopped nuts, and the other requires 3 cups of chopped nuts. How many cups of chopped nuts will you need in all?

4. You are walking along a trail that you know to be 3 miles long. After a bit, you read a sign saying that you have already walked $\frac{3}{4}$ mile. How many miles farther do you have to walk?

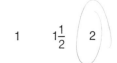

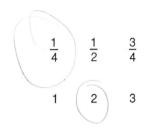

$\frac{1}{4}$ $\frac{1}{2}$ $\frac{3}{4}$

1   2   3

5. Three children are eating pizza. They all eat the same amount and altogether they eat $\frac{3}{4}$ pizza. How much of the pizza does each one eat?

6. You have 3 dozen eggs but only $\frac{3}{4}$ of them are not broken. How many dozen are whole?

Children should also be encouraged to make rough sketches representing the situation. Which of the preceding problems do these sketches suggest?

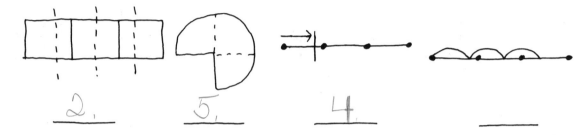

2,   5,   4

What symbolic expressions underlie each of the situations above? Write the number of the problem which corresponds to each of the following expressions:

$\frac{3}{4} + 3$ $3 - \frac{3}{4}$ $3 \times \frac{3}{4}$ $\frac{3}{4} \times 3$ $3 \div \frac{3}{4}$ $\frac{3}{4} \div 3$

($\frac{3}{4}$ of eggs)

3,   4   1,   6.   2   5

In writing symbolic expressions for these fraction problems, you probably relied on your understanding of the operations as developed with whole numbers. Of course the meanings of the operations addition, subtraction, multiplication, and division for fractions are closely related to those for whole numbers; yet some interpretations are easier to apply than others.

Addition and Subtraction

Addition and subtraction are usually understood as joining and taking apart, or as going forward or backward on a number line (for example, as in problems (3) and (4) above). These interpretations present no difficulty for work with fractions — although it is usually easier to think in terms of joining lengths, areas, or volumes rather than sets. The number line interpretation is especially easy. Write number sentences for each of these diagrams.

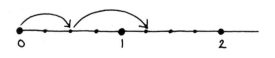

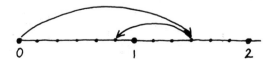

Multiplication

Multiplication is often presented initially as repeated addition — $3 \times 2 = 2 + 2 + 2$. This interpretation works well with multiplications such as $3 \times \frac{3}{4} = \frac{3}{4} + \frac{3}{4} + \frac{3}{4}$ (as in problem (1), page 517); however it is not as easy to define $\frac{3}{4} \times 3$ as "3 added to itself $\frac{3}{4}$ times." The usual interpretation of $\frac{3}{4} \times 3$ is as in problem (6), $\frac{3}{4}$ *of* 3 — that is, divide 3 into 4 equal parts and take 3 of them. Similarly, $\frac{1}{2} \times \frac{1}{4}$ can be read as "_____ of _____ which is _____." In a later section we will see that this interpretation is particularly easy to show in terms of an area or region model.

Division

Division is perhaps the most difficult operation on fractions for which to find meaningful problem situations. Certain types of problems do translate nicely from whole number division. For example, division by a whole number, such as $\frac{3}{4} \div 3$, can be interpreted as sharing (as in problem 5). That is, $\frac{3}{4} \div 3 = \square$ can be interpreted "How much in each share, if $\frac{3}{4}$ is shared among 3?" This is the *partitive* concept of division.

However, $3 \div \frac{3}{4}$ cannot easily be interpreted in this way. How can you share something among $\frac{3}{4}$ people? It is more natural for this problem to use the *measurement* concept of division that interprets $3 \div \frac{3}{4} = \square$ as "How many $\frac{3}{4}$'s are in 3?" (See problem 2 above.) Similarly, $\frac{1}{2} \div \frac{1}{4} = \square$ would be read "How many _____'s are in _____?" and so $\frac{1}{2} \div \frac{1}{4} = $ _____.

Some division examples, however, do not naturally fit either measurement or partitive interpretation such as $\frac{1}{3} \div \frac{1}{2} = \square$. We could ask "How many $\frac{1}{2}$'s are in $\frac{1}{3}$?" but it is difficult to visualize this interpretation. Such examples may be most conveniently treated by translating to the related multiplication: just as $6 \div 2 = \square$ corresponds to $2 \times \square = 6$, so $\frac{1}{3} \div \frac{1}{2} = \square$ corresponds to $\frac{1}{2} \times \square = \frac{1}{3}$. That is, $\frac{1}{3} \div \frac{1}{2} = \square$ can be read "$\frac{1}{2}$ of what number is $\frac{1}{3}$?"

You have been finding number sentences to match certain problem situations. Now do this in reverse. Try to write problem situations that match each of the following number sentences. Try to vary the types of models for fractions, and make your problems believable and realistic. Draw rough sketches to show an appproximate solution to your problem.

Number Sentence	Problem Situation	Sketch
1. $\dfrac{3}{8} + \dfrac{3}{4} = \square$		
2. $1\dfrac{1}{2} - \dfrac{5}{8} = \square$		
3. $5 \times \dfrac{3}{8} = \square$		
4. $\dfrac{3}{4} \times \dfrac{1}{2} = \square$		
5. $3 \div \dfrac{1}{2} = \square$		
6. $\dfrac{1}{2} \div 3 = \square$		
7. $\dfrac{3}{4} \div \dfrac{1}{8} = \square$		

A Closer Look at Various Models for Fractions

In order to help children abstract the idea of rational number and to bridge the gap between real-world situations and symbolic expressions, it is helpful to give various experiences first with concrete materials (as you did in Activities 1 and 2 with pattern blocks and Cuisenaire rods), and then with semiconcrete models. In this section, we will look at area, length, and set or discrete models more closely. Each model has some unique mathematical direction: *area models* can call upon and reinforce geometry concepts; *length models* are related to measurement with rulers; and set or *discrete models* relate to operations of multiplication and division on whole numbers.

Area Models for Fractions

Geometric shapes are often used as units in work with fractions. Can you divide each shape into *congruent* parts to show each of the fractions listed? (To find congruent parts for thirds, for example, you must have three pieces that would fit exactly on top of each other.) Try it in pencil first. You will probably find that six of them are quite difficult. Compare your results with someone else's. Are there any shapes on which you agreed completely? Do your results show anything about equivalent fractions? (**Hint:** If you are stuck, the puzzles in Activity 3 with pattern blocks might help you.)

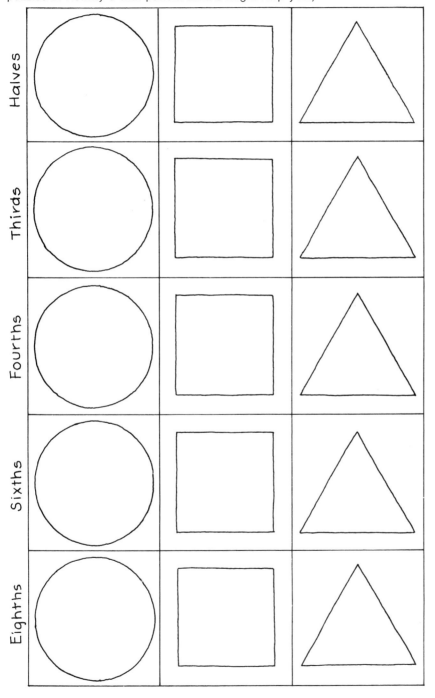

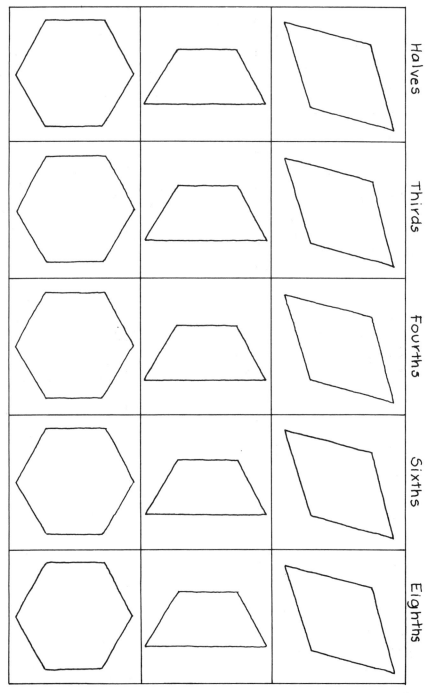

Children may find it easier to do this type of activity through folding
paper. They could work with just one or two larger cutout shapes. Which of

your results here could be done by folding paper? Which shapes would be best to use in this way?

In this activity, you found fractional parts that were congruent. Children at first usually associate fractions with congruent parts of the whole, yet congruence is not essential. For example, the shaded region in diagram a does represent $\frac{1}{4}$ of the rectangle. This shaded triangle is not congruent to all of the other three triangles — however all four triangles do have the same area. It may be difficult to see this, unless a few more lines are drawn (see diagram b). Now the rectangle is divided into eight *congruent* regions, and you can see that the shaded part represents $\frac{2}{8}$ or $\frac{1}{4}$ of the area. Recognizing that this shaded region does represent $\frac{1}{4}$ of the area of the rectangle calls on some deeper knowledge of geometry.

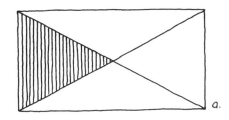

a.

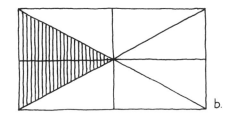

b.

When using a triangle to show thirds, you might have tried to do it as shown here (that is, by dividing the base into three equal lengths.) Of course this does not suit the problem, because the three regions are not congruent. (Why?) Do these three regions in fact have the same area? _____ Can you explain why? (**Hint:** Do these three triangles have the same height? Do they have the same base? See Chapter 8, Geometry on a Geoboard, pages 370–372.)

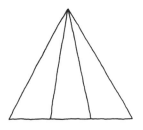

It is correct to use noncongruent parts as models for fractions so long as all parts have the same area. However, unless children can clearly see why the areas are the same, they will miss the point of the area model for fractions. Since the concept of fraction is introduced to children long before they have the geometric skills necessary to recognize noncongruent regions of the same area, early area models for fractions should use only congruent parts.

Length Models for Fractions

1. Look at a ruler (preferably the kind that has inches on one side and centimeters on the other). The inch side probably looks like this. **Note:** The ruler has been enlarged. Tell by how much.

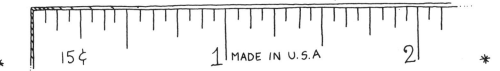

Why are the little vertical lines of different lengths?

Would you buy a ruler on which all of the markings were of the *same* length? What difficulties might you have with such a ruler?

Take a piece of paper, and lay it over the picture of the ruler on the previous page so that the bottom edge of the paper goes through the two stars (*). Now gradually slide the paper upwards to uncover the whole picture. What did you see?

Use your ruler to measure this length: ━━━━━ Write the length in inches in four different ways suggested by the marks on the ruler. _____,
_____, _____, _____

Now look at the other edge of your ruler, which probably looks like this. (Again the ruler has been enlarged. Tell by how much.)

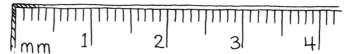

What does the "mm" mean? _____ Do the numbers stand for mm's? ___ What would you call the smallest subdivision in fractional terms? _____ Try the same activity as before, sliding up a piece of paper over the picture of the ruler. How many "steps" do you see this time?

2. Cut a strip of paper that is as long as this line segment.

0   1

Fold your strip of paper in half. This should allow you to mark where $\frac{1}{2}$ is on the line above. What other fractions can you make by folding? (Do not use a ruler for this.) Being as exact as possible, mark fractions on the line, and list the ones you can locate by folding. _____ Which fractions are difficult to find? _____

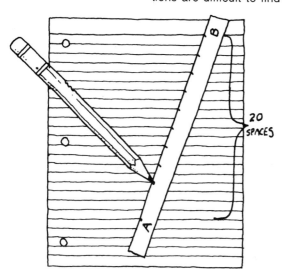

3. By folding paper you may be able to approximate where certain fractions lie on the line segment. You can get a much more precise location by a simple trick using a sheet of ruled paper. The fact that the lines are regularly spaced allows you to divide lengths into various fractional parts. For example, to divide the length between points A and B marked on the paper strip (drawn to the right) into tenths, count off 10 rows (or some multiple of 10 if this is too small). Then arrange the strip so that A is on the bottom line and B is on the top line marked. Then use the lines to mark off 10 segments of equal length.

Now use this method with your strip of paper from part (2). Divide the length from 0 to 1 on the line segment into five equal lengths, and mark the points corresponding to $\frac{1}{5}$, $\frac{2}{5}$, $\frac{3}{5}$, and $\frac{4}{5}$.

4. In fact, the length in part (2) is the same as the length of the unit in the chart below. Do your marks for fractions on your strip or line segment correspond to the marks on the chart? This chart, similar to the one you drew in Activity 4 with Cuisenaire rods, can be used to demonstrate many facts about rational numbers. Use the chart to answer the questions. You will probably find it useful to use a straightedge vertically on the chart.

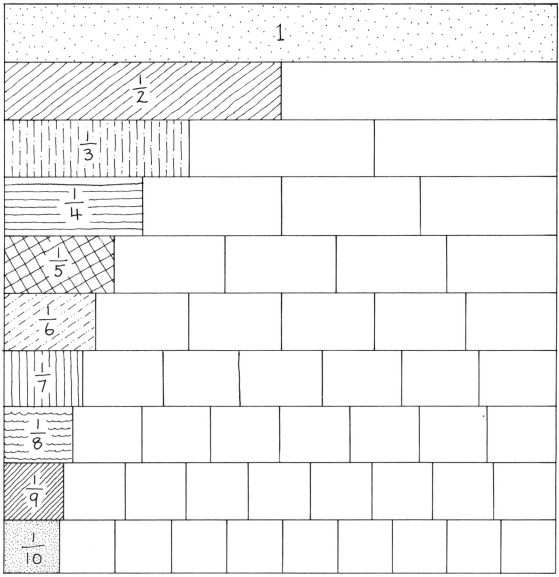

a. Which is greater, $\frac{1}{7}$ or $\frac{1}{8}$? Which is greater, $\frac{2}{3}$ or $\frac{5}{7}$?

b. Does $\frac{2}{3} = \frac{6}{9}$? Fill in the blanks. $\frac{1}{2} = \frac{}{4} = \frac{}{6} = \frac{}{8} = \frac{}{10}$

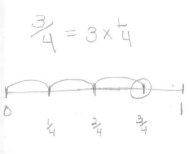

c. Use the chart to find two fractions that are equivalent to $\frac{2}{3}$.

d. Can you see the difference between $\frac{1}{9}$ and $\frac{1}{10}$? Do you think that you could see the difference between $\frac{1}{20}$ and $\frac{1}{21}$?

e. Can you find a decimal for $\frac{3}{5}$? $\frac{3}{5} = \frac{}{10} = .\underline{\hspace{1cm}}$

f. Is $\frac{2}{3}$ closer to $\frac{3}{7}$ or $\frac{4}{7}$?

Is $\frac{1}{8}$ closer to .1 or .2?

Is $\frac{6}{7}$ closer to .8 or .9?

Children could make such a chart from colored strips of paper, and use the cut-up strips to do approximate additions, subtractions, multiplications, and divisions (in the same way that you used Cuisenaire rods in Activity 8).

5. There is another meaning for a fraction. If you were asked to mark $\frac{2}{3}$ on the number line below, you would probably divide the interval 0 to 1 into three parts of equal length, and then count off two of them.

You are thinking of $\frac{2}{3}$ as $2 \times \frac{1}{3}$, which is how the notation $\frac{2}{3}$ is usually introduced. Another interpretation would be $\frac{2}{3} = \frac{1}{3} \times 2$. This would suggest dividing the interval from 0 to 2 into three parts of equal length, and taking one of them; or thinking of $\frac{2}{3}$ as $2 \div 3$, as shown below.

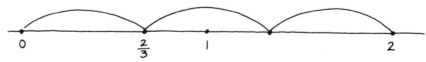

This interpretation is sometimes not taught in early work with fractions, yet children will certainly encounter it if they attempt to work with fractions on a calculator, since $\frac{2}{3}$ is entered by pushing successively buttons for 2, ÷, 3.

Try using this procedure to find $\frac{3}{4}$ on the number line below.

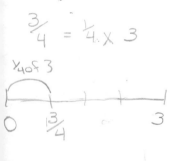

A Discrete Model for Fractions

The following activities show how a discrete or set model can be used to develop various fraction concepts. Imagine doing them with red and black checkers, and fill in the blanks.

A Pattern

Use red (◯) and black (●) checkers to make the patterns below. Draw in the next pattern.

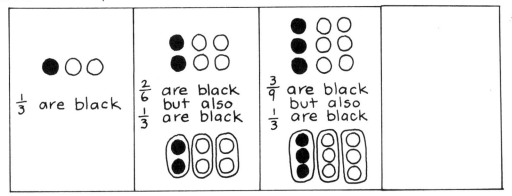

$\frac{1}{3}$ are black

$\frac{2}{6}$ are black but also $\frac{1}{3}$ are black

$\frac{3}{9}$ are black but also $\frac{1}{3}$ are black

Comparison

Lay out 12 checkers (cookies?) like this.

If 3 people share them, each gets

If 4 people share them, each gets

Do you get more if 3 people share, or if 4 people share? _____

You can write this as $\frac{1}{3} > \frac{1}{4}$.

Describe below how to use checkers to find out which is bigger, $\frac{1}{2}$ or $\frac{2}{3}$.

Addition

Lay out 12 checkers. Take $\frac{1}{3}$ of the 12 checkers (_____ checkers).

Take $\frac{1}{6}$ of the 12 checkers (_____ checkers). How many altogether?

_____

What fraction is this of the 12 checkers _____ You can write

$$\frac{1}{3} + \frac{1}{6} = \frac{\square}{\square}$$

Describe below how you could use checkers to find $\frac{1}{5} + \frac{1}{2}$. (How many checkers would you need? _____

Do you find using a discrete model as clear as using a length model or an area model for showing equivalent fractions? _____ for comparing fractions ? _____ for addition of fractions? _____

Many educators feel that this discrete model for operations on fractions is more difficult than a continuous one — perhaps because so many numbers are involved. (For example, $\frac{1}{2}$ of 12 plus $\frac{1}{3}$ of 12 is equal to $6 + 4$ or 10 which is equal to $\frac{10}{12}$ or $\frac{5}{6}$ of 12.) However fractions often do arise in a discrete model; for example, in probability. If children toss a coin a large number of times, they will find that out of 50 tosses, about 25 are heads; out of 100 tosses, about 50 are heads; out of 200 tosses about 100 are heads, and so forth. They encounter the number 1/2 — the probability of tossing a head — as the ratio of the number of heads tossed to the total number of tosses. Work with this discrete model for fractions is often delayed until after children have become secure with operations on fractions using continuous models such as regions or lengths.

Developing Algorithms for Fractions

This chapter so far has primarily concerned introducing the concept of fractions and relating operations on them to real-world situations and manipulation of concrete objects (or drawings of such manipulations). Usually during

grades 4–6, children are expected to associate systematic symbolic procedures, or algorithms, with these informal processes. (According to the scope
and sequence chart on page 513, algorithms for finding equivalent fractions are developed in grade 4, for addition and subtraction of fractions in
grade 5, and for multiplication and division in grade 6.) In this section we will
examine how algorithms can be developed through the use of appropriate
models for fractions.

Equivalent Fractions

Already in this chapter you have seen how children can show equivalent
fractions with various materials, as in Activity 4 with pattern blocks and with
Cuisenaire rods, with a length model, and with a discrete model. Now we
will examine a more systematic procedure that helps children to make the
transition from manipulative experience to semiconcrete to symbolic algorithm. The exercises below use a rectangular area model for fractions. (Children might first do these exercises by folding paper squares before drawing
the subdivisions.) Try these exercises, using the method of the example in the
upper left corner.

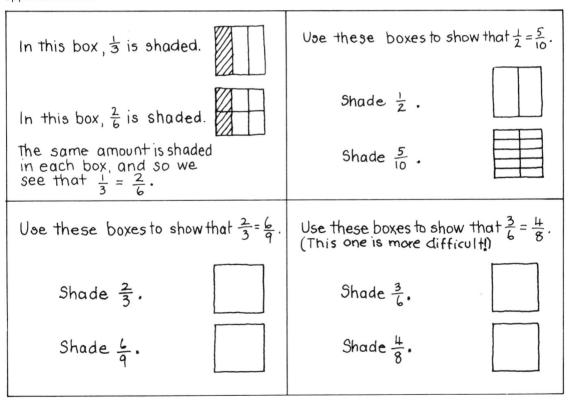

Through exercises like these, children can collect information about pairs of
equivalent fractions. They can be encouraged to look for a pattern or rule.
They might be helped by questions such as the following: When looking at

$\frac{1}{2} = \frac{5}{10}$, what do you do to the 1 to get 5? to the 2 to get 10? Does it work on other pairs of equivalent fractions? Children will probably notice that when numerator and denominator are multiplied by the same number, the result is an equivalent fraction. Symbolically stated, for any fraction $\frac{a}{b}$ and for any number k ($k = 1, 2, 3, \ldots$), $\frac{a}{b} = \frac{a \times k}{b \times k}$. In fact this model *shows* this. The effect of the horizontal slicing is to multiply both the *total* number of parts (*b*) and the number of *shaded* parts (*a*) by the same number (*k*).

You probably found it difficult to show $\frac{3}{6} = \frac{4}{8}$ using this model. One

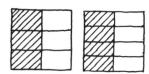

simple way is to draw the diagrams to the left and note that the same amount is shaded in each. When children are given a situation such as this, they will probably discover that in many cases it is easier to write a fraction in *simplest terms* — that is, to divide both numerator and denominator by the same number.

(For example, $\frac{3}{6} = \frac{3 \div 3}{6 \div 3} = \frac{1}{2}$ and $\frac{4}{8} = \frac{4 \div 4}{8 \div 4} = \frac{1}{2}$.)

Another technique is to search for a common denominator, which can always be found by taking the product of the two denominators.

(For example, $\frac{3}{6} = \frac{3 \times 8}{6 \times 8} = \frac{24}{48}$ and $\frac{4}{8} = \frac{4 \times 6}{8 \times 6} = \frac{24}{48}$.)

Children can discover another way to tell if two fractions are equivalent if the following question is posed. Write several pairs of equivalent fractions on the chalkboard and draw loops as shown. Ask children what they notice about the numbers in the loops.

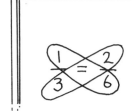

Complete the following: Fractions $\frac{a}{b}$ and $\frac{c}{d}$ are equivalent, that is $\frac{a}{b} = \frac{c}{d}$, if and only if _____. You may have written what is commonly called the *cross-product rule*. While formulating this rule is an attractive discovery activity for children, it is probably a mistake to teach it as a method for comparing fractions before the junior high school grades. This is because children are liable to learn it by rote and to apply it inappropriately in other situations.

In later work with fractions at the symbolic level, children may find the following device useful to show very quickly a family of equivalent fractions, for example, $\left\{\frac{2}{5}, \frac{4}{10}, \frac{6}{15}, \right\}$. They can fill out a multiplication table as shown below on heavy paper or cardboard, and then cut the inside part into horizontal strips. They select two strips (say the one beginning with 2 and the one beginning with 5), place one above the other, and read off equivalent fractions $\frac{2}{5}$, $\frac{4}{10}$, $\frac{6}{15}$, etc. Why does this work?

×	1	2	3	4	5	6	7	8	9	10
1	1	2	3	4	5	6	7	8	9	10
2	2	4	6	8	10	12	14	16	18	20
3	3	6	9	12	15	18	21	24	27	30
4	4	8	12	16	20	24	28	32	36	40
5	5	10	15	20	25	30	35	40	45	50
6	6	12	18	24	30	36	42	48	54	60
7	7	14	21	28	35	42	49	56	63	70
8	8	16	24	32	40	48	56	64	72	80
9	9	18	27	36	45	54	63	72	81	90
10	10	20	30	40	50	60	70	80	90	100

2	4	6	8	10	12	14	16	18	20
5	10	15	20	25	30	35	40	45	50

We have examined ways to see if two fractions are equivalent. A similar question is to find which of two nonequivalent fractions is the greater. For example, which is greater, $\frac{4}{7}$ or $\frac{3}{5}$? Children can do this with a semiconcrete model (such as the chart on page 525), however if they understand how to form equivalent fractions, they will see that they need only find equivalent fractions for $\frac{4}{7}$ and $\frac{3}{5}$ that have the same denominator. It is often easiest to take the product of the denominators, here 7 × 5. Thus $\frac{4}{7} = \frac{4 \times 5}{7 \times 5} = \frac{20}{35}$, while $\frac{3}{5} = \frac{}{35}$. Therefore, _____ is greater.

Addition and Subtraction of Fractions

Addition and subtraction of fractions are complicated algorithms, which seem difficult for children to remember unless they have a solid understanding of the meaning of fractions and equivalence of fractions. Many errors in these operations can be avoided by stressing reasonableness of answers and by relating problems to actions on materials or to semiconcrete models. Activity 6, with pattern blocks and with Cuisenaire rods, showed how addition and subtraction can be physically acted out with these materials. In this section, we will look at a systematic semiconcrete procedure (using shading of a square region) which can be related to the algorithm, and then how these ideas can be presented in other symbolic formats.

Read the procedure for the first exercise below, and then complete the others in a similar format. This procedure uses an area model and the aim is to find a common unit of measurement for the shaded regions.

To add $\frac{1}{2} + \frac{2}{3}$, follow the steps below.

$\frac{1}{2}$ is shaded [ ] or [ ] = $\frac{3}{6}$

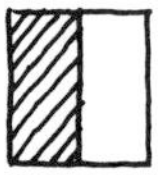

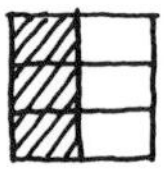

$+ \frac{2}{3}$ is shaded [ ] or [ ] = $\frac{4}{6}$

Here there are $3 + 4 = 7$ congruent rectangles shaded. So the sum is shaded below.

$1\frac{1}{6}$ or $\frac{7}{6}$ (Each small rectangle is $\frac{1}{6}$.)

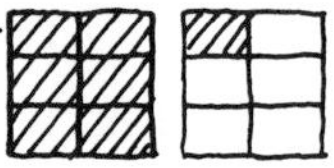

Fill in the missing parts in the following addition of $\frac{3}{4} + \frac{1}{3}$.

$\frac{3}{4}$ is shaded [ ] or [ ] = $\frac{\bigcirc}{\bigcirc}$

$+ \frac{1}{3}$ is shaded [ ] or [ ] = $\frac{\bigcirc}{\bigcirc}$

Here there are ___ + ___ = ___ congruent rectangles shaded. So the sum is shaded below.

$\bigcirc$ (Each small rectangle is $\frac{\bigcirc}{\bigcirc}$.)

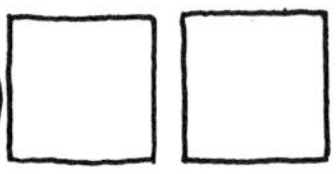

In the space below, repeat this procedure to find $\frac{3}{5} + \frac{3}{4}$.

Adapt this procedure to find $\frac{2}{3} - \frac{1}{2}$.

Notice that this procedure has two prerequisites: adding or subtracting fractions with the same denominator, and finding equivalent fractions with the same denominator.

Children should have many experiences — manipulative (such as with pattern blocks) or semiconcrete (such as with drawings of regions) — to develop the first understanding. Sometimes the verbal pattern "3 *fourths* plus 1 *fourth* equals 4 *fourths*" will help children to see that this addition of fractions with the same denominator is similar to "3 *cups* and 1 *cup* makes 4 *cups*" or "3 *cm* and 1 *cm* makes 4 *cm*" or any other such use of the fact $3 + 1 = 4$. Some teachers, however, feel that children should also see simple additions with unlike denominators (perhaps $\frac{1}{2} + \frac{1}{4}$) early in their work with the addition of fractions, so that they realize that numerators can only be added when the denominators are the same. This point was mentioned earlier as a possible cause for error; pattern 2, p. 515.

In the previous section we discussed developing the second understanding — finding equivalent fractions. Once children understand the importance of finding equivalent fractions with a common denominator, they might use shortcut symbolic procedures to find them. For example, to add $\frac{1}{2}$ and $\frac{2}{3}$ they might list equivalent fractions for each (possibly using the strips described on pages 530–531):

$$\left\{\frac{1}{2}, \frac{2}{4}, \boxed{\frac{3}{6}}, \frac{4}{8}, \frac{5}{10}, \frac{6}{12}, \ldots\right\} \text{ and } \left\{\frac{2}{3}, \boxed{\frac{4}{6}}, \frac{6}{9}, \frac{8}{12}, \ldots\right\}$$

Then they would look for a pair of fractions with a common denominator — of course, it is convenient if they use the *least* common denominator —and add them.

$$\frac{3}{6} + \frac{4}{6} = \frac{7}{6}$$

Eventually children will realize that it is not necessary to list so many equivalent fractions. The common denominator must be a multiple of the two denominators, and so it is only necessary to find some common multiple (usually the least common multiple or LCM is most convenient) and translate the example into one with this common multiple as the denominator of both fractions. They might think as follows:

Fill in similar blanks for this example.

Children might try to describe this procedure as a "flow diagram" for addition and subtraction of fractions. (The value of such a diagram lies in the children's construction of it. Try not to teach this as a method to be memorized.) Note the extra choice included in this general procedure to deal with fractions that already have a common denominator.

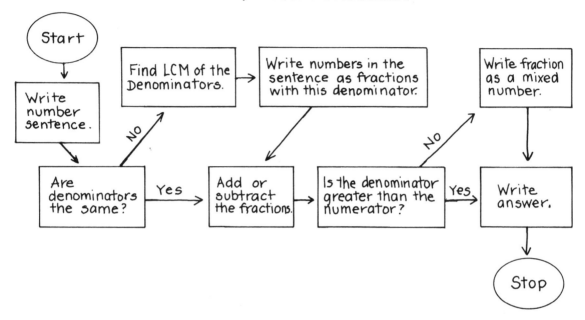

Try following this flow diagram with $\frac{3}{4} + \frac{1}{2}$ and $\frac{3}{4} - \frac{1}{2}$.

When doing $\frac{3}{4} + \frac{1}{2}$, did you write your answer as 5/4, or as $1\frac{1}{4}$? Both answers are correct, yet unfortunately many teachers feel that the answer must be expressed as a mixed number. This can cause difficulties for children who are just learning the algorithm for addition of fractions, because it introduces an additional step and possibility for error at the end of the exercise, and diverts attention from the process of addition. Actually in some situations it is more useful to have a fraction as an answer (5/4) and in other cases a mixed number.[2] Children should be comfortable with either.

Does the flow diagram above work for exercises involving mixed numbers such as $2\frac{1}{2} + 1\frac{1}{3}$? If not, could you modify it?

Children can do exercises involving mixed numbers by writing the mixed numbers as fractions, but sometimes this is inefficient. For example, to add $23\frac{1}{3} + 15\frac{1}{2}$ we could find that $23\frac{1}{3} = \frac{70}{3}$ and $15\frac{1}{2} = \frac{31}{2}$ and continue from there to find the sum $\frac{70}{3} + \frac{31}{2}$, but it is easier to write the addition in a vertical format, as the sum of two mixed numbers.

$$
\begin{array}{ccc}
23\frac{1}{3} & & 23\frac{2}{6} \\
& \rightarrow & \\
+\,15\frac{1}{2} & & +\,15\frac{3}{6} \\
\hline
& & 38\frac{5}{6}
\end{array}
$$

Similarly the subtraction $23\frac{1}{3} - 15\frac{1}{2}$ can be written vertically; however, here the difficulty arises that $\frac{1}{3}$ is less than $\frac{1}{2}$. How do we find $\frac{1}{3} - \frac{1}{2}$? The solution is to "regroup." Think of $23\frac{1}{3}$ as $22 + 1\frac{1}{3}$ or $22\frac{4}{3}$. Complete the vertical subtraction format shown to the right.

$$\begin{array}{r} 23\frac{1}{3} \\ -15\frac{1}{2} \\ \hline \end{array} \rightarrow$$

$$\begin{array}{r} 23\frac{1}{3} \\ -15\frac{1}{2} \\ \hline \end{array} \rightarrow \quad \begin{array}{r} 22\frac{4}{3} \\ -15\frac{1}{2} \\ \hline \end{array} \rightarrow \quad \begin{array}{r} 22 \text{---} \\ -15 \text{---} \\ \hline \\ \hline \end{array}$$

Multiplication of Fractions

Multiplication of fractions may seem easy because it is such a simple rule — just multiply the numerators and multiply the denominators. But children manage to forget an operation taught only as a rule, however simple, and also may apply a similar simple rule to addition where it is inappropriate. Using the procedure below, children can find the product of two fractions using a semiconcrete model — and then discover and formulate the rule or algorithm for themselves. Even if they do by chance forget the algorithm, they may remember this procedure and be able to reconstruct the correct process. Study the procedure in the first exercise, and then use this procedure to do the other two exercises. Again, children could first approach this technique through paper folding, and perhaps imagining cutting up a cake. (For example, interpret $\frac{2}{3} \times \frac{4}{5}$ as starting with $\frac{4}{5}$ of a square cake and then eating $\frac{2}{3}$ of it. How much of the whole cake did you eat?)

To find $\frac{2}{3} \times \frac{4}{5}$, follow the steps below. Think "$\frac{2}{3} \times \frac{4}{5}$ means $\frac{2}{3}$ of $\frac{4}{5}$."

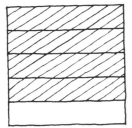

This square is sliced horizontally into fifths.
$\frac{4}{5}$ is shaded like ///.

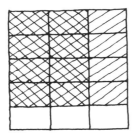

This square is sliced vertically into thirds.
$\frac{2}{3}$ of $\frac{4}{5}$ is shaded like \\\.

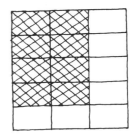

This square is now cut into 3×5 small rectangles. Of these, 2×4 are shaded, and so
$\frac{2}{3}$ of $\frac{4}{5} = \frac{2 \times 4}{3 \times 5} = \frac{8}{15}$.

Fill in the missing parts to find $\frac{3}{4} \times \frac{3}{5}$.

This square is sliced horizontally into fifths.

$\frac{3}{5}$ is shaded like ⧸⧸⧸.

This square is sliced vertically into

_____.

$\frac{3}{4}$ of $\frac{3}{5}$ is shaded like \\\\.

This square is now cut into _____ small rectangles. Of these, _____ are shaded, and so

$\frac{3}{4}$ of $\frac{3}{5}$ = _____ = _____.

In the space below, find $\frac{1}{2} \times \frac{3}{4}$ by this process.

Children who have frequently worked with the array model for multiplication will probably see that when the procedure is finished, the total number of small rectangles is the product of the denominators, while the total number of cross-shaded rectangles is the product of the numerators. Thus they can discover why the standard rule for multiplying fractions works.

In elementary school grades, fraction multiplication exercises should not be so complex that children cannot relate them to a model like the one above.

For example, exercises such as $\frac{53}{71} \times \frac{82}{97}$ are inappropriate until children have a firm understanding of the process of multiplication of fractions.

Division of Fractions

Division may be the most difficult operation on fractions to learn because it is often hard to give physical meaning to divisions. As with all operations, if taught by rote, division procedures are easily forgotten. Many mathematics educators feel that it is important to give children lots of informal concrete or semiconcrete experiences with division of fractions (as in Activity 8) before teaching the algorithm. For example, using circle pieces, children might be asked, "How many $\frac{1}{8}$ pieces will it take to cover up three $\frac{1}{4}$ pieces?" This

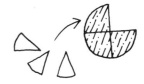

corresponds to the division sentence $\frac{3}{4} \div \frac{1}{8} = \square$.

Some divisions can be done by methods that are extensions of whole number procedures. Try the divisions below. Study the procedures, and then use each method to do the divisions to the right.

Repeated Subtraction $\frac{1}{2}\overline{)1\frac{1}{2}}$ $1\frac{1}{2} \div \frac{1}{2}$ $\begin{array}{r} -\frac{1}{2} \quad 1\times\frac{1}{2} \\ \hline 1 \\ -\frac{1}{2} \quad 1\times\frac{1}{2} \\ \hline \frac{1}{2} \\ -\frac{1}{2} \quad 1\times\frac{1}{2} \\ \hline 0 \quad 3 \end{array}$	$2\frac{2}{3} \div \frac{2}{3}$
Sharing Share $\frac{5}{6}$ of a square among 3. $\frac{5}{6} \div 3$ First shade $\frac{5}{6}$. Then share. Each share is $\frac{5}{18}$ of the square.	$\frac{2}{3} \div 4$
Number Line How many $\frac{1}{2}$'s are in $1\frac{2}{3}$? $1\frac{2}{3} \div \frac{1}{2}$ There are 3 halves and $\frac{1}{3}$ of a half left over, or $3\frac{1}{3}$.	$1\frac{1}{2} \div \frac{1}{3}$

The informal procedures should eventually be replaced by a symbolic algorithm which works for any type of division. Below are given examples of three methods for finding $\frac{3}{4} \div \frac{1}{3}$, which also show in some way *why* the answer is correct. The first depends on understanding that a fraction corresponds to a division — that is, $\frac{2}{3}$ means $2 \div 3$ — and that division by 1 leaves a number unchanged — that is, $\frac{6}{1} = 6$. The second relies on interpretation of division in terms of multiplication. Both require an understanding of multiplication of fractions. The third relates the division to a corresponding whole number division. Study the procedures, and then use each method to do the divisions to the right.

Complex Fraction Method

$$\frac{3}{4} \div \frac{1}{3} = \frac{\frac{3}{4}}{\frac{1}{3}} = \frac{\frac{3}{4} \times \frac{3}{1}}{\frac{1}{3} \times \frac{3}{1}} = \frac{\frac{3}{4} \times \frac{3}{1}}{1}$$

$$= \frac{3}{4} \times \frac{3}{1} = \frac{3 \times 3}{4 \times 1} = \frac{9}{4}$$

$$\frac{3}{2} \div \frac{1}{5} =$$

Missing Factor Method

$$\frac{3}{4} \div \frac{1}{3} = \boxed{} \quad \text{means} \quad \frac{1}{3} \times \boxed{} = \frac{3}{4}.$$

How can we fill in the box?

$$\frac{1}{3} \times \boxed{\frac{3}{1} \times \frac{3}{4}} = \frac{3}{4}$$

$$\left(\text{because}\left(\frac{1}{3} \times \frac{3}{1}\right) \times \frac{3}{4} = 1 \times \frac{3}{4} = \frac{3}{4}\right)$$

$$\frac{3}{2} \div \frac{1}{5} =$$

Common Denominator Method

$$\frac{3}{4} \div \frac{1}{3} = \frac{9}{12} \div \frac{4}{12}$$

"How many 4 twelfths are in 9 twelfths?" is the same question as "How many 4's are in 9?" The answer is $9 \div 4$ or $\frac{9}{4}$.

$$\frac{3}{2} \div \frac{1}{5} =$$

Which method do you prefer?

After using these procedures to divide fractions, children may discover and state their own rule. They may notice that in the first two methods $\frac{3}{4} \div \frac{1}{3} = \frac{3}{4} \times \frac{3}{1}$ and generalize to say that $\frac{a}{b} \div \frac{c}{d} = $ _____ × _____. This rule is, of course, often taught as *invert and multiply* — but without some understanding of the process, children are likely to make an error by inverting the wrong fraction.

Developing Algorithms for Decimals

In many ways, decimal notation for rational numbers is easier to deal with than fractional notation, because many decimal algorithms are simply extensions of algorithms learned for whole numbers. However, if children learn fraction algorithms first, they can build on their knowledge to understand just how the place-value algorithms apply. Children should realize that decimals and fractions are simply two different ways to represent the same rational number. In the future, when the metric system and hand-held calculators are used more commonly, we may find the place-value (that is, decimal) approach to rational numbers being taught first. However, at present, algorithms for decimals are often justified in terms of previous work with fractions.

We have seen in Chapter 7, Place Value, how various models for place value — chip trading, multibase blocks, measurement in the metric system — can be used to show decimal fractions. These materials can be used to act out many simple situations.

Addition and Subtraction of Decimals

These operations present no difficulties when acted out physically. To the right are shown two materials (squared material and a place-value chart) being used to show 1.2 + .34. The most common error that children make in the symbolic algorithm is to line up the last digits, instead of lining up the decimal point or place values. To avoid this difficulty, children might use expanded notation: $1.2 + .34 = \left(1 + \frac{2}{10}\right) + \left(\frac{3}{10} + \frac{4}{100}\right)$, and then it is clear that the tenths must be added.

Actually some teachers say that exercises involving "ragged decimals" (different numbers of places to the right of the decimal point) are unrealistic; that in real life, where decimals usually come from measurements, it is more natural to take all measurements to the same degree of accuracy. Thus the addition above, if it was about length, might be 1.20 m + .34 m, where the measurements were 120 cm and 34 cm to the nearest centimeter.

Multiplication of Decimals

Some multiplications (of a decimal by a whole number) are easy to act out with place-value materials. For example, children can find 3 × 1.42 by making three piles, each containing materials for 1.42, then combining and exchanging pieces to find the total.

Children can demonstrate multiplication of two decimals (such as 1.2 × 2.3) on squared paper. This model depends on children's prior experience with an area model for multiplication — they should know that a piece of paper 5 cm by 8 cm has area 5 × 8 or 40 square centimeters. In Chapter 9, Whole Number Algorithms and Their Uses, this model was used to show the multiplication of two two-digit numbers.

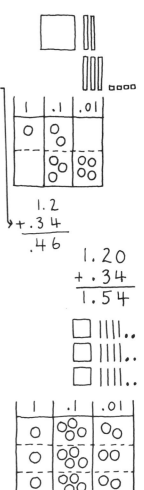

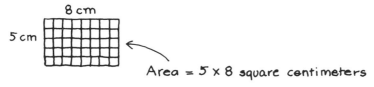

Area = 5 × 8 square centimeters

I square unit

To use this method for decimal multiplication, it is easiest to use graph paper in which every tenth line is thickened. The unit of length is then the distance between thickened lines (____1 unit____). The unit of area is the square which is one unit on a side. (See to the left.) Notice that the strip

(⬛⬛⬛⬛⬛⬛⬛⬛⬛⬛) has area $\frac{1}{10}$ square unit, and the small square (☐)

has area $\frac{1}{100}$ square unit. Do you see why? Study the procedure below, and use it to solve the second multiplication.

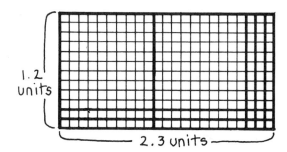

1.2 units

2.3 units

To multiply 1.2 × 2.3, construct a rectangle that measures 1.2 units by 2.3 units, and then find its area.

Notice that this rectangle is made up of 2 large squares, 7 strips, and 6 small squares. Thus the area is

$$(2 \times 1) + \left(7 \times \frac{1}{10}\right) + \left(6 \times \frac{1}{100}\right) \text{ square units, or}$$
2 + .7 + .06 square units
or 2.76 square units

Find 1.6 × 3.2 by this method.

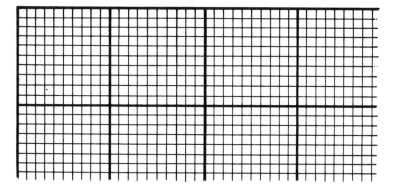

$$\begin{array}{r} 1.2 \\ \times\, 2.3 \\ \hline 3\,6 \\ 2\,4 \\ \hline 27.6 \end{array}$$

At the symbolic level, the multiplication algorithm for decimals closely resembles that for multiplication of whole numbers. The most common error specific to decimal multiplication is in the placement of the decimal point in the answer. One way to avoid this sort of error is to have children estimate their answers first. For example, 1.2 × 2.3 must be between 1 × 2 and 2 × 3 (why?) and so the erroneous answer 27.6 must be wrong.

Children can discover the rule for the correct placement of the decimal point using one of the procedures below. Study the procedures, and then use each method to do the multiplication to the right.

Using Fractions

$$1.2 \times 2.3 = \frac{12}{10} \times \frac{23}{10} = \frac{12 \times 23}{10 \times 10} \qquad 3.2 \times .16 =$$

$$= \frac{276}{100} = 2.76$$

Expanding as Decimals

$$1.2 \times 2.3 = (12 \times .1) \times (23 \times .1) \qquad 3.2 \times .16$$
$$= (12 \times 23) \times (.1 \times .1)$$
$$= 276 \times .01 = 2.76$$

(Notice that in the second method children must know that $.1 \times .1 = .01$, which they can see from the sequence of drawings below.)

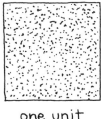

one unit

|

one-tenth of a unit

.|

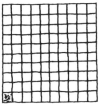

one-tenth of one-tenth of a unit, or one-hundredth

$.1 \times .1 = .01$

Which of the two methods above do you find clearer, Using Fractions or Expanding as Decimals?

Probably when you multiply 2.3×1.2, you do not use any of these explanations or procedures. Many adults would say: "Multiply as whole numbers, count up the total number of places to the right of the decimal point, and put the decimal point in the answer that many spaces from the right." Perhaps you learned this method by rote and could not explain why it works. However, even if you succeed in multiplying decimals this way, there are many people who have difficulty remembering such rote-taught rules. Algorithms such as this are most easily learned and remembered if they are explained and understood. Do you see how the step ". . . put the decimal point that many spaces from the right . . ." corresponds to dividing by 100 in Using Fractions and to multiplying by .01 in Expanding as Decimals?

Notice that multiplication of decimals differs from addition and subtraction of decimals in that numbers need not be lined up by place value. For example, if you write $3.2 \times .16$ in a vertical format, the "1" would be placed under the "3" even though the "1" stands for tenths and the "3" stands for units.

One common application of multiplication of decimals arises with percents. The symbol 15%, read as fifteen percent, means fifteen out of one hun-

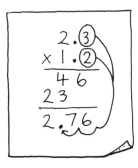

dred or $\frac{15}{100}$ or .15. The expression "15% of 40" means $\frac{15}{100} \times 40$, or .15 $\times$ 40, which is 6. (Do you see why?) Once children learn what "% of" means, percentage exercises become examples of decimal multiplication. Write a decimal multiplication for each of the following, and solve it.

25% of 3.20   _____ × _____
6.5% of 200   _____ · × _____
80% of 35   _____ × _____
150% of 200   _____ × _____

Could you write story problems that correspond to these four exercises? (**Hint:** Think of sales, banks, tests, . . .)

Division of Decimals

As with division of fractions, certain divisions of decimals can be done informally, with place-value models. Some divisions of decimals can be done by sharing. For example, 4.26 ÷ 3 can be acted out by taking materials for 4.26, and exchanging as necessary to share these materials among 3 piles. This can be represented in a diagram as shown to the left, which corresponds to a scaffolding algorithm for division.

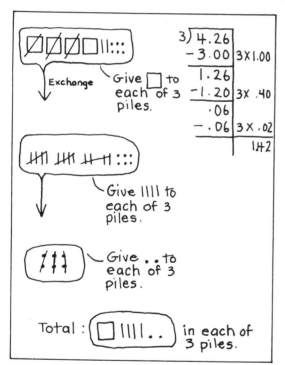

Other divisions can be acted out by repeated subtraction. For example, 2.8 ÷ .7 is done by taking materials for 2.8, and seeing how many times pieces for .7 can be taken away (exchanging when necessary). This can be shown by the algorithm to the left.

Try to do these two divisions by algorithms like the preceding ones. As you do them, imagine acting them out with place-value materials. Which one can be done by the sharing approach?

Children should do such divisions with concrete or semiconcrete materials, and learn to estimate to check the reasonableness of their answers, before working only symbolically.

$6.72 \div 4$	$6.72 \div 2.24$

The symbolic algorithm for division of decimals can be justified by the procedures with fractions shown below. Study the procedures, and then use each method to do the divisions to the right.

Division of Fractions	
$7.5 \div .15 = \dfrac{75}{10} \div \dfrac{15}{100} = \dfrac{75}{10} \times \dfrac{100}{15}$ $= \dfrac{7500}{150} = 50$	$1.56 \div 1.3$
Equivalent Fractions	
$7.5 \div .15 = \dfrac{7.5}{.15} = \dfrac{7.5 \times 100}{.15 \times 100}$ $= \dfrac{750}{15} = 50$	$1.56 \div 1.3$

Notice how the second method in particular shows why the standard procedure works — that is, "Move the decimal point the same number of spaces to the right in both divisor and dividend, so that the divisor is a whole number."

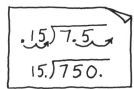

Review and Practice Activities

The Activities and Discussion Questions and Comments in this chapter have concentrated on motivating and building up concepts and developing algorithms for rational numbers. As seen in earlier chapters (especially Chapter 5 on basic facts and Chapter 9 on algorithms), while these are necessary first steps to building skill with operations, they by no means suffice. Once children understand what the operations mean, they must eventually move away from the concrete or semiconcrete model and develop some reasonable speed and accuracy with operations on rational numbers. Without some skill, children will not be able to apply their knowledge of fractions in many useful contexts.

Children can practice rational number skills in many ways. Perhaps most desirable and motivating are the incidental situations — where rational number problems arise in the course of other investigations. Also many interesting practice activities can be adapted from use with whole numbers. And finally, teachers can design special games to practice particular rational number skills.

Incidental Practice

Practice can arise incidentally in many measurement situations. When doubling or tripling recipes that use fractional measurements, children will multiply fractions by a whole number. In Activity 13, Around and Across (Chapter 6), children find the circumference and diameter of various round objects and then find the quotient in order to discover an appproximation for π. In doing this they will probably practice division of decimals (if the measurements are metric). Think of another incidental measurement situation where children might practice some skill with rational numbers.

Rational numbers might also arise in other mathematical topics. For example, you have seen how children can search for solutions to an open sentence, make a graph, and find some visual pattern (Chapter 10, pages 463–464). This activity can also provide self-checking practice with rational numbers. Complete the table below and make a graph of the missing points.

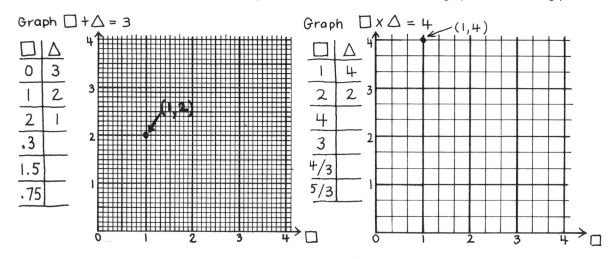

Adaptations of Practice Activities

Here are two practice ideas adapted from earlier chapters. Complete the exercises shown.

Add the numbers as indicated by the arrows. The puzzle on the left has been started. Try the ones in the middle, then fill in your own numbers and try the one on the right.

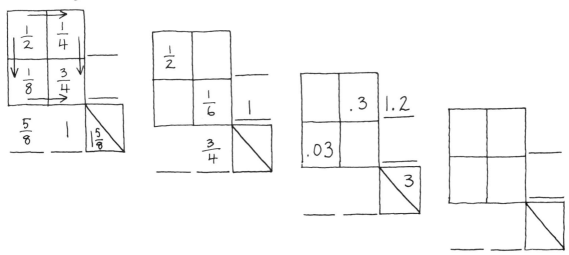

A Game

Materials: Spinner (marked 1,2,3,4,5,6), Die or Number Cards (1–6)

Directions: Each player draws a "frame," as shown here. One player chooses four numbers (1–6) using the spinner, die, or drawing cards, and calls them out. As they are called, players enter them in the spaces. No erasures are allowed, When all numbers are entered, players solve their own fraction problem. The greatest answer wins.

Suppose the numbers 2, 4, 6, 8 were chosen. What is the largest possible answer you could make? _____ What is the smallest? _____

Variations: Use different frames. ⬚+⬚   ⬚×⬚   ⬚÷⬚

Restrict the numbers chosen to 1, 2, 3, 4, 6, 12 (to simplify the computation).

Have the least answer win.

Play as a "solitaire" game — pick four numbers and arrange them to make the largest and smallest answer possible.

Bingo-type Games

In bingo-type games, each child has his own board and some markers. A caller chooses a clue card of some sort and shows it or calls it out. Children cover spaces on their board corresponding to the clues. The winner is the first to fill up a row, a column, a diagonal, or some other specified pattern. Below some sample games are described — a few clues and part of a sample game board. For each one, identify the appropriate grade level according to the scope and sequence chart on page 513.

Clues	Board	
"One-half," "one-third," "one-quarter,"....	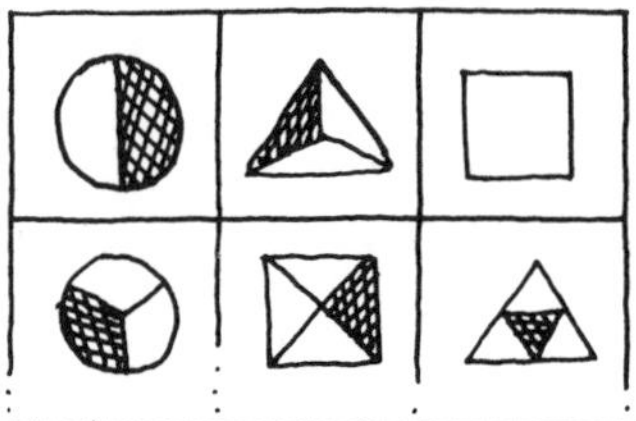	Grade ___
"$\frac{1}{2}$, $\frac{1}{3}$, $\frac{1}{4}$, ..."	Same board as above.	Grade ___
"$\frac{1}{2}$, $\frac{1}{3}$, $\frac{2}{3}$, ..."	$\frac{2}{4}$ $\frac{5}{5}$ $\frac{6}{8}$ $\frac{2}{8}$ $\frac{3}{9}$ $\frac{6}{9}$	Grade ___
"1, $1\frac{1}{2}$, 2, ..."	$\frac{1}{2}+\frac{1}{2}$ $1\frac{1}{4}+1\frac{1}{4}$ $\frac{3}{4}+\frac{9}{4}$ $1\frac{1}{4}+\frac{1}{2}$ $\frac{3}{8}+\frac{1}{8}$ $\frac{3}{2}+\frac{1}{4}$	Grade ___

Make up some sample clues and part of a sample game board that would be suitable for sixth grade.

Card Games

Many traditional card games can be adapted to provide practice with rational numbers. For these games you will need to make special decks of cards with appropriate fractions or decimals on them.

War

Directions: This game can be played with two to four people. The dealer gives a card to each player. The player whose card shows the greatest fraction wins that round, and collects the four cards. If two players are tied, each gets dealt another card and the player with the greatest fraction wins all of the cards on the table. If a player does not correctly claim a round, all of his cards are returned to the dealer. When the deck is exhausted, the player with the most cards wins.

For example, if these cards are dealt in one round, who wins? _____

A $\dfrac{5}{8}$ B $\dfrac{1}{2}$ C $\dfrac{4}{6}$ D $\dfrac{6}{10}$

Put in Order

Directions: This game can be played with two to six people. In this game each player gets dealt five cards face up in front of him. The cards cannot be moved or rearranged — however at each round a player can discard *one* of the five cards and have a new one dealt in its place. The first player to have five cards in order (smallest to largest) wins.

For example, if your cards looked like this, which would you discard?

$\dfrac{5}{6}$ $\dfrac{3}{12}$ $\dfrac{2}{3}$ $\dfrac{1}{2}$ $\dfrac{10}{12}$

Making Sets

Directions: This game can be played with three to six people. In games of this type, children are dealt some cards (perhaps six) and they try to make sets that belong together. On their turn they have a choice. They can draw a card from a central deck and discard an unwanted card, or they can pick up the entire discard pile if they can use the top card to make a complete set, and then discard an unwanted card. As sets are made, they should be put out in front of the players. The player with the most sets at the end is the winner.

You can design various "sets" that belong together — here is one idea, in which all of the sets have three cards.

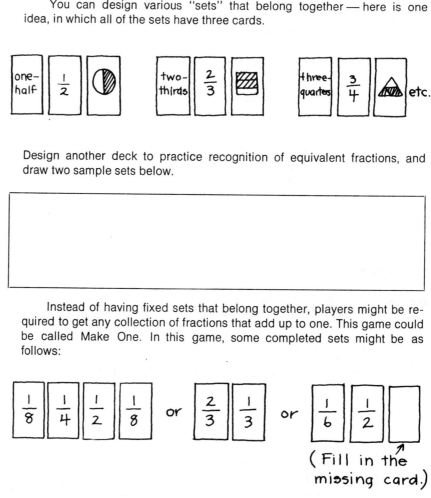

Design another deck to practice recognition of equivalent fractions, and draw two sample sets below.

Instead of having fixed sets that belong together, players might be required to get any collection of fractions that add up to one. This game could be called Make One. In this game, some completed sets might be as follows:

These ideas give only a hint of the many ways in which card games can provide practice with both rational number operations, and other mathematical skills (if the cards are appropriately designed).

Rational and Irrational Numbers

This chapter has concentrated primarily on fractional rather than decimal notation, because fractions present new and special difficulties to children, while work with the meaning of addition and subtraction of decimals can be treated as an extension of familiar place-value procedures. However fractions and decimals are simply different ways to write the same numbers — that is, the rational numbers. In this section we will examine how the two representations, fractions and decimals, are related. While some of this material is beyond the usual scope of the elementary school curriculum, it is nevertheless useful background knowledge for the teacher.

Writing Decimals as Fractions

Any decimal can be written easily either as a sum of fractions (by using expanded notation) or as a single fraction with a denominator being some power of ten. One example is provided below. Complete the others.

$$2.123 = \frac{2}{1} + \frac{1}{10} + \frac{2}{100} + \frac{3}{1000} = \frac{2123}{1000}$$

$.0142 = $ _____ $= $ _____

$22.63 = $ _____ $= $ _____

Writing Fractions as Decimals

Some fractions can be written easily as decimals. In fact, some fractions are memorized because they occur so often in everyday life — for example, in money, a quarter is written as $.25, and a half dollar is written as $.50. Sometimes we might need to perform a calculation to find equivalent fractions. For some fractions it is easy to find an equivalent fraction with denominators, such as 10, 100, 1000, as follows:

$$\frac{11}{25} = \frac{4 \times 11}{4 \times 25} = \frac{44}{100} = .44, \quad \frac{3}{4} = \frac{25 \times 3}{25 \times 4} = \frac{75}{100} = .75,$$
$$\frac{3}{8} = \frac{125 \times 3}{125 \times 8} = \frac{375}{1000} = .375$$

This method only works for fractions whose denominator divides the numbers 10, 100, or 1000, . . . evenly. It may not be practical in the third example, for $\frac{3}{8}$, because you may not remember that 8 does divide 1000 evenly. In general, we can think of any fraction as a division, for example $\frac{3}{8}$ as $3 \div 8$ and perform the division as shown here.
Write decimals for these fractions.

$\frac{3}{4} = $ _____ $\frac{5}{8} = $ _____ $\frac{6}{25} = $ _____ $\frac{2}{3} = $ _____

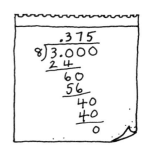

You probably found that $\frac{2}{3}$ is different from the other fractions given, in that we cannot apply the first procedure. We cannot fill in these boxes,

$$\frac{2}{3} = \frac{2 \times \square}{3 \times \square}$$ where the denominator $3 \times \square$ will be some power of 10.

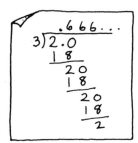

(Why? **Hint:** Remember that any number can be factored into primes in just one way. What is the prime factorization of a power of 10?) Also, if you try to apply the long division procedure, you will soon be convinced that the procedure will never end — The answer will be .66666 . . . where the three dots indicate that the process never stops. Sometimes a repeating decimal like this is written as $.\overline{6}$ where the bar over the 6 indicates that the 6 repeats forever.

Can you predict what fractions can be written as finite or terminating decimals?

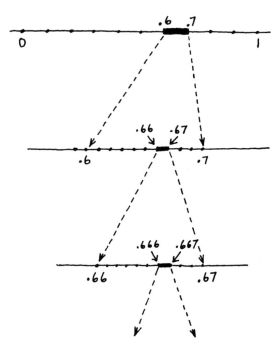

We might wonder if this infinite repeating decimal has any real meaning. If you think of numbers as points on a line, you can view a repeating decimal as giving you instructions about how to find a certain point. The first 6 in .6666 . . . tells you that the point described is to the right of .6 but to the left of .7 in the shaded interval in the diagram here. The next 6 locates the point as being between .66 and .67. (See diagram.) This process continues — the next 6 locates the point between .666 and .667. The more digits we consider, the better description we will have of the point. If we stop at any stage, we will just know approximately where the point is located, in some small interval. This approximation will quite soon be good enough for the naked eye — you probably cannot see the difference between .666 and .667 on the original number line — but under magnification it will be seen that these are different points with a whole interval between them. If the process of following directions given by each digit is continued infinitely, the exact point will be located.

Try writing these fractions as decimals. Use the bar notation to indicate the repeating part — that is, .31313131 . . ." would be as $.\overline{31}$.

$$\frac{1}{3} = \text{_____} \qquad \frac{5}{6} = \text{_____} \qquad \frac{1}{9} = \text{_____}$$

$$\frac{1}{11} = \text{_____} \qquad \frac{1}{7} = \text{_____}$$

You should have found a repeating pattern for each of these. In fact, *any* fraction will give a finite decimal or a repeating pattern, if you continue the division process long enough. (Do you see why? **Hint:** When you divide a number by 7, how many possible remainders are there?)

In fact there are other patterns to discover. You might use a calculator to find the first terms of these fractions when written as decimals. (Use the bar notation.) One has been done.
Do you notice anything?

$$\frac{1}{7} = \underline{\hspace{3cm}} \qquad \frac{2}{7} = \overline{.285714} \qquad \frac{3}{7} = \underline{\hspace{3cm}}$$

$$\frac{4}{7} = \underline{\hspace{3cm}} \qquad \frac{5}{7} = \underline{\hspace{3cm}} \qquad \frac{6}{7} = \underline{\hspace{3cm}}$$

Writing Infinite Repeating Decimals as Fractions

In the preceding section, you found that many fractions can be written as infinite repeating decimals. Can you do this in reverse? That is, do you know what fraction corresponds to .44444 . . .? or to .626262 . . .?

You might have guessed $\frac{4}{9}$ for .44444 . . . because it is 4 × .11111 . . . , and $\overline{.1}$ was seen to be $\frac{1}{9}$. But in general we cannot rely on memory. However there is a trick that allows us to find a fraction corresponding to *any* repeating decimal. Two examples are given below.

To find a fraction for $\overline{.62} = .626262 \ldots$; call this number $N = .626262 \ldots$.
Then $100 \times N = 62.626262 \ldots$. (Why?)
We may not know what either N or *100N* are as fractions, but we can find their difference.

$$\begin{array}{r} 100 \times N = 62.626262\ldots \\ - \quad 1 \times N = \quad .626262\ldots \\ \hline 99 \times N = 62 \end{array}$$

and so $N = \frac{62}{99}$, as you can check by long division.

To find a fraction for $\overline{.2341} = .2341341341 \ldots$; call this number $N = .2\overline{341}$.
Isolate the repeating part; that is, $10 \times N = 2.\overline{341}$.
Now we want to take a multiple of N that moves over the repeating pattern so that we can easily subtract: $1000 \times (10 \times N)$ gives $2341.\overline{341}$.
Now subtract.

$$\begin{array}{r} 10{,}000 \times N = 2341.\overline{341} \\ - \quad 10 \times N = \quad 2.\overline{341} \\ \hline 9{,}990 \times N = 2339 \end{array}$$

and so $N = \frac{2339}{9990}$, as you can again check by long division.

Use this procedure to find fractions for these repeating decimals.

$\overline{.41} = .414141 \ldots = \underline{\hspace{1.5cm}}, \quad .1\overline{7} = .177777 \ldots = \underline{\hspace{1.5cm}},$
$\overline{.2341} = \underline{\hspace{1.5cm}}, \quad .\overline{9} = \underline{\hspace{1.5cm}}.$

Other Numbers

The two preceding sections have shown that any rational number can be written either as a finite decimal or as an infinite repeating decimal. (Actually, as you saw, we can write 1 as .999..., and also as 1.00000..., and so finite decimals can be written as infinite repeating decimals also.) Any infinite repeating decimal represents a rational number. We might ask whether *all* numbers can be written this way. There are two approaches to this question. First (and more abstractly), we can ask if there are infinite decimals that do *not* repeat. Can you describe an infinite decimal that does not repeat?

Another more classical approach is to think of numbers as lengths or as points on a number line, and to try to find a number or length that is not rational. The following example was known to the ancient Greek mathematicians. Examine this right triangle with two sides of length 1. How long is the other side? You can see that the length is some number between 1 and 2.

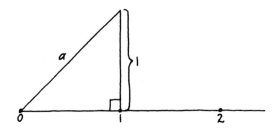

Using the Pythagorean theorem, you can see that $1^2 + 1^2 = a^2$, and so $a^2 = 2$, or $a = \sqrt{2}$. Is this number a rational number? If so, we must be able to write it as a fraction or decimal (finite or repeating). Such a fraction must be between 1 and 2, since $1^2 = 1$ and $2^2 = 4$. We might try some numbers — through experimentation, we see that $1.4^2 = 1.96$ and $1.5^2 = 2.25$, and so $\sqrt{2}$ is between 1.4 and 1.5. If we want a better approximation, we might find that $1.41^2 = 1.9881$ and $1.42^2 = 2.0164$, and so in fact $\sqrt{2}$ is between 1.41 and 1.42. Using a calculator, you can easily get better and better approximations to $\sqrt{2}$ but you will find that you cannot find a finite decimal or fraction which when multiplied by itself gives *exactly* 2.

We can show that $\sqrt{2}$ is *not* a rational number using a "proof by contradiction," by showing that it is impossible for $\sqrt{2}$ to be rational.

Suppose that $\sqrt{2}$ was rational. Then we could write it as a fraction $\sqrt{2} = \frac{p}{q}$, and we can assume that this fraction is in lowest terms — that is, p and q have no common divisors. Since $\sqrt{2} \times \sqrt{2} = 2$ (what is meant by the square root), we have $\frac{p}{q} \times \frac{p}{q} = 2$, or $\frac{p \times p}{q \times q} = 2$, and so $p \times p = 2 \times q \times q$. This shows that p is an *even* number. (Why? **Hint:** Could p be odd?) We can thus write p as $2 \times n$ for some whole number n. Substituting this expression for p into the equation $p \times p = 2 \times q \times q$, we have $2n \times 2n = 2 \times q \times q$, or $2 \times 2 \times n \times n = 2 \times q \times q$. We can divide both sides of this equation by 2 to get $2 \times n \times n = q \times q$. But this shows that q is also even (why?) which is impossible, since we assumed that $\frac{p}{q}$ was in lowest terms, and p is even. Thus $\sqrt{2}$ is *not* a rational number.

This fact startled the mathematicians in the school of Pythagoras; they tried to build all of mathematics on the whole numbers — yet numbers exist that cannot be expressed as ratios of whole numbers. In fact, the situation is worse than they imagined. It turns out that there are many such nonrational numbers, *irrational numbers* as they are called. Many arise as square roots ($\sqrt{3}$, $\sqrt{5}$, $\sqrt{6}$, $\sqrt{7}$, ...) but also, for example, π (the ratio of the circumference of a circle to its diameter) is an irrational number. This means that you can never describe π precisely as a decimal. One can approximate the value of π, and computers have calculated approximations to a huge number of decimal places, but any *finite* decimal expression is only an approximation. Also we cannot find a repeating pattern in its digits.

In the late nineteenth century, the Russian-German mathematician Georg Cantor formulated a theory of size or "cardinality" of infinite sets, and showed that there are different orders of infinity. He made it meaningful to say that some infinite sets are "larger" than others. The set of rational numbers is of the same cardinality as the set of counting numbers, but the set of irrational numbers has a different, greater cardinality.

The set of all numbers corresponding to the points on a line is called the set of *real numbers* and is composed of the set of rational numbers together with the set of irrational numbers.

Different Types of Number in the Elementary School

Children begin study of number with simple counting. First graders think of number as "1, 2, 3, . . ." and eventually also "0." As they learn to recognize number in more and more varied contexts, they will broaden their concept of number — perhaps to the integers, $\{. . . , -2, -1, 0, 1, 2, . . .\}$ to describe points on a number line which extends in both directions, to rational numbers to describe parts of things, or to measurement situations where an amount falls between whole number multiples of the unit. Rational numbers will probably suffice for an elementary school child's uses of number. The concept of irrational number is perhaps too abstract and subtle. Upper elementary school children may approach this idea in an informal way. They can experiment with looking for patterns in decimal expansions for fractions, and they can also use a calculator to try to find a number that when multiplied by itself gives 2. Formal study of irrational numbers will come later. Elementary school teachers should be aware of these topics and at all levels avoid teaching children false "facts" that they will later have to unlearn. For example:

Avoid stating in first grade that "2 − 3" can't be done." Children may formulate this statement themselves, but they mean "*I* can't do 2 − 3." Later they will learn to do such subtractions, and that in fact $2 - 3 = -1$. It is preferable to say "$2 - 3 = \square$ has no whole number solution."

Avoid giving third graders rules such as "Multiplying makes a number larger" or "Dividing makes a number smaller." While these "rules" are true for the counting numbers 2, 3, 4, . . . , they are not true for some fractions. Children who have been taught such rules will be alarmed when they find that multiplying by 1/2 makes a number smaller and dividing by 1/2 makes a number larger.

Avoid telling sixth graders that, for example, $\sqrt{2} = 1.42$ or $\pi = \frac{22}{7}$. They should be able to see that $1.42 \times 1.42 = 2.0164$, which is *close* to 2, but is not exactly 2. Rather, stress that these rational numbers are very good approximations for $\sqrt{2}$ and π.

Number Systems — A Structured Approach

Sometimes the logical development of mathematics does not exactly match the way in which children or adults learn about it. Children sometimes have an intuitive grasp of some aspect of rational numbers before they understand them completely. In this section we will give a brief summary of how the various number systems that we have been discussing and using can be developed logically by expanding one number system to another several times.

Beginning with the idea of a set, we can define the *whole numbers*, $\{0, 1, 2, 3, \ldots\}$. We say that two finite sets have the same (whole) number if they can be put into a one-to-one correspondence with each other. Addition, subtraction, multiplication, and division can be defined on these numbers (in terms of sets)[3] so that they have properties such as the following: The sum and product of any two whole numbers is a whole number. (This is called the *closure* property of addition and multiplication, respectively, on the whole numbers.) Addition and multiplication are commutative and associative. Multiplication is distributive over addition. 0 is the identity for addition, and 1 is the identity for multiplication. The whole numbers will in fact be contained in every expanded number system, and in each new system these (and other) properties will still hold.

In the set of whole numbers, we can certainly solve number sentences or equations of the type $a + b = \square$ and $a \times b = \square$, but we cannot always find whole number solutions to certain other equations. Each expansion of the number system can be viewed as finding new numbers to solve such equations.

For example, sometimes we can find a whole number solution to an equation of the form $a + \square = b$ (for example, $1 + \square = 5$ has the solution 4) but sometimes we cannot (for example, $5 + \square = 1$ has no whole number solution). To be able to solve such an equation, we can expand our number system to the *integers*, $\{\ldots {}^-2, {}^-1, 0, 1, 2, \ldots\}$, which include the whole numbers and on which we can define addition and multiplication so that all of the properties mentioned above hold. But now we can also solve any equation of the form $a + \square = b$ (for example, $5 + \square = 1$ has the solution ${}^-4$). In particular, you can find a number that is the solution to $a + \square = 0$. This number is called the *additive inverse* of a. Every integer has an additive inverse that is also an integer. (The additive inverse of 2 is ${}^-2$, and the additive inverse of ${}^-3$ is 3.)

In the system of integers, some equations still have no integer solutions; for example, $a \times \square = b$ sometimes has an integer solution ($2 \times \square = 6$ or ${}^-2 \times \square = 6$), but sometimes there is no integer solution (for example, $2 \times \square = 3$ or ${}^-2 \times \square = 3$). To be able to solve equations of this type also we can expand our number system to the set of rational numbers; all numbers of the form $\frac{b}{a}$ where

a and b are integers and a is not zero. Again, the integers are included in the rational numbers $(2 = \frac{2}{1}$ and $^-3 = \frac{^-3}{1})$, and we can define addition and multiplication on the rational numbers so that all of the same properties hold. But now in the rational numbers every equation of the form $a \times \square = b$ has a solution except when $a = 0$. (Do you see why a cannot be 0?) For example, $2 \times \square = 3$ has the solution $\frac{3}{2}$. In particular, the equation $a \times \square = 1$ always has a rational number solution (*unless* $a = 0$) that is called the *multiplicative inverse* of a, or the reciprocal of a. For example the reciprocal of $\frac{2}{3}$ is $\frac{3}{2}$, of 2 is _____, and of $\frac{5}{7}$ is _____. In the set of rational numbers, every number has an additive inverse, and every number except 0 has a multiplicative inverse. These properties form the basis for much later work in algebra.

In the system of rational numbers there are still equations that we cannot solve, for example, $\square \times \square = 2$. If we extend the set of rational numbers to the set of *real numbers* — corresponding to all points on a number line — we can solve this equation and many similar ones, and still all of the properties described for the earlier number systems hold.

Even in the set of real numbers, there are equations that do not have real number solutions. Some — for example, $\square \times 0 = 1$ — cannot be solved in *any* number system with the properties mentioned above, but others lead to a still further extension of the real number system. Do you see why the equation $\square \times \square = ^-1$ has no real number solution? (**Hint:** What is the product of two positive numbers? of two negative numbers?) Mathematicians have constructed a new system, which again includes the real numbers and also a new number called "i," a so-called *imaginary number*. The set of all numbers made up from sums of real numbers and real number multiples of "i" forms a new set, the *complex numbers*. These numbers are very important in higher mathematics and in applications to physics, and they are usually introduced only late in high school. But perhaps the eventual appearance of complex numbers in this way motivates the consideration of number systems as expansions of old systems in order to solve new equations.

TEST YOUR UNDERSTANDING

1. Write a problem situation corresponding to each of these exercises, and draw a diagram showing how to solve them.

   a. $\frac{3}{4} + \frac{1}{3}$ b. $2\frac{1}{2} - \frac{3}{4}$ c. $\frac{2}{3} \times 3\frac{1}{2}$ d. $4 \div \frac{1}{3}$ e. $4\frac{1}{2} \div 3$

2. Show that $\frac{2}{3}$ is equivalent to $\frac{4}{6}$ using these models: pattern blocks, Cuisenaire rods, number line, checkers, and one other of your choice. Show how to find $\frac{2}{3} + \frac{3}{2}$ using these models: pattern blocks, number line, and one other of your choice.

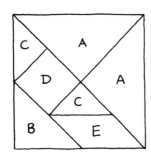

3. Show how to find $4 \times \frac{2}{3}$ using pattern blocks and one other material. Show how to find $\frac{1}{4} \times \frac{3}{5}$ and $\frac{2}{3} \times \frac{3}{2}$ using a square region.

4. Show how to find $\frac{3}{2} \div \frac{1}{4}$ using a number line, and $\frac{3}{2} \div 6$ using an area model. Show how to find $\frac{2}{3} \div \frac{3}{2}$ using the *Complex fraction* method and using the *Missing factor* method.

5. Put the following fractions in order, least to greatest: $\frac{1}{2}, \frac{3}{8}, \frac{3}{4}, \frac{2}{3}, \frac{7}{12}$. (Would the chart on page 525 help?)

6. The classical tangram puzzle is shown here. (See page 97.) If the large square has area 1, give the area of each of the pieces. How could you use the pieces to show $2 \times \frac{1}{8}$ and $\frac{1}{4} \div \frac{1}{16}$?

7. List three different types of models that you can use for fractions. Where do these models arise in real life? Why should children use more than one?   .

8. What is meant by parallel activities and why should children experience them?

9. Describe how children might be able to discover a method for determining when two fractions are equivalent.

10. Describe three common error patterns that children develop with fractions. Why might these errors arise, and how could you help children avoid them?

11. Solve the exercises below, and in each case draw a model or give an explanation of why your procedure works. Which exercises couldn't you do with a place-value material such as squared material or chips?

    a. $23.2 + 1.43$
    b. $23.2 - 1.43$
    c. 4×3.12
    d. 1.3×2.4
    e. $2.4 \div 6$
    f. $2.4 \div .6$
    g. $3.25 \div .6$

Check your answers by estimation.

12. What effects might the introduction of the metric system and hand-held calculators have on the place of rational numbers in the elementary school?

13. Fill in the blanks.

Fraction	$\frac{3}{8}$		$\frac{4}{3}$	$\frac{1}{7}$	
Decimal		.20			.313131 . . .

14. Explain the meaning of these words and the relationships between them: fraction, decimal, numerator, denominator, rational number, irrational number, real number.

Inserts for Bean-toss Device
(See note on page 491.)

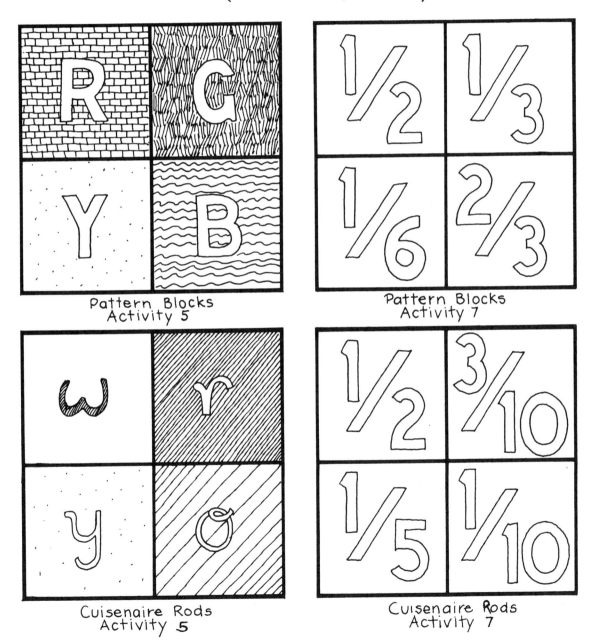

Pattern Blocks
Activity 5

Pattern Blocks
Activity 7

Cuisenaire Rods
Activity 5

Cuisenaire Rods
Activity 7

FURTHER READINGS AND PROJECTS

1. As mentioned on page 491, pattern blocks can provide children with a rich variety of informal geometry experiences. Examine *Pattern Block Activities Books A* and *B* by Marian Pasternack and Linda Silvey (Creative Publications). Which activities do you think children would particularly enjoy? What are some of the mathematical topics that can be developed through pattern blocks?

2. Examine *Fraction Bars* by Albert Bennet, Jr. and Patricia Davidson (Fort Collins, Col.: Scott Resources, Inc.). It is a program of games, activities, objectives, worksheets, and tests for teaching fractions. Fraction bars are similar to the fraction rods described on page 508. Look at the three sets of activities: Fraction Bars Introductory Card Set, which develops readiness for fractions and their operations; Card Set I, designed to teach specific fraction topics; Card Set II, which contains challenging games to provide review and practice. Also look at *Fraction Bars Teacher's Guide.* How could you use the ideas in these materials for teaching fractions?

3. Examine *Experiencing Fractions* by Stanley M. Jencks and Donald M. Peck (Washington, D.C.: Curriculum Development Associates, 1973). This booklet describes a sequence of activities for developing fractions, largely using the idea of sharing parts of an egg carton. Describe how the authors use egg cartons to show equivalent fractions $\left(\frac{2}{3} = \frac{4}{6}\right)$ and addition of fractions $\left(\frac{2}{3} + \frac{4}{6}\right)$. They also use regions on a pegboard as a model for fractions, especially for multiplication and division. Do you see how this model resembles the idea of shading rectangles presented in this chapter on pages 529, 532, and 535–536?

4. Read "Fun with Fractions for Special Education" by Ruth S. Jacobson, in *The Arithmetic Teacher* 18:6 (October 1971), pp. 417–419, which describes procedures for using acetate fraction strips on a fraction chart similar to the one on page 525 to teach addition and subtraction of fractions. How is addition to be done? subtraction? Describe a procedure for adding fractions with unlike denominators (for example, $\frac{1}{2} + \frac{1}{4} = \frac{2}{4} + \frac{1}{4} = \frac{3}{4}$).

5. On pages 515–516 you saw some error patterns for fractional numbers commonly made by children. Examine *Error Patterns in Computation: A Semi-Programmed Approach,* 2nd Edition, by Robert B. Ashlock (Columbus, Ohio: Charles E. Merrill, 1976). On pages 37–51 of that book, you will find more error patterns concerned with fraction and decimal computations. Try to identify the error patterns, then (following the directions in that book) turn to a later page (69–80) to check your identification. Finally, think of some activities to help in each case and compare your suggestions with those given on pages 106–118.

6. As suggested on page 515, the role of fractions in the elementary school mathematics curriculum is likely to change because of the use of the metric system and the availability of calculators. Examine the following articles about possible changes in the years ahead. You might also look at a recent textbook series to see if any of these changes are already taking place.

Donald H. Firl, "Fractions, Decimals, and Their Futures," *The Arithmetic Teacher,* 24:3 (March 1977), pp. 238–240.

W. George Cathcart, "Metric Measurement: Important Curricular Considerations," *The Arithmetic Teacher,* 24:2 (February 1977), pp. 158–160.

7. Examine the material on fractions in a current textbook series and teacher's guide. What types of models for fractions are used when fractions are first introduced? Are diagrams used to explain addition of fractions? multiplication? Do suggestions for teaching fractions in the teacher's guide reflect the three principles discussed on pages 513–514?

8. Flow-charting procedures, such as addition of fractions (see page 534), can provide children with a way of analyzing a new procedure and then using it. Examine the following articles about ways to use flow charts, such as adding integers, doing addition on an adding machine, solving a missing-addend situation as well as other situations.

Sherry P. Hubbard and Robert B. Ashlock, "Using Flowcharts with First Graders," *The Arithmetic Teacher,* 24:1 (January 1977), pp. 23–29.

Grayson H. Wheatley and Alan Van Duinen, "Mathematical Road Maps: A Teaching Technique," *The Arithmetic Teacher,* 23:1 (January 1976), pp. 18–20.

Bernard M. Kessler, "A Discovery Approach to the Introduction of Flow-charting in the Elementary Grades," *The Arithmetic Teacher,* 17:3 (March 1970), pp. 220–224.

Make a flow diagram or road map for some mathematical procedure involving fractions and for some everyday procedure such as buying a newspaper or getting dressed.

9. A brief discussion was given on pages 554–555 about how number systems can be constructed formally, beginning with whole numbers, then expanding this system to the integers, then to the rational numbers, and finally to the real numbers. This development is done carefully in Irving Adler's book *A New Look at Arithmetic* (New York: New American Library, 1965). In particular, Chapter 6 deals with the concept of real numbers and how we can define the operations of arithmetic on them. Read the last two sections of this chapter to find a convenient way to calculate the square root of any number and to construct the lengths $\sqrt{1}$, $\sqrt{2}$, $\sqrt{3}$.

NOTES

1. Materials like these, known as Fraction Bars, are available commercially from Scott Resources, Fort Collins, Colorado.

2. An unfortunate aspect of our mathematical language is that fractions greater than one are called *improper* or, in Britain, *vulgar.* These terms may in part be responsible for teachers' low opinion of them as suitable answers.

3. For example, to define the sum of two numbers, find disjoint sets A and B, each with one of these numbers of elements, and find the union A $\cup$ B. The sum is the number of elements in A $\cup$ B.

APPENDIX

CALCULATORS IN THE ELEMENTARY SCHOOL

Do you have a calculator of your own? Does a friend or family member have one? Do you think that many elementary school children are likely to have one in their home? If you had one easily available, would you use it to do whatever calculations you need to do?

The modern calculator is small and convenient to carry (some have been designed to fit in a checkbook, on your wrist, or on the end of a pencil), and the simplest ones are inexpensive — their price is comparable to that of a wrist watch. However with even the most basic calculator in your hands, you have the capability to do in seconds problems that would probably take you many minutes to do on paper, and that would have taken you much longer to do during your elementary school years. The effects of this technological revolution have hardly been felt in our schools yet, but eventually there are bound to be changes in the elementary school curriculum as a result of the availability of inexpensive hand-held calculators.

Some teachers and parents view the widespread use of calculators with apprehension. Will their use reduce children's motivation to learn arithmetic, both basic facts and paper-and-pencil algorithms? Will we see a further decline in "basic skills"? Some who fear these results would ban calculators entirely from elementary school classrooms, at least until children have mastered arithmetic. However others look forward to the new possibilities this innovation will make available.

Before discussing these issues, you should be familiar with some of the things you can do on a basic calculator, one which children might soon be using in elementary schools. Activities for you to do with a calculator will show some of the possible ways in which children can use calculators to learn and explore mathematics. As you do these activities, think about how children can use a calculator not only to perform direct computations but also to experience various mathematical processes: estimation, searching for patterns, problem solving, analyzing procedures, and forming and checking hypotheses.

For the activities you will need a calculator with the four operations (or *functions* as they are often called), $+$, $-$, $\times$, $\div$, and that works according to what is called *algebraic logic.* To find $2 + 3$, for instance, you push in order the buttons for 2, $+$, 3, $=$, and the answer, 5, will appear on the display. Perhaps the calculator will look much like the illustration. A button marked "C" clears what is on the display. It is also very convenient to have a button

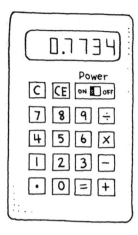

marked "CE," which simply clears the entry you have just punched in (in case you make a mistake) without clearing any previous computation. Be sure to begin each calculation by punching "C."

Even the most basic calculators vary a great deal from manufacturer to manufacturer, and so directions and results in the activities are not very detailed. The intention is that you should develop a feel for what such a device can do. Of course, you may well have a much more elaborate calculator with many more buttons or functions, in which case you might just ignore the extra buttons for the activities that follow (except where their use is indicated).

Some Basic Arithmetic

The first step in learning to use a calculator is to find out how to "speak" to it. Try these exercises on a calculator.

$104 + 53 =$ _____ $5 \times 99 =$ _____ $65 - 9 =$ _____ $69 \div 3 =$ _____

Rather than being told how to do computations on the calculator, children might be challenged to figure out how the buttons work themselves. They might first experiment with exercises which they can easily do mentally.

Now that you know the basics, try the following exercises. First, write what answer you think the calculator should provide. Then do the exercise using your calculator. (Push the buttons in the order shown.) Is your calculator ever wrong? If so, do you see why?

	Predicted answer	Calculator's answer
$1 \times 8 \div 8 =$	_____	_____
$1 \div 8 \times 8 =$	_____	_____
$1 \times 3 \div 3 =$	_____	_____
$1 \div 3 \times 3 =$	_____	_____
$2 + 3 \times 5 =$	_____	_____
$3 \times 5 + 2 =$	_____	_____

Fill in all of the spaces on your displays with 9's. Now add 1. Now subtract 1 from the result.

_____	_____
_____	_____

$0 \div 6 =$	_____	_____
$6 \div 0 =$	_____	_____
$0 \div 0 =$	_____	_____

Different calculators show different results when you try to divide by zero. Many calculators indicate that something is wrong by showing an overflow symbol. Does yours?

You might have said that the calculator should say that $2 + 3 \times 5$ is 17, because we have the convention that this expression means $2 + (3 \times 5)$. Children learn that when we write expressions involving several operations, we assume that they will be done in a certain order (that is, first multiplication and division and then addition and subtraction). But the calculator speaks a different language. Children must learn that the machine has no understanding of order of operations and does exactly what we say in the order given: it will find $(2 + 3) \times 5$, or 25.

Fractions

Can your calculator compute with fractions? First, you must communicate the fraction. $\frac{a}{b}$ can be entered as $a \div b$. Of course the result is a decimal. Try these exercises. Can you do them in different ways using a calculator? Are they easy to perform on the calculator?

$$1 + \frac{1}{2} = \text{_____} \qquad 1\frac{1}{2} - \frac{3}{4} = \text{_____} \qquad \frac{1}{2} \times \frac{1}{3} = \text{_____} \qquad \frac{1}{2} \div \frac{2}{3} = \text{_____}$$

Children will probably conclude that it is easier to think of fractions in decimal terms; instead of trying to "punch in" $\frac{1}{2} + \frac{1}{4}$, they might skip some steps and "think decimal," trying $.5 + .25$.

This fact that rational numbers are more easily dealt with as decimals than as fractions, together with the advent of the metric system of measurement, may eventually bring about earlier introduction of decimals in elementary school, and less stress on algorithms for fractions.

Decimals

Try these exercises.

$2.5 + .25 = \text{_____}$ $1.2 - .15 = \text{_____}$ $.20 \times 3 = \text{_____}$
$.4000 \div 4 = \text{_____}$ $.400 \div 4 = \text{_____}$ $.4 \div 4 \;\; = \text{_____}$

What is the smallest (positive) number that you can enter on your calculator? What happens if you divide this number by 2 on your calculator?

Integers

What happens when you try to subtract a number from a number greater than it? Try $3 - 5 = \text{_____}$. Is the answer correct?
Does your calculator handle integers? Try these exercises. Which ones can't be done on your calculator?

$^-2 - 5 = \text{_____}$ $^-3 \times 2 = \text{_____}$ $^-2 + 5 = \text{_____}$
$^-3 \times {}^-2 = \text{_____}$

Using a Calculator to Check Answers

Children can use a calculator to provide an immediate self-check of their own paper-and-pencil computations. This can help to build self-reliance and self-confidence, and also to catch errors early. Try these.

Suppose a child had done the multiplication as shown here. Is the solution correct? Use your calculator to find out just *where* the error was made.

$$367 R 55$$
$$58\overline{)21,331}$$
$$\underline{-174}$$
$$393$$
$$\underline{-348}$$
$$451$$
$$\underline{-406}$$
$$55$$

This next example is a bit more difficult. Use a calculator to find out the following:

1. Why is the answer wrong? How did you do this?

2. Where was the error made?

As in these examples, checking can involve more than determining if the answer is correct or not. Children can also be encouraged to apply their understanding of the meaning of an operation or a step in an algorithm. For example, in the multiplication, to find where the error was made, children must know where each row of partial products comes from. In the division, to check the answer, children may apply the relationship of this division to a multiplication and addition, and check to see if (58 × 367) + 55 is equal to 21,331.

Children might also use a calculator to check computations done by a new algorithm presented as enrichment; for example, lattice multiplication, or Russian Peasant multiplication (see pages 398–400).

Some calculators are specially designed to present random exercises to children. (You can select the operation and level of difficulty.) Children punch in their answers, and the calculator will tell them if the answer is correct, and also keep track of the total number of correct answers. These devices can provide an intriguing alternative to traditional pages of exercises.

Can you check this? What difficulties do you have?

$$\frac{7}{9} + \frac{7}{12} = 2\frac{7}{72}$$

On a basic calculator, you may have done this by first finding 7 ÷ 9, writing it down; then finding 7 ÷ 12, adding the result to 7 ÷ 9 and writing the sum down; then finding 7 ÷ 72, adding the result to 2, and comparing the result to what you had last written down. Can you think of a shorter way to do this?

If your calculator has a memory, you could save time by using it instead of paper and pencil. The key "M+" will add what is in the display to the memory, and the key "MR" will show you what is in the memory. If you have a memory on your calculator, write the sequence of buttons you would push to check the exercise involving addition of fractions above.

Estimation and the Calculator

When you use a calculator for complicated calculations, you may have doubts about whether or not you punched in each number correctly. (It is difficult to be sure, since the calculator does not keep a record of entries and only shows the final result of each calculation on its display panel.) Estimation is an important skill when you are using a calculator. It can help to reassure you that numbers have been correctly entered.

For example, you might try to calculate 3.56 × 41,200 and get the answer 1,466,720. To check this by estimation, you might think that 3.56 is close to 4, and 41,200 is close to 40,000 and so the desired product is somewhere near

4 × 40,000 or 160,000. Thus the answer on the calculator must be incorrect. (How do you think that this mistake was made when entering the numbers?)

Whenever children use a calculator they should be encouraged to think about whether the results are reasonable by estimating. Children can also use a calculator to practice and build up their skill in estimation, as in these examples. Try them.

Cross out one number in each addition so that the answer is correct. The first has been done. Check with your calculator.

$$
\begin{array}{r}
3274 \\
158 \\
654 \\
-2790- \\
+1234 \\
\hline
5320
\end{array}
\qquad
\begin{array}{r}
652 \\
122 \\
68 \\
34 \\
+\ 354 \\
\hline
1108
\end{array}
\qquad
\begin{array}{r}
54 \\
31 \\
12 \\
+\ 82 \\
\hline
167
\end{array}
$$

In each exercise, the decimal point is missing in the circled number. By *estimating*, put the decimal point where it should be. Then check with your calculator.

$3.766 \div .7 \ = \ \fbox{538}$

$12.734 \times \fbox{210} = 26.7414$

$\fbox{14445} \div 32.1 = 4.5$

These exercises can be done by trial and error, but it is more efficient to first estimate.

Some Special Features of a Calculator

So far we have used only the buttons for numbers, decimal point, and the four operations +, −, ×, ÷, and =. Most calculators have some further features built in.

Repeating Constants

Some calculators have a feature called *repeating constant*. (If there is a button marked "K," push it for this activity.) To see if yours does, try this.

Push 2 × 3	=	you get _____
Now again push =		you get _____
And again	=	you get _____
And again	=	you get _____

What is happening?

In case nothing happened on your calculator, *some* calculators give the answers 6, 12, 24, 48 in the exercise above. What would this calculator — or yours — do if you pushed

3 × 2	=	you get _____
Now again push =		you get _____
And again	=	you get _____

On some calculators, the same sort of thing happens for other operations. Try the following:

Push 2 + 3 =   you get _____   9 − 3 = you get _____

=   _____   =   _____

=   _____   =   _____

Push 12 ÷ 2 =   you get _____   Does this feature work in the

=   _____   same way for all four operations

=   _____   on your calculator?

Try pushing the buttons as indicated below. Do you see what the calculator is doing, if anything?

3 + = = = = _____   (**Note:** Some calculators will answer 15 to the

3 − = = = = _____   first one. Do you see what such a calculator

2 × = = = = _____   is doing?)

2 ÷ = = = = _____

This repeating constant feature can be used in another way. Try these. Write what is displayed after each "=" below.

2 × 3 = _____

5 = _____

11 = _____

26 = _____

100 = _____

If a calculator has a repeating constant feature, discovering how it works can be an interesting challenge for children.

The repeating constant feature can be particularly useful when children are memorizing tables. For example, you might punch in as follows:

3 + = (6) = (9) = (12) . . .

Each time before children push the "=" they should *say* the answer aloud; that is,

"2 × 3 is 6" (push "=" to check), "3 × 3 is 9" (push "=" to check) . . .

Try it yourself with the 13 times table (which you may not know very well). Punch in 13 + =, then repeatedly push the = button.

Does your calculator have other special feature buttons? If so, try some of them. What do they do?

Finding Patterns with a Calculator

Many interesting number patterns can be discovered by children. Some depend on collecting a large amount of data, possibly through extensive calculation. It is possible to collect this data by having each child in a class contribute one calculation to the whole class, but calculators make it possible for an individual child to become involved in a search for pattern that would otherwise be much too time consuming to be of much interest.

Some examples of such patterns have been given earlier. Activity 5, part 6, on page 404, had children choose a favorite digit, and multiply it first by 3, then 7, then 11, then 13, and finally by 37. They might be intrigued enough by seeing their original digit repeated in the answer to wonder if this works for any digit, or to see what happens if they start with a *two*-digit number. The calculator might make it much easier to explore these questions. Children could also design their own number tricks of this sort. For example, can you give instructions for someone to start with a two-digit number (say 16), and multiply by a series of numbers to get as a result three copies of the same two digits (that is, 161,616)?

Another chapter where computational patterns arose was Chapter 11, Rational Numbers, when we examined the relation between fractions and repeating decimals.

Try these patterns. (Remember that each is really an infinite repeating decimal, but of course the calculator will show only a few digits.) As soon as you see a pattern, *predict* the next one before trying it.

$$\frac{1}{11} = .09090909\ldots \qquad \frac{2}{11} = \underline{\hspace{2cm}} \qquad \frac{3}{11} = \underline{\hspace{2cm}}$$

$$\frac{4}{11} = \underline{\hspace{2cm}} \qquad \frac{5}{11} = \underline{\hspace{2cm}} \qquad \frac{6}{11} = \underline{\hspace{2cm}}$$

(Optional) Try $\dfrac{1}{13}, \dfrac{2}{13}, \dfrac{3}{13}, \ldots$. Do you see a pattern?)

Find $\dfrac{1}{9} = \underline{\hspace{2cm}}, \quad \dfrac{1}{99} = \underline{\hspace{2cm}}, \quad \dfrac{1}{999} = \underline{\hspace{2cm}}$

Predict the next: $\dfrac{1}{9999} = \underline{\hspace{2cm}}$

Find $6 \times 6 = \underline{\hspace{2cm}}, \quad 66 \times 66 = \underline{\hspace{2cm}}, \quad 666 \times 666 = \underline{\hspace{2cm}}$

Predict the next: $6666 \times 6666 = \underline{\hspace{2cm}}$

There are many amusing number tricks described in the literature of recreational mathematics. Try this one, for example, on your calculator.

Take *any* three-digit number (with the 100's digit at least 2 more than the units digit); for example, 351.
Reverse the digits and subtract.
Reverse the digits of the result and add.
What do you get? Write down your answer and try it again.

$$\begin{array}{r} 3\,5\,1 \\ -1\,5\,3 \\ \hline 1\,9\,8 \\ +8\,9\,1 \\ \hline 1\,0\,8\,9 \end{array}$$

When children see the pattern here, they might consider some "What if . . ." questions, such as "What if you use *any* three digit number?"

Using a Calculator to Solve Everyday Problems

If you have a calculator readily available, you will probably find that you soon develop a habit of using it whenever faced with numerical problems which you cannot do mentally. Possible uses might be in balancing a checkbook, planning purchases and computing taxes on them, working out income taxes, planning costs of a trip, or averaging test scores. With calculator in hand, you have vastly increased power to consider alternatives quickly. Calculation becomes a means to an end.

Children's interests may not be the same as adults'. At first they may be eager to use a calculator just because it is a new device, but eventually they should also appreciate its power as a tool in solving problems that interest them. Teachers can pick up on various numerical concerns of children, perhaps baseball averages or other sports records, prices of bicycles, comparing growth of animals. Some upper elementary children are interested in "adult" topics, perhaps having a term project of planning how to invest $1000 in stocks, and computing how their imaginary portfolios do over the year.

Try this one yourself. (If this problem situation does not interest you, think of another which does.)

Suppose you want to buy some peanut butter and jelly for sandwiches. You want to get both at the same store, but find that the prices vary a great deal. You don't want to spend more than $2. Assume (unrealistically!) that all peanut butters and jellies taste the same. Which would you rather buy, where, and why?

The availability of calculators in the classroom may enable children to investigate new areas of mathematics earlier. For example, probability experiments can be much more easily analyzed if computation need not all be done by hand. Children can more easily check to see if large numbers are prime. Also many realistic application situations will be easier to consider. Numbers arising in real-life situations will often lead to calculations that are very tedious without a calculator.

Games, Tricks, and Puzzles

Calculators can be a tool in many games which encourage children to practice skills, especially estimation, and to understand concepts. Here are some examples. Try them with someone else if you can.

Square Roots

Two children each pick a three-digit number. They take turns on a calculator, each trying to find the square root of the other's number. The first to guess a number whose square agrees with the other player's number up to two zeroes after the decimal point wins.

Staying Less

Players take turns on a calculator. Each can press only the 1, 2, 3, 4, or 5 key and add it to the total. The first to get 50 or over loses. The keys to be pushed can be varied, as well as the "target" number. If two players play, there is a simple strategy to be discovered.

(This is a variation of the game Poison Apple on page 182 and of Activity 5, part 4, on page 403.)

Estimation

Two numbers are chosen (maybe by spinning, drawing cards, or asking the teacher), possibly one with three digits and one with two digits. Each player tries to guess the quotient, the larger divided by the smaller, in a given fairly short time. (No paper and pencil are allowed!) Players then check the answer on a calculator. Each player's score is the difference between his guess and the correct answer. The lowest score wins.

(This is a variation of Activity 5, part 3, page 403. The game can also be played for other operations and other types of numbers, perhaps addition of three two-digit numbers or subtraction of two four-digit numbers.)

The calculator can also be a tool in many tricks and puzzles. Try these.

Find this number:

$$.02 \times \left(\frac{100 - 72.256}{3.2} + 30 \right)$$

Turn your calculator upside down. What do you see?
(**Hint:** The display should look like the picture on page 562.)

Children often enjoy these word puzzles. Perhaps you can make up some others. The letters E, I, O, G, H, L, and S can all more or less be made upside down on the calculator display panel. What words can you spell with these letters? Children might be encouraged to make up their own puzzles.

The next puzzle is a calculator variation of a classic challenge, to make all of the numbers from 1 to 100 using only four 4's.

You can get the number 3 by pushing the buttons

$4 + 4 + 4 \div 4 =$

Can you get the number 1 by pushing *only* the 4 button four times, and the buttons $+$, $-$, $\times$, $\div$, ., $=$ as often as you wish? Write how you would do this. Try to get each of the numbers from 1 to 10 in this way.

Implications

You have seen many possible uses of calculators. What role do *you* think they will have in the elementary school mathematics curriculum?

The issue of calculators in schools can be an emotional one. Teachers should be aware that some parents are violently opposed to their children having access to a calculator until basic skills are mastered. They fear a further decline in computational ability. Other parents will let their children do all of their homework on a calculator. Much research needs to be done on how extensive use of calculators will affect children's mastery of skills, but studies to date seem to indicate clearly that use of a calculator either has no effect or increases the mastery of skills of children. Certainly, calculators can build children's confidence in their ability to deal with numbers and can be a valuable self-checking device while building skills. Some mathematics educators have observed that children who use calculators regularly do not become slavishly attached to them, and even realize that in many cases mental computation is faster and more efficient.

Perhaps the deeper issue here is just what skills *are* basic in modern life? In many situations where people used to compute mentally or by hand, calculating devices have now taken over — at the grocery checkout and the bank teller's window to name two. Estimation is often a more important skill in these situations than exact computation. (Do I have more than $20 worth of groceries in my basket?) We are entering an age where calculators and computers will be more and more important. Calculators can give children experience with communicating with a machine, with translating human thought into a set of procedures that a machine can follow. Elementary school work with calculators may be important groundwork for later secondary school study of computers.

In 1976 the National Council of Supervisors of Mathematics published a position paper on basic mathematical skills.[1] Ten basic skill areas were listed. These skills were felt to be essential for access to further educational opportunities and desirable employment. Notice that computational skill is only one skill area out of ten. We have seen that a calculator can be used to build up and practice several of the other skill areas listed, especially problem solving, applying mathematics to everyday situations, alertness to the reasonableness of results, estimation and approximation, using mathematics to predict, and computer literacy. If basic skills are viewed in this way, the calculator can be a valuable skill-building tool.

The calculator is bound to affect the elementary school curriculum whether or not parents and teachers wish it, because its availability will affect our everyday uses of numbers and computation. The challenge to the teacher will be to use calculators to expand children's mathematical horizons.

TEN BASIC SKILL AREAS

Problem Solving
Learning to solve problems is the principal reason for studying mathematics. Problem solving is the process of applying previously acquired knowledge to new and unfamiliar situations. Solving word problems in texts is one form of problem solving, but students also should be faced with nontextbook problems. Problem-solving strategies involve posing questions, analyzing situations, translating results, illustrating results, drawing diagrams, and using trial and error. In solving problems, students need to be able to apply the rules of logic necessary to arrive at valid conclusions. They must be able to determine which facts are relevant. They should be unfearful of arriving at tentative conclusions and they must be willing to subject these conclusions to scrutiny.

Applying Mathematics to Everyday Situations
The use of mathematics is interrelated with all computation activities. Students should be encouraged to take everyday situations, translate them into mathematical expressions, solve the mathematics, and interpret the result in light of the initial situation.

Alertness to the Reasonableness of Results
Due to arithmetic errors or other mistakes, results of mathematical work are sometimes wrong. Students should learn to inspect all results and to check for reasonableness in terms of the original problem. With the increase in the use of calculating devices in society, this skill is essential.

Estimation and Approximation
Students should be able to carry out rapid approximate calculations by first rounding off numbers. They should acquire some simple techniques for estimating quantity, length, distance, weight, etc. It is also necessary to decide when a particular result is precise enough for the purpose at hand.

Appropriate Computational Skills
Students should gain facility with addition, subtraction, multiplication, and division with whole numbers and decimals. Today it must be recognized that long, complicated computations will usually be done with a calculator. Knowledge of single-digit number facts is essential and mental arithmetic is a valuable skill. Moreover, there are everyday situations which demand recognition of, and simple computations with, common fractions.

Because consumers continually deal with many situations that involve percentage, the ability to recognize and use percents should be developed and maintained.

Geometry
Students should learn the geometric concepts they will need to function effectively in the 3-dimensional world. They should have knowledge of concepts such as point, line, plane, parallel, and perpendicular. They should know basic properties of simple geometric figures, particularly those proper-

ties which relate to measurement and problem-solving skills. They also must be able to recognize similarities and differences among objects.

Measurement

As a minimum skill, students should be able to measure distance, weight, time, capacity, and temperature. Measurement of angles and calculations of simple areas and volumes are also essential. Students should be able to perform measurement in both metric and customary systems using the appropriate tools.

Reading, Interpreting, and Constructing Tables, Charts, and Graphs

Students should know how to read and draw conclusions from simple tables, maps, charts, and graphs. They should be able to condense numerical information into more manageable or meaningful terms by setting up simple tables, charts, and graphs.

Using Mathematics to Predict

Students should learn how elementary notions of probability are used to determine the likelihood of future events. They should learn to identify situations where immediate past experience does not affect the likelihood of future events. They should become familiar with how mathematics is used to help make predictions such as election forecasts.

Computer Literacy

It is important for all citizens to understand what computers can and cannot do. Students should be aware of the many uses of computers in society, such as their use in teaching/learning, financial transactions, and information storage and retrieval. The "mystique" surrounding computers is disturbing and can put persons with no understanding of computers at a disadvantage. The increasing use of computers by government, industry, and business demands an awareness of computer uses and limitations.

NOTE

1. See *The Arithmetic Teacher* 25:1 (October 1977), pp. 19–22.

SELECTED ANSWERS

Chapter 1
Page 21.   Dot Cards, $3 \times 3 \times 3 = 27$ pieces in all; People Pieces, $2 \times 2 \times 2 \times 2 = 16$; Solids: Height (tall, short), Base (square, triangle, circle), Shape (prismlike, pyramidlike), $2 \times 3 \times 2 = 12$ pieces in all.

Page 30.   (1) Sort by size (2 piles), shape (4 piles), shading (3 piles), etc. (2) 24 pieces; 6 triangles; 6 squares; 12 straight-sided; 12 curved. (3) no, yes.

Page 38.   (1) A ∪ B = [1,2,3,4,5,6,10,12,20]
A ∩ B = [1,2,4] A/B = [3,6,12]
Greatest Common Divisor

(2) B ∩ S have a brother and a sister.
B ∪ S have a brother or a sister, or both.
B/S have a brother, but not a sister.
4 children have a brother and a sister.

(3) B ∩ Y   B ∪ Y   B/Y

Page 40.   (1a) unions: [s,c,i,e,n,m,a,t,h]
[s,c,i,e,n,m,u] [m,a,t,h,u,s,i,c]
intersections: [ ] [s,i,c] [m]
(1b) 5,4,9,0; 5,5,7,3; 4,5,8,1
(1c) 9

Page 41.   (2a) B = [1,2,4,8] C = [1,2,3,4]
(2b) A/B = [6]
(2d) yes, no (2f) 1,2,3,6 are always true.

Page 42.   (3) A ∩ C′,   A ∪ B ∪ C,   A/C,

A′ ∪ C′ or (A ∩ C)′, B′ ∩ C

Chapter 2
Page 78.   (1) c, (2) none, (3) a, (4) b, d
Page 82.   Outcomes are: Tiles [1,2, . . . ,10]; Six Lima Beans [0,1,2, . . . ,6]; Top-type Spinner [1,2, . . . ,6]; Results can be expected to be equally likely for Tiles, Top-type Spinner
Page 83.   Experiment 2. Even numbers: [2,4,6,8,10],

5/10. Getting a 10: [10], 1/10. Getting a 0: [   ], 0/10 or 0.

Page 84.   Experiment 3. Getting a 5: 6/40. Getting an odd number: 18/40. Getting a number less than 10: 40/40 or 1.
The triangular numbers are 1,3,6,10,15,21,28, . . . (and their differences are 2,3,4,5, . . .). The square numbers are 1,4,9,16,25,36,49, . . . (and their differences are 3,5,7,9,11,13, . . .)

Page 85.   Lines in Circles. The number of chords gives the pattern 1,3,6,10, . . . (triangular numbers). There would be 21 chords for 7 points and 45 chords for 10 points.
Shapes. The number patterns should all be square numbers 1,4,9,16, . . .

Page 86.   Secret Agent Teams. 1-1, 2-3, 3-6, 5-6, 21. The pattern is the triangular numbers.

Chapter 3
Page 95.   (3) The smallest number of shapes from which you can build a solid is 4. While a solid can be made from only squares, only smaller triangles, only larger triangles, one cannot be made from only the rectangles. It is possible to make solids for any of the combinations of two shapes listed except the larger triangle and rectangle.

Page 96.   A square pyramid has 5 faces, 5 vertices, 8 edges. Pentagonal pyramid, 6, 6, 10. Hexagonal pyramid, 7, 7, 12. Triangular prism, 5, 6, 9. Square prism, 6, 8, 12. Pentagonal prism, 7, 10, 15. Hexagonal prism, 8, 12, 18. In general, if F is the number of faces, V the number of vertices and E the number of edges, $F + V - E = 2$, or $F + V = E + 2$. (This is known as Euler's formula.)

Page 100.   (3b) B,C,D:2; E,4. (3c) B,C,D:4; E,8. A,B,C:6; E,12. A,B,C: 1/2; E,2

Page 101.   (1b) Possible color combinations: all the same color (equilateral): WWW, GGG, RRR, YYY; two of the same color, third different (isosceles): WWG, <u>WWR</u>, <u>WWY</u>, GGW, GGR, GGY, RRW, RRG, RRY, YYW, YYG, YYR; all different colors (scalene): WGR, <u>WGY</u>, WRY, GRY.
If two sticks together are shorter than a third stick, then one *can't* make a triangle. In a triangle, the sum of the lengths of any two sides is greater than the length of the third side.

Page 102.   (1d) All equilateral triangles are similar. With the sticks of the sizes given, you cannot construct any similar but not congruent triangles (which are not equilateral).

Page 104.   (2d) pentagon 2; hexagon 3; n-gon $(n-3)$

Page 106.   A relationship involving d, e and f: any polygon with four angles whose angles are congruent must have all angles right angles. The incorrect definition is "A square is a four-sided polygon whose sides are all of equal length." (Any rhombus or "diamond" satisfies this.) Note: Read the first one as "a polygon with four angles all of which are right angles. . . ."

Page 108.   In the Creature Card, a and c are polyhedra. A polyhedron is a three-dimensional surface made up of faces each of which is a polygonal region of a plane. Solids a, b, c, and d could be solutions to the puzzle.

Page 114.   Isosceles triangle, 1 line of symmetry; equilateral, 3; scalene, 0. Square, 4. Rectangle and rhombus, 2. Trapezoid and kite, 1. Parallelogram, quadrilateral I, and quadrilateral II, 0.

Page 115.   Regular pentagon has 5 lines; Hexagon I, 2; Hexagon II (regular), 6. Regular octagon, 8. Oval, 2. Circles, infinite. Face, 1. Flower, 6.

Page 119.   Mouse is "safe" when the number of intersections is odd; "in danger" if this number is even. In the Creature Card, a and d are tracers.

Page 120.   b and c are closed curves. (A closed curve is one which ends where it began.) a, b and c are simple. (A simple curve does not intersect itself, except possibly the two ends could be the same.) The curves belong, in order, in regions a, c, b, c, d.

Page 122.   Networks 1, 2, 4, 6 and 8 can be traced. In general, a network can be traced if the number of odd vertices is 0 or 2.

Page 131.   The pattern for rays is 2, 4, 6, 8, . . . (even numbers). The pattern for angles is 1, 3, 6, 10, . . . (triangular numbers). There are 30 line segments in the star.

Page 132.   Three dimensions: examples do exist for 1, 3, 4, 5, 6; 7, yes; 8, no; 9, no. Intersections: (1) yes, yes, no, no; (2) yes, no, no, yes; (3) yes, no, no, yes

Chapter 4

Page 148.   Activity 11. Parts 1 and 2 both give triangular numbers (1,3,6,10, . . .).

Page 154.   (c), (e), (f), (a), (b), (h), (j), (d), (g), (i)

Page 158.   2, 4, 5, 3, 6, 1

Page 161. $3 \times 2 = \square$ is D; C; B; E; A; F

Page 163.   Diagrams show: $2 + 4 = 6$, $\frac{1}{2} + 1 = 1\frac{1}{2}$; $.2 + .4 = .6$; $10 + 20 = 30$

Page 170.   (top) Subtraction, division, and average do not always yield a counting number.
(1) Sentences that cannot be solved: $y - y = \square$, $w - y = \square$, $w - p = \square$.

Page 171.   (4) $6 - \square = 2$ or $\square + 2 = 6$; $\square - 6 = 2$ or $6 + 2 = \square$

Page 174.   (top) Not commutative: subtraction, division

(bottom) Not associative: subtraction, division, average

Chapter 5

Page 193.   Activity 8. (2) $2n + 2$ or $2(n + 1)$
(Optional) $n \rightarrow (n - 2) \div 2$ or $(n \div 2) - 1$

Page 194.   (3c) Double and add 3; add 1, double, add 1
(3d) Rule: $(n + 3) \times 2$ (not the same)
(4a) $n \rightarrow n$; (4b) "-5" (4c) adding and subtracting the same amount (e.g. $+4$, -4); multiplying or dividing by the same amount, for example

Page 208.   Solutions like A: D, H; like B, F; like E, none.

Page 212. $\square + 7 = 7 + \square$ is A; S, A, S, A, A, N, S, A, A;
$1 \div \square = \square$ is S; A, A, A, S, S.

Page 213. $6 + 4 = 10$: addend, addend, sum; $12 - 8 = 4$: minuend, subtrahend, difference; $6 \times 4 = 24$: factor, factor, product; $24 \div 3 = 8$: dividend, divisor, quotient

Chapter 6

Page 260.   (bottom) I — 1; II — 2,3,4; III — 4,5; IV — 4 (Part 4), 9; V — 6; VI — 7,8,9,10

Page 265.   Type I — 4; II — 2; III — 5; IV — 1; V — 3; VI — 6

Pages 267–268.   (1) 2 cm: begins at 1, not 0. (2) 7 cm: ruler used backwards. (3) 50 mm: measures to the nearest 10 mm, not mm; for example, 50 mm instead of 46 mm

Page 277.   About 4 square dm fit on the page; 400 white rods; the page measures about 4 sq. dm or 400 sq. cm.

Page 278.   Chestnut, 8 cc; Marble, 2 cc; Cup, 175 mL; Quart, 946 mL; Orange rod, 10 cc; Gas tank, 38 L

Page 283.   (top) .6 m = 6 dm = 60 cm = 600 mm;
1.2 m = 12 dm = 120 cm = 1200 mm;
.12 m = 1.2 dm = 12 cm = 120 mm;
.132 m = 1.32 dm = 13.2 cm = 132 mm;
2.2 L = 2200 mL; 750 mL = .750 L

Chapter 7

Page 301.   (3) 13, 25, 69. (4) 16, 26, 81

Page 302.   (7) 20_F, 43_F, 100_F, 400_F, 130_F, 304_F

Page 303.   (4) 110_T, 222_T

Page 304.   Activity 8. (2) 625, 125, 25, 5, 1. (3) c. (4) 44444_F

Page 305.   (6) 81, 27, 9, 3, 1; 22222_T

Page 316.   (1) Base five: 4 longs, 4 units. (2) Base five: 4 flats, 4 longs, 4 units

Page 327.   (top) 1012_F, 334_F, 1044_F, 313_F.
(2) $3 \times 123_F = 424_F$

Page 328. $233_F \div 32_F = 4$, $233_F \div 2 = 114_F$

Page 329.   (top) sharing divisions: 5,6

Page 330.   (bottom) $30 + 1 + .2 + .06 = 31.26$
Page 332.   (bottom) 256, 64, 16, 4, 1
Page 335. $25 = 11,001_{Two} = 31_{Eight}$ (Note $11_{Two} = 3$). $35 = 100,011_{Two} = 43_{Eight}$ (Note $100_{Two} = 4$, $011_{Two} = 3$). $99 = 1,100,011_{Two} = 143_{Eight}$
Page 339.   The numbers in the right-hand column of the table should read 1, 2, 3, 4, 5, 6, 5, 4, 3, 2, 1.
Page 340.   (bottom) Egyptian numerals: 350, 3025
Page 341.   Roman numerals: 708, CCLIX, 299, MCMLXXVI. Chinese numerals: 726, 850

Chapter 8
Page 370.   Area of a right triangle $= \frac{1}{2}b \times h$
Page 371.   Area of a parallelogram $= b \times h$
Page 372.   Area of any triangle $= \frac{1}{2}b \times h$
Page 373.   Area of a trapezoid $= \frac{1}{2}h \times (t + b)$ or $(t \times h) + \frac{1}{2}(b - t) \times h$
Page 376.   The sum of the measures of the angles of a triangle is 180°; of a quadrilateral, 360°.
Page 383. $A = \frac{1}{2}B + I - 1$
Page 385.   The slide transformation is described symbolically by $(\square, \triangle) \rightarrow (\square + 5, \triangle + 2)$.

Chapter 9
Page 400.

~~14~~ ~~11~~   ~~20~~ ~~36~~
  7   22   ~~10~~   ~~72~~
  3   44   5   144
  1   88   ~~2~~   ~~288~~
     ―――   ―――
      154   1   576
                   ―――
                   720

Column I; divide by 2 (and disregard the remainder). Column II; double. A row is crossed off if the number in Column I is even. Numbers added are those not crossed off in Column II.
Page 413.   (bottom) Form 3 more groups of 48, giving 4 groups of 48, yielding 192.
Page 414.   (bottom) Divide 55 into 4 groups (1 long, 3 units) and 3 left over.
Page 431.   (bottom) M1 − a; M2 − b; M3 − h; M4 − e; M5 − d; M6 − c; M7 − f; M8 − g; M9 − i
Page 433.   (2) a − D3; b − D5; c − D4; d − D1, D2, D4

Chapter 10
Page 454.   12 has 6 divisors. 4 and 8 have 3 divisors.
Page 455.   (bottom) Vertical patterns will be given by all factors of the number N of spaces in each row. Diagonal patterns ($\nearrow$) will be given by all factors of $N - 1$; and diagonal patterns ($\searrow$) will be given by all factors of $N + 1$.
Page 459.   In Activity 5, the second player *must* subtract 1 since 97 is prime and the only other factor is 97. Since you cannot leave $97 - 97 = 0$, the only possibility is $97 - 1 = 96$. Now the first player has a choice of subtracting any factor of 96.
Page 467.   (1) Numbers with exactly 3 factors are all

of the form p^2 where p is a prime, for example, 4, 9, 25, 49, ... (2) Numbers with exactly 4 factors are *either* of the form p^3 where p is a prime (for example, 8 or 27) or else of the form $p \times q$ where p and q are different primes. (3) Numbers with an odd number of factors are all square numbers (for example, 1, 4, 9, 16, 25, ...). Challenge: A number of the form p^n has $n + 1$ factors. A number of the form $q \times p^n$ has $2(n + 1)$ factors. In general, to find the number of factors of a number, write its prime factorization, add 1 to each exponent, and multiply. For example, $120 = 2^3 \times 3^1 \times 5^1$. Adding 1 to each exponent gives $3 + 1$, $1 + 1$, and $1 + 1$. Multiplying these sums gives $4 \times 2 \times 2 = 16$. 120 has 16 factors. Can you find them all?
Page 469. $437 = 19 \times 23$, 937 is prime, $1073 = 29 \times 37$
Page 471.   (1) 14, 78, 37.
(2) 22, 33, 56; 13, 24, 47;
↓↓↓↓→→, ↑, ←, ↑↑←
(3) ↓←, ↑→. (4) 16, $\nearrow$ means ↑→ or →↑ or subtract 9, $\searrow$ means add 11.
(8) 24, 24, 24, 24, 23, 23.
Page 474. $T_n + T_{n+1} = S_{n+1}$
Page 477.   (2) Top left: any two primes will work. Top right: impossible because 1 is a common factor. Bottom left: impossible. Bottom right: many possibilities; for example 6, 10, 15.
(4) Right, as shown.

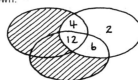

Page 478.   Arrow Diagrams: rules are multiply, take LCM, take GCF. Tables: $6 * 4 = 2$; $1 * 12 = 1$; $3 * 6 = 3$. (1) Yes.
Page 479.   (2) Yes, identity is 12. (3) Yes. (4) Yes.
Page 481.   (3) Always true. $b = ax$, $c = ay$, and so $b - c = ax - ay = a(x - y)$.
(4) Always true. $b = ax$ and so $bc = (ax)c = a(xc)$.
(5) Not always true; 4 divides 6×10 but does not divide either 6 or 10.
Page 482.   Divisibility rule for 4: 4 divides a number if and only if 4 divides the number shown by the last two digits of the number. Divisibility rule for 9: 9 divides a number if and only if 9 divides the sum of the digits of the number.

Chapter 11
Page 500.   Activity 8: a, h, d, e, c, g, i, b, f.
Page 506.   Activity 8: g, c, d, a, f, b, e.
Page 507.   One cannot easily represent the following fractions with pattern blocks: 1/4, 1/5, 1/7, 1/8, 1/9, 1/10. However one can easily represent any of the fractions with Cuisenaire rods.

Page 512.   56 rational numbers are represented.
Pages 521–522.

Page 529.   3/6 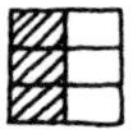 is the same as 1/2

which is the same as 4/8

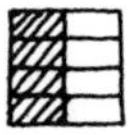

Page 530.   a/b = c/d if and only if a × d = b × c
Page 541.   3.2 × .16 = (32 × .1) × (16 × .01)
            = (32 × 16) × (.1 × .01)
            = 512 × .001 = .512
Page 542.   (top) .25 × 3.20 = .80, 13, 28, 300
Page 544.   (bottom) Tables for graphs include, left:
            (.3, 2.7), (1.5, 1.5), (.75, 2.25); right: (4, 1), (3,
            4/3), (4/3, 3), (5/3, 12/5)
Page 549.   .0142 = 0/10 + 1/100 + 4/1000 +
            2/10,000 = 142/10,000
            22.63 = 22/1 + 6/10 + 3/100 = 2263/100
            (bottom) .75, .625, .24, .666666 . . .
Page 550.   (bottom) $.\overline{3}$, $.8\overline{3}$, $.\overline{1}$, $.\overline{09}$, $.\overline{142857}$
Page 551.   (top) 3/7 = $.\overline{428571}$, 4/7 = $.\overline{571428}$,
            6/7 = $.\overline{857142}$
            (bottom) $.\overline{41}$ = 41/99, $.1\overline{7}$ = 16/90, $.\overline{2341}$ =
            2341/9999, $.\overline{9}$ =9/9 or 1

BIBLIOGRAPHY

Many references are included throughout this book in the Further Readings and Projects sections, which are designed to help you pursue your own particular interests in mathematics and teaching mathematics. In much the same spirit, the following bibliography of selected articles from several professional journals for teachers and from various mathematics and mathematics education books is included here to help you: (1) explore in greater depth topics in mathematics content, learning theory, and general strategies for teaching mathematics; (2) find ideas and suggestions for teaching topics in the elementary school mathematics curriculum, for using specific manipulative materials, and for teaching mathematics to special populations of children (for example, early childhood, special education); and (3) become familiar with some of the types of resources about teaching mathematics that are available to the classroom teacher.

The bibliography is organized in two parts. The first contains articles from several professional journals for teachers. The second lists books about mathematics, learning theory, and methods of teaching, including several which describe games, puzzles, and activities for use with children.

ARTICLES FROM PROFESSIONAL JOURNALS

A majority of the references listed are from *The Arithmetic Teacher*, published by the National Council of Teachers of Mathematics. It contains a variety of articles for elementary school mathematics teachers, including suggestions for specific classroom activities and sample activity worksheets. *The Arithmetic Teacher* also contains sections that review new curriculum materials, audio-visuals, and metric resources. More general journals for teachers are also represented in the bibliography (for example, *Early Years* and *Instructor*). They usually contain a section or column devoted to mathematics teaching and often include articles that present general suggestions that can be used in teaching several subjects; for example, the design and use of review-practice games. Also included are several articles about providing mathematics instruction for special education children who are being included in increasing numbers in mainstreaming and special education classroom situations.

These entries are organized into seven subsections. *The numbers in parentheses are the chapters of the book to which the articles are mainly related.*

(1) Classification and Mathematical Thinking (1)
(2) Number Concepts (2, 7, 10)
(3) Basic Facts (4, 5, 9)
(4) Whole Number Algorithms (9)
(5) Fractions and Decimals (7, 11)
(6) Geometry: Informal Geometry and Measurement (3, 6, 8)
(7A) The Mathematics Laboratory Approach
  (B) Games for Review and Practice
  (C) Evaluation
  (D) Calculators

AT = The Arithmetic Teacher

1. Classification and Mathematical Thinking
Adler, I. "Mental Growth and the Art of Teaching," *AT*, 13:7 (November 1966), 576–584.

Bruni, J. V., and Silverman, H. J. "Making and Using Attribute Materials," *AT*, 22:2 (February 1975), 88–95.

—————. "Using Classification to Interpret Consumer Information," *AT*, 24:1 (January 1977), 4–12.

Cruikshank, D. E. "Sorting, Classifying, and Logic," *AT*, 21:7 (November 1974), 588–598.

Geddes, D., and Lipsey, S. "Sets — Natural, Necessary, (K)nowable?" *AT*, 15:4 (April 1968), 337–340.

Newman, A. M., and Sanders, R. A. "Take a New Look at Your Classroom with Piaget as a Guide," *Young Children*, 32:4 (May 1977), 62–72.

Peterson, J. C., and Dolson, G. "Property Games," *AT*, 24:1 (January 1977), 36–38.

Piaget, J. "How Children Form Mathematical Concepts," *Scientific American*, (November 1953), 74–79.

Shumway, R. J. "Students Should See 'Wrong' Examples: An Idea from Research on Learning," *AT*, 21:4 (April 1974), 344–348.

Sternberg, L. "Pattern Recognition Training: A Key to Mathematics and Language Skill Development," *Teaching Exceptional Children*, 7:2 (Winter 1975), 61–63.

Vance, J. H. "The Large-Blue Triangle: A Matter of Logic," *AT*, 22:3 (March 1975), 237–240.

Weaver, J. F. "Classification and Mathematical Learning," *AT*, 14:5 (May 1967), 398–409.

2. Number Concepts
Armstrong, J., and Schmidt, H. "Simple Materials for Teaching Early Number Concepts to Trainable-

Level Mentally Retarded Pupils,'' *AT*, 19:2 (February 1972), 149–153.

Bradford, C. L. ''Keith's Secret Discovery of the Sieve of Eratosthenes,'' *AT*, 21:3 (March 1974), 239–241.

Bruni, J. V., and Silverman, H. J. ''Developing the Concept of Grouping,'' *AT*, 21:6 (October 1974), 474–479.

——————. ''Graphing as a Communication Skill,'' *AT*, 22:5 (May 1975), 354–366.

Cowle, I. M. ''Ancient Systems of Numeration — Stimulating and Illuminating,'' *AT*, 17:5 (May 1970), 413–416.

Dana, M. E., and Lindquist, M. M. ''Let Squares Do Their Share,'' *AT*, 26:2 (October 1978), 6–10.

Frame, M. R. ''Hamanns' Conjecture,'' *AT*, 23:1 (January 1976), 34–35.

Frye, S. ''Realistic Experiences to Find 'How many' and 'How much',''' *Instructor*, 87:9 (April 1978), 101–103.

Grossman, R. ''Lorena and Molly and Maths and Me,'' *Mathematics Teaching*, 68 (September 1974), 4–6.

Jones, M., and Litwiller, B. ''Practice and Discovery: Starting with the Hundred Board,'' *AT*, 20:5 (May 1973), 360–364.

Kiraly, J., and Morishima, A. ''Developing Mathematical Skills by Applying Piaget's Theory,'' *Education and Training of the Mentally Retarded*, 9:2 (April 1974), 62–65.

Liedtke, W. ''Rational Counting,'' *AT*, 26:2 (October 1978), 20–27.

Lindquist, M. M., and Dana, M. E. ''Making Counting Really Count — Counting Projects for First and Second Grades,'' *AT*, 25:8 (May 1978), 4–11.

Moser, J. M. ''Grouping of Objects as a Major Idea at the Primary Level,'' *AT*, 18:5 (May 1971), 301–305.

Needham, D. ''Multidisciplinary: Kids Dig Egypt,'' *Teacher*, 95:4 (April 1978), 82–86.

O'Brien, T. C., and Richards, J. ''Interviews to Assess Number Knowledge,'' *AT*, 18:5 (May 1971), 322–326.

Oliver, C. ''Gus' Magic Numbers: A Key to the Divisibility Tests for Primes,'' *AT*, 19:3 (March 1972), 183–189.

Pincus, M., and Morgenstern, F. ''Graphs in the Primary Grades,'' *AT*, 17:6 (October 1970), 499–501.

Randolph, W., and Jeffers, V. G. ''A New Look for the Hundreds Chart,'' *AT*, 21:3 (March 1974), 203–208.

Ronshausen, N. L. ''Introducing Place Value,'' *AT*, 25:4 (January 1978), 38–41.

Silverman, H. ''Teacher-made Materials for Teaching Number and Counting,'' *AT*, 19:6 (October 1972), 431–433.

Smith, R. F. ''Diagnosis of Pupil Performance on Place Value Tasks,'' *AT*, 20:5 (May 1973), 403–408.

Steinberg, E. R. ''Teaching Tens to Timmy — or a

Caution in Teaching with Physical Models,'' *AT*, 20:8 (December 1973), 620–625.

Swerdlin, R. ''The Numerical Coding of Information,'' *AT*, 21:4 (April 1974), 301–305.

3. Basic Facts

Ashlock, R. B. ''Teaching Basic Facts: Three Classes of Activities,'' *AT*, 18:6 (October 1971), 359–364.

Bennett, A. B., and Musser, G. L. ''A Concrete Approach to Integer Addition and Subtraction,'' *AT*, 23:5 (May 1976), 332–336.

Broome, K., and Wambold, C. L. ''Teaching Basic Math Facts to EMR Children through Individual and Small Group Instruction, Pupil Teaming, Contingency Contracting and Learning Center Activities,'' *Education and Training of the Mentally Retarded*, 12:2 (April 1977), 120–123.

Brown, V. ''Numbers Are Friends You Can Count On,'' *Early Years*, 6:8 (April 1976), 50–53.

Bruni, J. V., and Silverman, H. J. ''The Multiplication Facts: Once More, with Understanding,'' *AT*, 23:6 (October 1976), 402–409.

Callahan, J., and Jacobson, R. ''An Experiment with Retarded Children and Cuisenaire Rods,'' *AT*, 14:1 (January 1967), 10–13.

Cochran, B. S., Barson, A., and Davis, R. ''Child-created Mathematics,'' *AT*, 17:3 (March 1970), 211–215.

Cruikshank, D. E., and McGovern, J. ''Math Projects Build Skills,'' *Instructor*, 87:3 (October 1977), 194–198.

Dashiell, W. H., and Yawkey, T. D. ''Using Pan and Mathematical Balances with Young Children,'' *AT*, 21:1 (January 1974), 61–65.

Davidson, J. E. ''The Language Experience Approach to Story Problems,'' *AT*, 25:1 (October 1977), 28.

Davidson, P. ''Rods Can Help Children Learn at All Grade Levels,'' *Learning*, 6:3 (November 1977), 86–88.

Frank, A. R. ''Teaching Money Skills with a Number Line,'' *Teaching Exceptional Children*, 10:2 (Winter 1978), 46–47.

Grove, J. ''A Pocket Multiplier,'' *AT*, 25:6 (March 1978), 54.

Hutchenson, J. W., and Hutchenson, C. E. ''Homemade Device for Quick Recall of Number Facts,'' *AT*, 24:4 (January 1978), 54–55.

Jencks, S. M., and Peck, D. M. ''Hot and Cold Cubes,'' *AT*, 24:1 (January 1977), 70–71.

Johnson, D. C., and Cohen, L. ''Functions,'' *AT*, 17:4 (April 1970), 305–315.

Karlin, M. ''Machines,'' *AT*, 12:4 (April 1965), 327–334.

Kaufman, B. A., and Haag, V. H. ''New Math or Old Math? — The Wrong Question,'' *AT*, 24:3 (April 1977), 287–292.

Kindle, E. ''Droopy, the Number Line, and Multiplication of Integers,'' *AT*, 23:6 (December 1976), 647–650.

Kokaska, S. ''A Notation System in Arithmetic Skills,''

Education and Training of the Mentally Retarded, 10:2 (April 1975), 96–101.

Lindquist, M. M., and Dana, M. E. "Recycle Your Math with Magazines," *AT,* 25:3 (December 1977), 4–8.

Litwiller, B. E., and Duncan, D. R. "Patterns in a Diamond," *Teacher,* 91:2 (October 1973), 68–72.

March, R. "Georges Cuisenaire and His Rainbow Rods," *Learning,* 6:3 (November 1977), 81–86.

Metzner, S., and Sharp, R. M. "Cardematics I — Using Playing Cards as Reinforcers and Motivators in Basic Operations," *AT,* 21:5 (May 1974), 419–421.

Myers, A. C., and Thornton, C. A. "The Learning Disabled Child — Learning Basic Facts," *AT,* 25:3 (December 1977), 46–50.

Ogletree, E. J., and Ujaki, V. "A Motoric Approach to Teaching Multiplication to the Mentally Retarded Child," *Education and Training of the Mentally Retarded,* 11:2 (April 1976), 129–134.

Orans, S. "Going Shopping! Problem-solving Activities for the Primary Grades with Provisions for Individualization," *AT,* 17:7 (November 1970), 621–623.

Perl, T. "String Sculpture in the Mathematics Laboratory," *AT,* 23:8 (December 1976), 612–616.

Radeka, N. "Manual Manipulation — A Hand-y Way of Multiplying," *Education and Training of the Mentally Retarded,* 10:2 (April 1975), 102–103.

Shafer, D. M. "Multiplication Mastery via the Tape Recorder," *AT,* 17:7 (November 1970), 581–582.

Thompson, C. S., and Dunlop, W. P. "Basic Facts: Do Your Children Understand or Do They Memorize?" *AT,* 25:3 (December 1977), 14–16.

Thornton, C. "Helping the Special Child Measure Up in Basic Fact Skills," *Teaching Exceptional Children,* 9:2 (Winter 1977), 54–55.

Tredway, D. "Out of Balance," *AT,* 24:1 (January 1977), 14–16.

Underhill, R. G. "Teaching Word Problems to First Graders," *AT,* 25:2 (November 1977), 54–56.

Wheatley, G. H., and Wheatley, C. L. "How Shall We Teach Column Addition?" *AT,* 25:4 (January 1978), 18–19.

Wilhelm, C. M. "Photographing Story Problems," *Instructor,* 87:4 (November 1977), 141–143.

4. Whole Number Algorithms

Bachrach, B. "Using Money to Clarify the Decomposition Subtraction Algorithm," *AT,* 23:4 (April 1976), 244–246.

Bensman, K. H. "Mail-order Math," *AT,* 25:3 (December 1977), 9.

Bradford, J. W. "Methods and Materials for Learning Subtraction," *AT,* 25:5 (February 1978), 18–20.

Cacha, F. B. "Understanding Multiplication and Division of Multi-digit Numbers," *AT,* 19:5 (May 1972), 349–354.

—————. "Subtraction: Regrouping with Flexibility," *AT,* 22:5 (May 1975), 402–404.

Carpenter, T., *et al.* "Notes from National Assessment: Word Problems," *AT,* 23:5 (May 1976), 389–393.

Cox, L. S. "Diagnosing and Remediating Systematic Errors in Addition and Subtraction Computations," *AT,* 22:2 (February 1975), 151–157.

Dana, M. E., and Lindquist, M. M. "Food for Thought," *AT,* 25:7 (April 1978), 6–11.

Earp, N. W. "Procedures for Teaching Reading in Mathematics," *AT,* 17:7 (November 1970), 575–579.

Goodstein, H. A. "The Performance of Educable Mentally Retarded Children on Subtraction Word Problems," *Education and Training of the Mentally Retarded,* 8:4 (December 1973), 197–202.

Hall, D. E., and Hall, C. T. "The Odometer in the Addition Algorithm," *AT,* 24:1 (January 1977), 18–21.

Hater, M. A., Kane, R. B., and Byrne, M. A. "Building Reading Skills in the Mathematics Class," *AT,* 21:8 (December 1974), 662–668.

Hazenkamp, D. W. "Teaching Multiplication and Division Algorithms," in *Developing Computational Skills,* 1978 Yearbook of the National Council of Teachers of Mathematics. Reston, Va.: NCTM, 1978, 96–128.

Heddens, J. W., and Lazerick, B. "So 3 'Guzinta' 5 Once! So What!!" *AT,* 22:7 (November 1975), 576–578.

Henney, M. "Improving Mathematical Verbal Problem-solving Ability through Reading Instruction," *AT,* 18:4 (April 1971), 223–229.

Herald, P. J. "Helping the Child Who 'Can't Do Math'," *Teacher,* 91:7 (March 1974), 46–47, 89.

Ikeda, H., and Ando, M. "A New Algorithm for Subtraction?" *AT,* 21:8 (December 1974), 716–719.

Hutchings, B. "Low Stress Algorithms," in *Measurement in School Mathematics,* 1976 Yearbook of the National Council of Teachers of Mathematics. Reston, Va.: NCTM, 1976, 218–239.

Merseth, K. "Using Materials and Activities in Teaching Addition and Subtraction Algorithms," in *Developing Computational Skills,* 1978 Yearbook of the National Council of Teachers of Mathematics. Reston, Va.: NCTM, 1978, 61–77.

Moyer, J., and Moyer, M. "Computation: Implications for Learning Disabled Children" in *Developing Computational Skills,* 1978 Yearbook of the National Council of Teachers of Mathematics. Reston, Va.: NCTM, 1978, 78–95.

Richardson, L. I. "The Role of Strategies for Teaching Pupils to Solve Verbal Problems," *The Arithmetic Teacher,* 22:5 (May 1975), 414–421.

Suydam, M. N., and Weaver, J. F. "Research on Problem Solving: Implications for Elementary School Classrooms," *AT,* 25:2 (November 1977), 40–42.

Swart, W. L. "A Diary of Remedial Instruction in Division — Grade Seven," *AT,* 22:8 (December 1975), 614–622.

Wilderman, A. "Math Skills for Survival in the Real World," *Teacher*, 94:6 (February 1977), 68–70.

5. Fractions and Decimals

Bohan, H. "Paper Folding and Equivalent Fractions — Bridging a Gap," *AT*, 18:4 (April 1971), 245–249.

Bruni, J. V., and Silverman, H. J. "An Introduction to Fractions," *AT*, 22:7 (November 1975), 538–545.

——————. "Using Rectangles and Squares to Develop Fraction Concepts," *AT*, 24:2 (February 1977), 96–102.

Carpenter, T. P., Coburn, T. G., Reys, R. E., and Wilson, J. W. "Notes from National Assessment: Addition and Multiplication with Fractions," *AT*, 23:2 (February 1976), 137–142.

Cole, B. L. and Weissenfluh, H. S. "An Analysis of Teaching Percentages," *AT*, 21:3 (March 1974) 226–228.

Ellerbruch, L. W., and Payne, J. N. "A Teaching Sequence from Initial Fraction Concepts through the Addition of Fractions," in *Developing Computational Skills*, 1978 Yearbook of the National Council of Teachers of Mathematics. Reston, Va.: NCTM, 1978, 129–147.

Firl, D. H. "Fractions, Decimals, and Their Futures," *AT*, 24:3 (March 1977), 238–240.

Hubbard, S. P., and Ashlock, R. B. "Using Flowcharts with First Graders," *AT*, 24:1 (January 1977), 23–29.

Jacobson, R. S. "Fun with Fractions for Special Education," *AT*, 18:6 (October 1971), 417–419.

Jencks, S. M., and Peck, D. M. *Experiencing Fractions*. Washington, D.C.: Curriculum Development Associates, 1973.

Kessler, B. M. "A Discovery Approach to the Introduction of Flow-charting in the Elementary Grades," *AT*, 17:3 (March 1970), 220–224.

Post, T. R. "An Energy Crisis: An Opportunity for Meaningful Arithmetic Excursions," *AT*, 22:1 (January 1975), 61–64.

Rubidoux, D., and Montefusco, N. "An Easy Way to Change Repeating Decimals to Fractions — Nick's Method," *AT*, 24:1 (January 1977), 81–82.

Wassmansdorf, M. "Reducing Fractions Can Be Easy, Maybe Even Fun," *AT*, 21:2 (February 1974), 99–102.

Wheatley, G. H., and Van Duien, A. "Mathematical Road Maps: A Teaching Technique," *AT*, 23:1 (January 1976), 18–20.

Wilson, G. H. "Decimal-Common Fraction Sequence Versus Conventional Sequence," *School 'Science and Mathematics*, 72 (October 1972), 589–592.

Zullie, E. *Fractions and Pattern Blocks*. Palo Alto, Cal.: Creative Publications, 1975.

6. Informal Geometry and Measurement

Aman, G. "Discovery on a Geoboard," *AT*, 21:4 (April 1974), 267–272.

Black, J. M. "Geometry Alive in the Primary Classrooms," *AT*, 14:2 (February 1967), 90–93.

Bitter, G. G., and Geer, C. P. "A Metric Bibliography," in *Measurement in School Mathematics*, 1976 Yearbook of the National Council of Teachers of Mathematics. Reston, Va.: NCTM, 1976, 210–217.

Bruni, J. V., and Silverman, H. J. "Developing the Concept of Linear Measurement," *AT*, 21:8 (November 1974), 570–577.

——————. "Using Geostrips for Arithmetic," *AT*, 22:1 (January 1975), 4–11.

——————. "Using Geostrips and 'Angle Fixers' to Develop Ideas about Shapes and Angles," *AT*, 22:4 (April 1975), 256–268.

——————. "Making the Holidays a Solid Success," *AT*, 22:8 (December 1975), 604–611.

——————. "An Introduction to Weight Measurement," *AT*, 23:1 (January 1976), 4–10.

Carpenter, T. P., Coburn, T. G., Reys, R. E., and Wilson, J. W. "Notes from National Assessment: Basic Concepts of Area and Volume," *AT*, 22:6 (October 1975), 501–507.

——————. "Notes from National Assessment: Perimeter and Area," *AT*, 22:7 (November 1975), 586–590.

——————. "Notes from National Assessment: Recognizing and Naming Solids," *AT*, 23:1 (January 1976), 62–66.

Cathcart, W. G. "Metric Measurement: Important Curricular Considerations," *AT*, 24:2 (February 1977), 158–160.

Clason, R. G. "1866 When the United States Accepted the Metric System," *AT*, 24:1 (January 1977), 56–62.

Dennis, J. R. "Informal Geometry through Symmetry," *AT*, 16:6 (October 1969), 433–436.

Dickoff, S. S. "Paper Folding and Cutting a Set of Tangram Pieces," *AT*, 18:4 (April 1971), 250–252.

Egsgard, J. C. "Geometry All Around Us — K–12," *AT*, 16:6 (October 1969), 437–445.

Gardner, M. "Mathematical Games, On the Fanciful History and the Creative Challenges of the Puzzle Game of Tangrams," *Scientific American* (August 1974), 98–103.

Hensel, N. "Back to Basics with Block Play," *Day Care and Early Education*, 5:1 (Fall 1977), 36–38, 41.

Hirstein, J. J., Lamb, C. E., and Osborne, A. "Student Misconceptions about Area Measure," *AT*, 25:6 (March 1978), 10–16.

Ibe, M. D. "Mathematics and Art from One Shape," *AT*, 18:3 (March 1971), 183–184.

Immerzeel, G. "Geometric Activities for Early Childhood Education," *AT*, 20:6 (October 1973), 438–443.

Johnson, M. L. "Generating Patterns from Transformations," *AT*, 24:3 (March 1977), 191–195.

Karnowski, P. "How Long Is a Belgian Classroom?" *Instructor*, 85:3 (November 1975), 117–121.

Klein, J. S. "Build a Better Geoboard," *AT*, 24:1 (January 1977), 85–86.

Krutzer, R. O., and Allen, B. A. "Geoboard Activities for Primary Grades," *AT*, 22:8 (December 1975), 625–627.

Liedtke, W. "Experiences with Blocks in Kindergarten," *AT*, 22:5 (May 1975), 406–412.

—————. "Geoboard Mathematics," *AT*, 21:4 (April 1974), 273–277.

Lindquist, M. M. "Problem Solving with Five Easy Pieces," *AT*, 25:2 (November 1977), 6–10.

May, L. "Footsteps before Meters," *Early Years*, 7:5 (January 1977), 22–25, 58–59.

Meggison, G. W. "Rays and Angles," *AT*, 21:5 (May 1974), 433–435.

Mendoza, L. P. "1 + 2 + 3 + 4 . . . : A Geometric Pattern?" *AT*, 22:2 (February 1975), 97–100.

Ogletree, E. "Geometry: An Artistic Approach," *AT*, 16:6 (October 1969), 457–461.

Read, R. C. *Tangrams, 330 Puzzles*. New York: Dover, 1965.

Sanok, G. "Living in a World of Transformations," *AT*, 25:6 (April 1978), 36–40.

Sengstock, W. L., and Wyatt, K. E. "Meters, Liters, and Grams: The Metric System and Its Implications for Curriculum for Exceptional Children," *Teaching Exceptional Children*, 8:2 (Winter 1976), 58–65.

Swadener, M. "Pictures, Graphs, and Transformations — A Distorted View of Plane Figures for Middle Grades," *AT*, 21:5 (May 1974), 383–389.

Todd, R. M., Houck, C., and Canon, J. "Metric Concepts for Children with Specific Learning Disabilities," *Science and Children*, 13:8, (May 1976), 19–20.

Trafton, P. R., and LeBlanc, J. F. "Informal Geometry in Grades K–6," in *Geometry in the Mathematics Curriculum*, 36th Yearbook of the National Council of Teachers of Mathematics. Washington, D.C.: NCTM, 1973, 11–51.

Volkmor, C. B., and Langstaff, A. L. "Developing Visual Perceptual Abilities," *Teaching Exceptional Children*, 4:1 (Fall 1971), 29–33.

Walter, M. "An Example of Informal Geometry: Mirror Cards," *AT*, 13:6 (October 1966), 448–452.

—————. "Some Mathematical Ideas Involved in the Mirror Cards," *AT*, 14:2 (February 1967), 115–125.

Webb, L., and Ost, D. "Unifying Science and Mathematics in the Elementary School: One Approach," *AT*, 22:1 (January 1975), 67–72.

Wenninger, M. J. *Polyhedron Models for the Classroom*. Washington, D.C.: National Council of Teachers of Mathematics, 1966.

Wilderman, A. M. "The Metrics Are Coming," *Early Years*, 5:8 (April 1975), 51–59.

Williams, D. E., and Wolfson, B. "Metric Play — Games to Help Kids Think Metric,' *Instructor*, 86:8 (April 1977), 62–66.

7A. The Mathematics Laboratory Approach

Barson, A. "Task Cards," *AT*, 26:2 (October 1978), 53–54.

Biggs, E. E., and Hartung, M. L. "What is Your Position On — The Role of Experience in the Learning of Mathematics," *AT*, 18:5 (May 1971), 278–295.

Burns, S. "Apparatus for Special Schools," *Mathematics Teaching*, 68 (September 1974), 26–29.

Cathcart, W. G. (Ed.). *The Mathematics Laboratory: Readings from the Arithmetic Teacher*. Reston, Va.: National Council of Teachers of Mathematics, 1977.

Davidson, P. S. "An Annotated Bibliography of Suggested Manipulative Devices," *AT*, 15:6 (October 1968), 509–524.

Davidson, P. S., and Fair, A. W. "A Mathematics Laboratory — from Dream to Reality," *AT*, 17:2 (February 1970), 105–110.

Dunn, R., and Dunn, K. "How to Create Hands-on Materials," *Instructor*, 87:8 (March 1978), 134–140.

Goodman, L. "Meeting Children's Needs Through Materials Modification," *Teaching Exceptional Children*, 10:3 (Spring 1978), 92–93.

Higgins, J. L., and Sachs, L. A. *Mathematics Laboratories: 150 Activities and Games for Elementary Schools*. Reston, Va.: National Council of Teachers of Mathematics, 1974.

Post, T. R. "A Model for the Construction and Sequencing of Laboratory Activities," *AT*, 21:7 (November 1974), 616–622.

Reys, R. E. "Mathematics, Multiple Embodiments, and Elementary Teachers," *AT*, 19:6 (October 1972), 489–493.

—————. "Considerations for Teachers in Using Manipulative Materials," *AT*, 18:8 (December 1971), 551–558.

Smith, E. E., and Backman, C. A. (Eds.). *Teacher-Made Aids for Elementary School Mathematics: Readings from the Arithmetic Teacher*. Reston, Va.: NCTM, 1974.

Vance, J., and Kieren, T. "Laboratory Settings in Mathematics: What Does the Research Say to the Teacher?" *AT*, 18:8 (December 1971), 585–589.

7B. Games for Review-Practice

Bruni, J. V., and Silverman, H. J. "Using Indoor Games to Motivate Mathematics Learning," *AT*, 23:3 (March 1976), 154–162.

—————. "Making and Using Board Games," *AT*, 22:3 (March 1975), 172–179.

Crimm, J. "Handle with Flair," *Early Years*, 7:5 (January 1977), 36–39.

Dana, M. E., and Lindquist, M. M. "Thinking Up Your Own Practice Games," *AT*, 25:5 (February 1978), 4–10.

Frye, S. "New Ways to Math Drill," *Instructor*, 87:5 (December 1977), 81–84.

Golden, S. "Fostering Enthusiasm Through Child-created Games,'' *AT,* 17:2 (February 1970), 111–115.

Green, G. ''Distinguishing Drill with Manipulatives,'' *Instructor,* 86:5 (January 1977), 128–132.

Hamilton, G. ''Painless Drilling,'' *Early Years,* 8:5 (January 1978), 66–67, 72.

Hoffman, R. I. ''Tie Games to Concepts,'' *Instructor,* 85:8 (April 1976), 71–72.

Irwin, D. M. ''Make Your Own Games,'' *Day Care and Early Education,* 4:5 (May/June 1977), 32–33.

Kevra, B., Brey, R., and Schimmel, B. ''Success for Slow Learners, or Rx: Relax . . . and Play,'' *AT,* 19:5 (May 1972), 335–343.

Krulik, S., and Wilderman, A. ''More Than Just Play,'' *Teacher,* 95:3 (November 1977), 84–90.

May, L. ''Station to Station Math,'' *Early Years,* 8:5 (January 1978), 62–63, 74.

Simpson, M. J. ''Frame-a-Game,'' *Instructor,* 86:1 (August/September 1976), 88–92.

Smith, S. E., and Backman, C. A. (Eds.). *Games and Puzzles for Elementary and Middle School Mathematics: Readings from the Arithmetic Teacher.* Reston, Va.: National Council of Teachers of Mathematics, 1975.

Tahta, D. ''An Alphabet of Games,'' *Mathematics Teaching,* 73 (December 1975), 21–23.

Taylor, G. R., and Watkins, S. T. ''Active Games: An Approach to Teaching Mathematical Skills to the Educable Mentally Retarded,'' *AT,* 21:8 (December 1974), 674–678.

7C. Evaluation

Ashlock, R. B. ''A Test of Understanding for the Primary Grades,'' *AT,* 15:5 (May 1968), 438–441.

Beatty, L. S., and Madden, R. ''Using Test Results to Teach,'' *Early Years,* 8:6 (February 1978), 64–69.

Buros, O. K. (Ed.). *Mathematics Tests and Reviews.* Highland Park, N.J.: Gryphon Press, 1975.

Callahan, L. G. ''Test-Item Tendencies: Curiosity and Caution,'' *AT,* 25:3 (December 1977), 10–13.

Carry, L. R. ''A Critical Assessment of Published Tests for Elementary School Mathematics,'' *AT,* 21:1 (January 1974), 14–18.

Epstein, M. ''Testing in Mathematics: Why? What? How?'' *AT,* 15:4 (April 1968), 311–319.

Homan, D. R. ''The Child with a Learning Disability in Arithmetic,'' *AT,* 17:3 (March 1970), 199–203.

Hopkins, M. H. ''The Diagnosis of Learning Styles in Arithmetic,'' *AT,* 25:7 (April 1978), 47–50.

Houser, L. L., and Heimer, R. T. ''A Model for Evaluating Individualized Mathematics Learning Systems,'' *AT,* 26:4 (December 1978), 54–55.

Lankford, F. G. ''What Can A Teacher Learn about a Pupil's Thinking Through Oral Interviews?'' *AT,* 21:1 (January 1974), 26–32.

Michaels, L. A., and Forsyth, R. A. ''Measuring Attitudes toward Mathematics? Some Questions to Consider,'' *AT,* 26:4 (December 1978), 22–25.

O'Brien, T. C., and Richard, J. V. ''Interviews to Assess Number Knowledge,'' *AT,* 18:5 (May 1971), 322–326.

Peck, D., and Jencks, S. ''What the Tests Don't Tell,'' *AT,* 24:1 (January 1977), 54–55.

Pincus, M., *et al.* ''If You Don't Know How Children Think, How Can You Help Them?'' *AT,* 22:7 (November 1975), 580–585.

Suydam, M. N. *Evaluation in the Mathematics Classroom: From What and Why to How and Where.* Reston, Va.: The National Council of Teachers of Mathematics, 1974.

7D. Calculators

Beardslee, E. C. ''Teaching Computational Skills with a Calculator,'' in *Developing Computational Skills,* 1978 Yearbook of the National Council of Teachers of Mathematics. Reston, Va.: NCTM, 1978, 226–241.

Bell, M., Esty, E., Payne, J., and Suydam, M. ''Hand-held Calculators: Past, Present, and Future,'' in *Organizing for Mathematics Instruction,* 1977 Yearbook of the National Council of Teachers of Mathematics. Reston, Va.: NCTM, 1977, 224–240.

Bitter, G. ''The Calculator and the Curriculum,'' *Teacher,* 94:6 (February 1977), 64–67.

Immerzeel, G. ''It's 1986 and Every Student Has a Calculator,'' *Instructor,* 85:8 (April 1976), 46–51.

Koller, E. Z., and Mulhern, T. J. ''Use of a Pocket Calculator to Train Arithmetic Skills with Trainable Adolescents,'' *Education and Training of the Mentally Retarded,* 12:4 (December 1977), 332–335.

Martin, J. P. ''Problem Solving with Calculators,'' *AT,* 25:7 (April 1978), 24–26.

National Council of Teachers of Mathematics. *Calculator Information Resources.* Reston, Va.: NCTM, 1977.

BOOKS IN MATHEMATICS AND MATHEMATICS EDUCATION

The books listed below are grouped into three categories: (1) books about mathematics to strengthen or extend your understanding of content or to broaden your perspective about the nature of mathematics; (2) general references in education and learning theory, which have been cited in the book; (3) references on general approaches and specific methods for teaching mathematics, and activities for children, including innovative curriculum materials.

1. Mathematics

Adler, I. *A New Look at Arithmetic.* New York: New American Library, 1964.

Asimov, I. *Realm of Numbers.* New York: Fawcett World Library, 1959.

Banwell, C. S., Saunders, K. D., and Tahta, D. G.

Starting Points. London: Oxford University Press, 1972.

Berganini, D. *Mathematics: Life Science Library.* Morristown, N.J.: Silver Burdett, 1963.

Campbell, D. M. *The Whole Craft of Numbers.* Boston: Prindle, Weber, and Schmidt, 1976.

DelGrande, J. J. *Geoboards and Motion Geometry for Elementary Teachers.* Glenview, Ill.: Scott Foresman, 1972.

Dubisch, R. *Basic Concepts of Mathematics for Elementary Teachers.* Menlo Park, Cal.: Addison Wesley, 1977.

Gardner, M. *The Scientific American Book of Mathematical Puzzles and Diversions.* New York: Simon and Schuster, 1959.

——————. *Mathematical Carnival.* New York: Knopf, 1975.

Heddens, J. W. *Today's Mathematics* (3rd ed.). Chicago: Science Research Associates, 1974.

Hogben, L. *The Wonderful World of Mathematics.* Garden City, N.Y.: Doubleday, 1955.

Johnson, D., *et al. Applications in Mathematics Course A* (series, including *Functions and Graphs, Relations and Geometry, Sampling and Statistics, Estimation and Measurement, Prediction and Probability, Algebra*). Glenview, Ill.: Scott, Foresman, 1972.

Knaupp, J., Smith, L. T., Shoecraft, P. J., and Warkentin, G. D. *Patterns and Systems of Elementary Mathematics.* Boston: Houghton Mifflin, 1977.

Newman, J. R. *The World of Mathematics.* 4 vols. New York: Simon and Schuster, 1956.

O'Daffer, P., and Clemens, S. *Geometry: An Investigative Approach.* Menlo Park, Cal.: Addison-Wesley, 1976.

Page, D. A. "Probability," in *The Growth of Mathematical Ideas Grades K–12,* 24th Yearbook of the National Council of Teachers of Mathematics. Washington, D.C.: NCTM, 1959, 229–271.

Smith, D. E., and Ginsburg, J. *Numbers and Numerals.* Washington, D.C.: NCTM, 1937.

Stein, R. G. *Mathematics: An Exploratory Approach.* New York: McGraw-Hill, 1975.

2. General Education and Learning Theory

Biggs, E. E., and MacLean, J. R. *Freedom to Learn.* Reading, Mass.: Addison-Wesley, 1969.

Bruner, J. *The Process of Education.* New York: Random House, 1960.

Bruner, J., Goodnow, J., and Austin, G. *A Study of Thinking.* New York, John Wiley, 1956.

Dienes, Z. P. *Building Up Mathematics.* London: Hutchinson Educational Ltd., 1960.

Elkind, D. *Child Development and Education — A Piagetian Perspective.* New York: Oxford University Press, 1976.

Ginsburg, H., and Opper, S. *Piaget's Theory of Intellectual Development.* Englewood Cliffs, N.J.: Prentice-Hall, 1969.

Holt, J. *How Children Fail.* New York: Dell, 1964.

Kamii, C., and DeVries, R. *Piaget, Children and Number.* Washington, D.C.: National Association for the Education of Young Children, 1976.

Kline, M. *Why Johnny Can't Add: The Failure of the New Math.* New York: St. Martin's Press, 1973.

Lavatelli, C. S. *Piaget's Theory Applied to Early Childhood Curriculum.* Boston: American Science and Engineering, 1970.

Mager, R. F. *Preparing Instructional Objectives.* Palo Alto, Cal.: Fearon Publishers, 1962.

Piaget, J. *The Child's Conception of Number.* New York: Norton, 1965.

——————. *The Child's Conception of Space.* New York: Humanities Press, 1963.

Piaget, J., and Inhelder, B. *The Early Growth of Logic in the Child.* New York: Norton, 1969.

——————. *The Psychology of the Child.* New York: Basic Books, 1965.

Standing, E. M. *The Montessori Revolution.* New York: Schocken Books, 1966.

3. Mathematics Education, and Teaching Mathematics

Methods and Activities

Ashlock, R. B. *Error Patterns in Computation.* Columbus, Ohio: Charles E. Merrill, 1976.

Baratta-Lorton, M. *Mathematics Their Way.* Menlo Park, Cal.: Addison-Wesley, 1976.

——————. *Workjobs.* Menlo Park, Cal.: Addison-Wesley, 1972.

Bennet, A., and Davidson, P. *Fraction Bars.* Fort Collins, Col.: Scott Resources, n.d.

Buckeye, D., Ewbank, W., and Ginther, J. *Cloudburst of Math Lab Experiments.* 3 vols. Birmingham, Mich.: Midwest Publications, 1971.

Burns, M. *The I Hate Mathematics Book.* Boston: Little, Brown, 1975.

Cuisenaire Company of America. *Using the Cuisenaire Rods — A Photo/Text Guide for Teachers.* New Rochelle, N.Y.: Cuisenaire Company of America, 1969.

Davidson, P. *Idea Book for Cuisenaire Rods at the Primary Level.* New Rochelle, N.Y.: Cuisenaire Company of America, 1977.

Davis, R. *Explorations in Mathematics — A Text for Teachers.* Palo Alto, Cal.: Addison-Wesley, 1967.

——————. *Discovery in Mathematics — A Text for Teachers.* Menlo Park, Cal.: Addison-Wesley, 1964.

DeVito, A., and Krockover, G. H. *Creative Sciencing: Ideas and Activities for Teachers and Children.* Boston: Little, Brown, 1976.

Dienes, Z. P., and Golding, E. W. *Learning Logic, Logical Games.* New York: Herder and Herder, 1966.

Dumas, Enoch. *Math Activities for Child Involvement.* Boston: Allyn and Bacon, 1971.

Greenes, C. E., Willcut, R. E., and Spikell, M. A. *Problem Solving in the Mathematics Laboratory.* Boston: Prindle, Weber and Schmidt, 1972.

Hainstock, E. *Teaching Montessori in the Home (The School Years).* New York: Random House, 1971.

Hirsch, E. S. *The Block Book.* Washington, D.C.: National Association for the Education of Young Children, 1974.

Holt, M., and Dienes, Z. P. *Let's Play Maths.* Harmondsworth, Eng.: Penguin Books, 1973.

Immerzeel, G., and Ockenga, E. *Calculator Activities for the Classroom.* Palo Alto, Cal.: Creative Publications, 1977.

Johnson, D. *Games for Learning Mathematics* (revised edition). Portland, Me.: J. Weston Walch, 1973.

Johnson, S. J. *Arithmetic and Learning Disabilities.* Boston: Allyn and Bacon, 1979.

Judd, W. *Patterns to Play on a Hundred Chart.* Palo Alto, Cal.: Creative Publications, 1975.

——————. *Games, Tricks, and Puzzles for a Hand Calculator.* Menlo Park, Cal.: Dymax, 1974.

Kelly, S. J. *Learning Mathematics Through Activities.* Cupertino, Cal.: James E. Freel, 1973.

Kennedy, L. *Guiding Discovery in Mathematics* (2nd ed.). Belmont, Cal.: Wadsworth, 1975.

Kennedy, L., and Michon, R. L. *Games for Individualizing Mathematics Learning.* Columbus, Ohio: Charles E. Merrill, 1973.

Kohl, H. R. *Math, Writing and Games in the Open Classroom.* New York: The New York Review, 1974.

Marks, J. L., Purdy, C. R., Kinney, L. B., and Hiatt, A. A. *Teaching Elementary School Mathematics for Understanding.* New York: McGraw-Hill, 1975.

Members of the Association of Teachers of Mathematics. *Notes on Mathematics in the Primary School.* London: Cambridge University Press, 1968.

Page, D. *Maneuvers on Lattices, An Example of "Intermediate Intervention."* Watertown, Mass.: Educational Services Inc., 1965.

Pasternack, M., and Silvey, L. *Pattern Block Activities Books.* Palo Alto, Cal.: Creative Publications, 1975.

Pearson, C., and Marfuggi, J. *Creating and Using Learning Games.* Palo Alto, Cal.: Education Today Company, 1975.

Peterson, D. L. *Functional Mathematics for the Mentally Retarded.* Columbus, Ohio: Charles E. Merrill, 1973.

Reys, R. E., and Post, T. R. *The Mathematics Laboratory — Theory to Practice.* Boston: Prindle, Weber and Schmidt, 1973.

Stern, C., and Stern, M. *Children Discover Arithmetic.* New York: Harper and Row, 1971.

Schlossberg, E., and Brockman, J. *The Pocket Calculator Game Book.* New York: Bantam Books, 1975.

Williams, E., and Shuard, H. *Elementary Mathematics Today: A Resource for Teachers.* Menlo Park, Cal.: Addison-Wesley, 1970.

Wirtz, R. *Mathematics for Everyone.* Washington, D.C.: Curriculum Development Associates, 1974.

Selected Yearbooks of the National Council of Teachers of Mathematics, Reston, Va.

1963, *Enrichment Mathematics for the Grades*
1969, *Historical Topics for the Math Classroom*
1972, *The Slow Learner in Mathematics*
1975, *Mathematics Learning in Early Childhood*
1976, *Measurement in School Mathematics*
1977, *Organizing for Mathematics Instruction*
1978, *Developing Computational Skills*

Elementary School Mathematics Curriculum Resources

Cawley, John, *et al. Project Math Levels I–IV.* A program for children with handicaps to learning, grades 1–6. Tulsa, Okla.: Educational Development Corporation, P. O. Box 45663.

CEMREL. *Comprehensive School Mathematics Program.* St. Louis: CEMREL, 1975.

——————. *Teacher's Guide to CSMP Mathematics for the Upper Primary Grades.* St. Louis: CEMREL, 1975.

Developing Mathematical Processes (DMP Program). Chicago: Rand McNally, 1974.

Educational Development Center. *Unified Science and Mathematics for Elementary Schools* (USMES). Newton, Mass.: Education Development Center, 1973.

Elementary Science Study. *Attribute Games and Problems, Mirror Cards, Tangrams.* St. Louis: Webster Division, McGraw-Hill Book Company.

Lavatelli, C. *Early Childhood Curriculum — A Piaget Program Teacher's Guide.* Boston: American Science and Engineering, 1970.

Mason, M. *Mason Math Program* and film, "Math for 5 Year Olds." Princeton, N.J.: Miss Mason's School, P.O. Box 456.

MINNEMAST. *Minnesota Mathematics and Science Teaching Program.* Minneapolis, Minn.: Science and Mathematics Project, University of Minnesota, 1968.

Nuffield Mathematics Project. *Beginnings* (1968), *Environmental Geometry* (1968), *I Do and I Understand* (1967), *Number Patterns* (1973), *Pictorial Representations* (1967), *Size and Shape 2* (1968), *Size and Shape 3* (1968), *Probability and Statistics* (1969), *Mathematics: The First 3 Years* (1970). New York: Wiley.

Stern, C. *Discovering Arithmetic.* Boston: Houghton Mifflin, 1952.

Wirtz, R. *Drill and Practice at the Problem-Solving Level, Individualized Computation, Patterns and Problems, Mathematics for Everyone.* Washington, D.C.: Curriculum Development Associates, 1974.

INDEX

Abacus, 308–309, 319, 411–412
Abstract mode, 217–218
Activities
  calculator, 565–566
  discovery, 465–466
  enrichment, 332, 335–337, 464
  modifying, 107–110, 155–156
  parallel, 490, 506–509
  workbook, 65–66
Activities, for teaching. *See also*
    Cuisenaire rods
  addition, 143–144, 154–158,
    165–167, 188, 339, 471
  algorithms, 397–404, 433–442
  attributes, 3–10, 13–14
  basic facts, 182–194, 216–220,
    224–235, 339
  counting, 48–54, 59, 64–65, 69,
    73–74, 84–86
  decimals, 440–441, 544–548
  division, 185–186, 404, 433,
    439–440
  factors, 466–468
  fractions, 493–498, 500–509,
    520–524, 527–528, 544–545
  GCF, 476, 478
  geometry, 92–105, 107–118,
    121–123, 125, 131–134, 350–
    390, 491
  LCM, 477–478
  measurement, 50–51, 58, 244–
    273, 275–290, 354–359
  multiples, 452–455, 459, 462–463
  multiplication, 185–186, 404
  number(s), 23–25
  patterns, 5, 112, 116, 358, 452–
    476, 566–567
  place value, 301–302, 310–313,
    315–316, 320–321, 471
  prime numbers, 453, 456–457,
    463
  probability, 51–54, 81–84, 337–
    340
  problem solving, 440–441
  rational numbers, 512

sorting, 3, 8, 17–22, 30–31, 95,
  98, 353
subtraction, 170–171, 325–327,
  412
Addition. *See also* Algorithm(s);
    Basic facts
  activities, 143–144, 154–158,
    165–167, 188, 339, 471
  algorithm, 397–401, 409, 411–
    412, 429–430
  with bases, 302, 322–325, 332
  basic facts of, 199, 219–222,
    339
  concepts, 170–172, 199, 219–
    221, 518, 528
  with Cuisenaire rods, 143–144,
    154–155, 157–164, 170
  of decimals, 63, 331, 439, 539
  errors with, 400
  of fractions, 497–498, 504–505,
    518, 528, 531–535
  games, 159–160, 313–314, 401–
    403, 434
  higher-decade, 430
  materials for teaching, 155, 160–
    166, 322–325, 409, 411–412,
    497–498, 504–505, 528
  of mixed numbers, 534–535
  models for, 160–165
  and multiplication, relationship,
    172, 188
  on the number line, 165–167
  and problem solving, 199
  properties of, 174–176, 209–211,
    219–220
  scope and sequence of, 429–430
  and subtraction, relationship,
    170–171, 221
Addition of Fractions, 497–498,
    504–505, 515
Additive inverse, 554–555
Additive property of 0. *See* Identity
    property
Algorithm(s), 405
  activities, 397–404, 433–442

addition, decimals, 539
addition, fractions, 531–535
addition, whole numbers, 397–
  401, 409, 411–412, 429–430
and the calculator, 403, 410,
  426–427
decimals, 539–543
division, decimals, 542–543
division, fractions, 537–538
division, whole numbers, 401,
  406, 414–415, 421–428, 432–
  433
errors with whole number, 400–
  401, 405–408, 410
fractions, 528–538
games, 401–403, 413–415, 434,
  440–441
learning, 408–410
materials for teaching, 410–414,
  417–418, 422–424, 426–427,
  562–570
mixed numbers, 534–535
multiplication, decimals, 539–
  542
multiplication, fractions, 535–537
multiplication, whole numbers,
  398–401, 406, 413–421, 431–
  432
and puzzles, 440–441
scope and sequence of whole
  number, 428–433
self-checking, 439–441
subtraction, decimals, 539
subtraction, fractions, 531–535
subtraction, whole numbers,
  395, 400, 406, 412, 431
whole numbers, 397–448
and word problems, 396–397,
  402–403, 442–445
Angle(s), 129–131, 374–376
Applications, 214–215, 273, 409–
  410, 461, 509–510, 544. *See
  also* Problem solving; Word
  problems